Praise for the First Edition

More Praise for the First Edition

Outstanding...comprehensive and up-to-date ...grab this book and learn how to leverage Lucene's potential.
　　　　　　—Val's blog

...the code examples are useful and reusable.
　　　　　　—Scott Ganyo, Lucene Java Committer

...packed with examples and advice on how to effectively use this incredibly powerful tool.
　　　　　　—Brian Goetz, Quiotix Corporation

...it unlocked for me the amazing power of Lucene.
　　　　　　—Reece Wilton, Walt Disney Internet Group

...code samples as JUnit test cases are incredibly helpful.
　　　　　　—Norman Richards, co-author *XDoclet in Action*

A quick and easy guide to making Lucene work.
　　　　　　—Books-On-Line

A comprehensive guide...The authors of this book are experts in this field...they have unleashed the power of Lucene ...the best guide to Lucene available so far.
　　　　　　—JavaReference.com

Lucene in Action

Second Edition

MICHAEL McCANDLESS
ERIK HATCHER
OTIS GOSPODNETIĆ

MANNING

Greenwich
(74° w. long.)

For online information and ordering of this and other Manning books, please visit
www.manning.com. The publisher offers discounts on this book when ordered in quantity.
For more information, please contact

Special Sales Department
Manning Publications Co.
180 Broad St.
Suite 1323
Stamford, CT 06901
Email: orders@manning.com

Manning Publications Co.   Development editor: Sebastian Stirling
180 Broad St.   Copyeditor: Liz Welch
Suite 1323   Typesetter: Dottie Marsico
Stamford, CT 06901   Cover designer: Marija Tudor

ISBN 978-1-933988-17-7
Printed in the United States of America
1 2 3 4 5 6 7 8 9 10 – MAL – 15 14 13 12 11 10

brief contents

v

contents

vii

11 Lucene administration and performance tuning 345

PART 3 CASE STUDIES 381

12 Case study 1: Krugle
Krugle: Searching source code 383

foreword

Lucene started as a self-serving project. In late 1997, my job uncertain, I sought something of my own to market. Java was the hot new programming language, and I needed an excuse to learn it. I already knew how to write search software, and thought I might fill a niche by writing search software in Java. So I wrote Lucene.

In 2000, I realized that I didn't like to market stuff. I had no interest in negotiating licenses and contracts, and I didn't want to hire people and build a company. I liked writing software, not selling it. So I tossed Lucene up on SourceForge, to see if open source might let me keep doing what I liked.

A few folks started using Lucene right away. In 2001, folks at Apache offered to adopt Lucene. The number of daily messages on the Lucene mailing lists grew steadily. Code contributions started to trickle in. Most were additions around the edges of Lucene: I was still the only active developer who fully grokked its core. Still, Lucene was on the road to becoming a real collaborative project.

Now, in 2010, Lucene has a pool of active developers with deep understanding of its core. I'm no longer involved in day-to-day development; substantial additions and improvements are regularly made by this strong team.

Through the years, Lucene has been translated into several other programming languages, including C++, C#, Perl, and Python. In the original Java, and in these other incarnations, Lucene is used much more widely than I ever would have dreamed. It powers search in diverse applications like discussion groups at Fortune 100 companies, commercial bug trackers, email search supplied by Microsoft, and a web search engine that scales to billions of pages. When, at industry events, I am introduced to someone as the "Lucene guy," more often than not folks tell me how they've used Lucene in a project. I figure I've only heard about a small fraction of all Lucene applications.

Lucene is much more widely used than it ever would have been if I had tried to sell it. Application developers seem to prefer open source. Instead of having to contact technical support when they have a problem (and then wait for an answer, hoping they were correctly understood), they can frequently just look at the source code to diagnose their problems. If that's not enough, the free support provided by peers on the mailing lists is better than most commercial support. A functioning open-source project like Lucene makes application developers more efficient and productive.

Lucene, through open source, has become something much greater than I ever imagined it would. I set it going, but it took the combined efforts of the Lucene community to make it thrive.

So what's next for Lucene? I can't predict the future. What I do know is that even after over 10 years in existence, Lucene is still going strong, and its user and development communities are bigger and busier than ever, in part thanks to the first edition of *Lucene in Action* making it easier for more people to get started with Lucene. With every new release Lucene is getting better, more mature, more feature-rich, and faster.

Since the first edition of *Lucene in Action* was published in 2004, Lucene internals and its API have gone through radical changes that called for more than just minor book updates. In this totally revised second edition, the authors bring you up to speed on the latest improvements and new APIs in Lucene.

Armed with the second edition of *Lucene in Action*, you too are now a member of the Lucene community, and it's up to you to take Lucene to new places. Bon voyage!

DOUG CUTTING
FOUNDER OF LUCENE,
NUTCH, AND HADOOP

preface

I first started with Lucene about a year after the first edition of *Lucene in Action* was published. I already had experience building search engines, but didn't know much about Lucene in particular. So, I picked up a copy of *Lucene in Action* by Erik and Otis and read it, cover to cover, and I was hooked!

As I used Lucene, I found small improvements here and there, so I started contributing small patches, updating javadocs, discussing topics on Lucene's mailing lists, and so forth. I eventually became an active core committer and PMC member, committing many changes over the years.

It has now been five-and-a-half years since the first edition of *Lucene in Action* was published, which is practically an eternity in the fast-paced world of open source development! Lucene has gone through two major releases, and now has all sorts of new functionality such as numeric fields, the reusable analysis API, payloads, near-real-time search, and transactional APIs for indexing and searching, and so on.

When Manning first approached me, it was clear that a second edition was sorely needed. Furthermore, as one of the active core committers largely responsible for committing so many of these changes, I felt rather obligated to create the second edition. So I said yes, and then worked fiendishly to cover Lucene's changes, and I'm quite happy with the results. I hope this Second Edition of *Lucene in Action* will serve you well as you create your search applications, and I look forward to seeing you on the user and developer lists, asking your own interesting questions, and continuing to drive Lucene's relentless growth!

MICHAEL MCCANDLESS

preface to the first edition

From Erik Hatcher

I've been intrigued with searching and indexing from the early days of the Internet. I have fond memories (circa 1991) of managing an email list using majordomo, MUSH (Mail User's Shell), and a handful of Perl, awk, and shell scripts. I implemented a CGI web interface to allow users to search the list archives and other users' profiles using grep tricks under the covers. Then along came Yahoo!, AltaVista, and Excite, all which I visited regularly.

After my first child, Jakob, was born, my digital photo archive began growing rapidly. I was intrigued with the idea of developing a system to manage the pictures so that I could attach meta-data to each picture, such as keywords and date taken, and, of course, locate the pictures easily in any dimension I chose. In the late 1990s, I prototyped a filesystem-based approach using Microsoft technologies, including Microsoft Index Server, Active Server Pages, and a third COM component for image manipulation. At the time, my professional life was consumed with these same technologies. I was able to cobble together a compelling application in a couple of days of spare-time hacking.

My professional life shifted toward Java technologies, and my computing life consisted of less and less Microsoft Windows. In an effort to reimplement my personal photo archive and search engine in Java technologies in an operating system–agnostic way, I came across Lucene. Lucene's ease of use far exceeded my expectations—I had experienced numerous other open-source libraries and tools that were far simpler conceptually yet far more complex to use.

In 2001, Steve Loughran and I began writing *Java Development with Ant* (Manning). We took the idea of an image search engine application and generalized it as a document search engine. This application example is used throughout the Ant book and can be customized as an image search engine. The tie to Ant comes not only from a simple compile-and-package build process but also from a custom Ant task, <index>, we created that indexes files during the build process using Lucene. This Ant task now lives in Lucene's Sandbox and is described in section 8.4 of the first edition.

This Ant task is in production use for my custom blogging system, which I call BlogScene (http://www.blogscene.org/erik). I run an Ant build process, after creating a blog entry, which indexes new entries and uploads them to my server. My blog server consists of a servlet, some Velocity templates, and a Lucene index, allowing for rich queries, even syndication of queries. Compared to other blogging systems, Blog-Scene is vastly inferior in features and finesse, but the full-text search capabilities are very powerful.

I'm now working with the Applied Research in Patacriticism group at the University of Virginia (http://www.patacriticism.org), where I'm putting my text analysis, indexing, and searching expertise to the test and stretching my mind with discussions of how quantum physics relates to literature. "Poets are the unacknowledged engineers of the world."

From Otis Gospodnetić

My interest in and passion for information retrieval and management began during my student years at Middlebury College. At that time, I discovered an immense source of information known as the Web. Although the Web was still in its infancy, the long-term need for gathering, analyzing, indexing, and searching was evident. I became obsessed with creating repositories of information pulled from the Web, began writing web crawlers, and dreamed of ways to search the collected information. I viewed search as the killer application in a largely uncharted territory. With that in the back of my mind, I began the first in my series of projects that share a common denominator: gathering and searching information.

In 1995, fellow student Marshall Levin and I created WebPh, an open-source program used for collecting and retrieving personal contact information. In essence, it was a simple electronic phone book with a web interface (CGI), one of the first of its kind at that time. (In fact, it was cited as an example of prior art in a court case in the late 1990s!) Universities and government institutions around the world have been the primary adopters of this program, and many are still using it. In 1997, armed with my WebPh experience, I proceeded to create Populus, a popular white pages at the time. Even though the technology (similar to that of WebPh) was rudimentary, Populus carried its weight and was a comparable match to the big players such as WhoWhere, Bigfoot, and Infospace.

After two projects that focused on personal contact information, it was time to explore new territory. I began my next venture, Infojump, which involved culling high-quality information from online newsletters, journals, newspapers, and magazines. In addition to my own software, which consisted of large sets of Perl modules and scripts, Infojump utilized a web crawler called Webinator and a full-text search product called Texis. The service provided by Infojump in 1998 was much like that of FindArticles.com today.

Although WebPh, Populus, and Infojump served their purposes and were fully functional, they all had technical limitations. The missing piece in each of them was a powerful information-retrieval library that would allow full-text searches backed by inverted indexes. Instead of trying to reinvent the wheel, I started looking for a solution that I suspected was out there. In early 2000, I found Lucene, the missing piece I'd been looking for, and I fell in love with it.

I joined the Lucene project early on when it still lived at SourceForge and, later, at the Apache Software Foundation when Lucene migrated there in 2002. My devotion to Lucene stems from its being a core component of many ideas that had queued up in my mind over the years. One of those ideas was Simpy, my latest pet project. Simpy is a feature-rich personal web service that lets users tag, index, search, and share information found online. It makes heavy use of Lucene, with thousands of its indexes, and is powered by Nutch, another project of Doug Cutting's (see chapter 10 of the first edition). My active participation in the Lucene project resulted in an offer from Manning to co-author *Lucene in Action* with Erik Hatcher.

Lucene in Action is the most comprehensive source of information about Lucene. The information contained in the chapters encompasses all the knowledge you need to create sophisticated applications built on top of Lucene. It's the result of a very smooth and agile collaboration process, much like that within the Lucene community. Lucene and *Lucene in Action* exemplify what people can achieve when they have similar interests, the willingness to be flexible, and the desire to contribute to the global knowledge pool, despite the fact that they have yet to meet in person.

acknowledgments

We are sincerely and humbly indebted to Doug Cutting. Without Doug's generosity to the world, there would be no Lucene. Without the other Lucene committers, Lucene would have far fewer features, more bugs, and a much tougher time thriving with its growing adoption. Many thanks to all the committers, past and present. Similarly, we thank all those who contributed the case studies that appear in chapters 12, 13 and 14: Michele Catasta, Renaud Delbru, Mikkel Kamstrup Erlandsen, Toke Eskildsen, Robert Fuller, Grant Glouser, Ken Krugler, Jake Mannix, Nickolai Toupikov, Giovanni Tummarello, Mads Villadsen, and John Wang. We'd also like to thank Doug Cutting for penning the foreword to the second edition.

Our thanks to the staff at Manning, including Marjan Bace, Jeff Bleiel, Sebstian Stirling, Karen Tegtmeyer, Liz Welch, Elizabeth Martin, Dottie Marsico, Mary Piergies, and Marija Tudor. Manning rounded up a great set of reviewers, whom we thank for improving our drafts into the book you now read. The reviewers include Chad Davis, Dave Pawson, Rob Allen, Rick Wagner, Michele Galli, Robi Sen, Stuart Caborn, Jeremy Flowers, Robert Hanson, Rodney Woodruff, Anton Mazkovoi, Ramarao Kanneganti, Matt Payne, Curtis Miller, Nathan Levesque, Cos DiFazio, and Andy Dingley. Extra-special thanks go to Shai Erera for his technical editing. Thank you to all our MEAP readers who posted feedback on Manning's forums.

Michael McCandless

Writing a book is not easy. Writing a book about something as technically rich as Lucene is especially challenging. Writing a book about a successful, active, and fast moving open-source project is nearly impossible! Many things had to happen right for me to start and finish this book.

I would never have been part of this book without Doug having the initial itch, technical strength, and generosity to open-source his idea, without a vibrant community relentlessly pushing Lucene forward, without a forward-looking IBM supporting my involvement with Lucene and this book, and without Erik and Otis writing the first edition.

My four kids—Mia, Kyra, Joel, Kyle—always inspire me, with everything they do. Their boundless energy, free thinking, infinite series of insightful questions, amazing happiness, insatiable curiosity, gentle persistence, free sense of humor, sheer passion, temper tantrums, and sharp minds keep me very young at heart and inspire me to tackle big projects like this. You should strive, always, to remain a child.

I thank my wife, Jane, for convincing me to pursue this when Manning came knocking, and for her unmatched skills in efficiently running our busy family. Remarkably, she has made lots of time for me to work, write this book and still pursue all my crazy hobbies, and I can see that this ability is very rare.

My parents, all four of them, raised me with the courage to always stretch myself in what I try to tackle, but also with the discipline and persistence to finish what I start. They taught me integrity: if you commit to do something, you do it well. Always under-promise and overdeliver. They also led by example, showing me that individuals can do big things when they work hard. More importantly, they taught me that you should spend your life doing the things you love. Life is far too short to do otherwise.

Erik Hatcher

First, and really only, heartfelt thanks go to none other than Mike McCandless. He has pretty much single-handedly revised this book from its 1.0 release to the current spiffy "3.0" state. Mike approaches Lucene, this book, and life in general enthusiastically, with eagerness to tackle any task at hand. The first edition acknowledgments also very much apply here, as these influences are timelessly felt.

I personally thank Otis for his efforts with this book. Although we've yet to meet in person, Otis has been a joy to work with. He and I have gotten along well and have agreed on the structure and content on this book throughout. Thanks to Java Java in Charlottesville, Virginia, for keeping me wired and wireless; thanks, also, to Greenberry's for staying open later than Java Java and keeping me out of trouble by not having internet access (update: they now have wi-fi, much to the dismay of my productivity). The people I've surrounded myself with enrich my life more than anything. David Smith has been a life-long mentor, and his brilliance continues to challenge me; he gave me lots of food for thought regarding Lucene visualization (most of which I'm still struggling to fully grasp, and I apologize that it didn't make it into this manuscript). Jay Zimmerman and the No Fluff, Just Stuff symposium circuit have been dramatically influential for me. The regular NFJS speakers, including Dave Thomas, Stuart Halloway, James Duncan Davidson, Jason Hunter, Ted Neward, Ben

Galbraith, Glenn Vanderburg, Venkat Subramaniam, Craig Walls, and Bruce Tate, have all been a great source of support and friendship. Rick Hightower and Nick Lesiecki deserve special mention: they both were instrumental in pushing me beyond the limits of my technical and communication abilities. Words do little to express the tireless enthusiasm and encouragement Mike Clark has given me throughout writing *Lucene in Action*. Technically, Mike contributed the JUnitPerf performance-testing examples, but his energy, ambition, and friendship were far more pivotal. I extend gratitude to Darden Solutions for working with me through my tiring book and travel schedule and allowing me to keep a low-stress part-time day job. A Darden co-worker, Dave Engler, provided the CellPhone skeleton Swing application that I've demonstrated at NFJS sessions and JavaOne; thanks, Dave! Other Darden coworkers, Andrew Shannon and Nick Skriloff, gave us insight into Verity, a competitive solution to using Lucene. Amy Moore provided graphical insight. My great friend Davie Murray patiently endured several revision requests for a figure he created. Daniel Steinberg is a personal friend and mentor, and he allowed me to air Lucene ideas as articles at java.net. Simon Galbraith, a great friend and now a search guru, and I had fun bouncing search ideas around in email.

Otis Gospodnetić

I hate cheesy acknowledgments, but I really can't thank Margaret enough for being so supporting and patient with me. I owe her a lifetime supply of tea and rice. My parents Sanja and Vito opened my eyes early in my childhood by showing me as much of the world as they could, and that made a world of difference. They were also the ones who suggested I write my first book, which eliminated the fear of book-writing early in my life. Of course, I have to thank Doug Cutting, whose decision to open-source Lucene made a huge impact in my life, and to Michael McCandless for the amazing effort he has been putting into both *Lucene in Action, Second Edition* and Lucene. I think Mike actually has a few clones of him working 24/7 in his basement. No wonder I haven't met him in person yet!

about this book

Lucene in Action, Second Edition delivers details, best practices, caveats, tips, and tricks for using the best open-source search engine available.

This book assumes the reader is familiar with basic Java programming. Lucene's core itself is a single Java Archive (JAR) file, less than 1MB and with no dependencies, and integrates into the simplest Java stand-alone console program as well as the most sophisticated enterprise application.

Roadmap

We organized part 1 of this book to cover the core Lucene Application Programming Interface (API) in the order you're likely to encounter it as you integrate Lucene into your applications:

- In chapter 1, you meet Lucene. We introduce basic information-retrieval terminology and describe the components of modern search applications. Without wasting any time, we immediately build simple indexing and searching applications that you can put right to use or adapt to your needs. This example application opens the door for exploring the rest of Lucene's capabilities.
- Chapter 2 familiarizes you with Lucene's indexing operations. We describe the various field types and techniques for indexing numbers and dates. Tuning the indexing process, optimizing an index, using near real-time search and handling thread-safety are covered.
- Chapter 3 takes you through basic searching, including details of how Lucene ranks documents based on a query. We discuss the fundamental query types as

well as how they can be created through human-entered query expressions using Lucene's `QueryParser`.

- Chapter 4 delves deep into the heart of Lucene's indexing magic, the analysis process. We cover the analyzer building blocks including tokens, token streams, and token filters. Each of the built-in analyzers gets its share of attention and detail. We build several custom analyzers, showcasing synonym injection and metaphone (like soundex) replacement. Analysis of non-English languages is covered, with specific examples of analyzing Chinese text.

- Chapter 5 picks up where the searching chapter left off, with analysis now in mind. We cover several advanced searching features, including sorting, filtering, and term vectors. The advanced query types make their appearance, including the spectacular `SpanQuery` family. Finally, we cover Lucene's built-in support for querying multiple indexes, even in parallel.

- Chapter 6 goes well beyond advanced searching, showing you how to extend Lucene's searching capabilities. You'll learn how to customize search results sorting, extend query expression parsing, implement hit collecting, and tune query performance. Whew!

Part 2 goes beyond Lucene's built-in facilities and shows you what can be done around and above Lucene:

- In chapter 7, we show how to use Tika, another open-source project under the same Apache Lucene umbrella, to parse documents in many formats, in order to extract their text and metadata.

- Chapter 8 shows the important and popular set of extensions and tools around Lucene. Most of these are referred to as "contrib modules", in reference to the contrib subdirectory that houses them in Lucene's source control system. We start with Luke, an amazingly useful standalone tool for interacting with a Lucene index, and then move on to contrib modules that enable highlighting search terms and applying spelling correction, along with other goodies like non-English-language analyzers and several new query types.

- Chapter 9 covers additional functionality offered by Lucene's contrib modules, including chaining multiple filters together, storing an index in a Berkeley database, and leveraging synonyms from WordNet. We show two fast options for storing an index entirely in RAM, and then move on to xml-query-parser which enables creating queries from XML. We see how to do spatial searching with Lucene, and touch on a new modular `QueryParser`, plus a few odds and ends.

- Chapter 10 demonstrates how to access Lucene functionality from various programming languages, such as C++, C#, Python, Perl and Ruby.

- Chapter 11 covers the administrative side of Lucene, including how to understand disk, memory, and file descriptor usage. We see how to tune Lucene for various metrics like indexing throughput and latency, show you to make a hot backup of the index without pausing indexing, and how to easily take advantage of multiple threads during indexing and searching.

Part 3 (chapters 12, 13, and 14) brings all the technical details of Lucene back into focus with case studies contributed by those who have built interesting, fast, and scalable applications with Lucene at their core.

What's new in the second edition?

Much has changed in Lucene in the 5 years since this book was originally published. As is often the case with a successful open-source project with a strong technical architecture, a robust community of users and developers has thrived over time, and from all that energy has emerged a number of amazing improvements. Here's a sampling of the changes:

- Using near real-time searching
- Using Tika to extract text from documents
- Indexing with `NumericField` and performing fast numeric range querying with `NumericRangeQuery`
- Updating and deleting documents using `IndexWriter`
- Working with `IndexWriter`'s new transactional semantics (commit, rollback)
- Improving search concurrency with read-only `IndexReaders` and `NIOFS-Directory`
- Enabling pure Boolean searching
- Adding payloads to your index and using them with `BoostingTermQuery`
- Using `IndexReader.reopen` to efficiently open a new reader from an existing one
- Understanding resource usage, like memory, disk, and file descriptors
- Using Function queries
- Tuning for performance metrics like indexing and searching throughput
- Making a hot backup of your index without pausing indexing
- Using new ports of Lucene to other programming languages
- Measuring performance using the "benchmark" contrib package
- Understanding the new reusable `TokenStream` API
- Using threads to gain concurrency during indexing and searching
- Using `FieldSelector` to speed up loading of stored fields
- Using `TermVectorMapper` to customize how term vectors are loaded
- Understanding simplifications to Lucene's locking
- Using custom `LockFactory`, `DeletionPolicy`, `IndexDeletionPolicy`, `Merge-Policy`, and `MergeScheduler` implementations
- Using new contrib modules, like `XMLQueryParser` and Local Lucene search
- Debugging common problems

Entirely new case studies have been added, in Chapters 12, 13 and 14. A new chapter (11) has been added to cover the administrative aspects of Lucene. Chapter 7, which previously described a custom framework for parsing different document types, has been rewritten entirely based on Tika. In addition all code samples have been updated to Lucene's 3.0.1 APIs. And of course lots of great feedback from our readers has been folded in (thank you, and please keep it coming!).

Who should read this book?

Developers who need powerful search capabilities embedded in their applications should read this book. *Lucene in Action, Second Edition* is also suitable for developers who are curious about Lucene or indexing and search techniques, but who may not have an immediate need to use it. Adding Lucene know-how to your toolbox is valuable for future projects—search is a hot topic and will continue to be in the future.

This book primarily uses the Java version of Lucene (from Apache), and the majority of the code examples use the Java language. Readers familiar with Java will be right at home. Java expertise will be helpful; however, Lucene has been ported to a number of other languages including C++, C#, Python, and Perl. The concepts, techniques, and even the API itself are comparable between the Java and other language versions of Lucene.

Code examples

The source code for this book is available from Manning's website at http://www.manning.com/LuceneinActionSecondEdition or http://www.manning.com/hatcher3. Instructions for using this code are provided in the README file included with the source-code package.

The majority of the code shown in this book was written by us and is included in the source-code package, licensed under the Apache Software License (http://www.apache.org/licenses/LICENSE-2.0). Some code (particularly the case-study code, and the examples from Lucene's ports to other programming languages) isn't provided in our source-code package; the code snippets shown there are owned by the contributors and are donated as is. In a couple of cases, we have included a small snippet of code from Lucene's codebase, which is also licensed under Apache Software License 2.0.

Code examples don't include package and import statements, to conserve space; refer to the actual source code for these details. Likewise, in the name of brevity and keeping examples focused on Lucene's code, there are numerous places where we simply declare `throws Exception`, while for production code you should declare and catch only specific exceptions and implement proper handling when exceptions occur. In some cases there are fragments of code, inlined in the text, that are not full standalone examples; these cases are included in source files named Fragments.java, under each subdirectory.

Why JUnit?

We believe code examples in books should be top-notch quality and real-world applicable. The typical "hello world" examples often insult our intelligence and generally do little to help readers see how to really adapt to their environment.

We've taken a unique approach to the code examples in *Lucene in Action, Second Edition*. Many of our examples are actual JUnit test cases (http://www.junit.org), version 4.1. JUnit, the de facto Java unit-testing framework, easily allows code to assert that a particular assumption works as expected in a repeatable fashion. It also cleanly separates what we are trying to accomplish, by showing the small test case up front, from how we accomplish it, by showing the source code behind the APIs invoked by the test case. Automating JUnit test cases through an IDE or Ant allows one-step (or no steps with continuous integration) confidence building. We chose to use JUnit in this book because we use it daily in our other projects and want you to see how we really code. Test Driven Development (TDD) is a development practice we strongly espouse.

If you're unfamiliar with JUnit, please read the JUnit primer section. We also suggest that you read *Pragmatic Unit Testing in Java with JUnit* by Dave Thomas and Andy Hunt, followed by Manning's *JUnit in Action* by Vincent Massol and Ted Husted, a second edition of which is in the works by Petar Tahchiev, Felipe Leme, Vincent Massol, and Gary Gregory.

Code conventions and downloads

Source code in listings or in text is in a `fixed width font` to separate it from ordinary text. Java method names, within text, generally won't include the full method signature.

In order to accommodate the available page space, code has been formatted with a limited width, including line continuation markers where appropriate.

We don't include import statements and rarely refer to fully qualified class names—this gets in the way and takes up valuable space. Refer to Lucene's Javadocs for this information. All decent IDEs have excellent support for automatically adding import statements; Erik blissfully codes without knowing fully qualified classnames using IDEA IntelliJ, Otis and Mike both use XEmacs. Add the Lucene JAR to your project's classpath, and you're all set. Also on the classpath issue (which is a notorious nuisance), we assume that the Lucene JAR and any other necessary JARs are available in the classpath and don't show it explicitly. The lib directory, with the source code, includes JARs that the source code uses. When you run the ant targets, these JARs are placed on the classpath for you.

We've created a lot of examples for this book that are freely available to you. A .zip file of all the code is available from Manning's web site for *Lucene in Action*: http://www.manning.com/hatcher3. Detailed instructions on running the sample code are provided in the main directory of the expanded archive as a README file.

Our test data

Most of our book revolves around a common set of example data to provide consistency and avoid having to grok an entirely new set of data for each section. This example data consists of book details. Table 1 shows the data so that you can reference it and make sense of our examples.

The data, besides the fields shown in the table, includes fields for ISBN, URL, and publication month. When you unzip the source code available for download at

The data, besides the fields shown in the table, includes fields for ISBN, URL, and publication month. When you unzip the source code available for download at www.manning.com/hatcher3, the books are represented as *.properties files under the `data` sub-directory, and the command-line tool at `src/lia/common/Create-TestIndex.java` is used to create the test index used throughout the book. The fields for category and subject are our own subjective values, but the other information is objectively factual about the books.

Table 1 Sample data used throughout this book

Title / Author	Category	Subject
A Modern Art of Education Rudolf Steiner	/education/pedagogy	education philosophy psychology practice Waldorf
Lipitor, Thief of Memory Duane Graveline, Kilmer S. McCully, Jay S. Cohen	/health	cholesterol,statin,lipitor
Nudge: Improving Decisions About Health, Wealth, and Happiness Richard H. Thaler, Cass R. Sunstein	/health	information architecture,decisions,choices
Imperial Secrets of Health and Longevity Bob Flaws	/health/alternative/Chinese	diet chinese medicine qi gong health herbs
Tao Te Ching 道德經 Stephen Mitchell	/philosophy/eastern	taoism
Gödel, Escher, Bach: an Eternal Golden Braid Douglas Hofstadter	/technology/computers/ai	artificial intelligence number theory mathematics music
Mindstorms: Children, Computers, And Powerful Ideas Seymour Papert	/technology/computers/ programming/education	children computers powerful ideas LOGO education
Ant in Action Steve Loughran, Erik Hatcher	/technology/computers/ programming	apache ant build tool junit java development
JUnit in Action, Second Edition Petar Tahchiev, Felipe Leme, Vincent Massol, Gary Gregory	/technology/computers/ programming	junit unit testing mock objects
Lucene in Action, Second Edition Michael McCandless, Erik Hatcher, Otis Gospodnetić	/technology/computers/ programming	lucene search java
Extreme Programming Explained Kent Beck	/technology/computers/ programming/methodology	extreme programming agile test driven development methodology
Tapestry in Action Howard Lewis-Ship	/technology/computers/ programming	tapestry web user interface components
The Pragmatic Programmer Dave Thomas, Andy Hunt	/technology/computers/ programming	pragmatic agile methodology developer tools

Author Online

The purchase of *Lucene in Action, Second Edition* includes free access to a web forum run by Manning Publications, where you can discuss the book with the authors and other readers. To access the forum and subscribe to it, point your web browser to http://www.manning.com/LuceneinActionSecondEdition. This page provides information on how to get on the forum once you are registered, what kind of help is available, and the rules of conduct on the forum.

About the title

By combining introductions, overviews, and how-to examples, the *In Action* books are designed to help learning *and* remembering. According to research in cognitive science, the things people remember are things they discover during self-motivated exploration.

Although no one at Manning is a cognitive scientist, we are convinced that for learning to become permanent it must pass through stages of exploration, play, and, interestingly, re-telling of what is being learned. People understand and remember new things, which is to say they master them, only after actively exploring them. Humans learn *in action*. An essential part of an *In Action* guide is that it is example-driven. It encourages the reader to try things out, to play with new code, and explore new ideas.

There is another, more mundane, reason for the title of this book: our readers are busy. They use books to do a job or solve a problem. They need books that allow them to jump in and jump out easily and learn just what they want just when they want it. They need books that aid them *in action*. The books in this series are designed for such readers.

About the cover illustration

The figure on the cover of *Lucene in Action, Second Edition* is "An inhabitant of the coast of Syria." The illustration is taken from a collection of costumes of the Ottoman Empire published on January 1, 1802, by William Miller of Old Bond Street, London. The title page is missing from the collection and we have been unable to track it down to date. The book's table of contents identifies the figures in both English and French, and each illustration bears the names of two artists who worked on it, both of whom would no doubt be surprised to find their art gracing the front cover of a computer programming book?two hundred years later.

The collection was purchased by a Manning editor at an antiquarian flea market in the "Garage" on West 26th Street in Manhattan. The seller was an American based in Ankara, Turkey, and the transaction took place just as he was packing up his stand for the day. The Manning editor did not have on his person the substantial amount of cash that was required for the purchase and a credit card and check were both politely turned down.

With the seller flying back to Ankara that evening the situation was getting hope-less. What was the solution? It turned out to be nothing more than an old-fashioned verbal agreement sealed with a handshake. The seller simply proposed that the money be transferred to him by wire and the editor walked out with the seller's bank informa-tion on a piece of paper and the portfolio of images under his arm. Needless to say, we transferred the funds the next day, and we remain grateful and impressed by this unknown person's trust in one of us. It recalls something that might have happened a long time ago.

The pictures from the Ottoman collection, like the other illustrations that appear on our covers, bring to life the richness and variety of dress customs of two centuries ago. They recall the sense of isolation and distance of that period—and of every other historic period except our own hyperkinetic present.

Dress codes have changed since then and the diversity by region, so rich at the time, has faded away. It is now often hard to tell the inhabitant of one continent from another. Perhaps, trying to view it optimistically, we have traded a cultural and visual diversity for a more varied personal life. Or a more varied and interesting intellectual and technical life.

We at Manning celebrate the inventiveness, the initiative, and, yes, the fun of the computer business with book covers based on the rich diversity of regional life of two centuries ago—brought back to life by the pictures from this collection.

JUnit primer

This section is a quick and admittedly incomplete introduction to JUnit. We'll provide the basics needed to understand our code examples. First, JUnit test cases extend `junit.framework.TestCase`. Our concrete test classes adhere to a naming convention: we suffix class names with *Test*. For example, our `QueryParser` tests are in `Query-ParserTest.java`.

JUnit automatically executes all methods with the signature `public void test-XXX()`, where `XXX` is an arbitrary but meaningful name. JUnit test methods should be concise and clear, keeping good software design in mind (such as not repeating yourself, creating reusable functionality, and so on).

Assertions

JUnit is built around a set of `assert` statements, freeing you to code tests clearly and letting the JUnit framework handle failed assumptions and reporting the details. The most frequently used `assert` statement is `assertEquals`; there are a number of overloaded variants of the `assertEquals` method signature for various data types. An example test method looks like this:

```
public void testExample() {
 SomeObject obj = new SomeObject();
 assertEquals(10, obj.someMethod());
}
```

The `assert` methods throw a runtime exception if the expected value (10, in this example) isn't equal to the actual value (the result of calling `someMethod` on `obj`, in this example). Besides `assertEquals`, there are several other `assert` methods for convenience. We also use `assertTrue(expression)`, `assertFalse(expression)`, and `assertNull(expression)` statements. These test whether the expression is true, false, and null, respectively.

The `assert` statements have overloaded signatures that take an additional `String` parameter as the first argument. This `String` argument is used entirely for reporting purposes, giving the developer more information when a test fails. We use this `String` message argument to be more descriptive (or sometimes comical).

By coding our assumptions and expectations in JUnit test cases in this manner, we free ourselves from the complexity of the large systems we build and can focus on fewer details at a time. With a critical mass of test cases in place, we can remain confident and agile. This confidence comes from knowing that changing code, such as optimizing algorithms, won't break other parts of the system, because if it did, our automated test suite would let us know long before the code made it to production. Agility comes from being able to keep the codebase clean through refactoring. Refactoring is the art (or is it a science?) of changing the internal structure of the code so that it accommodates evolving requirements without affecting the external interface of a system.

JUnit in context

Let's take what we've said so far about JUnit and frame it within the context of this book. One of our test cases (from chapter 3) is shown here:

```
public class BasicSearchingTest extends TestCase {
  public void testTerm() throws Exception {
    IndexSearcher searcher;                          TestUtil provides
    Directory dir = TestUtil.getBookIndexDirectory();  directory
    searcher = new IndexSearcher(dir,
                      true);                    Create IndexSearcher

    Term t = new Term("subject", "ant");
    Query query = new TermQuery(t);
    TopDocs docs = searcher.search(query, 10);     One hit expected for
    assertEquals("Ant in Action", 1, docs.totalHits); search for "ant"

    t = new Term("subject", "junit");
    docs = searcher.search(new TermQuery(t), 10);  Two hits expected
    assertEquals(2, docs.totalHits);               for "junit"

    searcher.close();
  }
}
```

Of course, we'll explain the Lucene API used in this test case later. Here we'll focus on the JUnit details. The `TestUtil` class, from `lia/common/TestUtil.java`, contains a few utility methods used frequently throughout the book. Each time we use such a method for the first time, we show its source code. Here's `getBookIndexDirectory`:

```
public static String getBookIndexDirectory() {
  // The build.xml ant script sets this property for us:
  return System.getProperty("index.dir");
}
```

That method returns the path to where our sample data index resides in the filesystem. While we don't use it in this test, JUnit provides an initialization hook that executes prior to every test method; this hook is a method with the `public void setUp()` signature.

If our first `assert` in `testTerm` fails, we see an exception like this:

```
junit.framework.AssertionFailedError:
    Ant in Action expected:<1> but was:<0>
      at lia.searching.BasicSearchingTest.testTerm(BasicSearchingTest.java:20)
```

This failure indicates our test data is different than what we expect.

Testing Lucene

The majority of the tests in this book test Lucene itself. In practice, is this realistic? Isn't the idea to write test cases that test our own code, not the libraries themselves? There is an interesting twist to Test Driven Development used for learning an API: Test Driven Learning. It's immensely helpful to write tests directly to a new API in order to learn how it works and what you can expect from it. This is precisely what we've done in most of our code examples, so that tests are testing Lucene itself. Don't throw these learning tests away, though. Keep them around to ensure your expectations of the API hold true when you upgrade to a new version of the API, and refactor them when the inevitable API change is made.

Mock objects

In a couple of cases, we use mock objects for testing purposes. Mock objects are used as probes sent into real business logic in order to assert that the business logic is working properly. For example, in chapter 4, we have a `SynonymEngine` interface (see section 4.6). The real business logic that uses this interface is an analyzer. When we want to test the analyzer itself, it's unimportant what type of `SynonymEngine` is used, but we want to use one that has well defined and predictable behavior. We created a `MockSynonymEngine`, allowing us to reliably and predictably test our analyzer. Mock objects help simplify test cases such that they test only a single facet of a system at a time rather than having intertwined dependencies that lead to complexity in troubleshooting what really went wrong when a test fails. A nice effect of using mock objects comes from the design changes it leads us to, such as separation of concerns and designing using interfaces instead of direct concrete implementations.

about the authors

MICHAEL MCCANDLESS has been building search engines for over a decade. In 1999, with three other people, he founded iPhrase Technologies, a startup providing user-centric enterprise search engine software, written in Python and C++. After IBM acquired iPhrase in 2005, Michael became involved in Lucene and started contributing patches, becoming a committer in 2006 and PMC member in 2008. Michael received his B.S., M.S and Ph.D. from MIT, and now lives in Lexington, MA along with his wonderful wife, Jane, and four delightful kids, Mia, Kyra, Joel and Kyle. Michael's blog is at http://chbits.blogspot.com.

ERIK HATCHER codes, writes, and speaks on technical topics that he finds fun and challenging. He has written software for a number of diverse industries using many different technologies and languages. Erik coauthored *Java Development with Ant* (Manning, 2002) with Steve Loughran, a book that has received industry acclaim. Since the release of Erik's first book, he has spoken at numerous venues including the No Fluff, Just Stuff symposium circuit, JavaOne, O'Reilly's Open Source Convention, JavaZone, devoxx, user groups, and even sometimes webinars. As an Apache Software Foundation member, he is an active contributor and committer on several Apache projects including Lucene and Solr. Erik proudly presents his favorite technologies passionately, recently notables are Solr, Solritas, Flare, Blacklight, and solr-ruby—preferring to dabble at the intersection of user experiences and Solr. Erik cofounded Lucid Imagination, where he helps carry the torch for open-source search goodness. Erik keeps fit and serene in central Virginia.

OTIS GOSPODNETIĆ has been a Lucene developer since before Lucene became Apache Lucene. He is the co-founder of Sematext, a company that focuses on providing services and products around search (focusing on Lucene, Solr, and Nutch) and analytics (think BigData, Hadoop, etc.). Otis has given talks about Lucene and Solr over the years and some of his previous technical publications include articles about Lucene, published by O'Reilly Network and IBM developerWorks. Years ago, Otis also wrote *To Choose and Be Chosen: Pursuing Education in America*, a guidebook for foreigners wishing to study in the United States; it's based on his own experience. Otis currently lives in New York City where he runs the NY Search & Discovery Meetup.

Part 1

Core Lucene

The first half of this book covers out-of-the-box (errr… out of the JAR) Lucene. Chapter 1, "Meet Lucene," provides a general overview, and you'll develop a complete indexing and searching application. Each successive chapter systematically delves into specific areas. "Building a search index," chapter 2, and "Adding search to your application," chapter 3, are the first steps to using Lucene. Returning to a glossed-over indexing process, "Lucene's analysis process," chapter 4, will round out your understanding of what happens to the text indexed with Lucene.

After those four chapters you'll have a good sense of Lucene's basic capabilities. But searching is where Lucene really shines, and so this part concludes with two additional chapters on searching: chapter 5, "Advanced search techniques," using only the built-in features, and "Extending search," chapter 6, showcasing Lucene's extensibility for custom purposes.

Meet Lucene

1

This chapter covers

- Learning about Lucene
- Understanding the typical search application architecture
- Using the basic indexing API
- Working with the search API

Lucene is a powerful Java search library that lets you easily add search to any application. In recent years Lucene has become exceptionally popular and is now the most widely used information retrieval library: it powers the search features behind many websites and desktop applications. Although it's written in Java, thanks to its popularity and the determination of zealous developers you now have at your disposal a number of ports or integrations to other programming languages (C/C++, C#, Ruby, Perl, Python, and PHP, among others).

One of the key factors behind Lucene's popularity is its simplicity, but don't let that fool you: under the hood sophisticated, state-of-the-art information retrieval techniques are quietly at work. The careful exposure of its indexing and searching API is a sign of the well-designed software. You don't need in-depth knowledge about how Lucene's information indexing and retrieval work in order to start using it. Moreover, Lucene's straightforward API requires using only a handful of classes to get started. Finally, for those of you tired of bloatware, Lucene's core JAR is refreshingly tiny—only 1 MB—and it has no dependencies!

In this chapter we cover the overall architecture of a typical search application and where Lucene fits. It's crucial to recognize that Lucene is simply a search library, and you'll need to handle the other components of a search application (crawling, document filtering, runtime server, user interface, administration, etc.) as your application requires. We show you how to perform basic indexing and searching with ready-to-use code examples. We then briefly introduce all the core elements you need to know for both of these processes. We start with the modern problem of information explosion, to understand why we need powerful search functionality in the first place.

NOTE Lucene is an active open source project. By the time you read this, likely Lucene's APIs and features will have changed. This book is based on the 3.0.1 release of Lucene, and thanks to Lucene's backward compatibility policy, all code samples should compile and run fine for future 3.x releases. If you encounter a problem, send an email to java-user@lucene.apache.org and Lucene's large, passionate, and responsive community will surely help.

1.1   *Dealing with information explosion*

To make sense of the perceived complexity of the world, humans have invented categorizations, classifications, genuses, species, and other types of hierarchical organizational schemes. The Dewey decimal system for categorizing items in a library collection is a classic example of a hierarchical categorization scheme.

The explosion of the internet and digital repositories has brought large amounts of information within our reach. With time, the amount of data available has become so vast that we need alternate, more dynamic ways of finding information (see figure 1.1). Although we can classify data, trawling through hundreds or thousands of categories and subcategories of data is no longer an efficient method for finding information.

The need to quickly locate certain information out of the sea of data isn't limited to the internet realm—desktop computers store increasingly more data on multi-terabyte hard drives. Changing directories and expanding and collapsing hierarchies of folders isn't an effective way to access stored documents. Furthermore, we no longer use computers only for their raw computing abilities: they also serve as communication devices, multimedia players, and media storage devices. Those uses require the ability to quickly find a specific piece of data; what's more, we need to make rich media—such as images, video, and audio files in various formats—easy to locate.

With this abundance of information, and with time one of the most precious commodities for most people, we must be able to make flexible, free-form, ad hoc queries that can quickly cut across rigid category boundaries and find exactly what we're after while requiring the least effort possible.

To illustrate the pervasiveness of searching across the internet and the desktop, figure 1.1 shows a search for *lucene* at Google. Figure 1.2 shows the Apple Mac OS X

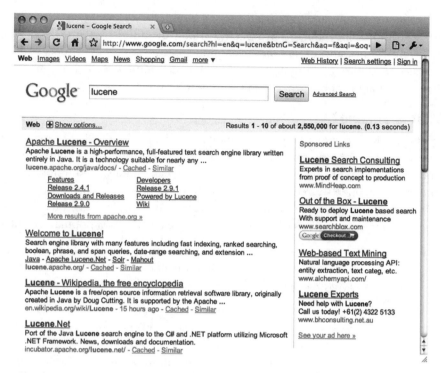

Figure 1.1 Searching the internet with Google

Finder (the counterpart to Microsoft's Explorer on Windows) and the search feature embedded at the upper right. The Mac OS X music player, iTunes, also has embedded search capabilities, as shown in figure 1.3.

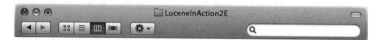

Figure 1.2 Mac OS X Finder with its embedded search capability

Search is needed everywhere! All major operating systems have embedded searching. The Spotlight feature in Mac OS X integrates indexing and searching across all file types, including rich metadata specific to each type of file, such as emails, contacts, and more.[1]

Figure 1.3 Apple's iTunes intuitively embeds search functionality.

---

[1] Erik and Mike freely admit to fondness of all things Apple.

Different people are fighting the same problem—information overload—using different approaches. Some have been working on novel user interfaces, some on intelligent agents, and others on developing sophisticated search tools and libraries like Lucene. Before we jump into action with code samples, we'll give you a high-level picture of what Lucene is, what it isn't, and how it came to be.

1.2   What is Lucene?

Lucene is a high-performance, scalable information retrieval (IR) library. IR refers to the process of searching for documents, information within documents, or metadata about documents. Lucene lets you add searching capabilities to your applications. It's a mature, free, open source project implemented in Java, and a project in the Apache Software Foundation, licensed under the liberal Apache Software License. As such, Lucene is currently, and has been for quite a few years, the most popular free IR library.

NOTE   Throughout the book, we'll use the term *information retrieval* (or its acronym *IR*) to describe search tools like Lucene. People often refer to IR libraries as *search engines*, but you shouldn't confuse IR libraries with web search engines.

As you'll soon discover, Lucene provides a simple yet powerful core API that requires minimal understanding of full-text indexing and searching. You need to learn about only a handful of its classes in order to start integrating Lucene into an application. Because Lucene is a Java library, it doesn't make assumptions about what it indexes and searches, which gives it an advantage over a number of other search applications. Its design is compact and simple, allowing Lucene to be easily embedded into desktop applications.

Beyond Lucene's core JAR are a number of extensions modules that offer useful add-on functionality. Some of these are vital to almost all applications, like the spellchecker and highlighter modules. These modules are housed in a separate area called contrib, and you'll see us referring to such contrib modules throughout the book. There are so many modules that we have two chapters, 8 and 9, to cover them!

Lucene's website, at http://lucene.apache.org/java, is a great place to learn more about the current status of Lucene. There you'll find the tutorial, Javadocs for Lucene's API for all recent releases, an issue-tracking system, links for downloading releases, and Lucene's wiki (http://wiki.apache.org/lucene-java), which contains many community-created and -maintained pages.

You've probably used Lucene without knowing it! Lucene is used in a surprisingly diverse and growing number of places: NetFlix, Digg, MySpace, LinkedIn, Fedex, Apple, Ticketmaster, SalesForce.com, the Encyclopedia Britannica CD-ROM/DVD, the Eclipse IDE, the Mayo Clinic, *New Scientist* magazine, Atlassian (JIRA), Epiphany, MIT's OpenCourseWare and DSpace, the Hathi Trust Digital Library, and Akamai's Edge-Computing platform. Your name may be on this list soon, too! The "powered by" Lucene page on Lucene's wiki has even more examples.

1.2.1 What Lucene can do

People new to Lucene often mistake it for a ready-to-use application like a file-search program, a web crawler, or a website search engine. That isn't what Lucene is: Lucene is a software library, a toolkit if you will, not a full-featured search application. It concerns itself with text indexing and searching, and it does those things very well. Lucene lets your application deal with business rules specific to its problem domain while hiding the complexity of indexing and searching behind a simple-to-use API. Lucene is the core that the application wraps around.

A number of full-featured search applications have been built on top of Lucene. If you're looking for something prebuilt or a framework for crawling, document handling, and searching, the "powered by" page on Lucene's wiki lists some of these options.

Lucene allows you to add search capabilities to your application. Lucene can index and make searchable any data that you can extract text from. Lucene doesn't care about the source of the data, its format, or even its language, as long as you can derive text from it. This means you can index and search data stored in files: web pages on remote web servers, documents stored in local file systems, simple text files, Microsoft Word documents, XML or HTML or PDF files, or any other format from which you can extract textual information.

Similarly, with Lucene's help you can index data stored in your databases, giving your users rich, full-text search capabilities that many databases provide only on a limited basis. Once you integrate Lucene, users of your applications can perform searches by entering queries like `+George +Rice -eat -pudding`, `Apple -pie +Tiger`, `animal:monkey AND food:banana`, and so on. With Lucene, you can index and search email messages, mailing-list archives, instant messenger chats, your wiki pages...the list goes on. Let's recap Lucene's history.

1.2.2 History of Lucene

Lucene was written by Doug Cutting;[2] it was initially available for download from its home at the SourceForge website. It joined the Apache Software Foundation's Jakarta family of high-quality open source Java products in September 2001 and became its own top-level Apache project in February 2005. It now has a number of subprojects, which you can see at http://lucene.apache.org. This book is primarily about the Java subproject, at http://lucene.apache.org/java, though many people refer to it simply as "Lucene."

With each release, the project has enjoyed increased visibility, attracting more users and developers. As of March 2010, the most recent release of Lucene is 3.0.1. Table 1.1 shows Lucene's release history.

---

[2] *Lucene* is Doug's wife's middle name; it's also her maternal grandmother's first name.

Table 1.1 Lucene's release history

Version	Release date	Milestones
0.01	March 2000	First open source release (SourceForge)
1.0	October 2000	
1.01b	July 2001	Last SourceForge release
1.2	June 2002	First Apache Jakarta release
1.3	December 2003	Compound index format, `QueryParser` enhancements, remote searching, token positioning, extensible scoring API
1.4	July 2004	Sorting, span queries, term vectors
1.4.1	August 2004	Bug fix for sorting performance
1.4.2	October 2004	`IndexSearcher` optimization and miscellaneous fixes
1.4.3	November 2004	Miscellaneous fixes
1.9.0	February 2006	Binary stored fields, `DateTools`, `NumberTools`, `RangeFilter`, `RegexQuery`; requires Java 1.4
1.9.1	March 2006	Bug fix in `BufferedIndexOutput`
2.0	May 2006	Removed deprecated methods
2.1	February 2007	Delete/update document in `IndexWriter`, locking simplifications, `QueryParser` improvements, benchmark contrib module
2.2	June 2007	Performance improvements, function queries, payloads, pre-analyzed fields, custom deletion policies
2.3.0	January 2008	Performance improvements, custom merge policies and merge schedulers, background merges by default, tool to detect index corruption, `IndexReader.reopen`
2.3.1	February 2008	Bug fixes from 2.3.0
2.3.2	May 2008	Bug fixes from 2.3.1
2.4.0	October 2008	Further performance improvements, transactional semantics (rollback, commit), `expungeDeletes` method, delete by query in `IndexWriter`
2.4.1	March 2009	Bug fixes from 2.4.0
2.9	September 2009	New per-segment Collector API, faster search performance, near real-time search, attribute-based analysis
2.9.1	November 2009	Bug fixes from 2.9
2.9.2	February 2010	Bug fixes from 2.9.1
3.0.0	November 2009	Removed deprecated methods, fixed some bugs
3.0.1	February 2010	Bug fixes from 3.0.0

NOTE Lucene's creator, Doug Cutting, has significant theoretical and practical experience in the field of IR. He's published a number of research papers on IR topics and has worked for companies such as Excite, Apple, Grand Central and Yahoo!. In 2004, worried about the decreasing number of web search engines and a potential monopoly in that realm, he created Nutch, the first open source World Wide Web search engine (http://lucene.apache.org/nutch); it's designed to handle crawling, indexing, and searching of several billion frequently updated web pages. Not surprisingly, Lucene is at the core of Nutch. Doug is also actively involved in Hadoop (http://hadoop.apache.org), a project that spun out of Nutch to provide tools for distributed storage and computation using the map/reduce framework.

Doug Cutting remains a strong force behind Lucene, and many more developers have joined the project with time. As of this writing, Lucene's core team includes about half a dozen active developers, three of whom are authors of this book. In addition to the official project developers, Lucene has a fairly large and active technical user community that frequently contributes patches, bug fixes, and new features.

One way to judge the success of open source software is by the number of times it's been ported to other programming languages. Using this metric, Lucene is quite a success! Although Lucene is written entirely in Java, as of this writing there are Lucene ports and bindings in many other programming environments, including Perl, Python, Ruby, C/C++, PHP, and C# (.NET). This is excellent news for developers who need to access Lucene indices from applications written in diverse programming languages. You can learn more about many of these ports in chapter 10.

To understand how Lucene fits into a search application, including what Lucene can and can't do, in the next rather large section we review the architecture of a "typical" modern search application.

1.3   *Lucene and the components of a search application*

It's important to grasp the big picture so that you have a clear understanding of which parts Lucene can handle and which parts your application must separately handle. A common misconception is that Lucene is an entire search application, when in fact it's simply the core indexing and searching component.

We'll see that a search application starts with an indexing chain, which in turn requires separate steps to retrieve the raw content; create documents from the content, possibly extracting text from binary documents; and index the documents. Once the index is built, the components required for searching are equally diverse, including a user interface, a means for building up a programmatic query, query execution (to retrieve matching documents), and results rendering.

Modern search applications have wonderful diversity. Some run quietly, as a small component deeply embedded inside an existing tool, searching a specific set of content (local files, email messages, calendar entries, etc.). Others run on a remote website, on a dedicated server infrastructure, interacting with many users via a web browser or mobile device, perhaps searching a product catalog or a known and clearly scoped set of documents. Some run inside a company's intranet and search a massive collection of documents visible inside the company. Still others index a large subset of the entire web and must deal with unbelievable scale both in content and in simultaneous search traffic. Yet despite all this variety, search engines generally share a common overall architecture, as shown in figure 1.4.

When designing your application, you clearly have strong opinions on what features are necessary and how they should work. Be forewarned: modern popular web search engines (notably Google) have pretty much set the baseline requirements that all users will expect the first time they interact with your search application. If your search can't meet this baseline, users will be disappointed right from the start. Google's spell correction is amazing, the dynamic summaries with highlighting under each result are accurate, and the response time is well under a second. When in doubt, look to Google for inspiration and guidance on which basic features your search application must provide. Imitation is the sincerest form of flattery!

Let's walk through a search application, one component at a time. As you're reading along, think through what your application requires from each of these components to understand how you could use Lucene to achieve your search goals. We'll also clearly point out which components Lucene can handle (the shaded boxes in figure 1.4) and which will be up to your application or other open source software. We'll then wrap up with a summary of Lucene's role in your search application.

Starting from the bottom of figure 1.4 and working up is the first part of all search engines, a concept called *indexing*: processing the original data into a highly efficient cross-reference lookup in order to facilitate rapid searching.

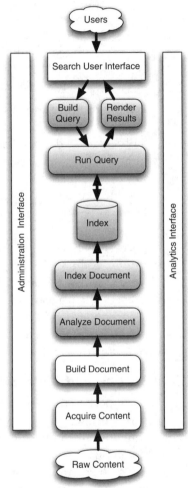

Figure 1.4   Typical components of search application; the shaded components show which parts Lucene handles.

1.3.1   Components for indexing

Suppose you need to search a large number of files, and you want to find files that contain a certain word or a phrase. How would you go about writing a program to do this? A naïve approach would be to sequentially scan each file for the given word or phrase. Although this approach would work, it has a number of flaws, the most obvious of which is that it doesn't scale to larger file sets or cases where files are very large. Here's where indexing comes in: to search large amounts of text quickly, you must first index that text and convert it into a format that will let you search it rapidly, eliminating the slow sequential scanning process. This conversion process is called *indexing*, and its output is called an *index*.

You can think of an index as a data structure that allows fast random access to words stored inside it. The concept behind it is analogous to an index at the end of a book, which lets you quickly locate pages that discuss certain topics. In the case of Lucene, an index is a specially designed data structure, typically stored on the file system as a set of index files. We cover the structure of separate index files in detail in appendix B, but for now think of a Lucene index as a tool that allows quick word lookup.

When you take a closer look, you discover that indexing consists of a sequence of logically distinct steps which we'll explore next. First, you must gain access to the content you need to search.

ACQUIRE CONTENT

The first step, at the bottom of figure 1.4, is to acquire content. This process, which involves using a crawler or spider, gathers and scopes the content that needs to be indexed. That may be trivial, for example, if you're indexing a set of XML files that resides in a specific directory in the file system or if all your content resides in a well-organized database. Alternatively, it may be horribly complex and messy if the content is scattered in all sorts of places (file systems, content management systems, Microsoft Exchange, Lotus Domino, various websites, databases, local XML files, CGI scripts running on intranet servers, and so forth).

Using entitlements (which means allowing only specific authenticated users to see certain documents) can complicate content acquisition, because it may require "superuser" access when acquiring the content. Furthermore, the access rights or access control lists (ACLs) must be acquired along with the document's content, and added to the document as additional fields used during searching to properly enforce the entitlements. We cover security filters during searching in section 5.6.7.

For large content sets, it's important that this component be efficiently incremental, so that it can visit only changed documents since it was last run. It may also be "live," meaning it's a continuously running service, waiting for new or changed content to arrive and loading that content the moment it becomes available.

Lucene, as a core search library, doesn't provide any functionality to support acquiring content. This is entirely up to your application, or a separate piece of software. A number of open source crawlers are available, among them the following:

- Solr (http://lucene.apache.org/solr), a sister project under the Apache Lucene umbrella, has support for natively ingesting relational databases and XML feeds, as well as handling rich documents through Tika integration. (We cover Tika in chapter 7.)
- Nutch (http://lucene.apache.org/nutch), another sister project under the Apache Lucene umbrella, has a high-scale crawler that's suitable for discovering content by crawling websites.
- Grub (http://www.grub.org) is a popular open source web crawler.
- Heritrix is Internet Archive's open source crawler (http://crawler.archive.org).
- Droids, another subproject under the Apache Lucene umbrella, is currently under Apache incubation at http://incubator.apache.org/droids.
- Aperture (http://aperture.sourceforge.net) has support for crawling websites, file systems, and mail boxes and for extracting and indexing text.
- The Google Enterprise Connector Manager project (http://code.google.com/p/google-enterprise-connector-manager) provides connectors for a number of nonweb repositories.

If your application has scattered content, it might make sense to use a preexisting crawling tool. Such tools are typically designed to make it easy to load content stored in various systems, and sometimes provide prebuilt connectors to common content stores, such as websites, databases, popular content management systems, and file systems. If your content source doesn't have a preexisting connector for the crawler, it's likely easy enough to build your own.

The next step is to create bite-sized pieces, called documents, out of your content.

BUILD DOCUMENT

Once you have the raw content that needs to be indexed, you must translate the content into the *units* (usually called *documents*) used by the search engine. The document typically consists of several separately named fields with values, such as *title, body, abstract, author,* and *url.* You'll have to carefully design how to divide the raw content into documents and fields as well as how to compute the value for each of those fields. Often the approach is obvious: one email message becomes one document, or one PDF file or web page is one document. But sometimes it's less clear: how should you handle attachments on an email message? Should you glom together all text extracted from the attachments into a single document, or make separate documents, somehow linked back to the original email message, for each attachment?

Once you've worked out this design, you'll need to extract text from the original raw content for each document. If your content is already textual in nature, with a known standard encoding, your job is simple. But more often these days documents are binary in nature (PDF, Microsoft Office, Open Office, Adobe Flash, streaming video and audio multimedia files) or contain substantial markups that you must remove before indexing (RDF, XML, HTML). You'll need to run document filters to extract text from such content before creating the search engine document.

Interesting business logic may also apply during this step to create additional fields. For example, if you have a large "body text" field, you might run semantic analyzers to pull out proper names, places, dates, times, locations, and so forth into separate fields in the document. Or perhaps you tie in content available in a separate store (such as a database) and merge this for a single document to the search engine.

Another common part of building the document is to inject boosts to individual documents and fields that are deemed more or less important. Perhaps you'd like your press releases to come out ahead of all other documents, all things being equal? Perhaps recently modified documents are more important than older documents? Boosting may be done statically (per document and field) at indexing time, which we cover in detail in section 2.5, or dynamically during searching, which we cover in section 5.7. Nearly all search engines, including Lucene, automatically statically boost fields that are shorter over fields that are longer. Intuitively this makes sense: if you match a word or two in a very long document, it's quite a bit less relevant than matching the same words in a document that's, say, three or four words long.

Lucene provides an API for building fields and documents, but it doesn't provide any logic to build a document because that's entirely application specific. It also doesn't provide any document filters, although Lucene has a sister project at Apache, Tika, which handles document filtering very well (see chapter 7). If your content resides in a database, projects like DBSight, Hibernate Search, LuSQL, Compass, and Oracle/Lucene integration make indexing and searching your tables simple by handling the Acquire Content and Build Document steps seamlessly.

The textual fields in a document can't be indexed by the search engine just yet. In order to do that, the text must first be analyzed.

ANALYZE DOCUMENT

No search engine indexes text directly: rather, the text must be broken into a series of individual atomic elements called *tokens*. This is what happens during the Analyze Document step. Each token corresponds roughly to a "word" in the language, and this step determines how the textual fields in the document are divided into a series of tokens. There are all sorts of interesting questions here: how do you handle compound words? Should you apply spell correction (if your content itself has typos)? Should you inject synonyms inlined with your original tokens, so that a search for "laptop" also returns products mentioning "notebook"? Should you collapse singular and plural forms to the same token? Often a stemmer, such as Dr. Martin Porter's Snowball stemmer (covered in section 8.2.1) is used to derive roots from words (for example, runs, running, and run, all map to the base form *run*). Should you preserve or destroy differences in case? For non-Latin languages, how can you even determine what a "word" is? This component is so important that we have a whole chapter, chapter 4, describing it.

Lucene provides an array of built-in analyzers that give you fine control over this process. It's also straightforward to build your own analyzer, or create arbitrary analyzer chains combining Lucene's tokenizers and token filters, to customize how tokens are created. The final step is to index the document.

INDEX DOCUMENT

During the indexing step, the document is added to the index. Lucene provides everything necessary for this step, and works quite a bit of magic under a surprisingly simple API. Chapter 2 takes you through all the nitty-gritty steps for performing indexing.

We're done reviewing the typical indexing steps for a search application. It's important to remember that indexing is something of a necessary evil that you must undertake in order to provide a good search experience: you should design and customize your indexing process only to the extent that you improve your users' search experience. We'll now visit the steps involved in searching.

1.3.2   *Components for searching*

Searching is the process of looking up words in an index to find documents where they appear. The quality of a search is typically described using *precision* and *recall* metrics. Recall measures how well the search system finds relevant documents; precision measures how well the system filters out the irrelevant documents. Appendix C describes how to use Lucene's benchmark contrib module to measure precision and recall of your search application.

You must consider a number of other factors when thinking about searching. We already mentioned speed and the ability to quickly search large quantities of text. Support for single and multiterm queries, phrase queries, wildcards, fuzzy queries, result ranking, and sorting are also important, as is a friendly syntax for entering those queries. Lucene offers a number of search features, bells, and whistles—so many that we had to spread our search coverage over three chapters (chapters 3, 5, and 6).

Let's work through the typical components of a search engine, this time working top down in figure 1.4, starting with the search user interface.

SEARCH USER INTERFACE

The user interface is what users actually see, in the web browser, desktop application, or mobile device, when they interact with your search application. The UI is the most important part of your search application! You could have the greatest search engine in the world under the hood, tuned with fabulous state-of-the-art functionality, but with one silly mistake, the UI will lack consumability, thus confusing your precious and fickle users who will then quietly move on to your competitors.

Keep the interface simple: don't present a lot of advanced options on the first page. Provide a ubiquitous, prominent search box, visible everywhere, rather than requiring a two-step process of first clicking a search link and then entering the search text (this is a common mistake).

Don't underestimate the importance of result presentation. Simple details, like failing to highlight matches in the titles and excerpts, or using a small font and cramming too much text into the results, can quickly kill a user's search experience. Be sure the sort order is clearly called out and defaults to an appropriate starting point (usually relevance). Be fully transparent: if your search application is doing something "interesting," such as expanding the search to include synonyms, using boosts to influence sort order, or automatically correcting spelling, say so clearly at the top of the search results and make it easy for the user to turn it off.

NOTE   The worst thing that can happen, and it happens quite easily, is to erode the user's trust in the search results. Once this happens, your users will quietly move on and you may never again have the chance to earn back that trust.

Most of all, eat your own dog food: use your own search application extensively. Enjoy what's good about it, but aggressively correct what's bad. Almost certainly your search interface should offer spell correction. Lucene has a contrib module, spellchecker, covered in section 8.5, that you can use. Likewise, providing dynamic excerpts (sometimes called summaries) with hit highlighting under each search result is important, and Lucene's contrib directory offers two such modules, highlighter and fast vector highlighter, covered in sections 8.3 and 8.4, to handle this.

Lucene doesn't provide any default search UI; it's entirely up to your application to build one. Once a user interacts with your search interface, she or he submits a search request, which first must be translated into an appropriate Query object for the search engine.

BUILD QUERY

When you manage to entice a user to use your search application, she or he issues a search request, often as the result of an HTML form or Ajax request submitted by a browser to your server. You must then translate the request into the search engine's Query object. We call this the Build Query step.

Query objects can be simple or complex. Lucene provides a powerful package, called QueryParser, to process the user's text into a query object according to a common search syntax. We'll cover QueryParser and its syntax in chapter 3, but it's also fully described at http://lucene.apache.org/java/3_0_0/queryparsersyntax.html. The query may contain Boolean operations, phrase queries (in double quotes), or wildcard terms. If your application has further controls on the search UI, or further interesting constraints, you must implement logic to translate this into the equivalent query. For example, if there are entitlement constraints that restrict which set of documents each user is allowed to search, you'll need to set up filters on the query, which we visit in section 5.6.

Many applications will at this point also modify the search query so as to boost or filter for important things, if the boosting wasn't done during indexing. Often an e-commerce site will boost categories of products that are more profitable, or filter out products presently out of stock (so you don't see that they're out of stock and then go elsewhere to buy them). Resist the temptation to heavily boost and filter the search results: users will catch on and lose trust.

Lucene's default QueryParser is often sufficient for an application. Sometimes, you'll want to use the output of QueryParser but then add your own logic afterward to further refine the query object. Still other times you want to customize the QueryParser's syntax, or customize which Query instances it actually creates, which, thanks to Lucene's open source nature, is straightforward. We discuss customizing QueryParser in section 6.3. Now, you're ready to execute the search request to retrieve results.

SEARCH QUERY

Search Query is the process of consulting the search index and retrieving the documents matching the Query, sorted in the requested sort order. This component covers the complex inner workings of the search engine, and Lucene handles all of it for you. Lucene is also wonderfully extensible at this point, so if you'd like to customize how results are gathered, filtered, sorted, and so forth, it's straightforward. See chapter 6 for details.

There are three common theoretical models of search:

- *Pure Boolean model*—Documents either match or don't match the provided query, and no scoring is done. In this model there are no relevance scores associated with matching documents, and the matching documents are unordered; a query simply identifies a subset of the overall corpus as matching the query.
- *Vector space model*—Both queries and documents are modeled as vectors in a high dimensional space, where each unique term is a dimension. Relevance, or similarity, between a query and a document is computed by a vector distance measure between these vectors.
- *Probabilistic model*—In this model, you compute the probability that a document is a good match to a query using a full probabilistic approach.

Lucene's approach combines the vector space and pure Boolean models, and offers you controls to decide which model you'd like to use on a search-by-search basis. Finally, Lucene returns documents that you next must render in a consumable way for your users.

RENDER RESULTS

Once you have the raw set of documents that match the query, sorted in the right order, you then render them to the user in an intuitive, consumable manner. The UI should also offer a clear path for follow-on searches or actions, such as clicking to the next page, refining the search, or finding documents similar to one of the matches, so that the user never hits a dead end.

We've finished reviewing the components of both the indexing and searching paths in a search application, but we aren't done. Search applications also often require ongoing administration.

1.3.3   *The rest of the search application*

There's still quite a bit more to a typical fully functional search engine, especially a search engine running on a website. You must include administration, in order to keep track of the application's health, configure the different components, and start and stop servers. You must also include analytics, allowing you to use different views to see how your users are searching, thus giving you the necessary guidance on what's working and what's not. Finally, for large search applications, scaling—so that your application can handle larger and larger content sizes as well as higher and higher numbers of simultaneous search queries—is a very important feature. Spanning the left side of figure 1.4 is the administration interface.

ADMINISTRATION INTERFACE

A modern search engine is a complex piece of software and has numerous controls that need configuration. If you're using a crawler to discover your content, the administration interface should let you set the starting URLs, create rules to scope which sites the crawler should visit or which document types it should load, set how quickly it's allowed to read documents, and so forth. Starting and stopping servers, managing replication (if it's a high-scale search, or if high availability failover is required), culling search logs, checking overall system health, and creating and restoring from backups are all examples of what an administration interface might offer.

Lucene has a number of configuration options that an administration interface would expose. During indexing you may need to tune the size of the RAM buffer, how many segments to merge at once, how often to commit changes, or when to optimize and purge deletes from the index. We'll cover these topics in detail in chapter 2. Searching also has important administration options, such as how often to reopen the reader. You'll probably also want to expose some basic summary information of the index, such as segment and pending deletion counts. If some documents failed to be indexed properly, or queries hit exceptions while searching, your administration API would detail them.

Many search applications, such as desktop search, don't require this component, whereas a full enterprise search application may have a complex administration interface. Often the interface is primarily web based, but it may also consist of additional command-line tools. On the right side of figure 1.4 is the analytics interface.

ANALYTICS INTERFACE

Spanning the right side is the analytics interface, which is often a web-based UI, perhaps running under a separate server hosting a reporting engine. Analytics is important: you can gain a lot of intelligence about your users and why they do or do not buy your widgets through your website, by looking for patterns in the search logs. Some would say this is the most important reason to deploy a good search engine! If you run an e-commerce website, incredibly powerful tools—that let you see how your users run searches, which searches failed to produce satisfactory results, which results users clicked on, and how often a purchase followed or did not follow a search—enable you to optimize the buying experience of your users.

Lucene-specific metrics that could feed the analytics interface include:

- How often which kinds of queries (single term, phrase, Boolean queries, etc.) are run
- Queries that hit low relevance
- Queries where the user didn't click on any results (if your application tracks click-throughs)
- How often users are sorting by specified fields instead of relevance
- The breakdown of Lucene's search time

You may also want to see indexing metrics, such as documents indexed per second or byte size of documents being indexed.

Lucene, since it's a search library, doesn't provide any analytics tools. If your search application is web based, Google Analytics is a fast way to create an analytics interface. If that doesn't fit your needs, you can also build your own custom charts based on Google's visualization API. The final topic we visit is scaling.

SCALING

One particularly tricky area is scaling of your search application. The vast majority of search applications don't have enough content or simultaneous search traffic to require scaling beyond a single computer. Lucene indexing and searching through-put allows for a sizable amount of content on a single modern computer. Still, such applications may want to run two identical computers to ensure there's no single point of failure (no downtime) in the event of hardware failure. This approach also enables you to pull one computer out of production to perform maintenance and upgrades without affecting ongoing searches.

There are two dimensions to scaling: net amount of content, and net query throughput. If you have a tremendous amount of content, you must divide it into shards, so that a separate computer searches each shard. A front-end server sends a single incoming query to all shards, and then coalesces the results into a single result set. If instead you have high search throughput during your peak traffic, you'll have to take the same index and replicate it across multiple computers. A front-end load balancer sends each incoming query to the least loaded back-end computer. If you require both dimensions of scaling, as a web scale search engine will, you combine both of these practices.

A number of complexities are involved in building such an architecture. You'll need a reliable way of replicating the search index across computers. If a computer has some downtime, planned or not, you need a way to bring it up-to-date before putting it back into production. If there are transactional requirements, so that all searchers must "go live" on a new index commit simultaneously, that adds complexity. Error recovery in a distributed setting can be complex. Finally, important functionality like spell correction and highlighting, and even how term weights are computed for scoring, are impacted by such a distributed architecture.

Lucene provides no facilities for scaling. However, both Solr and Nutch, projects under the Apache Lucene umbrella, provide support for index sharding and replication. The Katta open source project, hosted at http://katta.sourceforge.net and based on Lucene, also provides this functionality. Elastic search, at http://www.elastic-search.com, is another option that's also open source and based on Lucene. Before you build your own approach, it's best to have a solid look at these existing solutions.

We've finished reviewing the components of a modern search application. Now it's time to think about whether Lucene is a fit for your application.

1.3.4   *Where Lucene fits into your application*

As you've seen, a modern search application can require many components. Yet the needs of a specific application from each of these components vary greatly. Lucene covers many of these components well (the gray shaded ones from figure 1.4), but other components are best covered by complementary open source software or by your own custom application logic. It's possible your application is specialized enough to not require certain components. You should at this point have a good sense of what we mean when we say Lucene is a search library, not a full application.

If Lucene isn't a direct fit, it's likely one of the open source projects that complements or builds upon Lucene does fit. For example, Solr runs within an application server and exposes an administration interface, both dimensions of scaling, the ability to index content from a database, and important end-user functionality like faceted navigation, all built on top of Lucene. Lucene is the search library whereas Solr provides most components of an entire search application.

In addition, some web application frameworks also provide search plug-ins based on Lucene. For example, there's a searchable plug-in for Grails (http://www.grails.org/Searchable+Plugin), based on the Compass Search Engine Framework, which in turn uses Lucene under the hood.

Now let's see a concrete example of using Lucene for indexing and searching.

1.4   *Lucene in action: a sample application*

It's time to see Lucene in action. To do that, recall the problem of indexing and searching files, which we described in section 1.3. To show you Lucene's indexing and searching capabilities, we'll use a pair of command-line applications: Indexer and Searcher. First we'll index files in a directory; then we'll search the created index.

These example applications will familiarize you with Lucene's API, its ease of use, and its power. The code listings are complete, ready-to-use command-line programs. If file indexing/searching is the problem you need to solve, you can copy the code listings and tweak them to suit your needs. In the chapters that follow, we'll describe each aspect of Lucene's use in much greater detail.

Before we can search with Lucene, we need to build an index, so we start with our Indexer application.

1.4.1   *Creating an index*

In this section you'll see a simple class called `Indexer`, which indexes all files in a directory ending with the .txt extension. When Indexer completes execution, it leaves behind a Lucene index for its sibling, Searcher (presented next in section 1.4.2).

We don't expect you to be familiar with the few Lucene classes and methods used in this example—we'll explain them shortly. After the annotated code listing, we show you how to use Indexer; if it helps you to learn how Indexer is used before you see how it's coded, go directly to the usage discussion that follows the code.

USING INDEXER TO INDEX TEXT FILES

Listing 1.1 shows the Indexer command-line program, originally written for Erik's introductory Lucene article on java.net. It takes two arguments:

- A path to a directory where we store the Lucene index
- A path to a directory that contains the files we want to index

Listing 1.1   Indexer, which indexes .txt files

```
public class Indexer {

  public static void main(String[] args) throws Exception {
    if (args.length != 2) {
      throw new IllegalArgumentException("Usage: java " +
  Indexer.class.getName()
        + " <index dir> <data dir>");
    }
    String indexDir = args[0];
    String dataDir = args[1];

    long start = System.currentTimeMillis();
    Indexer indexer = new Indexer(indexDir);
    int numIndexed;
    try {
      numIndexed = indexer.index(dataDir, new TextFilesFilter());
    } finally {
      indexer.close();
    }
    long end = System.currentTimeMillis();

    System.out.println("Indexing " + numIndexed + " files took "
      + (end - start) + " milliseconds");
  }

  private IndexWriter writer;

  public Indexer(String indexDir) throws IOException {
    Directory dir = FSDirectory.open(new File(indexDir));
    writer = new IndexWriter(dir,
              new StandardAnalyzer(
                Version.LUCENE_30),
              true,
              IndexWriter.MaxFieldLength.UNLIMITED);
  }

  public void close() throws IOException {
    writer.close();
  }

  public int index(String dataDir, FileFilter filter)
    throws Exception {

    File[] files = new File(dataDir).listFiles();

    for (File f: files) {
      if (!f.isDirectory() &&
          !f.isHidden() &&
          f.exists() &&
          f.canRead() &&
          (filter == null || filter.accept(f))) {
        indexFile(f);
      }
    }

    return writer.numDocs();
  }
```

❶ Create index in this directory

❷ Index *.txt files from this directory

❸ Create Lucene IndexWriter

❹ Close IndexWriter

❺ Return number of documents indexed

```
private static class TextFilesFilter implements FileFilter {
  public boolean accept(File path) {
    return path.getName().toLowerCase()
          .endsWith(".txt");
  }
}

protected Document getDocument(File f) throws Exception {
  Document doc = new Document();
  doc.add(new Field("contents", new FileReader(f)));
  doc.add(new Field("filename", f.getName(),
          Field.Store.YES, Field.Index.NOT_ANALYZED));
  doc.add(new Field("fullpath", f.getCanonicalPath(),
          Field.Store.YES, Field.Index.NOT_ANALYZED));
  return doc;
}

private void indexFile(File f) throws Exception {
  System.out.println("Indexing " + f.getCanonicalPath());
  Document doc = getDocument(f);
  writer.addDocument(doc);
}
}
```

6 Index .txt files only, using FileFilter

7 Index file content

8 Index filename

9 Index file full path

10 Add document to Lucene index

Indexer is simple. The static main method parses **1**, **2** the incoming arguments, creates an Indexer instance, locates **6** *.txt in the provided data directory, and prints how many documents were indexed and how much time was required. The code involving the Lucene APIs includes creating **3** and closing **4** the IndexWriter, creating **7**, **8**, **9** the document, adding **10** the document to the index, and returning the number of documents indexed **5**.

This example intentionally focuses on plain text files with .txt extensions to keep things simple, while demonstrating Lucene's usage and power. In chapter 7, we'll show you how to index other common document types, such as Microsoft Word or Adobe PDF, using the Tika framework. Before seeing how to run Indexer, let's talk a bit about the Version parameter you see as the first argument to StandardAnalyzer.

VERSION PARAMETER

As of version 2.9, a number of classes now accept a parameter of type Version (from the org.apache.lucene.util package) during construction. This class defines enum constants, such as LUCENE_24 and LUCENE_29, referencing Lucene's minor releases. When you pass one of these values, it instructs Lucene to match the settings and behavior of that particular release. Lucene will also emulate bugs present in that release and fixed in later releases, if the Lucene developers felt that fixing the bug would break backward compatibility of existing indexes. For each class that accepts a Version parameter, you'll have to consult the Javadocs to see what settings and bugs are changed across versions. All examples in this book use LUCENE_30.

Although some may see the Version argument as polluting Lucene's API, it is in fact a demonstration of both Lucene's maturity and how seriously the Lucene developers take backward compatibility. The Version parameter gives Lucene the freedom to fix bugs and improve default settings for new users, over time, while still achieving backward compatibility when it's important. It also places the choice—latest and greatest versus strict backward compatibility—in your hands.

Let's use Indexer to build our first Lucene search index!

RUNNING INDEXER

The simplest way to run Indexer is to use Apache Ant. You'll first have to unpack the zip file containing source code with this book, which you can download from Manning's site at http://www.manning.com/hatcher3, and change to the directory lia2e. If you don't see the file build.xml in your working directory, you're not in the right directory. If this is the first time you've run any targets, Ant will compile all the example sources, build the test index, and finally run Indexer, first prompting you for the index and document directory, in case you'd like to change the defaults. It's also fine to run Indexer using Java from the command line; just ensure your classpath includes the JARs under the lib subdirectory as well as the build/classes directory.

By default the index will be placed under the subdirectory indexes/MeetLucene, and the sample documents under the directory src/lia/meetlucene/data will be indexed. This directory contains a sampling of modern open source licenses.

Go ahead and type ant Indexer, and you should see output like this:

```
% ant Indexer

Index *.txt files in a directory into a Lucene index.
Use the Searcher target to search this index.

Indexer is covered in the "Meet Lucene" chapter.

Press return to continue...

Directory for new Lucene index: [indexes/MeetLucene]

Directory with .txt files to index: [src/lia/meetlucene/data]

Overwrite indexes/MeetLucene? (y, n) y
Running lia.meetlucene.Indexer...
Indexing /Users/mike/lia2e/src/lia/meetlucene/data/apache1.0.txt
Indexing /Users/mike/lia2e/src/lia/meetlucene/data/apache1.1.txt
Indexing /Users/mike/lia2e/src/lia/meetlucene/data/apache2.0.txt
Indexing /Users/mike/lia2e/src/lia/meetlucene/data/cpl1.0.txt
Indexing /Users/mike/lia2e/src/lia/meetlucene/data/epl1.0.txt
Indexing /Users/mike/lia2e/src/lia/meetlucene/data/freebsd.txt
Indexing /Users/mike/lia2e/src/lia/meetlucene/data/gpl1.0.txt
Indexing /Users/mike/lia2e/src/lia/meetlucene/data/gpl2.0.txt
Indexing /Users/mike/lia2e/src/lia/meetlucene/data/gpl3.0.txt
Indexing /Users/mike/lia2e/src/lia/meetlucene/data/lgpl2.1.txt
Indexing /Users/mike/lia2e/src/lia/meetlucene/data/lgpl3.txt
Indexing /Users/mike/lia2e/src/lia/meetlucene/data/lpgl2.0.txt
Indexing /Users/mike/lia2e/src/lia/meetlucene/data/mit.txt
Indexing /Users/mike/lia2e/src/lia/meetlucene/data/mozilla1.1.txt
Indexing /Users/mike/lia2e/src/lia/meetlucene/data/
➥ mozilla_eula_firefox3.txt
Indexing /Users/mike/lia2e/src/lia/meetlucene/data/
➥ mozilla_eula_thunderbird2.txt
Indexing 16 files took 757 milliseconds

BUILD SUCCESSFUL
```

Indexer prints the names of files it indexes, so you can see that it indexes only files with the .txt extension. When it completes indexing, Indexer prints the number of files it indexed and the time it took to do so. Because the reported time includes both file-directory listing and indexing, you shouldn't consider it an official performance measure. In our example, each of the indexed files was small, but roughly 0.8 seconds to index a handful of text files is reasonably impressive. Indexing throughput is clearly important, and we cover it extensively in chapter 11. But generally, searching is far more important since an index is built once but searched many times.

1.4.2 Searching an index

Searching in Lucene is as fast and simple as indexing; the power of this functionality is astonishing, as chapters 3, 5, and 6 will show you. For now, let's look at Searcher, a command-line program that we'll use to search the index created by Indexer. Keep in mind that our Searcher serves the purpose of demonstrating the use of Lucene's search API. Your search application could also take the form of a web or desktop application with a GUI, a web application, and so on.

In the previous section, we indexed a directory of text files. The index in this example resides in a directory of its own on the file system. We instructed Indexer to create a Lucene index in the indexes/MeetLucene directory, relative to the directory from which we invoked Indexer. As you saw in listing 1.1, this index contains the indexed contents of each file, along with the absolute path. Now we need to use Lucene to search that index in order to find files that contain a specific piece of text. For instance, we may want to find all files that contain the keyword *patent* or *redistribute*, or we may want to find files that include the phrase *modified version*. Let's do some searching now.

USING SEARCHER TO IMPLEMENT A SEARCH

The Searcher program, originally written for Erik's introductory Lucene article on java.net, complements Indexer and provides command-line searching capability. Listing 1.2 shows Searcher in its entirety. It takes two command-line arguments:

- The path to the index created with Indexer
- A query to use to search the index

Listing 1.2 Searcher, which searches a Lucene index

```
public class Searcher {

  public static void main(String[] args) throws IllegalArgumentException,
        IOException, ParseException {
    if (args.length != 2) {
      throw new IllegalArgumentException("Usage: java " +
      Searcher.class.getName()
        + " <index dir> <query>");
    }

    String indexDir = args[0];
    String q = args[1];
```

❶ Parse provided index directory

❷ Parse provided query string

```
    search(indexDir, q);
  }

  public static void search(String indexDir, String q)
    throws IOException, ParseException {

    Directory dir = FSDirectory.open(new File(indexDir));      ❸ Open
    IndexSearcher is = new IndexSearcher(dir);                      index

    QueryParser parser = new QueryParser(Version.LUCENE_30,
                    "contents",                                ❹ Parse
                    new StandardAnalyzer(                          query
                      Version.LUCENE_30));
    Query query = parser.parse(q);
    long start = System.currentTimeMillis();               ❺ Search
    TopDocs hits = is.search(query, 10);                        index
    long end = System.currentTimeMillis();

    System.err.println("Found " + hits.totalHits +
      " document(s) (in " + (end - start) +                 ❻ Write
      " milliseconds) that matched query '" +                   search
      q + "':");                                                 stats

    for(ScoreDoc scoreDoc : hits.scoreDocs) {              ❼ Retrieve
      Document doc = is.doc(scoreDoc.doc);                     matching document
      System.out.println(doc.get("fullpath"));
    }                                                      ❽ Display
                                                              filename
    is.close();                          ❾ Close
  }                                         IndexSearcher
}
```

Searcher, like its Indexer sibling, is quite simple and has only a few lines of code dealing with Lucene:

❶ ❷ We parse command-line arguments (index directory, query string).

❸ We use Lucene's `Directory` and `IndexSearcher` classes to open our index for searching.

❹ We use `QueryParser` to parse a human-readable search text into Lucene's `Query` class.

❺ Searching returns hits in the form of a `TopDocs` object.

❻ Print details on the search (how many hits were found and time taken)

❼ ❽ Note that the `TopDocs` object contains only references to the underlying documents. In other words, instead of being loaded immediately upon search, matches are loaded from the index in a lazy fashion—only when requested with the Index-Searcher.doc(int) call. That call returns a `Document` object from which we can then retrieve individual field values.

❾ Close the `IndexSearcher` when we're done.

RUNNING SEARCHER

Let's run Searcher and find documents in our index using the query `'patent'`:

```
% ant Searcher

Search an index built using Indexer.
```

```
Searcher is described in the "Meet Lucene" chapter.

Press return to continue...

Directory of existing Lucene index built by
➥ Indexer:  [indexes/MeetLucene]

Query:  [patent]

Running lia.meetlucene.Searcher...
Found 8 document(s) (in 11 milliseconds) that
➥ matched query 'patent':
/Users/mike/lia2e/src/lia/meetlucene/data/cpl1.0.txt
/Users/mike/lia2e/src/lia/meetlucene/data/mozilla1.1.txt
/Users/mike/lia2e/src/lia/meetlucene/data/epl1.0.txt
/Users/mike/lia2e/src/lia/meetlucene/data/gpl3.0.txt
/Users/mike/lia2e/src/lia/meetlucene/data/apache2.0.txt
/Users/mike/lia2e/src/lia/meetlucene/data/lpgl2.0.txt
/Users/mike/lia2e/src/lia/meetlucene/data/gpl2.0.txt
/Users/mike/lia2e/src/lia/meetlucene/data/lgpl2.1.txt

BUILD SUCCESSFUL
Total time: 4 seconds
```

The output shows that 8 of the 16 documents we indexed with Indexer contain the word *patent* and that the search took a meager 11 milliseconds. Because Indexer stores files' absolute paths in the index, Searcher can print them. It's worth noting that storing the file path as a field was our decision and appropriate in this case, but from Lucene's perspective, it's arbitrary metadata included in the indexed documents.

You can use more sophisticated queries, such as 'patent AND freedom' or 'patent AND NOT apache' or '+copyright +developers', and so on. Chapters 3, 5, and 6 cover various aspects of searching, including Lucene's query syntax.

Our example indexing and searching applications give you a taste of what Lucene makes possible. Its API usage is simple and unobtrusive. The bulk of the code (and this applies to all applications interacting with Lucene) is plumbing relating to the business purpose—in this case, Indexer's parsing of command-line arguments and directory listings to look for text files and Searcher's code that prints matched filenames based on a query to the standard output. But don't let this fact, or the conciseness of the examples, tempt you into complacence: there's a lot going on under the covers of Lucene.

To effectively leverage Lucene, you must understand how it works and how to extend it when the need arises. The remainder of this book is dedicated to giving you these missing pieces.

Next we'll drill down into the core classes Lucene exposes for indexing and searching.

1.5 *Understanding the core indexing classes*

As you saw in our Indexer class, you need the following classes to perform the simplest indexing procedure:

- `IndexWriter`
- `Directory`
- `Analyzer`
- `Document`
- `Field`

Figure 1.5 shows how these classes each participate in the indexing process. What follows is a brief overview of each of these classes, to give you a rough idea of their role in Lucene. We'll use these classes throughout this book.

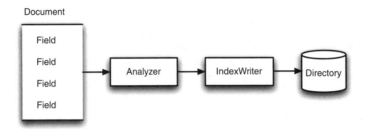

Figure 1.5   Classes used when indexing documents with Lucene

1.5.1   *IndexWriter*

`IndexWriter` is the central component of the indexing process. This class creates a new index or opens an existing one, and adds, removes, or updates documents in the index. Think of `IndexWriter` as an object that gives you write access to the index but doesn't let you read or search it. `IndexWriter` needs somewhere to store its index, and that's what `Directory` is for.

1.5.2   *Directory*

The `Directory` class represents the location of a Lucene index. It's an abstract class that allows its subclasses to store the index as they see fit. In our Indexer example, we used `FSDirectory.open` to get a suitable concrete `FSDirectory` implementation that stores real files in a directory on the file system, and passed that in turn to `Index-Writer`'s constructor.

Lucene includes a number of interesting `Directory` implementations, covered in section 2.10. `IndexWriter` can't index text unless it's first been broken into separate words, using an analyzer.

1.5.3   *Analyzer*

Before text is indexed, it's passed through an analyzer. The analyzer, specified in the `IndexWriter` constructor, is in charge of extracting those tokens out of text that should be indexed and eliminating the rest. If the content to be indexed isn't plain text, you should first extract plain text from it before indexing. Chapter 7 shows how to use Tika to extract text from the most common rich-media document formats. `Analyzer` is an abstract class, but Lucene comes with several implementations of it. Some of them deal with skipping *stop words* (frequently used words that don't help distinguish one document from the other, such as *a, an, the, in,* and *on*); some deal with conversion of tokens to lowercase letters, so that searches aren't case sensitive; and so on. Analyzers are an important part of Lucene and can be used for much more than simple input filtering. For a developer integrating Lucene into an application, the choice of analyzer(s) is a critical element of application design. You'll learn much more about them in chapter 4.

The analysis process requires a document, containing separate fields to be indexed.

1.5.4　*Document*

The `Document` class represents a collection of fields. Think of it as a virtual document—a chunk of data, such as a web page, an email message, or a text file—that you want to make retrievable at a later time. Fields of a document represent the document or metadata associated with that document. The original source (such as a database record, a Microsoft Word document, a chapter from a book, and so on) of document data is irrelevant to Lucene. It's the text that you extract from such binary documents, and add as a `Field` instance, that Lucene processes. The metadata (such as author, title, subject and date modified) is indexed and stored separately as fields of a document.

NOTE　When we refer to a document in this book, we mean a Microsoft Word, RTF, PDF, or other type of a document; we aren't talking about Lucene's `Document` class. Note the distinction in the case and font.

Lucene only deals with text and numbers. Lucene's core doesn't itself handle anything but `java.lang.String`, `java.io.Reader`, and native numeric types (such as int or float). Although various types of documents can be indexed and made searchable, processing them isn't as straightforward as processing purely textual or numeric content. You'll learn more about handling nontext documents in chapter 7.

In our Indexer, we're concerned with indexing text files. So, for each text file we find, we create a new instance of the `Document` class, populate it with fields (described next), and add that document to the index, effectively indexing the file. Similarly, in your application, you must carefully design how a Lucene document and its fields will be constructed to match specific needs of your content sources and application.

A document is simply a container for multiple fields; `Field` is the class that holds the textual content to be indexed.

1.5.5　*Field*

Each document in an index contains one or more named fields, embodied in a class called `Field`. Each field has a name and corresponding value, and a bunch of options, described in section 2.4, that control precisely how Lucene will index the field's value. A document may have more than one field with the same name. In this case, the values of the fields are appended, during indexing, in the order they were added to the document. When searching, it's exactly as if the text from all the fields were concatenated and treated as a single text field.

You'll apply this handful of classes most often when using Lucene for indexing. To implement basic search functionality, you need to be familiar with an equally small and simple set of Lucene search classes.

1.6   *Understanding the core searching classes*

The basic search interface that Lucene provides is as straightforward as the one for indexing. Only a few classes are needed to perform the basic search operation:

- `IndexSearcher`
- `Term`
- `Query`
- `TermQuery`
- `TopDocs`

The following sections provide a brief introduction to these classes. We'll expand on these explanations in the chapters that follow, before we dive into more advanced topics.

1.6.1   *IndexSearcher*

`IndexSearcher` is to searching what `IndexWriter` is to indexing: the central link to the index that exposes several search methods. You can think of `IndexSearcher` as a class that opens an index in a read-only mode. It requires a `Directory` instance, holding the previously created index, and then offers a number of search methods, some of which are implemented in its abstract parent class `Searcher`; the simplest takes a `Query` object and an `int  topN` count as parameters and returns a `TopDocs` object. A typical use of this method looks like this:

```
Directory dir = FSDirectory.open(new File("/tmp/index"));
IndexSearcher searcher = new IndexSearcher(dir);
Query q = new TermQuery(new Term("contents", "lucene"));
TopDocs hits = searcher.search(q, 10);
searcher.close();
```

We cover the details of `IndexSearcher` in chapter 3, along with more advanced information in chapters 5 and 6. Now we'll visit the fundamental unit of searching, `Term`.

1.6.2   *Term*

A `Term` is the basic unit for searching. Similar to the `Field` object, it consists of a pair of string elements: the name of the field and the word (text value) of that field. Note that `Term` objects are also involved in the indexing process. However, they're created by Lucene's internals, so you typically don't need to think about them while indexing. During searching, you may construct `Term` objects and use them together with `TermQuery`:

```
Query q = new TermQuery(new Term("contents", "lucene"));
TopDocs hits = searcher.search(q, 10);
```

This code instructs Lucene to find the top 10 documents that contain the word *lucene* in a field named contents, sorting the documents by descending relevance. Because the TermQuery object is derived from the abstract parent class Query, you can use the Query type on the left side of the statement.

1.6.3 Query

Lucene comes with a number of concrete Query subclasses. So far in this chapter we've mentioned only the most basic Lucene Query: TermQuery. Other Query types are BooleanQuery, PhraseQuery, PrefixQuery, PhrasePrefixQuery, TermRangeQuery, NumericRangeQuery, FilteredQuery, and SpanQuery. All of these are covered in chapters 3 and 5. Query is the common, abstract parent class. It contains several utility methods, the most interesting of which is setBoost(float), which enables you to tell Lucene that certain subqueries should have a stronger contribution to the final relevance score than other subqueries. The setBoost method is described in section 3.5.12. Next we cover TermQuery, which is the building block for most complex queries in Lucene.

1.6.4 TermQuery

TermQuery is the most basic type of query supported by Lucene, and it's one of the primitive query types. It's used for matching documents that contain fields with specific values, as you've seen in the last few paragraphs. Finally, wrapping up our brief tour of the core classes used for searching, we touch on TopDocs, which represents the result set returned by searching.

1.6.5 TopDocs

The TopDocs class is a simple container of pointers to the top N ranked search results—documents that match a given query. For each of the top N results, TopDocs records the int docID (which you can use to retrieve the document) as well as the float score. Chapter 3 describes TopDocs in more detail.

1.7 Summary

In this chapter, you've gained some healthy background knowledge on the architecture of search applications, as well as some initial Lucene knowledge. You now know that Lucene is an information retrieval library, not a ready-to-use standalone product, and that it most certainly doesn't contain a web crawler, document filters, or a search user interface, as people new to Lucene sometimes think. However, as confirmation of Lucene's popularity, there are numerous projects that integrate with or build on Lucene, and that could be a good fit for your application. In addition, you can choose among numerous ways to access Lucene's functionality from programming environments other than Java. You've also learned a bit about how Lucene came to be and about the key people and the organization behind it.

In the spirit of Manning's *in Action* books, we showed you two real, standalone applications, Indexer and Searcher, which are capable of indexing and searching text files stored in a file system. We then briefly described each of the Lucene classes used in these two applications.

Search is everywhere, and chances are that if you're reading this book, you're interested in search becoming an integral part of your applications. Depending on your needs, integrating Lucene may be trivial, or it may involve challenging architectural considerations.

We've organized the next couple of chapters as we did this chapter. The first thing we need to do is index some documents; we discuss this process next in detail in chapter 2.

Building a search index

This chapter covers

- Performing basic index operations
- Boosting documents and fields during indexing
- Indexing dates, numbers, and sortable fields
- Advanced indexing topics

So you want to search files stored on your hard disk, or perhaps search your email, web pages, or even data stored in a database. Lucene can help you do that. But before you can search something, you'll have to index it, and Lucene will help you do that as well, as you'll learn in this chapter.

In chapter 1, you saw a simple indexing example. This chapter goes further and teaches you about index updates, parameters you can use to tune the indexing process, and more advanced indexing techniques that will help you get the most out of Lucene. Here you'll also find information about the structure of a Lucene index, important issues to keep in mind when accessing a Lucene index with multiple threads and processes, the transactional semantics of Lucene's indexing API, sharing an index over remote file systems, and the locking mechanism that Lucene employs to prevent concurrent index modification.

Despite the great detail we'll go into, don't forget the big picture: indexing is simply a means to an end. What matters is the search experience your applications present to your users; indexing is "merely" the necessary evil you must go through in order to enable a strong user search experience. So although there are fun details here about indexing, your time is generally better spent working on how to improve the search experience. In nearly every application, the search features are far more important than the details of indexing. That being said, implementing search features requires important corresponding steps during indexing, as you'll see here.

Be warned: this is a rather long chapter. The length is necessary because Lucene exposes many details of indexing. The good news is that most applications don't need to use any of Lucene's advanced indexing options. In fact, sections 2.1, 2.2, and 2.3 may be all that's needed for many applications, or to simply get started. If you're the curious type, and you just won't leave any stone unturned, or your application needs to use all the bells and whistles, the rest of this chapter is for you!

Let's begin now with Lucene's conceptual model for content.

2.1   How Lucene models content

Let's first walk through its conceptual approach to modeling content. We'll start with Lucene's fundamental units of indexing and searching, documents and fields, then move on to important differences between Lucene and the more structured model of modern databases.

2.1.1   Documents and fields

A document is Lucene's atomic unit of indexing and searching. It's a container that holds one or more fields, which in turn contain the "real" content. Each field has a name to identify it, a text or binary value, and a series of detailed options that describe what Lucene should do with the field's value when you add the document to the index. To index your raw content sources, you must first translate it into Lucene's documents and fields. Then, at search time, it's the field values that are searched; for example, users could search for "title:lucene" to find all documents whose title field value contains the term *lucene*.

At a high level, there are three things Lucene can do with each field:

- The value may be indexed (or not). A field must be indexed if you intend to search on it. Only text fields may be indexed (binary valued fields may only be stored). When a field is indexed, tokens are first derived from its text value, using a process called analysis, and then those tokens are enrolled into the index. See section 2.4.1 for options that control how the field's value is indexed.

- If it's indexed, the field may also optionally store term vectors, which are collectively a miniature inverted index for that one field, allowing you to retrieve all of its tokens. This enables certain advanced use cases, like searching for documents similar to an existing one (more uses are covered in section 5.7). See section 2.4.3 for options that control how term vectors are indexed.

- Separately, the field's value may be stored, meaning a verbatim copy of the unanalyzed value is written away in the index so that it can later be retrieved. This is useful for fields you'd like to present unchanged to the user, such as the document's title or abstract. See section 2.4.2 for options that control how the field's values are stored.

How you factor your raw content sources into Lucene's documents and fields is typically an iterative design process that's application dependent. Lucene couldn't care less which fields you use, what their names are, and so forth. Documents usually have quite a few fields, such as title, author, date, abstract, body text, URL, and keywords. Sometimes a catchall field is used, combining all text into a single field for searching. Once you've created your document, you add it to your index. Then, at search time, you can retrieve the documents that match each query and use their stored fields to present results to the end user.

Lucene is often compared to a database, because both can store content and retrieve it later. But there are important differences. The first one is Lucene's flexible schema.

NOTE When you retrieve a document from the index, only the stored fields will be present. For example, fields that were indexed but not stored won't be in the document. This behavior is frequently a source of confusion.

2.1.2 *Flexible schema*

Unlike a database, Lucene has no notion of a fixed global schema. In other words, each document you add to the index is a blank slate and can be completely different from the document before it: it can have whatever fields you want, with any indexing and storing and term vector options. It need not have the same fields as the previous document you added. It can even have the same fields, with different options, than in other documents.

This feature is quite powerful: it allows you to take an iterative approach to building your index. You can jump right in and index documents without having to predesign the schema. If you change your mind about your fields, start adding additional fields later on and then go back and reindex previously added documents, or rebuild the index.

Lucene's flexible schema also means a single index can hold documents that represent different entities. For instance, you could have documents that represent retail products with fields such as name and price, and documents that represent people with fields such as name, age, and gender. You could also include unsearchable "meta" documents, which simply hold metadata about the index or your application (such as what time the index was last updated or which product catalog was indexed) but are never included in search results.

The second major difference between Lucene and databases is that Lucene requires you to flatten, or denormalize, your content when you index it.

2.1.3   Denormalization

One common challenge is resolving any "mismatch" between the structure of your documents versus what Lucene can represent. For example, XML can describe a recursive document structure by nesting tags within one another. A database can have an arbitrary number of joins, via primary and secondary keys, relating tables to one other. Microsoft's Object Linking & Embedding (OLE) documents can reference other documents for embedding. Yet Lucene documents are flat. Such recursion and joins must be denormalized when creating your documents. Open source projects that build on Lucene, like Hibernate Search, Compass, LuSQL, DBSight, Browse Engine, and Oracle/Lucene integration, each has different and interesting approaches for handling this denormalization.

Now that you understand how Lucene models documents at a conceptual level, it's time to visit the steps of the indexing process at a high level.

2.2   *Understanding the indexing process*

As you saw in chapter 1, only a few methods of Lucene's public API need to be called in order to index a document. As a result, from the outside, indexing with Lucene looks like a deceptively simple and monolithic operation. But behind the simple API lies an interesting and relatively complex set of operations that we can break down into three major and functionally distinct groups, as described in the following sections and shown in figure 2.1.

During indexing, the text is first extracted from the original content and used to create an instance of `Document`, containing `Field` instances to hold the content. The text in the fields is then analyzed to produce a stream of tokens. Finally, those tokens are added to the index in a segmented architecture. Let's talk about text extraction first.

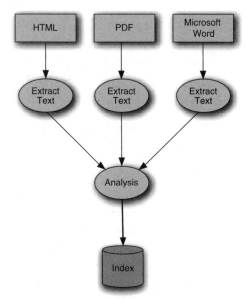

Figure 2.1   Indexing with Lucene breaks down into three main operations: extracting text from source documents, analyzing it, and saving it to the index.

2.2.1   *Extracting text and creating the document*

To index data with Lucene, you must extract plain text from it, the format that Lucene can digest, and then create a Lucene document. In chapter 1, we limited our examples to indexing and searching .txt files, which allowed us to easily slurp their content and use it to populate `Field` instances. But things aren't always that simple: the Build Document step from figure 1.4 has quite a bit of work hidden behind it.

Suppose you need to index a set of manuals in PDF format. To prepare these manuals for indexing, you must first find a way to extract the textual information from the PDF documents and use that extracted text to create Lucene documents and their fields. No methods would accept a PDF Java type, even if such a type existed. You face the same situation if you want to index Microsoft Word documents or any document format other than plain text. Even when you're dealing with XML or HTML documents, which use plain-text characters, you still need to be smart about preparing the data for indexing, to avoid indexing the XML elements or HTML tags and index only the real text.

The details of text extraction are in chapter 7 where we describe the Tika framework, which makes it almost too simple to extract text from documents in diverse formats. Once you have the text you'd like to index, and you've created a document with all fields you'd like to index, all text must then be analyzed.

2.2.2 *Analysis*

Once you've created Lucene documents populated with fields, you can call `Index-Writer`'s `addDocument` method and hand your data off to Lucene to index. When you do that, Lucene first analyzes the text, a process that splits the textual data into a stream of *tokens*, and performs a number of optional operations on them. For instance, the tokens could be lowercased before indexing, to make searches case insensitive, using Lucene's `LowerCaseFilter`. Typically it's also desirable to remove all stop words, which are frequent but meaningless tokens, from the input (for example *a, an, the, in, on*, and so on, in English text) using `StopFilter`. Similarly, it's common to process input tokens to reduce them to their roots, for example by using `Porter-StemFilter` for English text (similar classes exist in Lucene's contrib analysis module, for other languages). The combination of an original source of tokens, followed by the series of filters that modify the tokens produced by that source, make up the analyzer. You are also free to build your own analyzer by chaining together Lucene's token sources and filters, or your own, in customized ways.

This important step, covered under the Analyze Document step in figure 1.4, is called analysis. The input to Lucene can be analyzed in so many interesting and useful ways that we cover this process in detail in chapter 4. The analysis process produces a stream of tokens that are then written into the files in the index.

2.2.3 *Adding to the index*

After the input has been analyzed, it's ready to be added to the index. Lucene stores the input in a data structure known as an inverted index. This data structure makes efficient use of disk space while allowing quick keyword lookups. What makes this structure inverted is that it uses tokens extracted from input documents as lookup keys instead of treating documents as the central entities, much like the index of this book references the page number(s) where a concept occurs. In other words, rather than trying to answer the question "What words are contained in this document?" this structure is optimized for providing quick answers to "Which documents contain word *X*?"

If you think about your favorite web search engine and the format of your typical query, you'll see that this is exactly the query that you want to be as quick as possible. The core of today's web search engines are inverted indexes.

Lucene's index directory has a unique segmented architecture, which we describe next.

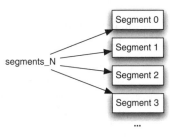

Figure 2.2 Segmented structure of a Lucene inverted index

INDEX SEGMENTS

Lucene has a rich and detailed index file format that has been carefully optimized with time. Although you don't need to know the details of this format in order to use Lucene, it's still helpful to have some basic understanding at a high level. If you find yourself curious about all the details, see appendix B.

Every Lucene index consists of one or more segments, as depicted in figure 2.2. Each segment is a standalone index, holding a subset of all indexed documents. A new segment is created whenever the writer flushes buffered added documents and pending deletions into the directory. At search time, each segment is visited separately and the results are combined.

Each segment, in turn, consists of multiple files, of the form _X.<ext>, where X is the segment's name and <ext> is the extension that identifies which part of the index that file corresponds to. There are separate files to hold the different parts of the index (term vectors, stored fields, inverted index, and so on). If you're using the compound file format (which is enabled by default but you can change using `Index-Writer.setUseCompoundFile`), then most of these index files are collapsed into a single compound file: _X.cfs. This reduces the number of open file descriptors during searching, at a small cost of searching and indexing performance. Chapter 11 covers this trade-off in more detail.

There's one special file, referred to as the *segments* file and named segments_<N>, that references all live segments. This file is important! Lucene first opens this file, and then opens each segment referenced by it. The value <N>, called "the generation," is an integer that increases by one every time a change is committed to the index.

Naturally, over time the index will accumulate many segments, especially if you open and close your writer frequently. This is fine. Periodically, `IndexWriter` will select segments and coalesce them by merging them into a single new segment and then removing the old segments. The selection of segments to be merged is governed by a separate `MergePolicy`. Once merges are selected, their execution is done by the `MergeScheduler`. These classes are advanced topics, covered in section 2.13.6.

Let's now walk through the basic operations (add, update, delete) you do when indexing.

2.3   *Basic index operations*

We've covered Lucene's conceptual approach to modeling documents, and then we described the logical steps of the indexing process. Now it's time to look at some real code, using Lucene's APIs to add, remove, and update documents. We start with adding documents to an index since that's the most frequent operation.

2.3.1 *Adding documents to an index*

Let's look at how to create a new index and add documents to it. There are two methods for adding documents:

- addDocument(Document)—Adds the document using the default analyzer, which you specified when creating the IndexWriter, for tokenization.
- addDocument(Document, Analyzer)—Adds the document using the provided analyzer for tokenization. But be careful! In order for searches to work correctly, you need the analyzer used at search time to "match" the tokens produced by the analyzers at indexing time. See section 4.1.2 for more details.

Listing 2.1 shows all the steps necessary to create a new index and add two tiny documents. In this example, the content for the documents is contained entirely in the source code as Strings, but in the real world the content for your documents would typically come from an external source. The setUp() method is called by the JUnit framework before every test.

Listing 2.1   Adding documents to an index

```
public class IndexingTest extends TestCase {
  protected String[] ids = {"1", "2"};
  protected String[] unindexed = {"Netherlands", "Italy"};
  protected String[] unstored = {"Amsterdam has lots of bridges",
                                 "Venice has lots of canals"};
  protected String[] text = {"Amsterdam", "Venice"};

  private Directory directory;

  protected void setUp() throws Exception {        ① Run before every test
    directory = new RAMDirectory();

    IndexWriter writer = getWriter();              ② Create
                                                     IndexWriter
    for (int i = 0; i < ids.length; i++)
    {                                              ③ Add documents
      Document doc = new Document();
      doc.add(new Field("id", ids[i],
                        Field.Store.YES,
                        Field.Index.NOT_ANALYZED));
      doc.add(new Field("country", unindexed[i],
                        Field.Store.YES,
                        Field.Index.NO));
      doc.add(new Field("contents", unstored[i],
                        Field.Store.NO,
                        Field.Index.ANALYZED));
      doc.add(new Field("city", text[i],
                        Field.Store.YES,
                        Field.Index.ANALYZED));
      writer.addDocument(doc);
    }
```

```
      writer.close();
    }                                                          Create IndexWriter  ❷
    private IndexWriter getWriter() throws IOException {
      return new IndexWriter(directory, new WhitespaceAnalyzer(),
                          IndexWriter.MaxFieldLength.UNLIMITED);
    }                                                          Create new searcher  ❹
    protected int getHitCount(String fieldName, String searchString)
      throws IOException {
      IndexSearcher searcher = new IndexSearcher(directory);
      Term t = new Term(fieldName, searchString);
      Query query = new TermQuery(t);                              Build simple
      int hitCount = TestUtil.hitCount(searcher, query);          single-term
      searcher.close();                                    ❺      query
      return hitCount;
    }                                      Get number of hits  ❻

    public void testIndexWriter() throws IOException {
      IndexWriter writer = getWriter();
      assertEquals(ids.length, writer.numDocs());
      writer.close();                                  Verify writer
    }                                              ❼  document count

    public void testIndexReader() throws IOException {
      IndexReader reader = IndexReader.open(directory);
      assertEquals(ids.length, reader.maxDoc());
      assertEquals(ids.length, reader.numDocs());  ❽  Verify reader
      reader.close();                                 document count
    }
  }
```

❶ The setUp() method first creates a new RAMDirectory, to hold the index.

❷ Next, it creates an IndexWriter on this Directory. We created the getWriter convenience method because we need to get the IndexWriter in many places.

❸ Finally, setUp() iterates over our content, creating a Document and Fields, and then adds the Document to the index.

❹ ❺ ❻ We create the IndexSearcher and execute a basic single-term query with the specified string, returning the number of documents that matched.

❼ ❽ We verify the documents counts according to IndexReader and IndexWriter matches how many documents we added.

The index contains two documents, each representing a country and a city in that country, whose text is analyzed with WhitespaceAnalyzer. Because setUp() is called before each test is executed, each test runs against a freshly created index.

In the getWriter method, we create the IndexWriter with three arguments:

- Directory, where the index is stored.
- The analyzer to use when indexing tokenized fields (analysis is covered in chapter 4).

- MaxFieldLength.UNLIMITED, a required argument that tells IndexWriter to index all tokens in the document (section 2.7 describes this setting in more detail).

IndexWriter will detect that there's no prior index in this Directory and create a new one. If there were an existing index, IndexWriter would simply add to it.

NOTE The IndexWriter constructors that don't take an explicit boolean create argument will first check whether an index already exists in the provided Directory. If one exists, IndexWriter will append to that index. Otherwise, it will create a new index in the Directory.

There are numerous IndexWriter constructors. Some explicitly take a create argument, allowing you to force a new index to be created over an existing one. More advanced constructors allow you to specify your own IndexDeletionPolicy or Index-Commit for expert use cases, as described in section 2.13.

Once the index is created, we construct each document using the for loop. It's quite simple: first we create a new empty Document, then one by one we add each Field we'd like to have on the document. Each document gets four fields, each with different options (Field options are described in section 2.4). Finally, we call writer.addDocument to index the document. After the for loop, we close the writer, which commits all changes to the directory. We could also have called commit(), which would commit the changes to the directory but leave the writer open for further changes.

Notice how we use the static method TestUtil.getHitCount to get the number of hits for a query. TestUtil is a utility class, included with the book's source code, that includes a small number of common methods that we reuse throughout the book. Its methods are self-explanatory, and as we use each for the first time we'll show you the source code. For example, this is the one-line method hitCount:

```
public static int hitCount(IndexSearcher searcher, Query query)
  throws IOException {
  return searcher.search(query, 1).totalHits;
}
```

This method runs the search and returns the total number of hits that matched. Next let's look at the opposite of adding documents: deleting them.

2.3.2 Deleting documents from an index

Although most applications are more concerned with getting documents into a Lucene index, some also need to remove them. For instance, a newspaper publisher may want to keep only the last week's worth of news in its searchable indexes. Other applications may want to remove all documents that contain a certain term or replace an old version of a document with a newer one whenever the original source of the document has changed. IndexWriter provides various methods to remove documents from an index:

- deleteDocuments(Term) deletes all documents containing the provided term.
- deleteDocuments(Term[]) deletes all documents containing any of the terms in the provided array.
- deleteDocuments(Query) deletes all documents matching the provided query.
- deleteDocuments(Query[]) deletes all documents matching any of the queries in the provided array.
- deleteAll() deletes all documents in the index. This is exactly the same as closing the writer and opening a new writer with create=true, without having to close your writer.

If you intend to delete a single document by Term, you must ensure you've indexed a Field on every document and that all field values are unique so that each document can be singled out for deletion. This is the same concept as a *primary key* column in a database table, but in no way is it enforced by Lucene. You can name this field anything you want (ID is common). This field should be indexed as an unanalyzed field (see section 2.4.1) to ensure the analyzer doesn't break it up into separate tokens. Then, use the field for document deletion like this:

```
writer.deleteDocuments(new Term("ID", documentID));
```

Be careful with these methods! If you accidentally specify the wrong Term (for example, a Term from an ordinary indexed text field instead of your unique ID field), you could easily and quickly delete a great many documents from your index. In each case, the deletes aren't done immediately. Instead, they're buffered in memory, just like the added documents, and periodically flushed to the directory. As with added documents, you must call commit() or close() on your writer to commit the changes to the index. Even once the deletes are flushed to the directory, the disk space consumed by that document isn't immediately freed. Rather, the documents are simply marked as deleted. Section 2.13.2 describes this process in more detail.

Let's look at listing 2.2 to see deleteDocuments in action. We created two test cases to show the deleteDocuments methods and to illustrate the effect of optimizing after deletion.

Listing 2.2   Deleting documents from an index

```
public void testDeleteBeforeOptimize() throws IOException {
    IndexWriter writer = getWriter();                    Verify 2 docs in index
    assertEquals(2, writer.numDocs());
    writer.deleteDocuments(new Term("id", "1"));         Delete first document
    writer.commit();
    assertTrue(writer.hasDeletions());                   ❶ Verify index
    assertEquals(2, writer.maxDoc());                       contains deletions
    assertEquals(1, writer.numDocs());
    writer.close();                                      ❷ Verify I indexed
}                                                           doc, I deleted doc

public void testDeleteAfterOptimize() throws IOException {
    IndexWriter writer = getWriter();
```

```
    assertEquals(2, writer.numDocs());
    writer.deleteDocuments(new Term("id", "1"));        ❸ Optimize to
    writer.optimize();                                     compact deletions
    writer.commit();
    assertFalse(writer.hasDeletions());
    assertEquals(1, writer.maxDoc());                   Verify I indexed
    assertEquals(1, writer.numDocs());                  doc, 0 deleted doc
    writer.close();
}
```

❶ This test demonstrates the use of the `hasDeletions()` method to check if an index contains any documents marked for deletion.

❷ This code shows the difference between two methods that are often mixed up: `maxDoc()` and `numDocs()`. The former returns the total number of deleted or undeleted documents in the index, whereas the latter returns the number of undeleted documents in an index. Because our index contains two documents, one of which is deleted, `numDocs()` returns 1 and `maxDocs()` returns 2.

❸ In the method `testDeleteAfterOptimize()`, we force Lucene to merge index segments, after deleting one document, by optimizing the index. Then, the `maxDoc()` method returns 1 rather than 2, because after a delete and optimize, Lucene truly removes the deleted document. Only one document remains in the index.

NOTE Users often confuse the `maxDoc()` and `numDocs()` methods in `IndexWriter` and `IndexReader`. The first method, `maxDoc()` returns the total number of deleted or undeleted documents in the index, whereas `numDocs()` returns only the number of undeleted documents.

We've finished adding and deleting documents; now we'll visit updating documents.

2.3.3 Updating documents in the index

In many applications, after initially indexing a document you may still want to make further changes to it, requiring you to reindex it. For example, if your documents are crawled from a web server, one way to detect that the content has changed is to look for a changed ETag HTTP header. If it's different from when you last indexed the document, that means changes have been made to the content and you should update the document in the index.

In some cases you may want to update only certain fields of the document. Perhaps the title changed but the body was unchanged. Unfortunately, although this is a frequently requested feature, Lucene can't do that: instead, it deletes the entire previous document and then adds a new document to the index. This requires that the new document contains all fields, even unchanged ones, from the original document. `IndexWriter` provides two convenience methods to replace a document in the index:

- `updateDocument(Term, Document)` first deletes all documents containing the provided term and then adds the new document using the writer's default analyzer.

- updateDocument(Term, Document, Analyzer) does the same but uses the provided analyzer instead of the writer's default analyzer.

The updateDocument methods are probably the most common way to handle deletion because they're typically used to replace a single document in the index that has changed. Note that these methods are simply shorthand for first calling delete-Documents(Term) and then addDocument. Use updateDocument like this:

```
writer.updateDocument(new Term("ID", documenteId), newDocument);
```

Because updateDocument uses deleteDocuments under the hood, the same caveat applies: be sure the Term you pass in uniquely identifies the one document you intend to update. Listing 2.3 is an example.

Listing 2.3 Updating indexed Documents

```
public void testUpdate() throws IOException {

    assertEquals(1, getHitCount("city", "Amsterdam"));

    IndexWriter writer = getWriter();

    Document doc = new Document();                          ◁──┐
    doc.add(new Field("id", "1",
                    Field.Store.YES,
                    Field.Index.NOT_ANALYZED));            ◁──
    doc.add(new Field("country", "Netherlands",
                    Field.Store.YES,
                    Field.Index.NO));                      ◁── Create new
    doc.add(new Field("contents",                              document
                    "Den Haag has a lot of museums",          for "Haag"
                    Field.Store.NO,
                    Field.Index.ANALYZED));                ◁──
    doc.add(new Field("city", "Den Haag",
                    Field.Store.YES,
                    Field.Index.ANALYZED));                ◁──┘

    writer.updateDocument(new Term("id", "1"),    │ Replace with
                        doc);                      │ new version
    writer.close();
                                                              Verify old
    assertEquals(0, getHitCount("city", "Amsterdam"));  ◁── document is gone
    assertEquals(1, getHitCount("city", "Den Haag"));  ◁─┐
}                                                       Verify new
                                                        document is indexed
```

We create a new document that will replace the original document with id 1. Then we call updateDocument to replace the original one. We have effectively updated one of the documents in the index.

We've covered the basics on how to add, delete, and update documents. Now it's time to delve into all the interesting field-specific options available to you when you're creating a document.

2.4   *Field options*

Field is perhaps the most important class when indexing documents: it's the actual class that holds each value to be indexed. When you create a field, you can specify numerous options to control what Lucene should do with that field once you add the document to the index. We touched on these options at a high level at the start of this chapter; now it's time to revisit this topic and enumerate each in more detail.

The options break down into multiple independent categories, which we cover in each subsection which follows: indexing, storing, and using term vectors. After describing those options, we'll see other values (besides String) that you can assign to a field. Finally we'll show the common combinations of field options.

Let's start with the options to control how the field's value is added to the inverted index.

2.4.1   *Field options for indexing*

The options for indexing (Field.Index.*) control how the text in the field will be made searchable via the inverted index. Here are the choices:

- Index.ANALYZED—Use the analyzer to break the field's value into a stream of separate tokens and make each token searchable. This option is useful for normal text fields (body, title, abstract, etc.).

- Index.NOT_ANALYZED—Do index the field, but don't analyze the String value. Instead, treat the Field's entire value as a single token and make that token searchable. This option is useful for fields that you'd like to search on but that shouldn't be broken up, such as URLs, file system paths, dates, personal names, Social Security numbers, and telephone numbers. This option is especially useful for enabling "exact match" searching. We indexed the id field in listings 2.1 and 2.3 using this option.

- Index.ANALYZED_NO_NORMS—A variant of Index.ANALYZED that doesn't store norms information in the index. Norms record index-time boost information in the index but can be memory consuming when you're searching. Section 2.5.3 describes norms in detail.

- Index.NOT_ANALYZED_NO_NORMS—Just like Index.NOT_ANALYZED, but also doesn't store norms. This option is frequently used to save index space and memory usage during searching, because single-token fields don't need the norms information unless they're boosted.

- Index.NO—Don't make this field's value available for searching.

When Lucene builds the inverted index, by default it stores all necessary information to implement the Vector Space Model. This model requires the count of every term that occurred in the document, as well as the positions of each occurrence (needed, for example, by phrase searches). But sometimes you know the field will be used only for pure Boolean searching and need not contribute to the relevance score. Fields used only for filtering, such as entitlements or date filtering, are a common example.

In this case, you can tell Lucene to skip indexing the term frequency and positions by calling `Field.setOmitTermFreqAndPositions(true)`. This approach will save some disk space in the index, and may also speed up searching and filtering, but will silently prevent searches that require positional information, such as `PhraseQuery` and `SpanQuery`, from working. Let's move on to controlling how Lucene stores a field's value.

2.4.2   *Field options for storing fields*

The options for stored fields (`Field.Store.*`) determine whether the field's exact value should be stored away so that you can later retrieve it during searching:

- `Store.YES`—Stores the value. When the value is stored, the original `String` in its entirety is recorded in the index and may be retrieved by an `IndexReader`. This option is useful for fields that you'd like to use when displaying the search results (such as a URL, title, or database primary key). Try not to store very large fields, if index size is a concern, as stored fields consume space in the index.
- `Store.NO`—Doesn't store the value. This option is often used along with `Index.ANALYZED` to index a large text field that doesn't need to be retrieved in its original form, such as bodies of web pages, or any other type of text document.

Lucene includes a helpful utility class, `CompressionTools`, that exposes static methods to compress and decompress byte arrays. Under the hood it uses Java's built-in `java.util.Zip` classes. You can use `CompressionTools` to compress values before storing them in Lucene. Note that although doing so will save space in your index, depending on how compressible the content is, it will also slow down indexing and searching. You're spending more CPU in exchange for less disk space used, which for many applications isn't a good trade-off. If the field values are small, compression is rarely worthwhile.

Let's visit options for controlling how term vectors are indexed.

2.4.3   *Field options for term vectors*

Sometimes when you index a document you'd like to retrieve all its unique terms at search time. One common use is to speed up highlighting the matched tokens in stored fields. (Highlighting is covered more in sections 8.3 and 8.4.) Another use is to enable a link, "Find similar documents," that when clicked runs a new search using the salient terms in an original document. Yet another example is automatic categorization of documents. Section 5.9 shows concrete examples of using term vectors once they're in your index.

But what exactly are term vectors? Term vectors are a mix between an indexed field and a stored field. They're similar to a stored field because you can quickly retrieve all term vector fields for a given document: term vectors are keyed first by document ID. But then, they're keyed secondarily by term, meaning they store a miniature inverted index for that one document. Unlike a stored field, where the original `String` content is stored verbatim, term vectors store the actual separate terms that were produced by the analyzer, allowing you to retrieve all terms for each field, and the frequency of their occurrence within the document, sorted in lexicographic order. Because the tokens coming out of an analyzer also have position and offset information (see section 4.2.1), you can choose separately whether these details are also stored in your term vectors by passing these constants as the fourth argument to the `Field` constructor:

- `TermVector.YES`—Records the unique terms that occurred, and their counts, in each document, but doesn't store any positions or offsets information
- `TermVector.WITH_POSITIONS`—Records the unique terms and their counts, and also the positions of each occurrence of every term, but no offsets
- `TermVector.WITH_OFFSETS`—Records the unique terms and their counts, with the offsets (start and end character position) of each occurrence of every term, but no positions
- `TermVector.WITH_POSITIONS_OFFSETS`—Stores unique terms and their counts, along with positions and offsets
- `TermVector.NO`—Doesn't store any term vector information

Note that you can't index term vectors unless you've also turned on indexing for the field. Stated more directly: if `Index.NO` is specified for a field, you must also specify `TermVector.NO`.

We're done with the detailed options to control indexing, storing, and term vectors. Now let's see how you can create a field with values other than `String`.

2.4.4 *Reader, TokenStream, and byte[] field values*

There are a few other constructors for the `Field` object that allow you to use values other than `String`:

- `Field(String name, Reader value, TermVector termVector)` uses a `Reader` instead of a `String` to represent the value. In this case, the value can't be stored (the option is hardwired to `Store.NO`) and is always analyzed and indexed (`Index.ANALYZED`). This can be useful when holding the full `String` in memory might be too costly or inconvenient—for example, for very large values.
- `Field(String name, Reader value)`, like the previous value, uses a `Reader` instead of a `String` to represent the value but defaults `termVector` to `TermVector.NO`.
- `Field(String name, TokenStream tokenStream, TermVector termVector)` allows you to preanalyze the field value into a `TokenStream`. Likewise, such fields aren't stored and are always analyzed and indexed.
- `Field(String name, TokenStream tokenStream)`, like the previous value, allows you to preanalyze the field value into a `TokenStream` but defaults `termVector` to `TermVector.NO`.
- `Field(String name, byte[] value, Store store)` is used to store a binary field. Such fields are never indexed (`Index.NO`) and have no term vectors (`TermVector.NO`). The store argument must be `Store.YES`.

- Field(String name, byte[] value, int offset, int length, Store store), like the previous value, indexes a binary field but allows you to reference a sub-slice of the bytes starting at offset and running for length bytes.

It should be clear by now that Field is quite a rich class and exposes a number of options to express to Lucene precisely how its value should be handled. Let's see some examples of how these options are typically combined in practice.

2.4.5 Field option combinations

You've now seen all the options for the three categories (indexing, storing, and term vectors) you can use to control how Lucene handles a field. These options can nearly be set independently, resulting in a number of possible combinations. Table 2.1 lists commonly used options and their example usage, but remember you are free to set the options however you'd like.

Table 2.1   A summary of various field characteristics, showing you how fields are created, along with common usage examples

Index	Store	TermVector	Example usage
NOT_ANALYZED_NO_NORMS	YES	NO	Identifiers (filenames, primary keys), telephone and Social Security numbers, URLs, personal names, dates, and textual fields for sorting
ANALYZED	YES	WITH_POSITIONS_OFFSETS	Document title, document abstract
ANALYZED	NO	WITH_POSITIONS_OFFSETS	Document body
NO	YES	NO	Document type, database primary key (if not used for searching)
NOT_ANALYZED	NO	NO	Hidden keywords

Next let's see how to index fields we intend to sort on.

2.4.6 Field options for sorting

When returning documents that match a search, Lucene orders them by their score by default. Sometimes, you need to order results using other criteria. For instance, if you're searching email messages, you may want to order results by sent or received date, or perhaps by message size or sender. Section 5.2 describes sorting in more detail, but in order to perform field sorting, you must first index the fields correctly.

If the field is numeric, use NumericField, covered in section 2.6.1, when adding it to the document, and sorting will work correctly. If the field is textual, such as the sender's name in an email message, you must add it as a Field that's indexed but not analyzed using Field.Index.NOT_ANALYZED. If you aren't doing any boosting for the field, you should index it without norms, to save disk space and memory, using Field.Index.NOT_ANALYZED_NO_NORMS:

```
new Field("author", "Arthur C. Clark", Field.Store.YES,
        Field.Index.NOT_ANALYZED_NO_NORMS);
```

NOTE   Fields used for sorting must be indexed and must contain one token per
document. Typically this means using `Field.Index.NOT_ANALYZED` or
`Field.Index.NOT_ANALYZED_NO_NORMS` (if you're not boosting documents or fields), but if your analyzer will always produce only one token,
such as `KeywordAnalyzer` (covered in section 4.7.3), `Field.Index.`
`ANALYZED` or `Field.Index.ANALYZED_NO_NORMS` will work as well.

Now that we're done with the exhaustive indexing options for fields, let's visit one
final field topic, multivalued fields.

2.4.7   *Multivalued fields*

Suppose your documents have an author field, but sometimes there's more than one
author for a document. One way to handle this would be to loop through all the
authors, appending them into a single `String`, which you could then use to create a
Lucene field. Another, perhaps more elegant way is to keep adding the same `Field`
with different value, like this:

```
Document doc = new Document();
for (String author : authors) {
  doc.add(new Field("author", author,
                    Field.Store.YES,
                    Field.Index.ANALYZED));
}
```

This is perfectly acceptable and encouraged, as it's a natural way to represent a field
that legitimately has multiple values. Internally, whenever multiple fields with the
same name appear in one document, both the inverted index and term vectors will
logically append the tokens of the field to one another, in the order the fields were
added. You can use advanced options during analysis that control certain important
details of this appending, notably how to prevent searches from matching across two
different field values; see section 4.7.1 for details. But, unlike indexing, when the
fields are stored they're stored separately in order in the document, so that when you
retrieve the document at search time you'll see multiple `Field` instances.

We're done with our coverage of Lucene's field options. The wide variety of
options has evolved over time to accommodate the diverse application of Lucene. We
showed you the numerous specific options to control how a field is indexed, whether
a field is stored, and whether term vectors will be computed and stored. Besides
`Strings`, field values can also be binary values (for storing), a `TokenStream` value (for
preanalyzed fields), or a `Reader` (if holding the full `String` in memory is too costly or
inconvenient). Fields that will be used for sorting (covered more in section 5.2) must
be indexed properly. Finally, in this section we've seen that Lucene gracefully handles
fields with multiple values.

Next we cover another field capability, *boosting*, that controls how important specific fields and documents are during Lucene's scoring.

2.5   *Boosting documents and fields*

Not all documents and fields are created equal—or at least you can make sure that's the case by using boosting. Boosting may be done during indexing, as we describe here, or during searching, as described in section 5.7. Search-time boosting is more dynamic, because every search can separately choose to boost or not to boost with different factors, but also may be somewhat more CPU intensive. Because it's so dynamic, search-time boosting also allows you to expose the choice to the user, such as a checkbox that asks "Boost recently modified documents?".

Regardless of whether you boost during indexing or searching, take caution: too much boosting, especially without corresponding transparency in the user interface explaining that certain documents were boosted, can quickly and catastrophically erode the user's trust. Iterate carefully to choose appropriate boosting values and to ensure you're not doing so much boosting that your users are forced to browse irrelevant results. In this section we'll show you how to selectively boost documents or fields during indexing, then describe how boost information is recorded into the index using norms.

2.5.1   *Boosting documents*

Imagine you have to write an application that indexes and searches corporate email. Perhaps the requirement is to give company employees' emails more importance than other email messages when sorting search results. How would you go about doing this?

Document boosting is a feature that makes such a requirement simple to implement. By default, all documents have no boost—or, rather, they all have the same boost factor of 1.0. By changing a document's boost factor, you can instruct Lucene to consider it more or less important with respect to other documents in the index when computing relevance. The API for doing this consists of a single method, set-Boost(float), which can be used as shown in listing 2.4. (Note that certain methods, like getSenderEmail and isImportant, aren't defined in this fragment, but are included in the full examples sources included with the book.)

Listing 2.4   Selectively boosting documents and fields

```
Document doc = new Document();
String senderEmail = getSenderEmail();
String senderName = getSenderName();
String subject = getSubject();
String body = getBody();
doc.add(new Field("senderEmail", senderEmail,
                Field.Store.YES,
                Field.Index.NOT_ANALYZED));
doc.add(new Field("senderName", senderName,
                Field.Store.YES,
                Field.Index.ANALYZED));
doc.add(new Field("subject", subject,
                Field.Store.YES,
```

```
                      Field.Index.ANALYZED));
  doc.add(new Field("body", body,
                    Field.Store.NO,
                    Field.Index.ANALYZED));
  String lowerDomain = getSenderDomain().toLowerCase();
  if (isImportant(lowerDomain)) {
    doc.setBoost(1.5F);
  } else if (isUnimportant(lowerDomain)) {
    doc.setBoost(0.1F);
  }
  writer.addDocument(doc);
```

❶ Good domain boost factor: 1.5

❷ Bad domain boost factor: 0.1

In this example, we check the domain name of the email message sender to determine whether the sender is a company employee.

❶ When we index messages sent by an important domain name (say, the company's employees), we set their boost factor to 1.5, which is greater than the default factor of 1.0.

❷ When we encounter messages from a sender associated with a fictional bad domain, as checked by isUnimportant, we label them as nearly insignificant by lowering their boost factor to 0.1.

During searching, Lucene will silently increase or decrease the scores of documents according to their boost. Sometimes you need finer per-field boosting granularity, which Lucene also makes possible.

2.5.2 *Boosting fields*

Just as you can boost documents, you can also boost individual fields. When you boost a document, Lucene internally uses the same boost factor to boost each of its fields. Imagine that another requirement for the email-indexing application is to consider the subject field more important than the field with a sender's name. In other words, search matches made in the subject field should be more valuable than equivalent matches in the senderName field in our earlier example. To achieve this behavior, we use the setBoost(float) method of the Field class:

```
Field subjectField = new Field("subject", subject,
                               Field.Store.YES,
                               Field.Index.ANALYZED);
subjectField.setBoost(1.2F);
```

In this example, we arbitrarily picked a boost factor of 1.2, just as we arbitrarily picked document boost factors of 1.5 and 0.1 earlier. The boost factor values you should use depend on what you're trying to achieve; you'll need to do some experimentation and tuning to achieve the desired effect. But remember when you want to change the boost on a field or document, you'll have to fully remove and then read the entire document, or use the updateDocument method, which does the same thing.

It's worth noting that shorter fields have an implicit boost associated with them, due to the way Lucene's scoring algorithm works. While indexing, IndexWriter consults the Similarity.lengthNorm method to perform this computation. To override this logic, you can implement your own Similarity class and tell IndexWriter to use it by calling its setSimilarity method. Boosting is, in general, an advanced feature that many applications can work well without, so tread carefully!

Document and field boosting come into play at search time, as you'll learn in section 3.3.1. Lucene's search results are ranked according to how closely each document matches the query, and each matching document is assigned a score. Lucene's scoring formula consists of a number of factors, and the boost factor is one of them.

How does Lucene record these boost factors in the index? This is what norms are for.

2.5.3   *Norms*

During indexing, all sources of index-time boosts are combined into a single floating-point number for each indexed field in the document. The document may have its own boost; each field may have a boost; and Lucene computes an automatic boost based on the number of tokens in the field (shorter fields have a higher boost). These boosts are combined and then compactly encoded (quantized) into a single byte, which is stored per field per document. During searching, norms for any field being searched are loaded into memory, decoded back into a floating-point number, and used when computing the relevance score.

Even though norms are initially computed during indexing, it's also possible to change them later using IndexReader's setNorm method. setNorm is an advanced method that requires you to recompute your own norm factor, but it's a potentially powerful way to factor in highly dynamic boost factors, such as document recency or click-through popularity.

One problem often encountered with norms is their high memory usage at search time. This is because the full array of norms, which requires one byte per document per separate field searched, is loaded into RAM. For a large index with many fields per document, this can quickly add up to a lot of RAM. Fortunately, you can easily turn norms off by either using one of the NO_NORMS indexing options in Field.Index or by calling Field.setOmitNorms(true) before indexing the document containing that field. Doing so will potentially affect scoring, because no index-time boost information will be used during searching, but it's possible the effect is trivial, especially when the fields tend to be roughly the same length and you're not doing any boosting on your own.

Beware: if you decide partway through indexing to turn norms off, you must rebuild the entire index because if even a single document has that field indexed with norms enabled, then through segment merging this will "spread" so that all documents consume one byte even if they'd disabled norms. This happens because Lucene doesn't use sparse storage for norms.

We explore how to index numbers, dates, and times next.

2.6   *Indexing numbers, dates, and times*

Although most content is textual in nature, in many cases handling numeric or date/time values is crucial. In a commerce setting, the product's price, and perhaps other numeric attributes like weight and height, are clearly important. A video search engine may index the duration of each video. Press releases and articles have a time-stamp. These are just a few examples of important numeric attributes that modern search applications face.

In this section we'll show you how to handle such numbers with Lucene. There are two very different situations where applications need to handle numbers, and you'll learn how Lucene supports both. When Lucene indexes a number, it's actually building up a rich data structure in the index, which we'll touch on. Finally, we'll explore several approaches for handling dates and times.

2.6.1   *Indexing numbers*

There are two common scenarios in which indexing numbers is important. In one scenario, numbers are embedded in the text to be indexed, and you want to make sure those numbers are preserved and indexed as their own tokens so that you can use them later as ordinary tokens in searches. For instance, your documents may contain sentences like "Be sure to include Form 1099 in your tax return": you want to be able to search for the number 1099 just as you can search for the phrase "tax return" and retrieve the document that contains the exact number.

To enable this, simply pick an analyzer that doesn't discard numbers. As we discuss in section 4.2.3, `WhitespaceAnalyzer` and `StandardAnalyzer` are two possible candidates. If you feed them the "Be sure to include Form 1099 in your tax return" sentence, they'll extract 1099 as a token and pass it on for indexing, allowing you to later search for 1099 directly. On the other hand, `SimpleAnalyzer` and `StopAnalyzer` discard numbers from the token stream, which means the search for 1099 won't match any documents. If in doubt, use Luke, which is a wonderful tool for inspecting all details of a Lucene index, to check whether numbers survived your analyzer and were added to the index. Luke is described in more detail in section 8.1.

In the other scenario, you have a field that contains a single number and you want to index it as a numeric value and then use it for precise (equals) matching, range searching, and/or sorting. For example, you might be indexing products in a retail catalog, where each product has a numeric price and you must enable your users to be able to restrict a search by price range.

In past releases, Lucene could only operate on textual terms. This required careful preprocessing of numbers, such as zero-padding or advanced number-to-text encodings, to turn them into `Strings` so that sorting and range searching by the textual terms worked properly. Fortunately, as of version 2.9, Lucene includes easy-to-use built-in support for numeric fields, starting with the new `NumericField` class. You simply create a `NumericField`, use one of its set<Type>Value methods (accepting types int, long, float, and double, and then returning itself) to record the value, and then add the NumericField to your document just like any other Field. Here's an example:

```
doc.add(new NumericField("price").setDoubleValue(19.99));
```

Under the hood, Lucene works some serious magic to ensure numeric values are indexed to allow for efficient range searching and numeric sorting. Each numeric value is indexed using a *trie* structure, which logically assigns a single numeric value to larger and larger predefined brackets. Each bracket is assigned a unique term in the index, so that retrieving all documents within a single bracket is fast. At search time, the requested range is translated into an equivalent union of these brackets, resulting in a high-performance range search or filter.

Although each NumericField instance accepts only a single numeric value, you're allowed to add multiple instances, with the same field name, to the document. The resulting NumericRangeQuery and NumericRangeFilter will logically "or" together all the values. But the effect on sorting is undefined. If you require sorting by the field, you'll have to index a separate NumericField that has only one occurrence for that field name.

An advanced parameter, precisionStep, lets you control the gap (in bits) between each successive bracket. The default value is 4 bits. Smaller values result in more trie brackets, thus increasing the size of the index (usually by a minor amount) but allowing for potentially faster range searching. The Javadocs provide full details of these trade-offs, but likely the default value is sufficient for most applications. Section 3.5.4 describes how to search numeric fields.

NumericField can also easily handle dates and times by converting them to equivalent ints or longs.

2.6.2　*Indexing dates and times*

Email messages include sent and received dates, files have several timestamps associated with them, and HTTP responses have a Last-Modified header that includes the date of the requested page's last modification. Chances are, like many other Lucene users, you'll need to index dates and times. Such values are easily handled by first converting them to an equivalent int or long value, and then indexing that value as a number. The simplest approach is to use Date.getTime to get the equivalent value, in millisecond precision, for a Java Date object:

```
doc.add(new NumericField("timestamp")
    .setLongValue(new Date().getTime()));
```

Alternatively, if you don't require full millisecond resolution for your dates, you can simply quantize them. If you need to quantize down to seconds, minutes, hours, or days, it's straight division:

```
doc.add(new NumericField("day")
    .setIntValue((int) (new Date().getTime()/24/3600)));
```

If you need to quantize further, to month or year, or perhaps you'd like to index hour of day or day of week or month, you'll have to create a `Calendar` instance and get fields from it:

```
Calendar cal = Calendar.getInstance();
cal.setTime(date);
doc.add(new NumericField("dayOfMonth")
    .setIntValue(cal.get(Calendar.DAY_OF_MONTH)));
```

As you've seen, Lucene makes it trivial to index numeric fields. You've seen several approaches for converting dates and times into equivalent numeric values for indexing. Now let's visit one final topic related to fields: *truncation.*

2.7 *Field truncation*

Some applications index documents whose sizes aren't known in advance. As a safety mechanism to control the amount of RAM and hard disk space used, you may want to limit the amount of input they are allowed index per field. It's also possible that a large binary document is accidentally misclassified as a text document, or contains binary content embedded in it that your document filter failed to process, which quickly adds many absurd binary terms to your index, much to your horror. Other applications deal with documents of known size but you'd like to index only a portion of each. For example, you may want to index only the first 200 words of each document.

To support these diverse cases, `IndexWriter` allows you to truncate per-`Field` indexing so that only the first N terms are indexed for an analyzed field. When you instantiate `IndexWriter`, you must pass in a `MaxFieldLength` instance expressing this limit. `MaxFieldLength` provides two convenient default instances: `MaxField-Length.UNLIMITED`, which means no truncation will take place, and `MaxField-Length.LIMITED`, which means fields are truncated at 10,000 terms. You can also instantiate `MaxFieldLength` with your own limit.

After creating `IndexWriter`, you may alter the limit at any time by calling `setMax-FieldLength` or retrieve the limit with `getMaxFieldLength`. However, any documents already indexed will have been truncated at the previous value: changes to `maxField-Length` aren't retroactive. If multiple `Field` instances with the same name exist, the truncation applies separately to each of them, meaning each field has its first N terms indexed. If you're curious about how often the truncation is kicking in, call `Index-Writer.setInfoStream(System.out)` and search for any lines that say `"maxField-Length reached for field X, ignoring following tokens"`. (Note that the `infoStream` also receives many other diagnostic details, useful in their own right.)

Please think carefully before using any field truncation! It means that only the first N terms are available for searching, and any text beyond the Nth term is completely ignored. Searches that would've matched a document after the Nth term will silently fail to match the document. Eventually users will notice that your search engine fails to find certain documents in certain situations and will assume it's buggy. Many times someone asks the Lucene users list, "Why doesn't this search find this document?" and the answer is inevitably, "You'll have to increase your maxFieldLength."

NOTE   Use maxFieldLength sparingly! Because truncation means some documents' text will be completely ignored, and thus unavailable for searching, your users will eventually discover that your search fails to find some documents. This will quickly erode their trust in your application ("What else can't it find?"), which can be catastrophic to your user base and perhaps your whole business if search is its core. User trust is the most important thing to protect in your business.

We're done visiting all the interesting things you can do with fields. As you've seen, Lucene's Field class includes a rich array of options to support the many ways that a value can be handled. Next, we explore how to minimize the turnaround time between adding a document and then being able to search it.

2.8   *Near-real-time search*

New in Lucene 2.9 is an important feature called near-real-time search, which addresses a frequent challenge for all search engines: the ability to search on documents quickly after indexing them. Many applications have such a requirement, but it's a challenge for search engines to implement. Fortunately, Lucene now makes this simple, by providing this method in IndexWriter:

```
IndexReader getReader()
```

This method immediately flushes any buffered added or deleted documents, and then creates a new read-only IndexReader that includes those documents. We'll see how IndexReader is used for searching in the next chapter, but for now, just trust us! Under the hood, the newly opened reader is instantiated in an efficient manner, so that any old segments in common with the previously opened reader are shared. Thus, if only a few documents have been added, the turnaround time will generally be fast. Note that calling getReader necessarily slows down your indexing throughput because it causes the IndexWriter to immediately flush a new segment instead of waiting until its RAM buffer is full. Section 3.2.5 shows an example of searching using a near-real-time reader.

Next we describe the optimization process.

2.9   *Optimizing an index*

When you index documents, especially many documents or using multiple sessions with IndexWriter, you'll invariably create an index that has many separate segments. When you search the index, Lucene must search each segment separately and then combine the results. Although this works flawlessly, applications that handle large indexes will see search performance improvements by optimizing the index, which merges many segments down to one or a few segments. An optimized index also consumes fewer file descriptors during searching. After describing the optimization process and the available methods, we'll talk about disk space consumed during optimization.

NOTE Optimizing only improves searching speed, not indexing speed.

It's entirely possible that you get excellent search throughput without optimizing, so be sure to first test whether you need to consider optimizing. IndexWriter exposes four methods to optimize:

- optimize() reduces the index to a single segment, not returning until the operation is finished.
- optimize(int maxNumSegments), also known as *partial optimize*, reduces the index to at most maxNumSegments segments. Because the final merge down to one segment is the most costly, optimizing to, say, five segments should be quite a bit faster than optimizing down to one segment, allowing you to trade less optimization time for slower search speed.
- optimize(boolean doWait) is just like optimize, except if doWait is false then the call returns immediately while the necessary merges take place in the background. Note that doWait=false only works for a merge scheduler that runs merges in background threads, such as the default ConcurrentMergeScheduler. Section 2.13.6 describes merge schedulers in more detail.
- optimize(int maxNumSegments, boolean doWait) is a partial optimize that runs in the background if doWait is false.

Remember that index optimization consumes substantial CPU and input/output (I/O) resources, so use it judiciously. It is a trade-off of a large onetime cost for faster searching. If you update your index only rarely, and do lots of searching between updates, this trade-off is worthwhile. If a single computer is doing both indexing and searching, consider scheduling optimize after hours or over the weekend so that it doesn't interfere with ongoing searching.

Another important cost to be aware of is that optimizing requires substantial temporary disk space. Because Lucene must merge segments together, while the merge is running temporary disk space is used to hold the files for the new segment. But the old segments can't be removed until the merge is complete and the changes are committed, either by calling IndexWriter.commit or by closing the IndexWriter. This means you should expect the size of your index to roughly triple (temporarily) during optimization. Once optimization completes, and once you call commit(), disk usage will fall back to a lower level than the starting size. Any open readers on the index will also potentially impact the transient disk usage. Section 11.3.1 describes overall disk usage of Lucene in more detail.

NOTE During optimization, the index will require substantial temporary disk space, up to three times its starting size. After optimization completes, the index will consume less disk space than at the start.

Let's now look at some Directory implementations other than FSDirectory.

2.10 *Other directory implementations*

Recall from chapter 1 that the purpose of Lucene's abstract Directory class is to present a simple file-like storage API, hiding away the details of what underlying mechanism is performing the storage. Whenever Lucene needs to write to or read from files in the index, it uses the Directory methods to do so. Table 2.2 lists the five core Directory implementations available in Lucene 3.0.

Of these classes, three are concrete Directory implementations to read and write files from the file system. They're all subclasses of the abstract FSDirectory base class. Unfortunately, there's no single best FSDirectory implementation. Each has potentially serious limitations in certain situations:

- SimpleFSDirectory uses java.io.* APIs for access. Unfortunately, this Directory implementation doesn't scale during reading when multiple threads are in use because it must do internal locking to work around the lack of positional reads in java.io.*.

- NIOFSDirectory uses positional reads in java.nio.* APIs, and thus has no internal locking and scales very well with many threads when reading. Unfortunately, due to a longstanding Windows-only issue on Sun's JREs, NIOFSDirectory will perform badly, perhaps worse than SimpleFSDirectory, on Windows.

- MMapDirectory uses memory-mapped I/O when reading and also doesn't have any locking, so it scales well with threads. But because memory-mapped I/O consumes process address space equal to the size of your index, it's best to use it only on a 64-bit JRE, or on a 32-bit JRE if you're absolutely certain that your index size is very small relative to the actual portion of 32-bit address space available to your process (typically 2–3 GB, depending on the OS). Java doesn't provide a way to cleanly "unmap" memory-mapped sections of a file, which means it's only when garbage collection happens that the underlying file is closed and memory is freed. This means you could easily have many leftover maps, consuming large chunks of process address space and leaving the underlying index files open far longer than you'd expect. Furthermore, on 32-bit JREs, you may hit false OutOfMemoryError due to fragmentation issues. MMapDirectory provides the setMaxChunkSize method to work around this.

All of these Directory implementations share the same code (from SimpleFSDirectory, using java.io.*) for writing.

So which implementation should you use? One good approach is to use the static FSDirectory.open method. This method attempts to pick the best default FSDirectory implementation given your current OS and platform, and may improve its decision making with each Lucene release (though note that as of Lucene 3.0, it won't ever return an MMapDirectory). Alternatively, you can directly instantiate the precise class that you want, as long as you understand the previous issues (be sure to read the Javadocs for all the latest details!).

Table 2.2 Lucene's several core `Directory` implementations

Directory	Description
SimpleFSDirectory	A simplistic `Directory` that stores files in the file system, using `java.io.*` APIs. It doesn't scale well with many threads.
NIOFSDirectory	A `Directory` that stores files in the file system, using `java.nio.*` APIs. This does scale well with threads on all platforms except Microsoft Windows, due to a longstanding issue with Sun's Java Runtime Environment (JRE).
MMapDirectory	A `Directory` that uses memory-mapped I/O to access files. This is a good choice on 64-bit JREs, or on 32-bit JREs where the size of the index is relatively small.
RAMDirectory	A `Directory` that stores all files in RAM.
FileSwitchDirectory	A `Directory` that takes two directories in, and switches between these directories based on file extension.

Lucene also provides `RAMDirectory`, which is a `Directory` implementation that stores all "files" in memory instead of on disk. This makes reading and writing exceptionally fast, and is useful in cases where the index is small enough to fit in available memory and where the index is easily and quickly regenerated from the source documents. But if the computer has enough RAM, most OSs will use free RAM as an I/O cache. This means, after warming up, the `FSDirectory` will be about as fast as the `RAMDirectory` for searching. Lucene's unit tests make extensive use of `RAMDirectory` to create short-lived indexes for testing. To build a new index in `RAMDirectory`, instantiate your writer like this:

```
Directory ramDir = new RAMDirectory();
IndexWriter writer = new IndexWriter(ramDir, analyzer,
                        IndexWriter.MaxFieldLength.UNLIMITED);
```

You can then use the writer as you normally would to add, delete, or update documents. Just remember that once the Java Virtual Machine (JVM) exits, your index is gone!

Alternatively, you can copy the contents of another `Directory` otherDir into `RAMDirectory` like this:

```
Directory ramDir = new RAMDirectory(otherDir);
```

This is typically used to speed up searching of an existing on-disk index when it's small enough, though modern OSs do a good job of caching recently used bytes in the I/O cache so it's likely the gains in practice are minimal. A more general API is this static method, to copy all files between any two `Directory` instances:

```
Directory.copy(Directory sourceDir,
            Directory destDir,
            boolean closeDirSrc);
```

But be aware that this blindly replaces any existing files in destDir, and you must ensure no IndexWriter is open on the source directory because the copy method doesn't do any locking. If the destDir already has an index present and you'd like to add in all documents from srcDir, keeping all documents already indexed in otherDir, use IndexWriter.addIndexesNoOptimize instead:

```
IndexWriter writer = new IndexWriter(otherDir, analyzer,
                              IndexWriter.MaxFieldLength.UNLIMITED);
writer.addIndexesNoOptimize(new Directory[] {ramDir});
```

There are other addIndexes methods in IndexWriter, but each of them does its own optimize, which likely you don't need or want.

In past versions of Lucene, it was beneficial to control memory buffering by first batch-indexing into a RAMDirectory and then periodically adding the index into an index stored on disk. But as of Lucene 2.3, IndexWriter makes efficient use of memory for buffering changes to the index and this is no longer a win. See section 11.1.4 for other ways to improve indexing throughput.

The final Directory implementation, FileSwitchDirectory, switches between two Directory implementations you provide, based on the extension of the file. This implementation could be used to store certain index files in a RAMDirectory and others in a backing MMapDirectory, for example. But realize this is an advanced use and you must rely on the extensions of the current Lucene index file format, which is free to change between releases.

Let's discuss the complex topic of concurrency next.

2.11   Concurrency, thread safety, and locking issues

In this section, we cover three closely related topics: accessing an index from multiple JVMs, thread safety of IndexReader and IndexWriter, and the locking mechanism that Lucene uses to enforce these rules. A thorough understanding of these topics is essential, because it will eliminate surprises that can result when your indexing application starts serving multiple users simultaneously or when it scales up by parallelizing some of its operations.

2.11.1   Thread and multi-JVM safety

Lucene's concurrency rules are simple:

- Any number of read-only IndexReaders may be open at once on a single index. It doesn't matter if these readers are in the same JVM or multiple JVMs, or on the same computer or multiple computers. Remember, that within a single JVM it's best for resource utilization and performance reasons to share a single

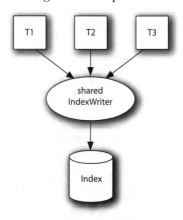

Figure 2.3   A single IndexWriter can be shared by multiple threads.

IndexReader instance for a given index using multiple threads. For instance, multiple threads or processes may search the same index in parallel.

- Only a single writer may be open on an index at once. Lucene uses a write lock file to enforce this (described in detail in section 2.11.3). As soon as an Index-Writer is created, a write lock is obtained. Only when that IndexWriter is closed is the write lock released. Note that if you use IndexReader to make changes to the index—for example, to change norms (section 2.5.3) or delete documents (section 2.13.1)—then that IndexReader acts as a writer: it must successfully obtain the write lock before making the first change, only releasing it once closed.

- IndexReaders may be open even while an IndexWriter is making changes to the index. Each IndexReader will always show the index as of the point in time that it was opened. It won't see any changes being done by the IndexWriter until the writer commits and the reader is reopened. It's even fine to open a new IndexWriter with create=true while an IndexReader is already open: that IndexReader will continue searching its point-in-time view of the index.

- Any number of threads can share a single instance of IndexReader or Index-Writer. These classes are not only thread safe but also thread friendly, meaning they generally scale well as you add threads (assuming your hardware has concurrency, because the amount of synchronized code inside these classes is kept to a minimum). Figure 2.3 depicts such a scenario. Sections 11.2.1 and 11.2.2 describe issues related to using multiple threads for indexing and searching.

As you can see, Lucene works well with multiple threads and multiple JVMs. But there are interesting challenges if you need to share an index over a remote file system.

2.11.2 *Accessing an index over a remote file system*

If you intend to have multiple JVMs, on different computers, accessing the same index, you'll have to expose access to that index over a remote file system. One common configuration is to have a single dedicated computer that writes to the index stored in a file system local to that computer, and then multiple computers that perform searching of that index via a remote file system. Such a configuration can be made to work, but the performance will usually be far worse than searching an index stored on a local file system (see table 2.3). It's possible to gain some performance back by mounting the remote file system as read-only, but to maximize performance it's best to replicate a copy of the index onto the local file system of each computer that will do searching. Solr, the enterprise search server built on top of Lucene, supports replication out of the box.

If you still intend to access the index over a remote file system, it's important to be aware of the possible limitations. Unfortunately, certain popular remote file systems are known to be problematic, as summarized in table 2.3. NFS, AFP, and Samba/CIFS 2.0 are known to have intermittent problems when opening or reopening an index

Table 2.3   Issues related to accessing a Lucene index across remote file systems

Remote file system	Notes
Samba/CIFS 1.0	The standard remote file system for Windows computers. Sharing a Lucene index works fine.
Samba/CIFS 2.0	The new version of Samba/CIFS that's the default for Windows Server 2007 and Windows Vista. Lucene has trouble due to incoherent client-side caches.
Networked File System (NFS)	The standard remote file systems for most Unix OSs. Lucene has trouble due to both incoherent client-side caches as well as how NFS handles deletion of files that are held open by another computer.
Apple File Protocol (AFP)	Apple's standard remote file system protocol. Lucene has trouble due to incoherent client-side caches.

due to incoherent client-side caching. The problem only occurs when the writer has just committed changes to an index, and then on another computer a reader or another writer is opened or reopened. Thus you're more likely to encounter this if you frequently try to reopen your readers and writer and often commit changes to the index. When you do encounter the issue, you'll see an unexpected `FileNotFound-Exception` inside the `open` or `reopen` methods. Fortunately, the workaround is quite simple: retry a bit later, because typically the client-side caches will correct themselves after a certain amount of time.

NFS in particular presents a further challenge because of how it handles deletion of files that are still held open on other computers. Most file systems protect open files from deletion. For example, Windows simply disallows deletion of an open file, whereas most native Unix file systems allow the deletion to proceed but the actual bytes of the file remain allocated on disk until all open file handles are closed (this is called "delete on last close" semantics). In both approaches, an open file handle can still be used to read all bytes in the file after the file deletion is attempted. NFS does neither of these, and simply removes the file, so that the next I/O operation attempted by a computer with an open file handle will encounter the much-dreaded "Stale NFS file handle" `IOException`.

To prevent this error from hitting your searchers, you must create your own `IndexDeletionPolicy` class to control deletion of previous commit points until all searchers on the index have reopened to the newer commit point. For example, a common approach is to remove an index commit only if it's older than, say, 4 hours, as long as you can ensure that every `IndexReader` reading the index reopens itself less than 4 hours after a commit. Alternatively, on hitting the "Stale NFS file handle" during searching, you could at that moment reopen your searcher and then redo the search. This is a viable approach only if reopening a searcher is not too time consuming. Otherwise, the unlucky query that hit the error will take unacceptably long to get results.

As you've seen, Lucene allows highly concurrent access to an index. Many readers can share an index, many threads can share an `IndexWriter` and `IndexReader`, and so forth. The only strong concurrency limitation is that no more than one writer may be open at once. We'll now describe how Lucene enforces this, and how you can control it, using Lucene's locking implementations. In general, locking is a complex topic, and even Lucene's simple exposure of locking options is no exception. So we spend even more time enumerating the choices than we did on all of Lucene's concurrency rules!

2.11.3 Index locking

To enforce a single writer at a time, which means an `IndexWriter` or an `IndexReader` doing deletions or changing norms, Lucene uses a file-based lock: if the lock file (`write.lock` by default) exists in your index directory, a writer currently has the index open. Any attempt to create another writer on the same index will hit a `LockObtain-FailedException`. This is a vital protection mechanism, because if two writers are accidentally created on a single index, that would quickly lead to index corruption.

Lucene allows you to change your locking implementation: any subclass of `Lock-Factory` can be set as your locking implementation by calling `Directory.setLock-Factory`. Be sure to call this before opening an `IndexWriter` on that `Directory` instance. Normally you don't need to worry about which locking implementation you're using. It's usually only those advanced applications that have multiple computers or JVMs that take turns performing indexing that may need to customize the locking implementation. Table 2.4 lists the core locking implementations provided with Lucene.

Table 2.4   Locking implementations provided by Lucene

Locking class name	Description
`NativeFSLockFactory`	This is the default locking for `FSDirectory`, using `java.nio` native OS locking, which will never leave leftover lock files when the JVM exits. But this locking implementation may not work correctly over certain shared file systems, notably NFS.
`SimpleFSLockFactory`	Uses Java's `File.createNewFile` API, which may be more portable across different file systems than `NativeFSLockFactory`. Be aware that if the JVM crashes or `IndexWriter` isn't closed before the JVM exits, this may leave a leftover `write.lock` file, which you must manually remove.
`SingleInstanceLockFactory`	Creates a lock entirely in memory. This is the default locking implementation for `RAMDirectory`. Use this when you know all `IndexWriter`s will be instantiated in a single JVM.
`NoLockFactory`	Disables locking entirely. Be careful! Only use this when you are absolutely certain that Lucene's normal locking safeguard isn't necessary—for example, when using a private `RAMDirectory` with a single `IndexWriter` instance.

Note that none of these locking implementations are "fair." For example, if a lock is already held by an existing writer, the new writer will simply retry, every one second by default, to obtain the lock. There's no queue that would allow the new writer to get the lock as soon as the old one releases it. If you have an application that requires such fairness, it's best to implement your own locking.

If you do choose to create your own locking implementation, be certain it works correctly. There's a simple but useful debugging tool, LockStressTest, which can be used in conjunction with LockVerifyServer and VerifyingLockFactory to verify that a given locking implementation is functioning properly. These classes are in the org.apache.lucene.store package; see their Javadocs for how to use them. If you aren't sure whether your new lock factory is working properly, use LockStressTest to find out.

You should be aware of two additional methods related to locking:

- IndexWriter's isLocked(Directory)—Tells you whether the index specified in its argument is locked. This method can be handy when an application needs to check whether the index is locked before attempting to create an IndexWriter.
- IndexWriter's unlock(Directory)—Does exactly what its name implies. Although this method gives you power to unlock any Lucene index at any time, using it is dangerous. Lucene creates locks for a good reason, and unlocking an index while it's being modified will quickly result in a corrupted and unusable index.

Although you now know about Lucene's write lock, you should resist touching this file directly. Instead, always rely on Lucene's API to manipulate it. If you don't, your code may break if Lucene starts using a different locking mechanism in the future, or even if it changes the name or location of its lock files.

To demonstrate locking, listing 2.6 shows how the write lock prevents more than one writer from accessing an index simultaneously. In the testWriteLock() method, Lucene blocks the second IndexWriter from opening an index that has already been opened by another IndexWriter. This is an example of write.lock in action.

> **Listing 2.5   Using file-based locks to enforce a single writer at a time**

```
public class LockTest extends TestCase {

  private Directory dir;

  protected void setUp() throws IOException {
    String indexDir =
      System.getProperty("java.io.tmpdir", "tmp") +
      System.getProperty("file.separator") + "index";
    dir = FSDirectory.open(new File(indexDir));
  }

  public void testWriteLock() throws IOException {

    IndexWriter writer1 = new IndexWriter(dir, new SimpleAnalyzer(),
                            IndexWriter.MaxFieldLength.UNLIMITED);
    IndexWriter writer2 = null;
```

```
    try {
      writer2 = new IndexWriter(dir, new SimpleAnalyzer(),
                                IndexWriter.MaxFieldLength.UNLIMITED);
      fail("We should never reach this point");
    }
    catch (LockObtainFailedException e) {        Handle expected
      e.printStackTrace();                    <-- exception
    }
    finally {
      writer1.close();
      assertNull(writer2);
    }
  }
}
```

When we run the code in listing 2.5, we see an exception stack trace caused by the locked index, which resembles the following stack trace:

```
org.apache.lucene.store.LockObtainFailedException: Lock obtain timed out:
  ➥ NativeFSLock@/var/tmp/index/write.lock
     at org.apache.lucene.store.Lock.obtain(Lock.java:84)
     at org.apache.lucene.index.IndexWriter.init(IndexWriter.java:1041)
```

As we mentioned earlier, new users of Lucene sometimes don't have a good understanding of the concurrency issues described in this section and consequently run into locking issues, such as the one shown in the previous stack trace. If you see similar exceptions in your applications, please don't disregard them if the consistency of your indexes is at all important to you. Lock-related exceptions are typically a sign of a misuse of the Lucene API; if they occur in your application, you should scrutinize your code to resolve them promptly.

Our next topic shows you how to gain insight into the internal operations `IndexWriter` is doing.

2.12 Debugging indexing

If you ever need to debug Lucene's index-writing process, remember that you can get Lucene to output information about its indexing operations by calling `IndexWriter`'s `setInfoStream` method, passing in a `PrintStream` such as `System.out`:

```
IndexWriter writer = new IndexWriter(dir, analyzer,
                                     IndexWriter.MaxFieldLength.UNLIMITED);
writer.setInfoStream(System.out);
```

This reveals detailed diagnostic information about segment flushes and merges, as shown here, and may help you tune indexing parameters described earlier in the chapter. If you're experiencing an issue during indexing, something you may believe to be a bug in Lucene, and you take your issue to the Lucene user's list at Apache, the first request you'll get back is someone asking you to post the output from setting `infoStream`. It will look something like this:

```
flush postings as segment _9 numDocs=1095
  oldRAMSize=16842752 newFlushedSize=5319835 docs/MB=215.832 new/old=31.585%
IFD [main]: now checkpoint "segments_1" [10 segments ; isCommit = false]
```

```
IW 0 [main]: LMP: findMerges: 10 segments
IW 0 [main]: LMP:    level 6.2247195 to 6.745619: 10 segments
IW 0 [main]: LMP:      0 to 10: add this merge
IW 0 [main]: add merge to pendingMerges: _0:C1010->_0 _1:C1118->_0
➡ _2:C968->_0 _3:C1201->_0 _4:C947->_0 _5:C1084->_0 _6:C1028->_0
➡ _7:C954->_0 _8:C990->_0 _9:C1095->_0 [total 1 pending]
IW 0 [main]: CMS: now merge
IW 0 [main]: CMS:    index: _0:C1010->_0 _1:C1118->_0 _2:C968->_0
➡ _3:C1201->_0 _4:C947->_0 _5:C1084->_0 _6:C1028->_0 _7:C954->_0
➡ _8:C990->_0 _9:C1095->_0 IW 0 [main]: CMS:    consider merge
➡ _0:C1010->_0 _1:C1118->_0 _2:C968->_0 _3:C1201->_0 _4:C947->_0
➡ _5:C1084->_0 _6:C1028->_0 _7:C954->_0 _8:C990->_0 _9:C1095->_0 into _a
IW 0 [main]: CMS:       launch new thread [Lucene Merge Thread #0]
IW 0 [main]: CMS:   no more merges pending; now return
IW 0 [Lucene Merge Thread #0]: CMS:    merge thread: start
IW 0 [Lucene Merge Thread #0]: now merge
  merge=_0:C1010->_0 _1:C1118->_0 _2:C968->_0 _3:C1201->_0 _4:C947->_0
➡ _5:C1084->_0 _6:C1028->_0 _7:C954->_0 _8:C990->_0 _9:C1095->_0 into _a
  index=_0:C1010->_0 _1:C1118->_0 _2:C968->_0 _3:C1201->_0 _4:C947->_0
➡ _5:C1084->_0 _6:C1028->_0 _7:C954->_0 _8:C990->_0 _9:C1095->_0
IW 0 [Lucene Merge Thread #0]: merging _0:C1010->_0 _1:C1118->_0
➡ _2:C968->_0 _3:C1201->_0 _4:C947->_0 _5:C1084->_0 _6:C1028->_0
➡ _7:C954->_0 _8:C990->_0 _9:C1095->_0 into _a
IW 0 [Lucene Merge Thread #0]: merge: total 10395 docs
```

In addition, if you need to peek inside your index once it's built, you can use Luke, a handy third-party tool that we discuss in section 8.1. Our final section covers some advanced indexing topics.

2.13 *Advanced indexing concepts*

We've covered many interesting topics in this chapter—you should be proud for getting this far. You've seen how Lucene models content, the steps for indexing at a high level, and the basics of how to add, delete, and update documents in an index. You understand all the field options that tell Lucene precisely what to do with each field's value, and you now know how to handle interesting cases like multivalued fields, field truncation, document/field boosting, and numeric and date/time values. We've covered why and how to optimize and index, and the liberal thread safety and locking customizability that Lucene supports. Very likely you can stop here and move on to the next chapter. But if you're still curious, read on.

We'll now drill down into the advanced topics in Lucene's indexing, including the surprising ability to use IndexReader for performing deletions, how Lucene decides when to create a new segment, and Lucene's transactional semantics. We'll show you how to eliminate wasted disk space consumed by deleted documents. Although these are undoubtedly advanced topics, and you could happily perform indexing without understanding these concepts, you may someday find yourself wondering exactly when and how changes made by IndexWriter become visible to new readers on the index. Let's begin by seeing when you may want to use IndexReader to perform deletions.

2.13.1 *Deleting documents with IndexReader*

`IndexReader` also exposes methods to delete documents. Why would you want two ways to do the same thing? Well, there are some interesting differences:

- `IndexReader` is able to delete by document number. This means you could do a search, step through matching document numbers, perhaps apply some application logic, then pick and choose which document numbers to delete. Although frequently requested, `IndexWriter` can't expose such a method because document numbers may change suddenly due to merging (see section 2.13.6).

- `IndexReader` can delete by `Term`, just like `IndexWriter`. But `IndexReader` returns the number of documents deleted; `IndexWriter` doesn't. This is due to a difference in the implementation: `IndexReader` determines immediately which documents were deleted, and is therefore able to count up the affected documents; `IndexWriter` simply buffers the deleted `Term` and applies it later.

- `IndexReader`'s deletions take effect immediately, if you use that same reader for searching. This means you can do deletion and immediately run a search, and the deleted documents will no longer appear in the search results. With `Index-Writer`, the deletions aren't visible until you open a new reader.

- `IndexWriter` is able to delete by `Query`, but `IndexReader` isn't (though it's not hard to run your own `Query` and simply delete every document number that was returned).

- `IndexReader` exposes a sometimes useful method, `undeleteAll`, which as you might infer reverses all pending deletions in the index. Note that this only reverses deletions that haven't been merged yet. This is possible because `Index-Writer` simply marks the document as deleted, but does not in fact remove the document from the index until the segment containing the document is merged, as described in the next section.

If you're tempted to use `IndexReader` for deletion, remember that Lucene allows only one "writer" to be open at once. Confusingly, an `IndexReader` that's performing deletions counts as a "writer." This means you are forced to close any open `IndexWriter` before doing deletions with `IndexReader`, and vice versa. If you find that you are quickly interleaving added and deleted documents, this will slow down your indexing throughput substantially. It's better to batch up your additions and deletions, using `IndexWriter`, to get better performance.

Generally, unless one of these differences is compelling for your application, it's best to simply use `IndexWriter` for all deletions. Let's look at the disk space consumed by deleted documents.

2.13.2 *Reclaiming disk space used by deleted documents*

Lucene uses a simple approach to record deleted documents in the index: the document is marked as deleted in a bit array, which is a quick operation, but the data corresponding to that document still consumes disk space in the index. This technique is necessary because in an inverted index, a given document's terms are scattered all over the place, and it'd be impractical to try to reclaim that space when the document is deleted. It's not until segments are merged, either by normal merging over time or by an explicit call to optimize, that these bytes are reclaimed. Section 2.13.6 describes how and when Lucene merges segments.

You can also call expungeDeletes to explicitly reclaim all disk space consumed by deleted documents. This call merges any segments that have pending deletions. Although this will generally be a lower-cost operation than optimizing, it's still quite costly and is likely only worthwhile when you know you've finished doing deletions for quite a while. In the worst case, if your deletions are scattered all over the segments so that all segments have deletions, then expungeDeletes does exactly the same thing as optimize: it merges all segments down to one. Let's see next how IndexWriter chooses to make a new segment.

2.13.3 *Buffering and flushing*

As shown in figure 2.4, when new documents are added to a Lucene index, or deletions are pending, they're initially buffered in memory instead of being immediately written to the disk. This buffering is done for performance reasons to minimize disk I/O. Periodically, these changes are flushed to the index Directory as a new segment.

IndexWriter triggers a flush according to three possible criteria, which are controlled by the application:

- To flush when the buffer has consumed more than a preset amount of RAM, use setRAMBufferSizeMB. The RAM buffer size shouldn't be taken as an exact maximum of memory usage because you should consider many other factors when measuring overall JVM memory usage. Furthermore, IndexWriter doesn't account for all of its RAM usage, such as the memory required by segment merging. Section 11.3.3 describes ideas to minimize overall JVM memory usage.
- It's also possible to flush after a specific number of documents have been added by calling setMaxBufferedDocs.
- You can trigger flushing whenever the total number of buffered deleted terms and queries exceeds a specified count by calling setMaxBufferedDeleteTerms.

Flushing happens whenever one of these triggers is hit, whichever comes first. There's a constant IndexWriter.DISABLE_ AUTO_FLUSH, which you can pass to any of these methods to prevent flushing by that criterion. By default, IndexWriter flushes only when RAM usage is 16 MB.

When a flush occurs, the writer creates new segment and deletion files in the `Directory`. However, these files are neither visible nor usable to a newly opened `IndexReader` until the writer commits the changes and the reader is reopened. It's important to understand this difference. Flushing is done to free up memory consumed by buffered changes to the index. Committing is done to make all changes (buffered or already flushed) persistent and visible in the index. This means `IndexReader` always sees the starting state of the index (when `IndexWriter` was opened), until the writer commits.

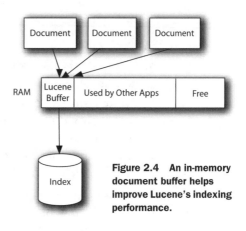

Figure 2.4   An in-memory document buffer helps improve Lucene's indexing performance.

NOTE   While an `IndexWriter` is making changes to the index, a newly opened `IndexReader` won't see any of these changes until `commit()` or `close()` is called and the reader is reopened. This even applies to opening a new `IndexWriter` with `create=true`. But a newly opened near-real-time reader (see section 2.8) is able to see the changes without requiring a `commit()` or `close()`.

Let's drill down to understand more about index commits.

2.13.4 Index commits

A new index commit is created whenever you invoke one of `IndexWriter`'s commit methods. There are two such methods: `commit()` creates a new index commit, and `commit(Map<String,String> commitUserData)` records the provided string map as opaque metadata into the commit for later retrieval. Closing the writer also calls `commit()`. Note that a newly opened or reopened `IndexReader` or `IndexSearcher` will only see the index as of the last commit, and all changes made by `IndexWriter` in between calls to commit are invisible to readers. The one exception to this is the near-real-time search functionality, covered in section 2.8, which is able to search changes made with the `IndexWriter` without first committing those changes to disk.

Note that commit can be a costly operation, and doing so frequently will slow down your indexing throughput. If for some reason you decide that you want to discard all changes, you can call `rollback()` to remove all changes in the current `Index-Writer` session since the last commit to the index. Here are the steps `IndexWriter` takes during commit:

1 Flush any buffered documents and deletions.
2 Sync all newly created files, including newly flushed files as well as any files produced by merges that have finished since `commit` was last called or since the

IndexWriter was opened. IndexWriter calls Directory.sync to achieve this, which doesn't return until all pending writes in the specified file have been written to stable storage on the underlying I/O system. This is usually a costly operation as it forces the OS to flush any pending writes. Different file systems also show wide variance in the cost of this operation.

3   Write and sync the next segments_N file. Once this completes, IndexReaders will suddenly see all changes done since the last commit.

4   Remove old commits by calling on IndexDeletionPolicy to remove old commits. You can create your own implementation of this class to customize which commits are deleted, and when.

Because old index files referenced only by the last commit aren't removed until a new commit is completed, waiting a long time between commits will necessarily consume more disk space than performing more frequent commits. If your Lucene index is interacting with an external transactional resource, such as a database, you may be interested in the advanced APIs that Lucene exposes to enable a two-phase commit.

TWO-PHASE COMMIT

For applications that need to commit a transaction involving a Lucene index and other external resources, such as a database, Lucene exposes the prepareCommit() and prepareCommit(Map<String,String> commitUserData) methods. Each method does steps 1 and 2 in our list, as well as most of step 3, but it stops short of making the new segments_N file visible to a reader. After prepareCommit() is called, you should either call rollback() to abort the commit or commit() to complete it. Commit() is a fast call if prepareCommit() was already called. If an error will be hit, such as "disk full," most likely prepareCommit() will hit the error, not commit(). The separation of these two phases of committing allows you to build a distributed two-phase commit protocol involving Lucene.

By default, after creating a new commit, IndexWriter removes all prior commits. But you can override this behavior by creating a custom IndexDeletionPolicy.

INDEXDELETIONPOLICY

IndexDeletionPolicy is the class that tells IndexWriter when it's safe to remove old commits. The default policy is KeepOnlyLastCommitDeletionPolicy, which always removes all prior commits whenever a new commit is complete. Most of the time you should use this default. But for some advanced applications where you'd like to keep an old point-in-time snapshot around even though further changes have been committed to the index, you may implement your own policy.

For example, when you're sharing an index over NFS, it may be necessary to customize the deletion policy so that a commit isn't deleted until all readers using the index have switched to the most recent commit, based on application specific logic (see section 2.11.2 for details). Another example is a retail company that would like to keep the last N versions of its catalog available for searching. Note that whenever your policy chooses to keep a commit around, that commit will necessarily consume additional disk space in the index.

If you keep multiple commits in your index, there are some useful APIs to help you tell them apart.

MANAGING MULTIPLE INDEX COMMITS

Normally, a Lucene index will have only a single commit present, which is the last commit. But by implementing a custom deletion policy, you can easily accumulate many commits in the index. You can use the static `IndexReader.listCommits()` method to retrieve all commits present in an index. Then, you can step through each and gather whatever details you need. For example, if you previously called `Index-Writer.commit(Map<String,String> commitUserData)`, then that string map is available from each commit by calling its `getUserData()` method. This string map may store something meaningful to your application, enabling you to pick out a particular commit of interest.

Once you've found a commit, you can open an `IndexReader` on it: several of the static open methods accept an `IndexCommit`. You could use this to explicitly search a previous version of the index.

Using the same logic, you can also open an `IndexWriter` on a prior commit, but the use case is different: it allows you to roll back to a previous commit and start indexing new documents from that point, effectively undoing all changes to the index that had happened after that commit. This is similar to `IndexWriter`'s rollback method, except that method only rolls back changes done within the current `IndexWriter` session, whereas opening on a prior commit lets you roll back changes that were already committed to the index, perhaps long ago.

Next we'll see that Lucene supports a simplified ACID transactional model.

2.13.5 *ACID transactions and index consistency*

Lucene implements the ACID transactional model, with the restriction that only one transaction (writer) may be open at once. Here's what ACID stands for, along with details about how Lucene meets it:

- *Atomic*—All changes done with the writer are either committed to the index, or none are; there is nothing in-between.
- *Consistency*—The index will also be consistent; for example, you'll never see a delete without the corresponding `addDocument` from `updateDocument`; you'll always see all or none of the indexes added from an `addIndexes` call.
- *Isolation*—While you are making changes with `IndexWriter`, no changes are visible to a newly opened `IndexReader` until you successfully commit. This even includes passing `create=true` to a newly opened `IndexWriter`. The `IndexReader` only sees the last successful commit.
- *Durability*—If your application hits an unhandled exception, the JVM crashes, the OS crashes, or the computer suddenly loses power, the index will remain consistent and will contain all changes included in the last successful commit. Changes done after that will be lost. Note that if your hard drive develops errors, or your RAM or CPU flips bits, that can easily corrupt your index.

NOTE   If your application, the JVM, the OS, or the machine crashes, the index
        won't be corrupted and will automatically roll back to the last successful
        commit. But Lucene relies on the OS and I/O system that holds the index
        to properly implement the `fsync` system call by flushing any OS or I/O
        write caches to the actual underlying stable storage. In some cases, it may
        be necessary to disable write caching on the underlying I/O devices.

Next we describe how Lucene merges segments, and what you can do to control this
process.

2.13.6 *Merging*

When an index has too many segments, `IndexWriter` selects some of the segments
and merges them into a single, large segment. Merging has a couple of important
benefits:

- It reduces the number of segments in the index because once the merge completes, all of the old segments are removed and a single large segment is added
  in their place. This makes searching faster since there are fewer segments to
  search, and also prevents hitting the file descriptor limit enforced by the OS.
- It reduces the size of the index. For example, if there were deletes pending on
  the merged segments, the merging process frees up the bytes consumed by
  deleted documents. Even if there are no pending deletions, a single merged
  segment will generally use fewer bytes to represent exactly the same set of
  indexed documents.

So when exactly is a merge necessary? What specifically does "too many segments"
mean? That's decided by the `MergePolicy`. But `MergePolicy` only decides which
merges should be done; it's up to `MergeScheduler` to carry out these merges. Let's
first drill into `MergePolicy`.

MERGEPOLICY

`IndexWriter` relies on a subclass of the abstract `MergePolicy` base class to decide
when a merge should be done. Whenever new segments are flushed, or a previously
selected merge has completed, the `MergePolicy` is consulted to determine if a merge
is now necessary, and if so, precisely which segments will be merged. Besides picking
"normal" segment merges to do, the `MergePolicy` also selects merges necessary to
optimize the index and to run `expungeDeletes`.

Lucene provides two core merge policies, both subclassing from `LogMergePolicy`.
The first, which is the default used by `IndexWriter`, is `LogByteSizeMergePolicy`. This
policy measures the size of a segment as the total size in bytes of all files for that segment. The second one, `LogDocMergePolicy`, makes the same merging decisions
except it measures size of a segment by the document count of the segment. Note that
neither merge policy takes deletions into account. If you have mixed document sizes,
it's best to use `LogByteSizeMergePolicy` because it's a more accurate measure of segment size.

If the core merge policies don't suit your application, you can subclass `Merge-Policy` to implement your own. For example, you could implement a time-dependent policy that defers large merges until off-peak hours, to ensure merging doesn't conflict with ongoing searches. Or perhaps you'd like a policy that tries harder to select segments with many pending deletions, so as to reclaim disk space sooner in the index.

Table 2.5 shows the parameters that control how `LogByteSizeMergePolicy` chooses merges. Some of these are also exposed as convenience methods in `Index-Writer`.

To understand these parameters we first must understand how both of these policies select merges. For each segment, its level is computed using this formula:

$$(int)\ log(max(minMergeMB, size))/log(mergeFactor)$$

Table 2.5 Parameters that control merge selection with the default `MergePolicy`, `LogByteSizeMergePolicy`

IndexWriter method	LogByteSizeMergePolicy Method	Default value	Description
setMergeFactor	setMergeFactor	10	Controls segment merge frequency and size
	setMinMergeMB	1.6 MB	Sets a floor on the smallest segment level
	setMaxMergeMB	Long.MAX_VALUE	Limits the size in bytes of a segment to be merged
setMaxMergeDocs	setMaxMergeDocs	Integer.MAX_VALUE	Limits the number of documents for a segment to be merged

This effectively groups the segments of roughly equal size (in log space) into the same level. Tiny segments, less than `minMergeMB`, are always forced into the lowest level to prevent too many tiny segments in the index. Each level contains segments that are up to `mergeFactor` times larger than the previous level. For example, when using `LogByte-SizeMergePolicy`, level 0 segments are up to `mergeFactor` bytes in size; level 1 segments are up to `mergeFactor^2` bytes in size, level 2 segments are up to `mergeFactor^3` bytes in size, and so on. When using `LogDocMergePolicy`, the same progression holds but the size is measured as number of documents in each segment, not byte size.

Once a given level has `mergeFactor` or more segments, they are merged. Thus, `mergeFactor` controls not only how segments are assigned to levels based on size, and thus when to trigger a merge, but also how many segments are merged at once. The larger this setting is, the more segments will exist in your index and the less frequently merges will be done, for a given number of documents in the index. Larger values generally result in faster indexing throughput, but may result in too many open file descriptors (see section 11.3.2 for details on controlling file descriptor usage). It's probably best to leave this at its default value (10) unless you see strong gains when testing different values. When the merge completes, a new segment at the next higher level replaces the merged segments. To prevent merges of large segments, set `max-MergeMB` or `maxMergeDocs`. If ever a segment is over `maxMergeMB` in byte size, or `max-MergeDocs` in its document count, that segment will never be merged. By setting `maxMergeDocs` you can force extremely large segments to remain separate forever in your index.

Besides selecting merges for normal ongoing maintenance of the index, `Merge-Policy` is responsible for selecting merges when `optimize` or `expungeDeletes` is called. In fact, it's up to the `MergePolicy` to define what these methods mean. For example, maybe during optimization you want to skip segments larger than a certain size. Or perhaps for `expungeDeletes` you only want to merge a segment if it has more than 10 percent of its documents deleted. These examples can be easily achieved by creating your own `MergePolicy` that subclasses `LogByteSizeMergePolicy`.

Over time, `LogByteSizeMergePolicy` produces an index with a logarithmic stair-case structure: you have a few very large segments, a few segments `mergeFactor` smaller, and so on. The number of segments in your index is proportional to the logarithm of the net size, in bytes or number of documents, of your index. This generally does a good job of keeping segment count low while minimizing the net merge cost. But some of these settings can be tuned to improve indexing throughput, as described in section 11.1.4.

MERGESCHEDULER

Selection of a merge is only the first step. The next step is the actual merging. `Index-Writer` relies on a subclass of `MergeScheduler` to achieve this. By default, `IndexWriter` uses `ConcurrentMergeScheduler`, which merges segments using background threads. There's also `SerialMergeScheduler`, which always merges segments using the caller's thread, which means you could suddenly see methods like `addDocu-ment` and `deleteDocuments` take a long time while it executes a merge. You could also implement your own `MergeScheduler`.

Generally, customizing `MergePolicy` settings, or implementing your own `Merge-Policy` or `MergeScheduler`, are extremely advanced use cases. For most applications, Lucene's default settings work very well. If you're curious about when `IndexWriter` is flushing and merging, you can call its `setInfoStream` method, as described in section 2.12. Finally, if for some reason you need to wait for all merges to finish, call `IndexWriter`'s `waitForMerges` method.

2.14   *Summary*

We've covered a lot of good ground in this chapter! Fear not: all of your hard work learning these juicy details of Lucene's indexing will shortly pay off, once you build search functionality on top of your index. You now have a solid understanding of how to make changes to a Lucene index. You saw Lucene's conceptual model for documents and fields, including a flexible but flat schema (when compared to a database).

We saw that the indexing process consists of gathering content, extracting text, creating documents and fields, analyzing the text into a token stream, and then handing it off to `IndexWriter` for addition to an index. We also briefly discussed the interesting segmented structure of an index.

You now know how to add, delete, and update documents. We delved into a great many interesting options for controlling how a field is indexed, including how the value is added to the inverted index, stored fields, and term vectors, and how a field can hold certain values other than a `String`. We described variations like multivalued fields, field and document boosting, and value truncation. You now know how to index dates, times, and numbers, as well as fields for sorting.

We discussed segment-level changes, like optimizing an index and using `expunge-Deletes` to reclaim disk space consumed by deleted documents. You now know of all the `Directory` implementations you could use to hold an index, such as `RAMDirectory` and `NIOFSDirectory`. We discussed Lucene's concurrency rules, and the locking it uses to protect an index from more than one writer.

Finally we covered a number of advanced topics: how and why to delete documents using `IndexReader` instead of `IndexWriter`; buffering, flushing, and committing; `IndexWriter`'s support for transactions; merging and the classes available for customizing it; using an index over remote file systems; and turning on `Index-Writer`'s `infoStream` to see details on the steps it's taking internally.

Much of this advanced functionality won't be needed by the vast majority of search applications; in fact, a few of `IndexWriter`'s APIs are enough to build a solid search application. By now you should be dying to learn how to search with Lucene, and that's what you'll read about in the next chapter.

Adding search to your application

This chapter covers

- Querying a Lucene index
- Using Lucene's diverse built-in queries
- Working with search results
- Understanding Lucene scoring
- Parsing human-entered query expressions

The previous chapter showed you in great detail how to build a search index in preparation for searching. As fun as indexing is, it's just a means to an end, a necessary evil, and its value only becomes clear once you enable searching on top of it. In this chapter, we'll show you how to capitalize on all your indexing efforts. For example, consider this scenario:

> Give me a list of all books published in the last 12 months on the subject of "Java" where "open source" or "Jakarta" is mentioned in the contents. Restrict the results to only books that are on special. Oh, and under the covers, also ensure that books mentioning "Apache" are picked up, because we explicitly specified "Jakarta." And make it snappy, on the order of milliseconds for response time.

Such scenarios are easily handled with Lucene, even when your content source consists of millions of documents, but it'll take us three search chapters to see the necessary functionality in Lucene to achieve this example in full. We start with the frequently used search APIs, described in this chapter. Indeed, the majority of applications using Lucene can provide excellent search functionality using only what's covered in this chapter. But a search engine is only as good as its search capabilities, and it's here where Lucene shines. After visiting analysis in chapter 4—important because it's used during both indexing and searching—we'll return to search in chapter 5, delving into Lucene's more advanced search capabilities, as well as in chapter 6, elaborating on ways to extend Lucene's classes for even greater, customized searching power.

In this chapter we begin with a simple example showing that the code you write to implement search is generally no more than a few lines long. Next we illustrate the scoring formula, providing a deep look into one of Lucene's most special attributes. With this example and a high-level understanding of how Lucene ranks search results, we'll spend most of the chapter exploring the diversity of Lucene's built-in search queries, including searching by specific term, by range (numeric or textual), by prefix or wildcard, by phrase, or by fuzzy term matching. We show how the powerful `Boolean-Query` can join any number of clauses together, including arbitrarily nested clauses, using Boolean constraints. Finally we show how simple it is to create a complex search query from a text search expression entered by the end user using Lucene's built-in `QueryParser`.

This is our first of three chapters about Lucene's search APIs, so we'll limit our discussion for now to the primary classes that you'll typically use for search integration, shown in table 3.1.

When you're *querying* a Lucene index, a `TopDocs` instance, containing an ordered array of `ScoreDoc`, is returned. The array is ordered by *score* by default. Lucene computes a score (a numeric value of relevance) for each document, given a query. The `ScoreDocs` themselves aren't the actual matching documents, but rather references, via an integer *document ID*, to the documents matched. In most applications that display

Table 3.1 Lucene's primary searching API

Class	Purpose
IndexSearcher	Gateway to searching an index. All searches come through an `IndexSearcher` instance using any of the several overloaded `search` methods.
Query (and subclasses)	Concrete subclasses encapsulate logic for a particular query type. Instances of `Query` are passed to an `IndexSearcher`'s `search` method.
QueryParser	Processes a human-entered (and readable) expression into a concrete `Query` object.
TopDocs	Holds the top scoring documents, returned by `IndexSearcher.search`.
ScoreDoc	Provides access to each search result in `TopDocs`.

search results, users access only the first few documents, so it isn't necessary to retrieve the full document for all results; you need to retrieve for the current page only the documents that will be presented to the user. In fact, for very large indexes, it often wouldn't even be possible, or would take far too long, to collect all matching documents into available physical computer memory.

Let's see how easy it is to search with Lucene.

3.1   Implementing a simple search feature

Suppose you're tasked with adding search to an application. You've tackled getting the data indexed, using the APIs we covered in the last chapter, but now it's time to expose the full-text searching to the end users. It's hard to imagine that adding search could be any simpler than it is with Lucene. Obtaining search results requires only a few lines of code—literally. Lucene provides easy and highly efficient access to those search results, too, freeing you to focus on your application logic and UI around those results.

When you search with Lucene, you'll have a choice of either programmatically constructing your query or using Lucene's QueryParser to translate text entered by the user into the equivalent Query. The first approach gives you ultimate power, in that your application can expose whatever UI it wants, and your logic translates interactions from that UI into a Query. But the second approach is wonderfully easy to use, and offers a standard search syntax that all users are familiar with. In this section we'll show you how to make the simplest programmatic query, searching for a single term, and then we'll see how to use QueryParser to accept textual queries. In the sections that follow, we'll take this simple example further by detailing all the query types built into Lucene. We begin with the simplest search of all: searching for all documents that contain a single term.

3.1.1   Searching for a specific term

IndexSearcher is the central class used to search for documents in an index. It has several overloaded search methods. You can search for a specific term using the most commonly used search method. A term is a String value that's paired with its containing field name—in our example, subject.

NOTE   The original text may have been normalized into terms by the analyzer, which may eliminate terms (such as stop words), convert terms to lowercase, convert terms to base word forms (*stemming*), or insert additional terms (*synonym processing*). It's crucial that the terms passed to Index-Searcher be consistent with the terms produced by analysis of the source documents during indexing. Chapter 4 discusses the analysis process in detail.

Using our example book data index, which is stored in the build/index subdirectory with the book's source code, we'll query for the words *ant* and *junit*, which are words we know were indexed. Listing 3.1 creates the term query, performs the search and asserts that the single expected document is found. Lucene provides several built-in Query types (see section 3.4), TermQuery being the most basic.

> **Listing 3.1 Simple searching with `TermQuery`**

```
public class BasicSearchingTest extends TestCase {
  public void testTerm() throws Exception {
    Directory dir = TestUtil.getBookIndexDirectory();       ◁─┐ Obtain directory
    IndexSearcher searcher = new IndexSearcher(dir);        ◁─┘ from TestUtil
                                                            ◁─┐ Create IndexSearcher
    Term t = new Term("subject", "ant");
    Query query = new TermQuery(t);
    TopDocs docs = searcher.search(query, 10);
    assertEquals("Ant in Action",                           │ Confirm one
                 1, docs.totalHits);                        │ hit for "ant"
    t = new Term("subject", "junit");
    docs = searcher.search(new TermQuery(t), 10);
    assertEquals("Ant in Action, " +                        │ Confirm two
                 "JUnit in Action, Second Edition",         │ hits for "junit"
                 2, docs.totalHits);
    searcher.close();
    dir.close();
  }
}
```

This is our first time seeing the `TestUtil.getBookIndexDirectory` method; it's quite simple:

```
public static Directory getBookIndexDirectory() throws IOException {
  return FSDirectory.open(new File(System.getProperty("index.dir")));
}
```

The `index.dir` property defaults to "build/index" in the build.xml ant script, so that when you run the tests using Ant from the command line, the index directory is set correctly. That index is built from the books under the data directory, using the `Create-TestIndex` tool (under the src/lia/common subdirectory). We use this method in many tests to retrieve the directory containing the index built from our test book data.

A `TopDocs` object is returned from our search. In a real application we'd step through the individual `ScoreDocs` representing the hits, but for this test we were only interested in checking that the proper number of documents were found.

Note that we close the searcher, and then the directory, after we are done. In general it's best to keep these open and share a single searcher for all queries that need to run. Opening a new searcher can be a costly operation because it must load and populate internal data structures from the index.

This example created a simple query (a single term). Next, we discuss how to transform a user-entered query expression into a `Query` object.

3.1.2 *Parsing a user-entered query expression: QueryParser*

Lucene's search methods require a `Query` object. *Parsing* a query expression is the act of turning a user-entered textual query such as "mock OR junit" into an appropriate `Query` object instance; in this case, the `Query` object would be an instance of `Boolean-Query` with two optional clauses, one for each term. The process is illustrated in figure 3.1. The code in listing 3.2 parses two query expressions and asserts that they

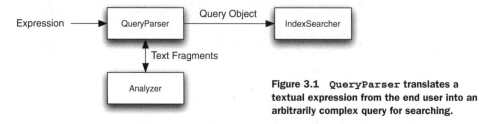

Figure 3.1 `QueryParser` translates a textual expression from the end user into an arbitrarily complex query for searching.

worked as expected. After returning the hits, we retrieve the title from the first document found.

NOTE   Query expressions are similar to SQL expressions used to query a database in that the expression must be parsed into something at a lower level that the database server can understand directly.

Listing 3.2   `QueryParser`, which makes it trivial to translate search text into a `Query`

```
public void testQueryParser() throws Exception {
  Directory dir = TestUtil.getBookIndexDirectory();
  IndexSearcher searcher = new IndexSearcher(dir);

  QueryParser parser = new QueryParser(Version.LUCENE_30,        Create
                                       "contents",              QueryParser
                                       new SimpleAnalyzer());

  Query query = parser.parse("+JUNIT +ANT -MOCK");
  TopDocs docs = searcher.search(query, 10);
  assertEquals(1, docs.totalHits);                              Parse
  Document d = searcher.doc(docs.scoreDocs[0].doc);             user's
  assertEquals("Ant in Action", d.get("title"));               text

  query = parser.parse("mock OR junit");
  docs = searcher.search(query, 10);
  assertEquals("Ant in Action, " +
               "JUnit in Action, Second Edition",
               2, docs.totalHits);

  searcher.close();
  dir.close();
}
```

Lucene includes an interesting built-in feature that parses query expressions, available through the `QueryParser` class. It parses rich expressions such as the two shown (`"+JUNIT +ANT -MOCK"` and `"mock OR junit"`) into one of the `Query` implementations. The resulting `Query` instances can be very rich and complex! Dealing with human-entered queries is the primary purpose of the `QueryParser`. Once you have the `Query` object returned by `QueryParser`, the rest of the searching is identical to how you'd search programmatically.

As you can see in figure 3.1, `QueryParser` requires an *analyzer* to break pieces of the query text into terms. In the first expression, the query was entirely uppercased. The terms of the contents field, however, were lowercased when indexed. `QueryParser`, in this example, uses `SimpleAnalyzer`, which lowercases the terms before constructing a `Query` object. (Analysis is covered in great detail in the next chapter, but it's intimately intertwined with indexing text and searching with `QueryParser`.) The main point regarding analysis to consider in this chapter is that you need to be sure to query on the actual terms indexed. `QueryParser` is the only searching piece that uses an analyzer. Querying through the API using `TermQuery` and the others discussed in section 3.4 doesn't require an analyzer but does rely on matching terms to what was indexed. Therefore, if you construct queries entirely programmatically you must ensure the terms included in all of your queries match the tokens produced by the analyzer used during indexing. In section 4.1.2, we talk more about the interactions of `QueryParser` and the analysis process.

Equipped with the examples shown thus far, you're more than ready to begin searching your indexes. There are, of course, many more details to know about searching. In particular, `QueryParser` requires additional explanation. Next is an overview of how to use `QueryParser`, which we return to in greater detail later in this chapter.

USING QUERYPARSER

Before diving into the details of `QueryParser` (which we do in section 3.5), let's first look at how it's used in a general sense. `QueryParser` is instantiated with `matchVersion` (`Version`), a field name (`String`), and an analyzer, which it uses to break the incoming search text into `Terms`:

```
QueryParser parser = new QueryParser(Version matchVersion,
                                     String field,
                                     Analyzer analyzer)
```

The `matchVersion` parameter instructs Lucene which release it should use for matching defaults and settings, in order to preserve backward compatibility. Note that in some cases, Lucene will emulate bugs from past releases. Section 1.4.1 describes `Version` in more detail.

The field name is the default field against which all terms will be searched, unless the search text explicitly requests matches against a different field name using the syntax "field:text" (more on this in section 3.5.11). Then, the `QueryParser` instance has a `parse()` method to allow for the simplest use:

```
public Query parse(String query) throws ParseException
```

The query String is the expression to be parsed, such as +cat +dog.

If the expression fails to parse, a `ParseException` is thrown, a condition that your application should handle in a graceful manner. `ParseException`'s message gives a reasonable indication of why the parsing failed; however, this description may be too technical for end users.

The `parse()` method is quick and convenient to use, but it may not be sufficient. There are various settings that can be controlled on a `QueryParser` instance, such as the default operator when multiple terms are used (which defaults to OR). These settings also include locale (for date parsing), default phrase slop (described in section 3.4.6), the minimum similarity and prefix length for fuzzy queries, the date resolution, whether to lowercase wildcard queries, and various other advanced settings.

HANDLING BASIC QUERY EXPRESSIONS WITH QUERYPARSER

QueryParser translates query expressions into one of Lucene's built-in query types. We'll cover each query type in section 3.4; for now, take in the bigger picture provided by table 3.2, which shows some examples of expressions and their translation.

Table 3.2 Expression examples that `QueryParser` handles

Query expression	Matches documents that...
java	Contain the term *java* in the default field
java junit	Contain the term *java* or *junit*, or both, in the default field[a]
java OR junit	
+java +junit	Contain both *java* and *junit* in the default field
java AND junit	
title:ant	Contain the term *ant* in the title field
title:extreme -subject:sports	Contain *extreme* in the title field and don't have *sports* in the subject field
title:extreme AND NOT subject:sports	
(agile OR extreme) AND methodology	Contain *methodology* and must also contain *agile* and/or *extreme*, all in the default field
title:"junit in action"	Contain the exact phrase "junit in action" in the title field
title:"junit action"~5	Contain the terms junit and *action* within five positions of one another, in the title field
java*	Contain terms that begin with *java*, like *javaspaces, javaserver, java.net*, and the exact tem *java* itself.
java~	Contain terms that are close to the word *java*, such as *lava*
lastmodified: [1/1/09 TO 12/31/09]	Have `lastmodified` field values between the dates January 1, 2009 and December 31, 2009

a. The default operator is OR. It can be set to AND (see section 3.5.6).

With this broad picture of Lucene's search capabilities, you're ready to dive into details. We'll revisit QueryParser in section 3.5, after we cover the more foundational pieces. Let's take a closer look at Lucene's IndexSearcher class.

3.2 *Using IndexSearcher*

Searching with Lucene is a surprisingly simple affair. You first create an instance of IndexSearcher, which opens the search index, and then use the search methods on that class to perform all searching. The returned TopDocs class represents the top results, and you use that to present results to the user. Next we discuss how to handle pagination, and finally we show how to use Lucene's new (as of version 2.9) near-real-time search capability for fast turnaround on recently indexed documents. Let's begin with the creation of an IndexSearcher.

3.2.1 Creating an IndexSearcher

Like the rest of Lucene's primary API, IndexSearcher is simple to use. The classes involved are shown in figure 3.2. First, as with indexing, we'll need a directory. Most often you're searching an index in the file system:

```
Directory dir = FSDirectory.open(new File("/path/to/index"));
```

Section 2.10 describes alternate Directory implementations. Next we create an IndexReader:

```
IndexReader reader = IndexReader.open(dir);
```

Finally, we create the IndexSearcher:

```
IndexSearcher searcher = new IndexSearcher(reader);
```

Directory, which we've already seen in the context of indexing, provides the abstract file-like API. IndexReader uses that API to interact with the index files stored during indexing, and exposes the low-level API that IndexSearcher uses for searching. Index-Searcher's APIs accept Query objects, for searching, and return TopDocs objects representing the results, as we discussed in section 3.2.3.

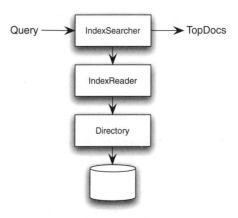

Note that it's IndexReader that does all the heavy lifting to open all index files and expose a low-level reader API, while Index-Searcher is a rather thin veneer. Because it's costly to open an IndexReader, it's best to reuse a single instance for all of your searches, and open a new one only when necessary.

Figure 3.2   The relationship between the common classes used for searching

NOTE   Opening an IndexReader is costly, so you should reuse a single instance for all of your searching when possible, and limit how often you open a new one.

It's also possible to directly create the IndexSearcher from a directory, which creates its own private IndexReader under the hood, as we saw in chapter 1. If you go this route, you can retrieve the underlying IndexReader by calling IndexSearcher's get-IndexReader method, but remember that if you close the searcher it will also close this IndexReader because it had opened it.

IndexReader always searches a point-in-time snapshot of the index as it existed when the IndexReader was created. If you need to search changes to the index, you'll have to open a new reader. Fortunately, the IndexReader.reopen method is a resource-efficient means of obtaining a new IndexReader that covers all changes to the index but shares resources with the current reader when possible. Use it like this:

```
IndexReader newReader = reader.reopen();
if (reader != newReader) {
  reader.close();
  reader = newReader;
  searcher = new IndexSearcher(reader);
}
```

The reopen method only returns a new reader if there were changes in the index, in which case it's your responsibility to close the old reader and create a new Index-Searcher. In a real application, where multiple threads may still be searching using the old reader, you'll have to protect this code to make it thread safe. Section 11.2.2 provides a useful drop-in class that does this for you. Section 3.2.5 shows how to obtain a near-real-time IndexReader from an IndexWriter, which is even more resource efficient in cases where you have access to the IndexWriter making changes to the index. Now that we have an IndexSearcher, let's see how to search!

NOTE   An IndexSearcher instance searches only the index as it existed at the time the IndexSearcher was instantiated. If indexing is occurring concurrently with searching, newer documents indexed won't be visible to searches. In order to see the new documents, you should open a new reader.

3.2.2   *Performing searches*

Once you have an IndexSearcher, simply call one of its search methods to perform a search. Under the hood, the search method does a tremendous amount of work, very quickly. It visits every single document that's a candidate for matching the search, only accepting the ones that pass every constraint on the query. Finally, it gathers the top results and returns them to you.

The main search methods available to an IndexSearcher instance are shown in table 3.3. In this chapter we only make use of the search(Query, int) method because many applications won't need to use the more advanced methods. The other search method signatures, including the filtering and sorting variants, are covered in chapter 5. Chapter 6 covers the customizable search methods that accept a Collector for gathering results.

Most of IndexSearcher's search methods return TopDocs, which we cover next, to represent the returned results.

3.2.3   *Working with TopDocs*

Now that we've called search, we have a TopDocs object at our disposal that we can use for efficient access to the search results. Typically, you'll use one of the search

Table 3.3 Primary IndexSearcher search methods

IndexSearcher.search method signature	When to use
TopDocs search(Query query, int n)	Straightforward searches. The int n parameter specifies how many top-scoring documents to return.
TopDocs search(Query query, Filter filter, int n)	Searches constrained to a subset of available documents, based on filter criteria.
TopFieldDocs search(Query query, Filter filter, int n, Sort sort)	Searches constrained to a subset of available documents based on filter criteria, and sorted by a custom Sort object
void search(Query query, Collector results)	Used when you have custom logic to implement for each document visited, or you'd like to collect a different subset of documents than the top N by the sort criteria.
void search(Query query, Filter filter, Collector results)	Same as previous, except documents are only accepted if they pass the filter criteria.

methods that return a TopDocs object, as shown in table 3.3. Results are ordered by relevance—in other words, by how well each document matches the query (sorting results in other ways is discussed in section 5.2).

The TopDocs class exposes a small number of methods and attributes for retrieving the search results; they're listed in table 3.4. The attribute TopDocs.totalHits returns the number of matching documents. The matches, by default, are sorted in decreasing score order. The TopDocs.scoreDocs attribute is an array containing the requested number of top matches. Each ScoreDoc instance has a float score, which is the relevance score, and an int doc, which is the document ID that can be used to retrieve the stored fields for that document by calling IndexSearcher.document (doc). Finally, TopDocs.getMaxScore() returns the best score across all matches; when you sort by relevance (the default), that will always be the score of the first result. But if you sort by other criteria and enable scoring for the search, as described in section 5.2, it will be the maximum score of all matching documents even when the best scoring document isn't in the top results by your sort criteria.

Table 3.4 TopDocs methods for efficiently accessing search results03_Ch03.fm

TopDocs method or attribute	Return value
totalHits	Number of documents that matched the search
scoreDocs	Array of ScoreDoc instances that contains the results
getMaxScore()	Returns best score of all matches, if scoring was done while searching (when sorting by field, you separately control whether scores are computed)

3.2.4   *Paging through results*

Presenting search results to end users most often involves displaying only the first 10 to 20 most relevant documents. Paging through ScoreDocs is a common requirement, although if you find users are frequently doing a lot of paging you should revisit your design: ideally the user almost always finds the result on the first page. That said, pagination is still typically needed. You can choose from a couple of implementation approaches:

- Gather multiple pages' worth of results on the initial search and keep the resulting ScoreDocs and IndexSearcher instances available while the user is navigating the search results.
- Requery each time the user navigates to a new page.

Requerying is most often the better solution. Requerying eliminates the need to store per-user state, which in a web application can be costly, especially with a large number of users. Requerying at first glance seems a waste, but Lucene's blazing speed more than compensates. Also, thanks to the I/O caching in modern operating systems, requerying will typically be fast because the necessary bits from disk will already be cached in RAM. Frequently users don't click past the first page of results anyway.

In order to requery, the original search is reexecuted, with a larger number of requested matches, and the results are displayed beginning on the desired page. How the original query is kept depends on your application architecture. In a web application where the user types in an expression that's parsed with QueryParser, the original expression could be made part of the links for navigating the pages and reparsed for each request, or the expression could be kept in a hidden HTML field or as a cookie.

Don't prematurely optimize your paging implementations with caching or persistence. First implement your paging feature with a straightforward requery approach; chances are you'll find this sufficient for your needs. Let's see an example of near-real-time search next.

3.2.5   *Near-real-time search*

One of the new features in Lucene's 2.9 release is near-real-time search, which enables you to rapidly search changes made to the index with an open IndexWriter, without having to first close or commit changes to that writer. Many applications make ongoing changes with an always open IndexWriter and require that subsequent searches quickly reflect these changes. If that IndexWriter instance is in the same JVM that's doing searching, you can use near-real-time search, as shown in listing 3.3.

This capability is referred to as *near*-real-time search, and not simply real-time search, because it's not possible to make strict guarantees about the turnaround time, in the same sense as a "hard" real-time OS is able to do. Lucene's near-real-time search is more like a "soft" real-time OS. For example, if Java decides to run a major garbage collection cycle, or if a large segment merge has just completed, or if your machine is struggling because there's not enough RAM, the turnaround time of the near-real-time reader can be much longer. But in practice the turnaround time can be very fast (tens of milliseconds or less), depending on your indexing and searching throughput, and how frequently you obtain a new near-real-time reader.

In the past, without this feature, you'd have to call commit on the writer, and then reopen on your reader, but this can be time consuming since commit must sync all new files in the index, an operation that's often costly on certain operating systems and file systems because it usually means the underlying I/O device must physically write all buffered bytes to stable storage. Near-real-time search enables you to search segments that are newly created but not yet committed. Section 11.1.3 gives some tips for further reducing the index-to-search turnaround time.

Listing 3.3 Near-real-time search

```
public class NearRealTimeTest extends TestCase {
  public void testNearRealTime() throws Exception {
    Directory dir = new RAMDirectory();
    IndexWriter writer = new IndexWriter(dir, new
     StandardAnalyzer(Version.LUCENE_30),
     IndexWriter.MaxFieldLength.UNLIMITED);
    for(int i=0;i<10;i++) {
      Document doc = new Document();
      doc.add(new Field("id", ""+i, Field.Store.NO,
     Field.Index.NOT_ANALYZED_NO_NORMS));
      doc.add(new Field("text", "aaa", Field.Store.NO,
     Field.Index.ANALYZED));
      writer.addDocument(doc);
    }
    IndexReader reader = writer.getReader();                    ← ❶ Create near-real-
    IndexSearcher searcher = new IndexSearcher(reader);              time reader
                                                               ← Wrap reader in
    Query query = new TermQuery(new Term("text", "aaa"));          IndexSearcher
    TopDocs docs = searcher.search(query, 1);
    assertEquals(10, docs.totalHits);                ←— Search returns 10 hits

    writer.deleteDocuments(new Term("id", "7"));          ←❷ Delete 1 document

    Document doc = new Document();
    doc.add(new Field("id",                                ❸ Add 1
                      "11",                                   document
                      Field.Store.NO,
                      Field.Index.NOT_ANALYZED_NO_NORMS));
    doc.add(new Field("text",
                      "bbb",
                      Field.Store.NO,
                      Field.Index.ANALYZED));
    writer.addDocument(doc);
                                                       ❹ Reopen reader
    IndexReader newReader = reader.reopen();              ←
    assertFalse(reader == newReader);               ←❺ Confirm reader is new
    reader.close();                                      ←
    searcher = new IndexSearcher(newReader);      ❻ Close old reader

    TopDocs hits = searcher.search(query, 10);         ❼ Verify 9 hits now
    assertEquals(9, hits.totalHits);
```

```
    query = new TermQuery(new Term("text", "bbb"));
    hits = searcher.search(query, 1);
    assertEquals(1, hits.totalHits);

    newReader.close();
    writer.close();
  }
}
```

⑧ Confirm new document matched

❶ `IndexWriter` returns a reader that's able to search all previously committed changes to the index, plus any uncommitted changes. The returned reader is always read-only.

❷ ❸ We make changes to the index but don't commit them.

❹ ❺ ❻ We ask the reader to reopen. Note that this simply calls `writer.getReader` again under the hood. Because we made changes, the `newReader` will be different from the old one so we must close the old one.

❼ ❽ The changes made with the writer are reflected in new searches.

The important method is `IndexWriter.getReader`. This method flushes any buffered changes to the directory, and then creates a new `IndexReader` that includes the changes. If further changes are made through the `IndexWriter`, you use the reopen method in the `IndexReader` to get a new reader. If there are changes, a new reader is returned, and you should then close the old reader. The reopen method is very efficient: for any unchanged parts of the index, it shares the open files and caches with the previous reader. Only newly created files since the last open or reopen will be opened. This results in very fast, often subsecond, turnaround. Section 11.2.2 provides further examples of how to use the reopen method with a near-real-time reader.

Next we look at how Lucene scores each document that matches the search.

3.3   *Understanding Lucene scoring*

Every time a document matches during search, it's assigned a score that reflects how good the match is. This score computes how similar the document is to the query, with higher scores reflecting stronger similarity and thus stronger matches. We chose to discuss this complex topic early in this chapter so you'll have a general sense of the various factors that go into Lucene scoring as you continue to read. We'll start with details on Lucene's scoring formula, and then show how you can see the full explanation of how a certain document arrived at its score.

3.3.1   *How Lucene scores*

Without further ado, meet Lucene's similarity scoring formula, shown in figure 3.3. It's called the similarity scoring formula because its purpose is to measure the similarity between a query and each document that matches the query. The score is computed for each document (d) matching each term (t) in a query (q).

$$\sum_{t\ in\ q} (tf(t\ in\ d) \times idf(t)^2 \times boost(t.field\ in\ d) \times lengthNorm(t.field\ in\ d)) \times coord(q,d) \times queryNorm(q)$$

Figure 3.3   Lucene uses this formula to determine a document score based on a query.

NOTE If this equation or the thought of mathematical computations scares you, you may safely skip this section. Lucene's scoring is top-notch as is, and a detailed understanding of what makes it tick isn't necessary to take advantage of Lucene's capabilities.

This score is the raw score, which is a floating-point number >= 0.0. Typically, if an application presents the score to the end user, it's best to first normalize the scores by dividing all scores by the maximum score for the query. The larger the similarity score, the better the match of the document to the query. By default Lucene returns documents reverse-sorted by this score, meaning the top documents are the best matching ones. Table 3.5 describes each of the factors in the scoring formula.

Boost factors are built into the equation to let you affect a query or field's influence on score. Field boosts come in explicitly in the equation as the `boost(t.field in d)` factor, set at indexing time. The default value of field boosts, logically, is 1.0. During indexing, a document can be assigned a boost, too. A document boost factor implicitly sets the starting field boost of all fields to the specified value. Field-specific boosts are multiplied by the starting value, giving the final value of the field boost factor. It's possible to add the same named field to a document multiple times, and in such situations the field boost is computed as all the boosts specified for that field and document multiplied together. Section 2.5 discusses index-time boosting in more detail.

In addition to the explicit factors in this equation, other factors can be computed on a per-query basis as part of the `queryNorm` factor. Queries themselves can have an

Table 3.5 Factors in the scoring formula

Factor	Description
`tf(t in d)`	Term frequency factor for the term (`t`) in the document (`d`)—how many times the term `t` occurs in the document.
`idf(t)`	Inverse document frequency of the term: a measure of how "unique" the term is. Very common terms have a low `idf`; very rare terms have a high `idf`.
`boost(t.field in d)`	Field and document boost, as set during indexing (see section 2.5). You may use this to statically boost certain fields and certain documents over others.
`lengthNorm(t.field in d)`	Normalization value of a field, given the number of terms within the field. This value is computed during indexing and stored in the index norms. Shorter fields (fewer tokens) get a bigger boost from this factor.
`coord(q, d)`	Coordination factor, based on the number of query terms the document contains. The coordination factor gives an AND-like boost to documents that contain more of the search terms than other documents.
`queryNorm(q)`	Normalization value for a query, given the sum of the squared weights of each of the query terms.

impact on the document score. Boosting a `Query` instance is sensible only in a multiple-clause query; if only a single term is used for searching, changing its boost would impact all matched documents equally. In a multiple-clause Boolean query, some documents may match one clause but not another, enabling the boost factor to discriminate between matching documents. Queries also default to a 1.0 boost factor.

Most of these scoring formula factors are controlled and implemented as a subclass of the abstract `Similarity` class. `DefaultSimilarity` is the implementation used unless otherwise specified. More computations are performed under the covers of `DefaultSimilarity`; for example, the term *frequency factor* is the square root of the actual frequency. Because this is an "in action" book, it's beyond the book's scope to delve into the inner workings of these calculations. In practice, it's extremely rare to need a change in these factors. Should you need to change them, please refer to `Similarity`'s Javadocs, and be prepared with a solid understanding of these factors and the effect your changes will have.

It's important to note that a change in index-time boosts or the `Similarity` methods used during indexing, such as `lengthNorm`, require that the index be rebuilt for all factors to be in sync.

Let's say you're baffled as to why a certain document got a good score to your `Query`. Lucene offers a nice feature to help provide the answer.

3.3.2 *Using explain() to understand hit scoring*

Whew! The scoring formula seems daunting—and it is. We're talking about factors that rank one document higher than another based on a query; that in and of itself deserves the sophistication going on. If you want to see how all these factors play out, Lucene provides a helpful feature called `Explanation`. `IndexSearcher` has an `explain` method, which requires a `Query` and a document ID and returns an `Explanation` object.

The `Explanation` object internally contains all the gory details that factor into the score calculation. Each detail can be accessed individually if you like; but generally, dumping out the explanation in its entirety is desired. The `.toString()` method dumps a nicely formatted text representation of the `Explanation`. We wrote a simple program to dump `Explanations`, shown in listing 3.4.

Listing 3.4   The `explain()` method

```
public class Explainer {
  public static void main(String[] args) throws Exception {
    if (args.length != 2) {
      System.err.println("Usage: Explainer <index dir> <query>");
      System.exit(1);
    }

    String indexDir = args[0];
    String queryExpression = args[1];

    Directory directory = FSDirectory.open(new File(indexDir));
```

```
QueryParser parser = new QueryParser(Version.LUCENE_30,
                              "contents", new SimpleAnalyzer());
Query query = parser.parse(queryExpression);

System.out.println("Query: " + queryExpression);

IndexSearcher searcher = new IndexSearcher(directory);
TopDocs topDocs = searcher.search(query, 10);

for (ScoreDoc match : topDocs.scoreDocs) {
  Explanation explanation
      = searcher.explain(query, match.doc);       Generate
                                                  Explanation

  System.out.println("----------");
  Document doc = searcher.doc(match.doc);          Output
  System.out.println(doc.get("title"));            Explanation
  System.out.println(explanation.toString());
}
searcher.close();
directory.close();
  }
}
```

Using the query `junit` against our sample index produced the following output; notice that the most relevant title scored best:

```
Query: junit
----------
JUnit in Action, Second Edition
0.7629841 = (MATCH) fieldWeight(contents:junit in 11), product of:
  1.4142135 = tf(termFreq(contents:junit)=2)     ◄┐
  2.466337 = idf(docFreq=2, maxDocs=13)           ❶
  0.21875 = fieldNorm(field=contents, doc=11)

----------
Ant in Action
0.61658424 = (MATCH) fieldWeight(contents:junit in 9), product of:
  1.0 = tf(termFreq(contents:junit)=1)            ◄┐
  2.466337 = idf(docFreq=2, maxDocs=13)           ❷
  0.25 = fieldNorm(field=contents, doc=9)
```

❶ *JUnit in Action, Second Edition* has the term *junit* twice in its contents field. The contents field in our index is a catchall field, aggregating all textual fields to allow a single field for searching.

❷ *Ant in Action* has the term *junit* only once in its contents field.

There's also a `.toHtml()` method that outputs the same hierarchical structure, except as nested HTML `<ul>` elements suitable for outputting in a web browser. In fact, the `Explanation` feature is a core part of the Nutch project, allowing for transparent ranking.

Explanations are handy to see the inner workings of the score calculation, but they expend the same amount of effort as a query. So, be sure not to use extraneous `Explanation` generation.

By now you have a strong foundation for getting your search application off the ground: we showed the most important ways of performing searches with Lucene. Now, it's time to drill down into detail on the numerous types of queries Lucene offers.

3.4 *Lucene's diverse queries*

As you saw in section 3.2, querying Lucene ultimately requires a call to one of Index-Searcher's search methods, using an instance of Query. Query subclasses can be instantiated directly, or, as we discussed in section 3.1.2, a Query can be constructed through the use of QueryParser, a front end that converts free text into each of the Query types we describe here. In each case we'll show you how to programmatically instantiate each Query, and also what QueryParser syntax to use to create the query.

Even if you're using QueryParser, combining a parsed query expression with an API-created Query is a common technique to augment, refine, or constrain a human-entered query. For example, you may want to restrict free-form parsed expressions to a subset of the index, like documents only within a category. Depending on your search's UI, you may have date pickers to select a date range, drop-downs for selecting a category, and a free-form search box. Each of these clauses can be stitched together using a combination of QueryParser and programmatically constructed queries.

Yet another way to create Query objects is by using the XML Query Parser package, contained in Lucene's contrib modules and described in section 9.5. This package allows you to express arbitrary queries directly as XML strings, which the package then converts into a Query instance. The XML could be created in any way, but one simple approach is to apply a transform to name-value pairs provided by an advanced search UI.

This section covers each of Lucene's built-in Query types, TermQuery, TermRange-Query, NumericRangeQuery, PrefixQuery, BooleanQuery, PhraseQuery, Wildcard-Query, FuzzyQuery, and the unusual yet aptly named MatchAllDocsQuery. We'll see how these queries match documents, and how to create them programmatically. There are still more queries under Lucene's contrib area, described in section 8.6. In section 3.5 we'll show how you can create each of these query types using QueryParser instead. We begin with TermQuery.

3.4.1 *Searching by term: TermQuery*

The most elementary way to search an index is for a specific term. A term is the smallest indexed piece, consisting of a field name and a text-value pair. Listing 3.1 provided an example of searching for a specific term. This code constructs a Term object instance:

```
Term t = new Term("contents", "java");
```

A TermQuery accepts a single Term:

```
Query query = new TermQuery(t);
```

All documents that have the word *java* in a contents field are returned from searches using this TermQuery. Note that the value is case sensitive, so be sure to match the case of terms indexed; this may not be the exact case in the original document text, because an analyzer (see chapter 4) may have indexed things differently.

TermQuerys are especially useful for retrieving documents by a key. If documents were indexed using Field.Index.NOT_ANALYZED, the same value can be used to retrieve these documents. For example, given our book test data, the following code retrieves the single document matching the ISBN provided:

```
public void testKeyword() throws Exception {
    Directory dir = TestUtil.getBookIndexDirectory();
    IndexSearcher searcher = new IndexSearcher(dir);

    Term t = new Term("isbn", "9781935182023");
    Query query = new TermQuery(t);
    TopDocs docs = searcher.search(query, 10);
    assertEquals("JUnit in Action, Second Edition",
                 1, docs.totalHits);

    searcher.close();
    dir.close();
}
```

A Field.Index.NOT_ANALYZED field doesn't imply that it's unique, though. It's up to you to ensure uniqueness during indexing. In our sample book data, isbn is unique among all documents.

3.4.2 *Searching within a term range: TermRangeQuery*

Terms are ordered lexicographically (according to String.compareTo) within the index, allowing for straightforward searching of textual terms within a range as provided by Lucene's TermRangeQuery. The beginning and ending terms may either be included or excluded. If either term is null, that end is open-ended. For example, a null lowerTerm means there is no lower bound, so all terms less than the upper term are included. Only use this query for textual ranges, such as for finding all names that begin with N through Q. NumericRangeQuery, covered in the next section, should be used for ranges on numeric fields.

The following code illustrates TermRangeQuery, searching for all books whose title begins with any letter from d to j. Our books data set has three such books. Note that the title2 field in our book index is simply the lowercased title, indexed as a single token using Field.NOT_ANALYZED_NO_NORMS:

```
public void testTermRangeQuery() throws Exception {
    Directory dir = TestUtil.getBookIndexDirectory();
    IndexSearcher searcher = new IndexSearcher(dir);
    TermRangeQuery query = new TermRangeQuery("title2", "d", "j",
                                              true, true);
    TopDocs matches = searcher.search(query, 100);
    assertEquals(3, matches.totalHits);
    searcher.close();
    dir.close();
}
```

The last two Booleans to the `TermRangeQuery` state whether the start and end points are inclusive (`true`) or exclusive (`false`). We passed `true`, for an inclusive search, but had we passed `false` instead there would be no change in the results because we have no books with the exact title d or j.

Because Lucene always stores its terms in lexicographic sort order (using `String.compareTo`, which compares by UTF16 code unit), the range defined by the beginning and ending terms is always according to this lexicographic order. However, `TermRangeQuery` can also accept a custom `Collator`, which is then used for range checking. Unfortunately, this process can be extremely slow for a large index because it requires enumerating every single term in the index to check if it's within bounds. The `CollationKeyAnalyzer`, a contrib module, is one way to gain back the performance.

Next we consider the numeric equivalent of `TermRangeQuery`.

3.4.3 *Searching within a numeric range: NumericRangeQuery*

If you indexed your field with `NumericField`, you can efficiently search a particular range for that field using `NumericRangeQuery`. Under the hood, Lucene translates the requested range into the equivalent set of brackets in the previously indexed *trie structure*. Each bracket is a distinct term in the index whose documents are OR'd together. The number of brackets required will be relatively small, which is what gives `NumericRangeQuery` such good performance when compared to an equivalent `TermRangeQuery`.

Let's look at an example based on the pubmonth field from our book index. We indexed this field as an integer with month precision, meaning March 2010 is indexed as a `NumericField` with the integer value 201,003. We can then do an inclusive range search like this:

```
public void testInclusive() throws Exception {
  Directory dir = TestUtil.getBookIndexDirectory();
  IndexSearcher searcher = new IndexSearcher(dir);
  // pub date of TTC was September 2006
  NumericRangeQuery query = NumericRangeQuery.newIntRange("pubmonth",
                                                          200605,
                                                          200609,
                                                          true,
                                                          true);

  TopDocs matches = searcher.search(query, 10);
  assertEquals(1, matches.totalHits);
  searcher.close();
  dir.close();
}
```

Just like `TermRangeQuery`, the last two Booleans to the `newIntRange` method state whether the start and end points are inclusive (`true`) or exclusive (`false`). There's only one book published in that range, which was published in September 2006. If we change the range search to be exclusive, the book is no longer found:

```
public void testExclusive() throws Exception {
  Directory dir = TestUtil.getBookIndexDirectory();
  IndexSearcher searcher = new IndexSearcher(dir);

  // pub date of TTC was September 2006
  NumericRangeQuery query = NumericRangeQuery.newIntRange("pubmonth",
                                                          200605,
                                                          200609,
                                                          false,
                                                          false);

  TopDocs matches = searcher.search(query, 10);
  assertEquals(0, matches.totalHits);
  searcher.close();
  dir.close();
}
```

NumericRangeQuery also optionally accepts the same precisionStep parameter as NumericField. If you had changed this value from its default during indexing, it's crucial that you provide an acceptable value (either the same value, or a multiple of the value used during indexing) when searching. Otherwise you'll silently get incorrect results. See the Javadocs for NumericRangeQuery for more details.

Now let's move on to another query that matches terms by prefix.

3.4.4 Searching on a string: PrefixQuery

PrefixQuery matches documents containing terms beginning with a specified string. It's deceptively handy. The following code demonstrates how you can query a hierarchical structure *recursively* with a simple PrefixQuery. The documents contain a category field representing a hierarchical structure, which is perfect for matching with a PrefixQuery, as shown in listing 3.5.

Listing 3.5 PrefixQuery

```
public class PrefixQueryTest extends TestCase {
  public void testPrefix() throws Exception {
    Directory dir = TestUtil.getBookIndexDirectory();
    IndexSearcher searcher = new IndexSearcher(dir);
    Term term = new Term("category",
                    "/technology/computers/programming");    Search,
    PrefixQuery query = new PrefixQuery(term);               including
                                                             subcategories
    TopDocs matches = searcher.search(query, 10);
    int programmingAndBelow = matches.totalHits;

    matches = searcher.search(new TermQuery(term), 10);    Search, without
    int justProgramming = matches.totalHits;               subcategories

    assertTrue(programmingAndBelow > justProgramming);
    searcher.close();
    dir.close();
  }
}
```

Our `PrefixQueryTest` demonstrates the difference between a `PrefixQuery` and a `TermQuery`. A methodology category exists below the `/technology/computers/ programming` category. Books in this subcategory are found with a `PrefixQuery` but not with the `TermQuery` on the parent category.

Our next query, `BooleanQuery`, is an interesting one because it's able to embed and combine other queries.

3.4.5 *Combining queries: BooleanQuery*

The query types discussed here can be combined in complex ways using `Boolean- Query`, which is a container of Boolean *clauses*. A clause is a subquery that can be required, optional, or prohibited. These attributes allow for logical AND, OR, and NOT combinations. You add a clause to a `BooleanQuery` using this API method:

```
public void add(Query query, BooleanClause.Occur occur)
```

where `occur` can be `BooleanClause.Occur.MUST`, `BooleanClause.Occur.SHOULD`, or `BooleanClause.Occur.MUST_NOT`.

A `BooleanQuery` can be a clause within another `BooleanQuery`, allowing for arbitrary nesting. Let's look at some examples. Listing 3.6 shows an AND query to find the most recent books on one of our favorite subjects, *search*.

Listing 3.6   Using `BooleanQuery` to combine required subqueries

```
public void testAnd() throws Exception {
    TermQuery searchingBooks =
        new TermQuery(new Term("subject", "search"));        ←--❶

    Query books2010 =
        NumericRangeQuery.newIntRange("pubmonth", 201001,
                                      201012,
                                      true, true);           ❷

    BooleanQuery searchingBooks2010 = new BooleanQuery();
    searchingBooks2010.add(searchingBooks, BooleanClause.Occur.MUST);   ❸
    searchingBooks2010.add(books2010, BooleanClause.Occur.MUST);

    Directory dir = TestUtil.getBookIndexDirectory();
    IndexSearcher searcher = new IndexSearcher(dir);
    TopDocs matches = searcher.search(searchingBooks2010, 10);

    assertTrue(TestUtil.hitsIncludeTitle(searcher, matches,
                           "Lucene in Action, Second Edition"));
    searcher.close();
    dir.close();
}
```

❶ This query finds all books containing the subject `"search"`.

❷ This query finds all books published in 2010.

❸ Here we combine the two queries into a single Boolean query with both clauses required (the second argument is `BooleanClause.Occur.MUST`).

In this test case, we used a new utility method, `TestUtil.hitsIncludeTitle`:

```
public static boolean hitsIncludeTitle(IndexSearcher searcher,
                                       TopDocs hits, String title)
  throws IOException {
  for (ScoreDoc match : hits.scoreDocs) {
    Document doc = searcher.doc(match.doc);
    if (title.equals(doc.get("title"))) {
      return true;
    }
  }
  System.out.println("title '" + title + "' not found");
  return false;
}
```

`BooleanQuery.add` has two overloaded method signatures. One accepts only a `BooleanClause`, and the other accepts a `Query` and a `BooleanClause.Occur` instance. A `BooleanClause` is simply a container of a `Query` and a `BooleanClause.Occur` instance, so we omit coverage of it. `BooleanClause.Occur.MUST` means exactly that: only documents matching that clause are considered. `BooleanClause.Occur.SHOULD` means the term is optional. `BooleanClause.Occur.MUST_NOT` means any documents matching this clause are excluded from the results. Use `Boolean-Clause.Occur.SHOULD` to perform an OR query, as shown in listing 3.7.

Listing 3.7 Using `BooleanQuery` to combine optional subqueries.

```
public void testOr() throws Exception {
  TermQuery methodologyBooks = new TermQuery(        Match lst category
          new Term("category",
            "/technology/computers/programming/methodology"));

  TermQuery easternPhilosophyBooks = new TermQuery(   Match 2nd
      new Term("category",                            category
        "/philosophy/eastern"));

  BooleanQuery enlightenmentBooks = new BooleanQuery();
  enlightenmentBooks.add(methodologyBooks,            Combine both
                    BooleanClause.Occur.SHOULD);      categories
  enlightenmentBooks.add(easternPhilosophyBooks
                    BooleanClause.Occur.SHOULD);

  Directory dir = TestUtil.getBookIndexDirectory();
  IndexSearcher searcher = new IndexSearcher(dir);
  TopDocs matches = searcher.search(enlightenmentBooks, 10);
  System.out.println("or = " + enlightenmentBooks);

  assertTrue(TestUtil.hitsIncludeTitle(searcher, matches,
                          "Extreme Programming Explained"));
  assertTrue(TestUtil.hitsIncludeTitle(searcher, matches,
                          "Tao Te Ching \u9053\u5FB7\u7D93"));
  searcher.close();
  dir.close();
}
```

It's fine to mix and match different clauses within a single `BooleanQuery`; simply specify the `BooleanClause.Occur` for each. You can create very powerful queries by doing so. For example, you could construct a query that must match "java" and "programming", must not match "ant", and should match "computers" as well as "flowers." Then, you'll know that every returned document will contain both "java" and "programming," won't contain "ant", and will contain either "computers" or "flowers", or both.

`BooleanQuerys` are restricted to a maximum number of clauses; 1,024 is the default. This limitation is in place to prevent queries from accidentally adversely affecting performance. A `TooManyClauses` exception is thrown if the maximum is exceeded. This had been necessary in past Lucene releases, because certain queries would rewrite themselves under the hood to the equivalent `BooleanQuery`. But as of 2.9, these queries are now executed in a more efficient manner. Should you ever have the unusual need of increasing the number of clauses allowed, there's a `setMaxClauseCount(int)` method on `BooleanQuery`, but be aware of the performance cost of executing such queries.

The next query, `PhraseQuery`, differs from the queries we've covered so far in that it pays attention to the positional details of multiple-term occurrences.

3.4.6 Searching by phrase: PhraseQuery

An index by default contains positional information of terms, as long as you didn't create pure Boolean fields by indexing with the `omitTermFreqAndPositions` option (described in section 2.4.1). `PhraseQuery` uses this information to locate documents where terms are within a certain distance of one another. For example, suppose a field contained the phrase *the quick brown fox jumped over the lazy dog*. Without knowing the exact phrase, you can still find this document by searching for documents with fields having *quick* and *fox* near each other. Sure, a plain `TermQuery` would do the trick to locate this document knowing either of those words, but in this case we only want documents that have phrases where the words are either exactly side by side (*quick fox*) or have one word in between (*quick* [irrelevant] *fox*).

The maximum allowable positional distance between terms to be considered a match is called *slop*. *Distance* is the number of positional moves of terms used to reconstruct the phrase in order. Let's take the phrase just mentioned and see how the slop factor plays out. First we need a little test infrastructure, which includes a `setUp()` method to index a single document, a `tearDown()` method to close the directory and searcher, and a custom `matched(String[], int)` method to construct, execute, and assert a phrase query matched the test document, shown in listing 3.8.

Listing 3.8 `PhraseQuery`

```
public class PhraseQueryTest extends TestCase {
  private Directory dir;
  private IndexSearcher searcher;
```

```
protected void setUp() throws IOException {
  dir = new RAMDirectory();
  IndexWriter writer = new IndexWriter(dir,
                              new WhitespaceAnalyzer(),
                              IndexWriter.MaxFieldLength.UNLIMITED);
  Document doc = new Document();
  doc.add(new Field("field",
          "the quick brown fox jumped over the lazy dog",   ← Add a single
          Field.Store.YES,                                     test document
          Field.Index.ANALYZED));
  writer.addDocument(doc);
  writer.close();

  searcher = new IndexSearcher(dir);
}

protected void tearDown() throws IOException {
  searcher.close();
  dir.close();
}

private boolean matched(String[] phrase, int slop)
    throws IOException {
  PhraseQuery query = new PhraseQuery();         ← Create initial
  query.setSlop(slop);                              PhraseQuery

  for (String word : phrase) {                   ← Add sequential
    query.add(new Term("field", word));             phrase terms
  }

  TopDocs matches = searcher.search(query, 10);
  return matches.totalHits > 0;
}
}
```

Because we want to demonstrate several phrase query examples, we wrote the matched method to simplify the code. Phrase queries are created by adding terms in the desired order. By default, a PhraseQuery has its slop factor set to zero, specifying an exact phrase match. With our setUp() and helper matched method, our test case succinctly illustrates how PhraseQuery behaves. Failing and passing slop factors show the boundaries:

```
public void testSlopComparison() throws Exception {
  String[] phrase = new String[] {"quick", "fox"};

  assertFalse("exact phrase not found", matched(phrase, 0));

  assertTrue("close enough", matched(phrase, 1));
}
```

Terms added to a phrase query don't have to be in the same order found in the field, although order does impact slop-factor considerations. For example, had the terms been reversed in the query (*fox* and then *quick*), the number of moves needed to match the document would be three, not one. To visualize this, consider how many moves it would take to physically move the word *fox* two slots past *quick*; you'll see that

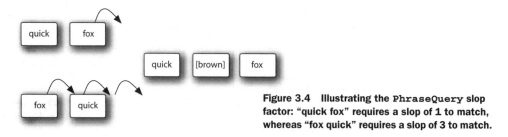

Figure 3.4   **Illustrating the `PhraseQuery` slop factor: "quick fox" requires a slop of 1 to match, whereas "fox quick" requires a slop of 3 to match.**

it takes one move to move *fox* into the same position as *quick* and then two more to move *fox* beyond *quick* sufficiently to match "quick brown fox."

Figure 3.4 shows how the slop positions work in both of these phrase query scenarios, and this test case shows the match in action:

```
public void testReverse() throws Exception {
  String[] phrase = new String[] {"fox", "quick"};

  assertFalse("hop flop", matched(phrase, 2));
  assertTrue("hop hop slop", matched(phrase, 3));
}
```

Let's now examine how multiple-term phrase queries work.

MULTIPLE-TERM PHRASES

`PhraseQuery` supports multiple-term phrases. Regardless of how many terms are used for a phrase, the slop factor is the maximum total number of moves allowed to put the terms in order. Let's look at an example of a multiple-term phrase query:

```
public void testMultiple() throws Exception {
  assertFalse("not close enough",
      matched(new String[] {"quick", "jumped", "lazy"}, 3));

  assertTrue("just enough",
      matched(new String[] {"quick", "jumped", "lazy"}, 4));

  assertFalse("almost but not quite",
      matched(new String[] {"lazy", "jumped", "quick"}, 7));

  assertTrue("bingo",
      matched(new String[] {"lazy", "jumped", "quick"}, 8));
}
```

Now that you've seen how phrase queries match, let's turn our attention to how phrase queries affect the score.

PHRASE QUERY SCORING

Phrase queries are scored based on the edit distance needed to match the phrase. More exact matches count for more weight than sloppier ones. The phrase query factor is shown in figure 3.5. The inverse relationship with distance ensures that greater distances have lower scores.

Figure 3.5   **Sloppy phrase scoring formula** $\dfrac{1}{distance + 1}$

NOTE Terms surrounded by double quotes in QueryParser-parsed expressions are translated into a PhraseQuery. The slop factor defaults to 0, but you can adjust the slop factor by adding a tilde (~) followed by an integer. For example, the expression "quick fox"~3 is a PhraseQuery with the terms quick and fox and a slop factor of 3. There are additional details about PhraseQuery and the slop factor in section 3.4.6. Phrases are analyzed by the analyzer passed to the QueryParser, adding another layer of complexity, as discussed in section 4.1.2.

Our next query, WildcardQuery, matches terms using wildcard characters.

3.4.7 Searching by wildcard: WildcardQuery

Wildcard queries let you query for terms with missing pieces but still find matches. Two standard wildcard characters are used: * for zero or more characters, and ? for zero or one character. Listing 3.9 demonstrates WildcardQuery in action. You can think of WildcardQuery as a more general PrefixQuery because the wildcard doesn't have to be at the end.

Listing 3.9 WildcardQuery

```java
private void indexSingleFieldDocs(Field[] fields) throws Exception {
  IndexWriter writer = new IndexWriter(directory,
      new WhitespaceAnalyzer(), IndexWriter.MaxFieldLength.UNLIMITED);
  for (Field f : fields) {
    Document doc = new Document();
    doc.add(f);
    writer.addDocument(doc);
  }
  writer.optimize();
  writer.close();
}

public void testWildcard() throws Exception {
  indexSingleFieldDocs(new Field[]
    { new Field("contents", "wild", Field.Store.YES,
            Field.Index.ANALYZED),
      new Field("contents", "child", Field.Store.YES,
            Field.Index.ANALYZED),
      new Field("contents", "mild", Field.Store.YES,
            Field.Index.ANALYZED),
      new Field("contents", "mildew", Field.Store.YES,
            Field.Index.ANALYZED) });

  IndexSearcher searcher = new IndexSearcher(directory);
  Query query = new WildcardQuery(new Term("contents", "?ild*"));    // Create WildcardQuery
  TopDocs matches = searcher.search(query, 10);
  assertEquals("child no match", 3, matches.totalHits);

  assertEquals("score the same", matches.scoreDocs[0].score,
                                 matches.scoreDocs[1].score, 0.0);
  assertEquals("score the same", matches.scoreDocs[1].score,
                                 matches.scoreDocs[2].score, 0.0);
  searcher.close();
}
```

Note how the wildcard pattern is created as a `Term` (the pattern to match) even though it isn't explicitly used as an exact term under the covers. Internally, it's used as a pattern to match terms in the index. A `Term` instance is a convenient placeholder to represent a field name and an arbitrary string.

WARNING   Performance degradations can occur when you use `WildcardQuery`. A larger prefix (characters before the first wildcard character) decreases the number of terms enumerated to find matches. Beginning a pattern with a wildcard query forces the term enumeration to search *all* terms in the index for matches.

Oddly, the closeness of a wildcard match has no effect on scoring. The last two assertions in listing 3.9, where *wild* and *mild* are closer matches to the pattern than *mildew*, demonstrate this.

Our next query is `FuzzyQuery`.

3.4.8   Searching for similar terms: FuzzyQuery

Lucene's `FuzzyQuery` matches terms *similar* to a specified term. The *Levenshtein distance* algorithm determines how similar terms in the index are to a specified target term. (See http://en.wikipedia.org/wiki/Levenshtein_Distance for more information about Levenshtein distance.) *Edit distance* is another term for Levenshtein distance; it's a measure of similarity between two strings, where distance is measured as the number of character deletions, insertions, or substitutions required to transform one string to the other string. For example, the edit distance between *three* and *tree* is 1, because only one character deletion is needed.

Levenshtein distance isn't the same as the distance calculation used in `Phrase-Query` and `PrefixQuery`. The phrase query distance is the number of term moves to match, whereas Levenshtein distance is an intraterm computation of character moves. The `FuzzyQuery` test demonstrates its usage and behavior:

```
public void testFuzzy() throws Exception {
  indexSingleFieldDocs(new Field[] { new Field("contents",
                                                "fuzzy",
                                                Field.Store.YES,
                                                Field.Index.ANALYZED),
                                new Field("contents",
                                                "wuzzy",
                                                Field.Store.YES,
                                                Field.Index.ANALYZED)
                                });

  IndexSearcher searcher = new IndexSearcher(directory);
  Query query = new FuzzyQuery(new Term("contents", "wuzza"));
  TopDocs matches = searcher.search(query, 10);
  assertEquals("both close enough", 2, matches.totalHits);

  assertTrue("wuzzy closer than fuzzy",
          matches.scoreDocs[0].score != matches.scoreDocs[1].score);

  Document doc = searcher.doc(matches.scoreDocs[0].doc);
```

```
    assertEquals("wuzza bear", "wuzzy", doc.get("contents"));
    searcher.close();
}
```

This test illustrates a couple of key points. Both documents match; the term searched for (*wuzza*) wasn't indexed but was close enough to match. FuzzyQuery uses a *threshold* rather than a pure edit distance. The threshold is a factor of the edit distance divided by the string length. Edit distance affects scoring; terms with less edit distance are scored higher. Other term statistics, such as the inverse document frequency, are also factored in, as described in section 3.3. Distance is computed using the formula shown in figure 3.6.

Figure 3.6 FuzzyQuery distance formula
$$1 - \frac{distance}{min(textlen, targetlen)}$$

WARNING FuzzyQuery enumerates all terms in an index to find terms within the allowable threshold. Use this type of query sparingly or at least with the knowledge of how it works and the effect it may have on performance.

3.4.9 *Matching all documents: MatchAllDocsQuery*

MatchAllDocsQuery, as the name implies, simply matches every document in your index. By default, it assigns a constant score, the boost of the query (default: 1.0), to all documents that match. If you use this as your top query, it's best to sort by a field other than the default relevance sort.

It's also possible to have MatchAllDocsQuery assign as document scores the boosting recorded in the index, for a specified field, like so:

```
Query query = new MatchAllDocsQuery(field);
```

If you do this, documents are scored according to how the specified field was boosted (as described in section 2.5).

We're done reviewing Lucene's basic core Query classes. Chapter 5 covers more advanced Query classes. Now we'll move on to using QueryParser to construct queries from a user's textual query.

3.5 *Parsing query expressions: QueryParser*

Although API-created queries can be powerful, it isn't reasonable that all queries should be explicitly written in Java code. Using a human-readable textual query representation, Lucene's QueryParser constructs one of the previously mentioned Query subclasses. Because the QueryParser already recognizes the standard search syntax that has become popular thanks to web search engines like Google, using Query-Parser is also an immediate and simple way for your application to meet that user expectation. QueryParser is also easily customized, as we'll see in section 6.3.

The constructed Query instance could be a complex entity, consisting of nested BooleanQuerys and a combination of almost all the Query types mentioned, but an expression entered by the user could be as readable as this:

```
+pubdate:[20100101 TO 20101231] Java AND (Lucene OR Apache)
```

This query searches for all books about Java that also include *Lucene* or *Apache* in their contents and were published in 2010.

NOTE   Whenever special characters are used in a query expression, you need to provide an escaping mechanism so that the special characters can be used in a normal fashion. QueryParser uses a backslash (\) to escape special characters within terms. The characters that require escaping are as follows:

```
\ + - ! ( ) : ^ ] { } ~ * ?
```

We've already seen a brief introduction to QueryParser in section 3.1.2 at the start of the chapter. In this section we'll first delve into the specific syntax for each of Lucene's core Query classes that QueryParser supports. We'll also describe some of the settings that control the parsing of certain queries. We'll wrap up with further syntax that QueryParser accepts for controlling grouping, boosting, and field searching of each query clause. This discussion assumes knowledge of the Query types discussed in section 3.4. Note that some of these subsections here are rather short; this is a reflection of just how powerful QueryParser is under the hood—it's able to take a simple-to-describe search syntax and easily build rich queries.

We begin with a handy way to glimpse what QueryParser does to expressions.

3.5.1 *Query.toString*

Seemingly strange things can happen to a query expression as it's parsed with Query-Parser. How can you tell what really happened to your expression? Was it translated properly into what you intended? One way to peek at a resultant Query instance is to use its toString() method.

All concrete core Query classes we've discussed in this chapter have a special toString() implementation. The standard Object.toString() method is overridden and delegates to a toString(String field) method, where field is the name of the default field. Calling the no-arg toString() method uses an empty default field name, causing the output to explicitly use field selector notation for all terms. Here's an example of using the toString() method:

```
public void testToString() throws Exception {
  BooleanQuery query = new BooleanQuery();
  query.add(new FuzzyQuery(new Term("field", "kountry")),
          BooleanClause.Occur.MUST);
  query.add(new TermQuery(new Term("title", "western")),
          BooleanClause.Occur.SHOULD);
  assertEquals("both kinds", "+kountry~0.5 title:western",
              query.toString("field"));
}
```

The toString() methods (particularly the String-arg one) are handy for visual debugging of complex API queries as well as getting a handle on how QueryParser interprets query expressions. Don't rely on the ability to go back and forth accurately between a Query.toString() representation and a QueryParser-parsed expression, though. It's generally accurate, but an analyzer is involved and may confuse things; this issue is discussed further in section 4.1.2. Let's begin, again, with the simplest Query type, TermQuery.

3.5.2   *TermQuery*

As you might expect, a single word is by default parsed into a TermQuery by Query-Parser, as long as it's not part of a broader expression recognized by the other query types. For example:

```
public void testTermQuery() throws Exception {
  QueryParser parser = new QueryParser(Version.LUCENE_30,
                                       "subject", analyzer);
  Query query = parser.parse("computers");
  System.out.println("term: " + query);
}
```

produces this output:

```
term: subject:computers
```

Note how QueryParser built the term query by appending the default field we'd provided when instantiating it, subject, to the analyzed term, computers. Section 3.5.11 shows how you can specify a field other than the default one. Note that the text for the word is passed through the analysis process, described in the next chapter, before constructing the TermQuery. In our QueryParserTest we're using an analyzer that simply splits words at whitespace. Had we used a more interesting analyzer, it could have altered the term—for example, by stripping the plural suffix, and perhaps reducing the word to its root form before passing it to the TermQuery. It's vital that this analysis done by QueryParser match the analysis performed during indexing. Section 4.1.2 delves into this tricky topic.

Let's see how QueryParser constructs range searches.

3.5.3   *Term range searches*

Text or date range queries use bracketed syntax, with TO between the beginning term and ending term. Note that TO must be all caps. The type of bracket determines whether the range is inclusive (square brackets) or exclusive (curly braces). Note that, unlike with the programmatic construction of NumericRangeQuery or TermRange-Query, you can't mix inclusive and exclusive: both the start and end term must be either inclusive or exclusive.

Our testRangeQuery() method, in listing 3.10, demonstrates both inclusive and exclusive range queries.

Listing 3.10   Creating a `TermRangeQuery` using `QueryParser`

```
public void testTermRangeQuery() throws Exception {
  Query query = new QueryParser(Version.LUCENE_30,          ◁─┐  Verify
                                "subject", analyzer)            │  inclusive range
                  .parse("title2:[Q TO V]");               ◁─┘
```

```
     assertTrue(query instanceof TermRangeQuery);

     TopDocs matches = searcher.search(query, 10);
     assertTrue(TestUtil.hitsIncludeTitle(searcher, matches,
               "Tapestry in Action"));

     query = new QueryParser(Version.LUCENE_30,
                 "subject",
                 analyzer)                                              Verify
           .parse("title2:{Q TO \"Tapestry in Action\" }");           exclusive range
     matches = searcher.search(query, 10);
     assertFalse(TestUtil.hitsIncludeTitle(searcher, matches,    ◁⎯    Exclude Tapestry
               "Tapestry in Action"));                                 in Action
   }
```

NOTE   Nondate range queries lowercase the beginning and ending terms as the
user entered them, unless `QueryParser.setLowercaseExpanded-`
`Terms(false)` has been called. The text isn't analyzed. If the start or end
terms contain whitespace, they must be surrounded with double quotes,
or parsing fails.

Let's look next at numeric and date ranges.

3.5.4   *Numeric and date range searches*

QueryParser won't create a `NumericRangeQuery` for you. This is because Lucene currently doesn't keep track of which of your fields were indexed with `NumericField`,
though it's possible this limitation has been corrected by the time you read this. QueryParser does include certain built-in logic for parsing dates when they appear as
part of a range query, but the logic doesn't work when you've indexed your dates
using `NumericField`. Fortunately, subclassing `QueryParser` to correctly handle
numeric fields is straightforward, as described in sections 6.3.3 and 6.3.4.

Next we'll see how QueryParser creates prefix and wildcard queries.

3.5.5   *Prefix and wildcard queries*

If a term contains an asterisk or a question mark, it's considered a `WildcardQuery`.
When the term contains only a trailing asterisk, QueryParser optimizes it to a `Prefix-`
`Query` instead. Both prefix and wildcard queries are lowercased by default, but this
behavior can be controlled:

```
public void testLowercasing() throws Exception {
  Query q = new QueryParser(Version.LUCENE_30,
          "field", analyzer).parse("PrefixQuery*");
  assertEquals("lowercased",
      "prefixquery*", q.toString("field"));

  QueryParser qp = new QueryParser(Version.LUCENE_30,
                                   "field", analyzer);
  qp.setLowercaseExpandedTerms(false);
  q = qp.parse("PrefixQuery*");
  assertEquals("not lowercased",
      "PrefixQuery*", q.toString("field"));
}
```

Wildcards at the beginning of a term are prohibited using `QueryParser` by default, which you can override at the expense of performance by calling the `setAllow-LeadingWildcard` method. Section 3.4.7 discusses more about the performance issue, and section 6.3.2 provides a way to prohibit `WildcardQuerys` entirely from parsed expressions.

Let's look next at `QueryParser`'s ability to create `BooleanQuerys`.

3.5.6 Boolean operators

Constructing Boolean queries textually via `QueryParser` is done using the operators AND, OR, and NOT. Note that these operators must be typed as all caps. Terms listed without an operator specified use an implicit operator, which by default is OR. The query `abc xyz` will be interpreted as either `abc OR xyz` or `abc AND xyz`, based on the implicit operator setting. To switch parsing to use AND:

```
QueryParser parser = new QueryParser(Version.LUCENE_30,
                                "contents", analyzer);
parser.setDefaultOperator(QueryParser.AND_OPERATOR);
```

Placing a NOT in front of a term excludes documents matching the following term. Negating a term must be combined with at least one non-negated term to return documents; in other words, it isn't possible to use a query like `NOT term` to find all documents that don't contain a term. Each of the uppercase word operators has shortcut syntax; table 3.6 illustrates various syntax equivalents.

Table 3.6 Boolean query operator shortcuts

Verbose syntax	Shortcut syntax
a AND b	+a +b
a OR b	a b
a AND NOT b	+a –b

We'll see how to construct a `PhraseQuery` next.

3.5.7 Phrase queries

Terms enclosed in double quotes create a `PhraseQuery`. The text between the quotes is analyzed; thus the resultant `PhraseQuery` may not be exactly the phrase originally specified. This process has been the subject of some confusion. For example, the query `"This is Some Phrase*"`, when analyzed by the `StandardAnalyzer`, parses to a `PhraseQuery` using the phrase "some phrase." The `StandardAnalyzer` removes the words *this* and *is* because they match the default stop word list and leaves positional holes recording that the words were removed (more in section 4.3.2 on `Standard-Analyzer`). A common question is why the asterisk isn't interpreted as a wildcard query. Keep in mind that surrounding text with double quotes causes the surrounded text to be analyzed and converted into a `PhraseQuery`. Single-term phrases are optimized to a `TermQuery`. The following code demonstrates both the effect of analysis on a phrase query expression and the `TermQuery` optimization:

```
public void testPhraseQuery() throws Exception {
  Query q = new QueryParser(Version.LUCENE_30,
                        "field",
```

```
                        new StandardAnalyzer(
                            Version.LUCENE_30))
                    .parse("\"This is Some Phrase*\"");

    assertEquals("analyzed",
        "\"? ? some phrase\"", q.toString("field"));

    q = new QueryParser(Version.LUCENE_30,
                    "field", analyzer)
                .parse("\"term\"");
    assertTrue("reduced to TermQuery", q instanceof TermQuery);
}
```

You can see that the query represents the positional holes left by the removed stop words, using a ? character. The default slop factor is 0, but you can change this default by calling QueryParser.setPhraseSlop. The slop factor can also be overridden for each phrase by using a trailing tilde (~) and the desired integer slop value:

```
public void testSlop() throws Exception {
    Query q = new QueryParser(Version.LUCENE_30,
        "field", analyzer)
            .parse("\"exact phrase\"");
    assertEquals("zero slop",
        "\"exact phrase\"", q.toString("field"));

    QueryParser qp = new QueryParser(Version.LUCENE_30,
                                "field", analyzer);
    qp.setPhraseSlop(5);
    q = qp.parse("\"sloppy phrase\"");
    assertEquals("sloppy, implicitly",
        "\"sloppy phrase\"~5", q.toString("field"));
}
```

A sloppy PhraseQuery, as noted, doesn't require that the terms match in the same order. But a SpanNearQuery (discussed in section 5.5.3) has the ability to guarantee an in-order match. In section 6.3.5, we extend QueryParser and substitute a SpanNear-Query when phrase queries are parsed, allowing for sloppy in-order phrase matches. The final queries we discuss are FuzzyQuery and MatchAllDocsQuery.

3.5.8 *Fuzzy queries*

A trailing tilde (~) creates a fuzzy query on the preceding term. Note that the tilde is also used to specify sloppy phrase queries, but the context is different. Double quotes denote a phrase query and aren't used for fuzzy queries. You can optionally specify a trailing floating point number to specify the minimum required similarity. Here's an example:

```
public void testFuzzyQuery() throws Exception {
    QueryParser parser = new QueryParser(Version.LUCENE_30,
                                    "subject", analyzer);
    Query query = parser.parse("kountry~");
    System.out.println("fuzzy: " + query);

    query = parser.parse("kountry~0.7");
    System.out.println("fuzzy 2: " + query);
}
```

This produces the following output:

```
fuzzy: subject:kountry~0.5
fuzzy 2: subject:kountry~0.7
```

The same performance caveats that apply to `WildcardQuery` also apply to fuzzy queries and can be disabled by customizing, as discussed in section 6.3.2.

3.5.9 *MatchAllDocsQuery*

`QueryParser` produces the `MatchAllDocsQuery` when you enter `*:*`.

This wraps up our coverage showing how `QueryParser` produces each of Lucene's core query types. But that's not the end of `QueryParser`: it also supports some very useful syntax to group clauses of a `Query`, boost clauses, and restrict clauses to specific fields. Let's begin with grouping.

3.5.10 *Grouping*

Lucene's `BooleanQuery` lets you construct complex nested clauses; likewise, `QueryParser` enables this same capability with textual query expressions via grouping. Let's find all the methodology books that are about either agile or extreme methodologies. We use parentheses to form subqueries, enabling advanced construction of `BooleanQuerys`:

```
public void testGrouping() throws Exception {
  Query query = new QueryParser(
      Version.LUCENE_30,
      "subject",
      analyzer).parse("(agile OR extreme) AND methodology");
  TopDocs matches = searcher.search(query, 10);

  assertTrue(TestUtil.hitsIncludeTitle(searcher, matches,
                              "Extreme Programming Explained"));
  assertTrue(TestUtil.hitsIncludeTitle(searcher,
                              matches,
                              "The Pragmatic Programmer"));
}
```

You can arbitrarily nest queries within other queries using this code. It's possible to build up some truly amazing queries by doing so. Figure 3.7 shows an example of the recursive structure produced by such rich queries.

Next, we discuss how a specific field can be selected. Notice that field selection can also leverage parentheses.

3.5.11 *Field selection*

`QueryParser` needs to know the field name to use when constructing queries, but it would generally be unfriendly to require users to identify the field to search (the end user may not need or want to know the field names). As you've seen, the default field name is provided when you create the `QueryParser` instance. Parsed queries aren't restricted, however, to searching only the default field. Using field selector notation, you can specify terms in nondefault fields. For example, if you set query parser to

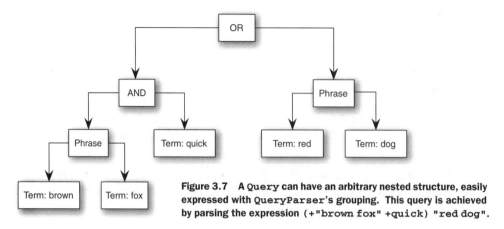

Figure 3.7 A `Query` can have an arbitrary nested structure, easily expressed with `QueryParser`'s grouping. This query is achieved by parsing the expression `(+"brown fox" +quick) "red dog"`.

search a catchall field by default, your users can still restrict the search to the `title` field using `title:lucene`. You can group field selection over multiple clauses. Using `field:(a b c)` will OR together (by default) the three term queries, where each term must appear in the specified field. Let's see how to boost a query clause next.

3.5.12 Setting the boost for a subquery

A caret (`^`) followed by a floating-point number sets the boost factor for the preceding query. For example, the query expression `junit^2.0 testing` sets the `junit` Term-Query to a boost of 2.0 and leaves the `testing` TermQuery at the default boost of 1.0. You can apply a boost to any type of query, including parenthetical groups.

3.5.13 To QueryParse or not to QueryParse?

`QueryParser` is a quick and effortless way to give users powerful query construction, but it isn't right for all scenarios. `QueryParser` can't create every type of query that can be constructed using the API. In chapter 5, we detail a handful of API-only queries that have no `QueryParser` expression capability. You must keep in mind all the possibilities available when exposing free-form query parsing to an end user; some queries have the potential for performance bottlenecks, and the syntax used by the built-in `QueryParser` may not be suitable for your needs. You can exert some limited control by subclassing `QueryParser` (see section 6.3.1).

Should you require different expression syntax or capabilities beyond what Query-Parser offers, technologies such as ANTLR (http://www.antlr.org) and JFlex (http://jflex.de/) are great options. We don't discuss the creation of a custom query parser, though we do explore extending `QueryParser` in chapter 6. The source code for Lucene's `QueryParser` is freely available for you to borrow from. The contrib area also contains an entirely new `QueryParser` framework, covered in section 9.9, that's designed for more modular extensibility. Another contrib option is the XML query parser, described in section 9.5, that's able to build arbitrary queries described as an XML string.

You can often obtain a happy medium by combining a `QueryParser`-parsed query with API-created queries as clauses in a `BooleanQuery`. For example, if users need to constrain searches to a particular category or narrow them to a date range, you can have the UI separate those selections into a category chooser or separate date-range fields.

3.6 *Summary*

Lucene provides highly relevant search results to queries—quickly. Most applications need only a few Lucene classes and methods to enable searching. The most fundamental things for you to take away from this chapter are an understanding of the basic query types and how to access search results.

Although it can be a bit daunting, Lucene's scoring formula (coupled with the index format discussed in appendix B and the efficient algorithms) provides the magic of returning the most relevant documents first. Lucene's `QueryParser` parses human-readable query expressions, giving rich full-text search power to end users. `QueryParser` immediately satisfies most application requirements—but it doesn't come without caveats, so be sure you understand the rough edges. Much of the confusion regarding `QueryParser` stems from unexpected analysis interactions; chapter 4 goes into great detail about analysis, including more on the `QueryParser` issues.

And yes, there's more to searching than we've covered in this chapter, but understanding the groundwork is crucial. After analysis in chapter 4, chapter 5 delves into Lucene's more elaborate features, such as constraining (or filtering) the search space of queries and sorting search results by field values; chapter 6 explores the numerous ways you can extend Lucene's searching capabilities for custom sorting and query parsing.

Lucene's analysis process

4

This chapter covers

- Understanding the analysis process
- Using Lucene's core analysis classes
- Writing custom analyzers
- Handling foreign languages

Analysis, in Lucene, is the process of converting field text into its most fundamental indexed representation, terms. These terms are used to determine what documents match a query during searching. For example, if you indexed this sentence in a field the terms might start with *for* and *example*, and so on, as separate terms in sequence. An analyzer is an encapsulation of the analysis process. An analyzer tokenizes text by performing any number of operations on it, which could include extracting words, discarding punctuation, removing accents from characters, low-ercasing (also called normalizing), removing common words, reducing words to a root form (stemming), or changing words into the basic form (lemmatization). This process is also called tokenization, and the chunks of text pulled from a stream of text are called tokens. Tokens, combined with their associated field name, are terms.

Lucene's primary goal is to facilitate information retrieval. The emphasis on retrieval is important. You want to throw gobs of text at Lucene and have them be richly searchable by the individual words within that text. In order for Lucene to know what "words" are, it analyzes the text during indexing, extracting it into terms. These terms are the primitive building blocks for searching.

Choosing the right analyzer is a crucial development decision with Lucene, and one size definitely doesn't fit all. Language is one factor, because each has its own unique features. Another factor to consider is the domain of the text being analyzed; different industries have different terminology, acronyms, and abbreviations that may deserve attention. Although we present many of the considerations for choosing analyzers, no single analyzer will suffice for all situations. It's possible that none of the built-in analysis options are adequate for your needs, and you'll have to invest in creating a custom analysis solution; fortunately, Lucene's building blocks make this quite easy.

In this chapter, we'll cover all aspects of the Lucene analysis process, including how and where to use analyzers, what the built-in analyzers do, and how to write your own custom analyzers using the building blocks provided by the core Lucene API. Custom analyzers are trivial to create, and many applications do so, so we'll cover examples such as synonym injection, sounds-like searching, stemming, and stop-word filtering. Let's begin by seeing when and how analyzers are used by Lucene.

4.1 *Using analyzers*

Before we get into the gory details of what lurks inside an analyzer, let's explore how an analyzer is used in Lucene. Analysis occurs any time text needs to be converted into terms, which in Lucene's core is at two spots: during indexing and when using Query-Parser for searching. If you highlight hits in your search results (which we strongly recommend because it gives a better end-user experience), you may need to analyze text at that point as well. Highlighting, enabled with two of Lucene's contrib modules, is covered in detail in chapter 8. In this section, we first detail how an analyzer is used in each of these scenarios, and then describe the important difference between *parsing* a document and *analyzing* it.

Before we begin with any code details, let's look at what the analysis process is all about. First we analyze the phrase "The quick brown fox jumped over the lazy dog," using each of the four built-in analyzers:

```
Analyzing "The quick brown fox jumped over the lazy dog"
  WhitespaceAnalyzer:
    [The] [quick] [brown] [fox] [jumped] [over] [the] [lazy] [dog]

  SimpleAnalyzer:
    [the] [quick] [brown] [fox] [jumped] [over] [the] [lazy] [dog]

  StopAnalyzer:
    [quick] [brown] [fox] [jumped] [over] [lazy] [dog]

  StandardAnalyzer:
    [quick] [brown] [fox] [jumped] [over] [lazy] [dog]
```

Each token is shown between brackets to make the separations apparent. During indexing, the tokens extracted during analysis are the terms indexed. And, most important, it's only the terms that are indexed that are searchable!

NOTE   Only the tokens produced by the analyzer are searchable, unless the field is indexed with `Field.Index.NOT_ANALYZED` or `Field.Index.NOT_ANALYZED_NO_NORMS`, in which case the entire field's value, as a single token, is searchable.

Next we analyze the phrase "XY&Z Corporation - xyz@example.com" with the same analyzers:

```
Analyzing "XY&Z Corporation - xyz@example.com"
  WhitespaceAnalyzer:
    [XY&Z] [Corporation] [-] [xyz@example.com]

  SimpleAnalyzer:
    [xy] [z] [corporation] [xyz] [example] [com]

  StopAnalyzer:
    [xy] [z] [corporation] [xyz] [example] [com]

  StandardAnalyzer:
    [xy&z] [corporation] [xyz@example.com]
```

You can see that the resulting tokens are very analyzer dependent. A few interesting things happen in these examples. Look at how the word *the* is treated, and likewise the company name *XY&Z* and the email address *xyz@example.com*; look at the special hyphen character (-) and the case of each token. Section 4.2.3 explains more of the details of what happened, and you can see the code that produced this output in listing 4.1 in section 4.24. In the meantime, here's a summary of each of these analyzers:

- `WhitespaceAnalyzer`, as the name implies, splits text into tokens on whitespace characters and makes no other effort to normalize the tokens. It doesn't lowercase each token.

- `SimpleAnalyzer` first splits tokens at nonletter characters, then lowercases each token. Be careful! This analyzer quietly discards numeric characters but keeps all other characters.

- `StopAnalyzer` is the same as `SimpleAnalyzer`, except it removes common words. By default, it removes common words specific to the English language (*the*, *a*, etc.), though you can pass in your own set.

- `StandardAnalyzer` is Lucene's most sophisticated core analyzer. It has quite a bit of logic to identify certain kinds of tokens, such as company names, email addresses, and hostnames. It also lowercases each token and removes stop words and punctuation.

Lucene doesn't make the results of the analysis process visible to the end user. Terms pulled from the original text are immediately and quietly added to the index. It's these terms that are matched during searching. When searching with `QueryParser`, the analysis process takes place again on the textual parts of the search query, in order to ensure the best possible matches.

Let's see how the analyzer is used during indexing.

4.1.1 Indexing analysis

During indexing, text contained in the document's field values must be converted into tokens, as shown in figure 4.1. You provide `IndexWriter` with an `Analyzer` instance up front:

```
Analyzer analyzer = new StandardAnalyzer(Version.LUCENE_30);
IndexWriter writer = new IndexWriter(directory, analyzer,
                    IndexWriter.MaxFieldLength.UNLIMITED);
```

Each analyzed field of every document indexed with the `IndexWriter` instance uses the analyzer specified by default. But if an individual document has special analysis needs, the analyzer may be specified on a per-document basis: both the `addDocument` and `updateDocument` methods in `IndexWriter` optionally accept an analyzer to be used for that one document.

To make sure the text is analyzed, specify `Field.Index.ANALYZED` or `Field.Index.ANALYZED_NO_NORMS` when creating the field. To index the entire field's value as a single token, like Field 3 in figure 4.1, pass `Field.Index.NOT_ANALYZED` or `Field.Index.NOT_ANALYZED_NO_NORMS` as the fourth argument. One example where this is usually required is if you intend to sort on the field, as covered in section 2.4.6.

NOTE `new Field(String, String, Field.Store.YES, Field.Index.ANALYZED)` creates a tokenized and stored field. Rest assured the original `String` value is stored. But the output of the designated `Analyzer` dictates what's indexed and available for searching.

The following code demonstrates indexing of a document where one field is analyzed and stored, and the second field is analyzed but not stored:

```
Document doc = new Document();
doc.add(new Field("title", "This is the title", Field.Store.YES,
                Field.Index.ANALYZED));
```

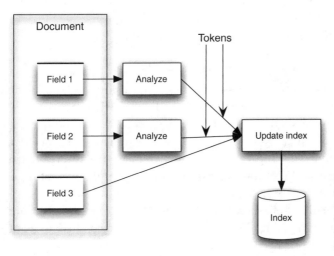

Figure 4.1 Analysis process during indexing. Fields 1 and 2 are analyzed, producing a sequence of tokens; Field 3 is unanalyzed, causing its entire value to be indexed as a single token.

```
doc.add(new Field("contents", "...document contents...", Field.Store.NO,
                  Field.Index.ANALYZED));
writer.addDocument(doc);
```

Both `"title"` and `"contents"` are analyzed using the `Analyzer` instance provided to the `IndexWriter`. `QueryParser` also uses an analyzer to parse fragments of the user's textual query.

4.1.2 *QueryParser analysis*

`QueryParser` is wonderful for presenting the end user with a free-form option of querying. To do its job, `QueryParser` uses an analyzer to break the text it encounters into terms for searching. You provide an analyzer when you instantiate the `QueryParser`:

```
QueryParser parser = new QueryParser(Version.LUCENE_30,
                                     "contents", analyzer);
Query query = parser.parse(expression);
```

The analyzer receives individual contiguous text pieces of the expression, not the expression as a whole, which in general may include operators, parentheses, and other special expression syntax to denote range, wildcard, and fuzzy searches. For example, when provided this query text:

```
"president obama" +harvard +professor
```

`QueryParser` will invoke the analyzer three separate times, first with the text *president obama*, then the text *harvard*, then *professor*. `QueryParser` analyzes all text equally, without knowledge of how it was indexed. This is a particularly thorny issue when you're querying for fields that were indexed without tokenization. We address this situation in section 4.7.3.

Should you use the same analyzer with `QueryParser` that you used during indexing? It depends. If you stick with the basic built-in analyzers, you'll probably be fine using the same analyzer in both situations. But when you're using more sophisticated analyzers, quirky cases can come up in which using different analyzers between indexing and `QueryParser` is necessary. We discuss this issue in more detail in section 4.5. Now we draw the difference between parsing and analyzing a document.

4.1.3 *Parsing vs. analysis: when an analyzer isn't appropriate*

An important point about analyzers is that they're used internally for textual fields enabled for analysis. Document formats such as HTML, Microsoft Word, XML, and others contain metadata such as the author, the title, the last modified date, and potentially much more. When you're indexing rich documents, this metadata should be separated and indexed as separate fields. Analyzers are used to analyze a specific field at a time and break things into tokens only within that field; creating new fields isn't possible within an analyzer.

Analyzers don't help in field separation because their scope is to deal with a single field at a time. Instead, parsing these documents prior to analysis is required. For example, it's a common practice to separate at least the <title> and <body> of HTML documents into separate fields. In these cases, the documents should be parsed, or preprocessed, into separate blocks of text representing each field. Chapter 7 covers this preprocessing step in detail.

Now that we've seen where and how Lucene uses analyzers, it's time to delve into just what an analyzer does and how it works.

4.2   *What's inside an analyzer?*

To understand the analysis process, we need to open the hood and tinker around a bit. Because it's possible that you'll be constructing your own analyzers, knowing the architecture and building blocks provided is crucial.

The `Analyzer` class is the abstract base class. Quite elegantly, it turns text into a stream of tokens enumerated by the `TokenStream` class. The single required method signature implemented by analyzers is

```
public TokenStream tokenStream(String fieldName, Reader reader)
```

The returned `TokenStream` is then used to iterate through all tokens.

Let's start "simply" with the `SimpleAnalyzer` and see what makes it tick. The following code is copied directly from Lucene's codebase:

```
public final class SimpleAnalyzer extends Analyzer {
  @Override
  public TokenStream tokenStream(String fieldName, Reader reader) {
    return new LowerCaseTokenizer(reader);
  }

  @Override
  public TokenStream reusableTokenStream(String fieldName, Reader reader
      throws IOException {
    Tokenizer tokenizer = (Tokenizer) getPreviousTokenStream();
    if (tokenizer == null) {
      tokenizer = new LowerCaseTokenizer(reader);
      setPreviousTokenStream(tokenizer);
    } else
      tokenizer.reset(reader);
    return tokenizer;
  }
}
```

The `LowerCaseTokenizer` divides text at nonletters (determined by `Character.isLetter`), removing nonletter characters and, true to its name, lowercasing each character.

The `reusableTokenStream` method is an additional, optional method that an analyzer can implement to gain better indexing performance. That method is allowed to reuse the same `TokenStream` that it had previously returned to the same thread. This approach can save a lot of allocation and garbage collection cost because every field of every document otherwise needs a new `TokenStream`. Two utility methods are implemented in the `Analyzer` base class, `setPreviousTokenStream` and `getPreviousTokenStream`, to store and retrieve a `TokenStream` in thread local storage. All the built-in Lucene analyzers implement this method: the first time the method is called from a given thread, a new `TokenStream` instance is created and saved. Subsequent calls return the previous `TokenStream` after resetting it to the new `Reader`.

In the following sections, we take a detailed look at each of the major players used by analyzers, including the `TokenStream` family, as well as the various attributes that represent the components of a token. We'll also show you how to visualize what an analyzer is actually doing, and describe the importance of the order of tokenizers. Let's begin with the basic unit of analysis, the token.

4.2.1   What's in a token?

A stream of tokens is the fundamental output of the analysis process. During indexing, fields designated for analysis are processed with the specified analyzer, and the important attributes from each token are then written into the index.

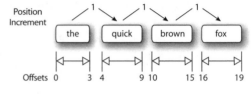

Figure 4.2   A token stream with positional and offset information

For example, let's analyze the text "the quick brown fox." Each token represents an individual word of that text. A token carries with it a text value (the word itself) as well as some metadata: the start and end character offsets in the original text, a token type, and a position increment. The token may also optionally contain application defined bit flags and an arbitrary `byte[]` payload, and can be easily extended to include any application specific attributes. Figure 4.2 shows the details of the token stream analyzing this phrase with the `SimpleAnalyzer`.

The start offset is the character position in the original text where the token text begins, and the end offset is the position just after the last character of the token text. These offsets are useful for highlighting matched tokens in search results, as described in chapter 8. The token type is a `String`, defaulting to `"word"`, that you can control and use in the token-filtering process if desired. As text is tokenized, the position relative to the previous token is recorded as the *position increment* value. Most of the built-in tokenizers leave the position increment at the default value of 1, indicating that all tokens are in successive positions, one after the other. Each token also has optional flags; a flag is a set of 32 bits (stored in an int) that's unused by Lucene's built-in analyzers but could be used by your application. Likewise, each token can have a `byte[]` recorded in the index, referred to as the payload. Using payloads is an advanced topic that we cover in section 6.5.

TOKENS INTO TERMS

After text is analyzed during indexing, each token is posted to the index as a term. The position increment, start, and end offsets and payload are the only additional metadata associated with the token that's recorded in the index. The token type and flags are discarded—they're only used during the analysis process.

POSITION INCREMENTS

The token position increment value relates the current token's position to the previous token's position. Position increment is usually 1, indicating that each word is in a unique and successive position in the field. Position increments factor directly into performing phrase queries (see section 3.4.6) and span queries (see section 5.5), which rely on knowing how far terms are from one another within a field.

Position increments greater than 1 allow for gaps and can be used to indicate where words have been removed. See section 4.6.1 for an example, where stop-word removal leaves gaps using position increments.

A token with a zero position increment places the token in the same position as the previous token. Analyzers that inject synonyms can use a position increment of zero for the synonyms. The effect is that phrase queries work regardless of which synonym was used in the query. See our SynonymAnalyzer in section 4.5 for an example that uses position increments of 0.

4.2.2 *TokenStream uncensored*

A TokenStream is a class that can produce a series of tokens when requested, but there are two very different styles of TokenStreams: Tokenizer and TokenFilter. They both inherit from the abstract TokenStream class, as shown in figure 4.3. Note the composite pattern used by TokenFilter to encapsulate another TokenStream (which could, of course, be another TokenFilter). A Tokenizer reads characters from a java. io.Reader and creates tokens, whereas a TokenFilter takes tokens in, and produces new tokens by either adding or removing whole tokens or altering the attributes of the incoming tokens.

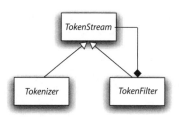

Figure 4.3   The hierarchy of classes used to produce tokens: TokenStream is the abstract base class; Tokenizer creates tokens from a Reader; and TokenFilter filters any other TokenStream.

When an analyzer returns a TokenStream from its tokenStream or reusableTokenStream method, it typically starts with a single Tokenizer, which creates the initial sequence of tokens, then chains together any number of TokenFilters to modify these tokens. This is referred to as the *analyzer chain*. Figure 4.4 shows an analyzer chain that has three TokenFilters.

Lucene's core tokenizers and analyzers

Figure 4.4   An analyzer chain starts with a Tokenizer, to produce initial tokens from the characters read from a Reader, then modifies the tokens with any number of chained TokenFilters.

Let's look at the core `Tokenizers` and `TokenFilters` in Lucene, shown in table 4.1. The corresponding class hierarchy is shown in figure 4.5.

Table 4.1   Analyzer building blocks provided in Lucene's core API

Class name	Description
TokenStream	Abstract `Tokenizer` base class.
Tokenizer	`TokenStream` whose input is a `Reader`.
CharTokenizer	Parent class of character-based tokenizers, with abstract `isTokenChar()` method. Emits tokens for contiguous blocks when `isTokenChar()` returns `true`. Also provides the capability to normalize (for example, lowercase) characters. Tokens are limited to a maximum size of 255 characters.
WhitespaceTokenizer	`CharTokenizer` with `isTokenChar()` true for all nonwhitespace characters.
KeywordTokenizer	Tokenizes the entire input string as a single token.
LetterTokenizer	`CharTokenizer` with `isTokenChar()` true when `Character.isLetter` is true.
LowerCaseTokenizer	`LetterTokenizer` that normalizes all characters to lowercase.
SinkTokenizer	A `Tokenizer` that absorbs tokens, caches them in a private list, and can later iterate over the tokens it had previously cached. This is used in conjunction with `TeeTokenizer` to "split" a `TokenStream`.
StandardTokenizer	Sophisticated grammar-based tokenizer, emitting tokens for high-level types like email addresses (see section 4.3.2 for more details). Each emitted token is tagged with a special type, some of which are handled specially by `StandardFilter`.
TokenFilter	`TokenStream` whose input is another `TokenStream`.
LowerCaseFilter	Lowercases token text.
StopFilter	Removes words that exist in a provided set of words.
PorterStemFilter	Stems each token using the Porter stemming algorithm. For example, country and countries both stem to *countri*.
TeeTokenFilter	Splits a `TokenStream` by passing each token it iterates through into a `SinkTokenizer`. It also returns the token unmmodified to its caller.
ASCIIFoldingFilter	Maps accented characters to their unaccented counterparts.
CachingTokenFilter	Saves all tokens from the input stream and can replay the stream once `reset` is called.
LengthFilter	Accepts tokens whose text length falls within a specified range.
StandardFilter	Designed to be fed by a `StandardTokenizer`. Removes dots from acronyms and 's (apostrophe followed by s) from words with apostrophes.

To illustrate the analyzer chain in code, here's a simple example analyzer:

```
public TokenStream tokenStream(String fieldName, Reader reader) {
    return new StopFilter(true,
                    new LowerCaseTokenizer(reader),
                    stopWords);
}
```

In this analyzer, `LowerCaseTokenizer` produces the initial set of tokens from a `Reader` and feeds them to a `StopFilter`. The `LowerCaseTokenizer` emits tokens that are adjacent letters in the original text, lowercasing each of the characters in the process. Non-letter characters form token boundaries and aren't included in any emitted token. Following this word tokenizer and lowercasing, `StopFilter` removes words in a stop-word list while preserving accurate `positionIncrements` (see section 4.3.1).

Buffering is a feature that's commonly needed in the `TokenStream` implementations. Low-level `Tokenizers` do this to buffer up characters to form tokens at boundaries such as whitespace or nonletter characters. `TokenFilters` that emit additional tokens into the stream they're filtering must queue an incoming token and the

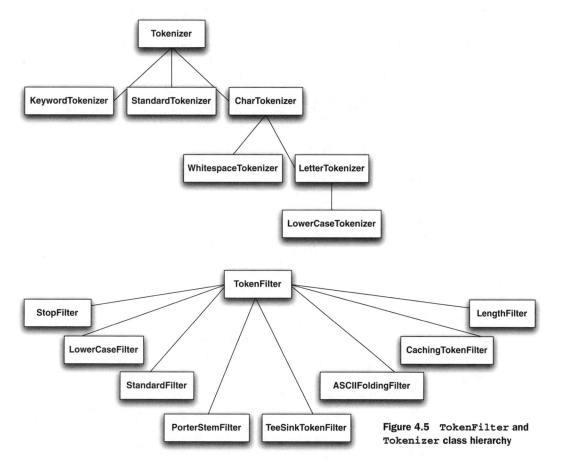

Figure 4.5 `TokenFilter` and `Tokenizer` class hierarchy

additional ones and emit them one at a time; our SynonymFilter in section 4.5 is an example of such a filter.

Most of the built-in TokenFilters alter a single stream of input tokens in some fashion, but one of them, TeeSinkTokenFilter, is more interesting. This is a filter that clones an incoming token stream into any number of output streams called *sinks*. It reads tokens from its single input source, then sends a copy of that token to all of its sink output streams as well as its output stream. Each of the sink streams can undergo its own further processing. This is useful when two or more fields would like to share the same initial analysis steps but differ on the final processing of the tokens.

Next we describe how to see the results of the analysis process.

4.2.3 *Visualizing analyzers*

Normally, the tokens produced by analysis are silently absorbed by indexing. Yet seeing the tokens is a great way to gain a concrete understanding of the analysis process. In this section we'll show you how to do just that. Specifically, we'll show you the source code that generated the token examples in section 4.1. Along the way we'll see that a token consists of several interesting attributes, including term, position-Increment, offset, type, flags, and payload.

We begin with listing 4.1, AnalyzerDemo, which analyzes two predefined phrases using Lucene's core analyzers. Each phrase is analyzed by all the analyzers, then the tokens are displayed with bracketed output to indicate what would be indexed.

Listing 4.1 AnalyzerDemo: seeing analysis in action

```java
public class AnalyzerDemo {
  private static final String[] examples = {
    "The quick brown fox jumped over the lazy dog",
    "XY&Z Corporation - xyz@example.com"
  };

  private static final Analyzer[] analyzers = new Analyzer[] {
    new WhitespaceAnalyzer(),
    new SimpleAnalyzer(),
    new StopAnalyzer(Version.LUCENE_30),
    new StandardAnalyzer(Version.LUCENE_30)
  };

  public static void main(String[] args) throws IOException {

    String[] strings = examples;
    if (args.length > 0) {          ◁─┐ Analyze command-
      strings = args;                  │ line strings
    }

    for (String text : strings) {
      analyze(text);
    }
  }

  private static void analyze(String text) throws IOException {
    System.out.println("Analyzing \"" + text + "\"");
```

```
    for (Analyzer analyzer : analyzers) {
      String name = analyzer.getClass().getSimpleName();
      System.out.println("  " + name + ":");
      System.out.print("    ");
      AnalyzerUtils.displayTokens(analyzer, text);    ◁——— Perform real work
      System.out.println("\n");
    }
  }
}
```

The real fun happens in `AnalyzerUtils` (listing 4.2), where the analyzer is applied to the text and the tokens are extracted. `AnalyzerUtils` passes text to an analyzer without indexing it and pulls the results in a manner similar to what happens during the indexing process under the covers of `IndexWriter`.

Listing 4.2 <code>AnalyzerUtils</code>: delving into an analyzer

```
public static void displayTokens(Analyzer analyzer,
                                   String text) throws IOException {
  displayTokens(analyzer.tokenStream("contents,"
                    new StringReader(text)));          ◁┐ Invoke analysis
}                                                        │ process
public static void displayTokens(TokenStream stream)
  throws IOException {

  TermAttribute term = stream.addAttribute(TermAttribute.class);
  while(stream.incrementToken()) {
    System.out.print("[" + term.term() + "] ");        ◁┐ Print token text
  }                                                       │ within brackets
}
```

Generally you wouldn't invoke the analyzer's `tokenStream` method explicitly except for this type of diagnostic or informational purpose. Note that the field name `contents` is arbitrary in the `displayTokens()` method. We recommend keeping a utility like this handy to see what tokens emit from your analyzers of choice. In fact, rather than write this yourself, you can use our `AnalyzerUtils` or the `AnalyzerDemo` code for experimentation. The `AnalyzerDemo` application lets you specify one or more strings from the command line to be analyzed instead of the embedded example ones:

```
%java lia.analysis.AnalyzerDemo "No Fluff, Just Stuff"

Analyzing "No Fluff, Just Stuff"
  org.apache.lucene.analysis.WhitespaceAnalyzer:
    [No] [Fluff,] [Just] [Stuff]

  org.apache.lucene.analysis.SimpleAnalyzer:
    [no] [fluff] [just] [stuff]

  org.apache.lucene.analysis.StopAnalyzer:
    [fluff] [just] [stuff]

  org.apache.lucene.analysis.standard.StandardAnalyzer:
    [fluff] [just] [stuff]
```

Let's now look deeper into what makes up a token.

LOOKING INSIDE TOKENS

We've seen that `TokenFilters` access and alter the attributes of tokens that flow through them. But exactly what attributes make up a token? We've added the `display-TokensWithFullDetails` utility method in `AnalyzerUtils`, shown in listing 4.3, to shed some light on this.

Listing 4.3 Seeing the term, offsets, type, and position increment of each token

```
public static void displayTokensWithFullDetails(Analyzer analyzer,
                                                String text)
      throws IOException {

  TokenStream stream = analyzer.tokenStream("contents",        ◁┘ Perform analysis
                                 new StringReader(text));

  TermAttribute term = stream.addAttribute(TermAttribute.class);
  PositionIncrementAttribute posIncr =                              Obtain
    stream.addAttribute(PositionIncrementAttribute.class);         attributes
  OffsetAttribute offset =                                         of interest
    stream.addAttribute(OffsetAttribute.class);
  TypeAttribute type = stream.addAttribute(TypeAttribute.class);

  int position = 0;                         ┐ Iterate through
  while(stream.incrementToken()) {        ◁┘ all tokens

    int increment = posIncr.getPositionIncrement();
    if (increment > 0) {
      position = position + increment;                             Compute
      System.out.println();                                       position, print
      System.out.print(position + ": ");
    }

    System.out.print("[" +
                    term.term() + ":" +
                    offset.startOffset() + "->" +          Print all
                    offset.endOffset() + ":" +             token details
                    type.type() + "] ");
  }
  System.out.println();
}
```

We display all token information on the example phrase using `SimpleAnalyzer`:

```
public static void main(String[] args) throws IOException {
  AnalyzerUtils.displayTokensWithFullDetails(new SimpleAnalyzer(),
      "The quick brown fox....");
}
```

Here's the output:

```
1: [the:0->3:word]
2: [quick:4->9:word]
3: [brown:10->15:word]
4: [fox:16->19:word]
```

Each token is in a successive position relative to the previous one (noted by the incrementing numbers 1, 2, 3, and 4). The word *the* begins at offset 0 and ends just before offset 3 in the original text. Each of the tokens has a type of word. We present a similar, but simpler, visualization of token position increments in section 4.6.1, and we provide a visualization of tokens sharing the same position. Each of these aspects of a token is recorded in its own `Attribute` class.

ATTRIBUTES

Notice that the `TokenStream` never explicitly creates a single object holding all attributes for the token. Instead, you interact with a separate reused attribute interface for each element of the token (term, offsets, position increments, etc.). Past versions of Lucene did use a standalone `Token` object, but in order to be more extensible, and to provide better analysis performance through reuse, Lucene switched to the attribute-based API as of version 2.9.

TokenStream subclasses from a class called `AttributeSource` (in `org.apache.lucene.util`). `AttributeSource` is a useful and generic means of providing strongly typed yet fully extensible attributes without requiring runtime casting, thus resulting in good performance. Lucene uses certain predefined attributes during analysis, as listed in table 4.2, but your application is free to add its own attributes by creating a concrete class implementing the `Attribute` interface. Note that Lucene will do nothing with your new attribute during indexing, so this is only currently useful in cases where one `TokenStream` early in your analysis chain wishes to send information to another `TokenStream` later in the chain.

Table 4.2   Lucene's built-in token attributes

Token attribute interface	Description
TermAttribute	Token's text
PositionIncrementAttribute	Position increment (defaults to 1)
OffsetAttribute	Start and end character offset
TypeAttribute	Token's type (defaults to word)
FlagsAttribute	Bits to encode custom flags
PayloadAttribute	Per-token byte[] payload (see section 6.5)

With this reusable API, you first obtain the attributes of interest by calling the `add-Attribute` method, which will return a concrete class implementing the requested interface. Then, you iterate through all tokens by calling `TokenStream.increment-Token`. This method returns `true` if it has advanced to a new token and `false` once you've exhausted the stream. You then interact with the previously obtained attributes to get that attribute's value for each token. When `incrementToken` returns `true`, all attributes within it will have altered their internal state to the next token.

If you're only interested in the position increment, you could do this:

```
TokenStream stream = analyzer.tokenStream("contents",
                                    new StringReader(text));
```

```
PositionIncrementAttribute posIncr =
  stream.addAttribute(PositionIncrementAttribute.class);
while (stream.incrementToken()) {
  System.out.println("posIncr=" + posIncr.getPositionIncrement());
}
```

Note that the core attribute classes in table 4.2 are bidirectional: you can use them to get and set the value for that attribute. Thus, a `TokenFilter` that alters only the position increment would grab and store the `PositionIncrementAttribute` from its input `TokenStream` when it's first instantiated, then implement the `incrementToken` method by first calling `incrementToken` on its input stream and calling `PositionIncrement-Attribute.setPositionIncrement` to change the value.

Sometimes you need to take a complete copy of all details for the current token and restore it later. You can do this by calling `captureState`, which returns a `State` object holding all state. You can later restore that state by calling `restoreState`. Note that this results in slower performance so you should avoid doing so, if possible, when creating your own `TokenFilters`.

WHAT GOOD ARE START AND END OFFSETS?

The start and end offset values, which record the original character offset at the start and end of each token's text, aren't used in the core of Lucene. Rather, they're treated as opaque integers for each token, and you could put any arbitrary integers you'd like into there.

If you index with `TermVectors`, as described in section 2.4.3, and specify that the offsets are stored, then at search time you can retrieve the `TermVectors` for a given document and access the offsets. Often this is used for highlighting, as discussed in chapter 8. It's also possible to reanalyze the text to do highlighting without storing `TermVectors`, in which case the start and end offsets are recomputed by the analyzer, then used in real time.

TOKEN TYPE USEFULNESS

You can use the token type to denote special lexical types for tokens. Under the covers of `StandardAnalyzer` is a `StandardTokenizer` that parses the incoming text into different types based on a grammar. Analyzing the phrase "I'll email you at xyz@example.com" with `StandardAnalyzer` produces this interesting output:

```
1: [i'll:0->4:<APOSTROPHE>]
2: [email:5->10:<ALPHANUM>]
3: [you:11->14:<ALPHANUM>]
5: [xyz@example.com:18->33:<EMAIL>]
```

Notice the token type of each token. The token `i'll` has an apostrophe, which `StandardTokenizer` notices in order to keep it together as a unit; and likewise for the email address. The word *at* was removed as a stop word. We cover the other `Standard-Analyzer` effects in section 4.3.2. `StandardAnalyzer` is the only built-in analyzer that leverages the token type data. Our metaphone and synonym analyzers, in sections 4.4 and 4.5, provide another example of token type usage. By default, Lucene doesn't record the token type into the index; thus, it only serves a purpose during analysis.

But you can use the `TypeAsPayloadTokenFilter` to record the type of each token as a payload. Section 6.5 describes payloads in more detail.

4.2.4 *TokenFilter order can be significant*

For certain `TokenFilters`, the order of events may be important during analysis. Each step may rely on the work of a previous step. A prime example is that of stop-word removal. `StopFilter` performs a case-sensitive lookup of each token in a set of stop words. It relies on being fed already lowercased tokens. As an example, we first write a functionally equivalent `StopAnalyzer` variant; we'll follow it with a flawed variant that reverses the order of the steps:

```
public class StopAnalyzer2 extends Analyzer {

  private Set stopWords;

  public StopAnalyzer2() {
    stopWords = StopAnalyzer.ENGLISH_STOP_WORDS_SET;
  }

  public StopAnalyzer2(String[] stopWords) {
    this.stopWords = StopFilter.makeStopSet(stopWords);
  }

  public TokenStream tokenStream(String fieldName, Reader reader) {
    return new StopFilter(true,
                  new LowerCaseFilter(
                    new LetterTokenizer(reader)),
                  stopWords);
  }
}
```

`StopAnalyzer2` uses a `LetterTokenizer` feeding a `LowerCaseFilter`, rather than just a `LowerCaseTokenizer`. A `LowerCaseTokenizer` has a performance advantage: it lowercases as it tokenizes, rather than dividing the process into two steps. This test case proves that our `StopAnalyzer2` works as expected, by using `AnalyzerUtils.tokens-FromAnalysis` and asserting that the stop word *the* was removed:

```
public void testStopAnalyzer2() throws Exception {
  AnalyzerUtils.assertAnalyzesTo(new StopAnalyzer2(),
                            "The quick brown...",
                            new String[] {"quick", "brown"});
}
```

We've added a utility method to our `AnalyzerUtils`. This method asserts that tokens match an expected list:

```
public static void assertAnalyzesTo(Analyzer analyzer, String input,
                                String[] output) throws Exception {
  TokenStream stream =
      analyzer.tokenStream("field", new StringReader(input));

  TermAttribute termAttr = stream.addAttribute(TermAttribute.class);
  for (String expected : output) {
    Assert.assertTrue(stream.incrementToken());
```

```
        Assert.assertEquals(expected, termAttr.term());
    }
    Assert.assertFalse(stream.incrementToken());
    stream.close();
}
```

To illustrate the importance that the order can make with token filtering, we've written a flawed analyzer that swaps the order of the StopFilter and the LowerCaseFilter:

```
public class StopAnalyzerFlawed extends Analyzer {
    private Set stopWords;

    public StopAnalyzerFlawed() {
        stopWords = StopAnalyzer.ENGLISH_STOP_WORDS_SET;
    }

    public TokenStream tokenStream(String fieldName, Reader reader) {
        return new LowerCaseFilter(
                new StopFilter(true, new LetterTokenizer(reader),
                               stopWords));
    }
}
```

The StopFilter presumes all tokens have already been lowercased and does a case-sensitive lookup. Another test case shows that *The* wasn't removed (it's the first token of the analyzer output), yet it was lowercased:

```
public void testStopAnalyzerFlawed() throws Exception {
    AnalyzerUtils.assertAnalyzesTo(new StopAnalyzerFlawed(),
                             "The quick brown...",
                             new String[] {"the", "quick", "brown"});
}
```

Lowercasing is just one example where order may matter. Filters may assume previous processing was done. For example, the StandardFilter is designed to be used in conjunction with StandardTokenizer and wouldn't make sense with any other Token-Stream feeding it. There may also be performance considerations when you order the filtering process. Consider an analyzer that removes stop words and injects synonyms into the token stream—it would be more efficient to remove the stop words first so that the synonym injection filter would have fewer terms to consider (see section 4.5 for a detailed example).

At this point you should have a solid grasp of the internals of the analysis process. An analyzer simply defines a specific chain of tokenizers, beginning with an original source of new tokens (TokenStream) followed by any number of TokenFilters that alter the tokens. A Token consists of values for a certain set of interesting attributes, which Lucene stores in different ways. Finally, we saw helpful methods for visualizing what an analyzer is doing. We'll now have a closer look at some example analyzers, beginning with the out-of-the-box analyzers that Lucene provides and followed by some of our own concoctions.

4.3 Using the built-in analyzers

Lucene includes several built-in analyzers, created by chaining together certain combinations of the built-in `Tokenizers` and `TokenFilters`. The primary ones are shown in table 4.3. We'll discuss certain language-specific contrib analyzers in section 4.8.2 and the special `PerFieldAnalyzerWrapper` in section 4.7.2.

Table 4.3   Primary analyzers available in Lucene

Analyzer	Steps taken
WhitespaceAnalyzer	Splits tokens at whitespace.
SimpleAnalyzer	Divides text at nonletter characters and lowercases.
StopAnalyzer	Divides text at nonletter characters, lowercases, and removes stop words.
KeywordAnalyzer	Treats entire text as a single token.
StandardAnalyzer	Tokenizes based on a sophisticated grammar that recognizes email addresses, acronyms, Chinese-Japanese-Korean characters, alphanumerics, and more. It also lowercases and removes stop words.

The built-in analyzers—`WhitespaceAnalyzer`, `SimpleAnalyzer`, `StopAnalyzer`, `KeywordAnalyzer`, and `StandardAnalyzer`—are designed to work with text in almost any Western (European-based) language. You can see the effect of each of these analyzers, except `KeywordAnalyzer`, in the output in section 4.1. `WhitespaceAnalyzer` and `SimpleAnalyzer` are truly trivial: the one-line description in table 4.3 pretty much sums them up, so we don't cover them further here. We cover `KeywordAnalyzer` in section 4.7.3. We explore the `StopAnalyzer` and `StandardAnalyzer` in more depth because they have nontrivial effects.

4.3.1 StopAnalyzer

`StopAnalyzer`, beyond doing basic word splitting and lowercasing, also removes special words called *stop words*. Stop words are words that are very common, such as *the*, and thus assumed to carry very little standalone meaning for searching since nearly every document will contain the word.

Embedded in `StopAnalyzer` is the following set of common English stop words, defined as `ENGLISH_STOP_WORDS_SET`. This default set is used unless otherwise specified:

```
"a", "an", "and", "are", "as", "at", "be", "but", "by",
"for", "if", "in", "into", "is", "it",  "no", "not", "of", "on",
"or", "such","that", "the", "their", "then", "there", "these",
"they", "this", "to", "was", "will", "with"
```

The `StopAnalyzer` has a second constructor that allows you to pass your own set instead.

Under the hood, `StopAnalyzer` creates a `StopFilter` to perform the filtering. Section 4.6.1 describes `StopFilter` in more detail.

4.3.2   *StandardAnalyzer*

StandardAnalyzer holds the honor as the most generally useful built-in analyzer. A JFlex-based[1] grammar underlies it, tokenizing with cleverness for the following lexical types: alphanumerics, acronyms, company names, email addresses, computer hostnames, numbers, words with an interior apostrophe, serial numbers, IP addresses, and Chinese and Japanese characters. StandardAnalyzer also includes stop-word removal, using the same mechanism as the StopAnalyzer (identical default English set, and an optional Set constructor to override). StandardAnalyzer makes a great first choice.

Using StandardAnalyzer is no different than using any of the other analyzers, as you can see from its use in section 4.1.1 and AnalyzerDemo (listing 4.1). Its unique effect, though, is apparent in the different treatment of text. For example, compare the different analyzers on the phrase "XY&Z Corporation - xyz@example.com" from section 4.1. StandardAnalyzer is the only one that kept XY&Z together as well as the email address xyz@example.com; both of these showcase the vastly more sophisticated analysis process.

4.3.3   *Which core analyzer should you use?*

We've now seen the substantial differences in how each of the four core Lucene analyzers works. How do you choose the right one for your application? The answer may surprise you: most applications don't use any of the built-in analyzers, and instead opt to create their own analyzer chain. For those applications that do use a core analyzer, StandardAnalyzer is likely the most common choice. The remaining core analyzers are usually far too simplistic for most applications, except perhaps for specific use cases (for example, a field that contains a list of part numbers might use Whitespace-Analyzer). But these analyzers are great for test cases, and are indeed used heavily by Lucene's unit tests.

Typically an application has specific needs, such as customizing the stop-words list, performing special tokenization for application-specific tokens like part numbers or for synonym expansion, preserving case for certain tokens, or choosing a specific stemming algorithm. In fact, Solr makes it trivial to create your own analysis chain by expressing the chain directly as XML in solrconfig.xml.

With that in mind, and now that you're equipped with a strong foundational knowledge of Lucene's analysis process, we'll move on to creating our own real-world analyzers. We'll show you how to implement a couple of frequently requested features: sounds-like querying and synonym expansion. Next, we create our own analyzer chain that normalizes tokens by their stems, removing stop words in the process, and discuss some challenges that result. After that we'll discuss some interesting field-specific variations that impact analysis. Finally we'll visit issues that arise when analyzing different languages, and we'll wrap up with a quick taste of how the Nutch project handles document analysis. Let's begin with sounds-like querying.

---

[1] JFlex is a sophisticated and high-performance lexical analyzer. See http://jflex.de.

4.4 Sounds-like querying

Have you ever played the game charades, cupping your hand to your ear to indicate that your next gestures refer to words that "sound like" the real words you're trying to convey? Neither have we. Suppose, though, that a high-paying client has asked you to implement a search engine accessible by Java 2 Micro Edition (J2ME)-enabled devices, such as a smart phone, to help during those tough charade matches. In this section, we'll implement an analyzer to convert words to a phonetic root using an implementation of the Metaphone algorithm from the Apache Commons Codec project. We chose the Metaphone algorithm as an example, but other algorithms are available, such as Soundex.

Let's start with a test case, shown in listing 4.4, showing the high-level goal of our search experience.

Listing 4.4 Searching for words that sound like one another

```java
public void testKoolKat() throws Exception {
  RAMDirectory directory = new RAMDirectory();
  Analyzer analyzer = new MetaphoneReplacementAnalyzer();

  IndexWriter writer = new IndexWriter(directory, analyzer, true,
                       IndexWriter.MaxFieldLength.UNLIMITED);

  Document doc = new Document();
  doc.add(new Field("contents",           ⟵  Index document
                "cool cat",
                Field.Store.YES,
                Field.Index.ANALYZED));
  writer.addDocument(doc);
  writer.close();

  IndexSearcher searcher = new IndexSearcher(directory);

  Query query = new QueryParser(Version.LUCENE_30,
                           "contents", analyzer)      │ Parse query text
                         .parse("kool kat");

  TopDocs hits = searcher.search(query, 1);
  assertEquals(1, hits.totalHits);           ⟵  Verify match
  int docID = hits.scoreDocs[0].doc;
  doc = searcher.doc(docID);
  assertEquals("cool cat", doc.get("contents"));   ⟵  Retrieve original value

  searcher.close();
}
```

It seems like magic! The user searched for "kool kat." Neither of those terms was in our original document, yet the search found the desired match. Searches on the original text would also return the expected matches. The trick lies in the Metaphone-ReplacementAnalyzer:

```java
public class MetaphoneReplacementAnalyzer extends Analyzer {
  public TokenStream tokenStream(String fieldName, Reader reader) {
    return new MetaphoneReplacementFilter(
```

```
                    new LetterTokenizer(reader));
    }
}
```

Because the Metaphone algorithm expects words that only include letters, the `Let-terTokenizer` is used to feed our metaphone filter. The `LetterTokenizer` doesn't lowercase, however. The tokens emitted are replaced by their metaphone equivalent, so lowercasing is unnecessary. Let's now dig into the `MetaphoneReplacementFilter` (listing 4.5), where the real work is done.

Listing 4.5   `TokenFilter` that replaces tokens with their metaphone equivalents

```
public class MetaphoneReplacementFilter extends TokenFilter {
  public static final String METAPHONE = "metaphone";

  private Metaphone metaphoner = new Metaphone();
  private TermAttribute termAttr;
  private TypeAttribute typeAttr;

  public MetaphoneReplacementFilter(TokenStream input) {
    super(input);
    termAttr = addAttribute(TermAttribute.class);
    typeAttr = addAttribute(TypeAttribute.class);
  }

  public boolean incrementToken() throws IOException {
    if (!input.incrementToken())              ◁─ Advance to next token
      return false;

    String encoded;
    encoded = metaphoner.encode(termAttr.term());   ◁─ Convert to Metaphone encoding
    termAttr.setTermBuffer(encoded);          ◁─ Overwrite with encoded text
    typeAttr.setType(METAPHONE);  ◁─ Set token type
    return true;
  }
}
```

The token emitted by our `MetaphoneReplacementFilter`, as its name implies, literally replaces the incoming token. This new token is set with the same position offsets as the original, because it's a replacement in the same position. The last line before returning the token sets the token type. The `StandardTokenizer`, as discussed in section 4.3.2, tags tokens with a type that is later used by the `StandardFilter`. The metaphone type isn't used in our examples, but it demonstrates that a later filter could be metaphone-token aware by calling `Token`'s `type()` method.

NOTE Token types, such as the `metaphone` type used in `MetaphoneReplace-mentFilter`, are carried through the analysis phase but aren't encoded into the index. Unless otherwise specified, the type `word` is used for tokens by default. Section 4.2.4 discusses token types further.

As always, it's good to view what an analyzer is doing with text. Using our `Analyzer-Utils`, two phrases that sound similar yet are spelled differently are tokenized and displayed:

```
public static void main(String[] args) throws IOException {
  MetaphoneReplacementAnalyzer analyzer =
                            new MetaphoneReplacementAnalyzer();
  AnalyzerUtils.displayTokens(analyzer,
              "The quick brown fox jumped over the lazy dog");

  System.out.println("");
  AnalyzerUtils.displayTokens(analyzer,
              "Tha quik brown phox jumpd ovvar tha lazi dag");
}
```

We get a sample of the metaphone encoder, shown here:

```
[0] [KK] [BRN] [FKS] [JMPT] [OFR] [0] [LS] [TKS]
[0] [KK] [BRN] [FKS] [JMPT] [OFR] [0] [LS] [TKS]
```

Wow—an exact match!

In practice, it's unlikely you'll want sounds-like matches except in special places; otherwise, far too many undesired matches may be returned.[2] In the "What would Google do?" sense, a sounds-like feature would be great for situations where a user misspelled every word and no documents were found but alternative words could be suggested. One implementation approach to this idea would be to run all text through a sounds-like analysis and build a cross-reference lookup to consult when a correction is needed.

Now let's walk through an analyzer that can handle synonyms during indexing.

4.5   *Synonyms, aliases, and words that mean the same*

How often have you searched for "spud" and been disappointed that the results didn't include "potato"? Okay, maybe that precise example doesn't happen often, but you get the idea: natural languages for some reason have evolved many ways to say the same thing. Such synonyms must be handled during searching, or your users won't find their documents.

Our next custom analyzer injects synonyms of words into the outgoing token stream during indexing but places the synonyms in the same position as the original word. By adding synonyms during indexing, searches will find documents that may not contain the original search terms but that match the synonyms of those words. We start with the test case showing how we expect our new analyzer to work, shown in listing 4.6.

Listing 4.6   Testing the synonym analyzer

```
public void testJumps() throws Exception {
  TokenStream stream =
    synonymAnalyzer.tokenStream("contents",        Analyze with
                      new StringReader("jumps"));    SynonymAnalyzer
```

---

[2] While working on this chapter, Erik asked his brilliant, then five-year-old son Jakob how he would spell *cool cat.* Jakob replied, "c-o-l c-a-t." What a wonderfully confusing language English is. Erik imagines that a "sounds-like" feature in search engines designed for children would be very useful. Metaphone encodes *cool, kool,* and *col* all as KL.

```
TermAttribute term = stream.addAttribute(TermAttribute.class);
PositionIncrementAttribute posIncr =
        stream.addAttribute(PositionIncrementAttribute.class);

int i = 0;
String[] expected = new String[]{"jumps",        ┃ Check for
                                 "hops",         ┃ correct synonyms
                                 "leaps"};
while(stream.incrementToken()) {
  assertEquals(expected[i], term.term());

  int expectedPos;
  if (i == 0) {
    expectedPos = 1;                              ┃
  } else {                                        ┃ Verify synonyms
    expectedPos = 0;                              ┃ positions
  }
  assertEquals(expectedPos,
            posIncr.getPositionIncrement());
  i++;
}
assertEquals(3, i);
}
```

Notice that our unit test shows not only that synonyms for the word *jumps* are emitted from the SynonymAnalyzer but also that the synonyms are placed in the same position (using an increment of 0) as the original word. Now that we see what behavior we expect of SynonymAnalyzer, let's see how to build it.

4.5.1   Creating SynonymAnalyzer

SynonymAnalyzer's purpose is to first detect the occurrence of words that have synonyms, and second to insert the synonyms at the same position. Figure 4.6 graphically shows what our SynonymAnalyzer does to text input, and listing 4.7 is the implementation.

Listing 4.7   SynonymAnalyzer implementation

```
public class SynonymAnalyzer extends Analyzer {
  private SynonymEngine engine;

  public SynonymAnalyzer(SynonymEngine engine) {
    this.engine = engine;
  }

  public TokenStream tokenStream(String fieldName, Reader reader) {
    TokenStream result = new SynonymFilter(
                      new StopFilter(true,
                        new LowerCaseFilter(
                          new StandardFilter(
                            new StandardTokenizer(
                              Version.LUCENE_30, reader))),
                          StopAnalyzer.ENGLISH_STOP_WORDS_SET),
                        engine
                        );
```

```
        return result;
    }
}
```

Once again, the analyzer code is minimal and simply chains a `Tokenizer` together with a series of `TokenFilters`; in fact, this is the `StandardAnalyzer` wrapped with an additional filter. (See table 4.1 for more on these basic analyzer building blocks.) The final `TokenFilter` in the chain is the new `SynonymFilter` (listing 4.8), which gets to the heart of the current discussion. When you're injecting terms, buffering is needed. This filter uses a `Stack` as the buffer.

Figure 4.6 `SynonymAnalyzer` visualized as factory automation

> **Listing 4.8 `SynonymFilter`: buffering tokens and emitting one at a time**

```
public class SynonymFilter extends TokenFilter {
    public static final String TOKEN_TYPE_SYNONYM = "SYNONYM";

    private Stack<String> synonymStack;
    private SynonymEngine engine;
    private AttributeSource.State current;

    private final TermAttribute termAtt;
    private final PositionIncrementAttribute posIncrAtt;

    public SynonymFilter(TokenStream in, SynonymEngine engine) {
        super(in);
        synonymStack = new Stack<String>();              ❶ Define synonym buffer
        this.engine = engine;

        this.termAtt = addAttribute(TermAttribute.class);
        this.posIncrAtt = addAttribute(PositionIncrementAttribute.class);
    }

    public boolean incrementToken() throws IOException {
        if (synonymStack.size() > 0) {                    ❷ Pop buffered
            String syn = synonymStack.pop();                 synonyms
            restoreState(current);
            termAtt.setTermBuffer(syn);
            posIncrAtt.setPositionIncrement(0);           ❸ Set position
            return true;                                     increment to 0
        }

        if (!input.incrementToken())                      ❹ Read next token
            return false;

        if (addAliasesToStack()) {                        ❺ Push synonyms onto stack
```

```
      current = captureState();                    ⑥ Save current token
    }

    return true;                          ⑦ Return current token
  }

  private boolean addAliasesToStack() throws IOException {
    String[] synonyms = engine.getSynonyms(termAtt.term());
    if (synonyms == null) {
      return false;
    }                                   Retrieve synonyms ⑧
    for (String synonym : synonyms) {
      synonymStack.push(synonym);              Push synonyms
    }                                  ⑨ onto stack
    return true;
  }
}
```

❶ We create a stack to hold the pending synonyms.

❷ ❸ The code successively pops the stack of buffered synonyms from the last streamed-in token until it's empty.

❹ After all previous token synonyms have been emitted, we read the next token.

❺ ❾ We push all synonyms of the current token onto the stack.

❻ We save details for the current token, if it has synonyms.

❼ We return the current (and original) token before its associated synonyms.

❽ Synonyms are retrieved from the SynonymEngine.

The design of SynonymAnalyzer allows for pluggable SynonymEngine implementations. SynonymEngine is a one-method interface:

```
public interface SynonymEngine {
  String[] getSynonyms(String s) throws IOException;
}
```

Using an interface for this design easily allows test implementations. We leave it as an exercise for you to create production-quality SynonymEngine implementations.[3] For our examples, we use a simple test that's hard-coded with a few synonyms:

```
public class TestSynonymEngine implements SynonymEngine {
  private static HashMap<String, String[]> map =

    new HashMap<String, String[]>();

  static {
    map.put("quick", new String[] {"fast", "speedy"});
    map.put("jumps", new String[] {"leaps", "hops"});
    map.put("over", new String[] {"above"});
    map.put("lazy", new String[] {"apathetic", "sluggish"});
    map.put("dog", new String[] {"canine", "pooch"});
  }
```

---

[3] It's cruel to leave you hanging with a mock implementation, isn't it? Actually, we've implemented a powerful SynonymEngine using the WordNet database. It's covered in section 9.3.2.

```
  public String[] getSynonyms(String s) {
    return map.get(s);
  }
}
```

Notice that the synonyms generated by TestSynonymEngine are one-way: *quick* has the synonyms *fast* and *speedy*, but *fast* has no synonyms. In a real production environment, you should ensure all synonyms list one another as alternate synonyms, but because we're using this for simple testing, it's fine.

Setting the position increment seems powerful, and indeed it is. You should only modify increments knowing of some odd cases that arise in searching, though. Because synonyms are indexed just like other terms, TermQuery works as expected. Also, PhraseQuery works as expected when we use a synonym in place of an original word. The SynonymAnalyzerTest test case in listing 4.9 demonstrates things working well using API-created queries.

Listing 4.9 SynonymAnalyzerTest: showing that synonym queries work

```
public class SynonymAnalyzerTest extends TestCase {
  private IndexSearcher searcher;
  private static SynonymAnalyzer synonymAnalyzer =
                    new SynonymAnalyzer(new TestSynonymEngine());

  public void setUp() throws Exception {
    RAMDirectory directory = new RAMDirectory();

    IndexWriter writer = new IndexWriter(directory,
                          synonymAnalyzer,
                          IndexWriter.MaxFieldLength.UNLIMITED);
    Document doc = new Document();
    doc.add(new Field("content",
                      "The quick brown fox jumps over the lazy dog",
                      Field.Store.YES,
                      Field.Index.ANALYZED));
    writer.addDocument(doc);

    writer.close();

    searcher = new IndexSearcher(directory);
  }

  public void tearDown() throws Exception {
    searcher.close();
  }

  public void testSearchByAPI() throws Exception {                    ❶ Search for
                                                                        "hops"
    TermQuery tq = new TermQuery(new Term("content", "hops"));   ←┘
    assertEquals(1, TestUtil.hitCount(searcher, tq));

    PhraseQuery pq = new PhraseQuery();
    pq.add(new Term("content", "fox"));                          ❷ Search for
    pq.add(new Term("content", "hops"));                           "fox hops"
    assertEquals(1, TestUtil.hitCount(searcher, pq));
  }
}
```

❶ A search for the word *hops* matches the document.

❷ A search for the phrase "fox hops" also matches.

The phrase "…fox jumps…" was indexed, and our `SynonymAnalyzer` injected hops in the same position as *jumps*. A `TermQuery` for *hops* succeeded, as did an exact `Phrase-Query` for "fox hops." Excellent!

Let's test it with `QueryParser`. We'll run two tests. The first one creates `Query-Parser` using our `SynonymAnalyzer` and the second one using `StandardAnalyzer`, as shown in listing 4.10.

Listing 4.10   Testing `SynonymAnalyzer` with `QueryParser`

```
public void testWithQueryParser() throws Exception {          SynonymAnalyzer
    Query query = new QueryParser(Version.LUCENE_30,              finds doc
                                  "content",
                                  synonymAnalyzer).parse("\"fox jumps\"");
    assertEquals(1, TestUtil.hitCount(searcher, query));
    System.out.println("With SynonymAnalyzer, \"fox jumps\" parses to " +
                                    query.toString("content"));

    query = new QueryParser(Version.LUCENE_30,               StandardAnalyzer
                            "content",                         also finds doc
                            new StandardAnalyzer(Version.LUCENE_30))
                  .parse("\"fox jumps\"");
    assertEquals(1, TestUtil.hitCount(searcher, query));
    System.out.println("With StandardAnalyzer, \"fox jumps\" parses to " +
                                    query.toString("content"));
}
```

Both analyzers find the matching document just fine, which is great. The test produces the following output:

```
With SynonymAnalyzer, "fox jumps" parses to "fox (jumps hops leaps)"
With StandardAnalyzer, "fox jumps" parses to "fox jumps"
```

As expected, with `SynonymAnalyzer`, words in our query were expanded to their synonyms. `QueryParser` is smart enough to notice that the tokens produced by the analyzer have zero position increment, and when that happens inside a phrase query, it creates a `MultiPhraseQuery`, described in section 5.3.

But this is wasteful and unnecessary: we only need synonym expansion during indexing or during searching, not both. If you choose to expand during indexing, the disk space consumed by your index will be somewhat larger, but searching may be faster because there are fewer search terms to visit. Your synonyms have been baked into the index, so you don't have the freedom to quickly change them and see the impact of such changes during searching. If instead you expand at search time, you can see fast turnaround when testing. These are simply trade-offs, and which option is best is your decision based on your application's constraints.

Next we improve our `AnalyzerUtils` class to more easily see synonyms expansion during indexing.

4.5.2   *Visualizing token positions*

Our `AnalyzerUtils.displayTokens` doesn't show us all the information when dealing with analyzers that set position increments other than 1. To get a better view of these types of analyzers, we add an additional utility method, `displayTokensWithPositions`, to `AnalyzerUtils`, as shown in listing 4.11.

Listing 4.11   Visualizing the position increment of each token

```
public static void displayTokensWithPositions
    (Analyzer analyzer, String text) throws IOException {

  TokenStream stream = analyzer.tokenStream("contents",
                                            new StringReader(text));
  TermAttribute term = stream.addAttribute(TermAttribute.class);
  PositionIncrementAttribute posIncr =
      stream.addAttribute(PositionIncrementAttribute.class);

  int position = 0;
  while(stream.incrementToken()) {
    int increment = posIncr.getPositionIncrement();
    if (increment > 0) {
      position = position + increment;
      System.out.println();
      System.out.print(position + ": ");
    }

    System.out.print("[" + term.term() + "] ");
  }
  System.out.println();
}
```

We wrote a quick piece of code to see what our `SynonymAnalyzer` is doing:

```
public class SynonymAnalyzerViewer {

  public static void main(String[] args) throws IOException {

  SynonymEngine engine = new TestSynonymEngine();

  AnalyzerUtils.displayTokensWithPositions(
    new SynonymAnalyzer(engine),
    "The quick brown fox jumps over the lazy dog");
  }
}
```

And we can now visualize the synonyms placed in the same positions as the original words:

```
2: [quick] [speedy] [fast]
3: [brown]
4: [fox]
5: [jumps] [hops] [leaps]
6: [over] [above]
8: [lazy] [sluggish] [apathetic]
9: [dog] [pooch] [canine]
```

Each number on the left represents the token position. The numbers here are continuous, but they wouldn't be if the analyzer left holes (as you'll see with the next custom analyzer). Multiple terms shown for a single position illustrate where synonyms were added.

4.6   Stemming analysis

Our final analyzer pulls out all the stops. It has a ridiculous, yet descriptive name: `PositionalPorterStopAnalyzer`. This analyzer removes stop words, leaving positional holes where words are removed, and leverages a stemming filter.

The `PorterStemFilter` is shown in the class hierarchy in figure 4.5, but it isn't used by any built-in analyzer. It stems words using the Porter stemming algorithm created by Dr. Martin Porter, and it's best defined in his own words:

> *The Porter stemming algorithm (or "Porter stemmer") is a process for removing the commoner morphological and inflexional endings from words in English. Its main use is as part of a term normalisation process that is usually done when setting up Information Retrieval systems.*[4]

In other words, the various forms of a word are reduced to a common root form. For example, the words *breathe, breathes, breathing,* and *breathed,* via the Porter stemmer, reduce to *breath.*

The Porter stemmer is one of many stemming algorithms. See section 8.2.1 for coverage of an extension to Lucene that implements the Snowball algorithm (also created by Dr. Porter). KStem is another stemming algorithm that has been adapted to Lucene (search Google for KStem and Lucene).

Next we'll show how to use `StopFilter` to remove words but leave a positional hole behind, and then we'll describe the full analyzer.

4.6.1   StopFilter leaves holes

Stop-word removal brings up an interesting issue: what happens to the holes left by the words removed? Suppose you index "one is not enough." The tokens emitted from `StopAnalyzer` will be *one* and *enough,* with *is* and *not* thrown away. By default, `StopAnalyzer` accounts for the removed words by incrementing the position increment. This is illustrated from the output of `AnalyzerUtils.displayTokensWithPositions`:

```
2: [quick]
3: [brown]
4: [fox]
5: [jump]
6: [over]
8: [lazi]
9: [dog]
```

Positions 1 and 7 are missing due to the removal of *the.* If you have a need to disable the holes so that position increment is always 1, use `StopFilter`'s `setEnablePositionIncrements` method. But be careful when doing so: your index won't

---

[4] Taken from the website http://tartarus.org/~martin/PorterStemmer/index.html

record the deleted words, so there can be surprising effects. For example, the phrase "one enough" will match the indexed phrase "one is not enough" if you don't preserve the holes!

Stepping back a bit, the primary reason to remove stop words is because these words typically have no special meaning; they are the "glue" words required in any language. The problem is, because we've discarded them, we've lost some information, which may or may not be a problem for your application. For example, nonexact searches can still match the document, such as "a quick brown fox."

There's an interesting alternative, called *shingles*, which are compound tokens created from multiple adjacent tokens. Lucene has a `TokenFilter` called `ShingleFilter` in the contrib analyzers module that creates shingles during analysis. We'll describe it in more detail in section 8.2.3. With shingles, stop words are combined with adjacent words to make new tokens, such as *the-quick*. At search time, the same expansion is used. This enables precise phrase matching, because the stop words aren't discarded. Using shingles yields good search performance because the number of documents containing *the-quick* is far fewer than the number containing the stop word *the* in any context. Nutch's document analysis, described in section 4.9, also uses shingles.

4.6.2 Combining stemming and stop-word removal

This custom analyzer uses a stop-word removal filter, enabled to maintain positional gaps and fed from a `LowerCaseTokenizer`. The results of the stop filter are fed to the Porter stemmer. Listing 4.12 shows the full implementation of this sophisticated analyzer. `LowerCaseTokenizer` kicks off the analysis process, feeding tokens through the stop-word removal filter and finally stemming the words using the built-in Porter stemmer.

Listing 4.12 `PositionalPorterStopAnalyzer`: stemming and stop word removal

```
public class PositionalPorterStopAnalyzer extends Analyzer {
  private Set stopWords;

  public PositionalPorterStopAnalyzer() {
    this(StopAnalyzer.ENGLISH_STOP_WORDS_SET);
  }

  public PositionalPorterStopAnalyzer(Set stopWords) {
    this.stopWords = stopWords;
  }

  public TokenStream tokenStream(String fieldName, Reader reader) {
    StopFilter stopFilter = new StopFilter(true,
                                           new LowerCaseTokenizer(reader),
                                           stopWords);
    stopFilter.setEnablePositionIncrements(true);
    return new PorterStemFilter(stopFilter);
  }
}
```

Next we describe field-specific issues with analysis.

4.7   Field variations

The fact that a document is composed of multiple fields, with diverse characteristics, introduces some interesting requirements to the analysis process. We'll first consider how analysis is impacted by multivalued fields. Next we'll discuss how to use different analyzers for different fields. Finally, we'll talk about skipping analysis entirely for certain fields.

4.7.1   Analysis of multivalued fields

Recall from chapter 2 that a document may have more than one `Field` instance with the same name, and that Lucene logically appends the tokens of these fields sequentially during indexing. Fortunately, your analyzer has some control over what happens at each field value boundary. This is important in order to ensure queries that pay attention to a `Token`'s position, such as phrase or span queries, don't inadvertently match across two separate field instances. For example, if one value is "it's time to pay income tax" and the next value is "return library books on time," then a phrase search for "tax return" will happily match this field!

To fix this, you'll have to create your own analyzer by subclassing the `Analyzer` class, then override the `getPositionIncrementGap` method (along with the `token-Stream` or `reusableTokenStream` method). By default, `getPositionIncrementGap` returns 0 (no gap), which means it acts as if the field values were directly appended to one another. Increase it to a large enough number (for example, 100) so that no positional queries could ever incorrectly match across the boundary.

It's also important to ensure that token offsets are computed properly for multivalued fields. If you intend to highlight such fields, as described in section 8.3, incorrect offsets will cause the wrong parts of the text to be highlighted. The token's `Offset-Attribute`, which exposes methods to retrieve the start and end offset, also has a special method `endOffset`, whose purpose is to return the final offset for the field. This is necessary for cases where a `TokenFilter` has stripped out one or more final tokens; Lucene would otherwise have no way to compute the final offset for that field value. The offsets of each `Field` instance are shifted by the sum of the `endOffset` of all fields before it. Lucene's core tokenizers all implement `endOffset` properly, but if you create your own tokenizer, it's up to you to do so. Similarly, if your application requires a gap to be added to offsets when a field has multiple values, you should override the `getOffsetGap` method of your custom analyzer.

Another frequently encountered analysis challenge is how to use a different analyzer for different fields.

4.7.2   Field-specific analysis

During indexing, the granularity of analyzer choice is at the `IndexWriter` or per-document level. With `QueryParser`, there's only one analyzer applied to all encountered text. Yet for many applications, where the documents have diverse fields, it would seem that each field may deserve unique analysis.

Internally, analyzers can easily act on the field name being analyzed, because that's passed as an argument to the `tokenStream` method. The built-in analyzers don't leverage this capability because they're designed for general-purpose use and field names are application specific, but you can easily create a custom analyzer that does so. Alternatively, Lucene has a helpful built-in utility class, `PerFieldAnalyzerWrapper`, that makes it easy to use different analyzers per field. Use it like this:

```
PerFieldAnalyzerWrapper analyzer = new PerFieldAnalyzerWrapper(
                                        new SimpleAnalyzer());
analyzer.addAnalyzer("body", new StandardAnalyzer(Version.LUCENE_30));
```

You provide the default analyzer when you create `PerFieldAnalyzerWrapper`. Then, for any field that requires a different analyzer, you call the `addAnalyzer` method. Any field that wasn't assigned a specific analyzer simply falls back to the default one. In the previous example, we use `SimpleAnalyzer` for all fields except body, which uses `StandardAnalyzer`.

Let's see next how `PerFieldAnalyzerWrapper` can be useful when you need to mix analyzed and unanalyzed fields.

4.7.3 *Searching on unanalyzed fields*

There are often cases when you'd like to index a field's value without analysis. For example, part numbers, URLs, and Social Security numbers should all be indexed and searched as a single token. During indexing this is easily done by specifying `Field.Index.NOT_ANALYZED` or `Field.Index.NOT_ANALYZED_NO_NORMS` when you create the field. You also want users to be able to search on these part numbers. This is simple if your application directly creates a `TermQuery`.

But a dilemma can arise if you use `QueryParser` and attempt to query on an unanalyzed field; this is because the fact that the field wasn't analyzed is only known during indexing. There's nothing special about such a field's terms once indexed; they're just terms. Let's see the issue exposed with a straightforward test case that indexes a document with an unanalyzed field and then attempts to find that document again, shown in listing 4.13.

> **Listing 4.13   Using `QueryParser` to match part numbers**

```
public class KeywordAnalyzerTest extends TestCase {

  private IndexSearcher searcher;

  public void setUp() throws Exception {
    Directory directory = new RAMDirectory();

    IndexWriter writer = new IndexWriter(directory,
                       new SimpleAnalyzer(),
                       IndexWriter.MaxFieldLength.UNLIMITED);

    Document doc = new Document();
    doc.add(new Field("partnum",
                    "Q36",
```

```
                    Field.Store.NO,
                    Field.Index.NOT_ANALYZED_NO_NORMS));
    doc.add(new Field("description",
                    "Illidium Space Modulator",
                    Field.Store.YES,
                    Field.Index.ANALYZED));
    writer.addDocument(doc);

    writer.close();

    searcher = new IndexSearcher(directory);
}

public void testTermQuery() throws Exception {
    Query query = new TermQuery(new Term("partnum", "Q36"));
    assertEquals(1, TestUtil.hitCount(searcher, query));
}

public void testBasicQueryParser() throws Exception {
    Query query = new QueryParser(Version.LUCENE_30,
                            "description",
                            new SimpleAnalyzer())
                    .parse("partnum:Q36 AND SPACE");
    assertEquals("note Q36 -> q",
                "+partnum:q +space",
                query.toString("description"));
    assertEquals("doc not found :(", 0,
                TestUtil.hitCount(searcher, query));
}
}
```

Don't analyze field

Don't analyze term

Verify document matches

❶

❷

❶ QueryParser analyzes each term and phrase of the query expression. Both *Q36* and *SPACE* are analyzed separately. SimpleAnalyzer strips nonletter characters and lowercases, so *Q36* becomes *q*. But at indexing time, *Q36* was left as is. Notice, also, that this is the same analyzer used during indexing, but because the field was indexed with Field.Index.NOT_ANALYZED_NO_NORMS, the analyzer wasn't used.

❷ Query has a nice toString() method (see section 3.3.2) to return the query as a QueryParser-like expression. Notice that *Q36* is gone.

The TermQuery worked fine, but QueryParser found no results. This issue of QueryParser encountering an unanalyzed field emphasizes a key point: indexing and analysis are intimately tied to searching. The testBasicQueryParser test shows that searching for terms created using Index.NOT_ANALYZED_NO_NORMS when a query expression is analyzed can be problematic. It's problematic because QueryParser analyzed the partnum field, but it shouldn't have. There are a few possible solutions:

- Change your UI so a user selects a part number separately from free-form queries. Generally, users don't want to know (and shouldn't need to know) about the field names in the index. This approach, while simple to implement, isn't generally recommended because it's poor practice to present more than one text entry box to the user: he or she may become confused.

- If part numbers or other textual constructs are common lexical occurrences in the text you're analyzing, consider creating a custom domain-specific analyzer that recognizes and preserves them.
- Subclass QueryParser and override one or both of the getFieldQuery methods to provide field-specific handling.
- Use PerFieldAnalyzerWrapper for field-specific analysis.

Designing a search UI is application-dependent; BooleanQuery (section 3.4.5) and filters (section 5.6) provide the support you need to combine query pieces in sophisticated ways. Section 9.5 shows how to present a forms-based search interface that uses XML to represent the full query. The information in this chapter provides the foundation for building domain-centric analyzers. We cover subclassing QueryParser in section 6.3. Of all these solutions, the simplest is to use PerFieldAnalyzerWrapper.

We'll use Lucene's KeywordAnalyzer to tokenize the part number as a single token. Note that KeywordAnalyzer and Field.Index.NOT_ANALYZED* are identical during indexing; it's only with QueryParser that using KeywordAnalyzer is necessary. We want only one field to be "analyzed" in this manner, so we leverage the PerField-AnalyzerWrapper to apply it only to the partnum field. First let's look at the Keyword-dAnalyzer in action as it fixes the situation:

```
public void testPerFieldAnalyzer() throws Exception {
  PerFieldAnalyzerWrapper analyzer = new PerFieldAnalyzerWrapper(
                                        new SimpleAnalyzer());
  analyzer.addAnalyzer("partnum", new KeywordAnalyzer());

  Query query = new QueryParser(Version.LUCENE_30,
                                "description", analyzer).parse(
                "partnum:Q36 AND SPACE");

  assertEquals("Q36 kept as-is",
               "+partnum:Q36 +space", query.toString("description"));
  assertEquals("doc found!", 1, TestUtil.hitCount(searcher, query));
}
```

We use PerFieldAnalyzerWrapper to apply the KeywordAnalyzer only to the partnum field, and SimpleAnalyzer to all other fields. This yields the same result as during indexing. The query now has the proper term for the partnum field, and the document is found as expected.

Given KeywordAnalyzer, we could streamline our code (in KeywordAnalyzer-Test.setUp) and use the same PerFieldAnalyzerWrapper used in testPerField-Analyzer during indexing. Using a KeywordAnalyzer on special fields during indexing would eliminate the use of Index.NOT_ANALYZED_NO_NORMS during indexing and replace it with Index.ANALYZED. Aesthetically, it may be pleasing to see the same analyzer used during indexing and querying, and using PerFieldAnalyzerWrapper makes this possible.

We've seen some interesting situations arising for different kinds of fields. Multi-valued fields require setting a position increment gap, to avoid matching across different values, while PerFieldAnalyzerWrapper lets us customize which analyzer is used for which field. Let's change topics now and discuss analyzing text from non-English languages.

4.8   *Language analysis issues*

Dealing with languages in Lucene is an interesting and multifaceted issue. How can text in various languages be indexed and subsequently retrieved? As a developer building Unicode-aware applications based on Lucene, what issues do you need to consider?

You must contend with several issues when analyzing text in various languages. The first hurdle is ensuring that character-set encoding is done properly so that external data, such as files, are read into Java properly. During the analysis process, different languages have different sets of stop words and unique stemming algorithms. Perhaps accents and other diacritics should be removed from characters as well, which would be language-dependent. Finally, you may require language detection if you aren't sure what language is being used. Each of these issues is ultimately up to the developer to address, with only basic building-block support provided by Lucene. A number of analyzers and additional building blocks such as `Tokenizers` and `TokenStreams` are available in the contrib directory (discussed in section 8.2) and elsewhere online.

We'll first describe the Unicode character encoding, then discuss options for analyzing non-English languages, and in particular Asian languages, which present unique challenges. Finally we'll investigate options for mixing multiple languages in one index. Let's begin with a brief introduction to Unicode and character encodings.

4.8.1   *Unicode and encodings*

Internally, Lucene stores all characters in the standard UTF-8 encoding. Java frees us from many struggles by automatically handling Unicode within `Strings`, represented as UTF16 code points, and providing facilities for reading in external data in the many encodings. You, however, are responsible for getting external text into Java and Lucene. If you're indexing files on a file system, you need to know what encoding the files were saved as in order to read them properly. If you're reading HTML or XML from an HTTP server, encoding issues get a bit more complex. Encodings can be specified in an HTTP content-type header or specified within the document itself in the XML header or an HTML `<meta>` tag.

We won't elaborate on these encoding details, not because they aren't important, but because they're separate issues from Lucene. Please refer to appendix D for several sources of more detailed information on encoding topics. In particular, if you're new to I18N issues, read Joel Spolsky's excellent article "The Absolute Minimum Every Software Developer Absolutely, Positively Must Know About Unicode and Character Sets (No Excuses!)" (http://www.joelonsoftware.com/articles/Unicode.html) and the Java language Internationalization tutorial (http://java.sun.com/docs/books/tutorial/i18n/intro/).

We'll proceed with the assumption that you have your text available as Unicode, and move on to the Lucene-specific language concerns.

4.8.2 Analyzing non-English languages

All the details of the analysis process apply when you're dealing with text in non-English languages. Extracting terms from text is the goal. With Western languages, where whitespace and punctuation are used to separate words, you must adjust stop-word lists and stemming algorithms to be specific to the language of the text being analyzed. You may also want to use the `ASCIIFoldingFilter`, which replaces non-ASCII Unicode characters with their ASCII equivalents, when possible.

Beyond the built-in analyzers we've discussed, the contrib directory provides many language-specific analyzers, under contrib/analyzers. These analyzers generally employ language-specific stemming and stop word removal. Also freely available is the `SnowballAnalyzer` family of stemmers, which supports many European languages. We discuss `SnowballAnalyzer` in section 8.2.1.

Next we see an advanced capability in Lucene that enables filtering of characters even before the `Tokenizer` sees them.

4.8.3 Character normalization

As of version 2.9, Lucene makes it possible to normalize the character stream seen by the `Tokenizer`. This normalization fits in between the `Reader` and the `Tokenizer`, filtering the characters produced by the `Reader`, as shown in figure 4.7. What's crucial about this API is it properly accounts for the necessary corrections to the start and end offsets of `Tokens` whenever the filtering adds or removes characters. This means highlighting will work correctly in the original input string.

When would you want to filter characters? One example usage might be mapping between the hiragana and katakana in Japanese character streams. Another is mapping traditional Chinese to simplified Chinese. Most applications don't need to filter the character stream, but if yours does you'll be happy to know it's simple.

Regardless of your reasons, Lucene provides a set of character filtering classes that mirrors their token-based counterparts. The `CharStream` abstract base class simply adds one method, `correctOffset`, to the `Reader` class. `CharReader` wraps a normal `Reader` and creates a `CharStream`, whereas `CharFilter` chains any `CharStream` together. Using these building blocks, you can create a character filter chain, beginning with a single `CharReader` followed by any number of `CharFilters`, before tokenization even gets started. Figure 4.7 shows an initial `CharReader` followed by three `CharFilters`.

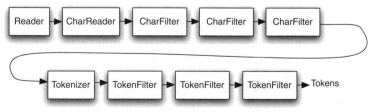

**Figure 4.6
Analysis chain that
includes character
normalization**

Lucene provides a single core concrete implementation of `CharFilter`, called `MappingCharFilter`, that allows you to enroll input and output pairs of substrings. Whenever one of the input substrings is seen in the input character stream, it's replaced with the corresponding output string. Although you can use this class as is, if you want to perform simple substring replacement keep in mind that it has a potentially high performance cost. That's because the current implementation allocates many temporary objects during analysis.

None of the core analyzers perform character filtering. You'll have to create your own analyzer that builds a chain starting with a `CharReader` followed by any number of `CharFilters`, then a `Tokenizer` and `TokenFilter` chain. Let's see what support Lucene provides for analyzing Asian languages next.

4.8.4   *Analyzing Asian languages*

Asian languages, such as Chinese, Japanese, and Korean (also denoted as CJK), generally use ideograms rather than an alphabet to represent words. These pictorial words may or may not be separated by whitespace and thus require a different type of analysis that recognizes when tokens should be split. The only built-in analyzer capable of doing anything useful with Asian text is the `StandardAnalyzer`, which recognizes some ranges of the Unicode space as CJK characters and tokenizes them individually.

Three analyzers in the Lucene contrib directory are suitable for Asian language analysis (see section 8.2 for more details on Lucene's contrib analyzers): `CJKAnalyzer`, `ChineseAnalyzer`, and `SmartChineseAnalyzer`. In our sample book data, the Chinese characters for the book *Tao Te Ching* were added to the title. Because our data originates in Java properties files, Unicode escape sequences are used:[5]

```
title=Tao Te Ching \u9053\u5FB7\u7D93
```

We used `StandardAnalyzer` for all tokenized fields in our index, which tokenizes each English word as expected (*tao, te,* and *ching*) as well as each of the Chinese characters as separate terms (*tao te ching*) even though there's no space between them. Our `ChineseTest` demonstrates that searching by the word *tao* using its Chinese representation works as desired:

```
public class ChineseTest extends TestCase {
  public void testChinese() throws Exception {
    Directory dir = TestUtil.getBookIndexDirectory();
    IndexSearcher searcher = new IndexSearcher(dir);
    Query query = new TermQuery(new Term("contents", "道"));
    assertEquals("tao", 1, TestUtil.hitCount(searcher, query));
  }
}
```

Note that our ChineseTest.java file was saved in UTF-8 format and compiled using the UTF-8 encoding switch (`-encoding utf8`) for the Javac compiler. We had to ensure

---

[5]   `java.util.Properties` loads properties files using the ISO-8859-1 encoding but allows characters to be encoded using standard Java Unicode \u syntax. Java includes a native2ascii program that can convert natively encoded files into the appropriate format.

that the representations of the Chinese characters are encoded and read properly and use a CJK-aware analyzer.

Similar to the `AnalyzerDemo` in listing 4.2, we created a `ChineseDemo` (listing 4.14) program to illustrate how various analyzers work with Chinese text. This demo uses Abstract Window Toolkit (AWT) Label components to properly display the characters regardless of your locale and console environment.

Listing 4.14 `ChineseDemo`: illustrates what analyzers do with Chinese text

```
public class ChineseDemo {                              Analyze
  private static String[] strings = {"道德經"};      ←┘ this text

  private static Analyzer[] analyzers = {
    new SimpleAnalyzer(),
    new StandardAnalyzer(Version.LUCENE_30),         Test these
    new ChineseAnalyzer (),                        ←┘ analyzers
    new CJKAnalyzer (Version.LUCENE_30),
    new SmartChineseAnalyzer (Version.LUCENE_30)
  };

  public static void main(String args[]) throws Exception {

    for (String string : strings) {
      for (Analyzer analyzer : analyzers) {
        analyze(string, analyzer);
      }
    }

  }

  private static void analyze(String string, Analyzer analyzer)
        throws IOException {
    StringBuffer buffer = new StringBuffer();

    TokenStream stream = analyzer.tokenStream("contents",
                                   new StringReader(string));
    TermAttribute term = stream.addAttribute(TermAttribute.class);

    while(stream.incrementToken()) {                ←  Retrieve
      buffer.append("[");                              tokens
      buffer.append(term.term());
      buffer.append("] ");
    }

    String output = buffer.toString();

    Frame f = new Frame();
    f.setTitle(analyzer.getClass().getSimpleName() + " : " + string);
    f.setResizable(false);

    Font font = new Font(null, Font.PLAIN, 36);
    int width = getWidth(f.getFontMetrics(font), output);

    f.setSize((width < 250) ? 250 : width + 50, 75);
    Label label = new Label(output);                ←  Display
    label.setSize(width, 75);                          analysis
    label.setAlignment(Label.CENTER);
```

```
      label.setFont(font);
      f.add(label);

      f.setVisible(true);
    }

    private static int getWidth(FontMetrics metrics, String s) {
      int size = 0;
      int length = s.length();
      for (int i = 0; i < length; i++) {
        size += metrics.charWidth(s.charAt(i));
      }

      return size;
    }
  }
```

CJKAnalyzer, ChineseAnalyzer, and SmartChineseAnalyzer are analyzers found in the Lucene contrib directory; they aren't included in the core Lucene distribution. ChineseDemo shows the output using an AWT Label component to avoid any confusion that might arise from console output encoding or limited fonts mangling things; you can see the output in figure 4.8.

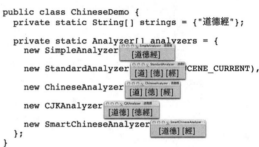

Figure 4.7 **ChineseDemo illustrating analysis of the title *Tao Te Ching***

The CJKAnalyzer pairs characters in overlapping windows of two characters each. Many CJK words are two characters. By pairing characters in this manner, words are likely to be kept together (as well as disconnected characters, increasing the index size). The ChineseAnalyzer takes a simpler approach and, in our example, mirrors the results from the built-in StandardAnalyzer by tokenizing each Chinese character. Words that consist of multiple Chinese characters are split into terms for each component character. Finally, SmartChineseAnalyzer uses probabilistic knowledge to find the optimal word segmentation for Simplified Chinese text.

4.8.5   *Zaijian*[6]

A major hurdle remains when you're dealing with various languages in a single index: handling text encoding. The StandardAnalyzer is still the best built-in general-purpose analyzer, even accounting for CJK characters; however, the contrib SmartChineseAnalyzer seems better suited for Chinese language analysis.

When you're indexing documents in multiple languages into a single index, using a per-document analyzer is appropriate. You may also want to add a field to documents indicating their language; this field can be used to filter search results or for

---

[6]   *Zaijian* means *good-bye* in Chinese.

display purposes during retrieval. In section 6.3.4, we'll show you how to retrieve the locale from a user's web browser, which could be used to select an appropriate analyzer during searching.

One final topic is language detection. This, like character encodings, is outside the scope of Lucene, but it may be important to your application. We don't cover language-detection techniques in this book, but it's an active area of research with several implementations to choose from (see appendix D).

4.9 *Nutch analysis*

We don't have the source code to Google, but we do have the open source project Nutch, created by Lucene's creator Doug Cutting. Nutch takes an interesting approach to analyzing text, specifically how it handles stop words, which it calls common terms. If all words are indexed, an enormous number of documents become associated with each common term, such as *the*. Querying for *the* is practically a nonsensical query, given that the majority of documents contain that term. When common terms are used in a query, but not within a phrase, such as *the quick brown* with no other adornments or quotes, they are discarded. However, if a series of terms is surrounded by double quotes, such as "the quick brown," a fancier trick is played, which we detail in this section.

Nutch combines an index-time analysis bigram (grouping two consecutive words as a single token) technique with a query-time optimization of phrases. This results in a far smaller document space considered during searching; for example, far fewer documents have *the quick* side by side than contain *the*. Using the internals of Nutch, we created a simple example to demonstrate the Nutch analysis trickery. The shingles contrib package offers the same capability. Listing 4.15 first analyzes the phrase "The quick brown…" using the NutchDocumentAnalyzer, then parses a query of "the quick brown" to demonstrate the Lucene query created.

> **Listing 4.15 NutchExample: demonstrating Nutch analysis and query parsing**

```
public class NutchExample {

  public static void main(String[] args) throws IOException {      Define ❶
    Configuration conf = new Configuration();                      custom
    conf.addResource("nutch-default.xml");                         analyzer
    NutchDocumentAnalyzer analyzer = new NutchDocumentAnalyzer(conf);  ◁┘

    TokenStream ts = analyzer.tokenStream("content",
                          new StringReader("The quick brown fox..."));
    int position = 0;
    while(true) {                              ◁┐  Display
      Token token = ts.next();                  ❷  token details
      if (token == null) {
        break;
      }
      int increment = token.getPositionIncrement();

      if (increment > 0) {
```

```
        position = position + increment;
        System.out.println();
        System.out.print(position + ": ");
    }

    System.out.print("[" +
                token.termText() + ":" +
                token.startOffset() + "->" +
                token.endOffset() + ":" +
                token.type() + "] ");
    }                                                              Parse to   ❸
    System.out.println();                                         Nutch's Query

    Query nutchQuery = Query.parse("\"the quick brown\"", conf);  ◁
    org.apache.lucene.search.Query luceneQuery;
    luceneQuery = new QueryFilters(conf).filter(nutchQuery);   ◁┐ Create
    System.out.println("Translated: " + luceneQuery);            │ translated
    }                                                            │ Lucene Query
}
```

❶ Nutch uses a custom analyzer, `NutchDocumentAnalyzer`. Note that Nutch internally embeds an earlier version (2.4) of Lucene, which explains why it's using the old analysis API based on the `Token` class and the `next()` method of `TokenStream`. These old deprecated APIs have been replaced with the attributes-based API as of version 3.0.

❷ We iterate through the tokens and print the details.

❸ We create the Nutch query, and use Nutch's `QueryFilters` to translate the `Query` into the rewritten Lucene `Query`.

The analyzer output shows how "the quick" becomes a bigram, but the word *the* isn't discarded. The bigram resides in the same token position as the:

```
1: [the:0->3:<WORD>] [the-quick:0->9:gram]
2: [quick:4->9:<WORD>]
3: [brown:10->15:<WORD>]
4: [fox:16->19:<WORD>]
```

Because additional tokens are created during analysis, the index is larger, but the benefit of this trade-off is that searches for exact-phrase queries are much faster. And there's a bonus: no terms were discarded during indexing.

During querying, phrases are also analyzed and optimized. The query output (recall from section 3.3.2 that `Query`'s `toString()` is handy) of the Lucene `Query` instance for the query expression "the quick brown" is:

```
Translated: +(url:"the quick brown"^4.0 anchor:"the quick brown"^2.0
  content:"the-quick quick brown" title:"the quick
  brown"^1.5 host:"the quick brown"^2.0)
```

A Nutch query expands to search in the url, anchor, title, and host fields as well, with higher boosts for those fields using the exact phrase. The content field clause is optimized to only include the bigram of a position that contains an additional <WORD> type token.

This was a quick view of what Nutch does with indexing analysis and query construction. Nutch continues to evolve, optimize, and tweak the various techniques for indexing and querying. The bigrams aren't taken into consideration except in the content field, but as the document base grows, whether optimizations are needed on other fields will be reevaluated. You can use the shingles contrib module, covered in section 8.2.3, to take the same approach as Nutch.

4.10 Summary

Analysis, while only a single facet of using Lucene, is the aspect that deserves the most attention and effort. The words that can be searched are those emitted during indexing analysis: nothing more, nothing less. Sure, using `StandardAnalyzer` may do the trick for your needs, and it suffices for many applications. But it's important to understand the analysis process. Users who take analysis for granted often run into confusion later when they try to understand why searching for "to be or not to be" returns no results (perhaps due to stop-word removal).

It takes less than one line of code to incorporate an analyzer during indexing. Many sophisticated processes may occur under the covers, such as stop word removal and stemming of words. Removing words decreases your index size but can have a negative impact on precision querying.

Because one size doesn't fit all when it comes to analysis, you may need to tune the analysis process for your application domain. Lucene's elegant analyzer architecture decouples each of the processes internal to textual analysis, letting you reuse fundamental building blocks to construct custom analyzers. When you're working with analyzers, be sure to use our `AnalyzerUtils`, or something similar, to see firsthand how your text is tokenized. If you're changing analyzers, you should rebuild your index using the new analyzer so that all documents are analyzed in the same manner.

Now, after four chapters, we've finished the first pass through the major components of Lucene: indexing, analysis, and searching. In the next chapter we'll dig deeper into search by describing Lucene's advanced search capabilities.

Advanced search techniques

This chapter covers
- Loading field values for all documents
- Filtering and sorting search results
- Span and function queries
- Leveraging term vectors
- Stopping a slow search

Many applications that implement search with Lucene can do so using the API introduced in chapter 3. Some projects, though, need more than the basic searching mechanisms. Perhaps you need to use security filters to restrict which documents are searchable for certain users, or you'd like to see search results sorted by a specific field, such as title, instead of by relevance. Using term vectors, you can find documents similar to an existing one, or automatically categorize documents. Function queries allow you to use arbitrary logic when computing scores for each hit, enabling you to boost relevance scores according to recency. We'll cover all of these examples in this chapter.

Rounding out our advanced topics are

- Creating span queries, advanced queries that pay careful attention to positional information of every term match within each hit
- Using `MultiPhraseQuery`, which enables synonym searching within a phrase
- Using `FieldSelector`, which gives fine control over which fields are loaded for a document
- Searching across multiple Lucene indexes
- Stopping a search after a specified time limit
- Using a variant of `QueryParser` that searches multiple fields at once

The first topic we'll visit is Lucene's field cache, which is a building block that underlies a number of Lucene's advanced features.

5.1 Lucene's field cache

Sometimes you need fast access to a certain field's value for every document. Lucene's normal inverted index can't do this, because it optimizes instead for fast access to all documents containing a specific term. Stored fields and term vectors let you access all field values by document number, but they're relatively slow to load and generally aren't recommended for more than a page's worth of results at a time.

Lucene's field cache, an advanced internal API, was created to address this need. Note that the field cache isn't a user-visible search feature; rather, it's something of a building block, a useful internal API that you can use when implementing advanced search features in your application. Often your application won't use the field cache directly, but advanced functionality you do use, such as sorting results by field values (covered in the next section), uses the field cache under the hood. Besides sorting, some of Lucene's built-in filters, as well as function queries, use the field cache internally, so it's important to understand the trade-offs involved.

There are also real-world cases when your application would directly use the field cache itself. Perhaps you have a unique identifier for every document that you'll need to access when searching, to retrieve values stored in a separate database or other store. Maybe you'd like to boost documents according to how recently they were published, so you need fast access to that date per document (we show this example in section 5.7.2). Possibly, in a commerce setting, your documents correspond to products, each with its own shipping weight (stored as a float or double, per document), and you'd like to access that to present the shipping cost next to each search result. These are all examples easily handled by Lucene's field cache API.

One important restriction for using the field cache is that all documents must have a single value for the specified field. This means the field cache can't handle multivalued fields as of Lucene 3.0, though it's possible this restriction has been relaxed by the time you're reading this.

NOTE   A field cache can only be used on fields that have a single term. This typically means the field was indexed with `Index.NOT_ANALYZED` or `Index.NOT_ANALYZED_NO_NORMS`, though it's also possible to analyze the fields as long as you're using an analyzer, such as `KeywordAnalyzer`, that always produces only one token.

We'll first see how to use a field cache directly, should you need access to a field's value for all documents, when building a custom filter or function query, for example. Then we'll discuss the important RAM and CPU trade-offs when using a field cache. Finally, we discuss the importance of accessing a field cache within the context of a single segment at a time. We begin with the field cache API.

5.1.1 *Loading field values for all documents*

You can easily use the field cache to load an array of native values for a given field, indexed by document number. For example, if every document has a field called "weight," you can get the weight for all documents like this:

```
float[] weights = FieldCache.DEFAULT.getFloats(reader, "weight");
```

Then, simply reference `weights[docID]` whenever you need to know a document's weight value. The field cache supports many native types: byte, short, int, long, float, double, strings, and the class `StringIndex`, which includes the sort order of the string values.

   The first time the field cache is accessed for a given reader and field, the values for all documents are visited and loaded into memory as a single large array, and recorded into an internal cache keyed on the reader instance and the field name. This process can be quite time consuming for a large index. Subsequent calls quickly return the same array from the cache. The cache entry isn't cleared until the reader is closed and completely dereferenced by your application (a `WeakHashMap`, keyed by the reader, is used under the hood). This means that the first search that uses the field cache will pay the price of populating it. If your index is large enough that this cost is too high, it's best to prewarm your `IndexSearchers` before using them for real queries, as described in section 11.2.2.

   It's important to factor in the memory usage of field cache. Numeric fields require the number of bytes for the native type, multiplied by the number of documents. For `String` types, each unique term is also cached for each document. For highly unique fields, such as title, this can be a large amount of memory, because Java's `String` object itself has substantial overhead. The `StringIndex` field cache, which is used when sorting by a string field, also stores an additional int array holding the sort order for all documents.

NOTE   The field cache may consume quite a bit of memory; each entry allocates an array of the native type, whose length is equal to the number of documents in the provided reader. The field cache doesn't clear its entries until you close your reader and remove all references to that reader from your application and garbage collection runs.

5.1.2 *Per-segment readers*

As of 2.9, Lucene drives all search results collection and sorting one segment at a time. This means the reader argument passed to the field cache by Lucene's core functionality will always be a reader for a single segment. This has strong benefits when reopening an `IndexReader`; only the new segments must be loaded into the field cache.

But this means you should avoid passing your top-level `IndexReader` to the field cache directly to load values, because you'd then have values double-loaded, thus consuming twice as much RAM. Typically, you require the values in an advanced customization, such as implementing a custom `Collector`, a custom `Filter`, or a custom `FieldComparatorSource`, as described in chapter 6. All of these classes are provided with the single-segment reader, and it's that reader that you should in turn pass to the field cache to retrieve values. If the field cache is using too much memory and you suspect that a top-level reader may have been accidentally enrolled, try using the `set-InfoStream` API to enable debugging output. Cases like this one, plus other situations such as the same reader and field loaded under two different types, will cause a detailed message to be printed to the `PrintStream` you provide.

NOTE   Avoid passing a top-level reader directly to the field cache API. This can result in consuming double the memory, if Lucene is also passing individual segments' readers to the API.

Now that we've seen how to use field cache directly, as a building block when creating your application, let's discuss a valuable Lucene capability that uses a field cache internally: field sorting.

5.2 *Sorting search results*

By default, Lucene sorts the matching documents in descending relevance score order, such that the most relevant documents appear first. This is an excellent default as it means the user is most likely to find the right document in the first few results rather than on page 7. However, often you'd like to offer the user an option to sort differently.

For example, for a book search you may want to display search results grouped into categories, and within each category the books should be ordered by relevance to the query, or perhaps a simple sort by title is what your users want. Collecting all results and sorting them programmatically as a second pass outside of Lucene is one way to accomplish this. Doing so, however, introduces a possible performance bottleneck if the number of results is enormous. In this section, we'll see both of these examples and explore various other ways to sort search results, including sorting by one or more field values in either ascending or descending order.

Remember that sorting under the hood uses the field cache to load values across all documents, so keep the performance trade-offs from section 5.1 in mind.

We'll begin by seeing how to specify a custom sort when searching, starting with two special sort orders: relevance (the default sort) and index order. Then we'll sort by a field's values, including optionally reversing the sort order. Next we'll see how to sort by multiple sort criteria. Finally we'll show you how to specify the field's type or locale, which is important to ensure the sort order is correct.

5.2.1 *Sorting search results by field value*

IndexSearcher contains several overloaded search methods. Thus far we've covered only the basic search(Query, int) method, which returns the top requested number of results, ordered by decreasing relevance. The sorting version of this method has the signature search(Query, Filter, int, Sort). Filter, which we'll cover in section 5.6, should be null if you don't need to filter the results.

By default, the search method that accepts a Sort argument won't compute any scores for the matching documents. This is often a sizable performance gain, and many applications don't need the scores when sorting by field. If scores aren't needed in your application, it's best to keep this default. If you need to change the default, use IndexSearcher's setDefaultFieldSortScoring method, which takes two Booleans: doTrackScores and doMaxScore. If doTrackScores is true, then each hit will have a score computed. If doMaxScore is true, then the max score across all hits will be computed. Note that computing the max score is in general more costly than the score per hit, because the score per hit is only computed if the hit is competitive. For our example, because we want to display the scores, we enable score tracking but not max score tracking.

Throughout this section we'll use the source code in listings 5.1 and 5.2 to show the effect of sorting. Listing 5.1 contains the displayResults method, which runs the search and prints details for each result. Listing 5.2 is the main method that invokes displayResults for each type of sort. You can run this by typing ant SortingExample in the book's source code directory.

Listing 5.1 Sorting search hits by field

```java
public class SortingExample {
  private Directory directory;

  public SortingExample(Directory directory) {
    this.directory = directory;
  }

  public void displayResults(Query query, Sort sort)        ◁──❶
      throws IOException {
    IndexSearcher searcher = new IndexSearcher(directory);

    searcher.setDefaultFieldSortScoring(true, false);        ◁──❷

    TopDocs results = searcher.search(query, null,           ❸
                                20, sort);

    System.out.println("\nResults for: " +        ◁──❹
        query.toString() + " sorted by " + sort);

    System.out.println(StringUtils.rightPad("Title", 30) +
        StringUtils.rightPad("pubmonth", 10) +
        StringUtils.center("id", 4) +
        StringUtils.center("score", 15));
```

```
PrintStream out = new PrintStream(System.out, true, "UTF-8");        ⬅ ❺

DecimalFormat scoreFormatter = new DecimalFormat("0.######");
for (ScoreDoc sd : results.scoreDocs) {
  int docID = sd.doc;
  float score = sd.score;
  Document doc = searcher.doc(docID);
  System.out.println(
      StringUtils.rightPad(
          StringUtils.abbreviate(doc.get("title"), 29), 30) +
      StringUtils.rightPad(doc.get("pubmonth"), 10) +               ❻
      StringUtils.center("" + docID, 4) +
      StringUtils.leftPad(
          scoreFormatter.format(score), 12));
  out.println("   " + doc.get("category"));
  //out.println(searcher.explain(query, docID));        ⬅ ❼
}

searcher.close();
}
```

The Sort object ❶ encapsulates an ordered collection of field sorting information. We ask IndexSearcher ❷ to compute scores per hit. Then we call the overloaded search method that accepts the custom Sort ❸. We use the useful toString method ❹ of the Sort class to describe itself, then create PrintStream that accepts UTF-8 encoded output ❺, and finally use StringUtils ❻ from Apache Commons Lang for nice columnar output formatting. Later you'll see a reason to look at the query explanation. For now, it's commented out ❼.

Now that you've seen how displayResults works, listing 5.2 shows how we invoke it to print the results as seen in the rest of this section.

Listing 5.2 Show results when sorting by different fields

```
public static void main(String[] args) throws Exception {
  Query allBooks = new MatchAllDocsQuery();

  QueryParser parser = new QueryParser(Version.LUCENE_30,        ❶ Create
                                       "contents",                  test
                                       new StandardAnalyzer(        query
                                           Version.LUCENE_30));
  BooleanQuery query = new BooleanQuery();
  query.add(allBooks, BooleanClause.Occur.SHOULD);
  query.add(parser.parse("java OR action"),
            BooleanClause.Occur.SHOULD);

  Directory directory = TestUtil.getBookIndexDirectory();        ❷ Create
  SortingExample example = new SortingExample(directory);           example
                                                                    runner
  example.displayResults(query, Sort.RELEVANCE);

  example.displayResults(query, Sort.INDEXORDER);

  example.displayResults(query,
      new Sort(new SortField("category", SortField.STRING)));

  example.displayResults(query,
      new Sort(new SortField("pubmonth", SortField.INT, true)));
```

```
    example.displayResults(query,
        new Sort(new SortField("category", SortField.STRING),
            SortField.FIELD_SCORE,
            new SortField("pubmonth", SortField.INT, true)
        ));

    example.displayResults(query,
        new Sort(new SortField[] {SortField.FIELD_SCORE,
        new SortField("category", SortField.STRING)}));
    directory.close();
}
```

The sorting example uses an unusual query ❶. This query was designed to match all results, and also to assign higher scores to some hits than others, so that we have some diversity when sorting by relevance. Next, the example runner is constructed from the sample book index included with this book's source code ❷.

Now that you've seen how to use sorting, let's explore ways search results can be sorted. We'll step through each of the invocations of displayResults from listing 5.2.

5.2.2   *Sorting by relevance*

Lucene sorts by decreasing relevance, also called the score, by default. Sorting by score works by either passing null as the Sort object or using the default sort behavior. Each of these variants returns results in the default score order. Sort.RELEVANCE is equivalent to new Sort():

```
example.displayResults(query, Sort.RELEVANCE);
example.displayResults(query, new Sort());
```

There's additional overhead involved in using a Sort object, though, so stick to using search(Query, int) if you simply want to sort by relevance. As shown in listing 5.2, this is how we sort by relevance:

```
example.displayResults(allBooks, Sort.RELEVANCE);
```

And here's the corresponding output (notice the decreasing score column):

```
Results for: *:* (contents:java contents:action) sorted by <score>
Title                        pubmonth   id      score
Lucene in Action, Second E... 201005     7       1.052735
    /technology/computers/programming
Ant in Action                 200707     9       1.052735
    /technology/computers/programming
Tapestry in Action            200403     10      0.447534
    /technology/computers/programming
JUnit in Action, Second Ed... 201005     11      0.429442
    /technology/computers/programming
Tao Te Ching 道德經             200609     0       0.151398
    /philosophy/eastern
Lipitor Thief of Memory       200611     1       0.151398
    /health
Imperial Secrets of Health... 199903     2       0.151398
    /health/alternative/chinese
Nudge: Improving Decisions... 200804     3       0.151398
```

```
    /health
Gödel, Escher, Bach: an Et... 199905      4      0.151398
    /technology/computers/ai
Extreme Programming Explained 200411      5      0.151398
    /technology/computers/programming/methodology
Mindstorms: Children, Comp... 199307      6      0.151398
    /technology/computers/programming/education
The Pragmatic Programmer      199910      8      0.151398
    /technology/computers/programming
A Modern Art of Education     200403     12      0.151398
    /education/pedagogy
```

The output of `Sort`'s `toString()` shows `<score>`, reflecting that we're sorting by relevance score, in descending order. Notice how many of the hits have identical scores, but within blocks of identical scores the sort is by document ID ascending. Lucene internally always adds an implicit final sort, by document ID, to consistently break any ties in the sort order that you specified.

5.2.3   *Sorting by index order*

If the order in which the documents were indexed is relevant, you can use `Sort.INDEXORDER`:

```
example.displayResults(query, Sort.INDEXORDER);
```

This results in the following output. Note the increasing document ID column:

```
Results for: *:* (contents:java contents:action) sorted by <doc>
Title                        pubmonth   id      score
Tao Te Ching 道德經            200609      0      0.151398
    /philosophy/eastern
Lipitor Thief of Memory      200611      1      0.151398
    /health
Imperial Secrets of Health... 199903      2      0.151398
    /health/alternative/chinese
Nudge: Improving Decisions... 200804      3      0.151398
    /health
Gödel, Escher, Bach: an Et... 199905      4      0.151398
    /technology/computers/ai
Extreme Programming Explained 200411      5      0.151398
    /technology/computers/programming/methodology
Mindstorms: Children, Comp... 199307      6      0.151398
    /technology/computers/programming/education
Lucene in Action, Second E... 201005      7      1.052735
    /technology/computers/programming
The Pragmatic Programmer      199910      8      0.151398
    /technology/computers/programming
Ant in Action                200707      9      1.052735
    /technology/computers/programming
Tapestry in Action           200403     10      0.447534
    /technology/computers/programming
JUnit in Action, Second Ed... 201005     11      0.429442
    /technology/computers/programming
A Modern Art of Education     200403     12      0.151398
    /education/pedagogy
```

Document order may be interesting for an index that you build up once and never change. But if you need to reindex documents, document order typically won't work because newly indexed documents receive new document IDs and will be sorted last. In our case, index order is unspecified.

So far we've only sorted by score, which was already happening without using the sorting facility, and document order, which is probably only marginally useful at best. Sorting by one of our own fields is what we're after.

5.2.4 *Sorting by a field*

Sorting by a textual field first requires that the field was indexed as a single token, as described in section 2.4.6. Typically this means using `Field.Index.NOT_ANALYZED` or `Field.Index.NOT_ANALYZED_NO_NORMS`. Separately, you can choose whether or not to store the field. In our book test index, the category field was indexed with `Field.Index.NOT_ANALYZED` and `Field.Store.YES`, allowing it to be used for sorting. `NumericField` instances are automatically indexed properly for sorting. To sort by a field, you must create a new `Sort` object, providing the field name:

```
example.displayResults(query,
    new Sort(new SortField("category", SortField.STRING)));
```

Here's the result when sorting by category. Note that the results are sorted by our category field in increasing alphabetical order:

```
Results for: *:* (contents:java contents:action)
➥    sorted by <string: "category">
Title                         pubmonth   id      score
A Modern Art of Education      200403     12      0.151398
    /education/pedagogy
Lipitor Thief of Memory        200611     1       0.151398
    /health
Nudge: Improving Decisions... 200804      3       0.151398
    /health
Imperial Secrets of Health... 199903      2       0.151398
    /health/alternative/chinese
Tao Te Ching 道德經              200609     0       0.151398
    /philosophy/eastern
Gödel, Escher, Bach: an Et... 199905      4       0.151398
    /technology/computers/ai
Lucene in Action, Second E... 201005      7       1.052735
    /technology/computers/programming
The Pragmatic Programmer       199910     8       0.151398
    /technology/computers/programming
Ant in Action                  200707     9       1.052735
    /technology/computers/programming
Tapestry in Action             200403     10      0.447534
    /technology/computers/programming
JUnit in Action, Second Ed... 201005      11      0.429442
    /technology/computers/programming
Mindstorms: Children, Comp... 199307      6       0.151398
    /technology/computers/programming/education
Extreme Programming Explained 200411      5       0.151398
    /technology/computers/programming/methodology
```

5.2.5 Reversing sort order

The default sort direction for sort fields (including relevance and document ID) is natural ordering. Natural order is descending for relevance but increasing for all other fields. The natural order can be reversed per Sort object by specifying true for the second argument. For example, here we list books with the newest publications first:

```
example.displayResults(allBooks,
        new Sort(new SortField("pubmonth", SortField.INT, true)));
```

In our book test index, the pubmonth field is indexed as NumericField, where the year and month are combined as an integer. For example, 201005 is indexed as integer 201,005. Note that pubmonth is now sorted in descending order:

```
Results for: *:* (contents:java contents:action)
      sorted by <int: "pubmonth">!
Title                            pubmonth    id      score
Lucene in Action, Second E... 201005         7     1.052735
      /technology/computers/programming
JUnit in Action, Second Ed... 201005        11     0.429442
      /technology/computers/programming
Nudge: Improving Decisions... 200804         3     0.151398
      /health
Ant in Action                 200707         9     1.052735
      /technology/computers/programming
Lipitor Thief of Memory       200611         1     0.151398
      /health
Tao Te Ching 道德經             200609         0     0.151398
      /philosophy/eastern
Extreme Programming Explained 200411         5     0.151398
      /technology/computers/programming/methodology
Tapestry in Action            200403        10     0.447534
      /technology/computers/programming
A Modern Art of Education     200403        12     0.151398
      /education/pedagogy
The Pragmatic Programmer      199910         8     0.151398
      /technology/computers/programming
Gödel, Escher, Bach: an Et... 199905         4     0.151398
      /technology/computers/ai
Imperial Secrets of Health... 199903         2     0.151398
      /health/alternative/chinese
Mindstorms: Children, Comp... 199307         6     0.151398
      /technology/computers/programming/education
```

The exclamation point in sorted by "pubmonth"! indicates that the pubmonth field is being sorted in reverse natural order (descending publication months, with newest first). Note that the two books with the same publication month are then sorted in document ID order due to Lucene's internal tie break by document ID.

5.2.6 Sorting by multiple fields

Sorting by multiple fields is important whenever your primary sort leaves ambiguity because there are equal values. Implicitly we've been sorting by multiple fields, because Lucene automatically breaks ties by document ID. You can control the sort fields explicitly by creating Sort with multiple SortFields. This example uses the category field as a primary alphabetic sort, with results within category sorted by score; finally, books with equal score within a category are sorted by decreasing publication month:

```
example.displayResults(query,
    new Sort(new SortField("category", SortField.STRING),
            SortField.FIELD_SCORE,
            new SortField("pubmonth", SortField.INT, true)
            ));
```

You can see in the results that we first sort by category, and second by score. For example, the category /technology/computers/programming has multiple books within it that are sorted first by decreasing relevance and second by decreasing publication month:

```
Results for: *:* (contents:java contents:action)
➡    sorted by <string: "category">,<score>,<int: "pubmonth">!
Title                           pubmonth   id      score
A Modern Art of Education        200403     12      0.151398
    /education/pedagogy
Nudge: Improving Decisions... 200804       3       0.151398
    /health
Lipitor Thief of Memory         200611     1       0.151398
    /health
Imperial Secrets of Health... 199903       2       0.151398
    /health/alternative/chinese
Tao Te Ching 道德經               200609     0       0.151398
    /philosophy/eastern
Gödel, Escher, Bach: an Et... 199905       4       0.151398
    /technology/computers/ai
Lucene in Action, Second E... 201005       7       1.052735
    /technology/computers/programming
Ant in Action                   200707     9       1.052735
    /technology/computers/programming
Tapestry in Action              200403     10      0.447534
    /technology/computers/programming
JUnit in Action, Second Ed... 201005       11      0.429442
    /technology/computers/programming
The Pragmatic Programmer         199910    8       0.151398
    /technology/computers/programming
Mindstorms: Children, Comp... 199307       6       0.151398
    /technology/computers/programming/education
Extreme Programming Explained 200411       5       0.151398
    /technology/computers/programming/methodology
```

The Sort instance internally keeps an array of SortFields, but only in this example have you seen it explicitly; the other examples used shortcuts to creating the Sort-Field array. A SortField holds the field name, a field type, and the reverse order flag. SortField contains constants for several field types, including SCORE, DOC, STRING, BYTE, SHORT, INT, LONG, FLOAT, and DOUBLE. SCORE and DOC are special types for sorting on relevance and document ID.

5.2.7 *Selecting a sorting field type*

By search time, the fields that can be sorted on and their corresponding types are already set. Indexing time is when the decision about sorting capabilities should be made, but custom sorting implementations can do so at search time, as you'll see in section 6.1. Section 2.4.6 discusses index-time sorting design. By indexing using a NumericField, you can base sorting on numeric values. Sorting by numeric values consumes less memory than by string values; section 5.1 discusses performance issues further.

When sorting by String values, you may need to specify your own locale, which we cover next.

5.2.8 *Using a nondefault locale for sorting*

When you're sorting on a SortField.STRING type, order is determined under the covers using String.compareTo by default. But if you need a different collation order, SortField lets you specify a Locale. A Collator instance is obtained for the provided locale using Collator.getInstance(Locale), and the Collator.compare method then determines the sort order. There are two overloaded SortField constructors for use when you need to specify locale:

```
public SortField (String field, Locale locale)
public SortField (String field, Locale locale, boolean reverse)
```

Both constructors imply the SortField.STRING type because the locale applies only to string-type sorting, not to numerics.

In this section, we've shown you how to precisely specify how Lucene should sort the search results. You've learned how to sort by relevance, which is Lucene's default, or by index order, as well as by field value. You know how to reverse the sort order and sort by multiple criteria. Often Lucene's default relevance sort is best, but for applications that need precise control, Lucene gives it to you. We'll now see an interesting alternative for performing phrase searches.

5.3 *Using MultiPhraseQuery*

The built-in MultiPhraseQuery is definitely a niche query, but it's potentially useful. MultiPhraseQuery is just like PhraseQuery except that it allows multiple terms per position. You could achieve the same logical effect, albeit at a high performance cost, by enumerating all possible phrase combinations and using a BooleanQuery to "OR" them together.

For example, suppose we want to find all documents about speedy foxes, with quick or fast followed by fox. One approach is to do a "quick fox" OR "fast fox" query. Another option is to use MultiPhraseQuery. In our example, shown in listing 5.3, two documents are indexed with similar phrases. One document uses "the quick brown fox jumped over the lazy dog" and the other uses "the fast fox hopped over the hound", as shown in our test setUp() method.

Listing 5.3   Setting up an index to test `MultiPhraseQuery`

```java
public class MultiPhraseQueryTest extends TestCase {
  private IndexSearcher searcher;

  protected void setUp() throws Exception {
    Directory directory = new RAMDirectory();
    IndexWriter writer = new IndexWriter(directory,
                                         new WhitespaceAnalyzer(),

    IndexWriter.MaxFieldLength.UNLIMITED);
    Document doc1 = new Document();
    doc1.add(new Field("field",
            "the quick brown fox jumped over the lazy dog",
            Field.Store.YES, Field.Index.ANALYZED));
    writer.addDocument(doc1);
    Document doc2 = new Document();
    doc2.add(new Field("field",
            "the fast fox hopped over the hound",
            Field.Store.YES, Field.Index.ANALYZED));
    writer.addDocument(doc2);
    writer.close();

    searcher = new IndexSearcher(directory);
  }
}
```

The test method in listing 5.4 demonstrates the mechanics of using the `MultiPhrase-Query` API by adding one or more terms to a `MultiPhraseQuery` instance in order.

Listing 5.4   Using `MultiPhraseQuery` to match more than one term at each position

```java
public void testBasic() throws Exception {
  MultiPhraseQuery query = new MultiPhraseQuery();
  query.add(new Term[] {
      new Term("field", "quick"),        // Allow either term, first
      new Term("field", "fast")
  });
  query.add(new Term("field", "fox"));   // Allow single term, second
  System.out.println(query);

  TopDocs hits = searcher.search(query, 10);
  assertEquals("fast fox match", 1, hits.totalHits);

  query.setSlop(1);
  hits = searcher.search(query, 10);
  assertEquals("both match", 2, hits.totalHits);
}
```

Just as with `PhraseQuery`, the slop factor is supported. In `testBasic()`, the slop is used to match `"quick brown fox"` in the second search; with the default slop of 0, it doesn't match. For completeness, listing 5.5 shows a test illustrating the described `BooleanQuery`, with a slop set for `"quick fox"`.

Listing 5.5 Mimicking `MultiPhraseQuery` using `BooleanQuery`

```
public void testAgainstOR() throws Exception {
  PhraseQuery quickFox = new PhraseQuery();
  quickFox.setSlop(1);
  quickFox.add(new Term("field", "quick"));
  quickFox.add(new Term("field", "fox"));

  PhraseQuery fastFox = new PhraseQuery();
  fastFox.add(new Term("field", "fast"));
  fastFox.add(new Term("field", "fox"));

  BooleanQuery query = new BooleanQuery();
  query.add(quickFox, BooleanClause.Occur.SHOULD);
  query.add(fastFox, BooleanClause.Occur.SHOULD);
  TopDocs hits = searcher.search(query, 10);
  assertEquals(2, hits.totalHits);
}
```

One difference between using `MultiPhraseQuery` and using `PhraseQuery`'s `Boolean-Query` is that the slop factor is applied globally with `MultiPhraseQuery`—it's applied on a per-phrase basis with `PhraseQuery`.

Of course, hard-coding the terms wouldn't be realistic, generally speaking. One possible use of a `MultiPhraseQuery` would be to inject synonyms dynamically into phrase positions, allowing for less precise matching. For example, you could tie in the WordNet-based code (see section 9.3 for more on WordNet and Lucene). As seen in listing 5.6, `QueryParser` produces a `MultiPhraseQuery` for search terms surrounded in double quotes when the analyzer it's using returns `positionIncrement` 0 for any of the tokens within the phrase.

Listing 5.6 Using `QueryParser` to produce a `MultiPhraseQuery`

```
public void testQueryParser() throws Exception {
  SynonymEngine engine = new SynonymEngine() {
      public String[] getSynonyms(String s) {
        if (s.equals("quick"))
          return new String[] {"fast"};
        else
          return null;
      }
    };

  Query q = new QueryParser(Version.LUCENE_30,
                            "field",
                            new SynonymAnalyzer(engine))
    .parse("\"quick fox\"");

  assertEquals("analyzed",
    "field:\"(quick fast) fox\"", q.toString());
  assertTrue("parsed as MultiPhraseQuery", q instanceof MultiPhraseQuery);
}
```

Next we'll visit `MultiFieldQueryParser`, which we'll use for querying on multiple fields.

5.4   *Querying on multiple fields at once*

In our book data, several fields were indexed to separately hold the title, category, author, subject, and so forth. But when searching a user would typically like to search across all fields at once. You could require users to spell out each field name, but except for specialized cases, that's requiring far too much work on your users' part. Users much prefer to search all fields, by default, unless a specific field is requested. We cover three possible approaches here.

The first approach is to create a multivalued catchall field to index the text from all fields, as we've done for the contents field in our book test index. Be sure to increase the position increment gap across field values, as described in section 4.7.1, to avoid incorrectly matching across two field values. You then perform all searching against the catchall field. This approach has some downsides: you can't directly control per-field boosting[1], and disk space is wasted, assuming you also index each field separately.

The second approach is to use `MultiFieldQueryParser`, which subclasses `Query-Parser`. Under the covers, it instantiates a `QueryParser`, parses the query expression for each field, then combines the resulting queries using a `BooleanQuery`. The default operator OR is used in the simplest parse method when adding the clauses to the `Boolean-Query`. For finer control, the operator can be specified for each field as required (`BooleanClause.Occur.MUST`), prohibited (`BooleanClause.Occur.MUST_NOT`), or normal (`BooleanClause.Occur.SHOULD`), using the constants from `BooleanClause`.

Listing 5.7 shows this heavier `QueryParser` variant in use. The `testDefault-Operator()` method first parses the query `"development"` using both the title and subject fields. The test shows that documents match based on either of those fields. The second test, `testSpecifiedOperator()`, sets the parsing to mandate that documents must match the expression in all specified fields and searches using the query `"lucene"`.

Listing 5.7   `MultiFieldQueryParser`, which searches on multiple fields at once

```
public void testDefaultOperator() throws Exception {
  Query query = new MultiFieldQueryParser(Version.LUCENE_30,
                                          new String[]
                                            {"title", "subject"},
     new SimpleAnalyzer()).parse("development");

  Directory dir = TestUtil.getBookIndexDirectory();
  IndexSearcher searcher = new IndexSearcher(
                   dir,
                   true);
  TopDocs hits = searcher.search(query, 10);

  assertTrue(TestUtil.hitsIncludeTitle(
        searcher,
```

---

[1]   Using payloads, an advanced topic covered in section 6.5, it is possible to retain per-field boost even within a catchall field.

```
              hits,
              "Ant in Action"));

   assertTrue(TestUtil.hitsIncludeTitle(
              searcher,                               Contains development
              hits,                                   in subject field
              "Extreme Programming Explained"));
   searcher.close();
   dir.close();
}

public void testSpecifiedOperator() throws Exception {
   Query query = MultiFieldQueryParser.parse(Version.LUCENE_30,
         "lucene",
         new String[]{"title", "subject"},
         new BooleanClause.Occur[]{BooleanClause.Occur.MUST,
                 BooleanClause.Occur.MUST},
         new SimpleAnalyzer());

   Directory dir = TestUtil.getBookIndexDirectory();
   IndexSearcher searcher = new IndexSearcher(
                                 dir,
                                 true);
   TopDocs hits = searcher.search(query, 10);

   assertTrue(TestUtil.hitsIncludeTitle(
              searcher,
              hits,
              "Lucene in Action, Second Edition "));
   assertEquals("one and only one", 1, hits.scoreDocs.length);
   searcher.close();
   dir.close();
}
```

MultiFieldQueryParser has some limitations due to the way it uses QueryParser. You can't control any of the settings that QueryParser supports, and you're stuck with the defaults, such as default locale date parsing and zero-slop default phrase queries.

If you choose to use MultiFieldQueryParser, be sure your queries are fabricated appropriately using the QueryParser and Analyzer diagnostic techniques shown in chapters 3 and 4. Plenty of odd interactions with analysis occur using QueryParser, and these are compounded when using MultiFieldQueryParser. An important downside of MultiFieldQueryParser is that it produces more complex queries, as Lucene must separately test each query term against every field, which will run slower than using a catchall field.

The third approach for automatically querying across multiple fields is the advanced DisjunctionMaxQuery, which wraps one or more arbitrary queries, OR'ing together the documents they match. You could do this with BooleanQuery, as Multi-FieldQueryParser does, but what makes DisjunctionMaxQuery interesting is how it scores each hit: when a document matches more than one query, it computes the score as the maximum score across all the queries that matched, compared to BooleanQuery, which sums the scores of all matching queries. This can produce better end-user relevance.

`DisjunctionMaxQuery` also includes an optional tie-breaker multiplier so that, all things being equal, a document matching more queries will receive a higher score than a document matching fewer queries. To use `DisjunctionMaxQuery` to query across multiple fields, you create a new field-specific `Query`, for each field you'd like to include, and then use `DisjunctionMaxQuery`'s add method to include that `Query`.

Which approach makes sense for your application? The answer is "It depends," because there are important trade-offs. The catchall field is a simple index time–only solution but results in simplistic scoring and may waste disk space by indexing the same text twice. Yet it likely yields the best searching performance. `MultiFieldQuery-Parser` produces `BooleanQuery`s that sum the scores (whereas `DisjunctionMaxQuery` takes the maximum score) for all queries that match each document, then properly implements per-field boosting. You should test all three approaches, taking into account both search performance and search relevance, to find the best.

We'll now move on to span queries, advanced queries that allow you to match based on positional constraints.

5.5   Span queries

Lucene includes a whole family of queries based on `SpanQuery`, loosely mirroring the normal Lucene `Query` classes. A span in this context is a starting and ending token position in a field. Recall from section 4.2.1 that tokens emitted during the analysis process include a position from the previous token. This position information, in conjunction with the new `SpanQuery` subclasses, allows for even more query discrimination and sophistication, such as all documents where "President Obama" is near "health care reform."

Using the query types we've discussed thus far, it isn't possible to formulate such a position-aware query. You could get close with something like `"president obama"` AND `"health care reform"`, but these phrases may be too distant from one another within the document to be relevant for our searching purposes. In typical applications, `Span-Query`s are used to provide richer, more expressive position-aware functionality than `PhraseQuery`. They're also commonly used in conjunction with payloads, covered in section 6.5, to enable access to the payloads created during indexing.

While searching, span queries track more than the documents that match: the individual spans, perhaps more than one per field, are also tracked. Contrasting with `TermQuery`, which simply matches documents, `SpanTermQuery` matches exactly the same documents but also keeps track of the positions of every term occurrence that matches. Generally this is more compute-intensive. For example, when `TermQuery` finds a document containing its term, it records that document as a match and immediately moves on, whereas `SpanTermQuery` must enumerate all the occurrences of that term within the document.

There are six subclasses of the base `SpanQuery`, shown in table 5.1. We'll discuss these `SpanQuery` types with a simple example, shown in listing 5.8: we'll index two documents, one with the phrase "the quick brown fox jumps over the lazy dog" and the other with the similar phrase "the quick red fox jumps over the sleepy cat." We'll

Table 5.1 `SpanQuery` family

SpanQuery type	Description
SpanTermQuery	Used in conjunction with the other span query types. On its own, it's functionally equivalent to `TermQuery`.
SpanFirstQuery	Matches spans that occur within the first part of a field.
SpanNearQuery	Matches spans that occur near one another.
SpanNotQuery	Matches spans that don't overlap one another.
FieldMaskingSpanQuery	Wraps another `SpanQuery` but pretends a different field was matched. This is useful for doing span matches across fields, which is otherwise not possible.
SpanOrQuery	Aggregates matches of span queries.

create a separate `SpanTermQuery` for each of the terms in these documents, as well as three helper assert methods. Finally, we'll create the different types of span queries to illustrate their functions.

Listing 5.8 `SpanQuery` demonstration infrastructure

```
public class SpanQueryTest extends TestCase {
  private RAMDirectory directory;
  private IndexSearcher searcher;
  private IndexReader reader;

  private SpanTermQuery quick;
  private SpanTermQuery brown;
  private SpanTermQuery red;
  private SpanTermQuery fox;
  private SpanTermQuery lazy;
  private SpanTermQuery sleepy;
  private SpanTermQuery dog;
  private SpanTermQuery cat;
  private Analyzer analyzer;

  protected void setUp() throws Exception {
    directory = new RAMDirectory();

    analyzer = new WhitespaceAnalyzer();
    IndexWriter writer = new IndexWriter(directory,
                                  analyzer,
                        IndexWriter.MaxFieldLength.UNLIMITED);

    Document doc = new Document();
    doc.add(new Field("f",
        "the quick brown fox jumps over the lazy dog",
        Field.Store.YES, Field.Index.ANALYZED));
    writer.addDocument(doc);

    doc = new Document();
    doc.add(new Field("f",
        "the quick red fox jumps over the sleepy cat",
```

```
        Field.Store.YES, Field.Index.ANALYZED));
    writer.addDocument(doc);

    writer.close();

    searcher = new IndexSearcher(directory);
    reader = searcher.getIndexReader();

    quick = new SpanTermQuery(new Term("f", "quick"));
    brown = new SpanTermQuery(new Term("f", "brown"));
    red = new SpanTermQuery(new Term("f", "red"));
    fox = new SpanTermQuery(new Term("f", "fox"));
    lazy = new SpanTermQuery(new Term("f", "lazy"));
    sleepy = new SpanTermQuery(new Term("f", "sleepy"));
    dog = new SpanTermQuery(new Term("f", "dog"));
    cat = new SpanTermQuery(new Term("f", "cat"));
}

private void assertOnlyBrownFox(Query query) throws Exception {
    TopDocs hits = searcher.search(query, 10);
    assertEquals(1, hits.totalHits);
    assertEquals("wrong doc", 0, hits.scoreDocs[0].doc);
}

private void assertBothFoxes(Query query) throws Exception {
    TopDocs hits = searcher.search(query, 10);
    assertEquals(2, hits.totalHits);
}

private void assertNoMatches(Query query) throws Exception {
    TopDocs hits = searcher.search(query, 10);
    assertEquals(0, hits.totalHits);
}
}
```

With this necessary bit of setup out of the way, we can begin exploring span queries. First we'll ground ourselves with SpanTermQuery.

5.5.1   *Building block of spanning, SpanTermQuery*

Span queries need an initial leverage point, and SpanTermQuery is just that. Internally, a SpanQuery keeps track of its matches: a series of start/end positions for each matching document. By itself, a SpanTermQuery matches documents just like TermQuery does, but it also keeps track of position of the same terms that appear within each document. Generally you'd never use this query by itself (you'd use TermQuery instead); you only use it as inputs to the other SpanQuery classes.

Figure 5.1 illustrates the SpanTermQuery matches for this code:

```
public void testSpanTermQuery() throws Exception {
    assertOnlyBrownFox(brown);
    dumpSpans(brown);
}
```

The brown SpanTermQuery was created in setUp() because it will be used in other tests that follow. We developed a method, dumpSpans, to visualize spans. The dump-Spans method uses lower-level SpanQuery APIs to navigate the spans; this lower-level

Figure 5.1 `SpanTermQuery` for brown

API probably isn't of much interest to you other than for diagnostic purposes, so we don't elaborate further. Each `SpanQuery` subclass sports a useful `toString()` for diagnostic purposes, which `dumpSpans` uses, as seen in listing 5.9.

Listing 5.9 `dumpSpans` method, used to see all spans matched by any `SpanQuery`

```java
private void dumpSpans(SpanQuery query) throws IOException {
  Spans spans = query.getSpans(reader);
  System.out.println(query + ":");
  int numSpans = 0;

  TopDocs hits = searcher.search(query, 10);
  float[] scores = new float[2];
  for (ScoreDoc sd : hits.scoreDocs) {
    scores[sd.doc] = sd.score;
  }
  while (spans.next()) {                          ⟵ Step through each span
    numSpans++;

    int id = spans.doc();
    Document doc = reader.document(id);           ⟵ Retrieve document

    TokenStream stream = analyzer.tokenStream("contents",
                    new StringReader(doc.get("f")));    ⟵ Reanalyze text
    TermAttribute term = stream.addAttribute(TermAttribute.class);

    StringBuilder buffer = new StringBuilder();
    buffer.append("   ");
    int i = 0;
    while(stream.incrementToken()) {              ⟵ Step through all tokens
      if (i == spans.start()) {
        buffer.append("<");
      }
      buffer.append(term.term());                 │ Print < and >
      if (i + 1 == spans.end()) {                 │ around span
        buffer.append(">");
      }
      buffer.append(" ");
      i++;
    }
    buffer.append("(").append(scores[id]).append(") ");
    System.out.println(buffer);
  }

  if (numSpans == 0) {
    System.out.println("   No spans");
  }
  System.out.println();
}
```

The output of dumpSpans(brown) is

```
f:brown:
    the quick <brown> fox jumps over the lazy dog (0.22097087)
```

More interesting is the dumpSpans output from a SpanTermQuery for "the":

```
dumpSpans(new SpanTermQuery(new Term("f", "the")));
```

```
f:the:
    <the> quick brown fox jumps over the lazy dog (0.18579213)
    the quick brown fox jumps over <the> lazy dog (0.18579213)
    <the> quick red fox jumps over the sleepy cat (0.18579213)
    the quick red fox jumps over <the> sleepy cat (0.18579213)
```

Not only were both documents matched, but also each document had two span matches highlighted by the brackets. The basic SpanTermQuery is used as a building block of the other SpanQuery types. Let's see how to match only documents where the terms of interest occur in the beginning of the field.

5.5.2 *Finding spans at the beginning of a field*

To query for spans that occur within the first specific number of positions of a field, use SpanFirstQuery. Figure 5.2 illustrates a SpanFirstQuery.

This test shows nonmatching and matching queries:

```
public void testSpanFirstQuery() throws Exception {
    SpanFirstQuery sfq = new SpanFirstQuery(brown, 2);
    assertNoMatches(sfq);

    dumpSpans(sfq);

    sfq = new SpanFirstQuery(brown, 3);
    dumpSpans(sfq);
    assertOnlyBrownFox(sfq);
}
```

No matches are found in the first query because the range of 2 is too short to find *brown*, but the range of 3 is just long enough to cause a match in the second query (see figure 5.2). Any SpanQuery can be used within a SpanFirstQuery, with matches for spans that have an ending position in the first specified number (2 and 3 in this case) of positions. The resulting span matches are the same as the original SpanQuery spans—in this case, the same dumpSpans() output for brown as you saw in section 5.5.1.

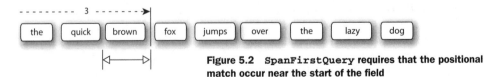

Figure 5.2 SpanFirstQuery requires that the positional match occur near the start of the field

5.5.3 *Spans near one another*

A `PhraseQuery` (see section 3.4.6) matches documents that have terms near one another, with a slop factor to allow for intermediate or reversed terms. `SpanNearQuery` operates similarly to `PhraseQuery`, with some important differences. `SpanNearQuery` matches spans that are within a certain number of positions from one another, with a separate flag indicating whether the spans must be in the order specified or can be reversed. The resulting matching spans span from the start position of the first span sequentially to the ending position of the last span. An example of a `SpanNearQuery` given three `SpanTermQuery` objects is shown in figure 5.3.

Using `SpanTermQuery` objects as the `SpanQuerys` in a `SpanNearQuery` is much like using a `PhraseQuery`. The `SpanNearQuery` slop factor is a bit less confusing than the `PhraseQuery` slop factor because it doesn't require at least two additional positions to account for a reversed span. To reverse a `SpanNearQuery`, set the `inOrder` flag (third argument to the constructor) to `false`. Listing 5.10 demonstrates a few variations of `SpanNearQuery` and shows it in relation to `PhraseQuery`.

> **Listing 5.10 Finding matches near one another using `SpanNearQuery`**

```
public void testSpanNearQuery() throws Exception {
  SpanQuery[] quick_brown_dog =
      new SpanQuery[]{quick, brown, dog};
  SpanNearQuery snq =
    new SpanNearQuery(quick_brown_dog, 0, true);        ◁──❶
  assertNoMatches(snq);
  dumpSpans(snq);

  snq = new SpanNearQuery(quick_brown_dog, 4, true);    ◁──❷
  assertNoMatches(snq);
  dumpSpans(snq);

  snq = new SpanNearQuery(quick_brown_dog, 5, true);    ◁──❸
  assertOnlyBrownFox(snq);
  dumpSpans(snq);

  // interesting - even a sloppy phrase query would require
  // more slop to match
  snq = new SpanNearQuery(new SpanQuery[]{lazy, fox}, 3, false);  ◁──❹
  assertOnlyBrownFox(snq);
  dumpSpans(snq);

  PhraseQuery pq = new PhraseQuery();                   ❺
  pq.add(new Term("f", "lazy"));
```

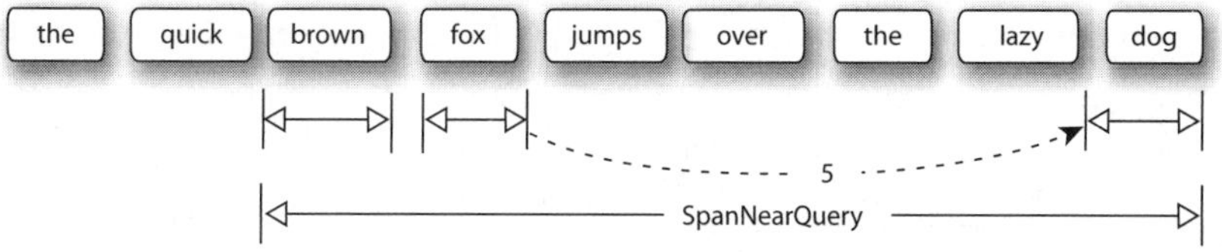

Figure 5.3 `SpanNearQuery` requires positional matches to be close to one another.

```
pq.add(new Term("f", "fox"));
pq.setSlop(4);
assertNoMatches(pq);

pq.setSlop(5);
assertOnlyBrownFox(pq);
}
```

❺

❻

❶ Querying for these three terms in successive positions doesn't match either document.

❷ Using the same terms with a slop of 4 positions still doesn't result in a match.

❸ With a slop of 5, the SpanNearQuery has a match.

❹ The nested SpanTermQuery objects are in reverse order, so the inOrder flag is set to false. A slop of only 3 is needed for a match.

❺ Here we use a comparable PhraseQuery, although a slop of 4 still doesn't match.

❻ A slop of 5 is needed for a PhraseQuery to match.

We've only shown SpanNearQuery with nested SpanTermQuerys, but SpanNearQuery allows for any SpanQuery type. A more sophisticated SpanNearQuery example is demonstrated later in listing 5.11 in conjunction with SpanOrQuery. Next we visit Span-NotQuery.

5.5.4 *Excluding span overlap from matches*

The SpanNotQuery excludes matches where one SpanQuery overlaps another. The following code demonstrates:

```
public void testSpanNotQuery() throws Exception {
  SpanNearQuery quick_fox =
      new SpanNearQuery(new SpanQuery[]{quick, fox}, 1, true);
  assertBothFoxes(quick_fox);
  dumpSpans(quick_fox);

  SpanNotQuery quick_fox_dog = new SpanNotQuery(quick_fox, dog);
  assertBothFoxes(quick_fox_dog);
  dumpSpans(quick_fox_dog);

  SpanNotQuery no_quick_red_fox =
      new SpanNotQuery(quick_fox, red);
  assertOnlyBrownFox(no_quick_red_fox);
  dumpSpans(no_quick_red_fox);
}
```

The first argument to the SpanNotQuery constructor is a span to include, and the second argument is a span to exclude. We've strategically added dumpSpans to clarify what's going on. Here's the output with the Java query annotated above each:

```
SpanNearQuery quick_fox =
        new SpanNearQuery(new SpanQuery[]{quick, fox}, 1, true);
spanNear([f:quick, f:fox], 1, true):
    the <quick brown fox> jumps over the lazy dog (0.18579213)
    the <quick red fox> jumps over the sleepy cat (0.18579213)
```

```
SpanNotQuery quick_fox_dog = new SpanNotQuery(quick_fox, dog);
spanNot(spanNear([f:quick, f:fox], 1, true), f:dog):
    the <quick brown fox> jumps over the lazy dog (0.18579213)
    the <quick red fox> jumps over the sleepy cat (0.18579213)

SpanNotQuery no_quick_red_fox =
        new SpanNotQuery(quick_fox, red);
spanNot(spanNear([f:quick, f:fox], 1, true), f:red):
    the <quick brown fox> jumps over the lazy dog (0.18579213)
```

The `SpanNearQuery` matched both documents because both have *quick* and *fox* within one position of each other. The first `SpanNotQuery`, `quick_fox_dog`, continues to match both documents because there's no overlap with the `quick_fox` span and dog. The second `SpanNotQuery`, `no_quick_red_fox`, excludes the second document because *red* overlaps with the `quick_fox` span. Notice that the resulting span matches are the original included span. The excluded span is only used to determine if there's an overlap and doesn't factor into the resulting span matches.

Our final query is useful for joining together multiple `SpanQuerys`.

5.5.5 *SpanOrQuery*

Finally let's talk about `SpanOrQuery`, which aggregates an array of `SpanQuerys`. Our example query, in English, is all documents that have "quick fox" near "lazy dog" or that have "quick fox" near "sleepy cat." The first clause of this query is shown in figure 5.4. This single clause is `SpanNearQuery` nesting two `SpanNearQuerys`, and each consists of two `SpanTermQuerys`.

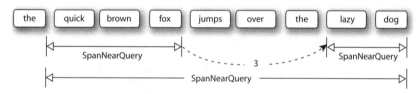

Figure 5.4   One clause of the `SpanOrQuery`

Our test case becomes a bit lengthier due to all the sub-`SpanQuerys` being built on (see listing 5.11). Using `dumpSpans`, we analyze the code in more detail.

Listing 5.11   Taking the union of two span queries using `SpanOrQuery`

```
public void testSpanOrQuery() throws Exception {
  SpanNearQuery quick_fox =
      new SpanNearQuery(new SpanQuery[]{quick, fox}, 1, true);

  SpanNearQuery lazy_dog =
      new SpanNearQuery(new SpanQuery[]{lazy, dog}, 0, true);

  SpanNearQuery sleepy_cat =
      new SpanNearQuery(new SpanQuery[]{sleepy, cat}, 0, true);

  SpanNearQuery qf_near_ld =
```

```
        new SpanNearQuery(
            new SpanQuery[]{quick_fox, lazy_dog}, 3, true);
    assertOnlyBrownFox(qf_near_ld);
    dumpSpans(qf_near_ld);

    SpanNearQuery qf_near_sc =
        new SpanNearQuery(
            new SpanQuery[]{quick_fox, sleepy_cat}, 3, true);
    dumpSpans(qf_near_sc);

    SpanOrQuery or = new SpanOrQuery(
        new SpanQuery[]{qf_near_ld, qf_near_sc});
    assertBothFoxes(or);
    dumpSpans(or);
}
```

We've used our handy dumpSpans a few times to allow us to follow the progression as the final OR query is built. Here's the output, followed by our analysis of it:

```
SpanNearQuery qf_near_ld =
        new SpanNearQuery(
            new SpanQuery[]{quick_fox, lazy_dog}, 3, true);
spanNear([spanNear([f:quick, f:fox], 1, true),
        spanNear([f:lazy, f:dog], 0, true)], 3, true):
   the <quick brown fox jumps over the lazy dog> (0.3321948)

SpanNearQuery qf_near_sc =
        new SpanNearQuery(
            new SpanQuery[]{quick_fox, sleepy_cat}, 3, true);
spanNear([spanNear([f:quick, f:fox], 1, true),
        spanNear([f:sleepy, f:cat], 0, true)], 3, true):
   the <quick red fox jumps over the sleepy cat> (0.3321948)

SpanOrQuery or = new SpanOrQuery(
        new SpanQuery[]{qf_near_ld, qf_near_sc});
spanOr([spanNear([spanNear([f:quick, f:fox], 1, true),
                spanNear([f:lazy, f:dog], 0, true)], 3, true),
        spanNear([spanNear([f:quick, f:fox], 1, true),
                spanNear([f:sleepy, f:cat], 0, true)], 3, true)]):
   the <quick brown fox jumps over the lazy dog> (0.6643896)
   the <quick red fox jumps over the sleepy cat> (0.6643896)
```

Two SpanNearQuerys are created to match "quick fox" near "lazy dog" (qf_near_ld) and "quick fox" near "sleepy cat" (qf_near_sc) using nested SpanNearQuerys made up of SpanTermQuerys at the lowest level. Finally, these two SpanNearQuery instances are combined within a SpanOrQuery, which aggregates all matching spans.

Both SpanNearQuery and SpanOrQuery accept any other SpanQuerys, so you can create arbitrarily nested queries. For example, imagine you'd like to perform a "phrase within a phrase" query, such as a subphrase query "Bob Dylan", with the slop factor 0 for an exact match, and an outer phrase query matching this phrase with the word *sings*, with a nonzero slop factor. Such a query isn't possible with PhraseQuery, because it only accepts terms. But you can easily create this query by embedding one SpanNearQuery within another.

5.5.6 *SpanQuery and QueryParser*

QueryParser doesn't currently support any of the SpanQuery types, but the surround QueryParser in Lucene's contrib modules does. We cover the surround parser in section 9.6.

Recall from section 3.4.6 that PhraseQuery is impartial to term order when enough slop is specified. Interestingly, you can easily extend QueryParser to use a SpanNearQuery with SpanTermQuery clauses instead, and force phrase queries to only match fields with the terms in the same order as specified. We demonstrate this technique in section 6.3.5.

We're now done with the advanced span query family. These are definitely advanced queries that give precise control over how the position of term matches within a document is taken into account. We'll now visit another advanced functionality: filters.

5.6 *Filtering a search*

Filtering is a mechanism of narrowing the search space, allowing only a subset of the documents to be considered as possible hits. They can be used to implement search-within-search features to successively search within a previous set of results or to constrain the document search space. A security filter allows users to only see search results of documents they "own," even if their query technically matches other documents that are off limits; we provide an example of a security filter in section 5.6.7.

You can filter any Lucene search using the overloaded search methods that accept a Filter instance. There are numerous built-in filter implementations:

- TermRangeFilter matches only documents containing terms within a specified range of terms. It's exactly the same as TermRangeQuery, without scoring.
- NumericRangeFilter matches only documents containing numeric values within a specified range for a specified field. It's exactly the same as Numeric-RangeQuery, without scoring.
- FieldCacheRangeFilter matches documents in a certain term or numeric range, using the FieldCache (see section 5.1) for better performance.
- FieldCacheTermsFilter matches documents containing specific terms, using the field cache for better performance.
- QueryWrapperFilter turns any Query instance into a Filter instance, by using only the matching documents from the Query as the filtered space, discarding the document scores.
- SpanQueryFilter turns a SpanQuery into a SpanFilter, which subclasses the base Filter class and adds an additional method, providing access to the positional spans for each matching document. This is just like QueryWrapperFilter but is applied to SpanQuery classes instead.
- PrefixFilter matches only documents containing terms in a specific field with a specific prefix. It's exactly the same as PrefixQuery, without scoring.

- CachingWrapperFilter is a decorator over another filter, caching its results to increase performance when used again.
- CachingSpanFilter does the same thing as CachingWrapperFilter, but it caches a SpanFilter.
- FilteredDocIdSet allows you to filter a filter, one document at a time. In order to use it, you must first subclass it and define the match method in your subclass.

Before you get concerned about mentions of caching results, rest assured that it's done with a tiny data structure (a DocIdBitSet) where each bit position represents a document.

Consider also the alternative to using a filter: aggregating required clauses in a BooleanQuery. In this section, we'll discuss each of the built-in filters as well as the BooleanQuery alternative, starting with TermRangeFilter.

5.6.1   TermRangeFilter

TermRangeFilter filters on a range of terms in a specific field, just like TermRange-Query minus the scoring. If the field is numeric, you should use NumericRangeFilter (described next) instead. TermRangeFilter applies to textual fields.

Let's look at title filtering as an example, shown in listing 5.12. We use the Match-AllDocsQuery as our query, and then apply a title filter to it.

Listing 5.12   Using `TermRangeFilter` to filter by title

```
public class FilterTest extends TestCase {
  private Query allBooks;
  private IndexSearcher searcher;

  protected void setUp() throws Exception {        ◄── ❶
    allBooks = new MatchAllDocsQuery();
    dir = TestUtil.getBookIndexDirectory();
    searcher = new IndexSearcher(dir);
  }

  protected void tearDown() throws Exception {
    searcher.close();
    dir.close();
  }

  public void testTermRangeFilter() throws Exception {
    Filter filter = new TermRangeFilter("title2", "d", "j", true, true);
    assertEquals(3, TestUtil.hitCount(searcher, allBooks, filter));
  }
}
```

The setUp() method ❶ establishes a baseline count of all the books in our index, allowing for comparisons when we use an all-inclusive date filter. The first parameter to both of the TermRangeFilter constructors is the name of the field in the index. In our sample data this field name is title2, which is the title of each book indexed lower-cased using Field.NOT_ANALYZED_NO_NORMS. The two final Boolean arguments to the constructor for TermRangeFilter, includeLower, and includeUpper determine whether the lower and upper terms should be included or excluded from the filter.

Ranges can also be optionally open-ended.

OPEN-ENDED RANGE FILTERING

`TermRangeFilter` also supports open-ended ranges. To filter on ranges with one end of the range specified and the other end open, just pass `null` for whichever end should be open:

```
filter = new TermRangeFilter("modified", null, jan31, false, true);
filter = new TermRangeFilter("modified", jan1, null, true, false);
```

`TermRangeFilter` provides two static convenience methods to achieve the same thing:

```
filter = TermRangeFilter.Less("modified", jan31);
filter = TermRangeFilter.More("modified", jan1);
```

5.6.2 *NumericRangeFilter*

`NumericRangeFilter` filters by numeric value. This is just like `NumericRangeQuery`, minus the constant scoring:

```
public void testNumericDateFilter() throws Exception {
  Filter filter = NumericRangeFilter.newIntRange("pubmonth",
                                                 201001,
                                                 201006,
                                                 true,
                                                 true);
  assertEquals(2, TestUtil.hitCount(searcher, allBooks, filter));
}
```

The same caveats as `NumericRangeQuery` apply here; for example, if you specify a `precisionStep` different from the default, it must match the `precisionStep` used during indexing.

Our next filter does the job of both `TermRangeFilter` and `NumericRangeFilter`, but is built on top of Lucene's field cache.

5.6.3 *FieldCacheRangeFilter*

`FieldCacheRangeFilter` is another option for range filtering. It achieves exactly the same filtering as both `TermRangeFilter` and `NumericRangeFilter`, but does so by using Lucene's field cache. This may result in faster performance in certain situations, since all values are preloaded into memory. But the usual caveats with field cache apply, as described in section 5.1.

`FieldCacheRangeFilter` exposes a different API to achieve range filtering. Here's how to do the same filtering on `title2` that we did with `TermRangeFilter`:

```
Filter filter = FieldCacheRangeFilter.newStringRange("title2",
    "d", "j", true, true);
assertEquals(3, TestUtil.hitCount(searcher, allBooks, filter));
```

To achieve the same filtering that we did with `NumericRangeFilter`:

```
filter = FieldCacheRangeFilter.newIntRange("pubmonth",
                                           201001,
                                           201006,
                                           true,
```

```
                                                    true);
   assertEquals(2, TestUtil.hitCount(searcher, allBooks, filter));
```

Let's see how to filter by an arbitrary set of terms.

5.6.4   *Filtering by specific terms*

Sometimes you'd simply like to select specific terms to include in your filter. For example, perhaps your documents have Country as a field, and your search interface presents a checkbox allowing the user to pick and choose which countries to include in the search. There are two ways to achieve this.

The first approach is FieldCacheTermsFilter, which uses field cache under the hood. (Be sure to read section 5.1 for the trade-offs of the field cache.) Simply instantiate it with the field (String) and an array of String:

```
public void testFieldCacheTermsFilter() throws Exception {
   Filter filter = new FieldCacheTermsFilter("category",
                    new String[] {"/health/alternative/chinese",
                                  "/technology/computers/ai",
                                  "/technology/computers/programming"});
   assertEquals("expected 7 hits",
                7,
                TestUtil.hitCount(searcher, allBooks, filter));
}
```

All documents that have any of the terms in the specified field will be accepted. Note that the documents must have a single term value for each field. Under the hood, this filter loads all terms for all documents into the field cache the first time it's used during searching for a given field. This means the first search will be slower, but subsequent searches, which reuse the cache, will be very fast. The field cache is reused even if you change which specific terms are included in the filter.

The second approach for filtering by terms is TermsFilter, which is included in Lucene's contrib modules and is described in more detail in section 8.6.4. TermsFilter doesn't do any internal caching, and it allows filtering on fields that have more than one term; otherwise, TermsFilter and FieldCacheTermsFilter are functionally identical. It's best to test both approaches for your application to see if there are any significant performance differences.

5.6.5   *Using QueryWrapperFilter*

QueryWrapperFilter uses the matching documents of a query to constrain available documents from a subsequent search. It allows you to turn a query, which does scoring, into a filter, which doesn't. Using a QueryWrapperFilter, we restrict the documents searched to a specific category:

```
public void testQueryWrapperFilter() throws Exception {
   TermQuery categoryQuery =
      new TermQuery(new Term("category", "/philosophy/eastern"));

   Filter categoryFilter = new QueryWrapperFilter(categoryQuery);
```

```
assertEquals("only tao te ching",
             1,
             TestUtil.hitCount(searcher, allBooks, categoryFilter));
}
```

Here we're searching for all the books (see setUp() in listing 5.12) but constraining the search using a filter for a category that contains a single book. Next we'll see how to turn a SpanQuery into a filter.

5.6.6   *Using SpanQueryFilter*

SpanQueryFilter does the same thing as QueryWrapperFilter, except that it's able to preserve the spans for each matched document. Here's a simple example:

```
public void testSpanQueryFilter() throws Exception {
  SpanQuery categoryQuery =
    new SpanTermQuery(new Term("category", "/philosophy/eastern"));

  Filter categoryFilter = new SpanQueryFilter(categoryQuery);

  assertEquals("only tao te ching",
               1,
               TestUtil.hitCount(searcher, allBooks, categoryFilter));
}
```

SpanQueryFilter adds a method, bitSpans, enabling you to retrieve the spans for each matched document. Only advanced applications will make use of spans (Lucene doesn't use them internally when filtering), so if you don't need this information, it's better (faster) to simply use QueryWrapperFilter.

Let's see how to use filters for applying security constraints, also known as entitlements.

5.6.7   *Security filters*

Another example of document filtering constrains documents with security in mind. Our example assumes documents are associated with an owner, which is known at indexing time. We index two documents; both have the term info in their keywords field, but each document has a different owner, as you can see in listing 5.13.

> **Listing 5.13   Setting up an index to use for testing the security filter**

```
public class SecurityFilterTest extends TestCase {

  private IndexSearcher searcher;

  protected void setUp() throws Exception {
    Directory directory = new RAMDirectory();
    IndexWriter writer = new IndexWriter(directory,
                           new WhitespaceAnalyzer(),
                           IndexWriter.MaxFieldLength.UNLIMITED);

    Document document = new Document();
    document.add(new Field("owner",          ❶ Elwood
                           "elwood",
```

```
                              Field.Store.YES,
                              Field.Index.NOT_ANALYZED));
     document.add(new Field("keywords",
                              "elwood's sensitive info",        ❶ Elwood
                              Field.Store.YES,
                              Field.Index.ANALYZED));
     writer.addDocument(document);

     document = new Document();
     document.add(new Field("owner",
                              "jake",
                              Field.Store.YES,                  ❷ Jake
                              Field.Index.NOT_ANALYZED));
     document.add(new Field("keywords",
                              "jake's sensitive info",
                              Field.Store.YES,
                              Field.Index.ANALYZED));
     writer.addDocument(document);

     writer.close();
     searcher = new IndexSearcher(directory);
   }
}
```

Using a TermQuery for info in the keywords field results in both documents found, naturally. Suppose, though, that Jake is using the search feature in our application, and only documents he owns should be searchable by him. Quite elegantly, we can easily use a QueryWrapperFilter to constrain the search space to only documents for which he's the owner, as shown in listing 5.14.

Listing 5.14   Securing the search space with a filter

```
public void testSecurityFilter() throws Exception {
  TermQuery query = new TermQuery(
                       new Term("keywords", "info"));          ❶

  assertEquals("Both documents match",
                2,                                             ❷
                TestUtil.hitCount(searcher, query));

  Filter jakeFilter = new QueryWrapperFilter(                  ❸
    new TermQuery(new Term("owner", "jake")));

  TopDocs hits = searcher.search(query, jakeFilter, 10);
  assertEquals(1, hits.totalHits);                             ❹
  assertEquals("elwood is safe",
                "jake's sensitive info",
       searcher.doc(hits.scoreDocs[0].doc)
               .get("keywords"));
}
```

❶ This is a general TermQuery for info.

❷ All documents containing info are returned.

❸ Here, the filter constrains document searches to only documents owned by jake.

❹ Only jake's document is returned, using the same info TermQuery.

If your security requirements are this straightforward, where documents can be associated with users or roles during indexing, using a `QueryWrapperFilter` will work nicely. But some applications require more dynamic enforcement of entitlements. In section 6.4, we develop a more sophisticated filter implementation that leverages external information; this approach could be adapted to a more dynamic custom security filter.

5.6.8 Using BooleanQuery for filtering

You can constrain a query to a subset of documents another way, by combining the constraining query to the original query as a required clause of a `BooleanQuery`. There are a couple of important differences, despite the fact that the same documents are returned from both. If you use `CachingWrapperFilter` around your `QueryWrapper-Filter`, you can cache the set of documents allowed, likely speeding up successive searches using the same filter. In addition, normalized document scores are unlikely to be the same. The score difference makes sense when you're looking at the scoring formula (see section 3.3) because the IDF (inverse document frequency) factor may be dramatically different. When you're using `BooleanQuery` aggregation, all documents containing the terms are factored into the equation, whereas a filter reduces the documents under consideration and impacts the inverse document frequency factor.

This test case demonstrates how to "filter" using `BooleanQuery` aggregation and illustrates the scoring difference compared to `testQueryFilter`:

```
public void testFilterAlternative() throws Exception {
  TermQuery categoryQuery =
    new TermQuery(new Term("category", "/philosophy/eastern"));

  BooleanQuery constrainedQuery = new BooleanQuery();
  constrainedQuery.add(allBooks, BooleanClause.Occur.MUST);
  constrainedQuery.add(categoryQuery, BooleanClause.Occur.MUST);

  assertEquals("only tao te ching",
               1,
               TestUtil.hitCount(searcher, constrainedQuery));
}
```

The technique of aggregating a query in this manner works well with `QueryParser` parsed queries, allowing users to enter free-form queries yet restricting the set of documents searched by an API-controlled query. We describe `PrefixFilter` next.

5.6.9 PrefixFilter

`PrefixFilter`, the corollary to `PrefixQuery`, matches documents containing `Terms` starting with a specified prefix. We can use `PrefixFilter` to restrict a search to all books under a specific category:

```
public void testPrefixFilter() throws Exception {
  Filter prefixFilter = new PrefixFilter(
                          new Term("category",
                                   "/technology/computers"));
  assertEquals("only /technology/computers/* books",
```

```
            8,
            TestUtil.hitCount(searcher,
                              allBooks,
                              prefixFilter));
  }
```

Next we show how to cache a filter for better performance.

5.6.10 *Caching filter results*

The biggest benefit from filters comes when they're cached and reused using `CachingWrapperFilter`, which takes care of caching automatically (internally using a `WeakHashMap`, so that externally dereferenced entries get garbage collected). You can cache any filter using `CachingWrappingFilter`. Filters cache by using the `IndexReader` as the key, which means searching should also be done with the same instance of `IndexReader` to benefit from the cache. If you aren't constructing `IndexReader` yourself but are creating an `IndexSearcher` from a directory, you must use the same instance of `IndexSearcher` to benefit from the caching. When index changes need to be reflected in searches, discard `IndexSearcher` and `IndexReader` and reinstantiate.

To demonstrate its usage, we return to the title filtering example. We want to use `TermRangeFilter`, but we'd like to benefit from caching to improve performance:

```
public void testCachingWrapper() throws Exception {
  Filter filter = new TermRangeFilter("title2",
                                      "d", "j",
                                      true, true);

  CachingWrapperFilter cachingFilter;
  cachingFilter = new CachingWrapperFilter(filter);
  assertEquals(3,
               TestUtil.hitCount(searcher,
                                 allBooks,
                                 cachingFilter));
  }
```

Successive uses of the same `CachingWrapperFilter` instance with the same `Index-Searcher` instance will bypass using the wrapped filter, instead using the cached results.

5.6.11 *Wrapping a filter as a query*

We saw how to wrap a filter as a query. You can also do the reverse, using `Constant-ScoreQuery` to turn any filter into a query, which you can then search on. The resulting query matches only documents that are included in the filter, and assigns all of them the score equal to the query boost.

5.6.12 *Filtering a filter*

The `FilteredDocIdSet` class is an abstract class that accepts a primary filter, and then, during matching whenever a document is being considered, the `match` method (of your subclass) is invoked to check whether the document should be allowed. This allows you to dynamically filter any other filter by implementing any custom logic in your `match` method. This approach is efficient because `FilteredDocIdSet` never fully materializes a bit set for the filter. Instead, each match is checked on demand.

This approach can be useful for enforcing entitlements, especially in cases where much of the enforcement is static (present in the index) but some amount of entitlement should be checked dynamically at runtime. For such a use case, you'd create a standard entitlements filter based on what's in the index, then subclass `FilteredDoc-IdSet`, overriding the `match` method, to implement your dynamic entitlements logic.

5.6.13   *Beyond the built-in filters*

Lucene isn't restricted to using the built-in filters. An additional filter found in the Lucene contrib modules, `ChainedFilter`, allows for complex chaining of filters. We cover it in section 9.1.

Writing custom filters allows external data to factor into search constraints, but a bit of detailed Lucene API know-how may be required to be highly efficient. We cover writing custom filters in section 6.4.

And if these filtering options aren't enough, Lucene adds another interesting use of a filter. The `FilteredQuery` filters a query, like `IndexSearcher`'s `search(Query, Filter, int)` can, except it is itself a query: therefore it can be used as a single clause within a `BooleanQuery`. Using `FilteredQuery` seems to make sense only when using custom filters, so we cover it along with custom filters in section 6.4.3.

We are done with filters. Our next advanced topic is function queries, which give you custom control over how documents are scored.

5.7   *Custom scoring using function queries*

Lucene's relevance scoring formula, which we discussed in chapter 3, does a great job of assigning relevance to each document based on how well it matches the query. But what if you'd like to modify or override how this scoring is done? In section 5.2 you saw how you can change the default relevance sorting to sort instead by one or more fields, but what if you need even more flexibility? This is where function queries come in.

Function queries give you the freedom to programmatically assign scores to matching documents using your own logic. All classes are from the `org.apache.lucene.search.function` package. In this section we first introduce the main classes used by function queries, and then see the real-world example of using function queries to boost recently modified documents.

5.7.1   *Function query classes*

The base class for all function queries is `ValueSourceQuery`. This is a query that matches all documents but sets the score of each document according to a `Value-Source` provided during construction. The function package provides `Field-CacheSource`, and its subclasses, to derive values from the field cache. You can also create your own `ValueSource`—for example, to derive scores from an external database. But probably the simplest approach is to use `FieldScoreQuery`, which subclasses

ValueSourceQuery and derives each document's score statically from a specific indexed field. The field should be a number, indexed without norms and with a single token per document. Typically you'd use Field.Index.NOT_ANALYZED_NO_NORMS. Let's look at a simple example. First, include the field "score" in your documents like this:

```
doc.add(new Field("score",
                  "42",
                  Field.Store.NO,
                  Field.Index.NOT_ANALYZED_NO_NORMS));
```

Then, create this function query:

```
Query q = new FieldScoreQuery("score", FieldScoreQuery.Type.BYTE);
```

That query matches all documents, assigning each a score according to the contents of its "score" field. You can also use the SHORT, INT, or FLOAT constants. Under the hood, this function query uses the field cache, so the important trade-offs described in section 5.1 apply.

Our example is somewhat contrived; you could simply sort by the score field, descending, to achieve the same results. But function queries get more interesting when you combine them using the second type of function query, CustomScoreQuery. This query class lets you combine a normal Lucene query with one or more other function queries.

We can now use the FieldScoreQuery we created earlier and a CustomScoreQuery to compute our own score:

```
Query q = new QueryParser(Version.LUCENE_30,
                          "content",
                          new StandardAnalyzer(
                            Version.LUCENE_30))
               .parse("the green hat");
FieldScoreQuery qf = new FieldScoreQuery("score",
                                         FieldScoreQuery.Type.BYTE);
CustomScoreQuery customQ = new CustomScoreQuery(q, qf) {
  public CustomScoreProvider getCustomScoreProvider(IndexReader r) {
    return new CustomScoreProvider(r) {
      public float customScore(int doc,
                               float subQueryScore,
                               float valSrcScore) {
        return (float) (Math.sqrt(subQueryScore) * valSrcScore);
      }
    };
  }
};
```

In this case we create a normal query q by parsing the user's search text. We next create the same FieldScoreQuery we used earlier to assign a static score to documents according to the score field. Finally, we create a CustomScoreQuery, overriding the getCustomScoreProvider method to return a class containing the customScore method to compute our score for each matching document. In this contrived case, we take the square root of the incoming query score and then multiply it by the static score provided by the `FieldScoreQuery`. You can use arbitrary logic to create your scores.

Note that the `IndexReader` argument provided to the `getCustomScoreProvider` method is per-segment, meaning the method will be called multiple times during searching if the index has more than one segment. This is important as it enables your scoring logic to efficiently use the per-segment reader to retrieve values in the field-cache. Let's see a more interesting use of function queries, using the field cache to boost matches by recency.

5.7.2 Boosting recently modified documents using function queries

A real-world use of `CustomScoreQuery` is to perform document boosting. You can boost according to any custom criteria, but for our example, shown in listing 5.15, we boost recently modified documents using a new custom query class, `Recency-BoostingQuery`. In applications where documents have a clear timestamp, such as searching a newsfeed or press releases, boosting by recency can be useful. The class requires you to specify the name of a numeric field that contains the timestamp of each document that you'd like to use for boosting.

Listing 5.15　Using recency to boost search results

```
static class RecencyBoostingQuery extends CustomScoreQuery {

  double multiplier;
  int today;
  int maxDaysAgo;
  String dayField;
  static int MSEC_PER_DAY = 1000*3600*24;

  public RecencyBoostingQuery(Query q, double multiplier,
                              int maxDaysAgo, String dayField) {
    super(q);
    today = (int) (new Date().getTime()/MSEC_PER_DAY);
    this.multiplier = multiplier;
    this.maxDaysAgo = maxDaysAgo;
    this.dayField = dayField;
  }

  private class RecencyBooster extends CustomScoreProvider {
    final int[] publishDay;

    public RecencyBooster(IndexReader r) throws IOException {
      super(r);
      publishDay = FieldCache.DEFAULT          Retrieve days
        .getInts(r, dayField);                 from field cache
    }

    public float customScore(int doc, float subQueryScore,
                             float valSrcScore) {            Compute
      int daysAgo = today - publishDay[doc];                elapsed days
      if (daysAgo < maxDaysAgo) {                 Skip old books
        float boost = (float) (multiplier *        Compute
                      (maxDaysAgo-daysAgo)         simple
                      / maxDaysAgo);              linear boost
```

```
            return (float) (subQueryScore * (1.0+boost));
        } else {
            return subQueryScore;                  ◁────┐ Return
        }                                                │ unboosted
    }                                                    │ score
}

    public CustomScoreProvider getCustomScoreProvider(IndexReader r)
        throws IOException {
      return new RecencyBooster(r);
    }
}
```

In our case, we previously indexed the pubmonthAsDay field, like this:

```
doc.add(new NumericField("pubmonthAsDay")
            .setIntValue((int) (d.getTime()/(1000*3600*24))));
```

See section 2.6.2 for options when indexing dates and times.

Once the index is set up, using RecencyBoostingQuery is straightforward, as shown in listing 5.16.

Listing 5.16   Testing recency boosting

```
public void testRecency() throws Throwable {
  Directory dir = TestUtil.getBookIndexDirectory();
  IndexReader r = IndexReader.open(dir);
  IndexSearcher s = new IndexSearcher(r);
  s.setDefaultFieldSortScoring(true, true);

  QueryParser parser = new QueryParser(
                          Version.LUCENE_30,
                          "contents",
                          new StandardAnalyzer(
                            Version.LUCENE_30));
  Query q = parser.parse("java in action");      ◁──── Parse query
  Query q2 = new RecencyBoostingQuery(q,          ◁───┐ Create recency
                             2.0, 2*365);              │ boosting query
  Sort sort = new Sort(new SortField[] {
      SortField.FIELD_SCORE,
      new SortField("title2", SortField.STRING)});
  TopDocs hits = s.search(q, null, 5, sort);

  for (int i = 0; i < hits.scoreDocs.length; i++) {
    Document doc = r.document(hits.scoreDocs[i].doc);
    System.out.println((1+i) + ": " +
                      doc.get("title") +
                      ": pubmonth=" +
                      doc.get("pubmonth") +
                      " score=" + hits.scoreDocs[i].score);
  }
  s.close();
  r.close();
  dir.close();
}
```

We first create a normal query, by parsing the search string "java in action", and then instantiate the RecencyBoostingQuery, giving a boost factor of up to 2.0 for any book published within the past two years. Then we run the search, sorting first by relevance score and second by title. The test as shown in listing 5.16 runs the unboosted query, producing this result:

```
1: Ant in Action: pubmonth=200707 score=0.78687847
2: Lucene in Action, Second Edition: pubmonth=201005 score=0.78687847
3: Tapestry in Action: pubmonth=200403 score=0.15186688
4: JUnit in Action, Second Edition: pubmonth=201005 score=0.13288352
```

If instead you run the search with q2, which boosts each result by recency, you'll see this:

```
1: Lucene in Action, Second Edition: pubmonth=201005 score=2.483518
2: Ant in Action: pubmonth=200707 score=0.78687847
3: JUnit in Action, Second Edition: pubmonth=201005 score=0.41940224
4: Tapestry in Action: pubmonth=200403 score=0.15186688
```

You can see that in the unboosted query, the top two results were tied based on relevance. But after factoring in recency boosting, the scores were different and the sort order changed (for the better, we might add!).

This wraps up our coverage of function queries. Although we focused on one compelling example, boosting relevance scoring according to recency, function queries open up a whole universe of possibilities. You're completely free to implement whatever scoring you'd like. We'll now look at support for searching across multiple Lucene indexes.

5.8   Searching across multiple Lucene indexes

Some applications need to maintain separate Lucene indexes, yet want to allow a single search to return combined results from all the indexes. Sometimes, such separation is done for convenience or administrative reasons—for example, if different people or groups maintain the index for different collections of documents. Other times it may be done due to high volume. For example, a news site may make a new index for every month and then choose which months to search over.

Whatever the reason, Lucene provides two useful classes for searching across multiple indexes. We'll first meet MultiSearcher, which uses a single thread to perform searching across multiple indexes. Then we'll see ParallelMultiSearcher, which uses multiple threads to gain concurrency.

5.8.1   Using MultiSearcher

With MultiSearcher, all indexes can be searched with the results merged in a specified (or descending-score, by default) order. Using MultiSearcher is comparable to using IndexSearcher, except that you hand it an array of IndexSearchers to search rather than a single directory (so it's effectively a decorator pattern and delegates most of the work to the subsearchers).

Listing 5.17 illustrates how to search two indexes that are split alphabetically by keyword. The index is made up of animal names beginning with each letter of the alphabet. Half the names are in one index, and half are in the other. A search is performed with a range that spans both indexes, demonstrating that results are merged together.

Listing 5.17   Securing the search space with a filter

```java
public class MultiSearcherTest extends TestCase {
  private IndexSearcher[] searchers;

  public void setUp() throws Exception {
    String[] animals = { "aardvark", "beaver", "coati",
                         "dog", "elephant", "frog", "gila monster",
                         "horse", "iguana", "javelina", "kangaroo",
                         "lemur", "moose", "nematode", "orca",
                         "python", "quokka", "rat", "scorpion",
                         "tarantula", "uromastyx", "vicuna",
                         "walrus", "xiphias", "yak", "zebra"};

    Analyzer analyzer = new WhitespaceAnalyzer();

    Directory aTOmDirectory = new RAMDirectory();        ❶ Create two
    Directory nTOzDirectory = new RAMDirectory();           directories

    IndexWriter aTOmWriter = new IndexWriter(aTOmDirectory,
                                             analyzer,
      IndexWriter.MaxFieldLength.UNLIMITED);
    IndexWriter nTOzWriter = new IndexWriter(nTOzDirectory,
                                             analyzer,
                          IndexWriter.MaxFieldLength.UNLIMITED);

    for (int i=animals.length - 1; i >= 0; i--) {
      Document doc = new Document();
      String animal = animals[i];
      doc.add(new Field("animal", animal,
              Field.Store.YES, Field.Index.NOT_ANALYZED));
      if (animal.charAt(0) < 'n') {
        aTOmWriter.addDocument(doc);                      ❷ Index halves of
      } else {                                               the alphabet
        nTOzWriter.addDocument(doc);
      }
    }

    aTOmWriter.close();
    nTOzWriter.close();

    searchers = new IndexSearcher[2];
    searchers[0] = new IndexSearcher(aTOmDirectory);
    searchers[1] = new IndexSearcher(nTOzDirectory);
  }

  public void testMulti() throws Exception {

    MultiSearcher searcher = new MultiSearcher(searchers);

    TermRangeQuery query = new TermRangeQuery("animal",    ❸ Search both
                                              "h",            indexes
                                              "t",
                                              true, true);
```

```
    TopDocs hits = searcher.search(query, 10);
    assertEquals("tarantula not included", 12, hits.totalHits);
}
```

This code uses two indexes ❶. The first half of the alphabet is indexed to one index, and the other half is indexed to the other index ❷. This query ❸ spans documents in both indexes.

The inclusive `TermRangeQuery` matches animal names that begin with *h* through animal names that begin with *t*, with the matching documents coming from both indexes. A related class, `ParallelMultiSearcher`, achieves the same functionality as `MultiSearcher` but uses multiple threads to gain concurrency.

5.8.2   *Multithreaded searching using ParallelMultiSearcher*

A multithreaded version of `MultiSearcher`, called `ParallelMultiSearcher`, spawns a new thread for each `Searchable` and waits for them all to finish when the search method is invoked. The basic search and search with filter options are parallelized, but searching with a `Collector` hasn't yet been parallelized. The exposed API is the same as `MultiSearcher`, so it's a simple drop-in.

Whether you'll see performance gains using `ParallelMultiSearcher` depends on your architecture. If the indexes reside on different physical disks and your computer has CPU concurrency, you should see improved performance. But there hasn't been much real-world testing to back this up, so be sure to test it for your application.

A cousin to `ParallelMultiSearcher` lives in Lucene's contrib/remote directory, enabling you to remotely search multiple indexes in parallel. We'll talk about term vectors next, a topic you've already seen on the indexing side in chapter 2.

5.9   *Leveraging term vectors*

Term vectors are an advanced means of storing the equivalent of an inverted index per document. They are a rather advanced topic, and there are many things you can do with term vectors, so this section is rather sizable. We'll work through two concrete examples illustrating what you can do at search time once you have term vectors in the index: finding similar documents and automatically categorizing documents.

Technically, a term vector is a collection of term-frequency pairs, optionally including positional information for each term occurrence. Most of us probably can't picture vectors in hyper-dimensional space, so for visualization purposes, let's look at two documents that contain only the terms *cat* and *dog*. These words appear various times in each document. Plotting the term frequencies of each document in X, Y coordinates looks something like figure 5.5. What gets interesting with term vectors is the angle between them, as you'll see in more detail in section 5.9.2.

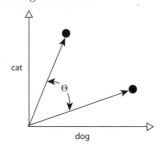

Figure 5.5   Term vectors for two documents containing the terms *cat* and *dog*

We showed how to enable indexing of term vectors in section 2.4.3. We indexed the title, author, subject, and contents fields with term vectors when indexing our book data. Retrieving term vectors for a field in a given document by ID requires a call to an `IndexReader` method:

```
TermFreqVector termFreqVector =
                    reader.getTermFreqVector(id, "subject");
```

A `TermFreqVector` instance has several methods for retrieving the vector information, primarily as matching arrays of `Strings` and `ints` (the term value and frequency in the field, respectively). If you had also stored offsets and/or positions information with your term vectors, using `Field.TermVector.WITH_POSITIONS_OFFSETS` for example, then you'll get a `TermPositionVector` back when you load the term vectors. That class contains offset and position information for each occurrence of the terms in the document.

You can use term vectors for some interesting effects, such as finding documents "like" a particular document, which is an example of latent semantic analysis. We'll show how to find books similar to an existing one, as well as a proof-of-concept categorizer that can tell us the most appropriate category for a new book, as you'll see in the following sections. We wrap up with the `TermVectorMapper` classes for precisely controlling how term vectors are read from the index.

5.9.1 Books like this

It'd be nice to offer other choices to the customers of our bookstore when they're viewing a particular book. The alternatives should be related to the original book, but associating alternatives manually would be labor-intensive and would require ongoing effort to keep up to date. Instead, we use Lucene's Boolean query capability and the information from one book to look up other books that are similar. Listing 5.18 demonstrates a basic approach for finding books like each one in our sample data.

Listing 5.18 Finding similar books to a specific example book

```
public class BooksLikeThis {

  public static void main(String[] args) throws IOException {
    Directory dir = TestUtil.getBookIndexDirectory();

    IndexReader reader = IndexReader.open(dir);
    int numDocs = reader.maxDoc();

    BooksLikeThis blt = new BooksLikeThis(reader);        ❶ Iterate over
    for (int i = 0; i < numDocs; i++) {                      every book
      System.out.println();
      Document doc = reader.document(i);
      System.out.println(doc.get("title"));

      Document[] docs = blt.docsLike(i, 10);               ❷ Look up
      if (docs.length == 0) {                                 books like this
        System.out.println("  None like this");
      }
```

```
      for (Document likeThisDoc : docs) {
        System.out.println("  -> " + likeThisDoc.get("title"));
      }
    }
    reader.close();
    dir.close();
  }

  private IndexReader reader;
  private IndexSearcher searcher;

  public BooksLikeThis(IndexReader reader) {
    this.reader = reader;
    searcher = new IndexSearcher(reader);
  }

  public Document[] docsLike(int id, int max) throws IOException {
    Document doc = reader.document(id);

    String[] authors = doc.getValues("author");
    BooleanQuery authorQuery = new BooleanQuery();
    for (String author : authors) {
      authorQuery.add(new TermQuery(new Term("author", author)),
          BooleanClause.Occur.SHOULD);
    }
    authorQuery.setBoost(2.0f);

    TermFreqVector vector =
        reader.getTermFreqVector(id, "subject");

    BooleanQuery subjectQuery = new BooleanQuery();
    for (String vecTerm : vector.getTerms()) {
      TermQuery tq = new TermQuery(
          new Term("subject", vecTerm));
      subjectQuery.add(tq, BooleanClause.Occur.SHOULD);
    }

    BooleanQuery likeThisQuery = new BooleanQuery();
    likeThisQuery.add(authorQuery, BooleanClause.Occur.SHOULD);
    likeThisQuery.add(subjectQuery, BooleanClause.Occur.SHOULD);

    likeThisQuery.add(new TermQuery(
        new Term("isbn", doc.get("isbn"))),
      BooleanClause.Occur.MUST_NOT);

    TopDocs hits = searcher.search(likeThisQuery, 10);
    int size = max;
    if (max > hits.scoreDocs.length) size = hits.scoreDocs.length;

    Document[] docs = new Document[size];
    for (int i = 0; i < size; i++) {
      docs[i] = reader.document(hits.scoreDocs[i].doc);
    }

    return docs;
  }
}
```

❸ Boost books by same author

❹ Use terms from "subject" term vectors

❺ Create final query

❻ Exclude current book

❶ As an example, we iterate over every book document in the index and find books like each one.

❷ Here we look up books that are like this one.

❸ Books by the same author are considered alike and are boosted so they will likely appear before books by other authors.

❹ Using the terms from the subject term vectors, we add each to a Boolean query.

❺ We combine the author and subject queries into a final Boolean query.

❻ We exclude the current book, which would surely be the best match given the other criteria, from consideration.

In ❸, we used a different way to get the value of the author field. It was indexed as multiple fields, and the original author string is a comma-separated list of author(s) of a book:

```
String[] authors = author.split(",");
for (String a : authors) {
  doc.add(new Field("author",
                    a,
                    Field.Store.YES,
                    Field.Index.NOT_ANALYZED,
                    Field.TermVector.WITH_POSITIONS_OFFSETS));
}
```

The output is interesting, showing how our books are connected through author and subject:

```
Tao Te Ching 道德經
  None like this

Lipitor Thief of Memory
  None like this

Imperial Secrets of Health and Longevity
  None like this

Nudge: Improving Decisions About Health, Wealth, and Happiness
  None like this

Gödel, Escher, Bach: an Eternal Golden Braid
  None like this

Extreme Programming Explained
  -> The Pragmatic Programmer
  -> Ant in Action

Mindstorms: Children, Computers, And Powerful Ideas
  -> A Modern Art of Education

Lucene in Action, Second Edition
  -> Ant in Action

The Pragmatic Programmer
  -> Extreme Programming Explained

Ant in Action
```

```
    -> Lucene in Action, Second Edition
    -> JUnit in Action, Second Edition
    -> Extreme Programming Explained

Tapestry in Action
  None like this

JUnit in Action, Second Edition
  -> Ant in Action

A Modern Art of Education
  -> Mindstorms: Children, Computers, And Powerful Ideas
```

If you'd like to see the actual query used for each, uncomment the output lines toward the end of the docsLike method.

The books-like-this example could've been done without term vectors, and we aren't using them as vectors in this case. We've only used the convenience of getting the terms for a given field. Without term vectors, the subject field could have been reanalyzed or indexed such that individual subject terms were added separately in order to get the list of terms for that field. Our next example also uses the frequency component to a term vector in a much more sophisticated manner.

Lucene's contrib modules contains a useful Query implementation, More-LikeThisQuery, doing the same thing as our BooksLikeThis class but more generically. BooksLikeThis is clearly hardwired to fields like subject and author from our books index. But MoreLikeThisQuery lets you set the field names, so it works well on any index. Section 8.6.1 describes this in more detail. The two highlighter contrib modules, described in sections 8.3 and 8.4, also use term vectors to find term occurrences for highlighting.

Let's see another example of using term vectors: automatic category assignment.

5.9.2 What category?

Each book in our index is given a single primary category: for example, this book is categorized as "/technology/computers/programming." The best category placement for a new book may be relatively obvious or (more likely) several possible categories may seem reasonable. You can use term vectors to automate the decision. We've written a bit of code that builds a representative subject vector for each existing category. This representative, archetypical, vector is the sum of all vectors for each document's subject field vector.

With these representative vectors precomputed, our end goal is a calculation that can, given some subject keywords for a new book, tell us what category is the best fit. Our test case uses two example subject strings:

```
public void testCategorization() throws Exception {
  assertEquals("/technology/computers/programming/methodology",
      getCategory("extreme agile methodology"));
  assertEquals("/education/pedagogy",
      getCategory("montessori education philosophy"));
}
```

The first assertion says that, based on our sample data, if a new book has the keywords "extreme agile methodology" in its subject, the best category fit is /technology/computers/programming/methodology. The best category is determined by finding the closest category angle-wise in vector space to the new book's subject.

The test setUp() builds vectors for each category:

```
protected void setUp() throws Exception {
  categoryMap = new TreeMap();

  buildCategoryVectors();
}
```

Our code builds category vectors by walking every document in the index and aggregating book subject vectors into a single vector for the book's associated category. Category vectors are stored in a map, keyed by category name. The value of each item in the category map is another map keyed by term, with the value an integer for its frequency, as seen in listing 5.19.

Listing 5.19   Build category vectors by aggregating for each category

```
private void buildCategoryVectors() throws IOException {
  IndexReader reader = IndexReader.open(TestUtil.getBookIndexDirectory());

  int maxDoc = reader.maxDoc();

  for (int i = 0; i < maxDoc; i++) {
    if (!reader.isDeleted(i)) {
      Document doc = reader.document(i);
      String category = doc.get("category");

      Map vectorMap = (Map) categoryMap.get(category);
      if (vectorMap == null) {
        vectorMap = new TreeMap();
        categoryMap.put(category, vectorMap);
      }

      TermFreqVector termFreqVector =
          reader.getTermFreqVector(i, "subject");

      addTermFreqToMap(vectorMap, termFreqVector);
    }
  }
}
```

A book's term frequency vector is added to its category vector in addTermFreqToMap. The arrays returned by getTerms() and getTermFrequencies() align with one another such that the same position in each refers to the same term, as listing 5.20 shows.

Listing 5.20   Aggregate term frequencies for each category

```
private void addTermFreqToMap(Map vectorMap,
                              TermFreqVector termFreqVector) {
  String[] terms = termFreqVector.getTerms();
  int[] freqs = termFreqVector.getTermFrequencies();
```

```
    for (int i = 0; i < terms.length; i++) {
      String term = terms[i];

      if (vectorMap.containsKey(term)) {
        Integer value = (Integer) vectorMap.get(term);
        vectorMap.put(term,
            new Integer(value.intValue() + freqs[i]));
      } else {
        vectorMap.put(term, new Integer(freqs[i]));
      }
    }
  }
}
```

That was the easy part—building the category vector maps— because it only involved addition.

$$\cos \Theta = \frac{A \cdot B}{\| A \| \| B \|}$$

Figure 5.6 Formula for computing the angle between two term vectors

Computing angles between vectors is more involved mathematically. In the simplest two-dimensional case, as shown in figure 5.5, two categories (A and B) have unique term vectors based on aggregation (as we've just done). The closest category, angle-wise, to a new book's subjects is the match we'll choose. Figure 5.6 shows the equation for computing an angle between two vectors.

Our `getCategory` method loops through all categories, computing the angle between each category and the new book. The smallest angle is the closest match, and the category name is returned, as shown in listing 5.21.

Listing 5.21 Finding the closest vector to match the best category

```
private String getCategory(String subject) {
  String[] words = subject.split(" ");

  Iterator categoryIterator = categoryMap.keySet().iterator();
  double bestAngle = Double.MAX_VALUE;
  String bestCategory = null;

  while (categoryIterator.hasNext()) {
    String category = (String) categoryIterator.next();

    double angle = computeAngle(words, category);

    if (angle < bestAngle) {
      bestAngle = angle;
      bestCategory = category;
    }
  }

  return bestCategory;
}
```

We assume that the subject string is in a whitespace-separated form and that each word occurs only once. Furthermore, we use `String.split` to extract tokens from the subject, which will only work with analyzers that don't alter the text of each token. If you're using an analyzer that does alter the tokens, such as one that includes `Porter-StemFilter`, you'll need to change the `String.split` to invoke your analyzer instead.

The angle computation takes these assumptions into account to simplify a part of the computation. Finally, computing the angle between an array of words and a specific category is done in computeAngle, shown in listing 5.22.

Listing 5.22   Computing term vector angles for a new book against a given category

```
private double computeAngle(String[] words, String category) {
  Map vectorMap = (Map) categoryMap.get(category);

  int dotProduct = 0;
  int sumOfSquares = 0;
  for (String word : words) {
    int categoryWordFreq = 0;

    if (vectorMap.containsKey(word)) {
      categoryWordFreq =
          ((Integer) vectorMap.get(word)).intValue();
    }

    dotProduct += categoryWordFreq;                        ◄——❶
    sumOfSquares += categoryWordFreq * categoryWordFreq;
  }

  double denominator;
  if (sumOfSquares == words.length) {
    denominator = sumOfSquares;                            ◄——❷
  } else {
    denominator = Math.sqrt(sumOfSquares) *
                  Math.sqrt(words.length);
  }

  double ratio = dotProduct / denominator;

  return Math.acos(ratio);
}
```

❶ The calculation is optimized with the assumption that each word in the words array has a frequency of 1.

❷ We multiply the square root of N by the square root of N to get N. This shortcut prevents a precision issue where the ratio could be greater than 1 (which is an illegal value for the inverse cosine function).

You should be aware that computing term vector angles between two documents or, in this case, between a document and an archetypical category, is computation intensive. It requires square-root and inverse cosine calculations and may be prohibitive in high-volume indexes. We finish our coverage of term vectors with the TermVector-Mapper class.

5.9.3   *TermVectorMapper*

Sometimes, the parallel array structure returned by IndexReader.getTermFreqVector may not be convenient for your application. Perhaps instead of sorting by Term, you'd like to sort the term vectors according to your own criteria. Or maybe you'd like to only load certain terms of interest. All of these can be done with a recent addition to Lucene, `TermVectorMapper`. This is an abstract base class that, when passed to `IndexReader.getTermFreqVector` methods, separately receives each term, with optional positions and offsets and can choose to store the data in its own manner. Table 5.2 describes the methods that a concrete `TermVectorMapper` implementation (subclass) must implement.

Table 5.2 Methods that a custom `TermVectorMapper` must implement

Method	Purpose
setDocumentNumber	Called once per document to tell you which document is currently being loaded.
setExpectations	Called once per field to tell you how many terms occur in the field, and whether positions and offsets are stored.
map	Called once per term to provide the actual term vectors data.
isIgnoringPositions	You should return `false` only if you need to see the positions data for the term vectors.
isIgnoringOffsets	You should return `false` only if you need to see the offsets data for the term vectors.

Lucene includes a few public core implementations of `TermVectorMapper`, described in table 5.3. You can also create your own implementation.

As we've now seen, term vectors are a powerful advanced functionality. We saw two examples where you might want to use them: automatically assigning documents to categories, and finding documents similar to an existing example. We also saw Lucene's advanced API for controlling exactly how term vectors are loaded. We'll now see how to load stored fields using another advanced API in Lucene: `FieldSelector`.

Table 5.3 Built-in implementations of `TermVectorMapper`

Method	Purpose
PositionBasedTermVectorMapper	For each field, stores a map from the integer position to terms and optionally offsets that occurred at that position.
SortedTermVectorMapper	Merges term vectors for all fields into a single `SortedSet`, sorted according to a `Comparator` that you specify. One comparator is provided in the Lucene core, `TermVectorEntryFreqSortedComparator`, which sorts first by frequency of the term and second by the term itself.
FieldSortedTermVectorMapper	Just like `SortedTermVectorMapper`, except the fields aren't merged together and instead each field stores its sorted terms separately.

5.10   *Loading fields with FieldSelector*

We've talked about reading a document from the index using an `IndexReader`. You know that the document returned differs from the original document indexed in that it has only those fields you chose to store at indexing time using `Field.Store.YES`. Under the hood, Lucene writes these fields into the index and `IndexReader` reads them.

Unfortunately, reading a document can be fairly time consuming, especially if you need to read many of them per search and if your documents have many stored fields. Often, a document may have one or two large stored fields, holding the actual textual content for the document, and a number of smaller "metadata" fields such as title, category, author, and published date. When presenting the search results, you might only need the metadata fields and so loading the very large fields is costly and unnecessary. This is where `FieldSelector` comes in. `FieldSelector`, which is in the `org.apache.lucene.document` package, allows you to load a specific restricted set of fields for each document. It's an interface with a single simple method:

```
FieldSelectorResult accept(String fieldName);
```

Concrete classes implementing this interface return a `FieldSelectorResult` describing whether the specified field name should be loaded, and how. `FieldSelectorResult` is an enum with seven values, described in table 5.4.

Table 5.4   `FieldSelectorResult` options when loading a stored field

Option	Purpose
`LOAD`	Load the field.
`LAZY_LOAD`	Load the field lazily. The actual contents of the field won't be read until `Field.stringValue()` or `Field.binaryValue()` is called.
`NO_LOAD`	Skip loading the field.
`LOAD_AND_BREAK`	Load this field and don't load any of the remaining fields.
`LOAD_FOR_MERGE`	Used internally to load a field during segment merging; this skips decompressing compressed fields.
`SIZE`	Read only the size of the field, then add a binary field with a 4-byte array encoding that size.
`SIZE_AND_BREAK`	Like `SIZE`, but don't load any of the remaining fields.

When loading stored fields with a `FieldSelector`, `IndexReader` steps through the fields one by one for the document, in the order they had originally been added to the document during indexing, invoking `FieldSelector` on each field and choosing to load the field (or not) based on the returned result.

There are several built-in concrete classes implementing `FieldSelector`, described in table 5.5. It's also straightforward to create your own implementation.

Table 5.5   Core FieldSelector implementations

Class	Purpose
LoadFirstFieldSelector	Loads only the first field encountered.
MapFieldSelector	You specify the String names of the fields you want to load; all other fields are skipped.
SetBasedFieldSelector	You specify two sets: the first set is fields to load and the second set is fields to load lazily.

Although FieldSelector will save time when loading fields, just how much time is application-dependent. Much of the cost when loading stored fields is in seeking the file pointers to the places in the index where all fields are stored, so you may find you don't save that much time skipping fields. Test on your application to find the right trade-off.

5.11   Stopping a slow search

Usually Lucene's searches are fast. But if you have a large index, or you create exceptionally complex searches, it's possible for Lucene to take too long to execute the search. Fortunately, Lucene has a special Collector implementation, TimeLimiting-Collector, that stops a search when it has taken too much time. We cover Collector in more detail in section 6.2.

TimeLimitingCollector delegates all methods to a separate Collector that you provide, and throws a TimeExceededException when the searching has taken too long. It's simple to use, as shown in listing 5.23.

Listing 5.23   Using TimeLimitingCollector to stop a slow search

```
public class TimeLimitingCollectorTest extends TestCase {
  public void testTimeLimitingCollector() throws Exception {
    Directory dir = TestUtil.getBookIndexDirectory();
    IndexSearcher searcher = new IndexSearcher(dir);
    Query q = new MatchAllDocsQuery();
    int numAllBooks = TestUtil.hitCount(searcher, q);

    TopScoreDocCollector topDocs = TopScoreDocCollector.create(10, false);
    Collector collector = new TimeLimitingCollector(topDocs,
                                          1000);
    try {
      searcher.search(q, collector);
      assertEquals(numAllBooks, topDocs.getTotalHits());
    } catch (TimeExceededException tee) {
      System.out.println("Too much time taken.");
    }
    searcher.close();
    dir.close();
  }
}
```

Wrap existing Collector

Verify all hits

Print timeout message

In this example we create a `TopScoreDocCollector`, which keeps the top 10 hits according to score, and wrap it with a `TimeLimitingCollector` that will abort the search if it takes longer than 1,000 msec (1.0 seconds). You'd obviously have to modify the exception handler to choose what to do when a timeout is hit. One option is to present the results collected so far, noting to the user that the results may not be accurate because the search took too long. This may be dangerous; the results are incomplete and the user could go on to make important decisions based on false results. Another option is to not show any results and simply ask users to rephrase or simplify their search.

There are a few couple of limitations to `TimeLimitingCollector`. First, it adds some of its own overhead during results collection (to check the timeout, per matched document) and that will make your searches run somewhat slower, though the impact should be small. Second, it only times out the search during collection, whereas it's possible that some queries take a very long time during `Query.rewrite()`. For such queries it's possible you won't hit the `TimeExceededException` until well after your requested timeout.

5.12 *Summary*

This chapter has covered some diverse Lucene functionality, highlighting Lucene's additional built-in search features. We touched on Lucene's internal field cache API, which allows you to load into memory an array of a given field's value for all documents. Sorting is a flexible way to control the ordering of search results.

We described a number of advanced queries. `MultiPhraseQuery` generalizes `PhraseQuery` by allowing more than one term at the same position within a phrase. The `SpanQuery` family leverages term-position information for greater searching precision. `MultiFieldQueryParser` is another `QueryParser` that matches against more than one field. Function queries let you programmatically customize how documents are scored.

Filters constrain document search space, regardless of the query, and you can either create your own filter (described in section 6.4), or use one of Lucene's many built-in ones. We saw how to wrap a query as a filter, and vice versa, as well as how to cache filters for fast reuse.

Lucene includes support for multiple index searching, including a parallel version to easily take advantage of concurrency. Term vectors enable interesting effects, such as "like this" term vector angle calculations. We showed how to fine-tune the loading of term vectors and stored fields by using `TermVectorMapper` and `FieldSelector`. Finally we showed you how to use `TimeLimitingCollector` to handle searches that could take too long to run.

As modern-day search applications become more diverse and interesting, and users more demanding, you'll find that Lucene's rich advanced capabilities we've covered here give you a strong arsenal for addressing your needs. We've only touched on what's possible with the examples in this chapter, because the possibilities with major features like sorting, filtering, and term vectors are so vast. Very likely whatever advanced needs your application encounters, they can be satisfied with what Lucene offers.

Yet this is still not quite the end of the searching story. Lucene also includes several ways to extend its searching behavior, such as custom sorting, positional payloads, filtering, and query expression parsing, which we cover in the next chapter.

Extending search

This chapter covers

- Creating a custom sort
- Using a `Collector`
- Customizing `QueryParser`
- Using positional payloads

Just when you thought we were done with searching, here we are again with even more on the topic! Chapter 3 discussed the basics of Lucene's built-in capabilities, and chapter 5 delved well beyond the basics into Lucene's more advanced searching features. In those two chapters, we explored only the built-in features. Lucene also has several powerful extension points, which we'll cover here.

Custom sorting lets you implement arbitrary sorting criteria when the built-in sort by relevance or field isn't appropriate. We'll show an example of sorting by geographic proximity to a user's current location. Custom collection lets you arbitrarily process each matching document yourself, in case you don't want the top documents according to a sort criterion. We'll also include examples of two custom collectors. `QueryParser` has many extension points to customize how each type of query is created, and we provide examples, including how to prevent certain query types and handling numeric and date fields. Custom filters let you arbitrarily restrict the allowed documents for matching. Finally, you can use payloads to separately boost specific occurrences of a given term within the same document. Armed with an understanding of these powerful extension points, you'll be able to customize Lucene's behavior in nearly arbitrary ways.

Let's begin with custom sorting.

6.1 Using a custom sort method

If sorting by score, ID, or field values is insufficient for your needs, Lucene lets you implement a custom sorting mechanism by providing your own subclass of the Field-ComparatorSource abstract base class. Custom sorting implementations are most useful in situations when the sort criteria can't be determined during indexing.

For this section we'll create a custom sort that orders search results based on geographic distance from a given location.[1] The given location is only known at search time, and could, for example, be the geographic location of the user doing the search if the user is searching from a mobile device with an embedded global positioning service (GPS). First we show the required steps at indexing time. Next we'll describe how to implement the custom sort during searching. Finally, you'll learn how to access field values involved in the sorting for presentation purposes.

6.1.1 Indexing documents for geographic sorting

We've created a simplified demonstration of this concept using the important question, "What Mexican food restaurant is nearest to me?" Figure 6.1 shows a sample of

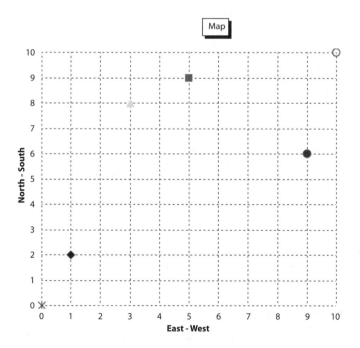

Figure 6.1 Which Mexican restaurant is closest to home (at 0,0) or work (at 10,10)?

---

[1] Thanks to Tim Jones (the contributor of Lucene's sort capabilities) for the inspiration.

restaurants and their fictitious grid coordinates on a sample 10 x 10 grid. Note that Lucene now includes the "spatial" package in the contrib modules, described in section 9.7, for filtering and sorting according to geographic distance in general.

The test data is indexed as shown in listing 6.1, with each place given a name, location in X and Y coordinates, and a type. The type field allows our data to accommodate other types of businesses and could allow us to filter search results to specific types of places.

Listing 6.1 Indexing geographic data

```
public class DistanceSortingTest extends TestCase {
  private RAMDirectory directory;
  private IndexSearcher searcher;
  private Query query;

  protected void setUp() throws Exception {
    directory = new RAMDirectory();
    IndexWriter writer =
        new IndexWriter(directory, new WhitespaceAnalyzer(),
                        IndexWriter.MaxFieldLength.UNLIMITED);
    addPoint(writer, "El Charro", "restaurant", 1, 2);
    addPoint(writer, "Cafe Poca Cosa", "restaurant", 5, 9);
    addPoint(writer, "Los Betos", "restaurant", 9, 6);
    addPoint(writer, "Nico's Taco Shop", "restaurant", 3, 8);

    writer.close();

    searcher = new IndexSearcher(directory);

    query = new TermQuery(new Term("type", "restaurant"));
  }

  private void addPoint(IndexWriter writer,
                        String name, String type, int x, int y)
    throws IOException {
    Document doc = new Document();
    doc.add(new Field("name", name, Field.Store.YES,
            Field.Index.NOT_ANALYZED));
    doc.add(new Field("type", type, Field.Store.YES,
            Field.Index.NOT_ANALYZED));
    doc.add(new Field("location", x + "," + y, Field.Store.YES,
            Field.Index.NOT_ANALYZED));
    writer.addDocument(doc);
  }
}
```

The coordinates are indexed into a single location field as a string x, y. The location could be encoded in numerous ways, but we opted for the simplest approach for this example.

6.1.2 *Implementing custom geographic sort*

Before we delve into the class that performs our custom sort, let's look at the test case that we're using to confirm that it's working correctly:

```
public void testNearestRestaurantToHome() throws Exception {
  Sort sort = new Sort(new SortField("location",
      new DistanceComparatorSource(0, 0)));

  TopDocs hits = searcher.search(query, null, 10, sort);

  assertEquals("closest",
               "El Charro",
               searcher.doc(hits.scoreDocs[0].doc).get("name"));
  assertEquals("furthest",
               "Los Betos",
               searcher.doc(hits.scoreDocs[3].doc).get("name"));
}
```

Home is at coordinates (0,0). Our test has shown that the first and last documents in the returned results are the ones closest and furthest from home. *Muy bien!* Had we not used a sort, the documents would've been returned in insertion order, because the score of each hit is equivalent for the restaurant-type query. The distance computation, using the basic distance formula, is done under our custom DistanceComparator-Source, shown in listing 6.2.

Listing 6.2   DistanceComparatorSource

```
public class DistanceComparatorSource
    extends FieldComparatorSource {                    ◄—❶
  private int x;
  private int y;

  public DistanceComparatorSource(int x, int y) {      ◄—❷
    this.x = x;
    this.y = y;
  }

  public FieldComparator newComparator(java.lang.String fieldName,
                                       int numHits, int sortPos,
                                       boolean reversed)                ❸
    throws IOException {
    return new DistanceScoreDocLookupComparator(fieldName,
                                                numHits);
  }

  private class DistanceScoreDocLookupComparator       ◄—❹
      extends FieldComparator {
    private int[] xDoc, yDoc;                           ◄—❺
    private float[] values;                             ◄—❻
    private float bottom;                  ◄—❼
    String fieldName;

    public DistanceScoreDocLookupComparator(
                String fieldName, int numHits) throws IOException {
      values = new float[numHits];
      this.fieldName = fieldName;
    }

    public void setNextReader(IndexReader reader, int docBase)
        throws IOException {
```

```
      xDoc = FieldCache.DEFAULT.getInts(reader, "x");          8
      yDoc = FieldCache.DEFAULT.getInts(reader, "y");
    }

    private float getDistance(int doc) {                        9
      int deltax = xDoc[doc] - x;
      int deltay = yDoc[doc] - y;
      return (float) Math.sqrt(deltax * deltax + deltay * deltay);
    }

    public int compare(int slot1, int slot2) {                 10
      if (values[slot1] < values[slot2]) return -1;
      if (values[slot1] > values[slot2]) return 1;
      return 0;
    }

    public void setBottom(int slot) {         <-- 11
      bottom = values[slot];
    }

    public int compareBottom(int doc) {                        12
      float docDistance = getDistance(doc);
      if (bottom < docDistance) return -1;
      if (bottom > docDistance) return 1;
      return 0;
    }

    public void copy(int slot, int doc) {                      13
      values[slot] = getDistance(doc);
    }

    public Comparable value(int slot) {                        14
      return new Float(values[slot]);
    }

    public int sortType() {
      return SortField.CUSTOM;
    }
  }

  public String toString() {
    return "Distance from ("+x+","+y+")";
  }
}
```

The sorting infrastructure within Lucene interacts with the FieldComparatorSource
and FieldComparator ❶, ❹ API in order to sort matching documents. For performance reasons, this API is more complex than you'd otherwise expect. In particular,
the comparator is made aware of the size of the queue (passed as the numHits argument to newComparator) ❸ being tracked within Lucene. In addition, the comparator is notified every time a new segment is searched (with the setNextReader
method).

   The constructor is provided with the origin location ❷ for computing distances.
With each call to setNextReader, we get all x and y values from the field cache ❺, ❽.
Be sure to understand the performance implications when a field cache is used, as
described in section 5.1. These values are also used by the getDistance method ❾

which computes the actual distance for a given document, and in turn the `value` method ⓮, which Lucene invokes to retrieve the actual value used for sorting.

While searching, when a document is competitive it's inserted into the queue at a given slot, as determined by Lucene. Your comparator is asked to compare hits within the queue (`compare` ⓾), set the bottom (worst scoring entry) slot in the queue (`set-Bottom` ❼, ⓫), compare a hit to the bottom of the queue (`compareBottom` ⓬), and copy a new hit into the queue (`copy` ⓭). The `values` array ❻ stores the distances for all competitive documents in the queue.

Sorting by runtime information such as a user's location is an incredibly powerful feature. At this point, though, we still have a missing piece: what's the distance from each of the restaurants to our current location? When using the `TopDocs`-returning `search` methods, we can't get to the distance computed. But a lower-level API lets us access the values used for sorting.

6.1.3 Accessing values used in custom sorting

The `IndexSearcher.search` method you use when sorting, covered in section 5.2, returns more information than the top documents:

```
public TopFieldDocs search(Query query, Filter filter,
                           int nDocs, Sort sort)
```

`TopFieldDocs` is a subclass of `TopDocs` that adds the values used for sorting each hit. The values are available via each `FieldDoc`, which subclasses `ScoreDoc`, contained in the array of returned results. `FieldDoc` encapsulates the computed raw score, document ID, and an array of `Comparables` with the value used for each `SortField`. Rather than concerning ourselves with the details of the API, which you can get from Lucene's Javadocs or the source code, let's see how to use it.

Listing 6.3's test case demonstrates the use of `TopFieldDocs` and `FieldDoc` to retrieve the distance computed during sorting, this time sorting from work at location (10,10).

Listing 6.3   Accessing custom sorting values for search results

```
public void testNeareastRestaurantToWork() throws Exception {
  Sort sort = new Sort(new SortField("unused",
     new DistanceComparatorSource(10, 10)));

  TopFieldDocs docs = searcher.search(query, null, 3, sort);      ⟵❶

  assertEquals(4, docs.totalHits);          ⟵❷
  assertEquals(3, docs.scoreDocs.length);        ⟵❸

  FieldDoc fieldDoc = (FieldDoc) docs.scoreDocs[0];        ⟵❹

  assertEquals("(10,10) -> (9,6) = sqrt(17)",
     new Float(Math.sqrt(17)),
     fieldDoc.fields[0]);        ⟵❺

  Document document = searcher.doc(fieldDoc.doc);          ⟵❻
  assertEquals("Los Betos", document.get("name"));
}
```

① This lower-level API requires that we specify the maximum number of hits returned.

② The total number of hits is still provided because all hits need to be determined to find the three best ones.

③ The total number of documents (up to the maximum specified) are returned.

④ docs.scoreDocs(0) returns a ScoreDoc and must be cast to FieldDoc to get sorting values.

⑤ The value of the first (and only, in this example) SortField computation is available in the first fields slot.

⑥ Getting the actual Document requires another call.

As you can see, Lucene's custom sorting capabilities empower you to build arbitrary sorting logic for those cases when sorting by relevance or by field value is insufficient. We delved into a basic example, sorting by geographic distance, but that's just one of many possibilities. We'll now switch to an even deeper extensions point inside Lucene: custom collection.

6.2   *Developing a custom Collector*

In most applications with full-text search, users are looking for the top documents when sorting by either relevance or field values. The most common usage pattern is such that only these ScoreDocs are visited. In some scenarios, though, users want more control over precisely which documents should be retained during searching.

Lucene allows full customization of what you do with each matching document if you create your own subclass of the abstract Collector base class. For example, perhaps you wish to gather every single document ID that matched the query. Or perhaps with each matched document you'd like to consult its contents or an external resource to collate additional information. We'll cover both of these examples in this section.

You might be tempted to run a normal search, with a very large numHits, and then postprocess the results. This strategy will work, but it's an exceptionally inefficient approach because these methods are spending sizable CPU computing scores, which you may not need, and performing sorting, which you also may not need. Using a custom Collector class avoids these costs.

We begin by delving into the methods that make up the custom Collector API (see table 6.1).

Table 6.1   Methods to implement for a custom Collector

Method name	Purpose
setNextReader(IndexReader reader, int docBase)	Notifies the collector that a new segment is being searched, and provides the segment's IndexReader and the starting base for documents.
setScorer(Scorer scorer)	Provides a Scorer to the Collector. This is also called once per segment. The Collector should call Scorer.score() from within its collect() method to retrieve the score for the current matched document.

Table 6.1 Methods to implement for a custom `Collector` (continued)

Method name	Purpose
`collect(int docID)`	Called for each document that matches the search. The `docID` is relative to the current segment, so `docBase` must be added to it to make it absolute.
`acceptsDocsOutOfOrder()`	Return `true` if your `Collector` can handle out-of-order `docID`s. Some `BooleanQuery` instances can collect results faster if this returns `true`.

6.2.1 *The Collector base class*

`Collector` is an abstract base class that defines the API that Lucene interacts with while doing searching. As with the `FieldComparator` API for custom sorting, `Collector`'s API is more complex than you'd expect, in order to enable high-performance hit collection. Table 6.1 shows the four methods with a brief summary.

All of Lucene's core search methods use a `Collector` subclass under the hood to do their collection. For example, when sorting by relevance, `TopScoreDocCollector` is used. When sorting by field, it's `TopFieldCollector`. Both of these are public classes in the `org.apache.lucene.search` package, and you can instantiate them yourself if needed.

During searching, when Lucene finds a matching document, it calls the `Collector`'s `collect(int docID)` method. Lucene couldn't care less what's done with the document; it's up to the `Collector` to record the match, if it wants. This is the hot spot of searching, so make sure your `collect` method does only the bare minimum work required.

Lucene drives searching one segment at a time, for higher performance, and notifies you of each segment transition by calling the `setNextReader(IndexReader reader, int docBase)`. The provided `IndexReader` is specific to the segment. It will be a different instance for each segment. It's important for the `Collector` to record the `docBase` at this point, because the `docID` provided to the `collect` method is relative within each segment. To get the absolute or global `docID`, you must add `docBase` to it. This method is also the place to do any segment-specific initialization required by your collector. For example, you could use the `FieldCache` API, described in section 5.1, to retrieve values corresponding to the provided `IndexReader`.

Note that the relevance score isn't passed to the `collect` method. This saves wasted CPU for `Collectors` that don't require it. Instead, Lucene calls the `setScorer(Scorer)` method on the `Collector`, once per segment in the index, to provide a `Scorer` instance. You should hold onto this `Scorer`, if needed, and then retrieve the relevance score of the currently matched document by calling `Scorer.score()`. That method must be called from within the `collect` method because it holds volatile data specific to the current `docID` being collected. Note that `Scorer.score()` will recompute the score every time, so if your `collect` method may invoke `score` multiple times, you should call it once internally and simply reuse the returned result. Alternatively,

Lucene provides the ScoreCachingWrapperScorer, which is a Scorer implementation that caches the score per document. Note also that Scorer is a rich and advanced API in and of itself, but in this context you should only use the score method.

The final method, acceptsDocsOutOfOrder(), which returns a Boolean, is invoked by Lucene to see whether your Collector can tolerate docIDs that arrive out of sorted order. Many collectors can, but some collectors either can't accept docIDs out or order, or would have to do too much extra work. If possible, you should return true, because certain BooleanQuery instances can use a faster scorer under the hood if given this freedom.

Let's look at two example custom Collectors: BookLinkCollector and AllDoc-Collector.

6.2.2   *Custom collector: BookLinkCollector*

We've developed a custom Collector, called BookLinkCollector, which builds a map of all unique URLs and the corresponding book titles matching a query. BookLinkCollector is shown in listing 6.4.

Listing 6.4   Custom Collector: collects all book links

```java
public class BookLinkCollector extends Collector {
  private Map<String,String> documents = new HashMap<String,String>();
  private Scorer scorer;
  private String[] urls;
  private String[] titles;

  public boolean acceptsDocsOutOfOrder() {
    return true;                              Accept docIDs
  }                                           out of order

  public void setScorer(Scorer scorer) {
    this.scorer = scorer;
  }

  public void setNextReader(IndexReader reader, int docBase)
      throws IOException {
    urls = FieldCache.DEFAULT.getStrings(reader, "url");       Load FieldCache
    titles = FieldCache.DEFAULT.getStrings(reader, "title2");  values
  }

  public void collect(int docID) {
    try {
      String url = urls[docID];               Store details for
      String title = titles[docID];           the match
      documents.put(url, title);
      System.out.println(title + ":" + scorer.score());
    } catch (IOException e) {
    }
  }

  public Map<String,String> getLinks() {
    return Collections.unmodifiableMap(documents);
  }
}
```

The collector differs from Lucene's normal search result collection in that it does not retain the matching document IDs. Instead, for each matching document, it adds a mapping of URL to title into its private map, then makes that map available after the search completes. For this reason, even though we are passed the docBase in setNextReader, there's no need to save it, as the urls and titles that we retrieve from the FieldCache are based on the per-segment document ID. Using our custom Collector requires the use of IndexSearcher's search method variant, as shown in listing 6.5.

Listing 6.5 Testing the `BookLinkCollector`

```
public void testCollecting() throws Exception {
    Directory dir = TestUtil.getBookIndexDirectory();
    TermQuery query = new TermQuery(new Term("contents", "junit"));
    IndexSearcher searcher = new IndexSearcher(dir);

    BookLinkCollector collector = new BookLinkCollector(searcher);
    searcher.search(query, collector);

    Map<String,String> linkMap = collector.getLinks();
    assertEquals("ant in action",
                 linkMap.get("http://www.manning.com/loughran"));;
    searcher.close();
    dir.close();
}
```

During the search, Lucene delivers each matching docID to our collector; after the search finishes, we confirm that the link map created by the collector contains the right mapping for "ant in action."

Let's look at a simple custom Collector, next.

6.2.3 *AllDocCollector*

Sometimes you'd like to simply record every single matching document for a search, and you know the number of matches won't be very large. Listing 6.6 shows a simple class, AllDocCollector, to do just that.

Listing 6.6 A collector that gathers all matching documents and scores into a `List`

```
public class AllDocCollector extends Collector {
    List<ScoreDoc> docs = new ArrayList<ScoreDoc>();
    private Scorer scorer;
    private int docBase;

    public boolean acceptsDocsOutOfOrder() {
        return true;
    }

    public void setScorer(Scorer scorer) {
        this.scorer = scorer;
    }

    public void setNextReader(IndexReader reader, int docBase) {
        this.docBase = docBase;
    }
```

```
public void collect(int doc) throws IOException {
  docs.add(
    new ScoreDoc(doc+docBase,              ◁── Create absolute docID
                 scorer.score())));        ◁── Record score
}
public void reset() {
  docs.clear();
}
public List<ScoreDoc> getHits() {
  return docs;
}
}
```

You simply instantiate it, pass it to the search, and use the getHits() method to retrieve all hits. But note that the resulting docIDs might be out of sorted order because acceptsDocsOutOfOrder() returns true. Just change that to false, if this is a problem.

As you've seen, creating a custom Collector is quite simple. Lucene passes you the docIDs that match and you're free to do what you want with them. We created one collector that populates a map, discarding the documents that match, and another that gathers all matching documents. The possibilities are endless!

Next we discuss useful ways to extend QueryParser.

6.3 Extending QueryParser

In section 3.5, we introduced QueryParser and showed that it has a few settings to control its behavior, such as setting the locale for date parsing and controlling the default phrase slop. QueryParser is also extensible, allowing subclassing to override parts of the query-creation process. In this section, we demonstrate subclassing Query-Parser to disallow inefficient wildcard and fuzzy queries, custom date-range handling, and morphing phrase queries into SpanNearQuerys instead of PhraseQuerys.

6.3.1 Customizing QueryParser's behavior

Although QueryParser has some quirks, such as the interactions with an analyzer, it does have extensibility points that allow for customization. Table 6.2 details the methods designed for overriding and why you may want to do so.

All of the methods listed return a Query, making it possible to construct something other than the current subclass type used by the original implementations of these methods. Also, each of these methods may throw a ParseException, allowing for error handling.

QueryParser also has extensibility points for instantiating each query type. These differ from the points listed in table 6.2 in that they create the requested query type and return it. Overriding them is useful if you only want to change which Query class is used for each type of query without altering the logic of what query is constructed. These methods are newBooleanQuery, newTermQuery, newPhraseQuery,

Table 6.2 QueryParser's extensibility points

Method	Why override?
getFieldQuery(String field, Analyzer analyzer, String queryText) or getFieldQuery(String field, Analyzer analyzer, String queryText, int slop)	These methods are responsible for the construction of either a `TermQuery` or a `PhraseQuery`. If special analysis is needed, or a unique type of query is desired, override this method. For example, a `SpanNearQuery` can replace `PhraseQuery` to force ordered phrase matches.
getFuzzyQuery(String field, String termStr, float minSimilarity)	Fuzzy queries can adversely affect performance. Override and throw a ParseException to disallow fuzzy queries.
getPrefixQuery(String field, String termStr)	This method is used to construct a query when the term ends with an asterisk. The term string handed to this method doesn't include the trailing asterisk and isn't analyzed. Override this method to perform any desired analysis.
getRangeQuery(String field, String start, String end, boolean inclusive)	Default range-query behavior has several noted quirks (see section 3.5.3). Overriding could lowercase the start and end terms, use a different date format, or handle number ranges by converting to a `NumericRangeQuery` (see section 6.3.3).
getBooleanQuery(List clauses) or getBooleanQuery(List clauses, boolean disableCoord)	Constructs a `BooleanQuery` given the clauses.
getWildcardQuery(String field, String termStr)	Wildcard queries can adversely affect performance, so overridden methods could throw a `ParseException` to disallow them. Alternatively, because the term string isn't analyzed, special handling may be desired.

newMultiPhraseQuery, newPrefixQuery, newFuzzyQuery, newRangeQuery, newMatch-AllDocsQuery and newWildcardQuery. For example, if whenever a TermQuery is created by QueryParser you'd like to instantiate your own subclass of TermQuery, simply override newTermQuery.

6.3.2 Prohibiting fuzzy and wildcard queries

The subclass in listing 6.7 demonstrates a custom query parser subclass that disables fuzzy and wildcard queries by taking advantage of the ParseException option.

Listing 6.7   Disallowing wildcard and fuzzy queries

```
public class CustomQueryParser extends QueryParser {
  public CustomQueryParser(Version matchVersion,
                           String field, Analyzer analyzer) {
    super(matchVersion, field, analyzer);
  }

  protected final Query getWildcardQuery(String field, String termStr)
      throws ParseException {
    throw new ParseException("Wildcard not allowed");
  }

  protected Query getFuzzyQuery(String field, String term,
                                float minSimilarity)
      throws ParseException {
    throw new ParseException("Fuzzy queries not allowed");
  }
}
```

To use this custom parser and prevent users from executing wildcard and fuzzy queries, construct an instance of CustomQueryParser and use it exactly as you would QueryParser, as shown in listing 6.8.

Listing 6.8   Using a custom `QueryParser`

```
public void testCustomQueryParser() {
  CustomQueryParser parser =
    new CustomQueryParser(Version.LUCENE_30,
                          "field", analyzer);
  try {
    parser.parse("a?t");
    fail("Wildcard queries should not be allowed");
  } catch (ParseException expected) {          ◁──┐
  }
                                                  │  Expected
  try {                                           │
    parser.parse("xunit~");                       │
    fail("Fuzzy queries should not be allowed");  │
  } catch (ParseException expected) {          ◁──┘
  }
}
```

With this implementation, both of these expensive query types are forbidden, giving you peace of mind in terms of performance and errors that may arise from these queries expanding into too many terms. Our next QueryParser extension enables creation of NumericRangeQuery.

6.3.3   *Handling numeric field-range queries*

As you learned in chapter 2, Lucene can handily index numeric and date values. Unfortunately, QueryParser is unable to produce the corresponding NumericRangeQuery instances at search time. Fortunately, it's simple to subclass QueryParser to do so, as shown in listing 6.9.

Listing 6.9 Extending `QueryParser` to properly handle numeric fields

```
class NumericRangeQueryParser extends QueryParser {
  public NumericRangeQueryParser(Version matchVersion,
                                 String field, Analyzer a) {
    super(matchVersion, field, a);
  }
  public Query getRangeQuery(String field,
                             String part1,
                             String part2,
                             boolean inclusive)
      throws ParseException {
    TermRangeQuery query = (TermRangeQuery)          Get super()'s default
      super.getRangeQuery(field, part1, part2,       TermRangeQuery
                          inclusive);
    if ("price".equals(field)) {
      return NumericRangeQuery.newDoubleRange(
                   "price",
                   Double.parseDouble(
                       query.getLowerTerm()),         Create matching
                   Double.parseDouble(                NumericRangeQuery
                       query.getUpperTerm()),
                   query.includesLower(),
                   query.includesUpper());
    } else {
      return query;          ◁─┐  Return default
    }                           │  TermRangeQuery
  }
}
```

Using this approach, you rely on QueryParser to first create the TermRangeQuery, and from that you construct the NumericRangeQuery as needed. Testing our NumericQuery-Parser, like this:

```
public void testNumericRangeQuery() throws Exception {
  String expression = "price:[10 TO 20]";

  QueryParser parser = new NumericRangeQueryParser(Version.LUCENE_30,
                                      "subject", analyzer);

  Query query = parser.parse(expression);
  System.out.println(expression + " parsed to " + query);
}
```

yields the expected output (note that the 10 and 20 have been turned into floating point values):

```
price:[10 TO 20] parsed to price:[10.0 TO 20.0]
```

As you've seen, extending QueryParser to handle numeric fields was straightforward. Let's do the same for date fields next.

6.3.4 *Handling date ranges*

QueryParser has built-in logic to detect date ranges: if the terms are valid dates, according to DateFormat.SHORT and lenient parsing within the default or specified locale, the dates are converted to their internal textual representation. By default, this conversion will use the older DateField.dateToString method, which renders each date with millisecond precision; this is likely not what you want. If you invoke Query-Parser's setDateResolution methods to state which DateTools.Resolution your field(s) were indexed with, then QueryParser will use the newer DateTools.dateTo-String method to translate the dates into strings with the appropriate resolution. If either term fails to parse as a valid date, they're both used as is for a textual range.

But despite these two built-in approaches for handling dates, QueryParsers's date handling hasn't been updated to handle date fields indexed as NumericField, which is the recommended approach for dates, as described in section 2.6.2. Let's see how we can once again override newRangeQuery, this time to translate our date-based range searches into the corresponding NumericRangeQuery, shown in listing 6.10.

Listing 6.10   Extending QueryParser to handle date fields

```
class NumericDateRangeQueryParser extends QueryParser {
  public NumericDateRangeQueryParser(Version matchVersion,
                                     String field, Analyzer a) {
    super(matchVersion, field, a);
  }
  public Query getRangeQuery(String field,
                             String part1,
                             String part2,
                             boolean inclusive)
    throws ParseException {
    TermRangeQuery query = (TermRangeQuery)
      super.getRangeQuery(field, part1, part2, inclusive);

    if ("pubmonth".equals(field)) {
      return NumericRangeQuery.newIntRange(
                "pubmonth",
                Integer.parseInt(query.getLowerTerm()),
                Integer.parseInt(query.getUpperTerm()),
                query.includesLower(),
                query.includesUpper());
    } else {
      return query;
    }
  }
}
```

In this case it's still helpful to use QueryParser's built-in logic for detecting and parsing dates. You simply build on that logic in your subclass by taking the further step to convert the query into a NumericRangeQuery. Note that in order to use this subclass you must call QueryParser.setDateResolution, so that the resulting text terms are created with DateTools, as shown in listing 6.11.

Listing 6.11 Testing date range parsing

```
public void testDateRangeQuery() throws Exception {
  String expression = "pubmonth:[01/01/2010 TO 06/01/2010]";

  QueryParser parser = new NumericDateRangeQueryParser(Version.LUCENE_30,
                                           "subject", analyzer);

  parser.setDateResolution("pubmonth", DateTools.Resolution.MONTH);
  parser.setLocale(Locale.US);                          ◁─── Tell QueryParser
                                                             date resolution
  Query query = parser.parse(expression);
  System.out.println(expression + " parsed to " + query);

  TopDocs matches = searcher.search(query, 10);
  assertTrue("expecting at least one result !", matches.totalHits > 0);
}
```

This test produces the following output:

```
pubmonth:[05/01/1988 TO 10/01/1988] parsed to pubmonth:[198805 TO 198810]
```

As you can see, QueryParser first parsed our textual date expressions (05/01/1988) into normalized form (198805), and then our NumericDateRangeQueryParser subclass translated those normalized forms into the equivalent NumericRangeQuery.

CONTROLLING THE DATE-PARSING LOCALE

To change the locale used for date parsing, construct a QueryParser instance and call setLocale(). Typically the client's locale would be determined and used instead of the default locale. For example, in a web application the HttpServletRequest object contains the locale set by the client browser. You can use this locale to control the locale used by date parsing in QueryParser, as shown in listing 6.12.

Listing 6.12 Using the client locale in a web application

```
public class SearchServletFragment extends HttpServlet {
  protected void doGet(HttpServletRequest request,
                     HttpServletResponse response)
    throws ServletException, IOException {

  QueryParser parser = new NumericDateRangeQueryParser(
                     Version.LUCENE_30,
                     "contents",
                     new StandardAnalyzer(Version.LUCENE_30));

  parser.setLocale(request.getLocale());
  parser.setDateResolution(DateTools.Resolution.DAY);

  Query query = null;
  try {
    query = parser.parse(request.getParameter("q"));
  } catch (ParseException e) {
    e.printStackTrace(System.err);            ◁─── Handle exception
  }

  TopDocs docs = searcher.search(query, 10);    ◁─┐ Perform search and
  }                                                │ render results
}
```

QueryParser's setLocale is one way in which Lucene facilitates internationalization (often abbreviated as I18N) concerns. Text analysis is another, more important, place where such concerns are handled. Further I18N issues are discussed in section 4.8.

Our final QueryParser customization shows how to replace the default Phrase-Query with SpanNearQuery.

6.3.5 *Allowing ordered phrase queries*

When QueryParser parses a single term, or terms within double quotes, it delegates the construction of the Query to a getFieldQuery method. Parsing an unquoted term calls the getFieldQuery method without the slop signature (slop makes sense only on multiterm phrase query); parsing a quoted phrase calls the getFieldQuery signature with the slop factor, which internally delegates to the nonslop signature to build the query and then sets the slop appropriately. The Query returned is either a TermQuery or a PhraseQuery, by default, depending on whether one or more tokens are returned from the analyzer.[2] Given enough slop, PhraseQuery will match terms out of order in the original text. There's no way to force a PhraseQuery to match in order (except with slop of 0 or 1). However, SpanNearQuery does allow in-order matching. A straightforward override of getFieldQuery allows us to replace a PhraseQuery with an ordered SpanNearQuery, shown in listing 6.13.

> **Listing 6.13 Translating PhraseQuery to SpanNearQuery**

```
protected Query getFieldQuery(String field, String queryText,
                              int slop)
    throws ParseException {
  Query orig = super.getFieldQuery(field, queryText, slop);        ← ❶

  if (!(orig instanceof PhraseQuery)) {              ❷
    return orig;
  }

  PhraseQuery pq = (PhraseQuery) orig;
  Term[] terms = pq.getTerms();                                    ← ❸
  SpanTermQuery[] clauses = new SpanTermQuery[terms.length];
  for (int i = 0; i < terms.length; i++) {
    clauses[i] = new SpanTermQuery(terms[i]);
  }

  SpanNearQuery query = new SpanNearQuery(                ❹
              clauses, slop, true);

  return query;
}
```

❶ We delegate to QueryParser's implementation for analysis and determination of query type.

❷ We override PhraseQuery and return anything else right away.

---

[2] A PhraseQuery could be created from a single term if the analyzer created more than one token for it.

③ We pull all terms from the original `PhraseQuery`.

④ We create a `SpanNearQuery` with all the terms from the original `PhraseQuery`.

Our test case shows that our custom `getFieldQuery` is effective in creating a `SpanNearQuery`:

```
public void testPhraseQuery() throws Exception {
    CustomQueryParser parser =
        new CustomQueryParser(Version.LUCENE_30,
                              "field", analyzer);

    Query query = parser.parse("singleTerm");
    assertTrue("TermQuery", query instanceof TermQuery);

    query = parser.parse("\"a phrase\"");
    assertTrue("SpanNearQuery", query instanceof SpanNearQuery);
}
```

Another possible enhancement would be to add a toggle switch to the custom query parser, allowing the in-order flag to be controlled by the user of the API.

As you can see, `QueryParser` is easily extended to alter its logic in producing queries from text. We'll switch now to an important extensions point for Lucene: custom filters.

6.4 Custom filters

If all the information needed to perform filtering is in the index, there's no need to write your own filter because the `QueryWrapperFilter` can handle it, as described in section 5.6.5.

But there are good reasons to factor external information into a custom filter. In this section we tackle the following example: using our book example data and pretending we're running an online bookstore, we want users to be able to search within our special hot deals of the day.

You might be tempted to simply store the specials flag as an indexed field, but keeping this up-to-date might prove too costly. Rather than reindex entire documents when specials change, we'll implement a custom filter that keeps the specials flagged in our (hypothetical) relational database. Then we'll see how to apply our filter during searching, and finally we'll explore an alternative option for applying the filter.

6.4.1 Implementing a custom filter

We start with abstracting away the source of our specials by defining this interface:

```
public interface SpecialsAccessor {
    String[] isbns();
}
```

The `isbns()` method returns those books that are currently specials. Because we won't have an enormous amount of specials at one time, returning all the ISBNs of the books on special will suffice.

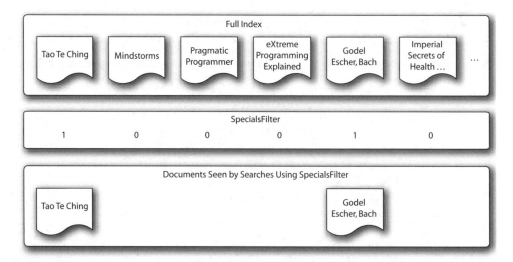

Figure 6.2 **A filter provides a bit for every document in the index. Only documents with 1 are accepted.**

Now that we have a retrieval interface, we can create our custom filter, SpecialsFilter. Filters extend from the org.apache.lucene.search.Filter class and must implement the getDocIdSet(IndexReader reader) method, returning a DocIdSet. Bit positions match the document numbers. Enabled bits mean the document for that position is available to be searched against the query, and unset bits mean the document won't be considered in the search. Figure 6.2 illustrates an example SpecialsFilter that sets bits for books on special (see listing 6.14).

Listing 6.14 Retrieving filter information from external source with SpecialsFilter

```
public class SpecialsFilter extends Filter {
  private SpecialsAccessor accessor;

  public SpecialsFilter(SpecialsAccessor accessor) {
    this.accessor = accessor;
  }

  public DocIdSet getDocIdSet(IndexReader reader) throws IOException {
    OpenBitSet bits = new OpenBitSet(reader.maxDoc());

    String[] isbns = accessor.isbns();          ◁── ❶

    int[] docs = new int[1];
    int[] freqs = new int[1];

    for (String isbn : isbns) {
      if (isbn != null) {
        TermDocs termDocs =
          reader.termDocs(new Term("isbn", isbn));   ◁── ❷
        int count = termDocs.read(docs, freqs);
        if (count == 1) {                         ❸
          bits.set(docs[0]);
        }
```

```
        }
      }

      return bits;
    }
  }
```

The filter is quite straightforward. First we fetch the ISBNs ❶ of the current specials. Next, we interact with the `IndexReader` API to iterate over all documents matching each ISBN ❷; in each case it should be a single document per ISBN because this is a unique field. The document was indexed with `Field.Index.NOT_ANALYZED`, so we can retrieve it directly with the ISBN. Finally, we record each matching document in an `OpenBitSet` ❸, which we return to Lucene. Let's test our filter during searching.

6.4.2 Using our custom filter during searching

To test that our filter is working, we created a simple `TestSpecialsAccessor` to return a specified set of ISBNs, giving our test case control over the set of specials:

```
public class TestSpecialsAccessor implements SpecialsAccessor {
  private String[] isbns;

  public TestSpecialsAccessor(String[] isbns) {
    this.isbns = isbns;
  }

  public String[] isbns() {
    return isbns;
  }
}
```

Here's how we test our `SpecialsFilter`, using the same `setUp()` that the other filter tests used:

```
public void testCustomFilter() throws Exception {
  String[] isbns = new String[] {"9780061142666", "9780394756820"};

  SpecialsAccessor accessor = new TestSpecialsAccessor(isbns);
  Filter filter = new SpecialsFilter(accessor);
  TopDocs hits = searcher.search(allBooks, filter, 10);
  assertEquals("the specials", isbns.length, hits.totalHits);
}
```

We use a generic query that is broad enough to retrieve all the books, making assertions easier to craft. But because our filter trimmed the search space, only the specials are returned. With this infrastructure in place, implementing a `SpecialsAccessor` to retrieve a list of ISBNs from a database should be easy; doing so is left as an exercise for the savvy reader.

Note that we made an important implementation decision *not* to cache the `DocIdSet` in `SpecialsFilter`. Decorating `SpecialsFilter` with a `CachingWrapperFilter` frees us from that aspect. Let's see an alternative means of applying a filter during searching.

6.4.3 An alternative: FilteredQuery

To add to the filter terminology overload, one final option is FilteredQuery.[3] FilteredQuery inverts the situation that searching with a filter presents. Using a filter, an IndexSearcher's search method applies a single filter during querying. Using the FilteredQuery, though, you can turn any filter into a query, which opens up neat possibilities, such as adding a filter as a clause to a BooleanQuery.

Let's take the SpecialsFilter as an example again. This time, we want a more sophisticated query: books in an education category on special, or books on Logo.[4] We couldn't accomplish this with a direct query using the techniques shown thus far, but FilteredQuery makes this possible. Had our search been only for books in the education category on special, we could've used the technique shown in the previous code snippet instead.

Our test case, in listing 6.15, demonstrates the described query using a Boolean-Query with a nested TermQuery and FilteredQuery.

Listing 6.15 Using a FilteredQuery

```
public void testFilteredQuery() throws Exception {
   String[] isbns = new String[] {"9780880105118"};      ←—①

   SpecialsAccessor accessor = new TestSpecialsAccessor(isbns);
   Filter filter = new SpecialsFilter(accessor);

   WildcardQuery educationBooks =
       new WildcardQuery(new Term("category", "*education*"));      ②
   FilteredQuery edBooksOnSpecial =
       new FilteredQuery(educationBooks, filter);

   TermQuery logoBooks =
       new TermQuery(new Term("subject", "logo"));      ③

   BooleanQuery logoOrEdBooks = new BooleanQuery();      ④
   logoOrEdBooks.add(logoBooks, BooleanClause.Occur.SHOULD);
   logoOrEdBooks.add(edBooksOnSpecial, BooleanClause.Occur.SHOULD);

   TopDocs hits = searcher.search(logoOrEdBooks, 10);
   System.out.println(logoOrEdBooks.toString());
   assertEquals("Papert and Steiner", 2, hits.totalHits);
}
```

① This is the ISBN number for Rudolf Steiner's *A Modern Art of Education.*

② We construct a query for education books on special, which only includes Steiner's book in this example.

③ We construct a query for all books with *logo* in the subject, which only includes *Mindstorms* in our sample data.

④ The two queries are combined in an OR fashion.

---

[3] We're sorry! We know that Filter, QueryWrapperFilter, FilteredQuery, and the completely unrelated TokenFilter names can be confusing.

[4] Erik began his programming adventures with Logo on an Apple IIe.

The getDocIdSet() method of the nested Filter is called each time a Filtered-Query is used in a search, so we recommend that you use a caching filter if the query is to be used repeatedly and the results of a filter don't change.

Filtering is a powerful means of overriding which documents a query may match, and in this section you've seen how to create custom filters and use them during searching, as well as how to wrap a filter as a query so that it may be used wherever a query may be used. Filters give you a lot of flexibility for advanced searching.

6.5   *Payloads*

Payloads, an advanced feature in Lucene, enable an application to store an arbitrary byte array for every occurrence of a term during indexing. This byte array is entirely opaque to Lucene: it's simply stored at each term position, during indexing, and then can be retrieved during searching. Otherwise the core Lucene functionality doesn't do anything with the payload or make any assumptions about its contents. This means you can store arbitrary encoded data that's important to your application, and then use it during searching, either to decide which documents are included in the search results or to alter how matched documents are scored or sorted.

All sorts of uses cases are enabled with payloads. One example, which we delve into in this section, is boosting the same term differently depending on where it occurred in the document. Another example is storing part-of-speech information for each term in the index, and altering how filtering, scoring, or sorting is done based on that. By creating a single-term field, you can store document-level metadata, such as an application-specific unique identifier. Yet another example is storing formatting information that was lost during analysis, such as whether a term was bold or italic, or what font or font size was used.

Position-specific boosting allows you to alter the score of matched documents when the specific occurrences of each term were "important." Imagine we're indexing mixed documents, where some of them are bulletins (weather warnings) and others are more ordinary documents. You'd like a search for "warning" to give extra boost when it occurs in a bulletin document. Another example is boosting terms that were bolded or italicized in the original text, or that were contained within a title or header tag for HTML documents. Although you could use field boosting to achieve this, that'd require you to separate all the important terms into entirely separate fields, which is often not feasible or desired. The payloads feature lets you solve this by boosting on a term-by-term basis within a single field.

Let's see how to boost specific term occurrences using payloads. We'll start with the steps required to add payloads to tokens during analysis. Then, we'll perform searches that take our custom payloads into account. Finally, we'll explore two other ways to interact with payloads in Lucene: first via SpanQuery and second by directly accessing Lucene's TermPositions API.

Let's begin with augmenting analysis to produce payloads.

6.5.1 *Producing payloads during analysis*

The first step is to create an analyzer that detects which tokens are important and attaches the appropriate payloads. The TokenStream for such an analyzer should define the PayloadAttribute, and then create a Payload instance when appropriate and set the payload using PayloadAttribute.setPayload inside the incrementToken method. Payloads are created with the following constructors:

```
Payload(byte[] data)
Payload(byte[] data, int offset, int length)
```

It's perfectly fine to set a null payload for some tokens. In fact, for applications where there's a common default value, it's best to represent that default value as a null payload, instead of a payload with the default value encoded into it, to save space in your index. Lucene simply records that there's no payload available at that position.

The analyzers contrib module includes several useful TokenFilters, as shown in table 6.3. These classes translate certain existing attributes of a Token, such as type and start/end offset, into a corresponding payload. The PayloadHelper class, which we'll use shortly in our use case, exposes useful functions to encode and decode numeric values to and from a byte[].

Table 6.3   TokenFilter in contrib/analyzers that encode certain TokenAttributes as payloads

Name	Purpose
NumericPayloadTokenFilter	Encodes a float payload for those tokens matching the specified token type
TypeAsPayloadTokenFilter	Encodes the token's type as a payload on every token
TokenOffsetPayloadTokenFilter	Encodes the start and end offset of each token into its payload
PayloadHelper	Static methods to encode and decode ints and floats into byte array payloads

Quite often, as is the case in our example, the logic you need to create a payload requires more customization. In our case, we want to create a payload for those term occurrences that should be boosted, containing the boost score, and set no payload for all other terms. Fortunately, it's straightforward to create your own TokenFilter to implement such logic. Listing 6.16 shows our own BulletinPayloadsAnalyzer and BulletinPayloadsFilter.

Our logic is quite simple: if the document is a bulletin, which is determined by checking whether the contents start with the prefix *Bulletin:*, we attach a payload that encodes a float boost to any occurrence of the term *warning*. We use PayloadHelper to encode the float into an equivalent byte array.

```
public class BulletinPayloadsFilter extends TokenFilter {

  private TermAttribute termAtt;
  private PayloadAttribute payloadAttr;
  private boolean isBulletin;
  private Payload boostPayload;

  BulletinPayloadsFilter(TokenStream in, float warningBoost) {
    super(in);
    payloadAttr = addAttribute(PayloadAttribute.class);
    termAtt = addAttribute(TermAttribute.class);
    boostPayload = new Payload(PayloadHelper.encodeFloat(warningBoost));
  }

  void setIsBulletin(boolean v) {
    isBulletin = v;
  }

  public final boolean incrementToken() throws IOException {
    if (input.incrementToken()) {
      if (isBulletin && termAtt.term().equals("warning")) {      Add payload
        payloadAttr.setPayload(boostPayload);                    boost
      } else {
        payloadAttr.setPayload(null);          ◁─── Clear payload
      }
      return true;
    } else {
      return false;
    }
  }
}
```

Using this analyzer, we can get our payloads into the index. But how do we use the payloads during searching to boost scores for certain matches?

6.5.2 *Using payloads during searching*

Fortunately, Lucene provides a built-in query `PayloadTermQuery`, in the package `org.apache.lucene.search.payloads`, for precisely this purpose. This query is just like `SpanTermQuery` in that it matches all documents containing the specified term and keeps track of the actual occurrences (spans) of the matches. But then it goes further by enabling you to contribute a scoring factor based on the payloads that appear at each term's occurrence. To do this, you'll have to create your own `Similarity` class that defines the `scorePayload` method, like this:

```
public class BoostingSimilarity extends DefaultSimilarity {
  public float scorePayload(int docID, String fieldName,
                            int start, int end, byte[] payload,
                            int offset, int length) {
    if (payload != null) {
      return PayloadHelper.decodeFloat(payload, offset);
    } else {
```

```
        return 1.0F;
    }
  }
}
```

We again use `PayloadHelper`, this time to decode the byte array back into a float. For every term occurrence, `PayloadTermQuery` invokes `scorePayload` to determine its payload score. Then, it aggregates these scores across all term matches for each matching document using a `PayloadFunction` instance that you provide. Lucene 2.9 offers three functions—`MinPayloadFunction`, `AveragePayloadFunction`, and `Max-PayloadFunction`—but you can easily create your own subclass if necessary. Finally, by default the aggregated payload score is multiplied by the normal score that `SpanTerm-Query` would otherwise provide, thus "boosting" the score for that document. If you'd rather entirely replace the score for the matching document with your payload score, use this constructor:

```
PayloadTermQuery(Term term, PayloadFunction function,
                 boolean includeSpanScore)
```

If you pass `false` for `includeSpanScore`, the score for each match will be the aggregated payload score. Now that we have all the pieces, let's pull it together into a test case, as shown in listing 6.17.

Listing 6.17 Using payloads to boost certain term occurrences

```
public class PayloadsTest extends TestCase {

  Directory dir;
  IndexWriter writer;
  BulletinPayloadsAnalyzer analyzer;

  protected void setUp() throws Exception {
    super.setUp();
    dir = new RAMDirectory();
    analyzer = new BulletinPayloadsAnalyzer(5.0F);       ◁─── Boost by 5.0
    writer = new IndexWriter(dir, analyzer,
                             IndexWriter.MaxFieldLength.UNLIMITED);
  }

  protected void tearDown() throws Exception {
    super.tearDown();
    writer.close();
  }

  void addDoc(String title, String contents) throws IOException {
    Document doc = new Document();
    doc.add(new Field("title",
                      title,
                      Field.Store.YES,
                      Field.Index.NO));
    doc.add(new Field("contents",
                      contents,
                      Field.Store.NO,
                      Field.Index.ANALYZED));
```

```
    analyzer.setIsBulletin(contents.startsWith("Bulletin:"));
    writer.addDocument(doc);
  }

  public void testPayloadTermQuery() throws Throwable {
    addDoc("Hurricane warning",
           "Bulletin: A hurricane warning was issued " +
           "at 6 AM for the outer great banks");
    addDoc("Warning label maker",
           "The warning label maker is a delightful toy for " +
           "your precocious seven year old's warning needs");
    addDoc("Tornado warning",
           "Bulletin: There is a tornado warning for " +
           "Worcester county until 6 PM today");

    IndexReader r = writer.getReader();
    writer.close();

    IndexSearcher searcher = new IndexSearcher(r);

    searcher.setSimilarity(new BoostingSimilarity());

    Term warning = new Term("contents", "warning");

    Query query1 = new TermQuery(warning);
    System.out.println("\nTermQuery results:");
    TopDocs hits = searcher.search(query1, 10);
    TestUtil.dumpHits(searcher, hits);                    Ranks first

    assertEquals("Warning label maker",
                 searcher.doc(hits.scoreDocs[0].doc).get("title"));

    Query query2 = new PayloadTermQuery(warning,
                                        new AveragePayloadFunction());
    System.out.println("\nPayloadTermQuery results:");
    hits = searcher.search(query2, 10);
    TestUtil.dumpHits(searcher, hits);              Ranks last after boosts

    assertEquals("Warning label maker",
                 searcher.doc(hits.scoreDocs[2].doc).get("title"));
    r.close();
    searcher.close();
  }
}
```

We index three documents, two of which are bulletins. Next, we do two searches, printing the results. The first search is a normal `TermQuery`, which should return the second document as the top result, because it contains two occurrences of the term *warning*. The second query is a `PayloadTermQuery` that boosts the occurrence of *warning* in each bulletin by 5.0 boost (passed as the single argument to `BulletinPayloadsAnalyzer`). Running this test produces this output:

```
TermQuery results:
0.2518424:Warning label maker
0.22259936:Hurricane warning
0.22259936:Tornado warning

BoostingTermQuery results:
```

```
0.7870075:Hurricane warning
0.7870075:Tornado warning
0.17807949:Warning label maker
```

Indeed, `PayloadTermQuery` caused the two bulletins (Hurricane warning and Tornado warning) to get much higher scores, bringing them to the top of the results!

Note that the payloads package also includes `PayloadNearQuery`, which is just like `SpanNearQuery` except it invokes `Similarity.scorePayload` just like `PayloadTermQuery`. In fact, all of the `SpanQuery` classes have access to payloads, which we describe next.

6.5.3 *Payloads and SpanQuery*

Although using `PayloadTermQuery` and `PayloadNearQuery` is the simplest way to use payloads to alter scoring of documents, all of the `SpanQuery` classes allow expert access to the payloads that occur within each matching span returned by the `getSpans` method. At this point, none of the `SpanQuery` classes, besides `SpanTermQuery` and `SpanNearQuery`, have subclasses that make use of the payloads. It's up to you to subclass a `SpanQuery` class and override the `getSpans` method if you'd like to filter documents that match based on payload, or override the `SpanScorer` class to provide custom scoring based on the payloads contained within each matched span. These are advanced use cases, and only a few users have ventured into this territory, so your best bet for inspiration is to spend some quality time on Lucene's users list.

The final exposure of payloads in Lucene's APIs is `TermPositions`.

6.5.4 *Retrieving payloads via TermPositions*

The final Lucene API that has been extended with payloads is the `TermPositions` iterator. This is an advanced internal API that allows you to step through the documents containing a specific term, retrieving each document that matched along with all positions, as well as their payload, of that term's occurrences in the document. `TermPositions` has these added methods:

```
boolean isPayloadAvailable()
int getPayloadLength()
byte[] getPayload(byte[] data, int offset)
```

Note that once you've called `getPayload()` you can't call it again until you've advanced to the next position by calling `nextPosition()`. Each payload can be retrieved only once.

Payloads are still under active development and exploration, in order to provide more core support to make use of payloads for either result filtering or custom scoring. Until the core support is fully fleshed out, you'll need to use the extension points described here to take advantage of this powerful feature. And stay tuned on the user's list!

6.6 *Summary*

Lucene offers developers extreme flexibility in searching capabilities, so much so that this is our third (and final!) chapter covering search. Custom sorting is useful when the built-in sorting by relevance or field values isn't sufficient. Custom `Collector` implementations let you efficiently do what you want with each matched document as it's found, while custom `Filters` allow you to pull in any external information to construct a filter.

In this chapter, you saw that by extending `QueryParser`, you can refine how it constructs queries, in order to prevent certain kinds of queries or alter how each `Query` is constructed. We also showed you how the advanced payloads functionality can be used for refined control over which terms in a document are more important than others, based on their positions.

Equipped with the searching features from this chapter and chapters 3 and 5, you have more than enough power and flexibility to integrate Lucene searching into your applications. Our next chapter explains how to extract text from diverse document formats using the Apache Tika project.

Part 2

Applied Lucene

Lucene itself is just a JAR, with the real fun and power coming from what you build around it. Part 2 explores ways to leverage Lucene. Projects commonly demand full-text searching of Microsoft Office, PDF, HTML, XML, and other document formats. "Extracting text with Tika" (chapter 7) illuminates ways to index these document types into Lucene. So many extensions have been developed to augment and extend Lucene that we dedicate two chapters, "Essential Lucene Extensions" (chapter 8) and "Further Lucene extensions" (chapter 9) to them. Although Java is the primary language used with Lucene, the index format is language neutral. "Using Lucene from other programming languages," (chapter 10) explores Lucene usage from languages such as C++, C#, Python, Perl, and Ruby. "Lucene administration and performance tuning" (chapter 11 and the final chapter in part 2) dives into the nitty-gritty details for managing Lucene's consumption of resources like memory, disk space, and file descriptors. You'll also learn how to improve indexing and searching performance metrics.

Extracting text with Tika

One of the more mundane yet vital steps when building a search application is extracting text from the documents you need to index. You might be lucky to have an application whose content is already in textual format or whose documents are always the same format, such as XML files or regular rows in a database. If you're unlucky, you must instead accept the surprisingly wide plethora of document formats that are popular today, such as Outlook, Word, Excel, PowerPoint, Visio, Flash, PDF, Open Office, Rich Text Format (RTF), and even archive file formats like TAR, ZIP, and BZIP2. Seemingly textual formats, like XML or HTML, present challenges because you must take care not to accidentally include any tags or JavaScript sources. The plain text format might seem simplest of all, yet determining its character set may not be easy.

In the past it was necessary to "go it alone": track down your own document filters, one by one, and interact with their unique and interesting APIs in order to extract the text you need. You'd also need to detect the document type and character encoding yourself. Fortunately, there's now an open source framework called Tika, under the Apache Lucene top-level project, that handles most of this work for you.

Tika has a simple-to-use API for providing a document source and then retrieving the text filtered from it. In this chapter we'll start with an overview of Tika, then delve into its logical design, API, and tools. After showing you how to install Tika, we'll discuss useful tools that let you filter a document without writing any Java code. Next we'll explore a class that extracts text programmatically and produces a corresponding Lucene document. After that, we'll examine two approaches for extracting fields from XML content, and then we'll wrap up by considering some of Tika's limitations and visiting a few alternative document filtering options.

7.1   *What is Tika?*

Tika was added to the Lucene umbrella in October 2008, after graduating from the Apache incubator, which is the process newly created projects go through to become an Apache project. The most recent release as of this writing is 0.6. Development continues at a rapid pace, and it's expected there will be non-backward-compatible changes in the march to the 1.0 release, so be sure to check Tika's website at http://lucene.apache.org/tika for the latest documentation.

Tika is a framework that hosts plug-in parsers for each supported document type. The framework presents the same standard API to the application for extracting text and metadata from a document, and under the hood the plug-in parser interacts with the external library using the custom API exposed by that library. This lets your application use the same uniform API regardless of document type. When you need to extract text from a document, Tika finds the right parser for the document (details on this shortly).

As a framework, Tika doesn't do any of the document filtering itself. Rather, it relies on external open source projects and libraries to do the heavy lifting. Table 7.1 lists the formats supported as of the 0.6 release, along with which project or library the document parser is based on. There's support for many common document formats and new formats are added frequently, so check online for the latest list.

In addition to extracting the body text for a document, Tika extracts metadata values for most document types. Tika represents metadata as a single String <-> String map, with constants exposed for the common metadata keys, listed in table 7.2. These constants are defined in the Metadata class in the org.apache.tika.metadata package. But not all parsers can extract metadata, and when they do, they may extract to different metadata keys than you expect. In general the area of metadata extraction is still in flux in Tika, so it's best to test parsing some samples of your documents to understand what metadata is exposed.

Let's drill down to learn how Tika models a document's logical structure and what concrete API is used to expose this.

Table 7.1 Supported document formats and the library used to parse them

Format	Library
Microsoft's OLE2 Compound Document Format (Excel, Word, PowerPoint, Visio, Outlook)	Apache POI
Microsoft Office 2007 OOXML	Apache POI
Adobe Portable Document Format (PDF)	PDFBox
Rich Text Format (RTF)—currently body text only (no metadata)	Java Swing API (`RTFEditorKit`)
Plain text character set detection	ICU4J library
HTML	CyberNeko library
XML	Java's `javax.xml` classes
ZIP Archives	Java's built-in zip classes, Apache Commons Compress
TAR Archives	Apache Ant, Apache Commons Compress
AR Archives	Apache Commons Compress
CPIO Archives	Apache Commons Compress
GZIP compression	Java's built-in support (`GZIPInputStream`) , Apache Commons Compress
BZIP2 compression	Apache Ant, Apache Commons Compress
Image formats (metadata only)	Java's `javax.imageio` classes
Java class files	ASM library (JCR-1522)
Java JAR files	Java's built-in zip classes and ASM library, Apache Commons Compress
MP3 audio (ID3v1 tags)	Implemented directly
Other audio formats (wav, aiff, au)	Java's built-in support (`javax.sound.*`)
OpenDocument	Parses XML directly
Adobe Flash	Parses metadata from FLV files directly
MIDI files (embedded text, eg song lyrics)	Java's built-in support (`javax.audio.midi.*`)
WAVE Audio (sampling metadata)	Java's built-in support (`javax.audio.sampled.*`)

Table 7.2 Metadata keys that Tika extracts

Metadata Constant	Description
RESOURCE_KEY_NAME	The name of the file or resource that contains the document. A client application can set this property to allow the parser to use filename heuristics to determine the format of the document. The parser implementation may set this property if the file format contains the canonical name of the file (for example, the GZIP format has a slot for the filename).
CONTENT_TYPE	The declared content type of the document. A client application can set this property based on an HTTP Content-Type header, for example. The declared content type may help the parser to correctly interpret the document. The parser implementation sets this property to the content type according to which document was parsed.
CONTENT_ENCODING	The declared content encoding of the document. A client application can set this property based on an HTTP Content-Type header, for example. The declared content type may help the parser to correctly interpret the document. The parser implementation sets this property to the content type according to which document was parsed.
TITLE	The title of the document. The parser implementation sets this property if the document format contains an explicit title field.
AUTHOR	The name of the author of the document. The parser implementation sets this property if the document format contains an explicit author field.
MSOffice.*	Defines additional metadata from Microsoft Office: APPLICATION_NAME, CHARACTER_COUNT, COMMENTS, KEYWORDS, LAST_AUTHOR, LAST_PRINTED, LAST_SAVED, PAGE_COUNT, REVISION_NUMBER, TEMPLATE, WORD_COUNT.

7.2 *Tika's logical design and API*

Tika uses the Extensible Hypertext Markup Language (XHTML) standard to model all documents, regardless of their original format. XHTML is a markup language that combines the best of XML and HTML: because an XHTML document is valid XML, it can be programmatically processed using standard XML tools. Further, because XHTML is mostly compatible with HTML 4 browsers, it can typically be rendered with a modern web browser. With XHTML, a document is cast to this logical top-level structure:

```
<html xmlns="http://www.w3.org/1999/xhtml">
  <head>
    <title>...</title>
  </head>
  <body>
    ...
  </body>
</html>
```

Within the <body>...</body> are other tags (such as <p>, <h1>, and <div>) representing internal document structure.

This is the logical structure of an XHTML document, but how does Tika deliver that to your application? The answer is SAX (Simple API for XML), another well-established standard used by XML parsers. With SAX, as an XML document is parsed, the parser invokes methods on an instance implementing the org.xml.sax.ContentHandler. This is a scalable approach for parsing XML documents because it enables the application to choose what should be done with each element as it's encountered. Arbitrarily large documents can be processed with minimal consumption of RAM.

The primary interface to Tika is the surprisingly simple parse method (in the org.apache.tika.parser.Parser class):

```
void parse(InputStream stream
        ContentHandler handler,
        Metadata metadata,
        ParseContext context)
```

Tika reads the bytes for the document from the InputStream but won't close it. We recommend you close the stream using a try/finally clause.

The document parser then decodes the bytes, translates the document into the logical XHTML structure, and invokes the SAX API via the provided ContentHandler. The third parameter, metadata, is used bidirectionally: input details, such as specified Content-Type (from an HTTP server) or filename (if known), are set before invoking parse, and then any metadata encountered while Tika is processing the document will be recorded and returned. The last parameter is used to pass in arbitrary programmatic configuration for parsers that require it.

You can see that Tika is simply a conduit: it doesn't do anything with the document text it encounters except invoke the ContentHandler. It's then up to your application to provide a ContentHandler that does something of interest with the resulting elements and text. But Tika includes helpful utility classes that implement ContentHandler for common cases. For example, BodyContentHandler gathers all text within the <body>...</body> part of the document and forwards it to another handler, OutputStream, Writer, or an internal string buffer for later retrieval.

If you know for certain which document type you're dealing with, you can directly create the right parser (for example, PDFParser, OfficeParser, or HtmlParser) and then invoke its parse method. If you're unsure of the document's type, Tika provides an AutoDetectParser, which is a Parser implementation that uses various heuristics to determine the document's type and apply the correct parser.

Tika tries to autodetect things like document format and the encoding of the character set (for text/plain documents). Still if you have preexisting information about your documents, such as the original filename (containing a possibly helpful extension) or the character encoding, it's best if you provide this information via the metadata input so Tika may use this. The filename should be added under Metadata.RESOURCE_NAME_KEY; content type should be added under Metadata.CONTENT_TYPE, and the content encoding should be added under Metadata.CONTENT_ENCODING.

It's time to get our feet wet! Let's walk through the installation process for Tika.

7.3   Installing Tika

You'll first need a build of Tika. The source code with this book includes the 0.6 release of Tika, in the lib directory, but likely you're staring at a newer release. The binary builds for Tika are included in the Maven 2 repository, which you may either download directly or reference in your application if you're already using Maven 2.

Building Tika from sources is also easy, although you should check "Getting Started" on the Tika website for any changes since this was written. Download the source release (for example, apache-tika-0.6-src.tar.gz for version 0.6) and extract it. Tika uses Apache's Maven 2 build system and requires Java 5 or higher, so you'll need to first install those dependencies. Then run `mvn install` from within the Tika source directory you unpacked. That command will download a bunch of dependencies into your Maven area, compile Tika's sources, run tests, and produce the resulting JARs. If all goes well, you'll see `BUILD SUCCESSFUL` printed at the end. If you encounter `OutOfMemoryError`, you can increase the heap size of the JVMs that maven spawns by setting the environment variable `MAVEN_OPTS` (for example, type `export MAVEN_OPTS="-Xmx2g"` for the bash shell).

Tika has a modular design, consisting of these components:

- tika-core contains the key interfaces and core functionality.
- tika-parsers contains all the adapters to external parser libraries.
- tika-app bundles everything together in a single executable JAR.

The sources for each of these components live in subdirectories by the same name. Once your build completes, you'll find a *target* subdirectory (under each of the component directories) containing the built JAR, such as tika-app-0.6.jar.

It's most convenient to use the tika-app-0.6.jar, because it has all dependencies, including the classes for all external parsers that Tika uses, contained within it. If for some reason that's not possible or you'd like to pick which external JARs your application requires, you can use Maven to gather all dependency JARs into the target/ dependency directory under each component directory.

NOTE   You can gather all required dependency JARs by running `mvn dependency:copy-dependencies`. This command will copy the required JARs out of your Maven area and into the target/dependency directory under each component directory. This command is useful if you intend to use Tika outside of Maven 2.

Now that we've built Tika, it's time to finally extract some text. We'll start with Tika's built-in text extraction tool.

7.4   Tika's built-in text extraction tool

Tika comes with a simple built-in tool allowing you to extract text from documents in the local file system or via URL. This tool creates an `AutoDetectParser` instance to filter the document, and then provides a few options for interacting with the results.

The tool can run either with a dedicated GUI or in a command line–only mode, allowing you to further process its output, using pipes, using other command-line tools. To run the tool with a GUI:

```
java -jar lib/tika-app-0.6.jar --gui
```

This command brings up a simple GUI window, in which you can drag and drop files in order to test how the filters work with them. Figure 7.1 shows the window after dragging the Microsoft Word document for chapter 2 of this book onto the window. The window has multiple tabs showing different text extracted during filtering:

- The Formatted Text tab shows the XHTML, rendered with Java's built-in `javax.swing.JEditorPane` as `text/html` content.
- The Plain Text tab shows only the text and whitespace parts, extracted from the XHTMLdocument.
- The Structured Text tab shows the raw XHTMLsource.
- The Metadata tab contains all metadata fields extracted from the document.
- The Errors tab describes any errors encountered while parsing the document.

Although the GUI tool is a great way to quickly test Tika on a document, it's often more useful to use the command line–only invocation:

```
cat Document.pdf | java -jar lib/tika-app-0.6.jar -
```

This command prints the full XHTML output from the parser (the extra - at the end of the command tells the tool to read the document from the standard input; you could also provide the filename directly instead of piping its contents into the command). This tool accepts various command-line options to change its behavior:

- `--help` or `-?` prints the full usage.
- `--verbose` or `-v` prints debug messages.

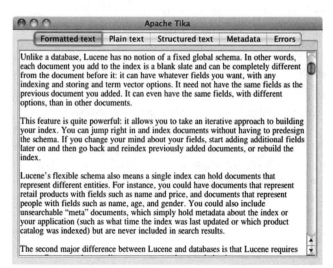

Figure 7.1 You can drag and drop any binary document onto Tika's built-in text extraction tool GUI in order to see what text and metadata Tika extracts.

- `--gui` or `-g` runs the GUI.

- `--encoding=X` or `-eX` specifies the output encoding to use.

- `--xml` or `-x` outputs the XHTML content (this is the default behavior). This corresponds to the Structured Text tab from the GUI.

- `--html` or `-h` outputs the HTML content, which is a simplified version of the XHTML content. This corresponds to the Formatted text (rendered as HTML) from the GUI.

- `--text` or `-t` outputs the plain-text content. This corresponds to the Plain Text tab from the GUI.

- `--metadata` or `-m` outputs only the metadata keys and values. This corresponds to the Metadata tab from the GUI.

You could use Tika's command-line tool as the basis of your text extraction solution. It's simple to use and fast to deploy. But if you need more control over which parts of the text are used, or which metadata fields to keep, you'll need to use Tika's programmatic API, which we cover next.

7.5   *Extracting text programmatically*

We've seen the signature for Tika's simple `parse` API, which is the core of any text extraction based on Tika. But what about the rest of the text extraction process? How can you build a Lucene document from a SAX `ContentHandler`? That's what we'll do now. We'll also see a useful utility class, aptly named `Tika`, that provides some methods that are particularly useful for integrating with Lucene. Finally, we'll show you how to customize which parser Tika chooses for each MIME type.

NOTE   Tika is advancing very quickly, so it's likely by the time you read this there is a good out-of-the-box integration of Lucene and Tika, so be sure to check at http://lucene.apache.org/tika. Solr already has a good integration: if you POST binary documents, such as PDFs or Microsoft Word documents, Solr will use Tika under-the-hood to extract and index text with flexible field mappings.

7.5.1   *Indexing a Lucene document*

Recall that the `Indexer` tool from chapter 1 has the serious limitation that it can only index plain-text files (with the extension .txt). `TikaIndexer`, shown in listing 7.1, fixes that! The basic approach is straightforward. You have a source for the document, which you open as an `InputStream`. Then you create an appropriate `ContentHandler` for your application, or use one of the utility classes provided with Tika. Finally, you build the Lucene `Document` instance from the metadata and text encountered by the `ContentHandler`.

Listing 7.1   Class to extract text from arbitrary documents and index it with Lucene

```
public class TikaIndexer extends Indexer {

  private boolean DEBUG = false;              <--1

  static Set<String> textualMetadataFields
        = new HashSet<String>();
  static {
    textualMetadataFields.add(Metadata.TITLE);
    textualMetadataFields.add(Metadata.AUTHOR);
    textualMetadataFields.add(Metadata.COMMENTS);             2
    textualMetadataFields.add(Metadata.KEYWORDS);
    textualMetadataFields.add(Metadata.DESCRIPTION);
    textualMetadataFields.add(Metadata.SUBJECT);
  }

  public static void main(String[] args) throws Exception {
    if (args.length != 2) {
      throw new IllegalArgumentException("Usage: java " +
        TikaIndexer.class.getName() +
        " <index dir> <data dir>");
    }

    TikaConfig config = TikaConfig.getDefaultConfig();
    List<String> parsers = new ArrayList<String>(config.getParsers()
                                  .keySet());
    Collections.sort(parsers);
    Iterator<String> it = parsers.iterator();               3
    System.out.println("Mime type parsers:");
    while(it.hasNext()) {
      System.out.println("  " + it.next());
    }
    System.out.println();

    String indexDir = args[0];
    String dataDir = args[1];

    long start = new Date().getTime();
    TikaIndexer indexer = new TikaIndexer(indexDir);
    int numIndexed = indexer.index(dataDir, null);
    indexer.close();
    long end = new Date().getTime();

    System.out.println("Indexing " + numIndexed + " files took "
      + (end - start) + " milliseconds");
  }

  public TikaIndexer(String indexDir) throws IOException {
    super(indexDir);
  }

  protected Document getDocument(File f) throws Exception {

    Metadata metadata = new Metadata();
    metadata.set(Metadata.RESOURCE_NAME_KEY, f.getName());    <--4

    InputStream is = new FileInputStream(f);      <--5
    Parser parser = new AutoDetectParser();         <--6
```

```
      ContentHandler handler = new BodyContentHandler();        ←──7
      ParseContext context = new ParseContext();                      8
      context.set(Parser.class, parser);

      try {
        parser.parse(is, handler, metadata,
                     new ParseContext());                             9
      } finally {
        is.close();
      }

      Document doc = new Document();

      doc.add(new Field("contents", handler.toString(),              10
                        Field.Store.NO, Field.Index.ANALYZED));

      if (DEBUG) {
        System.out.println("  all text: " + handler.toString());
      }

      for(String name : metadata.names()) {         ←──11
        String value = metadata.get(name);

        if (textualMetadataFields.contains(name)) {
          doc.add(new Field("contents", value,                     ←──12
                            Field.Store.NO, Field.Index.ANALYZED));
        }

        doc.add(new Field(name, value,                             13
                          Field.Store.YES, Field.Index.NO));

        if (DEBUG) {
          System.out.println("  " + name + ": " + value);
        }
      }

      if (DEBUG) {
        System.out.println();
      }

      doc.add(new Field("filename", f.getCanonicalPath(),       ←──14
              Field.Store.YES, Field.Index.NOT_ANALYZED));

      return doc;
    }
  }
```

In `TikaIndexer`, we simply subclass the original `Indexer` and override the static main and `getDocument` methods:

❶ Set debug flag to true for verbose output.

❷ ⑪ ⑫ List the metadata fields that we consider textual. After the document is parsed, we pull out any of these metadata fields that appeared in the document and include their values in the contents field on the document.

❸ Iterate through all of Tika's `Parsers` and print them, to see what document types it can currently handle.

❹ ⑬ ⑭ Create a `Metadata` instance using the `Tika.getFileMetadata()` method, which records the name of our file so Tika can use that to guess the document type. Any discovered fields in the document are returned in this same `Metadata` instance, and we store them in the document. We also separately store the file path.

5 **6** Open the file for reading, then use `AutoDetectParser` to find the appropriate parser.

7 **8** **9** **10** `BodyContentHandler` saves us from having to create our own content handler. It gathers all text in the body, which we then add to the contents field for the document. We set up the `ParseContext` and invoke the parser's `parse` method to do all the real work.

This example will work well, but you should fix a few things before using it in production:

- Catch and handle the exceptions that may be thrown by `parser.parse`. If the document is corrupted, you'll see a `TikaException`. If there was a problem reading the bytes from the `InputStream`, you'll encounter an `IOException`. You may see class loader exceptions if the required parser couldn't be located or instantiated.

- Be more selective about which metadata fields you want in your index and how you'd like to index them. Your choices are very much application dependent.

- Be more selective about which text is indexed. Right now `TikaIndexer` simply appends together all text from the document into the contents field by adding more than one instance of that field name to the document. You may instead want to handle different substructures of the document differently, and perhaps use an analyzer that sets a `positionIncrementGap` so that phrases and span queries can't match across two different contents fields.

- Add custom logic to filter out known "uninteresting" portions of text documents, such as standard headers and footer text that appear in all documents.

- If your document's text could be very large in size, consider using the `Tika.parse` utility method (described in the next section) instead.

As you can see, it's quite simple using Tika's programmatic APIs to extract text and build a Lucene document. In our example, we used the `parse` API from `AutoDetect-Parser`, but Tika also provides utility APIs that might be a useful alternate path for your application.

7.5.2 The Tika utility class

The `Tika` class, in the `org.apache.tika` package, is a utility class that exposes a number of helpful utility methods, shown in Table 7.3.

Table 7.3 Useful methods exposed by the `Tika` utility class

Method	Purpose
`String detect(…)`	Detects the media type of the provided `InputStream`, file, or URL, with optional metadata
`Reader parse(…)`	Parses the `InputStream`, file, or URL, returning a `Reader` from which you can read the text
`String parseToString(…)`	Parses the `InputStream`, file, or URL to a `String`

These methods often let you create a one-liner to extract the text from your document. One particularly helpful method for integrating with Lucene is the `Reader parse(…)` method, which parses the document but exposes a `Reader` to read the text. Lucene can index text directly from a `Reader`, making this is a simple way to index the text extracted from a document.

The returned `Reader` is an instance of `ParsingReader`, from the `org.apache.tika.parser` package, and it has a clever implementation. When created, it spawns a background thread to parse the document, using the `BodyContentHandler`. The resulting text is written to a `PipedWriter` (from `java.io`), and a corresponding `PipedReader` is returned to you. Because of this streaming implementation, the full text of the document is never materialized at once. Instead, the text is created as the `Reader` consumes it, with a small shared buffer. This means even documents that parse to an exceptionally large amount of text will use little memory during filtering.

During creation, `ParsingReader` also attempts to process all metadata for the document, so after it's created but before indexing the document you should call the `getMetadata()` method and add any important metadata to your document.

This class may be a great fit for your application. But because a thread is spawned for every document, and because `PipedWriter` and `PipedReader` are used, it's likely net indexing throughput is slower than if you simply materialize the full text yourself up front (say, with `StringBuilder`). Still, if materializing the full text up front is out of the question, because your documents may be unbounded in size, this method is a real lifesaver.

7.5.3   *Customizing parser selection*

Tika's `AutoDetectParser` first determines the MIME type of the document, through various heuristics, and then uses that MIME type to look up the appropriate parser. To do that lookup, Tika uses an instance of `TikaConfig`, which is a simple class that loads the mapping of MIME type to parser class via an XML file. The default `TikaConfig` class can be obtained with the static `getDefaultConfig` method, which in turn loads the file tika-config.xml that comes with Tika. Because this is an XML file, you can easily open it with your favorite text editor to see which MIME types Tika can presently handle. We also used `TikaConfig`'s `getParsers` method in listing 7.1 to list the MIME types.

If you'd like to change which parser is used for a given MIME type, or add your own parser to handle a certain MIME type, create your own corresponding XML file and instantiate your own `TikaConfig` from that file. Then, when creating `AutoDetectParser`, pass in your `TikaConfig` instance.

Now that we've seen all the nice things Tika can do, let's briefly touch on some known limitations.

7.6   *Tika's limitations*

As a new framework, Tika has a few known challenges that it's working through. Some of these issues are a by-product of its design and won't change with time without major changes, whereas others are solvable problems and will likely be resolved by the time you read this.

The first challenge is loss of document structure in certain situations. In general, some documents may have a far richer structure than the simple standard XHTML model used by Tika. In our example, addressbook.xml has a rich structure, containing two entries, each with rich specific fields. But Tika regularizes this down to a fixed XHTML structure, thus losing some information. Fortunately, there are other ways to create rich documents from XML, as you'll learn in the next section.

Another limitation is the astounding number of dependencies when using Tika. If you use the standalone JAR, this results in a large number of classes in that JAR. If you're not using the standalone JAR, you'll need many JAR files on your classpath. In part, this is because Tika relies on numerous external packages to do the actual parsing. But it's also because these external libraries often do far more than Tika requires. For example, PDFBox and Apache POI understand document fonts, layouts, and embedded graphics, and are able to create new documents in the binary format or modify existing documents. Tika only requires a small portion of this (the "extract text" part), yet these libraries don't typically factor that out as a standalone component. As a result, numerous excess classes and JARs end up on the classpath, which could cause problems if they conflict with other JARs in your application. To put this in perspective, Tika's 0.6 JAR weighs in at about 15MB, whereas Lucene's core JAR is about 1MB!

Another challenge is certain document parsers, such as Microsoft's OLE2 Compound Document Format, require full random access to the document's bytes, which `InputStream` doesn't expose. In such cases Tika currently copies all bytes from the stream into a temporary file, which is then opened directly for random access. A future improvement, possibly already done by the time you read this, will allow you to pass a random access stream directly to Tika (if your document is already stored and accessible via a random access file), to avoid this unnecessary copy.

Next you'll see how to extract text from XML content while preserving its full structure.

7.7   *Indexing custom XML*

XML is a useful markup language for representing document structure using your own schema or DTD. Unfortunately, Tika only supports simplistic handling of such content: it strips all tags, and extracts all text between the tags. In short, it discards all of the document's structure.

Typically this is not what you want; instead you need custom control over which tags within the XML are converted into fields of your document. To do this, you shouldn't use Tika at all, but rather build your own logic to extract the tags. In this section we'll describe two approaches for parsing XML content and creating Lucene documents. The first is to use an XML SAX parser. The second is to build a converter using the Apache Commons Digester project, which simplifies access to an XML document's structure.

As our working example throughout this section, listing 7.2 shows an XML snippet holding a single entry from an imaginary address book. It has a clear structure, recording the usual details about each contact. Notice, too, that the `<contact>` element has an attribute type. We'll extract this type, along with the text in all the elements, as separate fields in a Lucene document.

Listing 7.2   XML snippet representing an address book entry

```
<?xml version='1.0' encoding='utf-8'?>
<address-book>
    <contact type="individual">
        <name>Zane Pasolini</name>
        <address>999 W. Prince St.</address>
        <city>New York</city>
        <province>NY</province>
        <postalcode>10013</postalcode>
        <country>USA</country>
        <telephone>+1 212 345 6789</telephone>
    </contact>
</address-book>
```

7.7.1   *Parsing using SAX*

SAX defines an event-driven interface in which the parser invokes one of several methods supplied by the caller when a parsing event occurs. Events include beginnings and endings of documents and their elements, parsing errors, and so on. Listing 7.3 shows our solution for parsing the XML address book and converting it to a Lucene document.

Listing 7.3   Using the SAX API to parse an address book entry

```
public class SAXXMLDocument extends DefaultHandler {

  private StringBuilder elementBuffer = new StringBuilder();
  private Map<String,String> attributeMap = new HashMap<String,String> ();

  private Document doc;

  public Document getDocument(InputStream is)        ◁──❶ Start parser
    throws DocumentHandlerException {

    SAXParserFactory spf = SAXParserFactory.newInstance();
    try {
      SAXParser parser = spf.newSAXParser();
      parser.parse(is, this);
    } catch (Exception e) {
      throw new DocumentHandlerException(
        "Cannot parse XML document", e);
    }

    return doc;
  }
                                                    ❷ Create new
  public void startDocument() {                ◁──┘   document
    doc = new Document();
  }
```

```
  public void startElement(String uri, String localName,          ❸ Record
    String qName, Attributes atts)                                    attributes
    throws SAXException {

    elementBuffer.setLength(0);
    attributeMap.clear();
    int numAtts = atts.getLength();
    if (numAtts > 0) {
      for (int i = 0; i < numAtts; i++) {
        attributeMap.put(atts.getQName(i), atts.getValue(i));
      }
    }
  }

  public void characters(char[] text, int start, int length) {   ◁──┐ ❹ Gather
    elementBuffer.append(text, start, length);                          text
  }

  public void endElement(String uri, String localName,           ❺ Add fields
                         String qName)
    throws SAXException {
    if (qName.equals("address-book")) {
      return;
    }
    else if (qName.equals("contact")) {
      for (Entry<String,String> attribute : attributeMap.entrySet()) {
      String attName = attribute.getKey();
      String attValue = attribute.getValue();
      doc.add(new Field(attName, attValue, Field.Store.YES,
                                         Field.Index.NOT_ANALYZED));
      }
    }
    else {
      doc.add(new Field(qName, elementBuffer.toString(), Field.Store.YES,
       Field.Index.NOT_ANALYZED));
    }
  }

  public static void main(String args[]) throws Exception {
    SAXXMLDocument handler = new SAXXMLDocument();
    Document doc = handler.getDocument(
      new FileInputStream(new File(args[0])));
    System.out.println(doc);
  }
}
```

The five key methods in this listing are getDocument, startDocument, startElement, characters, and endElement. Also note the elementBuffer and the attributeMap. The former is used to store the textual representation of the CDATA enclosed by the current document element. Some elements may contain attributes, such as the <contact> element containing the attribute type, in our address book entry. The attributeMap is used for storing names and the value of the current element's attributes.

The getDocument method ❶ doesn't do much work: it creates a new SAX parser and passes it a reference to the InputStream of the XML document. From there, the parser implementation calls the other four key methods in this class, which together create a Lucene document instance that's eventually returned by the `getDocument` method.

In `startDocument` ❷, which is called when XML document parsing starts, we only create a new instance of the Lucene `Document`. This is the `Document` that we'll eventually populate with fields.

The `startElement` method ❸ is called whenever the beginning of a new XML element is found. We first erase the `elementBuffer` by setting its length to 0, and clear the `attributeMap` to remove data associated with the previous element. If the current element has attributes, we iterate through them and save their names and values in the `attributeMap`. In the case of the XML document in listing 7.2, this happens only when `startElement` method is called for the `<contact>` element, because only that element has an attribute.

The `characters` method ❹ may be called multiple times during the processing of a single XML element. In it we append to our `elementBuffer` the element contents passed into the method.

The last method of interest is `endElement` ❺, where you can finally see more of Lucene in action. This method is called when the parser processes the closing tag of the current element. Therefore, this is the method where we have all the information about the XML element that was just processed. We aren't interested in indexing the top-level element, `<address-book>`, so we immediately return from the method in that case. Similarly, we aren't interested in indexing the `<contact>` element. But we're interested in indexing that `<contact>`'s attributes, so we use `attributeMap` to get attribute names and values, and add them to the Lucene document. All other elements of our address book entry are treated equally, and we blindly index them as `Field.Index.NOT_ANALYZED`. Attribute values as well element data are indexed.

The final document returned is a ready-to-index Lucene document populated with fields whose names are derived from XML elements' names and whose values correspond to the textual content of those elements. You can run this tool by typing `ant` `SAXXMLDocument` at the command line in the root directory after unpacking the book's source code. It will produce output like this, showing you the document it created:

```
Document<stored,indexed<name:Zane Pasolini>
stored,indexed<address:999 W. Prince St.>
stored,indexed<city:New York>
stored,indexed<province:NY>
stored,indexed<postalcode:10013>
stored,indexed<country:USA>
stored,indexed<telephone:+1 212 345 6789>>
```

Although this code alone will let you index XML documents, let's look at another handy tool for parsing XML: Digester.

7.7.2 *Parsing and indexing using Apache Commons Digester*

Digester, available at http://commons.apache.org/digester/, is a subproject of the Apache Commons project. It offers a simple, high-level interface for mapping XML documents to Java objects; some developers find it easier to use than DOM or SAX XML parsers. When Digester finds developer-defined patterns in an XML document, it takes developer-specified actions.

The `DigesterXMLDocument` class in listing 7.4 parses XML documents, such as our address book entry (shown in listing 7.2), and returns a Lucene document with XML elements represented as fields.

Listing 7.4   Using Apache Commons Digester to parse XML

```
public class DigesterXMLDocument {

  private Digester dig;                                        Create ❷
  private static Document doc;                                 Contact

  public DigesterXMLDocument() {
                                                               Create ❶
    dig = new Digester();                          DigesterXMLDocument
    dig.setValidating(false);

    dig.addObjectCreate("address-book", DigesterXMLDocument.class);
    dig.addObjectCreate("address-book/contact", Contact.class);

    dig.addSetProperties("address-book/contact", "type", "type");

    dig.addCallMethod("address-book/contact/name",              Set type
                  "setName", 0);                               attribute ❸
    dig.addCallMethod("address-book/contact/address",
      "setAddress", 0);                           Set name
    dig.addCallMethod("address-book/contact/city",  ❹ property
      "setCity", 0);
    dig.addCallMethod("address-book/contact/province",
      "setProvince", 0);
    dig.addCallMethod("address-book/contact/postalcode",
      "setPostalcode", 0);
    dig.addCallMethod("address-book/contact/country",
      "setCountry", 0);
    dig.addCallMethod("address-book/contact/telephone",
      "setTelephone", 0);

    dig.addSetNext("address-book/contact", "populateDocument");
  }

  public synchronized Document getDocument(InputStream is)
    throws DocumentHandlerException {
                                                               Call
    try {                                             populateDocument ❺
      dig.parse(is);                     Parse XML
    }                                  ❻ InputStream
    catch (IOException e) {
      throw new DocumentHandlerException(
        "Cannot parse XML document", e);
    }
    catch (SAXException e) {
      throw new DocumentHandlerException(
        "Cannot parse XML document", e);
    }
```

```
        return doc;
    }

    public void populateDocument(Contact contact) {            7  Create Lucene
                                                                  document
        doc = new Document();

        doc.add(new Field("type", contact.getType(), Field.Store.YES,
                        Field.Index.NOT_ANALYZED));
        doc.add(new Field("name", contact.getName(), Field.Store.YES,
                        Field.Index.NOT_ANALYZED));
        doc.add(new Field("address", contact.getAddress(), Field.Store.YES,
                        Field.Index.NOT_ANALYZED));
        doc.add(new Field("city", contact.getCity(), Field.Store.YES,
                        Field.Index.NOT_ANALYZED));
        doc.add(new Field("province", contact.getProvince(), Field.Store.YES,
                        Field.Index.NOT_ANALYZED));
        doc.add(new Field("postalcode", contact.getPostalcode(),
                        Field.Store.YES, Field.Index.NOT_ANALYZED));
        doc.add(new Field("country", contact.getCountry(), Field.Store.YES,
                        Field.Index.NOT_ANALYZED));
        doc.add(new Field("telephone", contact.getTelephone(),
                        Field.Store.YES, Field.Index.NOT_ANALYZED));
    }

    public static void main(String[] args) throws Exception {
        DigesterXMLDocument handler = new DigesterXMLDocument();
        Document doc =
            handler.getDocument(new FileInputStream(new File(args[0])));
        System.out.println(doc);
    }
}
```

Note that the Contact class is a simple JavaBean (it has setters and getters for each element); we left it out of listing 7.4, but you can see it in the book's source code.

This is a lengthy piece of code, and it deserves a few explanations. In the Digester-XMLDocument constructor, we create an instance of Digester and configure it by specifying several rules. Each rule specifies an action and a pattern that will trigger the action when encountered.

The first rule ❶ tells Digester to create an instance of the DigesterXMLDocument class when the pattern address-book is found. It does that by using Digester's add-ObjectCreate method. Because <address-book> is the opening element in our XML document, this rule is triggered first.

The next rule ❷ instructs Digester to create an instance of class Contact when it finds the <contact> child element under the <address-book> parent, specified with the address-book/contact pattern.

To handle the <contact> element's attribute, we set the type property of the Contact instance when Digester finds the type attribute of the <contact> element ❸. To accomplish that, we use Digester's addSetProperties method. The Contact class is written as an inner class and contains only setter and getter methods.

Our DigesterXMLDocument class contains several similar-looking rules, all of which call Digester's addCallMethod method ❹. They're used to set various Contact properties. For instance, a call such as `dig.addCallMethod("address-book/contact/ name", "setName", 0)` calls the `setName` method of our `Contact` instance. It does this when Digester starts processing the `<name>` element, found under the parent `<address-book>` and `<contact>` elements. The value of the `setName` method parameter is the value enclosed by `<name>` and `</name>` tags. If you consider our sample address book from listing 7.2, this would call `setName("Zane Pasolini")`.

We use `Digester`'s `addSetNext` method ❺ to specify that the `populate-Document(Contact)` method should be called when the closing `</contact>` element is processed. The `getDocument` method takes an `InputStream` to the XML document to parse. Then we begin parsing the XML `InputStream` ❻. Finally, we populate a Lucene document with fields containing data collected by the Contact class during parsing ❼.

It's important to consider the order in which the rules are passed to Digester. Although we could change the order of various `addSetProperties()` rules in our class and still have properly functioning code, switching the order of `addObjectCreate()` and `addSetNext()` would result in an error.

As you can see, Digester provides a high-level interface for parsing XML documents. Because we've specified our XML parsing rules programmatically, our `DigesterXML-Document` can parse only our address book XML format. Luckily, Digester lets you specify these same rules declaratively using the XML schema described in the digester-rules DTD, which is included in the Digester distribution. By using such a declarative approach, you can design a Digester-based XML parser that can be configured at runtime, allowing for greater flexibility.

Under the covers, Digester uses Java's reflection features to create instances of classes, so you have to pay attention to access modifiers to avoid stifling Digester. For instance, the inner `Contact` class (not shown in the listing) is instantiated dynamically, so it must be public. Similarly, our `populateDocument(Contact)` method needs to be public because it, too, will be called dynamically. Digester also required that our `Document` instance be declared as static; in order to make `DigesterXMLDocument` thread-safe, we have to synchronize access to the `getDocument(InputStream)` method.

In our final section we briefly consider alternatives to Tika.

7.8 *Alternatives*

Although Tika is our favorite way to extract text from documents, there are some interesting alternatives. The Aperture open source project, hosted by SourceForge at http://aperture.sourceforge.net, has support for a wide variety of document formats and is able to extract text content and metadata. Furthermore, whereas Tika focuses only on text extraction, Aperture also provides crawling support, meaning it can connect to file systems, web servers, IMAP mail servers, Outlook, and iCal files and crawl for all documents within these systems.

There are also commercial document filtering libraries, such as Stellent's filters (also known as INSO filters, now part of Oracle), ISYS file readers, and KeyView filters (now part of Autonomy). These are closed solutions, and could be fairly expensive to license, so they may not be a fit for your application.

Finally, there are numerous individual open source parsers out there for handling document types. It's entirely possible your document type already has a good open source parser that simply hasn't yet been integrated with Tika. If you find one, you should consider building the Tika plug-in for it and donating it back, or even simply calling attention to the parser on Tika's developers mailing list.

7.9   Summary

There are a great many popular document formats in the world. In the past, extracting text from these documents was a real sore point in building a search application. But today, we have Tika, which makes text extraction surprisingly simple. We've seen Tika's command-line tool, which could be the basis of a quick integration with your application, as well as an example using Tika's APIs that with some small modifications could easily be the core of text extraction for your search application. Using Tika to handle text extraction allows you to spend more time on the truly important parts of your search application. In some cases, such as parsing XML, Tika isn't appropriate, and you've now seen how to create your own XML parser for such cases.

In the next chapter we'll look at Lucene's contrib modules, which provide a wide selection of interesting functionality that extends or builds on top of Lucene's core functionality.

8
Essential Lucene extensions

This chapter covers

- Highlighting hits in your search results
- Correcting the spelling of search text
- Viewing index details using Luke
- Using additional query, analyzer, and filter implementations

You've built an index, but can you browse or query it without writing code? Absolutely! In this chapter, we'll show you Luke, a useful tool that does just that. Do you need analysis beyond what the built-in analyzers provide? Several specialized analyzers for many languages are available in Lucene's contrib modules. How about providing term highlighting in search results? We've got two choices for that! We'll also show you how to offer suggestions for misspelled words.

This chapter examines the essential, most commonly used Lucene extensions, most of which are housed in the contrib subdirectory within Lucene's source code. Deliberate care was taken with the design of Lucene to keep the core source code cohesive yet extensible. We're taking the same care in this book by keeping an intentional separation between what's in the core of Lucene and the extensions packages that have been developed to augment it.

There are so many interesting packages that we've divided our coverage into two chapters. In this chapter we'll cover the more frequently used packages, and in the next chapter we'll describe the less popular, yet still interesting, long tail. The benchmark module is so useful we dedicate a separate appendix (C) to it.

Each package is at its own stage of development. Some packages are more mature, have stronger backward compatibility goals, have better documentation, and receive greater user and developer attention than others. Each package has its own Javadocs, at different degrees of completeness, so be sure to read them closely. Even if a given package isn't quite a drop-in fit for your application, you can always use its source code as a starting point or for inspiration. If you make improvements, please consider donating them back! This is how contrib came into existence in the first place.

If you ever find yourself baffled by why your searches are behaving a certain way, or you're confused about just what's inside your index, Luke, covered next, is a real life saver.

8.1   Luke, the Lucene Index Toolbox

Andrzej Bialecki created Luke (found at http://code.google.com/p/luke), an elegant Lucene index browser. This gem provides an intimate view inside a file system-based index from an attractive desktop Java application. We highly recommend having Luke handy when you're developing with Lucene because it allows for ad hoc querying and provides insight into the terms and structure in an index.

Luke has become a regular part of our Lucene development toolkit. Its tabbed and well-integrated UI allows for rapid browsing and experimentation. In this section we'll take you through most of what it can do, including browsing the terms and documents in an index, viewing overall index statistics, running ad hoc searches and seeing their explanations, and reconstructing documents. Luke can also make changes to the index, such as deleting or undeleting documents, as well as unlocking and optimizing the index. This is a tool that's targeted to developers or perhaps system administrators. And what a wonderful tool it is!

Luke is simple to use; it requires Java Runtime Environment (JRE) 1.5 or later to run. It's a single JAR file that can be launched directly (by double-clicking from a file system browser, if your system supports that) or by running `java -jar lukeall-<VERSION>.jar` from the command line. The latest version at the time of this writing is 0.9.9.1; it embeds Lucene 2.9.1. A source code release is also available. The first thing Luke needs is a path to the index file, as shown in the file selection dialog box in figure 8.1.

There are a number of interesting options you can control when opening the index. Luke's interface is nicely interconnected so that you can jump from one view to another in the same context. The interface is divided into five tabs: Overview, Documents, Search, Files, and Plugins. The Tools menu provides options for optimizing the current index, undeleting any documents flagged for deletion, and switching the index between compound and standard format.

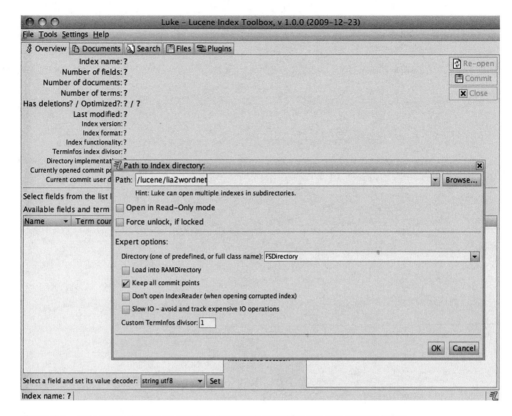

Figure 8.1 This Luke dialog box provides interesting options for opening the index.

8.1.1 Overview: seeing the big picture

Luke's Overview tab shows the major pieces of a Lucene index, including the number of fields, documents, and terms (figure 8.2). The top terms in one or more selected fields are shown in the Top Ranking Terms pane. Double-clicking a term opens the Documents tab for the selected term, where you can browse all documents containing that term. Right-clicking a term brings up a menu with three options:

- Show All Term Docs opens the Search tab for that term so all documents appear in a list.
- Browse Term Docs opens the Documents tab for the selected term.
- Copy to Clipboard copies the term to the clipboard so you can then paste it elsewhere.

8.1.2 Document browsing

The Documents tab is Luke's most sophisticated screen, where you can browse documents by document number and by term (see figure 8.3). Browsing by document number is straightforward; you can use the arrows to navigate through the documents

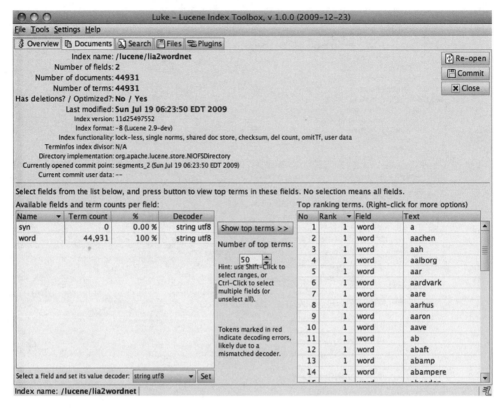

Figure 8.2   Luke's Overview tab allows you to browse fields and terms.

sequentially. The table at the bottom of the screen shows all stored fields for the currently selected document.

Browsing by term is trickier; you can go about it several ways. Clicking First Term navigates the term selection to the first term in the index for the specified field. You can scroll through terms by clicking the Next Term button. The number of documents containing a given term is shown in parentheses. To select a specific term, type all but the last character in the text box, click Next Term, and navigate forward until you find the desired term.

Just below the term browser is the term document browser, which lets you navigate through the documents containing the term you selected. The First Doc button selects the first document that contains the selected term, and as when you're browsing terms, Next Doc navigates forward.

The selected document, or all documents containing the selected term, can also be deleted from this screen (use caution if this is a production index, of course!).

Another feature of the Documents tab is the Copy Text to Clipboard feature. All fields shown, or the selected fields, may be copied to the clipboard.

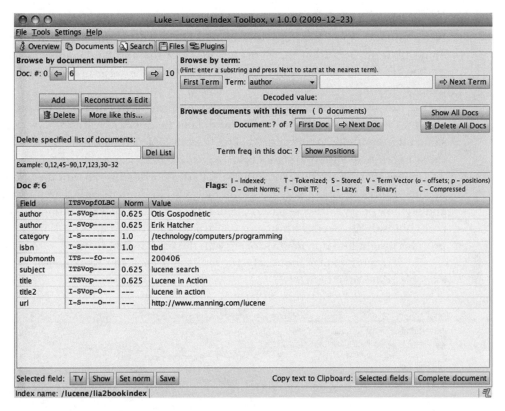

Figure 8.3 Luke's Documents tab shows all fields for the document you select.

NOTE Luke can only work within the constraints of a Lucene index, and unstored fields don't have the text available in its original form. The terms of those fields are navigable with Luke, but those fields aren't available in the document viewer or for copying to the clipboard (our contents field in this case).

Clicking the Show All Docs button shifts the view to the Search tab with a search on the selected term so that all documents containing this term are displayed. If a field's term vectors have been stored, the field's Term Vector button displays a window showing terms and frequencies.

One final feature of the Documents tab is the Reconstruct & Edit button. Clicking this button opens a document editor allowing you to edit (delete and readd) the document in the index or add a new document.

Luke reconstructs fields that were tokenized but not stored by aggregating in position order all the terms that were indexed. Reconstructing a field is a potentially lossy operation, and Luke warns of this when you view a reconstructed field (for example, if stop words were removed or tokens were stemmed during the analysis process, the original value can't be reconstructed).

8.1.3   *Using QueryParser to search*

We've already shown two ways to automatically arrive at the Search tab: choosing Show All Term Docs from the right-click menu of the Top Ranking Terms section of the Overview tab, and clicking Show All Docs from the term browser on the Documents tab.

You can also use the Search tab manually, entering `QueryParser` expression syntax along with your choice of `Analyzer` and default field. Click Search when the expression and other fields are as desired. The bottom table shows all the documents from the search hits, as shown in figure 8.4.

Double-clicking a document shifts back to the Documents tab with the appropriate document preselected. It's useful to interactively experiment with search expressions and see how `QueryParser` reacts to them. Luke shows all analyzers it finds in the classpath, but only analyzers with no-arg constructors may be used with Luke. Luke also provides insight into document scoring with the explanation feature.

To view score explanation, select a result and click the Explanation button; an example is shown in figure 8.5.

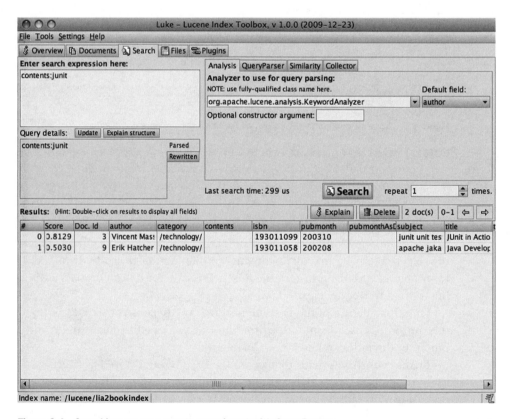

Figure 8.4   Searching: an easy way to experiment with QueryParser

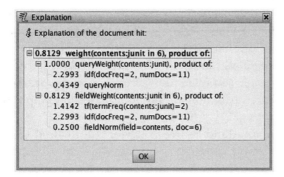

Figure 8.5 Lucene's scoring explanation details how the score for a specified document was computed.

8.1.4 Files and plugins view

The files view in Luke displays the files (and their sizes) that make up the internals of a Lucene index directory. The total index size is also shown.

As if the features already described about Luke weren't enough, Andrzej has gone the extra mile and added a plug-in framework so that others can add tools to Luke. Six plug-ins come built in, as shown in figure 8.6. Analyzer Tool has the same purpose as the `AnalyzerDemo` developed in section 4.2.4, showing the results of the analysis

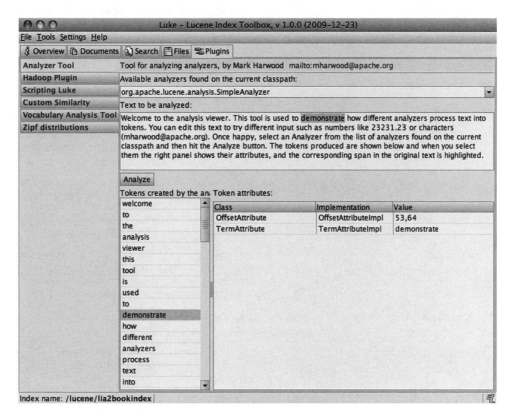

Figure 8.6 Luke includes several useful built-in plug-ins.

process on a block of text. Hadoop Plugin lets you open any Lucene index accessible via any file system supported by Hadoop. Scripting Luke lets you interactively run JavaScript code to access Luke's internals. Custom Similarity allows you to code up your own `Similarity` implementation in JavaScript, to customize how Lucene scores matching documents, which is then compiled and accessible in the Search panel. Vocabulary Analysis Tool and Zipf distribution are two tools that show graphs of term statistics from the index.

Consult the Luke documentation and source code for information on how to develop your own plug-in. Let's now switch to the numerous contrib options for analysis.

8.2   *Analyzers, tokenizers, and TokenFilters*

The more analyzers, the merrier, we always say. And the contrib modules don't disappoint in this area: they house numerous language-specific analyzers, a few related filters and tokenizers, and the slick Snowball algorithm analyzers. The analyzers are listed in table 8.1. The prefix `org.apache.lucene.analysis` is omitted from the class names.

Table 8.1   Contrib analyzers

Analyzer	`TokenStream` and `TokenFilter` chain
`ar.ArabicAnalyzer`	`ArabicLetterTokenizer > LowerCaseFilter > StopFilter > ArabicNormalizationFilter > ArabicStemFilter.`
`br.BrazilianAnalyzer`	`StandardTokenizer > StandardFilter >StopFilter` (custom stop table) `> BrazilianStemFilter > LowerCaseFilter.`
`cjk.CJKAnalyzer`	`CJKTokenizer > StopFilter` (custom English stop words ironically). Indexes Chinese text using bigrams of adjacent Chinese characters as tokens.
`cn.ChineseAnalyzer`	`ChineseTokenizer > ChineseFilter.` Indexes Chinese text by mapping each Chinese character to its own token.
`cn.smart.SmartChineseAnalyzer`	An alternative Chinese analyzer that attempts to segment Chinese text into words using a dictionary-based approach.
`compound.*`	Two different `TokenFilter`s that decompose compound words you find in many Germanic languages to the word parts. There are two approaches (one using hyphenation-based grammar to detect word parts, the other using a word-based dictionary).
`cz.CzechAnalyzer`	`StandardTokenizer > StandardFilter > LowerCaseFilter > StopFilter` (custom stop list).
`de.GermanAnalyzer`	`StandardTokenizer > StandardFilter > LowerCaseFilter > StopFilter` (custom stop list) `> GermanStemFilter.`
`el.GreekAnalyzer`	`StandardTokenizer > GreekLowerCaseFilter > StopFilter` (custom stop list).

Table 8.1   Contrib analyzers *(continued)*

Analyzer	`TokenStream` and `TokenFilter` chain
`fa.PersianAnalyzer`	`ArabicLetterTokenizer > LowerCaseFilter > ArabicNormalizationFilter > PersianNormalizationFilter > StopFilter.`
`fr.FrenchAnalyzer`	`StandardTokenizer > StandardFilter > StopFilter` (custom stop table) `> FrenchStemFilter > LowerCaseFilter.`
`miscellaneous.*`	Collection of miscellaneous `TokenStreams` and `TokenFilters`.
`ngram.*`	Breaks characters of a single word into a series of character ngrams. This can be useful for spell correction and live auto-completion.
`nl.DutchAnalyzer`	`StandardTokenizer > StandardFilter > StopFilter` (custom stop table)`> DutchStemFilter.`
`ru.RussianAnalyzer`	`RussianLetterTokenizer > RussianLowerCaseFilter > StopFilter` (custom stop list) `> RussianStemFilter.`
`th.ThaiAnalyzer`	`StandardFilter > ThaiWordFilter > StopFilter` (English stop words).
`analysis.WikipediaTokenizer`	Similar to `StandardTokenizer`, except it adds further specialization to process the Wikipedia-specific markup that appears in the XML export of the Wikipedia corpus. This produces additional Wikipedia-specific token types.
`shingle.*`	Tokenizers that create shingles (ngrams from multiple tokens) from another `TokenStream`.
`sinks.DateRecognizerSinkTokenizer`	A `SinkTokenizer` (see section 4.2.3) that only accepts tokens that are valid dates (using `java.text.DateFormat`).
`sinks.TokenRangeSinkTokenizer`	A `SinkTokenizer` (see section 4.2.3) that only accepts tokens within a certain range.
`sinks.TokenTypeSinkTokenizer`	A `SinkTokenizer` (see section 4.2.3) that only accepts tokens of a specific type as returned by `Token.type()`.
`payloads.*`	`TokenFilters` that carry over token attributes as payloads; these are described in section 6.5.
`position.PositionFilter`	Filter to set the position increment for all tokens.
`query.QueryAutoStopWordAnalyzer`	An analyzer that adds a `StopFilter` to any other analyzer.
`snowball.SnowballAnalyzer`	`StandardTokenizer > StandardFilter > LowerCaseFilter` [`> StopFilter`] `> SnowballFilter`
`ReverseStringFilter`	Reverses the text of each token that passes through it. For example, *country* becomes *yrtnuoc*. This is useful for doing efficient leading wildcard searches.

The language-specific analyzers vary in how they tokenize. The Brazilian and French analyzers use language-specific stemming and custom stop-word lists. The Czech analyzer uses standard tokenization, but also incorporates a custom stop-word list. The Chinese, CJK, and Smart Chinese analyzers take unique approaches; we saw the analysis of Chinese characters in section 4.8.4, illustrating how these three analyzers work.

Many of these analyzers, including the SnowballAnalyzer discussed next, let you customize the stop-word list just as the StopAnalyzer does (see section 4.3.1). Most of these analyzers do quite a bit in the filtering process. If the stemming or tokenization is all you need, borrow the relevant pieces, and construct your own custom analyzer from the parts here. Sections 4.4, 4.5, and 4.6 cover creating custom analyzers.

Most of the analyzers listed in table 8.1 don't require further explanation here. The language-dependent analyzers are straightforward: their purpose is to customize tokenization for their target language. ReverseStringFilter reverses every token it sees. DateRecognizerSinkTokenizer, TokenRangeSinkTokenizer, and TokenType-SinkTokenizer collect tokens fitting certain requirements. WikipediaTokenizer creates tokens from the Wikipedia XML export. The token filters under the compound package break words into their compound parts. The payloads package promotes token attribute values into payloads. We won't cover these analyzers and tokenizers any further here; please consult their Javadocs for any interesting gotchas.

We'll now give special attention to the snowball analyzers and shingle and ngram filters, because these analyzers and filters aren't quite as simple.

8.2.1 *SnowballAnalyzer*

The SnowballAnalyzer deserves special mention because it serves as a driver of an entire family of stemmers for different languages. Stemming was introduced in section 4.6. Martin Porter, who also developed the Porter stemming algorithm, created the Snowball algorithm.[1] The Porter algorithm was designed for English only; in addition, many "purported" implementations don't adhere to the definition faithfully.[2] To address these issues, Dr. Porter rigorously defined the Snowball system of stemming algorithms. Through these algorithmic definitions, accurate implementations can be generated. In fact, the snowball contrib module has a build process that can pull the definitions from Porter's site and generate the Java implementation.

One of the test cases demonstrates the result of the English stemmer stripping off the trailing *ming* from *stemming* and the *s* from *algorithms*:

```
public void testEnglish() throws Exception {
  Analyzer analyzer = new SnowballAnalyzer(Version.LUCENE_30,
                                           "English");
  AnalyzerUtils.assertAnalyzesTo(analyzer,
                                 "stemming algorithms",
                                 new String[] {"stem", "algorithm"});
}
```

---

[1] The name *Snowball* is a tribute to the string-manipulation language SNOBOL.
[2] From http://snowball.tartarus.org/texts/introduction.html

SnowballAnalyzer has two constructors; both accept the stemmer name, and one specifies a String[] stop-word list to use. Many unique stemmers exist for various languages. The non-English stemmers are Danish, Dutch, Finnish, French, German, German2, Hungarian, Italian, Kp (Kraaij-Pohlmann algorithm for Dutch), Norwegian, Portuguese, Romanian, Russian, Spanish, Swedish, and Turkish. There are a few English-specific stemmers named English, Lovins, and Porter. These exact names are the valid argument values for the name argument to the SnowballAnalyzer constructors. Here's an example using the Spanish stemming algorithm:

```
public void testSpanish() throws Exception {
  Analyzer analyzer = new SnowballAnalyzer(Version.LUCENE_30,
                                           "Spanish");
  AnalyzerUtils.assertAnalyzesTo(analyzer,
                                 "algoritmos",
                                 new String[] {"algoritm"});
}
```

If your project demands stemming, we recommend that you give the Snowball analyzer your attention first because an expert in the stemming field developed it. And, as already mentioned but worth repeating, you may want to use the clever piece of this analyzer (the SnowballFilter) wrapped in your own custom analyzer implementation. Sections 4.4, 4.5, and 4.6 discuss writing custom analyzers in great detail.

8.2.2 Ngram filters

The ngram filters take a single token and emit a series of letter ngram tokens, which are combinations of adjacent letters as separate tokens. Listing 8.1 shows how to use these unusual filters.

Listing 8.1 Creating combinations of adjacent letters with ngram filters

```
public class NGramTest extends TestCase {

  private static class NGramAnalyzer extends Analyzer {
    public TokenStream tokenStream(String fieldName, Reader reader) {
      return new NGramTokenFilter(new KeywordTokenizer(reader), 2, 4);
    }
  }

  private static class FrontEdgeNGramAnalyzer extends Analyzer {
    public TokenStream tokenStream(String fieldName, Reader reader) {
      return new EdgeNGramTokenFilter(new KeywordTokenizer(reader),
                EdgeNGramTokenFilter.Side.FRONT, 1, 4);
    }
  }

  private static class BackEdgeNGramAnalyzer extends Analyzer {
    public TokenStream tokenStream(String fieldName, Reader reader) {
      return new EdgeNGramTokenFilter(new KeywordTokenizer(reader),
                EdgeNGramTokenFilter.Side.BACK, 1, 4);
    }
  }
```

```
  public void testNGramTokenFilter24() throws IOException {
    AnalyzerUtils.displayTokensWithPositions(new NGramAnalyzer(), "lettuce");
  }

  public void testEdgeNGramTokenFilterFront() throws IOException {
    AnalyzerUtils.displayTokensWithPositions(new FrontEdgeNGramAnalyzer(),
                                  "lettuce");
  }

  public void testEdgeNGramTokenFilterBack() throws IOException {
    AnalyzerUtils.displayTokensWithPositions(new BackEdgeNGramAnalyzer(),
                                  "lettuce");
  }
}
```

The `testNGramTokenFilter24` method creates an `NGramTokenFilter` to generate all letter ngrams of length 2, 3, or 4, on the word *lettuce*. The resulting output looks like this:

```
 1: [le]
 2: [et]
 3: [tt]
 4: [tu]
 5: [uc]
 6: [ce]
 7: [let]
 8: [ett]
 9: [ttu]
10: [tuc]
11: [uce]
12: [lett]
13: [ettu]
14: [ttuc]
15: [tuce]
```

Note that each larger ngram series is positioned after the previous series. A more natural approach would be to have the ngram's position set to the character position where it starts in the word, but unfortunately at this time there's no option to do this (it's a known limitation, though, so maybe by the time you read this it'll be fixed).

The `EdgeNGramFilter` is similar, except it only generates ngrams anchored to the start or end of the word. Here's the output of the `testEdgeNGramTokenFilterFront`:

```
 1: [l]
 2: [le]
 3: [let]
 4: [lett]
```

And `testEdgeNGramTokenFilterBack`:

```
 1: [e]
 2: [ce]
 3: [uce]
 4: [tuce]
```

Next we consider shingle filters.

8.2.3 Shingle filters

Shingles are single tokens constructed from multiple adjacent tokens. They're similar to letter ngrams, used by the `spellchecker` package (section 8.5) and the ngram tokenizers (section 8.2.2) in that they make new tokens by combining multiple adjacent things. But whereas the ngram tokenizers operate on letters, shingles operate on whole words. For example, the sentence "please divide this sentence into shingles" might be tokenized into the shingles "please divide," "divide this," "this sentence," "sentence into," and "into shingles."

Why would you ever want to do such a thing? One common reason is to speed up phrase searches, especially for phrases involving common terms. Consider a search for the exact phrase "Wizard of Oz." Since the word *of* is incredibly common, including it in the phrase search will require Lucene to visit and filter out a great many occurrences that don't match the phrase, which is costly. If, instead, you'd indexed the tokens "wizard of" and "of oz," your phrase search would run quickly because those tokens occur far less frequently. The Nutch search engine, covered in section 4.9, creates shingles for exactly this reason. Because no stop words are discarded during indexing, shingles allows you to provide precisely correct phrase searching even for phrases containing stop words.

Another interesting use of shingles is document clustering, which lets you group similar or near-duplicate documents together. This is important for large collections of documents where duplicates may accidentally sneak in, which happens frequently when crawling for content through web servers that construct documents dynamically. Often slightly different URLs can yield the same underlying content, perhaps with a different header added in. Much like using term vectors to find similar documents (section 5.9.1), the approach is to represent each document by its salient shingles and then search for other documents that have similar shingles with similar frequency.

8.2.4 Obtaining the contrib analyzers

Depending on your needs, you may want JAR binary distributions of these analyzers or raw source code from which to borrow ideas. Section 8.7 provides details on how to access the contrib source code and build binary distributions. In the repository, the Snowball analyzer resides in contrib/snowball; the other analyzers discussed here are in contrib/analyzers. There are no external dependencies for these analyzers other than Lucene itself, so they're easy to incorporate. A test program called `TestApp` is included for the Snowball project. It's run in this manner:

```
> java -cp lib/lucene-snowball-3.0.1.jar org.tartarus.snowball.TestApp
Usage: TestApp <stemmer name> <input file> [-o <output file>]

> java -cp lib/lucene-snowball-3.0.1.jar org.tartarus.snowball.TestApp
    Lovins spoonful.txt
... output of stemmer applied to specified file
```

The Snowball `TestApp` bypasses `SnowballAnalyzer`. Only the Snowball stemmer itself is used with rudimentary text splitting at whitespace.

Next we show how to highlight matches in search results using the `Highlighter` package.

8.3   *Highlighting query terms*

The contrib highlighter module fragments and highlights text based on a Lucene query. `Highlighter` was originally contributed by Mark Harwood, but many others have since joined in. Giving end users some context around specific term hits from their searches is a powerful way for them to judge how relevant each hit is. Often, a brief glimpse of the surrounding context of the search terms is enough to know if that result is worth investigating further. Each hit includes some number of fragments of the matching document highlighting the terms of the query. Figure 8.7 shows an example of highlighting part of the text from chapter 3, based on a term query for term. The source code for this is shown in listing 8.2. Like spell correction, covered in section 8.5, the web search engines have established this feature as a baseline requirement that all other search engines are expected to have.

What's commonly referred to as highlighting in fact consists of two separate functions. First is dynamic fragmenting, which means picking a few choice sentences out of a large text that best match the search query. Some search applications skip this step and instead fall back on a static abstract or summary for each document, but that generally gives a worse user experience because it's static. The second function is highlighting, whereby specific words in context of their surrounding text are called out, often with bolding and a colored background, so the user's eyes can quickly jump to specific words that matched.

These two functions are fully independent. For example, you may apply highlighting to a title field without deriving fragments from it, because you always present the full title. Or, for a field that has a large amount of text, you'd first fragment it and then apply the highlighting. We'll begin with an overview of the components used during highlighting, and then show a simple example of highlighter in action, including how to use Cascading Style Sheets (CSS) to control the client-side mechanics of highlighting. We'll wrap up by showing you how to highlight search results.

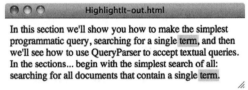

Figure 8.7   Highlighting matching query terms within text

8.3.1   *Highlighter components*

The Highlighter code is a sophisticated and flexible utility, and is well factored to break out the separate steps necessary during fragmentation and highlighting. Figure 8.8 shows the steps used by the `Highlighter` class to compute the highlighted text. Let's walk through each step.

TOKENSOURCES

Highlighting requires two separate inputs: the actual full original text (a `String`) to work on, and a `Token-Stream` derived from that text. Typically you'd store the full text as a stored field in the index, but if you have an alternate external store—for example, a database—that works fine as well. Just be sure that source can deliver the text for a page's worth of results quickly enough.

To create the `TokenStream`, you could reanalyze the text, using the same analyzer you had used during indexing. Alternatively, because you presumably had already analyzed the text during indexing, you can derive the `TokenStream` from previously stored term vectors (see section 2.4.3), as long as you used `Field.TermVector.WITH_POSITIONS_OFFSETS`. The convenient `TokenSources` class in the `Highlighter` package has static convenience methods that will extract a `Token-Stream` from an index using whichever of these sources is available. You can also create your own `TokenStream` separately if you'd like. Generally, term vectors will give you the fastest performance, but they do consume additional space in the index.

`Highlighter` relies on the start and end offset of each token from the token stream to locate the exact character slices to highlight in the original input text. So it's crucial that your analyzer sets `startOffset` and `endOffset` on each token correctly as character offsets! If these aren't right, you'll see nonword pieces of text highlighted, or you may hit an `InvalidTokenOffsets-`

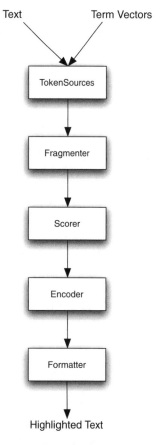

Text   Term Vectors

TokenSources

Fragmenter

Scorer

Encoder

Formatter

Highlighted Text

Figure 8.8   Java classes and interfaces used by Highlighter

`Exception` during highlighting. The core Lucene analyzers all set the offsets properly, so this normally isn't a problem unless you've created your own analyzer. The next component, `Fragmenter`, breaks the original text into small pieces called fragments.

FRAGMENTER

`Fragmenter` is a Java interface in the `Highlighter` package whose purpose is to split the original string into separate fragments for consideration. `NullFragmenter` is one concrete class implementing this interface that returns the entire string as a single fragment. This is appropriate for title fields and other short text fields, where you wish to show the full text. `SimpleFragmenter` is another concrete class that breaks up the text into fixed-size fragments by character length, with no effort to spot sentence boundaries. You can specify how many characters per fragment (the default is 100). But this fragmenter is a little too simple: it doesn't take into account positional constraints of the query when creating the fragments, which means for phrase queries and span queries, a matching span will easily be broken across two fragments.

Fortunately, the final fragmenter, SimpleSpanFragmenter, resolves that problem by attempting to make fragments that always include the spans matching each document. You'll have to pass in a QueryScorer (see the next section) so it knows where the span matches are.

If you don't set a Fragmenter on your Highlighter instance, it uses Simple-Fragmenter by default. Although it doesn't exist currently in the Highlighter package, a good implementation of Fragmenter would be one that attempts to produce fragments on sentence boundaries. Solr, covered in section 10.8, has RegexFragmenter (which fragments based on a provided regular expression) that could be used for rudimentary fragmenting by sentence.

Highlighter then takes each fragment produced by the fragmenter and passes each to the Scorer.

SCORER

The output of the Fragmenter is a series of text fragments from which Highlighter must pick the best one(s) to present. To do this, Highlighter asks the Scorer, a Java interface, to score each fragment. The Highlighter package provides two concrete implementations: QueryTermScorer, which scores each fragment based on how many terms from the provided Query appear in the fragment, and QueryScorer, which attempts to only assign scores to actual term occurrences that contributed to the match for the document. When combined with SimpleSpanFragmenter, QueryScorer is usually the best option because true matches are highlighted.

QueryTermScorer uses the terms from the query; it extracts them from primitive term, phrase, and Boolean queries and weighs them based on their corresponding boost factor. A query must be rewritten in its most primitive form for Query-TermScorer to be happy. For example, wildcard, fuzzy, prefix, and range queries rewrite themselves to a BooleanQuery of all the matching terms. Call Query.rewrite(IndexReader), which translates the query into primitive form, to rewrite a query prior to passing the Query to QueryTermScorer (unless you're sure the query is already a primitive one).

QueryScorer extracts matching spans for the query, then uses these spans to score each fragment. Fragments that didn't match the query, even if they contain a subset of the terms from the query, receive a score of 0.0. If you use the simpler Query-TermScorer, you'll find that a PhraseQuery can show fragments that don't show the entire phrase, which is terribly disconcerting and trust eroding to the end user. Note that QueryScorer is specific to each matching document (because it enumerates that document's matching spans), so it must be instantiated for every document you need to highlight. Because of these benefits, we strongly recommend that you use Query-Scorer instead of the simpler QueryTermScorer. All of the following examples use QueryScorer. The field name argument to QueryScorer specifies which field should be used for scoring the fragments; if you pass null, QueryScorer derives the field name(s) from the incoming Query.

At this point Highlighter chooses the best scoring fragments to present to the user. All that remains is to properly format them.

ENCODER

The `Encoder` Java interface has a simple purpose: to encode the original text into the external format. There are two concrete implementations: `DefaultEncoder`, which is used by default in `Highlighter`, does nothing with the text. `SimpleHTMLEncoder` encodes the text as HTML, escaping any special characters such as < and > and &, and non-ASCII characters. Once the encoder is done, the final step is to format the fragments for presentation.

FORMATTER

The `Formatter` Java interface takes each fragment of text as a `String`, as well as the terms to be highlighted, and renders the highlighting. `Highlighter` provides three concrete classes to choose from. `SimpleHTMLFormatter` wraps a begin and end tag around each hit. The default constructor will use the <b> (bold) HTML tag. `Gradient-Formatter` uses different shades of background color to indicate how strong each hit was, using the <font> HTML tag. `SpanGradientFormatter` does the same thing but uses the <span> HTML tag because some browsers may not render the <font> tag correctly. You can also create your own class implementing the `Formatter` API.

Now that we've explored all the components that go into highlighting, let's examine a complete example.

8.3.2　*Standalone highlighter example*

You understand the logical steps of the highlighting process, so let's look at some concrete examples. The simplest example of `Highlighter` returns the best fragment, surrounding each matching term with HTML <B> tags:

```
String text = "The quick brown fox jumps over the lazy dog";

TermQuery query = new TermQuery(new Term("field", "fox"));

TokenStream tokenStream =
    new SimpleAnalyzer().tokenStream("field",
        new StringReader(text));

QueryScorer scorer = new QueryScorer(query, "field");
Fragmenter fragmenter = new SimpleSpanFragmenter(scorer);
Highlighter highlighter = new Highlighter(scorer);
highlighter.setTextFragmenter(fragmenter);
assertEquals("The quick brown <B>fox</B> jumps over the lazy dog",
            highlighter.getBestFragment(tokenStream, text));
```

The previous code produces this output:

```
The quick brown <B>fox</B> jumps over the lazy dog
```

In this simple example, our text was a fixed string and we derived a `TokenStream` by using `SimpleAnalyzer`. To successfully highlight terms, the terms in the `Query` need to match `Tokens` emitted from the `TokenStream`. The same text must be used to generate the `TokenStream` as is used for the original text to highlight.

We then create a `QueryScorer` to score fragments. `QueryScorer` requires you to wrap the `TokenStream` in a `CachingTokenFilter` because it needs to process the tokens more than once. Using the `QueryScorer`, we create a `SimpleSpanFragmenter` to break the text into fragments. In this example, the text is small, so the fragmenter is pointless: the entire text will become the one and only fragment. We could've used `NullFragmenter` instead. Finally, we create `Highlighter`, set our fragmenter, and then ask it for the best scoring fragment.

Next we show how to use CSS to control how highlighting is done.

8.3.3   *Highlighting with CSS*

Using `<B>` tags to surround text that will be rendered by browsers is a reasonable default. Fancier styling should be done with CSS instead. Listing 8.2 shows our next example, `HighlightIt`, and was used to generate the highlighted result shown in figure 8.7. It uses custom begin and end tags to wrap highlighted terms with a `<span>` using the custom CSS class highlight. Using CSS attributes, the color and formatting of highlighted terms is decoupled from highlighting, permitting much more control over the end-user consumability of the interface.

Listing 8.2 also demonstrates the use of a custom `Fragmenter`, setting the fragment size to 70, and a custom `Formatter` to style highlights with CSS. Note that this is a contrived example; the content to be highlighted is a static string in the source code. In our first example, only the best fragment was returned, but `Highlighter` shines in returning multiple fragments. In this example we concatenate the best fragments with an ellipsis (…) separator; you could also have a `String[]` returned by not passing in a separator, so that your code could handle each fragment individually.

Listing 8.2   Highlighting terms using CSSs

```
public class HighlightIt {
  private static final String text =
    "In this section we'll show you how to make the simplest " +
    "programmatic query, searching for a single term, and then " +
    "we'll see how to use QueryParser to accept textual queries. " +
    "In the sections that follow, we'll take this simple example " +
    "further by detailing all the query types built into Lucene. " +
    "We begin with the simplest search of all: searching for all " +
    "documents that contain a single term.";

  public static void main(String[] args) throws Exception {

    if (args.length != 1) {
      System.err.println("Usage: HighlightIt <filename-out>");
      System.exit(-1);
    }

    String filename =
     args[0];
                                                     Create the query
    String searchText = "term";
    QueryParser parser = new QueryParser(Version.LUCENE_30,
                          "f",
                          new StandardAnalyzer(Version.LUCENE_30));
    Query query = parser.parse(searchText);
```

```
SimpleHTMLFormatter formatter =                          Customize
    new SimpleHTMLFormatter("<span class=\"highlight\">",   surrounding
                            "</span>");                      tags

TokenStream tokens = new StandardAnalyzer(Version.LUCENE_30)  Tokenize
    .tokenStream("f", new StringReader(text));                text

QueryScorer scorer = new QueryScorer(query, "f");   ◁─── Create QueryScorer

Highlighter highlighter                                   Create
            = new Highlighter(formatter, scorer);         highlighter
highlighter.setTextFragmenter(
            new SimpleSpanFragmenter(scorer));      Use
                                                    SimpleSpanFragmenter
String result =                                           Highlight best
    highlighter.getBestFragments(tokens, text, 3, "...");  3 fragments

FileWriter writer = new FileWriter(filename);
writer.write("<html>");
writer.write("<style>\n" +
    ".highlight {\n" +
    " background: yellow;\n" +
    "}\n" +                                 Write
    "</style>");                            highlighted
writer.write("<body>");                     HTML
writer.write(result);
writer.write("</body></html>");
writer.close();
  }
}
```

In neither of our examples did we perform a search and highlight actual hits. The text to highlight was hard-coded. This brings up an important issue when dealing with the Highlighter: where do you get the text to highlight in a real search application? We address this in the next section.

8.3.4   *Highlighting search results*

Whether to store the original field text in the index is up to you (see section 2.4 for field indexing options). If the original text isn't stored in the index (generally because of size considerations), you'll have to retrieve the text to be highlighted from its original source. Take care to ensure that the retrieved text is always identical to the text that had been indexed. This is a great reason to simply store the text during indexing. If the original text is stored with the field, it can be retrieved directly from the document obtained from the search, as shown in listing 8.3.

Listing 8.3   Highlighting matches in search results

```
public void testHits() throws Exception {
  IndexSearcher searcher = new
    IndexSearcher(TestUtil.getBookIndexDirectory());
  TermQuery query = new TermQuery(new Term("title", "action"));
  TopDocs hits = searcher.search(query, 10);

  QueryScorer scorer = new QueryScorer(query, "title");
```

```
Highlighter highlighter = new Highlighter(scorer);
highlighter.setTextFragmenter(
            new SimpleSpanFragmenter(scorer));

Analyzer analyzer = new SimpleAnalyzer();

for (ScoreDoc sd : hits.scoreDocs) {
  Document doc = searcher.doc(sd.doc);
  String title = doc.get("title");

  TokenStream stream =
   TokenSources.getAnyTokenStream(searcher.getIndexReader(),
                                              sd.doc,
                                              "title",
                                              doc,
                                              analyzer);

  String fragment =
      highlighter.getBestFragment(stream, title);

  System.out.println(fragment);
  }
}
```

With our sample book index, the output is

```
Ant in <B>Action</B>
Tapestry in <B>Action</B>
Lucene in <B>Action</B>, Second Edition
JUnit in <B>Action</B>, Second Edition
```

Notice that we use the convenient `TokenSources.getAnyTokenStream` method to derive a `TokenStream` from our original text. Under the hood, this method first tries to retrieve the term vectors from the index. As long as you indexed the document's field with `Field.TermVector.WITH_POSITIONS_OFFSETS`, term vectors are used to reconstruct the `TokenStream`. Otherwise, the analyzer you pass in is used to reanalyze the text. Whether to index term vectors or reanalyze the text is an application-dependent decision: run your own tests to measure the difference in runtime and index size for each approach. In our case, we did index the title field with term vectors in the books index, so term vectors are used to create the token stream. Note that by default, `Highlighter` will only process the first 50 KB characters in your document text. Use the `setMaxDocCharsToAnalyze` API to change this, but note that performance will be slower if you increase it. Note also that if the field is multivalued, as described in section 2.4.7, the tokens for all fields are logically concatenated as if they were one field. For highlighting to work correctly for such fields, you must ensure the start and end offsets of each token, as well as the end offset for each field value, are accurately set during analysis, as described in section 4.7.1.

Now let's visit an alternative highlighter, `FastVectorHighlighter`, which offers improved performance especially for larger documents.

8.4 *FastVectorHighlighter*

Contributed by KOJI SEKIGUCHI

As we saw in the previous section, `Highlighter` is one of the most fundamental tools for users to assess whether each result is worth investigating further. `Highlighter` is popular and widely used by Lucene applications, but when the documents are large, `Highlighter` can be quite time consuming if you increase the number of characters to analyze with `setMaxDocCharsToAnalyze`. An alternative highlighter, `FastVectorHighlighter`, was first added in Lucene's 2.9 release and offers faster performance.

As its name implies, `FastVectorHighlighter` is a fast highlighting tool, at the expense of more disk space consumption, because it relies on term vectors being present in the index. In contrib/benchmark (covered in appendix C), there's an algorithm file called highlight-vs-vector-highlight.alg that lets you see the difference between two highlighters in processing time. As of version 2.9, with modern hardware, that algorithm shows that `FastVectorHighlighter` is about two and a half times faster than `Highlighter`.

The advantages of `FastVectorHighlighter` over `Highlighter` are not only speed but also functionality. First, `FastVectorHighlighter` can support fields that are tokenized by ngram tokenizers. `Highlighter` can't support such fields very well. Second, more interesting is that `FastVectorHighlighter` can output the multicolored tag highlighting out of the box, as shown in figure 8.9. Third, `FastVectorHighlighter` can support "per phrase" tagging, rather than the "per term" tagging that `Highlighter` supports. For instance, if you search the phrase "lazy dog," `FastVectorHighlighter` produces `<b>lazy dog</b>` whereas `Highlighter` produces `<b>lazy</b> <b>dog</b>`.

Let's see how to use `FastVectorHighlighter`. After you run the program in listing 8.4, you should see the HTML page shown in figure 8.9.

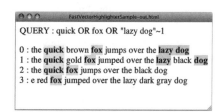

QUERY : quick OR fox OR "lazy dog"~1

0 : the **quick** brown **fox** jumps over the **lazy dog**
1 : the **quick** gold **fox** jumped over the **lazy** black **dog**
2 : the **quick fox** jumps over the black dog
3 : e red **fox** jumped over the lazy dark gray dog

Figure 8.9 `FastVectorHighlighter` **supports multicolored hit highlighting out of the box.**

Listing 8.4 Highlighting terms using `FastVectorHighlighter`

```
public class FastVectorHighlighterSample {
  static final String[] DOCS = {
    "the quick brown fox jumps over the lazy dog",
    "the quick gold fox jumped over the lazy black dog",
    "the quick fox jumps over the black dog",
    "the red fox jumped over the lazy dark gray dog"
  };
  static final String QUERY = "quick OR fox OR \"lazy dog\"~1";
  static final String F = "f";
  static Directory dir = new RAMDirectory();
  static Analyzer analyzer = new StandardAnalyzer(Version.LUCENE_30);
```

Index these
documents

Run this query

```
public static void main(String[] args) throws Exception {
  if (args.length != 1) {
    System.err.println("Usage: FastVectorHighlighterSample <filename>");
    System.exit(-1);
  }
  makeIndex();
  searchIndex(args[0]);
}

static void makeIndex() throws IOException {
  IndexWriter writer = new IndexWriter(dir, analyzer,
                                  true, MaxFieldLength.UNLIMITED);
  for(String d : DOCS){
    Document doc = new Document();
    doc.add(new Field(F, d, Store.YES, Index.ANALYZED,
                   TermVector.WITH_POSITIONS_OFFSETS));
    writer.addDocument(doc);
  }
  writer.close();
}

static void searchIndex(String filename) throws Exception {
  QueryParser parser = new QueryParser(Version.LUCENE_30,
                                   F, analyzer);
  Query query = parser.parse(QUERY);
  FastVectorHighlighter highlighter = getHighlighter();    <─┐  Get
  FieldQuery fieldQuery = highlighter.getFieldQuery(query);  <─┐ FastVectorHighlighter
  IndexSearcher searcher = new IndexSearcher(dir);
  TopDocs docs = searcher.search(query, 10);               Create FieldQuery

  FileWriter writer = new FileWriter(filename);
  writer.write("<html>");
  writer.write("<body>");
  writer.write("<p>QUERY : " + QUERY + "</p>");
  for(ScoreDoc scoreDoc : docs.scoreDocs) {
    String snippet = highlighter.getBestFragment(           Highlight top
        fieldQuery, searcher.getIndexReader(),              fragment
        scoreDoc.doc, F, 100 );
    if (snippet != null) {
      writer.write(scoreDoc.doc + " : " + snippet + "<br/>");
    }
  }
  writer.write("</body></html>");
  writer.close();
  searcher.close();
}

static FastVectorHighlighter getHighlighter() {
  FragListBuilder fragListBuilder = new SimpleFragListBuilder();
  FragmentsBuilder fragmentBuilder =
    new ScoreOrderFragmentsBuilder(
      BaseFragmentsBuilder.COLORED_PRE_TAGS,
      BaseFragmentsBuilder.COLORED_POST_TAGS);        Create
  return new FastVectorHighlighter(true, true,    FastVectorHighlighter
      fragListBuilder, fragmentBuilder);
}
}
```

The `makeIndex` method adds four static documents that are held in `DOCS` variable into the index. Note that any fields that will be highlighted must be indexed with `TermVec-tor.WITH_POSITIONS_OFFSETS`. The `searchIndex` method searches for `quick OR fox OR "lazy dog"~1` that's set in a constant `QUERY` and displays the highlighted results.

To get highlighted fragments, first you must get an instance of `FastVectorHigh-lighter`. Once you have the instance, create a `FieldQuery` from it. The `FieldQuery` will be necessary during highlighting (passed as the `fieldQuery` argument to `get-BestFragment`). To get an instance of `FastVectorHighlighter`, you can simply use the default constructor as follows:

```
FastVectorHighlighter highlighter = new FastVectorHighlighter();
```

You can't use the multicolored tag feature by using such `highlighter`, though. Because of this, we've provided the `getHighlighter` method in listing 8.4. In the method, to support the multicolored tag feature, `COLORED_PRE_TAGS` and `COLORED_POST_TAGS` constants are passed as arguments to the `ScoreOrderFragments-Builder` constructor; then the instance of the `FragmentsBuilder` is passed as an argument to `FastVectorHighlighter`.

As you've seen, `FastVectorHighlighter` has some compelling advantages over `Highlighter`. So should you always use `FastVectorHighlighter` and forget `High-lighter`? No, you can't, because `FastVectorHighlighter` also has some disadvantages. One of them is the additional consumption of disk space because the highlighting fields must be indexed with `TermVector.WITH_POSITIONS_OFFSETS`. Fur-thermore, the default `FragmentsBuilder` ignores word boundaries when building fragments. You can see this limitation in figure 8.9, with the last fragment that starts with the "e" from the word *the*. To avoid this inconvenience, you could implement a custom `FragmentsBuilder` that takes the word boundaries into account. Finally, `Fast-VectorHighlighter` can only support basic queries such as `TermQuery` and `Phrase-Query`. A `BooleanQuery` that consists of these basic queries is also supported. `Highlighter` supports almost all the queries in Lucene, including `WildcardQuery` and `SpanQuery`.

Each of the highlighters has strengths and weaknesses; you'll have to make an informed decision based on what's important to your application and your users.

Next we'll cover an important package that implements spell checking.

8.5 Spell checking

Spell checking is something users now take for granted in today's search engines. Enter a misspelled word into Google and you'll get back a helpful and nearly always accurate "Did you mean...?" with your typo corrected as a link that you can then click. Google's spell checking is so effective that you can rely on it to correct your typos. Spell checking is such a wonderfully simple and intuitive must-have feature to the end user. But, as a developer, just how do you implement it? Fortunately, Lucene has the spellchecker contrib module, created by David Spencer, for just this purpose.

Web search engines spend a lot of energy tuning their spell-checking algorithms, and it shows. Generally you get a good experience, and this sets a high bar for how all the world's search applications are expected to behave. Let's walk through the typical steps during spell checking, including generating possible suggestions, selecting the best one for each misspelled word, and presenting the choice to the user. We'll wrap up with some other possible ideas to explore. Along the way we'll see how the spellchecker contrib module tackles each.

8.5.1 Generating a suggestions list

You might assume the first step is to decide whether or not spell checking is even necessary. But that's hard to determine up front, and it's usually more effective to always run through the steps and then use the score of each potential suggestion to decide whether they should be presented to the user. The first step is to generate a raw set of possible suggestions. The spellchecker module works with one term at a time, so if the query has multiple terms you'll have to consider each separately (but see section 8.5.4 for some ideas on handling multiterm queries).

You'll need a source dictionary of "valid" words. You can try to use a generic known accurate dictionary, but it's difficult to find such dictionaries that will exactly match your search domain, and it's even harder to keep such a dictionary current over time. A more powerful means of deriving a dictionary is to use your search index to gather all unique terms seen during indexing from a particular field. This is the approach used by the spellchecker module.

Given the dictionary, you must enumerate the suggestions. You could use a phonetic approach, such as the "sounds like" matching we explored in section 4.4. Another approach, which is the one used by the spellchecker module, is to use letter ngrams to identify similar words. A letter ngram is all subsequences of adjacent letters in length, varying between a minimum and a maximum size. Using this approach, the ngrams for all words in the dictionary are indexed into a separate spellchecker index. This is usually a fast operation, and so the application's indexing process would rebuild the entire spellchecker index whenever the main index is updated.

Let's walk through an example. Say our dictionary contains the word *lettuce*. Table 8.2 shows the 3grams and 4grams that are added into the spellchecker index. In this case, our "document" is the word lettuce whose indexed tokens are the generated 3grams and 4grams. Next, imagine the user searches for *letuce*, whose ngrams are shown in table 8.3. To find the suggestions, the ngrams for *letuce* are used to run a search against the spellchecker index. Because many of the ngrams are shared (*let*, *tuc*, *uce*, and *tuce*), the correct word *lettuce* will be returned with a high relevance score.

Table 8.2 The ngrams for the word *lettuce*

Word	Lettuce
3gram	let, ett, ttu, tuc, uce
4gram	lett, ettu, ttuc, tuce

Table 8.3 The ngrams for the misspelled word *letuce*

Word	Lettuce
3gram	let, etu, tuc, uce
4gram	letu, etuc, tuce

Fortunately, the spellchecker module handles all this ngram processing for you, under the hood (though the `NGramTokenizer` and `EdgeNGramTokenizer`, described in section 8.2.2, let you create your own ngrams if you want to take a more custom approach). Creating the spellchecker index is surprisingly simple. Listing 8.5 shows how to do it, using the terms from an existing Lucene index. Run it with `ant Create-SpellCheckerIndex`. This creates a spellchecker index, stored in the local directory `indexes/spellchecker`, by enumerating all unique terms seen in the word field of the wordnet index, by default.

It produces output like this:

```
Now build SpellChecker index...
took 2431 milliseconds
```

Listing 8.5 Creating the spellchecker index

```java
public class CreateSpellCheckerIndex {

  public static void main(String[] args) throws IOException {

    if (args.length != 3) {
      System.out.println("Usage: java lia.tools.SpellCheckerTest " +
                         "SpellCheckerIndexDir IndexDir IndexField");
      System.exit(1);
    }

    String spellCheckDir = args[0];
    String indexDir = args[1];
    String indexField = args[2];

    System.out.println("Now build SpellChecker index...");
    Directory dir = FSDirectory.open(new File(spellCheckDir));     // Create SpellChecker
    SpellChecker spell = new SpellChecker(dir);
    long startTime = System.currentTimeMillis();

    Directory dir2 = FSDirectory.open(new File(indexDir));         // Open IndexReader
    IndexReader r = IndexReader.open(dir2);
    try {
      spell.indexDictionary(
              new LuceneDictionary(r, indexField));                // Add all words
    } finally {
      r.close();
    }
    dir.close();
    dir2.close();
    long endTime = System.currentTimeMillis();
    System.out.println("  took " + (endTime-startTime) + " milliseconds");
  }
}
```

Note that if you have an alternate source of words, or perhaps you'd like to use terms from a Lucene index but filter certain ones out, you can create your own class implementing the `Dictionary` interface (in the `org.apache.lucene.search.spell` package) and pass that to the `SpellChecker` instance instead. The next step is to pick the best suggestion.

8.5.2 *Selecting the best suggestion*

From the first step, using the letter ngram approach, we can now generate a set of suggestions for each term in the user's query. Listing 8.6 shows how to generate respellings with spellchecker, using the spellchecker index created by listing 8.5. Run it with ant SpellCheckerExample, which by default searches for corrections of the word *letuce*.

```
5 suggestions for 'letuce':
  lettuce
  letch
  deduce
  letup
  seduce
```

Not bad! Lettuce was the first choice. But how do we handle the other choices?

Listing 8.6 Finding the list of candidates using the spellchecker index

```
public class SpellCheckerExample {

  public static void main(String[] args) throws IOException {

    if (args.length != 2) {
      System.out.println("Usage: java lia.tools.SpellCheckerTest " +
                         "SpellCheckerIndexDir wordToRespell");
      System.exit(1);
    }

    String spellCheckDir = args[0];
    String wordToRespell = args[1];

    Directory dir = FSDirectory.open(new File(spellCheckDir));
    if (!IndexReader.indexExists(dir)) {
      System.out.println("\nERROR: No spellchecker index at path \"" +
                         spellCheckDir +
                         "\"; please run CreateSpellCheckerIndex first\n");
      System.exit(1);
    }
    SpellChecker spell = new SpellChecker(dir);          ◁┘ Create
                                                             SpellChecker
    spell.setStringDistance(new LevensteinDistance());   ◁┘ Set distance
                                                             metric
    String[] suggestions = spell.suggestSimilar(         Generate
                                 wordToRespell, 5);       candidates
    System.out.println(suggestions.length +
                       " suggestions for '" +
                       wordToRespell + "':");
    For (String suggestion : suggestions)
      System.out.println("  " + suggestion);
  }
}
```

Unfortunately, you don't usually have the luxury of showing many spelling suggestions to the user. Typically you can either present no choice (if you determine all terms in the query seem properly spelled, or there were no good spelling candidates found), or a single suggestion, back to the user.

Although the ngram approach is good for enumerating potential respellings, its relevance ranking is generally not good for selecting the best one. Typically, a different distance metric is used to resort the suggestions according to how similar each is to the original term. One common metric is the Levenshtein metric, which we used in section 3.4.8 to search for similar terms using FuzzyQuery. This is the default metric used by spellchecker, and generally it works well. You can also use the JaroWinkler class to select the Jaro-Winkler distance (see http://en.wikipedia.org/wiki/Jaro-Winkler), which is provided in the spellchecker package, or you could implement your own string similarity metric. The array of suggestions returned by SpellChecker.suggest-Similar is sorted by decreasing similarity according to the distance metric, so you simply pick the first result to present as the suggested spelling.

The final step is to present the spelling option to the user.

8.5.3 *Presenting the result to the user*

Once you have your single best spelling candidate, you first need to decide if it's good enough to present to the user. The SpellChecker class doesn't return the distance between each suggestion and the original user's term, though you could recompute that by calling the getDistance method on the StringDistance instance you're using. SpellChecker also has an alternative suggestSimilar method that takes additional arguments in order to restrict the suggestions to those terms that are more frequent than the original term; this way, you'll present a suggested spelling only if it occurred more frequently than the original term, which is a reasonable way to decide whether a candidate is worth presenting. It also has a setAccuracy method to set the minimum relevance of each suggestion.

Next, assuming you have a suggestion worth presenting, what exactly should your application do? One option, if you're confident of the spelling suggestion, is to automatically respell the term. But be sure to clearly tell the user at the top of the search results that this was done, and give the user a quick link to forcefully revert to her original search. Alternatively, you could search exactly as the user requested but present a "Did you mean…" with the spelling suggestion, as Google often does. Finally, you could search for both the original query plus the respelled query, OR'd together perhaps with different boosts.

Typically a search application will choose one of these options up front. But modern web search engines seem to make this choice dynamically, per query, depending on some measure of confidence of the spelling suggestion. Go ahead and try some searches in http://www.google.com and http://www.bing.com!

8.5.4 *Some ideas to improve spell checking*

Implementing spell checking is challenging, and we've touched on a few of the issues. The spellchecker contrib module gives you a great start. But you may want to explore some of the following improvements for your application:

- If you have high search traffic, consider using the terms from your user's queries to help rank the best suggestion. In applications whose dictionary changes quickly with time, such as a news search engine for current events, this strategy is especially compelling. This approach makes the assumption that most users know how to spell well, which so far seems to be a correct assumption!

- Instead of respelling each term separately, consider factoring in the other terms to bias the suggestions of each term. One way is to compute term co-occurrence statistics up front for every pair of terms X and Y, to measure how many documents or queries contain both terms X and Y. Then, when sorting the suggestions take these statistics into account with the other terms in the user's query. If a user enters the misspelled query "harry poter," you'd like to suggest "harry potter" instead of other choices like "harry poster."

- The dictionary you use for spell checking is critical. When you use terms from an existing index, you can easily import misspellings from the content you'd indexed if the content is "dirty." You can also accidentally import terms that you may never want to suggest, such as SKU numbers or stock ticker symbols. Try to filter such terms out, or only accept terms that occurred above a certain frequency.

- If you have high search traffic, you can train your spell checker according to how users click on the "Did you mean…" link, biasing future suggestions based on how users have accepted suggestions in the past. Use this as well to gather a test set for testing other improvements to your spell checking.

- If your search application has entitlements (restricting which content a user can see based on her entitlement), then take care to keep the spell-checker dictionary separate for different user classes. A single global dictionary can accidentally "leak" information across entitlement classes, which could cause serious problems.

- Tweak how you compute the confidence of each suggestion. The spellchecker module currently relies entirely on the `StringDistance` score for this, but you could imagine improving this by combining `StringDistance` with the frequency of this term in the index to gain a better confidence.

- One way to determine whether it's necessary to even present corrections is to first run the user's original search, and then if it returns 0, or very few, results, try the respelled search to see if it returns more, and use that to bias the decision.

As you've seen, despite seeming so simple when you use it, under the hood spell checking is quite challenging to implement. The spellchecker contrib module does much of this work for you, including creating a separate spellchecker index, enumerating candidate corrections, and ranking them by edit distance. Although it gives you a great start, we've left you with some suggestions on how to further improve on it.

Next we cover a slew of interesting `Query` implementations.

8.6   *Fun and interesting Query extensions*

The queries contrib module provides interesting additions to Lucene's core queries, contributed by Mark Harwood, including `MoreLikeThis`, `FuzzyLikeThisQuery`, `BoostingQuery`, `TermsFilter`, and `DuplicateFilter`.

8.6.1   *MoreLikeThis*

The `MoreLikeThis` class captures all the logic for finding similar documents to an existing document. In section 5.9.1 we saw the `BooksLikeThis` example to accomplish the same functionality, but `MoreLikeThis` is more general and will work with any Lucene index. Listing 8.7 shows how to do the same thing as `BooksLikeThis` using `MoreLikeThis`.

The approach is exactly the same: enumerate terms from the provided document and build a `Query` to find similar documents. `MoreLikeThis` is more flexible: if you give it a `docID` and an `IndexReader` instance, it will iterate through any field that's stored or that has indexed term vectors, to locate the terms for that document. For stored fields it must reanalyze the text, so be sure to set the analyzer first if the default `StandardAnalyzer` isn't appropriate. `MoreLikeThis` is able to find documents similar to an arbitrary `String` or the contents of a provided file or url as well.

Remember `MoreLikeThis` will usually return the same document (if your search was based on a document in the index), so be sure to filter it out in your presentation.

Listing 8.7   Using `MoreLikeThis` to find similar documents

```
public class BooksMoreLikeThis {
  public static void main(String[] args) throws Throwable {

    String indexDir = System.getProperty("index.dir");
    FSDirectory directory = FSDirectory.open(new File(indexDir));
    IndexReader reader = IndexReader.open(directory);

    IndexSearcher searcher = new IndexSearcher(reader);

    int numDocs = reader.maxDoc();

    MoreLikeThis mlt = new MoreLikeThis(reader);              ◁┘ Instantiate MoreLikeThis
    mlt.setFieldNames(new String[] {"title", "author"});      ◁┘ Lower default minimums
    mlt.setMinTermFreq(1);
    mlt.setMinDocFreq(1);

    for (int docID = 0; docID < numDocs; docID++) {          ◁┘ Iterate through all docs in index
      System.out.println();
      Document doc = reader.document(docID);
      System.out.println(doc.get("title"));

      Query query = mlt.like(docID);                          ◁┘ Build query to find similar docs
      System.out.println("  query=" + query);

      TopDocs similarDocs = searcher.search(query, 10);
      if (similarDocs.totalHits == 0)
        System.out.println("  None like this");
      for(int i=0;i<similarDocs.scoreDocs.length;i++) {
        if (similarDocs.scoreDocs[i].doc != docID) {          ◁┘ Don't show same doc
```

```
            doc = reader.document(similarDocs.scoreDocs[i].doc);
            System.out.println("  -> " + doc.getField("title").stringValue());
          }
        }
      }

      searcher.close();
      reader.close();
      directory.close();
    }
  }
```

8.6.2   *FuzzyLikeThisQuery*

FuzzyLikeThisQuery combines MoreLikeThis and FuzzyQuery. It allows you to build a query by adding arbitrary text, which is analyzed by default with StandardAnalyzer. The tokens derived from that analysis are then "fuzzed" using the same process that FuzzyQuery uses. Finally, from these terms the most differentiating terms are selected and searched on. This query can be a useful alternative when end users are unfamiliar with the standard QueryParser Boolean search syntax.

8.6.3   *BoostingQuery*

BoostingQuery allows you to run a primary Query but selectively demote search results matching a second Query. Use it like this:

```
Query balancedQuery = new BoostingQuery(positiveQuery,
                                        negativeQuery, 0.01f);
```

where positiveQuery is your primary query, negativeQuery matches those documents you'd like to demote, and 0.01f is the factor you'd like use when demoting. All documents matching negativeQuery alone won't be included in the results. All documents matching positiveQuery alone will be included with their original score. All documents matching both will have their score demoted by the specified factor.

BoostingQuery is similar to creating a Boolean query with the negativeQuery added as a NOT clause, except instead of excluding outright those documents matching negativeQuery, BoostingQuery still includes those documents, just with a weaker score.

8.6.4   *TermsFilter*

TermsFilter is a filter that matches any arbitrary set of terms you specify. It's like a TermRangeFilter that doesn't require the terms to be in a contiguous sequence. You simply construct the TermsFilter, add the terms one by one you'd like to filter on by calling the addTerm method, and then use that filter when searching. An example might be a collection of primary keys from a database query result or perhaps a choice of "category" labels picked by the end user.

8.6.5 *DuplicateFilter*

DuplicateFilter is a Filter that removes documents that have the same value for a specific unanalyzed field. For example, say you have a field KEY, which isn't analyzed but is indexed. Suppose a given document could be indexed multiple times in Lucene, perhaps once with only its "current version" and again with the "full revision history." There would now be two Lucene documents, each sharing the same KEY value. You could then do something like this:

```
DuplicateFilter df = new DuplicateFilter("KEY");
df.setKeepMode(DuplicateFilter.KM_USE_LAST_OCCURRENCE);
TopDocs hits = searcher.search(query, df, 10);
```

And the filter will keep only the last document added to the index that shares the same KEY value.

8.6.6 *RegexQuery*

RegexQuery, which is in the contrib/regex directory, allows you to specify an arbitrary regular expression for matching terms. Any document containing a term matching that regular expression will match. It's like WildcardQuery on steroids. Here's a simple example:

```
public void testRegexQuery() throws Exception {
    Directory directory = TestUtil.getBookIndexDirectory();
    IndexSearcher searcher = new IndexSearcher(directory);
    RegexQuery q = new RegexQuery(new Term("title", ".*st.*"));
    TopDocs hits = searcher.search(q, 10);
    assertEquals(2, hits.totalHits);
    assertTrue(TestUtil.hitsIncludeTitle(searcher, hits,
                                   "Tapestry in Action"));
    assertTrue(TestUtil.hitsIncludeTitle(searcher, hits,
              "Mindstorms: Children, Computers, And Powerful Ideas"));
    searcher.close();
    directory.close();
}
```

There are two books that match the cryptic regular expression .*st.*. By default RegexQuery uses Java's built-in regular expression syntax, from java.util.regex, but you can switch to Apache Jakarta's regular expression syntax (org.apache.regexp) by calling

```
RegexQuery.setRegexImplementation(new JakartaRegexpCapabilities());
```

The contrib/regex package also contains SpanRegexQuery, which combines Regex-Query and SpanQuery so that all matches also include the matching spans. The Span-Query family is described section 5.5.

Let's now see how to build contrib modules.

8.7   *Building contrib modules*

Most of Lucene's contrib modules are included in the standard Lucene releases, under the contrib directory. Each package generally has its own JAR files for the classes and the Javadocs.

Still, some packages aren't part of the build and release process. Further, there may be recent improvements not yet released that you'd like to use. To handle these cases, you'll need to access the source code and build the packages yourself. Fortunately, this is straightforward; you can easily obtain Lucene's source code directly (via Apache's SVN access or from the source code release). You can then either build the JAR files and incorporate the resulting binaries into your project or copy the desired source code into your project and build it directly into your own binaries.

8.7.1   *Get the sources*

The simplest way to obtain the sources for the contrib modules is to download the source release from http://lucene.apache.org. If you'd like to instead use the latest and greatest version you can check out the source code using a Subversion client (see http://subversion.tigris.org). Follow the instructions provided at the Apache site: http://wiki.apache.org/lucene-java/SourceRepository. Specifically, this step involves executing the following command from the command line:

```
svn checkout http://svn.apache.org/repos/asf/lucene/java/trunk lucene
```

This is read-only access to the repository. In your current directory, you'll now have a subdirectory named lucene-trunk. Under that directory is a contrib directory where all the goodies discussed here, and more, reside. Let's build the JARs.

8.7.2   *Ant in the contrib directory*

Next, let's build the components. You'll need Ant 1.7.0 or later in order to run the contrib build files. At the root of the lucene-trunk directory is a build.xml file. From the command line, with the current directory lucene-trunk, execute the following:

```
ant build-contrib
```

Most of the components will build and create a distributable JAR file in the build subdirectory. Now is also a good time to execute the Ant test, which runs all core and contrib unit tests, to confirm all Lucene's tests are passing.

Some components aren't currently integrated into this build process, so you may need to copy the necessary files into your project. Some outdated contributions are still there as well (these are the ones we didn't mention in this chapter), and additional contributions will probably arrive after we've written this.

Each contrib subdirectory, such as analyzers and Ant, has its own build.xml file. To build a single component, set your current working directory to the desired component's directory and execute ant. This is still a fairly crude way of getting your hands on these add-ons to Lucene, but it's useful to have direct access to the source. You may want to use the contrib modules for ideas and inspiration, not necessarily for the exact code.

8.8   *Summary*

Don't reinvent the wheel. Someone has no doubt encountered the same situation you're struggling with. The contrib modules and the other resources listed on the Lucene website should be your first stops.

In this chapter we've covered the truly essential extensions to Lucene. Google clearly sets a high bar as the baseline expectation of search users when it comes to spell checking and hit highlighting. Fortunately, Lucene's contrib modules include the spellchecker package and two packages for performing hit highlighting, giving you an excellent starting point for providing these functions to your users.

We saw Luke, which is an incredibly useful graphical tool for peeking into your index to see what terms and documents are present, as well as for running queries and basic index operations like optimization. Luke is an invaluable Swiss army knife of a tool that all Lucene applications should make use of.

If you're working with languages other than English, take advantage of the numerous analyzers for non-English languages; often you can choose from more than one analyzer to try per language. Beyond language-specific analyzers, we saw some other interesting analyzers like ngram, which creates tokens out of adjacent letters in each word, and shingle, which creates single tokens out of multiple adjacent words. Using the shingle filter is a particularly useful approach to allow phrase searches to include stop words.

We also saw a slew of interesting new Query implementations, including a generic MoreLikeThis class for finding documents similar to a specified original; Fuzzy-LikeThisQuery, which combines MoreLikeThis and FuzzyQuery; BoostingQuery, for mixing the scores of a positive and negative query; and RegexQuery, for matching documents containing terms that match a provided regular expression. The queries package also provides TermsFilter, to accept documents containing any of an arbitrary set of terms, and DuplicateFilter, to remove documents that seem to be duplicates of one another according to a specified field.

In the next chapter we continue our coverage of Lucene's contrib modules, visiting some of the less commonly used contrib modules.

Further
Lucene extensions

This chapter covers

- Searching indexes remotely using RMI
- Chaining multiple filters into one
- Storing an index in Berkeley DB
- Sorting and filtering according to geographic distance

In the previous chapter we explored a number of commonly used extensions to Lucene. In this chapter we'll round out that coverage by detailing some of the less popular yet still interesting and useful extensions.

ChainedFilter lets you logically chain multiple filters together into one Filter. The Berkeley DB package enables storing a Lucene index within a Berkeley database. There are two options for storing an index entirely in memory, which provide far faster search performance than RAMDirectory. We'll show three alternative QueryParser implementations, one based on XML, another designed to produce SpanQuery instances (something the core QueryParser can't do), and a final new query parser that's very modular. Spatial Lucene enables sorting and filtering based on geographic distance. You can perform remote searching (over RMI) using the contrib/remote module.

This chapter completes our coverage of Lucene's contrib modules, but remember that Lucene's sources are fast moving so it's likely new packages are available by the time you read this. If in doubt, you should always check Lucene's source code repository for the full listing of what new goodies are available.

Let's begin with chaining filters.

9.1 Chaining filters

Using a search filter, as we've discussed in section 5.6, is a powerful mechanism for selectively narrowing the document space to be searched by a query. The contrib directory contains an interesting meta-filter in the misc project, contributed by Kelvin Tan, which chains other filters together and performs AND, OR, XOR, and ANDNOT bit operations between them. ChainedFilter, like the built-in CachingWrapperFilter, isn't a concrete filter; it combines a list of filters and performs a desired bit-wise operation for each successive filter, allowing for sophisticated combinations.

Listing 9.1 shows the base test case we'll use to show ChainedFilter's functionality. It's slightly involved because it requires a diverse enough data set to showcase how the various scenarios work. We've set up an index with 500 documents, including a key field, with values 1 through 500; a date field, with successive days starting from January 1, 2009; and an owner field, with the first half of the documents owned by Bob and the second half owned by Sue.

Listing 9.1 Base test case to see `ChainedFilter` in action

```
public class ChainedFilterTest extends TestCase {
  public static final int MAX = 500;
  private RAMDirectory directory;
  private IndexSearcher searcher;
  private Query query;
  private Filter dateFilter;
  private Filter bobFilter;
  private Filter sueFilter;

  public void setUp() throws Exception {
    directory = new RAMDirectory();
    IndexWriter writer =
      new IndexWriter(directory, new WhitespaceAnalyzer(),
                  IndexWriter.MaxFieldLength.UNLIMITED);

    Calendar cal = Calendar.getInstance();
    cal.set(2009, 1, 1, 0, 0);                    ◁──── Set date to Jan 1 2009

    for (int i = 0; i < MAX; i++) {
      Document doc = new Document();
      doc.add(new Field("key", "" + (i + 1),
                      Field.Store.YES, Field.Index.NOT_ANALYZED));
      doc.add(new Field("owner", (i < MAX / 2) ? "bob" : "sue",
                      Field.Store.YES, Field.Index.NOT_ANALYZED));
      doc.add(new Field("date", DateTools.timeToString(
                              cal.getTimeInMillis(),
                            DateTools.Resolution.DAY),
                      Field.Store.YES, Field.Index.NOT_ANALYZED));
```

```
      writer.addDocument(doc);

      cal.add(Calendar.DATE, 1);
    }

    writer.close();

    searcher = new IndexSearcher(directory);

    BooleanQuery bq = new BooleanQuery();
    bq.add(new TermQuery(new Term("owner", "bob")),
          BooleanClause.Occur.SHOULD);
    bq.add(new TermQuery(new Term("owner", "sue")),
          BooleanClause.Occur.SHOULD);
    query = bq;

    cal.set(2099, 1, 1, 0, 0);
    dateFilter = TermRangeFilter.Less("date",
                      DateTools.timeToString(
                        cal.getTimeInMillis(),
                        DateTools.Resolution.DAY));

    bobFilter = new CachingWrapperFilter(
            new QueryWrapperFilter(
              new TermQuery(new Term("owner", "bob"))));

    sueFilter = new CachingWrapperFilter(
          new QueryWrapperFilter(
            new TermQuery(new Term("owner", "sue"))));
  }
}
```

Match all docs — (annotation for BooleanQuery block)

Match all docs, by date — (annotation for dateFilter block)

Match only Bob's docs — (annotation for bobFilter block)

Match only Sue's docs — (annotation for sueFilter block)

In addition to the test index, setUp defines an all-encompassing query and some filters for our examples. The query searches for documents owned by either Bob or Sue; used without a filter it will match all 500 documents. An all-encompassing DateFilter is constructed, as well as two QueryFilters, one to filter on owner Bob and the other on Sue.

Using a single filter nested in a ChainedFilter has no effect beyond using the filter without ChainedFilter, as shown here with two of the filters:

```
public void testSingleFilter() throws Exception {
  ChainedFilter chain = new ChainedFilter(
                                    new Filter[] {dateFilter});
  TopDocs hits = searcher.search(query, chain, 10);
  assertEquals(MAX, hits.totalHits);

  chain = new ChainedFilter(new Filter[] {bobFilter});
  assertEquals(MAX / 2, TestUtil.hitCount(searcher, query, chain),
    hits.totalHits);
}
```

The real power of ChainedFilter comes when we chain multiple filters together. The default operation is OR, combining the filtered space as shown when filtering on Bob or Sue:

```
public void testOR() throws Exception {
  ChainedFilter chain = new ChainedFilter(
            new Filter[] {sueFilter, bobFilter});
```

```
    assertEquals("OR matches all", MAX, TestUtil.hitCount(searcher, query,
        chain));
}
```

Rather than increase the document space, you can use AND to narrow the space:

```
public void testAND() throws Exception {
  ChainedFilter chain = new ChainedFilter(
          new Filter[] {dateFilter, bobFilter}, ChainedFilter.AND);
  TopDocs hits = searcher.search(query, chain, 10);
  assertEquals("AND matches just Bob", MAX / 2, hits.totalHits);
  Document firstDoc = searcher.doc(hits.scoreDocs[0].doc);
  assertEquals("bob", firstDoc.get("owner"));
}
```

The `testAND` test case shows that the `dateFilter` is AND'd with the `bobFilter`, effectively restricting the search space to documents owned by Bob because the `dateFilter` is all encompassing. In other words, the intersection of the provided filters is the document search space for the query. Filter bit sets can be XOR'd (exclusively OR'd, meaning one or the other, but not both) :

```
public void testXOR() throws Exception {
  ChainedFilter chain = new ChainedFilter(
    new Filter[]{dateFilter, bobFilter}, ChainedFilter.XOR);
  TopDocs hits = searcher.search(query, chain, 10);
  assertEquals("XOR matches Sue", MAX / 2, hits.totalHits);
  Document firstDoc = searcher.doc(hits.scoreDocs[0].doc);
  assertEquals("sue", firstDoc.get("owner"));
}
```

The `dateFilter` XOR'd with `bobFilter` effectively filters for owner Sue in our test data. The ANDNOT operation allows only documents that match the first filter but not the second filter to pass through:

```
public void testANDNOT() throws Exception {
  ChainedFilter chain = new ChainedFilter(
    new Filter[]{dateFilter, sueFilter},
      new int[] {ChainedFilter.AND, ChainedFilter.ANDNOT});

  TopDocs hits = searcher.search(query, chain, 10);
  assertEquals("ANDNOT matches just Bob",
              MAX / 2, hits.totalHits);
  Document firstDoc = searcher.doc(hits.scoreDocs[0].doc);
  assertEquals("bob", firstDoc.get("owner"));
}
```

In `testANDNOT`, given our test data, all documents in the date range except those owned by Sue are available for searching, which narrows it down to only documents owned by Bob.

Depending on your needs, the same effect can be obtained by combining query clauses into a `BooleanQuery` or using `FilteredQuery` (see section 6.4.3). Keep in mind the performance caveats to using filters; and, if you're reusing filters without changing the index, be sure you're using a caching filter. `ChainedFilter` doesn't cache, but wrapping it in a `CachingWrappingFilter` will take care of that.

Let's look at an alternative `Directory` implementation next.

9.2   *Storing an index in Berkeley DB*

The Chandler project (http://chandlerproject.org) is an ongoing effort to build an open source personal information manager. Chandler aims to manage diverse types of information such as email, instant messages, appointments, contacts, tasks, notes, web pages, blogs, bookmarks, photos, and much more. It's an extensible platform, not just an application. Search is a crucial component to the Chandler infrastructure.

The Chandler codebase uses Python primarily, with hooks to native code where necessary. We're going to jump right to how the Chandler developers use Lucene; refer to the Chandler site for more details on this fascinating project. Andi Vajda, one of Chandler's key developers, created PyLucene to enable full access to Lucene's APIs from Python. PyLucene is an interesting port of Lucene to Python; we cover it in full detail in section 10.7.

Chandler's underlying repository uses Oracle's Berkeley DB in a vastly different way than a traditional relational database, inspired by Resource Description Framework (RDF) and associative databases. Andi created a Lucene directory implementation that uses Berkeley DB as the underlying storage mechanism. An interesting side effect of having a Lucene index in a database is the transactional support it provides. Andi donated his implementation to the Lucene project, and it's maintained in the db/bdb area of the contrib directory.

Berkeley DB, at release 4.7.25 as of this writing, is written in C, but provides full Java API access via Java Native Interface (JNI). The db/bdb contrib module provides access via this API. Berkeley DB also has a Java edition, which is written entirely in Java, so no JNI access is required and the code exists in a single JAR file. Aaron Donovan ported the contrib/db/bdb to the "Java edition" under the contrib/db/bdb-je directory. Listing 9.2 shows how to use the Java edition version of Berkeley DB, but the API for the original Berkeley DB is similar. We provide the corresponding examples for both indexing and searching with the source code that comes with this book.

JEDirectory, which is a Directory implementation that stores its files in the Berkeley DB Java Edition, is more involved to use than the built-in RAMDirectory and FSDirectory. It requires constructing and managing two Berkeley DB Java API objects, EnvironmentConfig and DatabaseConfig. Listing 9.2 shows JEDirectory being used for indexing.

Listing 9.2   Storing an index in Berkeley DB, using `JEDirectory`

```
public class BerkeleyDbJEIndexer {
  public static void main(String[] args)
      throws IOException, DatabaseException {
    if (args.length != 1) {
      System.err.println("Usage: BerkeleyDbIndexer <index dir>");
      System.exit(-1);
    }

    File indexFile = new File(args[0]);
```

```
      if (indexFile.exists()) {                            Remove
        File[] files = indexFile.listFiles();              existing index,
        for (int i = 0; i < files.length; i++)             if present
          if (files[i].getName().startsWith("__"))
            files[i].delete();
        indexFile.delete();
      }

      indexFile.mkdir();

      EnvironmentConfig envConfig = new EnvironmentConfig();
      DatabaseConfig dbConfig = new DatabaseConfig();

      envConfig.setTransactional(true);                    Configure BDB's
      envConfig.setAllowCreate(true);                      environment, db
      dbConfig.setTransactional(true);
      dbConfig.setAllowCreate(true);B

      Environment env = new Environment(indexFile, envConfig);

      Transaction txn = env.beginTransaction(null, null);
      Database index = env.openDatabase(txn, "__index__", dbConfig);
      Database blocks = env.openDatabase(txn, "__blocks__", dbConfig);
      txn.commit();
      txn = env.beginTransaction(null, null);              Open db, transaction

      JEDirectory directory = new JEDirectory(txn, index, blocks);
                                                           Create JEDirectory
      IndexWriter writer = new IndexWriter(directory,
                             new StandardAnalyzer(Version.LUCENE_30),
                             true,
                             IndexWriter.MaxFieldLength.UNLIMITED);

      Document doc = new Document();
      doc.add(new Field("contents", "The quick brown fox...",
                    Field.Store.YES, Field.Index.ANALYZED));
      writer.addDocument(doc);

      writer.optimize();
      writer.close();

      directory.close();
      txn.commit();

      index.close();
      blocks.close();
      env.close();

      System.out.println("Indexing Complete");
  }
}
```

As you can see, there's a lot of Berkeley DB–specific setup required to initialize the database. Once you have an instance of JEDirectory, however, using it with Lucene is no different than using the built-in Directory implementations. Searching with JEDirectory uses the same mechanism (see BerkeleyDBJESearcher in the source code with this book). The next section describes using the WordNet database to include synonyms in your index.

9.3   *Synonyms from WordNet*

What a tangled web of words we weave. A system developed at Princeton University's Cognitive Science Laboratory, driven by psychology professor George Miller, illustrates the net of synonyms.[1] WordNet represents word forms that are interchangeable, both lexically and semantically. Google's define feature (type `define: word` as a Google search and see for yourself) often refers users to the online WordNet system, allowing you to navigate word interconnections. Figure 9.1 shows the results of searching for search at the WordNet site.

What does all this mean to developers using Lucene? With Dave Spencer's contribution to Lucene's contrib modules, the WordNet synonym database can be churned into a Lucene index. This allows for rapid synonym lookup—for example, for synonym injection during indexing or querying (see section 4.5 for such an implementation). We first see how to build an index containing WordNet's synonyms, then how to use these synonyms during analysis.

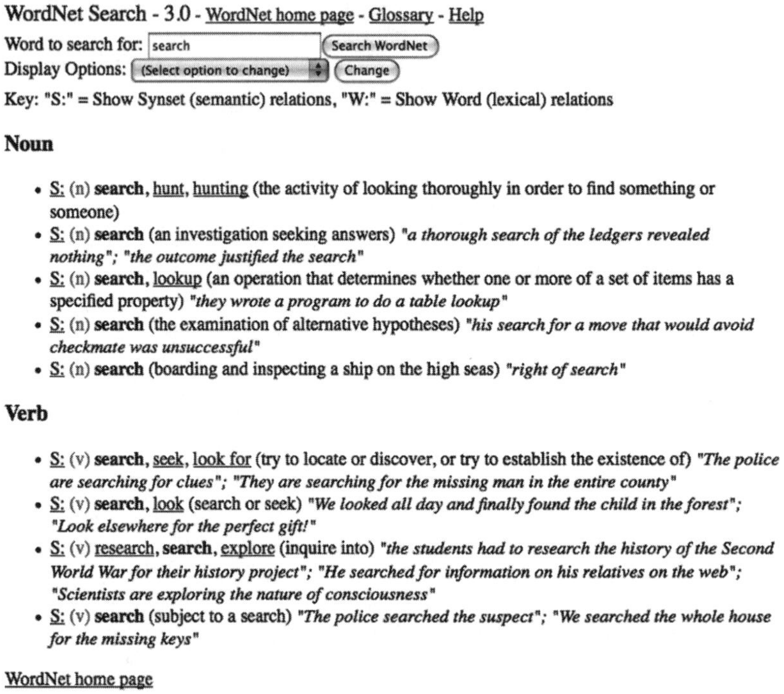

WordNet Search - 3.0 - WordNet home page - Glossary - Help

Word to search for: search   (Search WordNet)
Display Options: (Select option to change) ◆ (Change)
Key: "S:" = Show Synset (semantic) relations, "W:" = Show Word (lexical) relations

Noun

- S: (n) **search**, hunt, hunting (the activity of looking thoroughly in order to find something or someone)
- S: (n) **search** (an investigation seeking answers) *"a thorough search of the ledgers revealed nothing"; "the outcome justified the search"*
- S: (n) **search**, lookup (an operation that determines whether one or more of a set of items has a specified property) *"they wrote a program to do a table lookup"*
- S: (n) **search** (the examination of alternative hypotheses) *"his search for a move that would avoid checkmate was unsuccessful"*
- S: (n) **search** (boarding and inspecting a ship on the high seas) *"right of search"*

Verb

- S: (v) **search**, seek, look for (try to locate or discover, or try to establish the existence of) *"The police are searching for clues"; "They are searching for the missing man in the entire county"*
- S: (v) **search**, look (search or seek) *"We looked all day and finally found the child in the forest"; "Look elsewhere for the perfect gift!"*
- S: (v) research, **search**, explore (inquire into) *"the students had to research the history of the Second World War for their history project"; "He searched for information on his relatives on the web"; "Scientists are exploring the nature of consciousness"*
- S: (v) **search** (subject to a search) *"The police searched the suspect"; "We searched the whole house for the missing keys"*

WordNet home page

Figure 9.1   WordNet shows word interconnections, such as this entry for the word *search*.

---

[1]   Interestingly, this is the same George Miller who reported on the phenomenon of seven plus or minus two chunks in immediate memory.

9.3.1   *Building the synonym index*

To build the synonym index, follow these steps:

1   Download and expand the Prolog version of WordNet, currently distributed as the file WNprolog-3.0.tar.gz from the WordNet site at http://wordnet.princeton.edu/wordnet/download.

2   Obtain the binary (or build from source; see section 8.7) of the contrib Word-Net package.

3   Un-tar the file you downloaded. It should produce a subdirectory, prolog, that has many files. We're only interested in the wn_s.pl file. Build the synonym index using the `Syns2Index` program from the command line. The first parameter points to the wn_s.pl file and the second argument specifies the path where the Lucene index will be created:

```
java org.apache.lucene.wordnet.Syns2Index prolog/wn_s.pl wordnetindex
```

The `Syns2Index` program converts the WordNet Prolog synonym database into a standard Lucene index with an indexed field `word` and unindexed fields `syn` for each document. WordNet 3.0 produces 44,930 documents, each representing a single word; the index size is approximately 2.9MB, making it compact enough to load as a `RAM-Directory` for speedy access.

A second utility program in the WordNet contrib module lets you look up synonyms of a word. Here's a sample lookup of a word near and dear to our hearts:

```
java org.apache.lucene.wordnet.SynLookup indexes/wordnet search

Synonyms found for "search":
explore
hunt
hunting
look
lookup
research
seek
```

Figure 9.2 shows these same synonyms graphically using Luke.

To use the synonym index in your applications, borrow the relevant pieces from `SynLookup`, as shown in listing 9.3.

> **Listing 9.3   Looking up synonyms from a WordNet-based index**

```
public static void main(String[] args) throws IOException {
  if (args.length != 2) {
    System.out.println(
        "java org.apache.lucene.wordnet.SynLookup <index path> <word>");
  }

  FSDirectory directory = FSDirectory.open(new File(args[0]));
  IndexSearcher searcher = new IndexSearcher(directory);

  String word = args[1];
  Query query = new TermQuery(new Term(Syns2Index.F_WORD, word));
```

```
CountingCollector countingCollector = new CountingCollector();
searcher.search(query, countingCollector);

if (countingCollector.numHits == 0) {
  System.out.println("No synonyms found for " + word);
} else {
  System.out.println("Synonyms found for \"" + word + "\":");
}

ScoreDoc[] hits = searcher.search(query,
    countingCollector.numHits).scoreDocs;

for (int i = 0; i < hits.length; i++) {
  Document doc = searcher.doc(hits[i].doc);

  String[] values = doc.getValues(Syns2Index.F_SYN);

  for (int j = 0; j < values.length; j++) {
    System.out.println(values[j]);
  }
}

searcher.close();
directory.close();
}
```

Enumerate synonyms for word

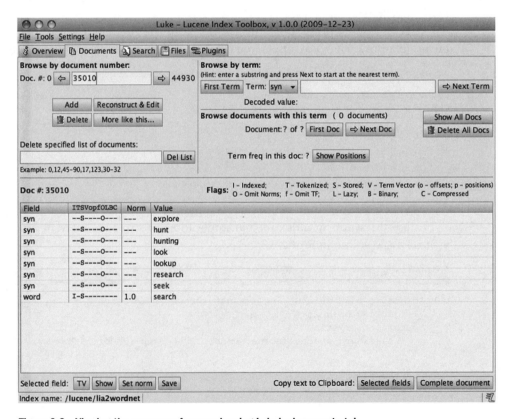

Figure 9.2   Viewing the synonyms for search using Luke's documents tab

The `SynLookup` program was written for this book, but it has been added into the WordNet contrib codebase.

9.3.2 Tying WordNet synonyms into an analyzer

The custom `SynonymAnalyzer` from section 4.5 can easily hook into WordNet synonyms using the `SynonymEngine` interface. Listing 9.4 contains the `WordNetSynonymEngine`, which is suitable for use with the `SynonymAnalyzer`.

Listing 9.4 `WordNetSynonymEngine` generates synonyms from WordNet's database

```java
public class WordNetSynonymEngine implements SynonymEngine {
  IndexSearcher searcher;
  Directory fsDir;

  public WordNetSynonymEngine(File index) throws IOException {
    fsDir = FSDirectory.open(index);
    searcher = new IndexSearcher(fsDir);
  }

  public void close() throws IOException {
    searcher.close();
    fsDir.close();
  }

  public String[] getSynonyms(String word) throws IOException {

    List<String> synList = new ArrayList<String>();

    AllDocCollector collector = new AllDocCollector();       // Collect every matching document

    searcher.search(new TermQuery(new Term("word", word)), collector);

    for (ScoreDoc hit : collector.getHits()) {               // Iterate over matching documents
      Document doc = searcher.doc(hit.doc);

      String[] values = doc.getValues("syn");

      for (String syn : values) {                            // Record synonyms
        synList.add(syn);
      }
    }

    return synList.toArray(new String[0]);
  }
}
```

We use the `AllDocCollector` from section 6.2.3 to keep all synonyms.

Adjusting the `SynonymAnalyzerViewer` from section 4.5.2 to use the `WordNetSynonymEngine`, our sample output looks like this:

```
1: [quick] [warm] [straightaway] [spry] [speedy] [ready] [quickly]
   [promptly] [prompt] [nimble] [immediate] [flying] [fast] [agile]
2: [brown] [embrown] [brownness] [brownish] [browned]
3: [fox] 2[trick] [throw] [slyboots] [fuddle] [fob] [dodger]
```

---

[2] We've apparently befuddled or outfoxed the WordNet synonym database because the synonyms injected for *fox* don't relate to the animal noun we intended.

```
       [discombobulate] [confuse] [confound] [befuddle] [bedevil]
4:  [jumps]
5:  [over] [terminated] [o] [ended] [concluded] [complete]
6:  [lazy] [slothful] [otiose] [indolent] [faineant]
7:  [dogs]
```

Interestingly, WordNet synonyms do exist for *jump* and *dog*, but only in singular form. Perhaps stemming should be added to our SynonymAnalyzer prior to the Synonym-Filter, or maybe the WordNetSynonymEngine should be responsible for stemming words before looking them up in the WordNet index. These are issues that need to be addressed based on your environment. This emphasizes again the importance of the analysis process and the fact that it deserves your attention.

We'll next see some alternative options for holding an index in RAM.

9.4   *Fast memory-based indices*

In section 2.10 we showed you how to use RAMDirectory to load an index entirely in RAM. This is especially convenient if you have a prebuilt index living on disk and you'd like to slurp the whole thing into RAM for faster searching. But because RAM-Directory still treats all data from the index as files, there's significant overhead during searching for Lucene to decode this file structure for every query. This is where two interesting contrib modules come in: MemoryIndex and InstantiatedIndex.

MemoryIndex, contributed by Wolfgang Hoschek, is a fast RAM-only index designed to test whether a single document matches a query. It's only able to index and search a single document. You instantiate the MemoryIndex, then use its addField method to add the document's fields into it. Then, use its search methods to search with an arbitrary Lucene query. This method returns a float relevance score; 0.0 means there was no match.

InstantiatedIndex, contributed by Karl Wettin, is similar, except it's able to index and search multiple documents. You first create an InstantiatedIndex, which is analogous to RAMDirectory in that it's the common store that a writer and reader share. Then, create an InstantiatedIndexWriter to index documents. Alternatively, you can pass an existing IndexReader when creating the InstantiatedIndex, and it will copy the contents of that index. Finally, create an InstantiatedIndexReader, and then an IndexSearcher from that, to run arbitrary Lucene searches.

Under the hood, both of these contributions represent all aspects of a Lucene index using linked in-memory Java data structures, instead of separate index files like RAMDirectory. This makes searching much faster than RAMDirectory, at the expense of more RAM consumption. In many cases, especially if the index is small, the documents you'd like to search have high turnover, the turnaround time after indexing and before searching must be low, and you have plenty of RAM, one of these classes may be a perfect fit.

Next we show how to build queries represented with XML.

9.5   *XML QueryParser:*
Beyond "one box" search interfaces

Contributed by MARK HARWOOD

The standard Lucene `QueryParser` is ideal for creating the classic single text input search interface provided by web search engines such as Google. But many search applications are more complex than this and require a custom search form to capture criteria with widgets such as the following:

- Drop-down list boxes, such as Gender: Male/Female
- Radio buttons or check boxes, such as Include Fuzzy Matching?
- Calendars for selecting dates or ranges of dates
- Maps for defining locations
- Separate free-text input boxes for targeting various fields, such as title or author

All of the criteria from these HTML form elements must be brought together to form a Lucene search request. There are fundamentally three approaches to constructing this request, as shown in figure 9.3.

Options 1 and 2 in figure 9.3 have drawbacks. The standard `QueryParser` syntax can only be used to instantiate a limited range of Lucene's available queries and filters. Option 2 embeds all the query logic in Java code, where it can be hard to read or maintain. Generally it's desirable to avoid using Java code to assemble complex collections of objects. Often a domain-specific text file provides a cleaner syntax and eases maintenance. Further examples include Spring configuration files, XML (Extensible Markup Language) UI (User Interface) Language (XUL) frameworks, Ant build files, or Hibernate database mappings. The contrib `XmlQueryParser` does exactly this, enabling option 3 from figure 9.3 for Lucene.

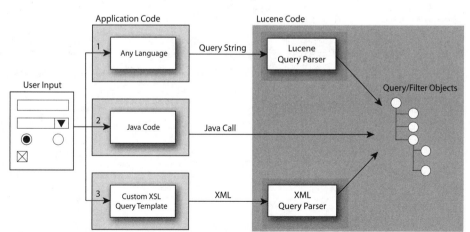

Figure 9.3   Three common options for building a Lucene query from a search UI

We'll start with a brief example, and then show a full example of how XmlQuery-Parser is used. We'll end with options for extending XmlQueryParser with new Query types. Here's a simple example XML query that combines a Lucene query and filter, enabling you to express a Lucene Query without any Java code:

```
<FilteredQuery>
  <Query>
    <UserQuery fieldName="text">"Swimming pool"</UserQuery>
  </Query>
  <Filter>
    <TermsFilter fieldName="dayOfWeek">monday friday</TermsFilter>
  </Filter>
</FilteredQuery>
```

XmlQueryParser parses such XML and produces a Query object for you, and the contrib module includes a full document type definition (DTD) to formally specify the out-of-the-box tags, as well as full HTML documentation, including examples, for all tags.

But how can you produce this XML from a web search UI in the first place? There are various approaches; one simple approach is to use the Extensible Stylesheet Language (XSL) to define query templates as text files that can be populated with user input at runtime. Let's walk through an example web application. This example is derived from the web demo available in the XmlQueryParser contrib sources.

9.5.1 *Using XmlQueryParser*

Consider the web-based form UI shown in figure 9.4. Let's create a servlet that can handle this job search form. The good news is this code should also work, unchanged, with your own choice of form.

Our Java servlet begins with some initialization code:

```
public void init(ServletConfig config) throws ServletException {
  super.init(config);
  try {
    openExampleIndex();

    queryTemplateManager = new QueryTemplateManager(
      getServletContext().getResourceAsStream("/WEB-INF/query.xsl"));

    xmlParser = new CorePlusExtensionsParser(defaultFldName,analyzer);

  } catch (Exception e) {
    throw new ServletException("Error loading query template",e);
  }
}
```

Figure 9.4   Advanced search user interface for a job search site, implemented with **XmlQueryParser**

The initialization code performs three basic operations:

- *Opening the search index*—Our method (not shown here) simply opens a standard `IndexSearcher` and caches it in our servlet's instance data.
- *Loading a Query template using the `QueryTemplateManager` class*—This class will be used later to help construct queries.
- *Creating an XML query parser*—The `CorePlusExtensionsParser` class used here provides an XML query parser that is preconfigured with support for all the core Lucene queries and filters and also those from Lucene's contrib modules (we'll examine how to add support for custom queries later).

Having initialized our servlet, we now add code to handle search requests, shown in listing 9.5.

Listing 9.5   Search request handler using XML query parser

```
protected void doPost(HttpServletRequest request, HttpServletResponse
    response)
  throws ServletException, IOException {

  Properties completedFormFields=new Properties();
  Enumeration pNames = request.getParameterNames();
  while(pNames.hasMoreElements()){                          Create
    String propName=(String) pNames.nextElement();          Properties
    String value=request.getParameter(propName);            object
    if((value!=null)&&(value.trim().length()>0)){
      completedFormFields.setProperty(propName, value);
    }
  }

  try{                                    Create XML document
    org.w3c.dom.Document xmlQuery=
      queryTemplateManager.getQueryAsDOM(completedFormFields);

    Query query=xmlParser.getQuery(xmlQuery.getDocumentElement());
                                                    Parse into
    TopDocs topDocs = searcher.search(query,10);    Lucene Query

    if(topDocs!=null) {
      ScoreDoc[] sd = topDocs.scoreDocs;
      Document[] results=new Document[sd.length];
      for (int i = 0; i < results.length; i++) {      Store
        results[i]=searcher.doc(sd[i].doc);           search
      }                                               results
      request.setAttribute("results", results);
    }
    RequestDispatcher dispatcher =
      getServletContext().getRequestDispatcher("/index.jsp");
    dispatcher.forward(request,response);
  }
  catch(Exception e){
    throw new ServletException("Error processing query",e);
  }
}
```

First, a `java.util.Properties` object is populated with all the form values where the user provided some choice of criteria. If `getParameter` is used, only one value for a given parameter is allowed; you could switch to `getParameterValues` instead to relax this limitation. The `Properties` object is then passed to the `QueryTemplateManager` to populate the search template and create an XML document that represents our query logic. The XML document is then passed to the query parser to create a `Query` object for use in searching. The remainder of the method is typical Servlet code used to package results and pass them on to a JavaServer Page (JSP) for display.

Having set up our servlet, we can now take a closer look at the custom query logic we need for our job search and how this is expressed in the query.xsl query template. The XSL language in the query template allows us to perform the following operations:

- Test for the presence of input values with `if` statements
- Substitute input values in the output XML document
- Manipulate input values, such as splitting strings and zero-padding numbers
- Loop around sections of content using `for each` statements

We won't attempt to document all the XSL language here, but clearly the previous list lets us perform the majority of operations that we typically need to transform user input into queries. The XSL statements that control the construction of our query clauses can be differentiated from the query clauses because they're all prefixed with the <xsl: tag. Our query.xsl is shown in listing 9.6.

Listing 9.6   Using XSL to transform the user's input into the corresponding XML query

```xml
<?xml version="1.0" encoding="ISO-8859-1"?>
<xsl:stylesheet version="1.0"
    xmlns:xsl="http://www.w3.org/1999/XSL/Transform">
  <xsl:template match="/Document">
    <BooleanQuery>
      <xsl:if test="type">                         ◁──❶
        <Clause occurs="must">
          <ConstantScoreQuery>
            <CachedFilter>
              <TermsFilter fieldName="type">
                <xsl:value-of select="type"/>
              </TermsFilter>
            </CachedFilter>
          </ConstantScoreQuery>
        </Clause>
      </xsl:if>

      <xsl:if test="description">                   ◁──❷
        <Clause occurs="must">
          <UserQuery fieldName="description">
            <xsl:value-of select="description"/>
          </UserQuery>
        </Clause>
      </xsl:if>

      <xsl:if test="South|North|East|West">         ◁──❸
```

```
          <Clause occurs="must">
            <ConstantScoreQuery>
              <BooleanFilter>
                <xsl:for-each select="South|North|East|West">
                  <Clause occurs="should">
                    <CachedFilter>
                      <TermsFilter fieldName="location">
                        <xsl:value-of select="name()"/>
                      </TermsFilter>
                    </CachedFilter>
                  </Clause>
                </xsl:for-each>
              </BooleanFilter>
            </ConstantScoreQuery>
          </Clause>
        </xsl:if>

        <xsl:if test="salaryRange">                    ◁──❹
          <Clause occurs="must">
            <ConstantScoreQuery>
              <RangeFilter fieldName="salary" >
                <xsl:attribute name="lowerTerm">
                  <xsl:value-of
select='format-number( substring-before(salaryRange,"-"), "000" )' />
                </xsl:attribute>
                <xsl:attribute name="upperTerm">
                  <xsl:value-of
select='format-number( substring-after(salaryRange,"-"), "000" )' />
                </xsl:attribute>
              </RangeFilter>
            </ConstantScoreQuery>
          </Clause>
        </xsl:if>
      </BooleanQuery>
  </xsl:template>
</xsl:stylesheet>
```

❶ If the user selects a preference for type of job, apply choice of permanent/contract filter and cache.

❷ Use standard Lucene query parser for any job description input.

❸ If any of the location fields are set, OR them all in a Boolean filter and cache individual filters.

❹ Translate salary range into a constant score range filter.

The template in listing 9.6 conditionally outputs clauses depending on the presence of user input. The logic behind each of the clauses is as follows:

- *Job type*—As a field with only two possible values (permanent or contract), this can be an expensive query clause to run because a search will typically match half of all the documents in our search index. If our index is very large, this can involve reading millions of document IDs from the disk. For this reason we use a cached filter for these search terms. Any filter can be cached in memory for reuse simply by wrapping it in a <CachedFilter> tag.

- *Job description*—As a free-text field, the standard Lucene query syntax is useful for allowing the user to express his criteria. The contents of the `<UserQuery>` tag are passed to a standard Lucene `QueryParser` to interpret the user's search.

- *Job location*—Like the job type field, the job location field is a field with a limited choice of values, which benefit from caching as a filter. Unlike the job type field, however, multiple choices of field values can be selected for a location. We use a `BooleanFilter` to OR multiple filter clauses together.

- *Job salary*—Job salaries are handled as a `RangeFilter` clause, which produces a Lucene `TermRangeFilter`. The input field from the search form requires some manipulation in the XSL template before it can be used. The salary range value arrives from our search form as a single string value such as 90–100. Before we can construct a Lucene request, we must split this into an Upper and Lower value, and make sure both values are zero-padded to comply with Lucene's requirement for these to be lexicographically ordered. Fortunately these operations can be performed using built-in XSL functions.

Let's see how to extend `XmlQueryParser`.

9.5.2 Extending the XML query syntax

Adding support for new tags in the query syntax or changing the classes that support the existing tags is a relatively simple task. As an example, we'll add support for a new XML tag to simplify the creation of date-based filters. Our new tag allows us to express date ranges in relation to today's date, such as "last week's news" or "people aged between 30 and 40." For example, in our job search application we might want to add a filter using syntax like this:

```
<Ago fieldName="dateJobPosted" timeUnit="days" from="0" to="7"/>
```

Each tag in the XML syntax has an associated `Builder` class, which is used to parse the content. The `Builders` are registered by adding the object with the name of the tag it supports to the parser. So in order to register a new builder for the `Ago` tag, we'd need to include a line like the following in the initialization method of our servlet:

```
xmlParser.addFilterBuilder("Ago", new AgoFilterBuilder());
```

The `AgoFilterBuilder` class, shown in listing 9.7, is a simple object that's used to parse any XML tags with the value `Ago`. For those familiar with the XML DOM interface, the code should be straightforward.

Listing 9.7 Extending the XML query parser with a custom `FilterBuilder`

```
public class AgoFilterBuilder implements FilterBuilder {

  static HashMap<String,Integer> timeUnits=new HashMap<String,Integer>();

  @Override                                      Extract field, time unit, from and to
  public Filter getFilter(Element element) throws ParserException {
    String fieldName = DOMUtils.getAttributeWithInheritanceOrFail(element,
                                                    "fieldName");
```

```
    String timeUnit = DOMUtils.getAttribute(element, "timeUnit", "days");
    Integer calUnit = timeUnits.get(timeUnit);
    if (calUnit == null) {
      throw new ParserException("Illegal time unit:"
                              +timeUnit+
                            " - must be days, months or years");
    }
    int agoStart = DOMUtils.getAttribute(element, "from",0);
    int agoEnd = DOMUtils.getAttribute(element, "to", 0);
    if (agoStart < agoEnd) {
      int oldAgoStart = agoStart;
      agoStart = agoEnd;
      agoEnd = oldAgoStart;
    }
    SimpleDateFormat sdf = new SimpleDateFormat("yyyyMMdd");

    Calendar start = Calendar.getInstance();
    start.add(calUnit, agoStart*-1);

    Calendar end = Calendar.getInstance();
    end.add(calUnit, agoEnd*-1);

    return NumericRangeFilter.newIntRange(
                fieldName,
                Integer.valueOf(sdf.format(start.getTime())),
                Integer.valueOf(sdf.format(end.getTime())),
                true, true);
  }
  static {
    timeUnits.put("days", Calendar.DAY_OF_YEAR);
    timeUnits.put("months",Calendar.MONTH);
    timeUnits.put("years", Calendar.YEAR);
  }
}
```

Extract field, time unit, from and to

Parse date/times

Create NumericRangeFilter

Our `AgoFilterBuilder` is called by the XML parser every time an `Ago` tag is encountered, and it's expected to return a Lucene `Filter` object given an XML DOM element. The class `DOMUtils` simplifies the code involved in extracting parameters. Our `AgoFilterBuilder` reads the `to`, `from`, and `timeUnit` attributes using `DOMUtils` to provide default values if no attributes are specified. Our code simplifies application logic for specifying `to` and `from` values by swapping the values if they're out of order.

An important consideration in coding `Builder` classes is that they should be thread-safe. For this reason our class creates a `SimpleDateFormat` object for each request rather than holding a single object in instance data because `SimpleDateFormat` isn't thread-safe.

Our `Builder` is relatively simple because the XML tag doesn't permit any child queries or filters to be nested inside it. The `BooleanQueryBuilder` class in Lucene's contrib module provides an example of a more complex XML tag that supports nested `Query` objects. These sorts of `Builder` classes must be initialized with a `QueryBuilderFactory`, which is used to find the appropriate `Builder` to handle each of the nested query tags.

Next we look at an alternate `QueryParser` that can produce span queries.

9.6   *Surround query language*

Contributed by PAUL ELSCHOT

As you saw in section 5.5, span queries offer some advanced possibilities for positional matching. Unfortunately, Lucene's `QueryParser` is unable to produce span queries. That's where the Surround `QueryParser` comes in. The Surround `QueryParser` defines an advanced textual language to create span queries.

Let's walk through an example to get a sense of the query language accepted by the Surround `QueryParser`. Suppose a meteorologist wants to find documents on "temperature inversion." In the documents, this "inversion" can also be expressed as "negative gradient," and each word can occur in various inflected forms.

This query in the Surround query language can be used for the "temperature inversion" concept:

```
5n(temperat*, (invers* or (negativ* 3n gradient*)))
```

This query will match the following sample texts:

- Even when the temperature is high, its inversion would...
- A negative gradient for the temperature.

But this won't match the following text, because there's nothing to match "gradient":

- A negative temperature.

This shows the power of spans: they allow word combinations in proximity ("negative gradient") to be treated as synonyms of single words ("inversion") or of other words in proximity.

You'll notice the Surround syntax is different from Lucene's built-in `QueryParser`. Operators, such as `5n`, may be in prefix notation, meaning they come first, followed by their subqueries in parentheses—for example, `5n(…,…)`. The parentheses for the prefix form gave the name Surround to the language, as they surround the underlying Lucene spans.

The `3n` operator is used in infix notation, meaning it's written between the two subqueries. Either notation is allowed in the Surround query language. The `5n` and `3n` operators create an unordered `SpanNearQuery` containing the specified subqueries, meaning they only match when their subqueries have spans within five or three positions of one another. If you replace n with w, then an ordered `SpanNearQuery` is created. The prefixed number may be from 1 to 99; if you leave off the number (and just type n or w), then the default is 1, meaning the subqueries have adjacent matching spans.

Continuing the example, suppose the meteorologist wants to find documents that match "negative gradient" and two more concepts: "low pressure" and "rain." In the documents, these concepts can be also expressed in plural or verb form and by synonyms such as "depression" for "low pressure" and "precipitation" for "rain." Also, all three concepts should occur at most 50 words away from each other:

```
50n( (low w pressure*) or depression*,
5n(temperat*, (invers* or (negativ* 3n gradient*)))),
rain* or precipitat*)
```

This matches the following sample texts:

- Low pressure, temperature inversion, and rain.
- When the temperature has a negative height gradient above a depression no precipitation is expected.

But it won't match this text because the word "gradient" is in the wrong place (further than three positions away), leading to improved precision in query results:

- When the temperature has a negative height above a depression no precipitation gradient is expected.

Just like the built-in `QueryParser`, Surround accepts parentheses to nest queries; `field:text` syntax to restrict the following search term to a specific field; * and ? as wildcards; Boolean AND, OR, and NOT operators; and the caret (^) for boosting subqueries. When no proximity is used, the Surround `QueryParser` produces the same Boolean and term queries as the built-in `QueryParser`. In proximity subqueries, wildcards and `or` map to `SpanOrQuery`, and single terms map to `SpanTermQuery`. Due to limitations of the Lucene `spans` package, the operators `and`, `not`, and `^` can't be used in subqueries of the proximity operators.

Note that the Lucene spans package is generally not as efficient as the phrase queries used by the standard query parser. And the more complex the query, the higher its execution time. Because of this, we recommend that you provide the user with the possibility of using filters.

Unlike the standard `QueryParser`, the Surround parser doesn't use an analyzer. This means that the user will have to know precisely how terms are indexed. For indexing texts to be queried by the Surround language, we recommend that you use a lowercasing analyzer that removes only the most frequently occurring punctuations. Such an analyzer is assumed in the previous examples. Using analyzers this way gives you good control over the query results, at the expense of having to use more wildcards during searching.

With the possibility of nested proximity queries; the need to know precisely what's indexed; the need to use parentheses, commas, and wildcards; and the preference for additional use of filters, the Surround query language isn't intended for the casual user. But for those users who are willing to spend more effort on their queries so they can achieve higher-precision results, this query language can be a good fit.

For a more complete description of the Surround query language, have a look at the README.txt file that comes with the source code. To use Surround, make sure that the surround contrib module is on the classpath and follow the example Java code to obtain a normal Lucene query:

```
String queryText = "5d(temperat*, (invers* or (negativ* 3d gradient*)))";
SrndQuery srndQuery = QueryParser.parse(queryText);
```

```
int maxBasicQueries = 1000;

BasicQueryFactory bqFactory = new BasicQueryFactory(maxBasicQueries);

String defaultFieldName = "txt";

Query luceneQuery = srndQuery.makeLuceneQueryField(
        defaultFieldName, bqFactory);
```

Our next contrib module is called Spatial Lucene.

9.7 Spatial Lucene

Contributed by PATRICK O'LEARY

Over the past decade, web search has transformed itself from finding a basic web page to finding specific results in a certain topic. Video search, medical search, image search, news, sports: each of these is referred to as a vertical search. One that stands out is local search, the use of specialized search techniques that allow users to submit geographically constrained searches against a structured database of local business listings.[3]

Lucene now contains a contrib module to enable local search: called Spatial Lucene, it started with the donation of local lucene from Patrick O'Leary (http://www.gissearch.com) and is expected to grow in capabilities over time. If you need to find "shoe stores that exist within 10 miles of location X," Spatial Lucene will do that.

Though by no means a full GIS (geographical information system) solution, Spatial Lucene supports these functions:

- Radial-based searching; for example, "show me only restaurants within 2 miles from a specified location." This defines a filter covering a circular area.
- Sorting by distance, so locations closer to a specified origin are sorted first.
- Boosting by distance, so locations closer to a specified origin receive a larger boost.

The real challenge with spatial search is that for every query that arrives, a different origin is required. Life would be simple if the origin were fixed, as we could compute and store all distances in the index. But because distance is a dynamic value, changing with every query as the origin changes, Spatial Lucene must take a dynamic approach that requires special logic during indexing as well as searching. We'll visit this logic here, as well as touch on some of the performance consideration implied by Spatial Lucene's approach. Let's first see how to index documents for spatial search.

9.7.1 Indexing spatial data

To use Spatial Lucene, you must first geo-code locations in your documents. This means a textual location, such as "77 Massachusetts Ave" or "the Louvre" must be translated into its corresponding latitude and longitude. Some methods for geo-coding are described at http://www.gissearch.com/geocode. This process must be done

---

[3] Wikipedia provides more details at http://en.wikipedia.org/wiki/Local_search_(Internet).

outside of Spatial Lucene, which only operates on locations represented as latitudes and longitudes.

Now what does Spatial Lucene do with each location? One simple approach would be to load each document's location, compute its distance on the fly, and use that for filtering, sorting, or boosting. This approach will work, but it results in rather poor performance. Instead, Spatial Lucene implements interesting transformations during indexing, including both projection and hierarchical tries and grids, that allow for faster searching.

PROJECTING THE GLOBE

To compute distances, we first must "flatten" the globe using a mathematical process called *projection*, depicted in figure 9.5. This is a necessary precursor so that we can represent any location on the surface of the earth using an equivalent two-dimensional coordinate system. This process is similar to having a light shine through a transparent globe and "projected" onto a flat canvas. By unfolding the globe into a flat surface, we make the methods for selecting bounding boxes much more uniform.

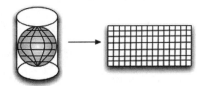

Figure 9.5 Projecting the globe's three-dimensional surface into two dimensions is necessary for spatial search.

There are two common projections. The first is the sinusoidal projection (http://en.wikipedia.org/wiki/Sinusoidal_projection), which keeps an even spacing of the projection. It will cause a distortion of the image, though, giving it a pinched look. The second projection is the Mercator projection (http://en.wikipedia.org/wiki/Mercator_projection), used because it gives a regular rectangular view of the globe. But it doesn't correctly scale to certain areas of the planet. If, for example, you look at a global projection of the earth on Google Maps and compare it to the spherical projection in Google Earth, you'll see that Greenland in Google Maps' rectangular projection is about the size of North America, whereas in Google Earth, it's about one third the size. Spatial Lucene has a built-in implementation for the sinusoidal projection, which we'll use in our example.

The next step is to map each location to a series of grid boxes.

TIERS AND GRID BOXES

Once each location is flattened through projection, it's mapped a hierarchical series of tiers and grid boxes as shown in figure 9.6. Tiers divide the 2D grid into smaller and smaller square grid boxes. Each grid box is assigned a unique ID; as each tier gets higher, the grid boxes become finer.

This arrangement allows for quick retrieval of locations stored at various levels of granularity. For instance, imagine you have 1 million documents representing different parts of the United States, and you want every document that has a location on the West Coast. If you were storing just the raw document locations, you'd have to iterate through every one of those million documents to see if its location is inside your

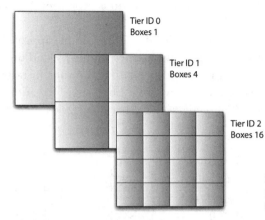

Tier ID 0
Boxes 1

Tier ID 1
Boxes 4

Tier ID 2
Boxes 16

Figure 9.6   Tiers and grid boxes recursively divide two dimensions into smaller and smaller areas.

search radius. But using grids, you can say, "My search radius is about 1,000 miles, so the tier that can best fit a 1,000-mile radius is tier 9, and grid reference –3.004 and –3.005 contain all the items I need." You then simply retrieve by two terms in Lucene to find the corresponding items. Two term retrievals versus 1 million iterations is a major cost and time savings.

Listing 9.8 shows how to index documents with Spatial Lucene. We use `Cartesian-TierPlotter` to create grid boxes for tiers 5 through 15.

Listing 9.8   Indexing a document for spatial search

```
public class SpatialLuceneExample {

  String latField = "lat";
  String lngField = "lon";
  String tierPrefix = "_localTier";

  private Directory directory;
  private IndexWriter writer;

  SpatialLuceneExample() throws IOException {
    directory = new RAMDirectory();
    writer = new IndexWriter(directory, new WhitespaceAnalyzer(),
                      MaxFieldLength.UNLIMITED);
  }

  private void addLocation(IndexWriter writer, String name, double lat,
                      double lng) throws IOException {

    Document doc = new Document();
    doc.add(new Field("name", name, Field.Store.YES,
              Field.Index.ANALYZED));

    doc.add(new Field(latField,
            NumericUtils.doubleToPrefixCoded(lat),
            Field.Store.YES, Field.Index.NOT_ANALYZED));
    doc.add(new Field(lngField,
            NumericUtils.doubleToPrefixCoded(lng),
            Field.Store.YES, Field.Index.NOT_ANALYZED));
```

Encode lat/lng as doubles

```
doc.add(new Field("metafile", "doc", Field.Store.YES,
                Field.Index.ANALYZED));
                                                        Use sinusoidal
IProjector projector = new SinusoidalProjector();      projection

int startTier = 5;                  Index around I
int endTier = 15;                   to I000 miles

for (; startTier <= endTier; startTier++) {
  CartesianTierPlotter ctp;
  ctp = new CartesianTierPlotter(startTier,            Compute
                          projector, tierPrefix);      bounding
                                                       box ID
  double boxId = ctp.getTierBoxId(lat, lng);
  System.out.println("Adding field " + ctp.getTierFieldName() + ":"
                + boxId);
  doc.add(new Field(ctp.getTierFieldName(), NumericUtils
                .doubleToPrefixCoded(boxId), Field.Store.YES,
                Field.Index.NOT_ANALYZED_NO_NORMS));
                                                       Add tier field
}

writer.addDocument(doc);
System.out.println("===== Added Doc to index ====");
  }
}
```

The most important part is the loop that creates the tiers for each location to be indexed. You start by creating a `CartesianTierPlotter` for the current tier:

```
ctp = new CartesianTierPlotter(startTier, projector, tierPrefix);
```

The parameters are as follows:

- `tierLevel`, in our case starting at 5 and going to 15.
- `projector` is the `SinusoidalProjector`, which is the method to project latitude and longitude to a flat surface.
- `tierPrefix` is the string used as the prefix of the field name, in our case "_localTier".

We then call `ctp.getTierBoxId(lat, lng)` with the latitude and longitude values. This returns the ID of the grid box that will contain the latitude and longitude values at this tier level, which is a double representing x,y coordinates. For example, adding field `_localTier11:-12.0016` would mean at zoom level 11, box –12.0016 contains the location you've added, at grid position x = –12, y = 16. This provides a rapid method for looking up values in an area and finding its nearest neighbors. The method `addLocation` is simple to use:

```
addLocation(writer, "TGIFriday", 39.8725000, -77.3829000);
```

This method will add somewhere called `"TGIFriday"` with its latitude and longitude coordinates to a Lucene spatial index. Let's now see how to search the spatial index.

9.7.2   *Searching spatial data*

Once you have your data indexed, you'll need to retrieve it; listing 9.9 shows how. We'll create a method to perform a normal text search that filters and sorts according to distance from a specific origin. This is the basis of a standard local search.

Listing 9.9   Sorting and filtering by spatial criteria

```
public void findNear(String what, double latitude, double longitude,
                     double radius)
  throws CorruptIndexException, IOException {
  IndexSearcher searcher = new IndexSearcher(directory);

  DistanceQueryBuilder dq;
  dq = new DistanceQueryBuilder(latitude,
                                longitude,
                                radius,             Create
                                latField,           distance
                                lngField,           query
                                tierPrefix,
                                true);

  Query tq;
  if (what == null)                                     Match all
    tq = new TermQuery(new Term("metafile", "doc"));    documents
  else
    tq = new TermQuery(new Term("name", what));

  DistanceFieldComparatorSource dsort;
  dsort = new DistanceFieldComparatorSource(      Create
              dq.getDistanceFilter());            distance sort
  Sort sort = new Sort(new SortField("foo", dsort));

  TopDocs hits = searcher.search(tq, dq.getFilter(), 10, sort);

  int numResults = hits.totalHits;

  Map<Integer,Double> distances =
      dq.getDistanceFilter().getDistances();      Get distances map

  System.out.println("Number of results: " + numResults);
  System.out.println("Found:");
  for(int i =0 ; i < numResults; i++) {
    int docID = hits.scoreDocs[i].doc;
    Document d = searcher.doc(docID);

    String name = d.get("name");
    double rsLat = NumericUtils.prefixCodedToDouble(d.get(latField));
    double rsLng = NumericUtils.prefixCodedToDouble(d.get(lngField));
    Double geo_distance = distances.get(docID);

    System.out.printf(name +": %.2f Miles\n", geo_distance);
    System.out.println("\t\t("+ rsLat +","+ rsLng +")");
  }
}
```

The key component during searching is `DistanceQueryBuilder`. The parameters are

- latitude and longitude of the center location (origin) for the search
- radius of your search
- latField and lngField, the names of the latitude and longitude fields in the index
- tierPrefix, the prefix of the spatial tiers in the index, which must match the tierPrefix used during indexing
- needPrecise, which is true if you intend to filter precisely by distance

Probably the only parameter whose purpose isn't obvious is needPrecise. To ensure that all results fit in a radius, the distance from the center location of your search may be calculated for every potential result. Sometimes that precision isn't needed. For instance, to filter for all locations on the West Coast, which is a fairly arbitrary request, a minimal bounding box could suffice in which case you'd leave needPrecise as false. If you need precisely filtered results, or you intend to sort by distance, you must specify true.

Distance is a dynamic field and not part of the index. That means we must use Spatial Lucene's DistanceSortSource, which takes the distanceFilter from the DistanceQueryBuilder, because it contains all the distances for the query. Note that the field name (foo, in our example) is unused; DistanceSortSource provides the sorting information. See section 6.1 to learn more about custom sorting. Let's finish our example.

FINDING THE NEAREST RESTAURANT

We've seen how to populate an index with the necessary information for spatial searching and how to construct a query that filters and sorts by distance. Let's put the finishing touches on it, combining what we've done so far with some spatial data, as shown in listing 9.10. We've added an addData method—to enroll a bunch of bars, clubs, and restaurants into the index—along with a main function that creates the index and then does a search for the nearest restaurant.

Listing 9.10 Finding restaurants near home with Spatial Lucene

```java
public static void main(String[] args) throws IOException {
  SpatialLuceneExample spatial = new SpatialLuceneExample();
  spatial.addData();
  spatial.findNear("Restaurant", 39.8725000, -77.3829000, 8);
}

private void addData() throws IOException {
  addLocation(writer, "McCormick & Schmick's Seafood Restaurant",
          39.9579000, -77.3572000);
  addLocation(writer, "Jimmy's Old Town Tavern", 39.9690000, -77.3862000);
  addLocation(writer, "Ned Devine's", 39.9510000, -77.4107000);
  addLocation(writer, "Old Brogue Irish Pub", 39.9955000, -77.2884000);
  addLocation(writer, "Alf Laylah Wa Laylah", 39.8956000, -77.4258000);
  addLocation(writer, "Sully's Restaurant & Supper", 39.9003000, -
      77.4467000);
  addLocation(writer, "TGIFriday", 39.8725000, -77.3829000);
```

```
    addLocation(writer, "Potomac Swing Dance Club", 39.9027000, -77.2639000);
    addLocation(writer, "White Tiger Restaurant", 39.9027000, -77.2638000);
    addLocation(writer, "Jammin' Java", 39.9039000, -77.2622000);
    addLocation(writer, "Potomac Swing Dance Club", 39.9027000, -77.2639000);
    addLocation(writer, "WiseAcres Comedy Club", 39.9248000, -77.2344000);
    addLocation(writer, "Glen Echo Spanish Ballroom", 39.9691000, -77.1400000);
    addLocation(writer, "Whitlow's on Wilson", 39.8889000, -77.0926000);
    addLocation(writer, "Iota Club and Cafe", 39.8890000, -77.0923000);
    addLocation(writer, "Hilton Washington Embassy Row", 39.9103000,
            -77.0451000);
    addLocation(writer, "HorseFeathers, Bar & Grill", 39.01220000000001,
            -77.3942);
    writer.close();
}
```

We add a list of named locations using `addData`. Then, we search for the word *Restaurant* in our index within 8 miles from location (39.8725000, −77.3829000). You can run search this by entering `ant SpatialLucene` at the command prompt. You should see the following result:

```
Number of results: 3
Found:
Sully's Restaurant & Supper: 3.94 Miles
        (39.9003,-77.4467)
McCormick & Schmick's Seafood Restaurant: 6.07 Miles
        (39.9579,-77.3572)
White Tiger Restaurant: 6.74 Miles
        (39.9027,-77.2638)
```

As our final topic, let's look at the performance of Spatial Lucene.

9.7.3   *Performance characteristics of Spatial Lucene*

Unlike standard text search, which relies heavily on an inverted index where duplication in words reduces the size of an index and improves retrieval time, spatial locations have a tendency to be unique. The introduction of a Cartesian grid with tiers provides the ability to "bucketize" the locations into nonunique grids of different size, thus improving retrieval time. But calculating distance still relies on visiting individual locations in the index. This presents several problems:

- Memory consumption can be high as both the latitude and longitude fields are accessed through the field cache (see section 5.1).
- Results can have varying density.
- Distance calculations are by nature complex and slow.

MEMORY

Memory can be reduced by using the `org.apache.lucene.spatial.geohash` methods, which condense the latitude and longitude fields into a single hash field.[4] The `DistanceQueryBuilder` supports geohash with its constructor:

---

[4] See http://en.wikipedia.org/wiki/Geohash for a good description of what a geohash is.

```
DistanceQueryBuilder(double lat, double lng, double miles,
                     String geoHashFieldPrefix,
                     String tierFieldPrefix,
                     boolean needPrecise)
```

There's a trade-off in the additional processing overhead, though, for encoding and decoding the geohash fields.

DENSITY OF RESULTS

As you can imagine, searches for pizza restaurants in Death Valley and New York City will have different characteristics. The more results you have, the more distance calculations you'll need to perform. Distribution and multithreading help; the more concurrent work you can spread across threads and CPUs, the quicker the response. Caching doesn't help here, although Spatial Lucene does cache overlapping locations, because the center location of your search may change more frequently than your search term.

NOTE Don't index all your data by regions—you'll find an uneven distribution of load. Cities will generally have more data than suburbs, thus taking more processing time. Furthermore, more people will search for results in cities compared to suburbs.

PERFORMANCE NUMBERS

As a rough performance test, we evaluated a textual query that filters and sorts by distance. A single thread was used, running on a 3.06 GHz, 1.5 Java virtual machine with a 500MB heap. The searcher was first warmed with 5 queries, and the time averaged five requests for all documents with varying radii. There were 647,860 total documents in the index.

Table 9.1 shows the results. The first column holds the number of documents returned by the query; the second column holds the amount of time for the boundary box calculation, without the precise distance calculation; and the third column indicates the additional time required to get the precise result.

Table 9.1 Searching and filtering time with varying result counts

Number of results	Time to find results	Time to filter by distance
9,959	7 ms	520 ms
14,019	10 ms	807 ms
80,900	12 ms	1,650 ms

It's clear from table 9.1 that large sets of spatial data can be retrieved from the index rapidly: 12 ms for 80,900 items in a Cartesian boundary box is quite fast. But a significant amount of time is consumed by calculating all the precise result distances to filter out any that might exist outside the radius and to enable sorting.

NOTE If your main concern is the search score, and a rough bounding box will suffice for precision—for example, all documents in the West Coast compared to all documents precisely within 1,000 miles sorted by distance—then use the `DistanceQueryBuilder` with `needPrecise` set to `false`. You can calculate distances at display time with `DistanceUtils.getInstance().getDistanceMi(search_lat, search_long, result_lat, result_lng);`.

Let's see a contrib module that enables remote searching using Java's RMI.

9.8   *Searching multiple indexes remotely*

The contrib directory includes remote index searching capability through Remote Method Invocation (RMI), under contrib/remote. Although it used to be core functionality inside Lucene, this capability was moved into the contrib area as of the 2.9 release. There are numerous other alternatives to exposing search remotely, such as through web services. This section focuses solely on Lucene's contrib capabilities; other implementations are left to your innovation.

An RMI server binds to an instance of `RemoteSearchable`, which is an implementation of the `Searchable` interface just like `IndexSearcher` and `MultiSearcher`. The server-side `RemoteSearchable` delegates to a concrete `Searchable`, such as a regular `IndexSearcher` instance.

Clients to the `RemoteSearchable` invoke search methods identically to search through an `IndexSearcher` or `MultiSearcher`, as shown throughout chapters 3, 5, and 6. Figure 9.7 illustrates one possible remote-searching configuration.

Other configurations are possible, depending on your needs. The client could instantiate a `ParallelMultiSearcher` over multiple remote (and/or local) indexes, and each server could search only a single index.

To demonstrate `RemoteSearchable`, we put together a multi-index server configuration, similar to figure 9.7, using both `Multi-Searcher` and `ParallelMultiSearcher` in order to compare performance. We split the WordNet index (a database of nearly 44,000 words and their synonyms) into 26 indexes representing A through Z, with each word in the index corresponding to its first letter. The server exposes two RMI client-accessible `Remo-teSearchables`, allowing clients to access either the serial `MultiSearcher` or the `Paral-lelMultiSearcher`.

`SearchServer` is shown in listing 9.11.

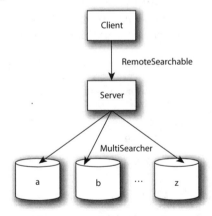

Figure 9.7   Remote searching through RMI, with the server searching multiple indexes

Listing 9.11 `SearchServer`: a remote search server using RMI

```
public class SearchServer {
  private static final String ALPHABET =
      "abcdefghijklmnopqrstuvwxyz";

  public static void main(String[] args) throws Exception {
    if (args.length != 1) {
      System.err.println("Usage: SearchServer <basedir>");
      System.exit(-1);
    }

    String basedir = args[0];                                          ← ❶
    Directory[] dirs = new Directory[ALPHABET.length()];
    Searchable[] searchables = new Searchable[ALPHABET.length()];
    for (int i = 0; i < ALPHABET.length(); i++) {
      dirs[i] = FSDirectory.open(new File(basedir, ""+ALPHABET.charAt(i)));
      searchables[i] = new IndexSearcher(
          dirs[i]);                                  ❷
    }

    LocateRegistry.createRegistry(1099);                          ← ❸

    Searcher multiSearcher = new MultiSearcher(searchables);
    RemoteSearchable multiImpl =
      new RemoteSearchable(multiSearcher);                            ❹
    Naming.rebind("//localhost/LIA_Multi", multiImpl);

    Searcher parallelSearcher =
        new ParallelMultiSearcher(searchables);
    RemoteSearchable parallelImpl =                                   ❺
        new RemoteSearchable(parallelSearcher);
    Naming.rebind("//localhost/LIA_Parallel", parallelImpl);

    System.out.println("Server started");

    for (int i = 0; i < ALPHABET.length(); i++) {
      dirs[i].close();
    }
  }
}
```

❶ Twenty-six indexes reside under the `basedir`, each named for a letter of the alphabet.

❷ A plain `IndexSearcher` is opened for each index.

❸ An RMI registry is created.

❹ A `MultiSearcher` over all indexes, named `LIA_Multi`, is created and published through RMI.

❺ A `ParallelMultiSearcher` over the same indexes, named `LIA_Parallel`, is created and published.

Querying through `SearchServer` remotely involves mostly RMI glue, as shown in `SearchClient` in listing 9.12. Because our access to the server is through a `Remote-Searchable`, which is a lower-level API than we want to work with, we wrap it inside a `MultiSearcher`. Why `MultiSearcher`? Because it's a wrapper over `Searchables`, making it as friendly to use as `IndexSearcher`.

Listing 9.12   `SearchClient` accesses RMI-exposed objects from `SearchServer`

```java
public class SearchClient {
  private static HashMap searcherCache = new HashMap();

  public static void main(String[] args) throws Exception {
    if (args.length != 1) {
      System.err.println("Usage: SearchClient <query>");
      System.exit(-1);
    }

    String word = args[0];

    for (int i=0; i < 5; i++) {
      search("LIA_Multi", word);                          ❶
      search("LIA_Parallel", word);
    }
  }

  private static void search(String name, String word)
      throws Exception {
    TermQuery query = new TermQuery(new Term("word", word));

    MultiSearcher searcher =                               ❷
      (MultiSearcher) searcherCache.get(name);

    if (searcher == null) {
      searcher =
        new MultiSearcher(                                 ❸
          new Searchable[]{lookupRemote(name)});
      searcherCache.put(name, searcher);
    }

    long begin = new Date().getTime();
    TopDocs hits = searcher.search(query, 10);            ❹
    long end = new Date().getTime();

    System.out.print("Searched " + name +
        " for '" + word + "' (" + (end - begin) + " ms): ");

    if (hits.scoreDocs.length == 0) {
      System.out.print("<NONE FOUND>");
    }

    for (ScoreDoc sd : hits.scoreDocs) {
      Document doc = searcher.doc(sd.doc);
      String[] values = doc.getValues("syn");
      for (String syn : values) {
        System.out.print(syn + " ");
      }
    }
    System.out.println();
    System.out.println();

  }                                                       ◁─❺

  private static Searchable lookupRemote(String name)
      throws Exception {
    return (Searchable) Naming.lookup("//localhost/" + name);  ◁─❻
  }
}
```

❶ We perform multiple identical searches to warm up the JVM and get a good sample of response time. The `MultiSearcher` and `ParallelMultiSearcher` are each searched.

❷ The searchers are cached, to be as efficient as possible.

❸ The remote `Searchable` is located and wrapped in a `MultiSearcher`.

❹ The searching process is timed.

❺ We don't close the searcher because it closes the remote searcher, thereby prohibiting future searches.

❻ Look up the remote interface.

WARNING   Don't `close()` the `RemoteSearchable` or its wrapping `MultiSearcher`. Doing so will prevent future searches from working because the server side will have closed its access to the index.

Let's see our remote searcher in action. For demonstration purposes, we ran it on a single machine in separate console windows. The server is started:

```
% ant SearchServer

Running lia.tools.remote.SearchServer...
Server started
Running lia.tools.remote.SearchClient...
Searched LIA_Multi for 'java' (78 ms): coffee

Searched LIA_Parallel for 'java' (36 ms): coffee

Searched LIA_Multi for 'java' (13 ms): coffee

Searched LIA_Parallel for 'java' (11 ms): coffee

Searched LIA_Multi for 'java' (11 ms): coffee

Searched LIA_Parallel for 'java' (16 ms): coffee

Searched LIA_Multi for 'java' (32 ms): coffee

Searched LIA_Parallel for 'java' (21 ms): coffee

Searched LIA_Multi for 'java' (8 ms): coffee

Searched LIA_Parallel for 'java' (15 ms): coffee
```

It's interesting to note the search times reported by each type of server-side searcher. The `ParallelMultiSearcher` is sometimes slower and sometimes faster than the `MultiSearcher` in our environment (four CPUs, single disk). Also, you can see the reason why we chose to run the search multiple times: the first search took much longer relative to the successive searches, which is probably due to JVM warmup and OS I/O caching. These results point out that performance testing is tricky business, but it's necessary in many environments. Because of the strong effect your environment has on performance, we urge you to perform your own tests with your own environment. Performance testing is covered in more detail in section 11.1.

If you choose to expose searching through RMI in this manner, you'll likely want to create a bit of infrastructure to coordinate and manage issues such as closing an index and how the server deals with index updates (remember, the searcher sees a snapshot of the index and must be reopened to see changes).

Let's explore yet another alternative for parsing queries, the newly added flexible `QueryParser`.

9.9 *Flexible QueryParser*

New in the 2.9 release is a modular alternative to Lucene's core `QueryParser`, under contrib/queryparser. This flexible `QueryParser` was donated to Lucene by IBM, where it's used in a number of internal products in order to share common query parsing infrastructure even when the supported syntax and query production vary substantially. By the time you read this, it's possible the core `QueryParser` will have been replaced with this more flexible one.

So what makes this new parser so flexible? It strongly decouples three phases of producing a `Query` object from an input `String`:

1. `QueryParser`—The incoming `String` is converted into a tree structured representation, where each `Query` is represented as a query node. This phase is intentionally kept minimal and hopefully is easily reused across many use cases. It's meant to be a thin veneer that does the initial rote translation of `String` into a rich query node tree.

2. `QueryNodeProcessor`—The query nodes are transformed into other query nodes or have their configuration altered. This phase is meant to do most of the heavy lifting—for example, taking into account what query types are allowed, what their default settings areand so forth.

3. `QueryBuilder`—This phase translates nodes in the query tree into the final `Query` instances that Lucene requires for searching. Like `QueryParser`, this is meant to be a thin veneer whose sole purpose is to render the query nodes into the appropriate Lucene `Query` objects.

There are two packages within the flexible `QueryParser`. First is the core framework, located under `org.apache.lucene.queryParser.core`. This package contains all the infrastructure for implementing the three phases of parsing. The second package contains the `StandardQueryParser`, located under `org.apache.lucene.query-Parser.standard`, and defines components for each of the three core phases of parsing for that match Lucene's core `QueryParser`. The `StandardQueryParser` is nearly a drop-in for any place that currently uses Lucene's core `QueryParser`:

```
Analyzer analyzer = new StandardAnalyzer(Version.LUCENE_30);
StandardQueryParser parser = new StandardQueryParser(analyzer);
Query q = parser.parse("(agile OR extreme) AND methodology", "subject");
System.out.println("parsed " + q);
```

Although the new parser is pluggable and modular, it does consist of many more classes than the core `QueryParser`, which can make initial customization more challenging. Listing 9.13 shows how to customize the flexible `QueryParser` to reject wildcard and fuzzy queries and produce span queries instead of phrase queries. We made these same changes in section 6.3.2 using the core `QueryParser`. Whereas the core `QueryParser` allows you to override one method to customize how each query is created, the flexible query parser requires you to create separate query processor or builder classes.

Listing 9.13 Customizing the flexible query parser

```
public class CustomFlexibleQueryParser extends StandardQueryParser {

  public CustomFlexibleQueryParser(Analyzer analyzer) {          Install custom
    super(analyzer);                                           node processor

    QueryNodeProcessorPipeline processors = (QueryNodeProcessorPipeline)
                         getQueryNodeProcessor();
    processors.addProcessor(new NoFuzzyOrWildcardQueryProcessor());   ◁─

    QueryTreeBuilder builders = (QueryTreeBuilder) getQueryBuilder();
    builders.setBuilder(TokenizedPhraseQueryNode.class,
                        new SpanNearPhraseQueryBuilder());
    builders.setBuilder(SlopQueryNode.class, new SlopQueryNodeBuilder());
  }
                                                              Install two custom
  private final class NoFuzzyOrWildcardQueryProcessor         query builders
      extends QueryNodeProcessorImpl {
    protected QueryNode preProcessNode(QueryNode node)
        throws QueryNodeException {
      if (node instanceof FuzzyQueryNode ||                   Prevent fuzzy,
          node instanceof WildcardQueryNode) {                wildcard queries
        throw new QueryNodeException(new MessageImpl("no"));
      }
      return node;
    }
    protected QueryNode postProcessNode(QueryNode node)
        throws QueryNodeException {
      return node;
    }
    protected List<QueryNode> setChildrenOrder(List<QueryNode> children) {
      return children;
    }
  }

  private class SpanNearPhraseQueryBuilder implements StandardQueryBuilder {
    public Query build(QueryNode queryNode) throws QueryNodeException {
      TokenizedPhraseQueryNode phraseNode =
          (TokenizedPhraseQueryNode) queryNode;
      PhraseQuery phraseQuery = new PhraseQuery();
                                                              Pull all terms
      List<QueryNode> children = phraseNode.getChildren();   ◁─  for phrase

      SpanTermQuery[] clauses;
      if (children != null) {
        int numTerms = children.size();
        clauses = new SpanTermQuery[numTerms];
        for (int i=0;i<numTerms;i++) {
          FieldQueryNode termNode = (FieldQueryNode) children.get(i);
          TermQuery termQuery = (TermQuery) termNode
            .getTag(QueryTreeBuilder.QUERY_TREE_BUILDER_TAGID);
```

```
            clauses[i] = new SpanTermQuery(termQuery.getTerm());
        }
    } else {                                                          Create
        clauses = new SpanTermQuery[0];                          SpanNearQuery
    }

    return new SpanNearQuery(clauses, phraseQuery.getSlop(), true);  ◁┘
    }
}                                                                     Override
                                                                 built-in builder
public class SlopQueryNodeBuilder implements StandardQueryBuilder {  ◁┘

    public Query build(QueryNode queryNode) throws QueryNodeException {
        SlopQueryNode phraseSlopNode = (SlopQueryNode) queryNode;

        Query query = (Query) phraseSlopNode.getChild().getTag(
                        QueryTreeBuilder.QUERY_TREE_BUILDER_TAGID);

        if (query instanceof PhraseQuery) {
            ((PhraseQuery) query).setSlop(phraseSlopNode.getValue());
        } else if (query instanceof MultiPhraseQuery) {
            ((MultiPhraseQuery) query).setSlop(phraseSlopNode.getValue());
        }

        return query;
    }
  }
}
```

In section 6.3 we were able to override single methods in QueryParser. But with the flexible QueryParser we create either a node processor, as we did to reject fuzzy and wildcard queries, or our own node builder, as we did to create a span query instead of a phrase query. Finally, we subclass StandardQueryParser to install our processors and builders.

In our last section, we'll cover some odds and ends available in the contrib/miscellaneous package.

9.10   *Odds and ends*

There are a great many other small packages available in the contrib/miscellaneous package, which we'll list briefly here:

- IndexSplitter and MultiPassIndexSplitter are two tools for taking an existing index and breaking it into multiple parts. IndexSplitter can only break the index according to its existing segments, but is fast because it does simple file-level copying. MultiPassIndexSplitter can break at arbitrary points (equally by document count), but is slower because it visits documents one at a time and makes multiple passes.

- BalancedSegmentMergePolicy is a custom MergePolicy that tries to avoid creating large segments while also avoiding allowing too many small segments to accumulate in the index. The idea is to prevent enormous merges from occurring, which because they are I/O- and CPU-intensive can affect ongoing search performance in a near-real-time search application. MergePolicy is covered in section 2.13.6.

- `TermVectorAccessor` enables you to access term vectors from an index even in cases where the document wasn't indexed with term vectors. You pass in a `Term-VectorMapper`, described in section 5.9.3, that will receive the term vectors. If term vectors were stored in the index, they're loaded directly and sent to the mapper. If not, the information is regenerated by visiting every term in the index and skipping to the requested document. Note that this regeneration process can be very slow on a large index.

- `FieldNormModifier` is a standalone tool (defines a static main method) that allows you to recompute all norms in your index according to a specified similarity class. It visits all terms in the inverted index for the field you specify, computing the length in terms of that field for all nondeleted documents, and then uses the provided similarity class to compute and set a new norm for each document. This is useful for fast experimentation of different ways to boost fields according to their length by using a custom `Similarity` class.

- `HighFreqTerms` is a standalone tool that opens the index at the directory path you provide, optionally also taking a specific field, and then prints out the top 100 most frequent terms in the index.

- `IndexMergeTool` is a standalone tool that opens a series of indexes at the paths you provide, merging them together using `IndexWriter.addIndexes`. The first argument is the directory that all subsequent directories will be merged into.

- `SweetSpotSimilarity` is an alternative `Similarity` implementation that provides a plateau of equally good lengths when computing field boost. You have to configure it to see the "sweet spot" typical length of your documents, but this can result in solid improvements to Lucene's relevance. http://wiki.apache.org/lucene-java/TREC_2007_Million_Queries_Track_IBM_Haifa_Team describes a set of experiments on the Trec 2007 Million Queries Track, including `Sweet-SpotSimilarity`, that provided sizable improvements to Lucene's relevance.

- `PrecedenceQueryParser` is an alternative `QueryParser` that tries to handle operator precedence in a more consistent manner.

- `AnalyzingQueryParser` is an extension to `QueryParser` that also passes the text for `FuzzyQuery`, `PrefixQuery`, `TermRangeQuery`, and `WildcardQuery` instances through the analysis process (the core `QueryParser` doesn't).

- `ComplexPhraseQueryParser` is an extension to `QueryParser` that permits embedding of wildcard and fuzzy queries within a phrase query, such as `(john jon jonathan~) peters*`.

9.11 Summary

This completes our coverage of all of Lucene's contrib modules!

Spatial Lucene is a delightful package that allows you to add geographic distance filters and sorting to your search application. `ChainedFilter` allows you to logically combine multiple filters into one.

We saw three alternative query parsers. `XmlQueryParser` aims to simplify creation of a rich search user interface by parsing XML into queries. The surround `QueryParser` enables a rich query language for span queries. The flexible QueryParser is a modular approach that strongly decouples three phases of query parsing and provides a drop-in replacement for the core QueryParser. Fast in-memory indices can be created using either MemoryIndex or InstantiatedIndex, or you can easily store your index in a Berkeley DB directory, giving you all the features of BDB, such as full transactions.

If you end up rolling up your sleeves and creating something new and generally useful, please consider donating it to the Lucene contrib repository or making it available to the Lucene community. We're all more than grateful for Doug Cutting's generosity for open sourcing Lucene itself. By also contributing, you benefit from a large number of skilled developers who can help review, debug, and maintain it; and, most important, you can rest easy knowing you have made the world a better place!

In the next chapter we'll cover the Lucene ports, which provide access to Lucene's functionality from programming languages and environments other than Java.

Using Lucene from other programming languages

This chapter covers
- Accessing Lucene from other programming languages
- Different styles of ports
- Comparing ports' APIs, features, and performance

Today, Lucene is the de facto standard open source IR library. Although Java is certainly a popular programming language, not everyone uses it. Many people prefer dynamic languages (such as Python, Ruby, Perl, or PHP). What do you do if you love Lucene but not Java? Fear not: you're in good company! Luckily, a number of options are available for accessing Lucene functionality from different programming languages, and we discuss them in this chapter.

Before we get started, let's discuss what we mean by the word *port*, as we're definitely taking liberty in broadening its usual meaning. We use the word port to mean any software that makes it possible to access Lucene's functionality from programming languages other than Java. Although port traditionally means a complete translation of the source code from one programming language to another, for this chapter we've been forced to modernize this definition. Many creative ways now exist for interacting with software from alternative programming languages. We'll first detail the four types of ports, and then we'll step through the popular Lucene ports we're aware of, in order by port type. In each case, we'll show which programming language(s) the port enables, and briefly describe the history, status, and trade-offs of that port. Please keep in mind that each port is an independent project with its own mailing lists, documentation, tutorials, user, and developer community that will be able to provide more detailed information.

10.1 Ports primer

Table 10.1 lists the different types of ports we'll see in this chapter.

A *native port* translates all of Lucene's sources into the target run time environment. This port type matches the traditional definition of the word port. Lucene.Net, which rewrites all of Lucene in C#, is a good example. Another example is Kino-Search, which provides Lucene-like functionality with a C core and Perl bindings. Because C or C++ is the accepted extensions language for many dynamic languages, such as Perl and Python, we count this as a native port. A native port can be a loose port, which means it doesn't precisely match all APIs of Lucene but retains the same general approach.

Table 10.1   Types of Lucene ports

Port type	Description	Ports	Pros	Cons
Native port	All of Lucene's sources are ported to the target environment.	Lucene.Net CLucene KinoSearch Ferret Lucy Zend Framework	Lightweight runtime. Direct access to full native environment.	Port is costly, so high release delay. Possibly higher chance of bugs. May be less compatible with Lucene Java (depends on port).
Reverse native port	The target language runs on a JVM.	Jython, JRuby	Lightweight runtime. 100% compatibility with Lucene.	Target language may lose some features, such as native extensions.
Local wrapper	A JVM is embedded into the native language's runtime, and a wrapper is used to expose Lucene's API.	PyLucene	Port is fast, so lower release delay, because only Lucene's APIs need to be exposed. 100% compatibility with Lucene.	Heavier, because two runtime environments are running side by side.
Client-server	A separate process, perhaps on a separate machine, runs Lucene Java and exposes a standard protocol for access. Clients in the target language are then created.	Solr + clients PHP Bridge Beagle	Clients are very fast to build. Solr provides functionality beyond Lucene and is actively developed. 100% compatibility with Lucene.	Much heavier weight since you now have a whole server to manage.

A reverse native port is the mirror image of a native port: the target runtime environment has been ported to run on a JVM. You write programs in your target language, such as Ruby, but the environment that runs your programs runs on a JVM and therefore has full access to any Java APIs, including Lucene. JRuby and Jython are good examples of this type of port. Such projects have nothing to do with Lucene; they simply enable access to any Java libraries from the target language, so none of the particular projects we discuss here are reverse native ports.

The local wrapper port runs a JVM under the hood, side by side with the "normal" runtime for the target language, and then only the APIs that need exposing are wrapped to the target environment. PyLucene is a good example.

In the client-server port, Lucene is running in a separate process, perhaps on another computer, and is accessible using a standard network-based protocol. The server could be just the JVM, as is the case with the PHP Bridge, or it may be a full server like Solr, which implements an XML over HTTP API for accessing Lucene and provides additional functionality beyond Lucene such as distributed search and faceted navigation. Clients are then developed, in multiple programming languages, to interact with the server over the network, using the target language.

Numerous differences exist between these types of ports, which we delve into next.

10.1.1 Trade-offs

Each type of port has important trade-offs, also summarized in table 10.1. The native port has the advantage of running only code for the target environment, within a single process. It's perhaps the cleanest, technically, and most lightweight approach, because a single runtime environment is running all code. But the downside is the cost of maintaining this port as Lucene's sources improve with time, which means longer release delay, higher chances that the port will differ from Lucene in API and index file format, and a higher risk that the project will be abandoned, as the efforts to continuously port source changes are significant. The native port is also likely to have substantially different performance characteristics, depending on whether the target environment is faster or slower than the JVM.

The reverse native port is a compelling option, assuming the runtime environment itself doesn't have problems running the target language. By using JRuby, you write Ruby code that has access to any Java code, but will generally lose access to Ruby extensions that are implemented in C. This option is also lightweight at runtime, because it runs in a single process and with a single (JVM) runtime environment.

The wrapper port is similarly a single process, but it embeds a JVM (to run the compiled Java bytecode from Lucene) as well as running the target environment's runtime, side by side, so it's somewhat heavier weight. The important trade-off is that much less work is required to stay current with Lucene's releases: only the API changes need to be ported, and not Lucene's entire implementation, so the work is in proportion to the net API "surface area" and the release delay can be much less. With PyLucene in particular, which autogenerates the wrapper code using the Java C Compiler

(JCC), the delay is essentially zero because the computer does all the work! If only other wrappers could use JCC.

Finally, the client-server port is the most strongly decoupled. Because a separate server runs and exposes Lucene's APIs via a standard network protocol, you can now share this server among multiple clients, possibly with different programming languages. But one potential downside is you now must manage a new standalone process or server, entirely different from your main application.

10.1.2 *Choosing the right port*

Having so many different types of ports may seem daunting at first, but in reality this gives a lot of flexibility to people who create the ports, which in turn gives you more options to choose from. If your application is already server-centric, and you're in love with PHP, then the client-server model (Solr as server and SolrPHP as client) is a no-brainer. In fact, server-based applications often require a client-server search architecture so that multiple front-end computers can share access to the search server(s). At the other end of the spectrum, if you're coding up a C++ desktop application and you can't afford a separate server, let alone a separate process, choose a native port like CLucene.

Ports have a tendency to come and go. Often it's one person driving the port, and if that person loses interest or can't afford the ongoing time, the port slowly dies. New ports, with new approaches, may surface and attract more interest. This is the natural evolution in the open source world. Although we do our best to describe the popular Lucene's ports, today, likely by the time you read this there will be other compelling options. We also mention briefly some other Lucene ports that aren't popular enough to merit full coverage. Be sure to do your due diligence, by searching the web and asking questions on users lists, before making your final decision.

Although each port tries to remain in sync with the latest Lucene version, they all necessarily lag behind Lucene's releases. Furthermore, most of the ports are relatively young, and from what we could gather, there's little developer community overlap. Each port takes some and omits some of the concepts from Lucene, but they all mimic its architecture. Each port has its own website, mailing lists, and everything else that typically goes along with open source projects. Each port also has its own group of founders and developers. There's also little communication between the ports' developers and Lucene's developers, although we're all aware of each project's existence.

With this said, let's look at each port, starting with CLucene.

10.2 *CLucene (C++)*

Contributed by BEN VAN KLINKEN *and* ITAMAR SYN-HERSHKO

CLucene is an open source native port of Lucene to C++, created by Ben van Klinken in 2003. Since then, many other developers have contributed to the project. The library's API and index file format are guaranteed to match those of the Java Lucene version it is based on. Table 10.2 shows its current status.

In its latest stable release, CLucene conforms to Lucene 1.9.1's API and index format, but ongoing development is active toward fixing issues and supporting more

Port feature	Port status
Port type	Native port
Programming languages	C++
Website	http://clucene.sourceforge.net/
Development status	Stable
Activity	Active development, active users
Last stable release	0.9.21b
Matching Lucene release	1.9.1
Compatible index format	Yes, 1.9.1
Compatible APIs	Yes
License	LGPL or Apache License 2.0

**Table 10.2
CLucene summary**

recent Lucene releases. As of this writing, development is proceeding on a source code branch toward full compatibility with Lucene's 2.3.2 release. Despite being officially marked unstable, the 2.3.2 branch seems quite stable and is already commonly used, although the APIs are still likely to change.

Adobe and Nero are believed to use CLucene in their products, as do other well-known open-source projects like Strigi, ht://Dig and kio-clucene.

10.2.1 *Motivation*

Many companies and developers use C/C++ exclusively and cannot take advantage of Lucene because it requires Java. CLucene offers the benefits of the Lucene world, while allowing those companies and developers to keep with the platforms and development tools they are most familiar with.

C++ developers are the main audience of CLucene. Since it is written in native code and has no prerequisites, it is also fairly easy to use the library from various high-level or scripting languages. Thanks to its flexible build system, native code, and small memory footprint, CLucene can also be used on embedded systems and mobile devices, where resources are tight and a JVM is usually not an option.

The project also aims to be attractive to people who like to use Lucene but want to increase performance or remove the overhead of using a JVM. Although the Java platform is constantly improving, basic operations like file handling and memory management will always be faster for C++ compiled code, since no underlying framework or Garbage Collection processes are involved. CLucene is guaranteed to provide better performance, even without the periodic code optimizations by its core team.

Although no current benchmarks are available to show this, those made with previous versions of Lucene and CLucene showed CLucene performed 5–10 times better than an equivalent version of Lucene, in terms of memory usage and execution speeds of indexing and searching operations. Both Lucene and CLucene have changed substantially since then.

10.2.2 API and index compatibility

The CLucene API is similar to Lucene's; code written in Java can be converted to C++ fairly easily. The drawback is that CLucene doesn't follow the generally accepted C++ coding standards. But due to the number of classes that would have to be redesigned and the difficulty it will pose for the process of keeping up with the original Lucene project, CLucene continues to follow a "Javaesque" coding standard. This approach also allows much of the user's code to be converted using macros and scripts.

Thanks to a full index-format compatibility, indexes built with Lucene are also searchable using CLucene and vice versa, as long as their index format version is supported by both. For example, as of this writing CLucene can read and write to indexes created by Lucene 2.3.2, but it will not work with indexes created or merged by Lucene 3+. Because backward compatibility is preserved in Lucene, even the most recent versions of Lucene can read indexes built with any version of CLucene, and those will still be readable by CLucene as long as they are not being written to by a more recent Lucene version.

Listing 10.1 shows a command-line program to perform basic indexing and searching. This program first indexes several documents with a single contents field. Following that, it runs a few searches against the generated in-memory index and prints the search results for each query.

Listing 10.1 Using CLucene's IndexWriter and IndexSearcher API

```
#include "CLucene.h"

using namespace lucene::analysis;
using namespace lucene::index;
using namespace lucene::document;
using namespace lucene::queryParser;
using namespace lucene::search;
using namespace lucene::store;

const TCHAR* docs[] = {
  _T("a b c d e"),
  _T("a b c d e a b c d e"),
  _T("a b c d e f g h i j"),        Index these
  _T("a c e"),                      documents
  _T("e c a"),
  _T("a c e a c e"),
  _T("a c e a b c"),
  NULL
};

const TCHAR* queries[] = {
  _T("a b"),
  _T("\"a b\""),
  _T("\"a b c\""),                  Run these
  _T("a c"),                        searches
  _T("\"a c\""),
  _T("\"a c e\""),
  NULL
```

```
};

int main( int32_t, char** argv )
{
  SimpleAnalyzer analyzer;                          Initialize
                                                    analyzer on stack

  try {

    Directory* dir = new RAMDirectory();

    IndexWriter* writer = new IndexWriter(dir, &analyzer, true);

    Document doc;                                   Reuse
                                                    Document
    for (int j = 0; docs[j] != NULL; ++j) {         instance
      doc.add( *_CLNEW Field(_T("contents"),
                             docs[j],                        Index document
                             Field::STORE_YES |
                             Field::INDEX_TOKENIZED) );
      writer->addDocument(&doc);
      doc.clear();
    }

    writer->close();
    delete writer;

    IndexReader* reader = IndexReader::open(dir);
    IndexSearcher searcher(reader);

    QueryParser parser(_T("contents"), &analyzer);
    parser.setPhraseSlop(4);

    Hits* hits = NULL;

    for (int j = 0; queries[j] != NULL; ++j)
      {                                             Parse
        Query* query = parser.parse(queries[j]);    query

        const wchar_t* qryInfo = query->toString(_T("contents"));
        _tprintf(_T("Query: %s\n"), qryInfo);
        delete[] qryInfo;

        hits = searcher.search(query);
        _tprintf(_T("%d total results\n"),
                 hits->length());                            Run search;
        for (size_t i=0; i < hits->length() && i<10; i++) {  print results
          Document* d = &hits->doc(i);
          _tprintf(_T("#%d. %s (score: %f)\n"),
                   i, d->get(_T("contents")),
                   hits->score(i));
        }

        delete hits;
        delete query;
      }

    searcher.close(); reader->close(); delete reader;
    dir->close(); delete dir;

  } catch (CLuceneError& e) {
    _tprintf(_T(" caught a exception: %s\n"), e.twhat());
```

```
    } catch (...){
      _tprintf(_T(" caught an unknown exception\n"));
    }
}
```

10.2.3 *Supported platforms*

Initially developed in Microsoft Visual Studio, CLucene also compiles in GCC, MinGW32, and the Borland C++ compiler. In addition to the Microsoft Windows platform, it has been successfully built on various Linux distributions (Red Hat, Ubuntu, and more), FreeBSD, Mac OS X and Debian. The code supports both 32- and 64-bit versions of these platforms.

Today, CLucene comes with CMake build scripts which simplify the build process, and allow it to be run on almost every platform. Both Unicode and non-Unicode builds are supported through it.

The CLucene team has made use of SourceForge's multiplatform compile farm to ensure that CLucene compiles and runs on as many platforms as possible. However, SourceForge has now closed its compile farm, so most cross-platform testing is done by contributors having physical access to various machines (even the rare ones), and by using virtual machines.

10.2.4 *Current and future work*

As part of the effort of being compatible with Java Lucene, the distribution package of CLucene includes many of the same components as Lucene, such as tests, contrib folder, and a demo application. This is the case also with the development repositories. Unfortunately, Lucene's rapid growth makes it very hard to keep up with it in real time, therefore many classes and tests may be missing.

CLucene once had several wrappers that allowed it to be used with other programming languages, such as Perl, Python, .NET and PHP. Most were made for previous versions of the library, and haven't been updated in some time. It is possible to bring them up to speed, or to use tools like SWIG to create one simple interface for many languages at once, should one needed to use them again.

Following a decision made during early development, no external libraries were incorporated for string handling, threading, and reference counting. The core team has begun to replace the custom code and macros used for those operations with Boost's C++ libraries. This update will make CLucene much more robust, and allow its developers to focus solely on porting more Lucene code, instead of worrying about platform-specific issues. Also, introduction of concepts like smart-pointers will make building of wrappers much easier.

10.3 *Lucene.Net (C# and other .NET languages)*

Contributed by GEORGE AROUSH, *creator of Apache Lucene.Net*

Apache Lucene.Net started as a project at SourceForge in 2004, as dotLucene. In April 2006, it was incubated into Apache, and by October 2009 it graduated as a subproject under Apache Lucene. As its main home page states:

Lucene.Net sticks to the APIs and classes used in the original Java implementation of Lucene. The API names as well as class names (including documentation and comments) are preserved with the intention of giving Lucene.Net the look and feel of the C# language and the .NET Framework. For example, the method IndexSearcher.search in the Java implementation now reads IndexSearcher.Search in the C# port.

In addition to the APIs and classes ported to C#, the algorithm of Java Lucene is ported to C# Lucene. This means an index created with Java Lucene is back-and-forth compatible with the C# Lucene; both at reading, writing and updating. In fact a Lucene index can be concurrently searched and updated using Lucene Java and Lucene.Net processes.

Lucene.Net's current status is summarized in table 10.3. Although the last official Apache release is 2.0, the trunk of the Lucene.Net subversion repository matches Lucene 1.4 up to 2.9.1 and all are quite stable and are used in a number of well-known environments such as MySpace and Beagle.

Beagle (http://beagle-project.org/Main_Page), a tool for searching your personal information space, including local files, email, images, calendar entries, and address book entries, is an interesting use case of Lucene.Net. Beagle is a large project in itself. Its design is just like Solr: there's a dedicated daemon process that exposes a network API, and then clients are available in various programming languages (currently at least C#, C, and Python). Beagle seems to be well adopted by Linux desktop environments as their standard local search implementation, running under Mono, the open source implementation of the .NET Framework.

Performance of Lucene.Net compares favorably with Lucene Java. The most recent testing, based on Lucene's 2.3.1 release, shows Lucene.Net to be about 5 percent faster than Lucene Java. The developers of Lucene.Net don't have any more recent performance numbers at this time. It would be safe to assume that Lucene.Net's performance is equal to that of Lucene Java.

The distribution package of Lucene.Net consists of the same components as the distribution package of Lucene. It includes the source code, tests, and the demo examples. In addition, some of the contrib components have been ported to C#.

Port feature	Port status
Port type	Native port
Programming languages	C#
Website	http://lucene.apache.org/lucene.net/
Development status	Stable
Activity	Active development, active users
Last stable release	2.9.1
Matching Lucene release	2.9.1
Compatible index format	Yes, 2.9.1
Compatible APIs	Yes
License	Apache License 2.0

Table 10.3
Lucene.Net summary

10.3.1 *API compatibility*

As stated earlier, although it's written in C#, Lucene.Net exposes an API that's virtually identical to that of Lucene. Consequently, code written for Lucene can be ported to C# with minimal effort. This compatibility also allows .NET developers to use documentation for the Java version, such as this book.

The difference is limited to the Java and C# naming styles. Whereas Java's method names begin with lowercase letters, the .NET version uses the C# naming style in which method names typically begin with uppercase letters. Listing 10.2 shows how to create an index using Lucene.Net.

Listing 10.2   C# code for indexing *.txt files with Lucene.Net

```csharp
class Indexer {
  String indexDir = args[0];
  String dataDir = args[1];

  public void Indexer(System.String indexDir) {
    Directory dir = FSDirectory.Open(new System.IO.FileInfo(indexDir));
    IndexWriter writer = new IndexWriter(
                      FSDirectory.Open(INDEX_DIR),
                      new StandardAnalyzer(Version.LUCENE_30),
                      true, IndexWriter.MaxFieldLength.UNLIMITED);
  }
```
Create IndexWriter
```csharp
  public void Close() {
    writer.Close();             // Close IndexWriter
  }

  public int Index(System.String dataDir) {
    System.String[] files =
        System.IO.Directory.GetFileSystemEntries(file.FullName);
    for (int i = 0; i < files.Length; i++) {
      IndexFile(new System.IO.FileInfo(files[i]));
    }
    return writer.NumDocs();
  }

  protected Document GetDocument(System.IO.FileInfo file) {
    Document doc = new Document();
    doc.Add(new Field("contents",
                    new System.IO.StreamReader(file.FullName,
                        System.Text.Encoding.Default)));
```
Index file content
```csharp
    doc.Add(new Field("filename",
                      file.Name,
                      Field.Store.YES,
                      Field.Index.NOT_ANALYZED));
    doc.Add(new Field("fullpath",
                      file.FullName,
                      Field.Store.YES,
                      Field.Index.NOT_ANALYZED));
```
Index filename and path
```csharp
    return doc;
  }

  private void IndexFile(System.IO.FileInfo file) {
```

```
    Document doc = GetDocument(file);                    Add document
    writer.AddDocument(doc);                         ◄─┘  to index
  }
}
```

As you can see, the source code is nearly identical to the corresponding indexing source code for Lucene java. The searching example, shown in listing 10.3, is also nearly identical. Both of these listings are extracted from the demo code that's included with Lucene.Net.

Listing 10.3   Searching an index with Lucene.Net

```
class Searcher {
  String indexDir = args[0];
  String q = args[1];
                                                            Open searcher
  public static void search(String indexDir, String q) {
    Directory dir = FSDirectory.Open(new System.IO.FileInfo(indexDir));
    IndexSearcher searcher = new IndexSearcher(dir);
    QueryParser parser = new QueryParser("contents",
                                    new
     StandardAnalyzer(Version.LUCENE_30));           Parse query        Search
    Query query = parser.Parse(q);                                      index
    Lucene.Net.Search.TopDocs hits = searcher.Search(query, 10);   ◄─┘
    System.Console.WriteLine("Found " +
                             hits.totalHits +
                             " document(s) that matched query '" + q + "':");
    for (int i = 0; i < hits.scoreDocs.Length; i++) {
      ScoreDoc scoreDoc = hits.ScoreDocs[i];                  Retrieve,
      Document doc = searcher.Doc(scoreDoc.doc);              display result
      System.Console.WriteLine(doc.Get("filename"));
    }
    searcher.Close();
    dir.Close();
  }
}
```

10.3.2 *Index compatibility*

Lucene.Net is fully compatible with Lucene at the index level: an index created by Lucene can be read by Lucene.Net, and vice versa. Of course, as Lucene evolves, indexes between versions of Lucene itself may not be portable, so this compatibility is currently limited to Lucene version 2.9.

10.4   *KinoSearch and Lucy (Perl)*

Perl is a popular programming language. Larry Wall, creator of Perl, has stated one of his goals in Perl is to offer many ways to accomplish a given task. Larry would be proud; there are quite a few choices for accessing Lucene's functionality from Perl.

We'll first visit the most popular choice, KinoSearch. After that we touch on Lucy, which is still under active development and hasn't had any releases yet but is nevertheless interesting. We finish with Solr's two Perl clients and CLucene's Perl bindings.

10.4.1 *KinoSearch*

KinoSearch, created and actively maintained by Marvin Humphrey, is a C and Perl loose native port of Lucene. This means its approach, at a high level, is similar to Lucene, but the architecture, APIs, and index file format aren't identical. The summary of its current status is shown in table 10.4. Marvin took the time to introduce interesting innovations to KinoSearch while porting to Perl and C; some of these innovations have inspired corresponding improvements back to Lucene, which is one of the delightful and natural "cross-fertilization" effects of open source development.

Port feature	Port status
Port type	Native port
Programming languages	C, Perl
Website	http://www.rectangular.com/kinosearch/
Development status	Alpha (though widely used and quite stable)
Activity	Active development, active users
Last stable release	0.163
Matching Lucene release	N/A (loose port)
Compatible index format	No
Compatible APIs	No
License	Custom

**Table 10.4
KinoSearch
summary**

KinoSearch is technically in the alpha stage of its development, but in practice is nevertheless extremely stable, bug free, and widely used in the Perl community. Development and users lists are active, and developers (mostly Marvin) are working toward the 1.0 first stable release. It's hard to gauge usage, but at least two well-known websites, Slashdot.org and Eventful.com, use it. When users find issues and post questions to the mailing lists, Marvin is always responsive.

KinoSearch also learned important lessons from an earlier port of Lucene to Perl, PLucene. PLucene, which has stopped development, suffered from performance problems, likely because it was implemented entirely in Perl; KinoSearch instead wraps Perl bindings around a C core. This allows the C core to do all the "heavy lifting," which results in much better performance. Early testing of KinoSearch showed its indexing performance to be close to Lucene's 1.9.1 release. But both KinoSearch and Lucene have changed quite a bit since then, so it's not clear how they compare today.

Probably the largest architectural difference is that KinoSearch requires you to specify field definitions up front when you first create the index (similarly to how you create a database table). The fields in documents then must match this preset schema. This allows KinoSearch to make internal simplifications, which gain performance, but at the cost of the full document flexibility that's available in Lucene.

There are also a number of API differences. For example, there's only one class, `InvIndexer`, for making changes to an index (whereas Lucene has two classes for doing so, `IndexWriter` and, somewhat confusingly, `IndexReader`). The index file format is also different, though similar. Listings 10.4 and 10.5 show examples for creating and search an index.

Listing 10.4   Creating an index with KinoSearch

```perl
use KinoSearch::InvIndexer;
use KinoSearch::Analysis::PolyAnalyzer;
my $analyzer
    = KinoSearch::Analysis::PolyAnalyzer->new( language => 'en' );

my $invindexer = KinoSearch::InvIndexer->new(
    invindex => '/path/to/invindex',
    create   => 1,
    analyzer => $analyzer,
);

$invindexer->spec_field(
    name  => 'title',
    boost => 3,
);
$invindexer->spec_field( name => 'bodytext' );

while ( my ( $title, $bodytext ) = each %source_documents ) {
    my $doc = $invindexer->new_doc;

    $doc->set_value( title    => $title );
    $doc->set_value( bodytext => $bodytext );

    $invindexer->add_doc($doc);
}

$invindexer->finish;
use KinoSearch::Searcher;
use KinoSearch::Analysis::PolyAnalyzer;

my $analyzer
    = KinoSearch::Analysis::PolyAnalyzer->new( language => 'en' );

my $searcher = KinoSearch::Searcher->new(
    invindex => '/path/to/invindex',
    analyzer => $analyzer,
);

my $hits = $searcher->search( query => "foo bar" );
while ( my $hit = $hits->fetch_hit_hashref ) {
    print "$hit->{title}\n";
}
```

Next we look at Lucy, a follow-on to KinoSearch.

10.4.2 Lucy

Lucy, at http://lucene.apache.org/lucy, is a new Lucene port. It plans to be a loose native port of Lucene to C, with a design that makes it simple to wrap the C code with APIs in different dynamic languages, with the initial focus on Perl and Ruby. Table 10.5 shows the summary of Lucy's current status.

Port feature	Port status
Port type	Native port
Programming languages	C with Perl, Ruby (and eventually others) bindings
Website	http://lucene.apache.org/lucy/
Development status	Design (no code/releases yet)
Activity	Active development
Last stable release	N/A
Matching Lucene release	N/A (loose port)
Compatible index format	No
Compatible APIs	No
License	Unknown

Table 10.5
Lucy summary

Lucy was started by the creator of KinoSearch, Marvin Humphrey, and the creator of Ferret (see section 10.5), David Balmain. Unfortunately, David became unavailable to work on the project, but Marvin and others have continued to actively work toward an initial release. Like Ferret and KinoSearch, Lucy is inspired by Lucene and derives much of its design from those two projects, aiming to achieve the best of both. Eventually other programming languages should be able to wrap Lucy's C core. Perl still offers more options.

10.4.3 Other Perl options

There are other ways to access Lucene's functionality from Perl. At least two clients are available for Solr: Solr.pm (see http://search.cpan.org/perldoc?Solr), which is separately developed from the Solr effort, and SolPerl, which is developed and distributed with Solr. Solr is a client-server port. If you have a strong preference for API- and index-compatible ports, and don't like that KinoSearch is a "loose" port, have a look at the Perl bindings in CLucene, which is also a native port of Lucene but with matching APIs and index file formats.

10.5 Ferret (Ruby)

The Ruby programming language, another dynamic language, has become quite popular recently. Fortunately, you can access Lucene from Ruby in various ways. The most popular port is Ferret, summarized in table 10.6.

Port feature	Port status
Port type	Native local wrapper
Programming languages	C, Ruby
Website	http://ferret.davebalmain.com/
Development status	Stable, though some serious bugs remain
Activity	Development stopped but users are active
Last stable release	0.11.6
Matching Lucene release	N/A (loose port)
Compatible index format	No
Compatible APIs	No
License	MIT-style license

Table 10.6
Ferret summary

Although independently developed, Ferret takes the same approach as KinoSearch, as a loose port of Lucene to C and Ruby. The C core does the heavy lifting, whereas the Ruby API exposes access to that core. Ferret was created by David Balmain, who has written a dedicated book about Ferret. There is also an acts_as_ferret plug-in for Ruby on Rails. Unfortunately, ongoing development on Ferret has ended.

User reports have shown Ferret's performance to be quite good, comparable at least to Lucene's 1.9 release. Even though development appears to have ended, usage of Ferret is still strong, especially for acts_as_ferret, (although there are reports of still open serious issues on the most recent release, so you should tread carefully).

Besides Ferret, you have a few other options for accessing Lucene from Ruby. solr-ruby, Solr's Ruby client, allows you to add, update, and delete documents as well as issue queries. Just install it with the command gem install solr-ruby. Here's a quick example:

```ruby
require 'solr'

# connect to the solr instance
conn = Solr::Connection.new('http://localhost:8983/solr', :autocommit => :on)

# add a document to the index
conn.add(:id => 123, :title_text => 'Lucene in Action, Second Edition')

# update the document
conn.update(:id => 123, :title_text => Ant in Action')

# print out the first hit in a query for 'action'
response = conn.query('action')
print response.hits[0]

# iterate through all the hits for 'action'
conn.query('action') do |hit|
  puts hit.inspect
end
```

```
# delete document by id
conn.delete(123)
```

Solr also provides a Ruby response format that produces valid Ruby Hash structure as the string response, which can be directly `eval`'d in Ruby even without the solr-ruby client. This enables a compact search solution. There's also an independently developed Rails plug-in, acts_as_solr, as well as Solr Flare (developed by Erik Hatcher), which is a feature-rich Rails plug-in that provides even more functionality than acts_as_solr. Finally, RSolr is a separately developed Solr Ruby client, available at http://github.com/mwmitchell/rsolr. It features transparent JRuby `DirectSolr-Connection` support and a simple hash-in, hash-out architecture.

NOTE   There's even a Common Lisp port called Montezuma, at http://code.google.com/p/montezuma. Development seems to have stopped after an initial burst of activity. In fact, Montezuma is a port of Ferret.

Another compelling option is to use JRuby, which is a reverse port of the Ruby language to run on a JVM. You still write Ruby code, but it's a JVM that's running your Ruby code, and thus any JAR, including Lucene, is accessible from Ruby. JRuby can access Lucene Java directly, and also work with Solr via solr-ruby, RSolr, or the native SolrJ library. The one downside to JRuby is that it can't run any Ruby extensions that are implemented in C (Lucene is entirely Java, so this would only affect apps that rely on other C-based Ruby extensions).

10.6   *PHP*

You have several interesting options if you'd like to use PHP. The first option is to use Solr with its PHP client, SolPHP, which is a client-server solution. As is the case for Ruby, Solr has a response format that produces valid PHP code, which can simply be `eval`'d in PHP.

The second option is CLucene's PHP bindings, included with CLucene's release, which is a pure native port. Another pure native port is Zend Framework.

10.6.1   *Zend Framework*

Zend Framework, summarized in table 10.7, is far more than a port of Lucene: it's a full open source object-oriented web application framework, implemented entirely in PHP 5. It includes a pure native port of Lucene to PHP 5 (described at http://framework.zend.com/manual/en/zend.search.lucene.html), and enables you to easily add full search to your web application.

There are some reports of slow performance during indexing (though this issue may have been resolved by more recent releases, so you should certainly test for yourself). Earlier releases didn't support Unicode content, but this has since been fixed.

Zend Framework may be a good fit for your application if you want a pure PHP solution, but if you don't require a native port and you'd like a lighter-weight solution instead, then PHP Bridge may be a good option.

Port feature	Port status
Port type	Pure native port
Programming languages	PHP 5
Website	http://framework.zend.com/
Development status	Stable
Activity	Active development and active users
Last stable release	1.7.3
Matching Lucene release	2.1
Compatible index format	Yes
Compatible APIs	Yes
License	BSD-style License

Table 10.7 Zend Framework summary

10.6.2 *PHP Bridge*

The PHP/Java Bridge, hosted at http://php-java-bridge.sourceforge.net/pjb/index.php, is technically a client-server solution. Normal Java Lucene runs in a stand-alone process, possibly on a different computer, and then the PHP runtime can invoke methods on Java classes through the PHP Bridge. It can also bridge to a running .NET process, so you could also use PHP to access Lucene.Net, for example. The release web archive (WAR) that you download from the website includes examples of indexing and searching with Lucene. For example, this is how you create an `IndexWriter`:

```
$tmp = create_index_dir();
$analyzer = new java("org.apache.lucene.analysis.standard.StandardAnalyzer");
$writer = new java("org.apache.lucene.index.IndexWriter",
                $tmp, $analyzer, true);
```

Because this is just a client-server wrapper around Lucene, you can tap directly into the latest release of Lucene. Performance should be close to Lucene's performance, except for the overhead of invoking methods over the bridge. Likely this affects indexing performance more so than searching performance.

10.7 *PyLucene (Python)*

Contributed by ANDI VAJDA, creator of PyLucene

In contrast to Perl, Guido van Rossum, the creator of Python, prefers to have one obvious way to do something, and in fact, there's one obvious choice for accessing Lucene from Python: PyLucene. Table 10.8 shows PyLucene's current status.

PyLucene is a "local wrapper" port, by adding Python bindings to the actual Lucene source code. PyLucene embeds a Java VM, that in turn executes the normal Lucene code, into a Python process. The PyLucene Python extension, a Python module called *lucene*, is machine-generated by a package called JCC, also included with the PyLucene sources. JCC is fascinating in its own right: it's written in Python and C++, and uses Java's reflection API, accessed via an embedded JVM, to peek at the public API for all classes in a JAR. Once it knows that API, it generates the appropriate C++ code that enables access to that API from Python through the Java Native Interface (JNI), using C++ as the common "bridge" language. Because JCC autogenerates all wrappers by inspecting Lucene's JAR file, the release latency is near zero.

Both PyLucene and JCC are released under the Apache 2.0 license and led by Andi Vajda, who also contributed Berkeley DbDirectory (see section 9.2) to the Lucene contrib codebase. PyLucene began as an indexing and searching component of Chandler (see section 9.2), an extensible open source PIM, but it was split into a separate project in June 2004. In January 2009, it was folded into Apache as a subproject of Lucene.

The performance of PyLucene should be similar to that of Lucene because the actual Lucene code is running in an embedded JVM in-process. The Python/Java barrier is crossed via the JNI and is reasonably fast. Virtually all the source code generated by JCC for PyLucene is C++. That code uses the Python VM for exposing Lucene objects to the Python interpreter, but none of the PyLucene code itself is interpreted Python.

PyLucene was first released in 2004. It has had a number of users over the years. Some Linux distributions, such as Debian, are now beginning to distribute PyLucene and JCC. Currently, the PyLucene developer mailing list has about 160 members. Traffic is moderate and usually involves build issues. Lucene issues while using PyLucene are usually handled on the Lucene user mailing list.

10.7.1 *API compatibility*

The source code for PyLucene is machine-generated by JCC. Therefore, all public APIs in all public classes available from Lucene are available from PyLucene. JCC exposes iterator and mapping access in Pythonic ways, making for a true Python experience while using Lucene. But here's a warning: once you've used Lucene from Python, it can be hard to go back to using Java!

As far as its structure is concerned, the API is virtually the same, which makes it easy for users of Lucene to learn how to use PyLucene. Another convenient side effect is that all existing Lucene documentation can be used for programming with PyLucene.

Port feature	Port status
Port type	Local wrapper
Programming languages	Python, C++, Java
Website	http://lucene.apache.org/pylucene/
Development status	Stable
Activity	Active development, active users
Last stable release	3.0
Matching Lucene release	3.0
Compatible index format	Yes
Compatible APIs	Yes
License	Apache Version 2.0

**Table 10.8
PyLucene summary**

PyLucene closely tracks the Lucene releases. The latest and greatest from Lucene is usually available via PyLucene a few days after a release.

10.7.2 *Other Python options*

PyLucene is our favorite option for using Lucene from Python, but there are other choices with different trade-offs:

- Solr, a client-server port, includes the SolPython client.
- If you prefer a native port, CLucene offers Python bindings.
- Beagle, described in section 10.3, also includes Python bindings. Like Solr, Beagle is a client-server solution, but the server runs in a .NET environment instead of a JVM.
- If you prefer a reverse port, you could simply use Jython, a port of the Python language to run on a JVM, which has full access to any Java APIs, including all releases of Lucene.

As you've seen, there are a number of ways to access Lucene from Python, the most popular being PyLucene.

10.8 *Solr (many programming languages)*

Solr, a sister project to Lucene and developed closely along with Lucene, is client-server architecture exposing access from many programming languages. Solr has comprehensive client-side support for many programming languages. Table 10.9 summarizes Solr's current status. In a nutshell, Solr is a server wrapper around Lucene. It provides a standard XML over HTTP interface for interacting with Lucene's APIs, and layers on further functionality not normally available in Lucene, such as distributed search, faceted navigation, and a field schema. Because Solr "translates" Lucene's Java-only API into a friendly network protocol, it's easy to create clients in different programming languages that speak this network protocol. For this reason, of all ways to access Lucene from other programming languages, Solr offers the least porting effort.

Port feature	Port status
Port type	Client-server
Programming languages	Java and many client wrappers
Website	http://lucene.apache.org/solr/
Development status	Stable
Activity	Active development, active users
Last stable release	1.3
Matching Lucene release	3.0
Compatible index format	Yes, 3.0
Compatible APIs	No
License	Apache License 2.0

Table 10.9
Solr summary

Name	Language/environment
SolRuby, acts_as_solr	Ruby/Rails
SolPHP	PHP
SolJava	Java
SolPython	Python
SolPerl, Solr.pm	Perl (http://search.cpan.org/perldoc?Solr)
SolJSON	JavaScript
SolrJS	JavaScript (http://solrjs.solrstuff.org/)
SolForrest	Apache Forrest/Cocoon
SolrSharp	C#
Solrnet	http://code.google.com/p/solrnet/
SolColdFusion	ColdFusion plug-in

Table 10.10
The many Solr clients
currently available

Solr has a delightful diversity of clients, shown in table 10.10. Be sure to check http://wiki.apache.org/solr/IntegratingSolr for the latest complete list. If you need to access Lucene from an exotic language, chances are there's already at least one Solr client. And if there isn't, it's easy to create one! Solr is actively developed and has excellent compatibility with Lucene because it uses Lucene under the hood. If your application can accept, or prefers, the addition of a standalone server, Solr is likely a good fit.

10.9   Summary

In this chapter, we discussed four types of ports, and we visited the popular existing Lucene ports known to us: CLucene, Lucene.Net, Pylucene, Solr and its many clients, KinoSearch, Ferret, the upcoming Lucy, and numerous PHP options. We looked at their APIs, supported features, Lucene compatibility, development and user activity, and performance as compared to Lucene, as well as some of the users of each port. The future may bring additional Lucene ports; the Lucene developers keep a list on the Lucene Wiki at http://wiki.apache.org/lucene-java/LuceneImplementations. As you can see, there are a great many ways to access Lucene from environments other than Java, each with its own trade-offs. Although this task may seem daunting, if you're trying to decide which of them to use, it's a great sign of Lucene's popularity and maturity that so many people have created all these options.

In the next chapter we'll visit administrative aspects of Lucene, including options for tuning Lucene for better performance.

Lucene administration
and performance tuning

This chapter covers

- Tuning for performance
- Effectively using threads
- Managing disk, file descriptors, memory usage
- Backing up and restoring your index
- Checking an index for corruption and repairing it
- Understanding common errors

You've seen diverse examples of how to use Lucene for indexing and searching, including many advanced use cases. In this chapter we cover the practical, hands-on administrative aspects of Lucene. Some say administrative details are a mundane and necessary evil, but at least one of your beloved authors would beg to differ! A well-tuned Lucene application is like a well-maintained car: it will operate for years without problems, requiring only a small, informed investment on your part. You can take pride in that! This chapter gives you all the tools you need to keep your Lucene application in tip-top shape.

Lucene has great out-of-the-box performance, but for some demanding applications, this is still not good enough. Fear not! There are many fun ways to tune for performance. Adding threads to your application is often effective, but the added complexity can make it tricky. We'll show you some simple drop-in classes that hide this complexity. Most likely you can tune Lucene to get the performance you need. We'll explore using hands-on examples for measuring performance.

Beyond performance, people are often baffled by Lucene's consumption of resources like disk space, file descriptors, and memory. Keeping tabs on this consumption over time as your index grows and application evolves is necessary to prevent sudden catastrophic problems. Fortunately, Lucene's use of these resources is simple to predict once you understand how. Armed with this information, you can easily prevent many problems.

Of course, what good is great performance if you have no more search index? Despite all your preventive efforts, things will eventually go wrong (thank you, Murphy's Law), and restoring from backup will be your only option. Lucene includes built-in support for making a hot backup of your index, even while you're still adding documents to it. You have no excuse to delay—just a bit of planning ahead will save you a lot of trouble later.

So, roll up your sleeves: it's time to get your hands dirty! Let's jump right in with performance tuning.

11.1   *Performance tuning*

Many applications achieve awesome performance with Lucene, out of the box. But you may find that as your index grows larger, and as you add new features to your application, or even as your website gains popularity and must handle higher and higher traffic, performance could eventually become an issue. Fortunately, you can try a number of things to improve Lucene's performance.

But first, be sure your application really does need faster performance from Lucene. Performance tuning can be a time-consuming and, frankly, rather addictive affair. It can also add complexity to your application, which may introduce bugs and make your application more costly to maintain. Ask yourself, honestly (use a mirror, if necessary): would your time be better spent improving the user interface or tuning relevance? You can always improve performance by simply rolling out more or faster hardware, so always consider that option first. Never sacrifice user experience in exchange for performance: keeping users happy, by providing the best experience humanly and "computerly" possible, should always be your top priority. These are the costs of performance tuning, so before you even start make sure you do need better performance. Still have your heart set on tuning performance? No problem: read on!

We'll begin with some basic steps you should always try no matter which performance metric you're optimizing for. Then, assuming you still require further tuning, we touch briefly on best practices for testing methodology. Without a solid and disciplined approach to testing, you have no way to measure your progress. Finally, we'll visit each of the important performance metrics in search applications: index-to-search delay, indexing throughput, search latency, and search throughput. We'll enumerate options to tune for each of these.

Which metric is important depends on your application and can vary with time. Often, indexing throughput is crucial while you're first building your index but then once the initial index is complete, index-to-search latency and search latency become more important. Be sure you know which metric matters to you because tuning for one is frequently at the expense of another! Trade-offs abound.

Let's begin with some simple steps to improve all metrics.

11.1.1 *Simple performance-tuning steps*

Before jumping into specific metrics, there are some simple steps that you should always follow regardless of what specific metric you need to tune:

- Use a solid-state disk (SSD), not magnetic platters, as your underlying storage device. Although solid-state disks are quite a bit more expensive per gigabyte, the stunning performance gains make the trade-off a no-brainer for most applications, and the price premium is quickly dropping with time.
- Upgrade to the latest release of Lucene. Lucene is always getting better: performance is improved, bugs are fixed, and new features are added. In version 2.3 in particular there were numerous optimizations to indexing, and version 2.9 has many optimizations for searching. The Lucene development community has a clear commitment to backward compatibility of the API: it's strictly kept across minor releases (such as 3.1 to 3.2) but not necessarily across major releases (such as 3.*x* to 4.*x*). A new minor release should just be a drop-in, so go ahead and try it!
- Upgrade to the latest release of Java; then try tuning the JVM's performance settings.
- Run your JVM with the -server switch; this generally configures the JVM for faster net throughput over time but at a possibly higher startup cost.
- Use a local file system for your index. Local file systems are generally quite a bit faster than remote ones. If you're concerned about local hard drives crashing, use a RAID array with redundancy. In any event, be sure to make backups of your index (see section 11.4): someday, something will inevitably go horribly wrong.
- Run a Java profiler, or collect your own rough timing using System.nanoTime, to verify your performance problem is in fact Lucene and not elsewhere in your application stack. For many applications, loading the document from a database or file system, filtering the raw document into plain text, and tokenizing that text, is time consuming. During searching, rendering the results from Lucene might be time consuming. You might be surprised!
- Do not reopen IndexWriter *or* IndexReader/IndexSearcher any more frequently than required. Share a single instance for a long time and reopen only when necessary.

- Use multiple threads. Modern computers have amazing concurrency in CPU, I/O, and RAM, and that concurrency is only increasing with time. Section 11.2 covers the tricky details when using threads.

- Use faster hardware. Fast CPU and fast I/O system (for large indices) will always help.

- Put as much physical memory as you can in your computers, and configure Lucene to take advantage of all of it (see section 11.3.3). But be sure Lucene isn't using so much memory that your computer is forced to constantly swap or the JVM is forced to constantly run garbage collection (GC).

- Budget enough memory, CPU, and file descriptors for your peak usage. This is typically when you're opening a new searcher during peak traffic perhaps while indexing a batch of documents.

- Turn off any fields or features that your application isn't using. Be ruthless!

- Group multiple text fields into a single text field. Then, you can search only that one field.

These best practices will take you a long ways toward better performance. It could be, after following these steps, you're done: if so, congratulations! If not, don't fear: there are still many options to try. We first need a consistent approach to testing performance.

11.1.2 *Testing approach*

You'll need to set up a simple repeatable test that allows you to measure the specific metrics you want to improve. Without this you can't know if you're improving things. The test should accurately reflect your application. Try to use true documents from your original content, and actual searches from your search logs, if available. Next, establish a baseline of your metric. If you see high variance on each run, you may want to run the test three or more times and record the best result (which is typically less noisy).

Finally, take an open-minded iterative approach: performance tuning is empirical and often surprising. Let the computer tell you what works and what doesn't. Make one change at a time, test it, and keep it only if the metric improved. Don't fall in love with some neat tuning before it demonstrates its value! Some changes will unexpectedly degrade performance, so don't keep those. Make a list of ideas to try, and sort them according to your best estimate of "bang for the buck": those changes that are quick to test and could be the biggest win should be tested first. Once you've improved your metric enough, stop and move on to other important things. You can always come back to your list later and keep iterating.

If all else fails, take your challenge to the Lucene java users list (java-user@lucene.apache.org). More than likely someone has already encountered and solved something similar to your problem and your question can lead to healthy discussion on how Lucene could be improved.

For our testing in this chapter we'll use the framework in contrib/benchmark, described in more detail in appendix C. This is an excellent tool for creating and running repeatable performance tests. It already has support for multiple runs of each test, changing Lucene configuration parameters, measuring metrics, and printing summary reports of the full test run. There are a large set of built-in tasks and document sources to choose from. Extending the framework with your own task is straightforward. You simply write an algorithm (.alg) file, using a simple custom scripting language, to describe the test. Then run it like this:

```
cd contrib/benchmark
ant run-task -Dtask-alg=<file.alg> -Dtask.mem=XXXM
```

That code prints great details about the metrics for each step of your test. Algorithm files also make it simple for others to reproduce your test results: you just send it to them and they run it!

APPLES AND ORANGES

When running indexing tests, there are a couple things you need to watch out for. First, because Lucene periodically merges segments, when you run two indexing tests with different settings it's quite possible that each resulting index could end in a different merge state. Maybe the first index has only 3 segments in it, because it just completed a large merge, and the other index has 17 segments. It's not fair to compare metrics from these two tests because in the first case Lucene did more work to make the index more compact. You're comparing apples and oranges.

To work around this, you could set mergeFactor to an enormous number, to turn off merging entirely. This will make the tests at least comparable, but just remember that the resulting numbers aren't accurate in an absolute sense, because in a real application you can't turn off merging. This is only worthwhile if you aren't trying to compare the cost of merging in the first place.

The second issue is to make sure your tests include the time it takes to call close on the IndexWriter. During close, IndexWriter flushes documents, may start new merges, and waits for any background merges to finish. Try to write your algorithm files so that the CloseIndex task is included in the report.

Let's look at specific metrics that you may need to tune.

11.1.3 Tuning for index-to-search delay

Index-to-search delay is the elapsed time from when you add, update, or delete documents in the index, until users see those changes reflected in their searches. For many applications, this is an important metric. But because a reader always presents the index as of the "point in time" when it was opened, the only way to reduce index-to-search delay is to reopen your reader more frequently.

Fortunately, the new near-real-time search feature added in Lucene 2.9, described in sections 2.8 and 3.2.5, is effective at keeping this turnaround time to a minimum, in practice often in the tens of milliseconds. After making changes using IndexWriter, you open a new reader by calling IndexWriter.getReader() or by using the previously obtained IndexReader's reopen method. But reopening the reader too frequently will slow down your indexing throughput as `IndexWriter` must flush its buffer to disk every time. Here are some tips for reducing the turnaround time:

- Call `IndexWriter.setMergedSegmentWarmer` to have `IndexWriter` warm up newly merged segments before making them available for searching. While this warming is happening (it takes place in a background thread as long as you're using the default `ConcurrentMergeScheduler`), new near-real-time readers can continue to be opened, using the segments from before the merge. This is especially important on completion of a large segment merge; it will reduce the subsequent latency on new searches against the near-real-time reader.

- Try switching `IndexWriter` to the `BalancedMergePolicy`, available in the miscellaneous contrib module (briefly covered in section 9.10). This `MergePolicy` was designed to minimize very large segment merges, which, because they are so CPU and I/O intensive, can have an adverse effect on search performance.

- Possibly set `IndexWriter`'s `maxBufferedDocs` to something small. That way, even when you aren't reopening the near-real-time reader, small segments are still being flushed. Although this may reduce your net indexing rate, in practice it also keeps reopen time to a minimum.

- If you know you're only adding documents, be sure to use `addDocument`, not `updateDocument`. There's a cost when using `updateDocument`, even if the specified term doesn't delete any documents: the `IndexWriter` must search for each deleted term while creating the new near-real-time reader.

On the bright side, many applications only require high indexing throughput while creating the initial index or doing bulk updates. During this time, the index-to-search latency doesn't matter because no searching is happening. But then once the index is built and in use in the application, the rate of document turnover is often low, while index-to-search latency becomes important. Next we'll see how to tune Lucene for high indexing throughput.

11.1.4 Tuning for indexing throughput

Indexing throughput measures how many documents per second you're able to add to your index, which determines how much time it will take to build and update your index. In the benchmark framework there are several built-in content sources we could choose from, including the Reuters corpus (`ReutersContentSource`), Wikipedia articles (`EnwikiContentSource`), and a simple document source that recursively finds all *.txt files under a directory (`DirContentSource`). We'll use Wikipedia as the document source for all our tests. This is obviously a large and diverse collection, so it makes for a good real-world test. For your own tests, create a document source subclassing `ContentSource`, and then use it for all your testing.

To minimize the cost of document construction, let's first preprocess the Wikipedia XML content into a single large text file that contains one article per line. We'll be following the steps shown in figure 11.1. There's a built-in `WriteLineDoc` task for exactly this purpose. Download the latest Wikipedia export from http://wikipedia.org. Leave it compressed as a bzip2 (.bz2) file; the benchmark framework can decompress it on the fly.

Next, save the following algorithm to createLineFile.alg:

```
content.source = org.apache.lucene.benchmark.byTask.feeds.EnwikiContentSource
docs.file = /x/lucene/enwiki-20090724-pages-articles.xml.bz2
line.file.out = wikipedia.lines.txt
content.source.forever = false

{WriteLineDoc() >: *
```

This algorithm uses the built-in `EnwikiContentSource`, which knows how to parse the XML format from Wikipedia, to produce one document at a time. Then, it runs the `WriteLineDoc` task over and over until there are no more documents, saving each document line by line to the file wikipedia.lines.txt.

Execute this by running `ant run-task -Dtask.alg=create-LineFile.alg` in a shell. It will take some time to run. Sit back and enjoy the sound of hard drives seeking away doing all the hard work for you—that is, if you're still not using a solid-state drive. It will print how many documents have been processed as it's running, and at the end will produce a large file, wikipedia.lines.txt, with one document per line. Great! Wasn't that easy?

Now that we're done with the onetime setup, let's run a real test, using the efficient `LineDocSource` as our content source. For the following tests, it's best to store wikipedia. lines.txt on a separate drive from the contrib/benchmark/work/index directory where the index is created so the I/O for reading the articles doesn't interfere with the I/O for writing the index. Go ahead and run the algorithm shown in listing 11.1.

Figure 11.1 Steps to test indexing throughput on Wikipedia articles

---

Listing 11.1 Testing indexing throughput using Wikipedia documents

```
analyzer=org.apache.lucene.analysis.standard.StandardAnalyzer
content.source=org.apache.lucene.benchmark.byTask.feeds.LineDocSource
directory=FSDirectory                    | Use stored fields
                                         ⤶ and term vectors
doc.stored = true
doc.term.vectors = true
docs.file=/x/lucene/enwiki-20090306-lines.txt

{ "Rounds"                      ⟵── Run test 3 times
  ResetSystemErase
  { "BuildIndex"
    -CreateIndex                              | Add first
    { "AddDocs" AddDoc > : 200000            ⤶ 200K docs
    -CloseIndex
  }
  NewRound
} : 3

RepSumByPrefRound BuildIndex     ⟵── Report results
```

This algorithm builds an index with the first 200,000 Wikipedia articles, three times, using `StandardAnalyzer`. At the end it prints a one-line summary of each run. If you were building a real index for Wikipedia, you should use an analyzer base on the Wikipedia tokenizer under contrib/wikipedia. This tokenizer understands the custom elements of Wikipedia's document format such as `[[Category:…]]`. Because we're only measuring indexing throughput here, `StandardAnalyzer` is fine for our purposes. You should see something like this as your final report:

```
Operation round runCnt recsPerRun rec/s elapsedSec avgUsedMem avgTotalMem
BuildIndex    0      1     200000 550.7    363.19  33,967,816  39,915,520
BuildIndex -  1  -   1  -  200000 557.3 -  358.85  24,595,904  41,435,136
BuildIndex    2      1     200000 558.4    358.17  23,531,816  41,435,136
```

Discarding the slowest and fastest run, our baseline indexing throughput is 557.3 documents/second. Not too shabby! As of Lucene 2.3, the out-of-the-box default indexing throughput has improved substantially. Here are some specific things to try to further improve your application's indexing throughput:

- Use many threads. This could be the single biggest impact change you can make, especially if your computer's hardware has a lot of concurrency. See section 11.2.1 for a drop-in threaded replacement for `IndexWriter`.

- Set `IndexWriter` to flush by memory usage and not document count. This is the default as of version 2.3, but if your application still calls `setMaxBufferedDocs`, change it to `setRAMBufferSizeMB` instead. Test different RAM buffer sizes. Typically larger is better, to a point. Make sure you don't go so high that the JVM is forced to GC too frequently, or the computer is forced to start swapping (see 11.3.3). Use the option `ram.flush.mb` in your algorithm to change the size of `IndexWriter`'s RAM buffer.

- Turn off compound file format (`IndexWriter.setUseCompoundFile(false)`). Creating a compound file takes some time during indexing. You'll also see a small performance gain during searching. But note that this will require many more file descriptors to be opened by your readers (see 11.3.2), so you may have to decrease `mergeFactor` to avoid hitting file descriptor limits. Set `compound=false` in your algorithm to turn off compound file format.

- Reuse `Document` and `Field` instances. As of version 2.3, a `Field` instance allows you to change its value. If your documents are highly regular (most are), create a single `Document` instance and hold onto its `Field` instances. Change only the `Field` values, and then call `addDocument` with the same `Document` instance. The `DocMaker` is already doing this, but you can turn it off by adding `doc.reuse.fields=false` to your algorithm.

- Test different values of `mergeFactor`. Higher values mean less merging cost while indexing, but slower searching because the index will generally have more segments. Beware: if you make this too high, and if compound file format is turned off, you can hit file descriptor limits on your OS (see section 11.3.2). As of version 2.3, segment merging is done in the background during indexing, so this is an automatic way to take advantage of concurrency. You may see faster performance with a high `mergeFactor`. But if you optimize the index in the end, a low `mergeFactor` should be faster as the merges will tend to be done concurrently while you're indexing. Test high and low values in your application and let the computer tell you which is best: you might be surprised!

- Use `optimize` sparingly; use the `optimize(maxNumSegments)` method instead. This method optimizes your index down to `maxNumSegments` (instead of always one segment), which can greatly reduce the cost of optimizing while still making your searches quite a bit faster. Optimizing takes a long time. If your searching performance is acceptable without optimizing, consider never optimizing.

- Index into separate indices, perhaps using different computers, and then merge them with `IndexWriter.addIndexesNoOptimize`. Don't use the older `addIndexes` methods; they make extra, often unnecessary, calls to `optimize`.

- Test the speed of creating the documents and tokenizing them by using the `ReadTokens` task in your algorithm. This task steps through each field of the document and tokenizes it using the specified analyzer. The document isn't indexed. This is an excellent way to measure the document construction and tokenization cost alone. Run this algorithm to tokenize the first 200K docs from Wikipedia using `StandardAnalyzer`:

```
analyzer=org.apache.lucene.analysis.standard.StandardAnalyzer

content.source=org.apache.lucene.benchmark.byTask.feeds.LineDocSource

docs.file=/x/lucene/enwiki-20090306-lines.txt

{ "Rounds"
  ResetSystemErase
  { ReadTokens > : 200000
  NewRound
} : 3

RepSumByPrefRound ReadTokens
```

which produces output like this:

```
Operation round run recsPerRun       rec/s elapsedSec avgUsedMem avgTotalMem
ReadTokens_N  0   1 161783312 1,239,927.9    130.48   2,774,040    2,924,544
ReadTokens_N  1 - 1 161783312 1,259,857.2  - 128.41   2,774,112  - 2,924,544
ReadTokens_N  2   1 161783312 1,253,862.0    129.03   2,774,184    2,924,544
```

- Discarding the fastest and slowest runs, we see that simply retrieving and tokenizing the documents takes 129.03 seconds, which is about 27 percent of the total indexing time from our baseline. This number is very low, because we're using `LineDocSource` as our content source. In a real application, creating, filtering, and tokenizing the document would be much more costly. Try it with your own `ContentSource`!

Let's combine the previous suggestions. We'll index the same 200,000 documents from Wikipedia but change the settings to try to improve indexing throughput. We'll turn off `compound`, increase `mergeFactor` to 30 and `ram.flush.mb` to 128, and use five threads to do the indexing. The resulting algorithm file is shown in listing 11.2.

Listing 11.2 Indexing with threads, compound, extra RAM, and larger `mergeFactor`

```
analyzer=org.apache.lucene.analysis.standard.StandardAnalyzer
content.source=org.apache.lucene.benchmark.byTask.feeds.LineDocSource
directory=FSDirectory

docs.file=/x/lucene/enwiki-20090306-lines.txt

doc.stored = true
doc.term.vector = true
ram.flush.mb = 128
compound = false
merge.factor = 30

log.step=1000

{ "Rounds"
  ResetSystemErase
  { "BuildIndex"
    -CreateIndex
    [ { "AddDocs" AddDoc > : 40000] : 5          Use 5 threads
    -CloseIndex                                   in parallel
  }
  NewRound
} : 3

RepSumByPrefRound BuildIndex
```

Running list 11.2 will produce output like this:

```
Operation   round runCnt recsPerRun rec/s elapsedSec  avgUsedMem avgTotalMem
BuildIndex    0      1     200000  879.5    227.40  166,013,008 205,398,016
BuildIndex  - 1  -   1  -  200000  899.7  - 222.29  167,390,016 255,639,552
BuildIndex    2      1     200000  916.8    218.15  174,252,944 276,684,800
```

Wow, the performance is even better: 899.7 documents per second! In your testing you should test each of these changes, one at a time, and keep only those that help.

There you have it! As we've seen, Lucene's out-of-the-box indexing throughput is excellent. But with some simple tuning ideas, you can make it even better. Let's look at search performance next.

11.1.5 *Tuning for search latency and throughput*

Search latency measures how long users must wait to see the results of their search. A user should never wait more than one second for search results, and ideally much less. Go run some Google searches and see how long you have to wait. Search throughput measures how many searches per second your application can service. These metrics, search latency and throughput, are two sides of one coin: improvements to search latency will also improve your search throughput, on the same hardware. It is a zero sum game, assuming you're running enough threads to fully saturate all resources available on the computer, which you definitely should!

The best way to measure your search latency and throughput is with a standalone load-testing tool, such as The Grinder or Apache JMeter. Such tools do a great job simulating multiple users and reporting latency and throughput results. They also test your application end to end, which is what a real user experiences when using your website. This is important, as it's common to pick up unexpected latency in the process of submitting the search, the processing performed by your web and application servers, the rendering of results performed by your application, the final HTML rendering in the web browser, and so forth. Remember that there are many cumulative delays in a modern search application, so be sure to measure all steps before and after Lucene is invoked to confirm that it's really Lucene that needs tuning.

Try to use real searches from real users when running search performance tests. If possible, cull search logs to get all searches, and run them in the same order and timing from the search logs. Use multiple threads to simulate multiple users, and verify you're fully utilizing the computer's concurrency. Include follow-on searches, like clicking through pages, in the test. The more "real world" your test is, the more accurate your test results are. For example, if you create your own small set of hand-crafted searches for testing, and run these over and over, you can easily see unexpectedly excellent performance because the OS has loaded all required bytes from disk into its I/O cache. To fix this, you may be tempted to flush the I/O cache before each test, which is possible. But then you're going too far in the other direction, by penalizing your results too heavily, since in your real application the I/O cache would legitimately help your performance.

Here are some steps to improve search performance:

- Use a read-only `IndexReader`, by calling `IndexReader.open(dir)` or `Index-Reader.open(dir, true)` (read-only is the default). Read-only `IndexReaders` have better concurrency because they can avoid synchronizing on certain internal data structures. This is now the default when you open an `IndexReader`.

- If you're not on Windows, use `NIOFSDirectory`, which has better concurrency, instead of `FSDirectory`. If you're running with a 64-bit JVM, try `MMapDirectory` as well.

- Make sure each step between the user and Lucene isn't adding unnecessary latency. For example, make sure your request queue is first-in, first-out and that all threads pull from this queue, so searches are answered in the order they originally arrived. Verify that rendering the results returned by Lucene is fast.

- Be sure you're using enough threads to fully utilize the computer's hardware (see section 11.2.2 for details). Increase the thread count until throughput no longer improves, but don't add so many threads that latency gets worse. There's a sweet spot—find it!

- Warm up your searchers before using them on real searches. The first time a certain sort is used, it must populate the `FieldCache`. Prewarm the searching by issuing one search for each of the sort fields that may be used (see section 11.1.2).

- Use `FieldCache` instead of stored fields, if you can afford the RAM. Field-Cache pulls all stored fields into RAM, whereas stored fields must go back to disk for every document. Populating a `FieldCache` is resource-consuming

(CPU and I/O), but it's done only once per field the first time it's accessed. Once it's populated, accessing it is very fast as long as the OS doesn't swap out the JVM's memory.

- Decrease `mergeFactor` so there are fewer segments in the index.
- Turn off compound file format.
- Limit your use of term vectors: retrieving them is quite slow. If you must, do so only for those hits that require it. Use `TermVectorMapper` (see section 5.9.3) to carefully select only the parts of the term vectors that you need.
- If you must load stored fields, use `FieldSelector` (see section 5.10) to restrict fields to exactly those that you need. Use lazy field loading for large fields so that the contents of the field are only loaded when requested.
- Run `optimize` or `optimize(maxNumSegments)` periodically on your index.
- Only request as many hits as you require.
- Only reopen the `IndexReader` when it's necessary.
- Call `query.rewrite().toString()` and print the result. This is the actual query Lucene runs. You might be surprised to see how queries like `FuzzyQuery` and `TermRangeQuery` rewrite themselves!
- If you're using `FuzzyQuery` (see section 3.4.8), set the minimum prefix length to a value greater than 0 (e.g., 3). Then you can increase the `minimumSimilarity`.

Note that quite a few of these options are in fact detrimental to indexing throughput: they're automatically at odds with one another. You have to find the right balance for your application.

We're done with performance tuning! You've seen how to measure performance, including the often conflicting metrics, and the many ways to tune Lucene's performance for different metrics. Next we'll see how to use threads to gain concurrency.

11.2 *Threads and concurrency*

Modern computers have highly concurrent hardware. Moore's law lives on, but instead of giving us faster clock speeds, we get more CPU cores. It's not just the CPU. Hard drives now provide *native command queuing*, which accepts many I/O requests at once and reorders them to make more efficient use of the disk heads. Even solid state disks do the same, and go further by using multiple channels to concurrently access the raw flash storage. The interface to RAM uses multiple channels. Then, there's concurrency across these resources: when one thread is stuck waiting for an I/O request to complete, another thread can use the CPU, and you'll gain concurrency.

Therefore, it's critical to use threads for indexing and searching. Otherwise, you're simply not fully utilizing the computer. It's like buying a Corvette and driving it no faster than 20 mph! Likely, switching to using threads is the single change you can make that will increase performance the most. You'll have to empirically test to find the right number of threads for your application and trade off search or indexing latency and throughput. Generally, at first, as you add more threads, you'll see latency stay about the same but throughput will improve. Then when you hit the right number of threads, adding more won't improve throughput and may hurt it somewhat due to context switching costs. But latency will increase.

Unfortunately, there's the dark side to threads, which if you've explored them in the past you've no doubt discovered: they can add substantial complexity to your application. Suddenly you must take care to make the right methods synchronized (but not too many!), change your performance testing to use threads, manage thread pools, and spawn and join threads at the right times. You'll spend lots of time reading the Javadocs in `java.util.concurrent`. Entirely new kinds of intermittent bugs become possible, such as deadlock if locks aren't acquired in the same order by different threads or `ConcurrentModificationException` and other problems if you're missing synchronization. Testing is difficult because the threads are scheduled at different times by the JVM every time you run a test. Are they really worth all this hassle?

Yes, they are! Lucene has been carefully designed to work well with many threads. Lucene is thread-safe: sharing `IndexSearcher`, `IndexReader`, `IndexWriter`, and so forth across multiple threads is perfectly fine. Lucene is also thread-friendly: synchronized code is minimized so that multiple threads can make full use of the hardware's concurrency. In fact, as of version 2.3, Lucene already makes use of concurrency right out of the box: `ConcurrentMergeScheduler` merges segments using multiple background threads so that adding and deleting documents in `IndexWriter` isn't blocked by merging. You can choose a merge scheduler in your algorithm by setting the `merge.scheduler` property. For example, to test indexing with the `SerialMergeScheduler` (which matches how segment merges were done before version 2.3), add `merge.scheduler = org.apache.lucene.index.Serial-MergeScheduler` to your algorithm.

In this section we'll show you how to leverage threads during indexing and searching, and provide a couple of drop-in classes to make it simple to gain concurrency.

11.2.1 Using threads for indexing

Figure 11.2 shows the design of a simple utility class, `ThreadedIndexWriter`, that extends `IndexWriter` and uses `java.util.concurrent` to manage multiple threads, adding and updating documents. The class simplifies multithreaded indexing because all details of these threads are hidden from you. It's also a drop-in for anywhere you're currently using the `IndexWriter` class, though you may need to modify it if you need to use one of `IndexWriter`'s expert constructors. Note that the class doesn't override `IndexWriter`'s `commit` or `prepareCommit` methods, which means you'll have to close it in order to commit all changes to the index.

The full source code is shown in listing 11.3. Specify how many threads to use, as well as the size of the

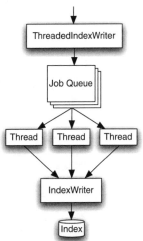

Figure 11.2
ThreadedIndexWriter
manages multiple threads for you.

queue, when you instantiate the class. Test different values to find the sweet spot for your application, but a good rule of thumb for numThreads is one plus the number of CPU cores in your computer that you'd like to consume on indexing, and then 4*numThreads for maxQueueSize. As you use more threads for indexing, you'll find that a larger RAM buffer size should help even more, so be sure to test different combinations of number of threads and RAM buffer size to reach your best performance. Check process monitor tools, like top or ps on Unix, Task Manager on Windows, or Activity Monitor on Mac OS X to verify that CPU utilization is near 100 percent.

Listing 11.3   Drop-in `IndexWriter` class to use multiple threads for indexing

```
public class ThreadedIndexWriter extends IndexWriter {

  private ExecutorService threadPool;
  private Analyzer defaultAnalyzer;                          Holds one doc
                                                         ◁┘ to be added
  private class Job implements Runnable {
    Document doc;
    Analyzer analyzer;
    Term delTerm;
    public Job(Document doc, Term delTerm, Analyzer analyzer) {
      this.doc = doc;
      this.analyzer = analyzer;
      this.delTerm = delTerm;
    }                                                 │ Does real work to
    public void run() {                             ◁┘ add, update doc
      try {
        if (delTerm != null) {
          ThreadedIndexWriter.super.updateDocument(delTerm, doc, analyzer);
        } else {
          ThreadedIndexWriter.super.addDocument(doc, analyzer);
        }
      } catch (IOException ioe) {
        throw new RuntimeException(ioe);
      }
    }
  }

  public ThreadedIndexWriter(Directory dir, Analyzer a,
                             boolean create, int numThreads,
                             int maxQueueSize,
                             IndexWriter.MaxFieldLength mfl)
      throws CorruptIndexException, IOException {
    super(dir, a, create, mfl);
    defaultAnalyzer = a;
    threadPool = new ThreadPoolExecutor(            ◁─── Create thread pool
        numThreads, numThreads,
        0, TimeUnit.SECONDS,
        new ArrayBlockingQueue<Runnable>(maxQueueSize, false),
        new ThreadPoolExecutor.CallerRunsPolicy());
  }
                                                        Have thread
  public void addDocument(Document doc) {               pool execute job
    threadPool.execute(new Job(doc, null, defaultAnalyzer));
  }                                                      ▽
```

```
public void addDocument(Document doc, Analyzer a) {
  threadPool.execute(new Job(doc, null, a));
}

public void updateDocument(Term term, Document doc) {
  threadPool.execute(new Job(doc, term, defaultAnalyzer));
}

public void updateDocument(Term term, Document doc, Analyzer a) {
  threadPool.execute(new Job(doc, term, a));
}

public void close()
    throws CorruptIndexException, IOException {
  finish();
  super.close();
}

public void close(boolean doWait)
    throws CorruptIndexException, IOException {
  finish();
  super.close(doWait);
}

public void rollback()
    throws CorruptIndexException, IOException {
  finish();
  super.rollback();
}

private void finish() {
  threadPool.shutdown();
  while(true) {
    try {
      if (threadPool.awaitTermination(Long.MAX_VALUE, TimeUnit.SECONDS)) {
        break;
      }
    } catch (InterruptedException ie) {
      Thread.currentThread().interrupt();
      throw new RuntimeException(ie);
    }
  }
}
}
```

Have thread pool execute job → (annotation pointing to the `execute` calls)

Shuts down thread pool → (annotation pointing to the `finish()` method)

The class overrides the addDocument and updateDocument methods: when one of these is called, a Job instance is created and added to the work queue in the thread pool. If the queue in the thread pool isn't full, control immediately returns back to the caller. Otherwise, the caller's thread is used to immediately execute the job. In the background, a worker thread wakes up, takes jobs from the front of the work queue, and does the real work. When you use this class, you can't reuse Document or Field instances, because you can't control precisely when a Document is done being indexed. The class overrides close and rollback methods, to first shut down the thread pool to ensure all adds and updates in the queue have completed.

Let's test `ThreadedIndexWriter` by using it in the benchmark framework, which makes it wonderfully trivial to extend with a new task. Make a `CreateThreadedIndex-Task.java`, as shown in listing 11.4.

Listing 11.4   Adding a new custom task to contrib/benchmark

```
public class CreateThreadedIndexTask extends CreateIndexTask {

  public CreateThreadedIndexTask(PerfRunData runData) {
    super(runData);
  }

  public int doLogic() throws IOException {
    PerfRunData runData = getRunData();
    Config config = runData.getConfig();
    IndexWriter writer = new ThreadedIndexWriter(
                        runData.getDirectory(),
                        runData.getAnalyzer(),
                        true,
                        config.get("writer.num.threads", 4),
                        config.get("writer.max.thread.queue.size",
                            20),
                        IndexWriter.MaxFieldLength.UNLIMITED);
    CreateIndexTask.setIndexWriterConfig(writer, config);
    runData.setIndexWriter(writer);
    return 1;
  }
}
```

Create an algorithm, derived from the baseline algorithm from section 11.2.3, with only these changes:

- Replace `CreateIndex` with `CreateThreadedIndex`.
- Add `doc.reuse.fields = false`, which tells `DocMaker` to not reuse fields.
- Optionally set `writer.num.threads` and `writer.max.thread.queue.size` to test different values.

Compile your `CreateThreadedIndexTask.java`, and run your algorithm like this so it knows where to find your new task:

```
ant run-task
  -Dtask.alg=indexWikiLine.alg
  -Dbenchmark.ext.classpath=/path/to/my/classes
```

You should see it finishes quite a bit faster than the original baseline. If your application already uses multiple threads while indexing, this class is unnecessary; this class is useful as a drop-in approach for taking advantage of threads in an application that doesn't already use multiple threads during indexing. Now you can drop this class in wherever you now use `IndexWriter` and take advantage of concurrency. Let's look next at using threads during searching.

11.2.2 *Using threads for searching*

Fortunately, a modern web or application server handles most of the threading issues for you: it maintains a first-in, first-out request queue, as well as a thread pool to service requests from the queue. This means much of the hard work is already done. All you have to do is create a query based on the details in the user's request, invoke your IndexSearcher, and render the results. It's so easy! If you aren't running Lucene in a web application, the thread pool support in java.util.concurrent should help you.

Be sure you tune the size of the thread pool to make full use of the computer's concurrency. Also, tune the maximum allowed size of the request queue for searching: when your website is suddenly popular and far too many searches per second are arriving, you want new requests to quickly receive an HTTP 500 Server Too Busy error, instead of waiting in the request queue forever. This also ensures that your application gracefully recovers once the traffic settles down again. Run a redline stress test to verify this.

There's one tricky aspect that the application server won't handle for you: reopening your searcher when your index has changed. Because an IndexReader only sees the index as of the point in time when it was opened, once there are changes to the index you must reopen your IndexReader to search them. Unfortunately, this can be a costly operation, consuming CPU and I/O resources. Yet, for some applications, minimizing index-to-search delay is worth that cost, which means you'll have to reopen your searcher frequently.

Threads make reopening your searcher challenging, because you can't close the old searcher until all searches are done with it, including iterating through the hits after IndexSearcher.search has returned. Beyond that, you may want to keep the old searcher around for long enough for all search sessions (the original search plus all follow-on actions like clicking through pages) to finish or expire. For example, consider a user who's stepping through page after page of results, where each page is a new search on your server. If you suddenly swap in a new searcher in between pages, then the documents assigned to each page could shift, causing the user to see duplicate results across pages or to miss some results. This unexpected behavior can erode your user's trust—pretty much the kiss of death for any search application. Prevent this by sending new pages for a previous search back to the original searcher when possible.

Listing 11.5 shows a useful utility class, SearcherManager, that hides the tricky details of reopening your searcher in the presence of multiple threads. It's able to open readers either from a Directory instance, in cases where you don't have direct access to the IndexWriter that's making changes, or from an IndexWriter by obtaining a near-real-time reader (see section 3.2.5 for details on near-real-time search).

> **Listing 11.5 Safely reopening IndexSearcher in a multithreaded world**

```
public class SearcherManager {                          Hold current
                                                        IndexSearcher
  private IndexSearcher currentSearcher;
  private IndexWriter writer;

  public SearcherManager(Directory dir) throws IOException {      ← ❶
```

```
  currentSearcher = new IndexSearcher(                    Create searcher
                          IndexReader.open(dir));         from Directory
  warm(currentSearcher);
}

public SearcherManager(IndexWriter writer) throws IOException {    ◁— ②
  this.writer = writer;
  currentSearcher = new IndexSearcher(             Create searcher from
                          writer.getReader());     near-real-time reader
  warm(currentSearcher);

  writer.setMergedSegmentWarmer(
      new IndexWriter.IndexReaderWarmer() {
        public void warm(IndexReader reader) throws IOException {     ③
          SearcherManager.this.warm(new IndexSearcher(reader));
        }
      });
}

public void warm(IndexSearcher searcher)          Implement
  throws IOException                              in subclass
{}

private boolean reopening;

private synchronized void startReopen()
  throws InterruptedException {
  while (reopening) {
    wait();
  }
  reopening = true;
}

private synchronized void doneReopen() {
  reopening = false;
  notifyAll();
}

public void maybeReopen()                         Reopen
  throws InterruptedException,                    searcher
          IOException {

  startReopen();

  try {
    final IndexSearcher searcher = get();
    try {
      IndexReader newReader = currentSearcher.getIndexReader().reopen();
      if (newReader != currentSearcher.getIndexReader()) {
        IndexSearcher newSearcher = new IndexSearcher(newReader);
        if (writer == null) {
          warm(newSearcher);
        }
        swapSearcher(newSearcher);
      }
    } finally {
      release(searcher);
    }
  } finally {
    doneReopen();
```

```
    }
  }
  public synchronized IndexSearcher get() {
    currentSearcher.getIndexReader().incRef();
    return currentSearcher;
  }

  public synchronized void release(
          IndexSearcher searcher)
    throws IOException {
    searcher.getIndexReader().decRef();
  }

  private synchronized void swapSearcher(IndexSearcher newSearcher)
    throws IOException {
    release(currentSearcher);
    currentSearcher = newSearcher;
  }

  public void close() throws IOException {
    swapSearcher(null);
  }
}
```

Return current searcher

Release searcher

This class uses the IndexReader.reopen API to efficiently open a new IndexReader that may share some SegmentReaders internally with the previous one. Instantiate this class once in your application—for example, naming it searcherManager—and then use it for access to the IndexSearcher whenever you need to run a search. Note that the class never closes the IndexSearcher. This is fine because Index-Searcher.close() is a no-op if you'd provided an already opened IndexReader when creating the IndexSearcher, as we've done.

If you have direct access to the IndexWriter that's making changes to the index, it's best to use the constructor that accepts IndexWriter ❷. You'll get faster reopen performance this way: SearcherManager uses IndexWriter's near-real-time getReader API, and you don't need to call IndexWriter.commit before reopening. Searcher-Manager also calls setMergedSegmentWarmer ❸ to ensure that newly merged segments are passed to the warm method.

Otherwise, use the constructor that takes a Directory instance ❶, which will open the IndexSearcher directly. Whenever you need a searcher, do this:

```
IndexSearcher searcher = searcherManager.get()
try {
  // do searching & rendering here…
} finally {
  searcherManager.release(searcher);
}
```

Every call to get must be matched with a corresponding call to release, ideally using a try/finally clause.

Note that this class doesn't do any reopening on its own. Instead, you must call maybeReopen every so often according to your application's needs. For example, a good time to call this is after making changes with the IndexWriter. If you passed Directory into SearcherManager, be sure you first commit any changes from the

IndexWriter before calling maybeReopen. You could also simply call maybeReopen during a search request, if upon testing you see the reopen time is fast enough. It's also possible to call maybeReopen from a dedicated background thread. In any event, you should create a subclass that implements the warm method to run the targeted initial searches against the new searcher before it's made available for general searching.

This concludes our coverage of using multiple threads with Lucene. Although adding threads to an application can sometimes bring unwanted complexity, the drop-in classes we provided should make it trivial to gain concurrency during indexing and searching. Let's move on now to exploring how Lucene uses resources.

11.3   *Managing resource consumption*

Like all software, Lucene requires certain precious resources to get its job done. A computer has a limited supply of things like disk storage, file descriptors, and memory. Often Lucene must share these resources with other applications. Understanding how Lucene uses resources and what you can do to control this lets you keep your search application healthy. You might assume Lucene's disk usage is proportional to the total size of all documents you've added, but you'll be surprised to see that often this is far from the truth. Similarly, Lucene's usage of simultaneous open file descriptors is unexpected: changes to a few Lucene configuration options can drastically change the number of required open files. Finally, to manage Lucene's memory consumption, you'll see why it's not always best to give Lucene access to all memory on the computer.

Let's start with everyone's favorite topic: how much disk space does Lucene require? Next we'll describe Lucene's open file descriptor usage and, finally, memory usage.

11.3.1 *Disk space*

Lucene's disk usage depends on many factors. An index with only a single pure indexed, typical text field will be about one third of the total size of the original text. At the other extreme, an index that has stored fields and term vectors with offsets and positions, with numerous deleted documents plus an open reader on the index, with an optimize running, can easily consume 10 times the total size of the original text! This wide range and seeming unpredictability makes it exciting to manage disk usage for a Lucene index.

Figure 11.3 shows the disk usage over time while indexing all documents from Wikipedia, finishing with an optimize call. The final disk usage was 14.2 GB, but the peak disk usage was 32.4 GB, which was reached while several large concurrent merges were running. You can immediately see how erratic it is. Rather than increasing gradually with time, as you add documents to the index, disk usage will suddenly ramp up during a merge and then quickly fall back again once the merge has finished, creating a sawtooth pattern. The size of this jump corresponds to how large the merge was (the net size of all segments being merged). Furthermore, with ConcurrentMerge-Scheduler, several large merges can be running at once and this will cause an even larger increase of temporary disk usage.

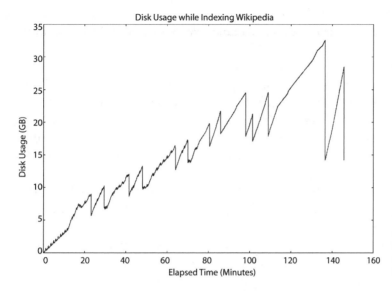

Figure 11.3
Disk usage while building an index of all Wikipedia documents, with `optimize` **called in the end**

How can you manage disk space when it has such wild swings? Fortunately, there's a method to this madness. Once you understand what's happening under the hood, you can predict and understand Lucene's disk usage. Also, you should know that in the event that your disk fills up while Lucene is writing to its index, the index won't become corrupt.

It's important to differentiate transient disk usage while the index is being built (shown in figure 11.3) versus final disk usage, when the index is completely built and optimized. It's easiest to start with the final size. Here's a coarse formula to estimate the final size based on the size of all text from the documents:

1/3 x indexed + 1 x stored +2 x term vectors

For example, if your documents have a single field that's indexed, with term vectors, and is stored, you should expect the index size to be around 3 1/3 times the total size of all text across all documents. Note that this formula is approximate. For example, documents with unusually diverse or unique terms, like a large spreadsheet that contains many unique product SKUs, will use more disk space.

You can reduce disk usage somewhat by turning off norms (section 2.5.3), turning off term frequency information for fields that don't need it (section 2.4.1), turning off positions and offsets when indexing term vectors (section 2.4.3), and indexing and storing fewer fields per document.

The transient disk usage depends on many factors. As the index gets larger, the size of each sawtooth will get larger as bigger merges are being done. Large merges also take longer to complete and will therefore tie up transient disk space for more time. When you optimize the index down to one segment, the final merge is the largest merge possible and will require one times the final size of your index in temporary disk space. Here are other things that will affect transient disk usage:

- Open readers prevent deletion of the segment files they're using. You should have only one open reader at a time, except when you are reopening it. Be sure to close the old reader!

- All segments that existed when the `IndexWriter` was first opened will remain in the directory, as well as those referenced by the current (in memory) commit point. If you commit frequently, less transient disk space will be used, but committing can be a costly operation, so this will impact your indexing throughput.

- If you frequently replace documents but don't run `optimize`, the space used by old copies of the deleted documents won't be reclaimed until those segments are merged.

- The more segments in your index, the more disk space will be used—more than if those segments were merged. This means a high `mergeFactor` will result in more disk space being used.

- Given the same net amount of text, many small documents will result in a larger index than fewer large documents.

- Don't open a new reader while `optimize`, or any other merges, are running; doing so will result in the reader holding references to segments that would otherwise be deleted. Instead, open after you have closed or committed your `IndexWriter`.

- Do open a new reader after making changes with `IndexWriter`, and close the old one. If you don't, the reader could be holding references to files that `IndexWriter` wants to delete, due to merging, which prevents the files from being deleted. Further, the existing reader will continue to work fine, but it won't see the newly committed changes from the `IndexWriter` until it's reopened.

- If you're running a hot backup (see section 11.4), the files in the snapshot being copied will also consume disk space until the backup completes and you release the snapshot.

Note that on Unix you may think disk space has been freed because the writer has deleted the old segments files, but in fact the files still consume disk space as long as those files are held open by an `IndexReader`. When you list the directory, you won't see the files, which is confusing—yet the files still consume bytes on disk. This is due to Unix's "delete on last close" semantics. Windows doesn't allow deletion of open files so you'll still see the files when you look at the directory. Don't be fooled!

So how can you make sense of all of this? A good rule of thumb is to measure the total size of your index. Let's call that *X*. Then, make sure at all times you have two times free disk space on the file system where the index is stored at all times. Let's consider file descriptor usage next.

11.3.2 *File descriptors*

Suppose you're happily tuning your application to maximize indexing throughput. You turned off compound file format. You cranked up `mergeFactor` and got awesome speedups, so you want to push it even higher. Unfortunately, there's a secret cost to these changes: you're drastically increasing how many files Lucene must hold open at once. At first you're ecstatic about your changes; everything seems fine. Then, as you add more documents, the index grows, Lucene will need more and more open files when one day—BOOM!—you hit the dreaded "Too many open files" `IOException`, and the OS stops you dead in your tracks. Faced with this silent and sudden risk, how can you possibly tune for the best indexing performance while staying under this limit?

Fortunately, there's hope! With a few simple steps you can take control of the situation. Start by running the following test:

```
public class OpenFileLimitCheck {
  public static void main(String[] args) throws IOException {
    List<RandomAccessFile> files = new ArrayList<RandomAccessFile>();
    try {
      while(true) {
        files.add(new RandomAccessFile("tmp" + files.size(), "rw"));
      }
    } catch (IOException ioe) {
      System.out.println("IOException after  " + files.size() + " open
    files:");
      ioe.printStackTrace(System.out);
      int i = 0;
      for (RandomAccessFile raf : files) {
        raf.close();
        new File("tmp" + i++).delete();
      }
    }
  }
}
```

When you run the test, it will always fail and then tell you how many files it was able to open before the OS cut it off. There's tremendous variation across OSs and JVMs. Running this under Mac OS X 10.6 and Java 1.5 shows that the limit is 98. Java 1.6 on Windows Server 2003 shows a limit of 9,994 open files. Java 1.5 on Debian Linux with Kernel 2.6.22 shows a limit of 1,018 open files. Java 1.6 on OpenSolaris allows 65,488 files.

Next, increase the limit to the maximum allowed by the OS. The exact command for doing so varies according to OS and shell (hello, Google, my old friend). Run the test again to make sure you've actually increased the limit.

Finally, monitor how many open files your JVM is actually using. There are OS level tools to do this. On Unix, use `lsof`. On Windows, use `Task Manager`. You'll have to add File Handles as a column, using the View > Select Columns menu. The sysinternals tools from Microsoft also include useful utilities like Process Monitor to see which specific files are held open by which processes.

To get more specifics about which files Lucene is opening, and when, use the class in listing 11.6. This class is a drop-in replacement for FSDirectory that adds tracking of open files. It reports whenever a file is opened or closed, for reading or writing, and lets you retrieve the current total count of open files.

Listing 11.6   Drop-in replacement for FSDirectory to track open files

```
public class TrackingFSDirectory extends SimpleFSDirectory {

  private Set<String> openOutputs = new HashSet<String>();        ◁─┐ Hold all open
  private Set<String> openInputs = new HashSet<String>();           │ filenames

  public TrackingFSDirectory(File path) throws IOException {
    super(path);
  }
                                                            ┌─ Return total
  synchronized public int getFileDescriptorCount() {   ◁───┘  open file count
    return openOutputs.size() + openInputs.size();
  }

  synchronized private void report(String message) {
    System.out.println(System.currentTimeMillis() + ": " +
                       message + "; total " + getFileDescriptorCount());
  }

  synchronized public IndexInput openInput(String name)                ◁─┐
      throws IOException {                                      Open    │
    return openInput(name, BufferedIndexInput.BUFFER_SIZE);  tracking   │
  }                                                             input    │

  synchronized public IndexInput openInput(String name, int bufferSize) │
      throws IOException {                                           ◁──┘
    openInputs.add(name);
    report("Open Input: " + name);
    return new TrackingFSIndexInput(name, bufferSize);
  }

  synchronized public IndexOutput createOutput(String name)
      throws IOException {                           ◁─┐ Open
    openOutputs.add(name);                             │ tracking
    report("Open Output: " + name);                    │ output
    File file = new File(getFile(), name);
    if (file.exists() && !file.delete())
      throw new IOException("Cannot overwrite: " + file);
    return new TrackingFSIndexOutput(name);
  }

  protected class TrackingFSIndexInput                   │ Track eventual close
      extends SimpleFSIndexInput {
    String name;
    public TrackingFSIndexInput(String name, int bufferSize)
        throws IOException {
      super(new File(getFile(), name), bufferSize, getReadChunkSize());
      this.name = name;
    }

    boolean cloned = false;
```

```
    public Object clone() {
      TrackingFSIndexInput clone = (TrackingFSIndexInput)super.clone();
      clone.cloned = true;
      return clone;
    }
    public void close() throws IOException {
      super.close();
      if (!cloned) {
        synchronized(TrackingFSDirectory.this) {
          openInputs.remove(name);
        }
      }
      report("Close Input: " + name);
    }
  }

  protected class TrackingFSIndexOutput        │  Track eventual close
      extends SimpleFSIndexOutput {            │
    String name;
    public TrackingFSIndexOutput(String name) throws IOException {
      super(new File(getFile(), name));
      this.name = name;
    }
    public void close() throws IOException {
      super.close();
      synchronized(TrackingFSDirectory.this) {
        openOutputs.remove(name);
      }
      report("Close Output: " + name);
    }
  }
}
```

Figure 11.4 shows the open file count while building a Wikipedia index, with compound file format turned off and mergeFactor left at its default (10). You can see that it follows a peaky pattern, with low usage when flushing segments and rather high usage while merges are running (because the writer holds open files for all segments being merged plus the new segment being created). This means mergeFactor, which sets the number of segments to merge at a time, directly controls the open file count during indexing. When two merges are running at once, which happens for three small merges starting around 7 minutes and then again for two small merges starting around 13 minutes, you'll see twice the file descriptor consumption.

Unlike indexing, where peak open file count is a simple multiple of mergeFactor, searching can require many more open files. For each segment in the index, the reader must hold open all files for that segment. If you're not using compound file format, that's seven files if no term vectors are indexed, or ten files if there are. For a quickly changing and growing index, this count can really add up. Figure 11.5 shows open file count for an IndexReader reading the same index from figure 11.4, while it's being built, reopening the reader every 10 seconds. During reopen, if the index has changed substantially because a merge has completed, the open file count will at first

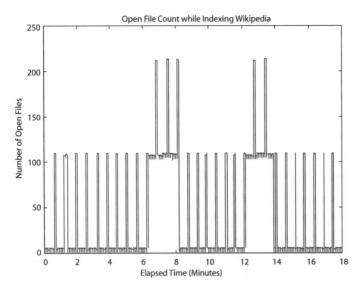

Open File Count while Indexing Wikipedia

**Figure 11.4
File descriptor
consumption while
building an index of
Wikipedia articles**

peak very high, because during this time both the old and new readers are in fact open. Once the old reader is closed, the usage drops down, in proportion to how many segments are in the index. When you use the IndexReader.reopen method, this spike is quite a bit smaller than if you open a new reader, because the file descriptors for segments that haven't changed are shared. As the index gets larger, the usage increases, though it's not a straight line because sometimes the reader catches the index soon after a large merge has finished. Armed with your new knowledge about open file consumption, here are some simple tips to keep them under control while still enjoying your indexing performance gains:

- Increase the IndexWriter buffer (setRAMBufferSizeMB). The less often the writer flushes a segment, the fewer segments there will be in the index.
- Use IndexReader.reopen instead of opening a whole new reader. This is a big reduction on peak open file count.
- Reduce mergeFactor—but don't reduce it so much that it substantially hurts indexing throughput.
- Consider reducing the maximum number of simultaneous merge threads. Do this by calling ConcurrentMergeScheduler.setMaxThreadCount.
- Optimize the index. A partial optimize, using the IndexWriter.optimize(int maxNumSegments) method, is a good compromise for minimizing the time it takes to optimize while still substantially reducing the number of segments in the index.
- Always budget for your peak usage. This is often when you're opening and warming a new reader, before you've closed the old one.
- If you run indexing and searching from a single JVM, you must add up the peak open file count for both. The peak often occurs when several concurrent merges

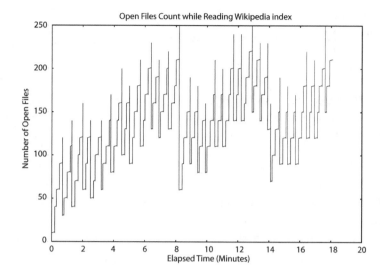

Figure 11.5   File descriptor usage by an `IndexReader` reopening every 30 seconds while Wikipedia articles are indexed

are running and you're reopening your reader. If possible, close your writer before reopening your reader to prevent this "perfect storm" of open files.

- Double-check that all other code also running in the same JVM isn't using too many open files—if it is, consider running a separate JVM for it.

- Double-check that you're closing your old `IndexReader` instances. Do this if you find you're still running out of file descriptors far earlier than you'd expect.

Striking the right balance between performance and the dreaded open file limit feels like quite an art. But now that you understand how Lucene uses open files, how to test and increase the limit on your OS, and how to measure exactly which files are held open by Lucene, you have all the tools you need to strike that perfect balance. It's now more science than art! We'll move next to another challenging resource: memory usage.

11.3.3   Memory

You've surely hit `OutOfMemoryError` in your Lucene application in the past? If you haven't, you will, especially when many of the ways to tune Lucene for performance also increase its memory usage. So you thought: no problem, just increase the JVMs' heap size and move on. Nothing to see here. You do that, and things seem fine, but little do you know you hurt the performance of your application because the computer has started swapping memory to disk. And perhaps a few weeks later you encounter the same error again. What's going on? How can you control this devious error and still keep your performance gains?

Managing memory usage is especially exciting, because there are two different levels of memory. First, you must control how the JVM uses memory from the OS. Second, you must control how Lucene uses memory from the JVM. And the two must be properly tuned together. Once you understand these levels, you'll have no trouble preventing memory errors and maximizing your performance at the same time.

You manage the JVM by telling it how large its heap should be. The option -Xms size sets the starting size of the heap and the option -Xmx size sets the maximum allowed size of the heap. In a production server environment, you should set both of these sizes to the same value, so the JVM doesn't spend time growing and shrinking the heap. Also, if there will be problems reaching the max (e.g., the computer must swap excessively), you can see these problems quickly on starting the JVM instead of hours later (at 2 a.m.) when your application suddenly needs to use all the memory. The heap size should be large enough to give Lucene the RAM that it needs, but not so large that you force the computer to swap excessively. Generally you shouldn't just give all RAM to the JVM: it's beneficial to leave excess RAM free to allow the OS to use as its I/O cache.

How can you tell if the computer is excessively swapping? Here are some clues:

- Listen to your hard drives, if your computer is nearby: they'll be noticeably grinding away, unless you're using solid-state disks.
- On Unix, run vmstat 1 to print virtual memory statistics, once per second. Then look for the columns for pages swapped in (typically si) and pages swapped out (typically so). On Windows, use Task Manager, and add the column Page Faults Delta, using the View > Select Columns menu. Check for high numbers in these columns (say, greater than 20).
- Ordinary interactive processes, like a shell or command prompt, or a text editor, or Windows Explorer, are not responsive to your actions.
- Using top on Unix, check the Mem: line. Check if the free number and the buffers number are both near 0. On Windows, use Task Manager and switch to the Performance tab. Check if the Available and System Cache numbers, under Physical Memory, are both near 0. The numbers tell you how much RAM the computer is using for its I/O cache.
- CPU usage of your process is unexpectedly low.

Note that modern OSs happily swap out processes that seem idle in order to use the RAM for the I/O cache. If you feel the OS is being too aggressive, you can try to tune it. For example, on Linux there is a kernel parameter called swappiness; setting it to 0 forces the OS to never swap out RAM for I/O cache. Some versions of Windows have an option to adjust for best performance of programs or system cache. But realize that some amount of swapping is normal. Excessive swapping, especially while you're indexing or searching, isn't good.

To manage how Lucene, in turn, uses memory from the JVM, you first need to measure how much memory Lucene needs. There are various ways, but the simplest is to specify the -verbose:gc and -XX:+PrintGCDetails options when you run Java, and then look for the size of the total heap after collection. This is useful because it excludes the memory consumed by garbage objects that aren't yet collected. If your Lucene application needs to use up nearly all of the memory allocated for the JVM's maximum heap size, it may cause excessive GC, which will slow things down. If you use even more memory than that, you'll eventually hit `OutOfMemoryError`.

During indexing, one big usage of RAM is the buffer used by `IndexWriter`, which you can control with `setRAMBufferSizeMB`. Don't set this too low as it will slow down indexing throughput. While a segment merge is running, some additional RAM is required, in proportion to the size of the segments being merged.

Searching is more RAM intensive. Here are some tips to reduce RAM usage during searching:

- Optimize your index to purge deleted documents.
- Limit how many fields you directly load into the `FieldCache`, which is entirely memory resident and time consuming to load (as described in section 5.1). Try not to load the `String` or `StringIndex FieldCache` entries as these are far more memory consuming than the native types (`int`, `float`, etc.).
- Limit how many fields you sort by. The first time a search is sorted by a given field, its values are loaded into the `FieldCache`. Similarly, try not to sort on `String` fields.
- Turn off field norms. Norms encode index-time boosting, which combines field boost, doc boost, and length boost into a single byte per document. Even documents without this field consume 1 byte because the norms are stored as a single contiguous array. This quickly works out to a lot of RAM if you have many indexed fields. Often norms aren't actually a big contributor to relevance scoring. For example, if your field values are all similar in length (e.g., a title field), and you aren't using field or document boosting, then norms are not necessary. Section 2.5.3 describes how to disable norms during indexing.
- Use a single "catchall" text field, combing text from multiple sources (such as title, body, or keywords), instead of one field per source. This reduces memory requirements within Lucene and could also make searching faster.
- Make sure your analyzer is producing reasonable terms. Use Luke to look at the terms in your index and verify these are legitimate terms that users may search on. It's easy to accidentally index binary documents, which can produce a great many bogus binary terms that would never be used for searching. These terms cause all sorts of problems once they get into your index, so it's best to catch them early by skipping or properly filtering the binary content. If your index has an unusually large number of legitimate terms—for example, if you're searching a large number of product SKUs—try specifying a custom `termInfos-IndexDivisor` when opening your `IndexReader` to reduce how many index terms are loaded into RAM. But note that this may slow down searching. There are so many trade-offs!
- Double-check that you're closing and releasing all previous `IndexSearcher`/ `IndexReader` instances. Accidentally keeping a reference to past instances can quickly exhaust RAM and file descriptors and even disk usage.
- Use a Java memory profiler to see what's using so much RAM.

Be sure to test your RAM requirements during searching while you are reopening a new reader because this will be your peak usage. If an IndexWriter shares the JVM, try to test while the IndexWriter is indexing and merging, to hit its peak usage.

Let's go back and rerun our fastest Wikipedia indexing algorithm, intentionally using a heap size that's too small to see what happens if you don't tune memory usage appropriately. Last time we ran it with a 512MB heap size, and we achieved 899.7 doc/sec throughput. This time let's give it only a 145MB heap size (anything below this will likely hit OutOfMemoryError). Run the algorithm, adding -Dtask.mem=145M, and you should see something like this:

```
Operation round runCnt recsPerRun rec/s elapsedSec  avgUsedMem  avgTotalMem
BuildIndex     0      1     200002 323.4      618.41 150,899,008 151,977,984
BuildIndex   - 1 -    1 -   200002 344.0    - 581.36 150,898,992 151,977,984
BuildIndex     2      1     200002 334.4      598.05 150,898,976 151,977,984
```

Whoa, that's 334.4 documents per second, which is 2.7 times slower than before! That slowdown is due to excessive GC that the JVM must do to keep memory usage under 145MB. You can see the importance of giving Lucene enough RAM.

Like any software, Lucene requires resources to get its job done, but you're now empowered to understand and control that usage. We'll now switch to a crucial topic for any high-availability application: backing up your index.

11.4   *Hot backups of the index*

So, it's 2 a.m., and you're having a pleasant dream about all the users who love your Lucene search application when, suddenly, you wake up to the phone ringing. It's an emergency call saying your search index is corrupted and the search application won't start. No problem, you answer: restore from the last backup! You do back up your search index, right?

Things will inevitably go wrong: a power supply fails, a hard drive crashes, your RAM becomes random. These events can suddenly render your index completely unusable, almost certainly at the worst possible time. Your final line of protection against such failures is a periodic backup of the index along with accessible steps to restore it. In this section we'll see a simple way to create and restore from backups.

11.4.1 *Creating the backup*

You can't simply copy the files in an index while an IndexWriter is still open, because the resulting copy can easily be corrupted, as the index can change during the copy. So, the most straightforward way to back up an index is to close your writer and make a copy of all files in the index directory. This approach will work, but it has some serious problems. During the copy, which could take a long time for a large index, you can't make any changes to the index. Many applications can't accept such a long downtime in their indexing. Another problem is that when a reader is open on the index, you'll copy more files than needed, if the reader is holding some files open that are no longer current. Finally, the I/O load of the copy can slow down searching. You might be tempted to throttle back the copy rate to compensate for this, but that will increase your indexing downtime. No wonder so many people just skip backups entirely, cross their fingers, and hope for the best!

As of Lucene 2.3, there's now a simple answer: you can easily make a "hot backup" of the index, so that you create a consistent backup image, with just the files referenced by the most recent commit point, without closing your writer. No matter how long the copying takes, you can still make updates to the index. The approach is to use the `SnapshotDeletionPolicy`, which keeps a commit point alive for as long it takes to complete the backup. Your backup program can take as long as it needs to copy the files. You could throttle its I/O or set it to low process or I/O priority to make sure it doesn't interfere with ongoing searching or indexing. You can spawn a subprocess to run `rsync`, `tar`, `robocopy`, or your favorite backup utility, giving it the list of files to copy. This can also be used to mirror a snapshot of the index to other computers.

The backup must be initiated by the JVM that has your writer, and you must create your writer using the `SnapshotDeletionPolicy`, like this:

```
IndexDeletionPolicy policy = new KeepOnlyLastCommitDeletionPolicy();
SnapshotDeletionPolicy snapshotter = new SnapshotDeletionPolicy(policy);
IndexWriter writer = new IndexWriter(dir, analyzer, snapshotter,
                                     IndexWriter.MaxFieldLength.UNLIMITED);
```

Note that you can pass any existing deletion policy into `SnapshotDeletionPolicy` (it doesn't have to be `KeepOnlyLastCommitDeletionPolicy`).

When you want to do a backup, just do this:

```
try {
  IndexCommit commit = snapshotter.snapshot();
  Collection<String> fileNames = commit.getFileNames();
  /*<iterate over & copy files from fileNames>*/
} finally {
  snapshotter.release();
}
```

Inside the `try` block, all files referenced by the commit point won't be deleted by the writer, even if the writer is still making changes, optimizing, and so forth as long as the writer isn't closed. It's fine if this copy takes a long time because it's still copying a single point-in-time snapshot of the index. While this snapshot is kept alive, the files that belong to it will hold space on disk. So while a backup is running, your index will use more disk space than it normally would (assuming the writer is continuing to commit changes to the index). Once you're done, call `release` to allow the writer to delete these files the next time it flushes or is closed.

Note that Lucene's index files are write-once. This means you can do an incremental backup by simply comparing filenames. You don't have to look at the contents of each file, nor its last modified timestamp, because once a file is written and referenced from a snapshot, it won't be changed. The only exception is the file segments.gen, which is overwritten on every commit, and so you should always copy this file. You shouldn't copy the write lock file (write.lock). If you're overwriting a previous backup, you should remove any files in that backup that aren't listed in the current snapshot, because they are no longer referenced by the current index.

`SnapshotDeletionPolicy` has a couple of small limitations:

- It only keeps one snapshot alive at a time. You could fix this by making a similar deletion policy that keeps track of more than one snapshot at a time.
- The current snapshot isn't persisted to disk. This means if you close your writer and open a new one, the snapshot will be deleted. So you can't close your writer until the backup has completed. This is also easy to fix: you could store and load the current snapshot on disk, then protect it on opening a new writer. This would allow the backup to keep running even if the original writer is closed and new one opened.

Believe it or not, that's all there is to it! Now let's move on to restoring your index.

11.4.2 Restoring the index

In addition to doing periodic backups, you should have a list simple of steps on hand to quickly restore the index from backup and restart your application. You should periodically test both backup and restore. Two o'clock in the morning is the worst time to find out you had a tiny bug in your backup process!

Here are the steps to follow when restoring an index:

1 Close any existing readers and writers on the index directory, so the file copies will succeed. In Windows, if there are still processes using those files, you won't be able to overwrite them.
2 Remove all existing files from the index directory. If you see an "Access is denied" error, double-check step 1.
3 Copy all files from your backup into the index directory. Be certain this copy doesn't encounter any errors, like a disk full, because that's a sure way to corrupt your index.
4 Speaking of corruption, let's talk next about common errors you may run into with Lucene.

11.5 Common errors

Lucene is wonderfully resilient to most common errors. If you fill up your disk, or see an `OutOfMemoryException`, you'll lose only the documents buffered in memory at the time. Documents already committed to the index will be intact, and the index will be consistent. The same is true if the JVM crashes, or hits an unhandled exception, or is explicitly killed, or if the OS crashes or the electricity to the computer is suddenly lost.

If you see a `LockObtainFailedException`, that's likely because there's a leftover write.lock file in your index directory that wasn't properly released before your application or JVM shut down or crashed. Consider switching to `NativeFSLockFactory`, which uses the OS provided locking (through the `java.nio.*` APIs) and will properly release the lock whenever the JVM exits normally or abnormally. You can safely remove the write.lock file, or use the `IndexReader.unlock` static method to do so. But first be certain there's no writer writing to that directory!

If you see `AlreadyClosedException`, double-check your code: this means you're closing the writer or reader but then continuing to use it.

11.5.1 *Index corruption*

So maybe you've seen an odd, unexpected exception in your logs, or maybe the computer is acting erratically, leading you to suspect a bad hard drive or RAM. Nervously, you bring your Lucene application back up, and all seems to be fine, so you just shrug and move on to the next crisis. But you can't escape the sinking sensation and burning question deep in your mind: is it possible my index is now corrupted? A month or two later, more strange exceptions start appearing. Corruption is insidious: it may silently enter your index but take quite a long time to be discovered, perhaps when the corrupted segment is next merged, or when a certain search term happens to hit on a corrupted part of the index. How can you manage this risk?

Unfortunately, there are certain known situations that can lead to index corruption. If this happens to you, try to get to the root cause of the corruption. Look through your logs and explain all exceptions. Otherwise, it may simply reoccur. Here are some typical causes of index corruption:

- *Hardware problems*—Bad power supply, slowly failing hard drive, bad RAM, and so forth.
- *Accidentally allowing two writers to write to the same index at the same time*—Lucene's locking normally prevents this. But if you use a different `LockFactory` inappropriately, or if you incorrectly removed a `write.lock` that in fact indicated that a writer was still open, that could lead to two writers open on the same index.
- *Errors when copying*—If you have a step in your indexing process where an index is copied from one place to another, an error in that copying can easily corrupt the target index.
- *A previously undiscovered bug in Lucene*—Take your case to the lists, or open an issue with as much detail as possible about what led to the corruption. The Lucene developers will jump on it!

Although you can't eliminate these risks, you can be proactive in detecting index corruption. If you see a `CorruptIndexException`, you know your index is corrupted. But all sorts of other unexplained exceptions are also possible. To proactively test your index for corruption, here are two things to try:

- Run Lucene with assertions enabled (`java -ea:org.apache.lucene`, when launching Java at the command line). This causes Lucene to perform additional tests at many points during indexing and searching, which could catch corruption sooner than you would otherwise.
- Run the `org.apache.lucene.index.CheckIndex` tool, providing the path to your index directory as the only command-line argument. This tool runs a thorough check of every segment in the index, and reports detailed statistics, and any corruption, for each. It produces output like this:

```
Opening index @ /lucene/work/index

Segments file=segments_2 numSegments=1
        version=FORMAT_SHARED_DOC_STORE [Lucene 2.3]
  1 of 1: name=_8 docCount=36845
    compound=false
    numFiles=11
    size (MB)=103.619
    docStoreOffset=0
    docStoreSegment=_0
    docStoreIsCompoundFile=false
    no deletions
    test: open reader........OK
    test: fields, norms.......OK [4 fields]
    test: terms, freq, prox...OK [612173 terms;
                                  20052335 terms/docs pairs;
                                  42702159 tokens]
    test: stored fields.......OK [147380 total field count;
                                  avg 4 fields per doc]
    test: term vectors........OK [110509 total vector count;
                                  avg 2.999 term/freq vector fields per doc]
No problems were detected with this index.
```

If you find your index is corrupted, first try to restore from backups. But what if all your backups are corrupted? This can easily happen because corruption may take a long time to detect. What can you do, besides rebuilding your full index from scratch? Fortunately, there's one final resort: use the CheckIndex tool to repair it.

11.5.2 *Repairing an index*

When all else fails, your final resort is the CheckIndex tool. In addition to printing details of your index, this tool can repair your index if you add the -fix command-line option:

```
java org.apache.lucene.index.CheckIndex <pathToIndex> -fix
```

That will forcefully remove those segments that hit problems. Note that this completely removes all documents that were contained in the corrupted segments, so use this option with caution and make a backup copy of your index first. You should use this tool just to get your search operational again on an emergency basis. Once you are back up, you should rebuild your index to recover the lost documents.

11.6 *Summary*

We've covered many important hands-on topics in this chapter! Think of this chapter like your faithful Swiss army knife: you now have the necessary tools under your belt to deal with all the important, real-world aspects of Lucene administration.

Lucene has great out-of-the-box performance, and now you know how to further tune that performance for specific metrics important to your application, using the powerful and extensible contrib/benchmark framework to set up repeatable tests. Unfortunately, tuning for one metric often comes at the expense of others, so you should decide up front which metric is most important to you. Sometimes this decision is not easy!

You've seen how crucial it is to use threads during indexing and searching to take advantage of the concurrency in modern computers, and now you have a couple of drop-in classes that make this painless during indexing and searching. Taking a hot backup of an index is a surprisingly simple operation.

Lucene's consumption of disk, file descriptors, and memory is no longer a mystery and is well within your control. Index corruption is not something to fear; you know what might cause it and you know how to detect and repair a corrupted index. The common errors that happen are easy to understand and fix.

This chapter wraps up our direct coverage of Lucene. You've learned a lot and you're now ready to go forth and build! The next three chapters describe several interesting real-world applications using Lucene.

Part 3

Case studies

Apicture is worth a thousand words. Examples of Lucene truly "in action" are invaluable. Readers of the first edition of this book loved the case studies chapter, so we've solicited a new set of case studies from the Lucene community for this new edition of the book. Lucene is the driving force behind many applications. There are countless proprietary or top-secret uses of Lucene that we may never know about, but there are also numerous applications that we can see in action online. Lucene's wiki has a section titled PoweredBy, at http://wiki.apache.org/lucene-java/PoweredBy, which lists many sites and products that use Lucene.

Lucene's API is straightforward, but the real magic happens when it's used cleverly. The case studies that follow are prime examples of intelligent uses of Lucene. Read between the lines of the implementation details of each and borrow the gems within. The study from Krugle.org, in chapter 12, shows several tricks they used for smart source code indexing and searching but that could be applied to situations other than source code. Chapter 13 describes SIREn, a set of Lucene extensions that enable efficient search on the semantic Web, also known as Web 3.0. SIREn makes heavy use of Lucene's extension points and is a great demonstration of what can be done using payloads (see section 6.5). Finally, chapter 14 describes two useful extensions to Lucene, the Bobo Browse faceted search system and the Zoie real-time search system.

If you're new to Lucene, read these case studies at a high level and gloss over any technical details or code listings; get a general feel for how Lucene is being used in a diverse set of applications. If you're an experienced Lucene developer or you've digested the previous chapters in this book, you'll enjoy the technical details; perhaps some are worth borrowing directly for your applications.

We're enormously indebted to the contributors of these case studies who took time out of their busy schedules to write what you see in the following chapters, but also to Lucene developers and numerous contributors who made it possible to build such a varied spectrum of search-related applications on top of the powerful yet flexible Lucene foundation.

Case study 1: Krugle

Krugle: Searching source code

Contributed by KEN KRUGLER *and* GRANT GLOUSER

Krugle.org provides an amazing service: it's a source-code search engine that continuously catalogs 4,000+ open source projects (including Lucene and its sister projects under the Apache Lucene umbrella), enabling you to search the source code itself as well as developers' comments in the source code control system. A search for *lucene* turns up matches not only from Lucene's source code, but from the many open source projects that use Lucene.

Krugle is built with Lucene, but there are some fun challenges that emerge when your documents are primarily source code. For example, a search for *deletion policy* must match tokens like `DeletionPolicy` in the source code. Punctuation like = and (, which in any other domain would be quickly discarded during analysis, must instead be carefully preserved so that a search like `for(int x=0` produces the expected results. Unlike a natural language where the frequent terms are classified as stop words that are then discarded, Krugle must keep all tokens from the source code.

These unique requirements presented a serious challenge, but as we saw in chapter 4, it's straightforward to create your own analysis chain with Lucene, and this is exactly what the Krugle team has done. A nice side effect of this process is Krugle's ability to identify which programming language is in use by each source file; this allows you to restrict searching to a specific language. Krugle also carefully crafts queries to match the tokenization done during analysis, such as controlling the position of each term within a `PhraseQuery`.

There's also much to learn about how Krugle handles the administrative aspects of Lucene: it must contend with tremendous scale, in both index size and query rate, yet still provide both searching and indexing on a single computer. You can do this by running dedicated, separate JREs for searching and indexing, carefully assigning separate hard drives for each, and managing the "snapshots" that are flipped between two environments. Krugle's approach for reducing memory usage during searching is also interesting.

The clever approach the Krugle team uses for self-testing—by randomly picking documents in the index to pass in as searches and asserting that the document is returned in the search results—is a technique most search applications could use to keep the end user's trust.

Without further ado, let's go through the intricacies of how Krugle.org uses Lucene to create a high-scale source code search engine.

12.1 Introducing Krugle

Krugle.org is a search engine for finding and exploring open source projects. The current version has information on the top 4,000+ open source projects, including project descriptions, licenses, SCM activity, and most importantly the source code—more than 400 million lines and growing. Figure 12.1 shows Krugle.org's search results for the query lucene indexsearcher.

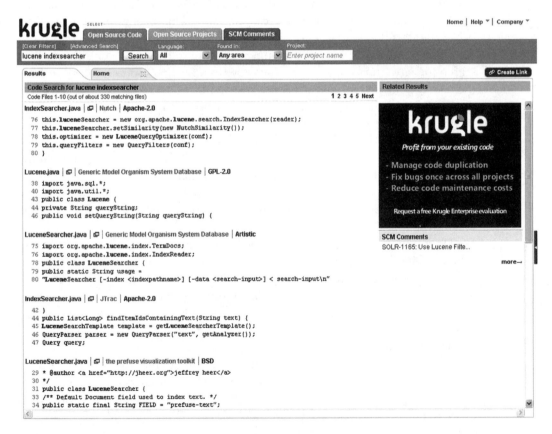

Figure 12.1   The Krugle.org search result page showing matches in multiple projects and multiple source code files

Krugle.org is a free public service, running on a single Krugle enterprise appliance. The appliance is sold to large companies for use inside the firewall. Enterprise development groups use a Krugle appliance to create a single, comprehensive catalog of source code, project metadata, and associated development organization information. This helps them increase code reuse, reduce maintenance costs, improve impact analysis, and monitor development activity across large and often distributed teams.

The most important functionality provided by a Krugle appliance is search, which is based on Lucene. For the majority of users, this means searching through their source code. In this case study we'll focus on how we used Lucene to solve some interesting and challenging requirements for source code search. Some of these problems often don't come into play in search applications that involve indexing and searching of human language you find in articles, books, emails, and so forth. But the "tricks" we've applied to source code analysis aren't limited to source code search.

We initially used Nutch to crawl technical web pages, collecting and extracting information about open source projects. We wound up running ten slave servers with one master server in a standard Hadoop configuration, and crawled roughly 50 million pages. The first version of the Krugle.org public site was implemented on top of Nutch, with four remote code searchers, four remote web page searchers, a back-end file server, and one master box that aggregated search results. This scaled easily to 150,000 projects and 2.6 billion lines of source code but wasn't a suitable architecture for a standalone enterprise product that could run reliably without daily care and feeding. In addition, we didn't have the commit comment data from the SCM systems that hosted the project source code, which was a highly valuable source of information for both searches and analytics.

So we created a workflow system (internally called "the Hub") that handled the crawling and processing of data, and converted the original multiserver search system into a single-server solution ("the API").

12.2 Appliance architecture

For an enterprise search appliance, a challenge is doing two things well at the same time: updating a live index and handling search requests. Both tasks can require extensive CPU, disk, and memory resources, so it's easy to wind up with resource contention issues that kill your performance.

We made three decisions that helped us avoid these issues. First, we pushed a significant amount of work "off the box" by putting a lot of the heavy lifting work into the hands of small clients called *source code management (SCM) interfaces (SCMIs)*. SCMIs run on external customer servers instead of on our appliance, and act as collectors of information about projects, SCM comments, source code, and other development-oriented information. The information is then partially digested before being sent back to the appliance via a typical HTTP Representational State Transfer (REST) protocol.

Second, we use separate JVMs for the data processing/indexing tasks and the searching/browsing tasks. This provides us with better controlled memory usage, at the cost of some wasted memory. The Hub data processing JVM receives data from the

SCMI clients; manages the workflow for parsing, indexing, and analyzing the results; and builds a new "snapshot." This snapshot is a combination of multiple Lucene indexes, along with all the content and other analysis results. When a new snapshot is ready, a "flip" request is sent to the API JVM that handles the search side of things, and this new snapshot is gracefully swapped in.

On a typical appliance, we have two 32-bit JVMs running, each with 1.5 GB of memory. One other advantage to this approach is that we can shut down and restart each JVM separately, which makes it easier to do live upgrades and debug problems.

Finally, we tune the disks being used to avoid seek contention. There are two drives devoted to snapshots: while one is serving up the current snapshot, the

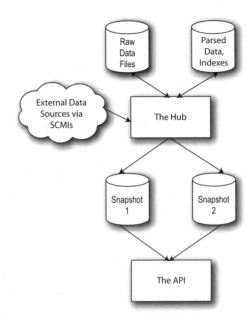

Figure 12.2   Krugle runs two JVMs in a single appliance and indexes content previously collected and digested by external agents.

other is being used to build the new snapshot. The Hub also uses two other drives for raw data and processed data, again to allow multiple tasks to run in a multithreaded manner without running into disk thrashing. The end result is an architecture depicted in figure 12.2.

12.3   *Search performance*

Due to the specific nature of the domain we're dealing with (programming languages), we uncovered some interesting areas to optimize. The first issue was the common terms in source code. On the first version of our public site, a search on `for (i = 0; i < 10; i++)` would bring it to a screeching halt, due to the high frequency of every term in the phrase. But we couldn't just strip out these common terms (or stop words)—that would prevent phrase queries.

So we borrowed a page from Nutch's playbook and combined common terms with subsequent terms while indexing and querying using a similar approach as the

Table 12.1   Combined terms, which improves performance for common single terms

Term #	Combined Term
1	for (
2	i =
3	0;
4	...
5	++)

shingle filter (covered in section 8.2.3). The `for loop` example results in the combined terms shown in table 12.1.

The individual terms are still indexed directly, in case you had to search on just i for some bizarre reason. Indexing combined terms results in many more unique terms in the index, but it means that the term frequencies drop—there are a lot fewer documents with 10; than just 10. The resulting list of common terms is shown in table 12.2.

Table 12.2 Most common single and combined terms in the source code index

Single Term	Combined Terms	Single Term	Combined Terms
.	) ;	<	. h
)	; }	1	("
(	({	/	= =
;	( )	:	0 ;
{	))	–	; return
}	} }	*	0)
=	if (	if	= "
,	# include	#	{ if
"	; if	return	# endif
>	")	...	...
0	= 0	add	> <

As an example, we have an index for our public site with just under 5 million source files (documents). This results in an index with the attributes shown in table 12.3, for the case where it doesn't use combined terms versus using 200 combined terms.

Table 12.3 Index file growth after combining high-frequency individual terms

Result	No combined terms	With combined terms
Unique terms	102 million	242 million
Total terms	3.7 billion	13.5 billion
Terms dictionary file size (*.tis)	1.1 GB	2.5 GB
Prox file size (*.prx)	10 GB	18 GB
Freq file size (*.frq)	3.5 GB	7.3 GB
Stored fields file size (*.fdt)	1.0 GB	1.0 GB

We had to switch to a 64-bit JVM and allocate 4 GB of RAM before we achieved reasonable performance with our index.

12.4 Parsing source code

During early beta testing, we learned a lot about how developers search in code, with two features in particular proving to be important. First, we needed to support semistructured searches—for example, where the user wants to limit the search to only find hits in class definition names.

To support this, we had to be able to parse the source code. But "parsing the source code" is a rather vague description. There are lots of compilers that obviously parse source code, but full compilation means that you need to know about include paths (or classpaths), compiler-specific switches, the settings for the macro preprocessor in C/C++, and so forth. The end result is that you effectively need to be able to build the project in order to parse it, and that in turn means you end up with a system that requires constant care and feeding to keep it running. Often that doesn't happen, so the end result is shelfware.

Early on we made a key decision that we had to be able to process files individually, without knowledge of such things as build settings and compiler versions. We also had to handle a wide range of languages. This in turn meant that the type of parsing we could do was constrained by what features we could extract from a fuzzy parse. We couldn't build a symbol table, for example, because that would require processing all includes and imports.

Depending on the language, the level of single-file parsing varies widely. Python, Java, and C# are examples of languages where you can generate a good parse tree, whereas C and C++ are at the other end of the spectrum. Dynamic languages like Ruby and Perl create their own unique problems, because the meaning of a term (is it a variable or a function?) sometimes isn't determined until runtime. So what we wind up with is a best guess, where we're right most of the time but we'll occasionally get it wrong.

We use ANTLR (Another Tool for Language Recognition) to handle most of our parsing needs. Terence Parr, the author of ANTLR, added memoization support to version 3.0, which allowed us to use fairly flexible rules without paying a huge performance penalty for frequent backtracking.

12.5   *Substring searching*

The second important thing we learned from our beta testing was that we had to support some form of substring searching. For example, when a user searches on *ldap*, she expects to find documents containing terms like *getLDAPConfig*, *ldapTimeout*, and *find_details_with_ldap*.

We could treat every search term as if it had implicit wildcards, like **ldap**, but that's both noisy and slow. The noise (false positive hits) comes from treating all contiguous runs of characters as potential matches, so a search for *heap* finds a term like *theAPI*.

The performance hit comes from having to

- Enumerate all terms in the index to find any that contain `<term>` as a substring
- Use the resulting set of matching terms in a (potentially very large) OR query

`BooleanQuery` allows a maximum of 1,024 clauses by default—searching on the Lucene mailing list shows many people have encountered this limit while trying to support wildcard queries.

There are a number of approaches to solving the wildcard search problem, some of which we covered in this book. For example, you can take every term and index it using all possible suffix substrings of the text. For example, *myLDAPhook* gets indexed as *myldaphook, yldaphook, ldaphook,* and so on. This then lets you turn a search for **ldap** into *ldap**, which cuts down on the term enumeration time by being able to do a binary search for terms starting with *ldap*, rather than enumerating all terms. But you still can end up with a very large number of clauses in the resulting OR query. And the index gets significantly larger, due to term expansion.

Another approach is to convert each term into ngrams—for example, using 3grams the term *myLDAPhook* would become *myl, yld, lda, dap,* and so on. Then a search for *ldap* becomes a search for *lda dap* in 3grams, which would match. This works as long as N (3, in this example) is greater than or equal to the minimum length of any substring you'd want to find. It also significantly increases the size of the index, and for long terms results in a large number of corresponding ngrams.

Another approach is to preprocess the index, creating a secondary index that maps each distinct substring to the set of all full terms that contain the substring. When a query runs, the first step is to use this secondary index to quickly find all possible terms that contain the query term as a substring, and then use that list to generate the set of subclauses for an OR query. This gives you acceptable query-time speed, at the cost of additional time during index generation. And you're still faced with potentially exceeding the maximum subclause limit.

We chose a fourth approach, based on the ways identifiers naturally decompose into substrings. We observed that arbitrary substring searches weren't as important as searches for whole subwords. For example, users expect a search for *ldap* to find documents containing *getLDAPConfig*, but it would be unusual for the user to search for *apcon* with the same expectation.

To implement this approach, we created a token filter that recognizes compound identifiers and splits them up into subwords, a process vaguely similar to stemming (chapter 4 shows how to create custom tokenizers and token filters for analysis). The filter looks for identifiers that follow common conventions like camelCase, or containing numbers or underscores. Some programming languages allow other characters in identifiers, sometimes any character; we stuck with letters, numbers, and underscores as the most common baseline. Other characters are treated as punctuation, so identifiers containing them are still split at those points. The difference is that the next step, subrange enumeration, won't cross the punctuation boundary.

When we encounter a suitable compound identifier, we examine it to locate the offsets of subword boundaries. For example, *getLDAPConfig* appears to be composed of the words *get, LDAP,* and *Config,* so the boundary offsets are at 0, 3, 7, and 13. Then we produce a term for each pair of offsets (i,j) such that i < j. All terms with a common

Start	End	Position	Term
0	3	1	get
0	7	1	getldap
0	13	1	getldapconfig
3	7	2	ldap
3	13	2	ldapconfig
7	13	3	config

Table 12.4 A case-aware token filter breaks a single token into multiple tokens when the case changes, making it possible to search on subtokens quickly without resorting to more expensive wildcards queries.

start offset share a common Lucene index position value; each new start offset gets a position increment of 1.

Table 12.4 shows a table of terms produced for the example *getLDAPConfig*.

An identifier with n subwords will produce n*(n+1)/2 terms by this method. Because *getLDAPConfig* has three subwords, we wind up with six terms. By comparison, the number of ngram grows only linearly with the length of the identifier. For example, *getLDAPConfig* would produce eleven 3grams because it decomposes into *get*, *etl*, *tld*, and so forth. The same level of expansion happens when you generate all suffix substring terms: you end up with *getladpconfig*, *etldapconfig*, *tldapconfig*, and so on until the length of the suffix string reaches your minimum length.

Usually, identifiers consist of at most three or four subwords, so our subrange enumeration produces fewer terms. Pathological cases do exist, resulting in far too many subwords for a given term, so it's crucial to set some bounds on the enumeration process. Three bounds we set are as follows:

- The maximum length in characters of the initial identifier.
- The maximum number of subwords.
- The maximum span of subwords (k) used to create terms. This limits the number of terms to O(kn).

Because we set the term positions in a nonstandard way while indexing (every compound identifier spans multiple term positions), we also set the term positions in queries. In the simple case, a single identifier, even a compound identifier, becomes a TermQuery. But what about a query that includes punctuation, something like getLDAPConfig()? This becomes a PhraseQuery, where the three terms are *getldapconfig*, *(*, and *)*. In the index, *getldapconfig* spans three term positions, but with a naïve PhraseQuery, Lucene will only match documents in which *getldapconfig* and a *(* are exactly one term position apart. Fortunately, the PhraseQuery API allows you to specify the position of each term using the add(term, position) method, and by counting the span of each term as we add them to the query, we can create a PhraseQuery that exactly matches the position pattern of the desired documents in the index. PhraseQuery is covered in section 3.5.7.

One final snag: occasionally, users are too impatient or lazy to capitalize their queries properly. When the user types `getldapconfig()` in the search field, we have no basis for calculating how many term positions were supposed to have been spanned by *getldapconfig*. In lieu of a smarter solution, we deal with this by adding setting the `PhraseQuery`'s slop (described in section 3.4.6) based on the number and length of such terms.

12.6   Query vs. search

One of the challenges we ran into was the fundamentally different perception of results. In pure search, the user doesn't know the full set of results and is searching for the most relevant matches. For example, when a user does a search for *lucene* using Google, he's looking for useful pages, but he has little to no idea about the exact set of matching pages.

In what we're calling a query-style search request, the user has more knowledge about the result set and expects to see all hits. He might not look at each hit, but if a hit is missing, the user will typically view this as a bug. For example, when one of our users searches for all callers of a particular function call in their company's source code, he typically doesn't know about every single source file where that API is used (otherwise users wouldn't need us), but users certainly do know of many files that should be part of the result set. And if that "well-known hit" is missing, we've got big problems.

So where did we run into this situation? When files are very large, the default setting for Nutch was to only process the first 10,000 terms using Lucene's field truncation (covered in section 2.7). This in general is okay for web pages but completely fails the query test when dealing with source code. Hell hath no fury like a developer who doesn't find a large file he knows should be a hit because the search term only exists near the end.

Another example is where we misclassified a file—for example, if file xxx.h was a C++ header instead of a C header. When the user filters search results by programming language, this can exclude files that she knows of and is expecting to see in the result set.

There wasn't a silver bullet for this problem, but we did manage to catch a lot of problems once we figured out ways to feed our data back on itself. For example, we'd take a large, random selection of source files from the http://www.krugle.org site and generate a list of all possible multiline searches in a variety of sizes (such as 1 to 10 lines). Each search is a small section of source code excised from a random file. We'd then verify that for every one of these code snippets, we got a hit in the original source document.

12.7   Future improvements

As with any project of significant size and complexity, there's always a long to-do list of future fixes, improvements, and optimizations. A few examples that help illustrate common issues with Lucene follow.

12.7.1 *FieldCache memory usage*

You know that Lucene's field cache is memory consuming (see section 5.1), and indeed we noticed on our public site server that more than 1.1 GB was being used by two Lucene field cache data structures. One of these contained the dates for SCM comments, and the other had the MD5 hashes of source files. We need dates to sort commit comments chronologically, and we need MD5s to remove duplicate source files when returning hits. For a thorough explanation about field cache and sorting, see chapter 5.

But a gigabyte is a lot of memory, and this grows to 1.6 GB during a snapshot flip, so we've looked into how to reduce the space required. The problems caused by a `FieldCache` with many unique values is one that's been discussed on the Lucene list in the past.

For dates, the easy answer is to use longs instead of ISO date strings. The only trick is to ensure that they're stored as strings with leading zeros so that they still sort in date order. Another option is the use of `NumericField`, which is described in section 2.6.1.

For MD5s, we did some tests and figured out that using the middle 60 bits of the 128-bit value still provided sufficient uniqueness for 10 million documents. In addition, we could encode 12 bits of data in each character of our string (instead of just 8 bits), so we only need five characters to store the 60 bits, rather than 32 characters for a hex-encoded 128-bit MD5 hash value.

12.7.2 *Combining indexes*

The major time hit during snapshot creation is merging many Lucene indexes. We cache an up-to-date index for each project, and combine all of these into a single index when generating a snapshot. With over 4,000 projects, this phase of snapshot generation takes almost five hours, or 80 percent of the total snapshot generation time.

Because we have a multicore box, the easiest first cut improvement is to fire off multiple merge tasks (one for each core). The result is many indexes, which we can easily use in the snapshot via a `ParallelMultiSearcher` (see section 5.8.2). A more sophisticated approach involves segmenting the projects into groups based on update frequency so that a typical snapshot generation doesn't require merging the project indexes for the projects that are infrequently updated.

12.8   *Summary*

In 2005 we were faced with a decision about which IR engine to use, and even which programming language made sense for developing Krugle. Luckily we got accurate and valuable input from a number of experienced developers, which answered our two main concerns:

- Java was "fast enough" for industrial-strength search.
- Lucene had both the power and flexibility we needed.

The flexibility of Lucene allowed us to handle atypical situations, such as queries that are actually code snippets or that include punctuation characters that other search engines are typically free to discard. We were also able to handle searches where query terms are substrings of input tokens by using a token filter that's aware of typical source code naming conventions and thus smart about indexing "compounds" often found in the source code. Without Lucene and the many other open source components we leveraged, there would have been no way to go from zero to beta in six months. So many thanks to our friends for encouraging us to use Lucene, and to the Lucene community for providing such an excellent search toolkit.

Case study 2: SIREn

Searching semistructured documents with SIREn

Contributed by RENAUD DELBRU, NICKOLAI TOUPIKOV, MICHELE CATASTA, ROBERT FULLER, *and* GIOVANNI TUMMARELLO

In this case study, the crew from the Digital Enterprise Research Institute (DERI; http://www.deri.ie) describes how they created the Semantic Information Retrieval Engine (SIREn) using Lucene. SIREn (which is open source and available at http://siren.sindice.com) searches the semantic web, also known as Web 3.0 or the "Web of Data," which is a quickly growing collection of semistructured documents available from web pages adopting the Resource Description Framework (RDF)[1] standard. With RDF, pages publicly available on the web encode structural relationships between arbitrary entities and objects via predicates. Although the standard has been defined for some time, it's only recently that websites have begun adopting it in earnest.

A publicly accessible demonstration of SIREn is running at http://sindice.com, covering more than 50 million crawled structured documents, resulting in over 1 billion entity, predicate, and object triples. SIREn is a powerful alternative to the more common RDF triplestores, typically backed by relational databases and thus often limited when it comes to full-text search.

One of the challenges when indexing RDF is the fact that there's no fixed schema: anyone can create new terms in their descriptions. This raises important challenges. As you'll see, SIREn first attempted to use a simplistic mapping of RDF subject, predicate, object triples to documents, where each predicate was a new field. But this led to performance challenges, because the number of fields is unbounded. To solve this, payloads (covered in section 6.5) were used to efficiently

---

[1] See http://en.wikipedia.org/wiki/Resource_Description_Framework.

encode the tuple information, and the resulting architecture provides a highly scalable schema free RDF search.

SIREn perhaps sets the record for making use of Lucene's customization APIs: it has created a number of Lucene extensions, including tokenizers (`TupleTokenizer`), token filters (`URINormalisationFilter`, `SirenPayloadFilter`), analyzers (`TupleAnalzyer`, `SPARQLQueryAnalyzer`), queries (`CellQuery`, `TupleQuery`), and its own query parser to handle SPARQL RDF queries (a standard query language for RDF content, defined by the W3C (World Wide Web Consortium). SIREn's analysis chain is a good example of using a token's type to record custom information per token, which is then consumed downstream by another token filter to create the right payloads. SIREn even includes integration with Solr. Such a componentized approach gives SIREn its open architecture, allowing developers to choose components to create their semantic web search application. Advanced stuff ahead!

13.1 Introducing SIREn

Although the specifications for RDF and Microformats[2] have been out for quite some time now, it's only in the last few years that many websites have begun to make use of them, thus effectively starting the Web of Data. Sites such as LinkedIn, Eventful, Digg, Last.fm, and others are using these specifications to share pieces of information that can be automatically reused by other websites or by smart clients. As an example, you can visit a Last.fm concert page[3] and automatically import the event in its calendar if an appropriate Microformats browser plug-in is used.

At DERI, we're developing the Sindice.com search engine. The goal of this project is to provide a search engine for the Web of Data. The challenge is that such an engine is expected not only to answer textual queries but also structured queries—that is, queries that use the structure of the data. To make things a bit more complex, the RDF specifications allow people to freely create new terms to use in their descriptions, making it effectively a schema-free indexing and structured answering problem.

Traditionally, querying graph-structured data has been done using ad hoc solutions, called triplestores, typically based on a database management system (DBMS) back-end. For Sindice, we needed something much more scalable than DBMSs and with the desirable features of the typical web search engines: top documents matching a query, real-time updates, full-text search, and distributed indexes.

Lucene has long offered these capabilities, but as you'll see in the next section, its native capabilities aren't intended for large semistructured document collections with different schemas. For this reason we developed SIREn, a Lucene extension to overcome these shortcomings and efficiently index and query RDF, as well as any textual document with an arbitrary number of metadata fields. Among other things, we developed custom tokenizers, token filters, queries, and scorers.

---

[2] See http://microformats.org/.
[3] See http://www.last.fm/events.

SIREn is today in use not only in Sindice.com but also within enterprise data integration projects where it serves as a large-scale schema-free semantic search engine to query across large volumes of documents and database records.

13.2   *SIREn's benefits*

The Web of Data is composed of RDF statements. Specifically, an RDF statement is a triple consisting of a subject, a predicate, and an object, and asserts that a subject has a property (the predicate) with some value (the object). A subject, or entity, has a reference that has the form of an URI (such as http://renaud.delbru.fr/rdf/foaf#me).

There are two kinds of statements:

- An attribute statement, A(e, v), where A is an attribute (foaf:name), e is an entity reference, and v is a literal (such as an integer, string, or date)
- A relation statement, R(e1, e2), where R is a relation (foaf:knows), and e1 and e2 are entity references

Those RDF statements intrinsically form a giant graph of interlinked entities (people, products, events, etc.). For example, figures 13.1 and 13.2 show a small RDF data set and how it can be split into three entities: renaud, giovanni, and DERI. Each entity graph forms a star composed of the incoming and outgoing relations of an entity node. Oval nodes represent entity references and rectangular ones represent literals. For space consideration, URIs have been replaced by their local names. In N-Triples syntax, URIs are enclosed in angle brackets (< and >), literals are written using double quotes, and a dot signifies the end of a triple. The following is a snippet of the N-Triples[4] syntax of the entity graph renaud:

```
http://renaud.delbru.fr/rdf/foaf#me
➡    <http://www.w3.org/1999/02/22-rdf-syntax-ns#type>
➡    <http://xmlns.com/foaf/0.1/Person> .
<http://renaud.delbru.fr/rdf/foaf#me
➡    http://xmlns.com/foaf/0.1/name
➡    "Renaud Delbru"
http://g1o.net#me
➡    <http://xmlns.com/foaf/0.1/knows>
➡    <http://renaud.delbru.fr/rdf/foaf#me>
```

SIREn follows an entity-centric view; its main purpose is to index and retrieve entities. To search and locate an entity on the Web of Data, SIREn offers the ability to ask star-shaped queries such as the one in figure 13.2. You could argue that Lucene already has the possibility to create such star-shaped queries as the document fields need not follow a fixed schema (see section 2.1.2). For example, each entity can be converted into a Lucene document, where each distinct predicate is a dynamic field and objects are values indexed into that field. Following this approach, a Lucene document will contain as many dynamic fields as the entity has predicates. But the use of dynamic

---

[4] N-Triples: http://www.w3.org/2001/sw/RDFCore/ntriples/

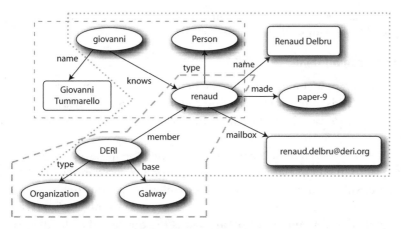

Figure 13.1   A visual representation of an RDF graph. The RDF graph is split (dashed lines) into three entities identified by the nodes `renaud`, `giovanni`, and `DERI`.

fields isn't suitable when dealing with semistructured information, as we'll explain in a moment, and a new data model like the one we proposed is necessary.

The web provides access to large data sources of all kinds. Some of these data sources contain raw data where the structure exists but has to be extracted. Some contain data that has structure but isn't as rigid and regular as data found in a database system. Data that's neither raw nor strictly typed is called *semistructured* data. Semistructured data can also arise when integrating several structured data sources because it's to be expected that the data sources won't follow the same schemas and the same conventions for their values.

SIREn is intended for indexing and querying large amounts of semistructured data. The use of SIREn is appropriate when

- You have data with a large schema or multiple schemas
- You have a rapidly evolving schema
- The type of data elements is eclectic

SIREn lets you efficiently perform complex structured queries (when the program or user is aware of the schema) as well as unstructured queries, such as simple keyword searches. Moreover, even in the case of unstructured queries, SIREn will be able to

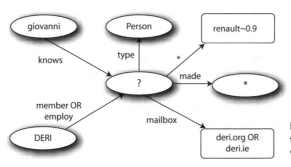

Figure 13.2   Star-shaped query matching the entity `renaud`, where `?` is the bound variable and `*` a wildcard

"respect" the data structure during the query processing to avoid false positive matches, as we'll explain in the next section.

13.2.1 *Searching across all fields*

With semistructured documents, the data schema is generally unknown and the number of different fields in the data collection can be large. Sometimes, we aren't able to know which field to use when searching. In that case, we can execute the search in every field.

The only way to search multiple fields at the same time in Lucene is to use the wildcard * pattern for the field element (WildcardQuery is covered in section 3.4.7). Internally, Lucene will expand the query by concatenating all the fields to each query terms. As a consequence, this will generally cause the number of query terms to increase significantly. A common workaround is to copy all other fields to a catchall search field. This solution can be convenient in certain cases, but it duplicates the information in the index and therefore increases the index size. Also, information structure is lost, because all values are concatenated inside one field.

13.2.2 *A single efficient lexicon*

Because data schemas are free, many identical terms can appear in different fields. Lucene maintains one lexicon per field by concatenating the field name with the term. If the same term appears in multiple fields, it will be stored in multiple lexicons. As SIREn primarily uses a single field, it has a single large lexicon and avoids term duplication in the dictionary.

13.2.3 *Flexible fields*

The data schema is generally unknown, and it's common to have many name variations for the same field. In SIREn, a field is a term as any other element of the data collection and can thus be normalized before indexing. In addition, this enables full-text search (Boolean operator, fuzzy operator, spelling suggestions, etc.) on a field name. For example, on the Web of Data, we generally don't know the exact terms (such as URIs) used as predicates when searching entities. By tokenizing and normalizing the predicate URI—for example, http://purl.org/dc/elements/1.1/author—we can search for all the predicates from one or more schemas containing the term author.

13.2.4 *Efficient handling of multivalued fields*

In Lucene, multivalued fields are handled by concatenating values together before indexing (see section 2.4.7). As a consequence, if two string values Mark James Smith and John Christopher Davis are indexed in a field author, the query author:"James AND Christopher" looking for an author called "James Christopher" will return a false positive. In SIREn, values in a multivalued property remain independent in the index and each one can be searched either separately or together.

13.3 Indexing entities with SIREn

To understand how SIREn indexes entities, you need to understand the following:

- The data model and how it's implemented on top of the Lucene framework
- The Lucene document schema that will index and store an entity
- How data is prepared before indexing

Let's take a look at each concept.

13.3.1 Data model

Given an entity, a way to represent its RDF description is to use two tables, each one having a tuple per RDF triple: in one table (outgoing relationships), the tuple key is the subject s (entity), the first cell is the predicate p (property), and the second one is the object o (value). In the second table (incoming relationships), the order is reversed; the key is the object o, and the second cell is the subject s. A generalized version of this accounting for multivalued predicates (such as multiple statements having the same s and p but different o) can be seen as two tuple tables composed by p and n values. This is shown in table 13.1. In SIREn, there's no limit on the number of cells and null values are free.

Each cell can be searched independently or together as one unit using full-text search operations such as Boolean, proximity, or fuzzy operators. By combining multiple cells, you can query a tuple pattern to retrieve a list of entity identifiers. It's also possible to combine tuples to query an entity description. The tuples listed in section 13.2 provide an example of combining query operators to match the entity described in table 13.1.

Table 13.1 Representation of an entity tuple table

Outgoing relations					
Subject	**Predicate**	**Object 1**	**Object 2**		**Object n**
id1	rdf:type	Person	Student	...	Thing
id1	foaf:name	Renaud Delbru	R. Delbru	...	
id1	foaf:mailbox	mail@deri.org		...	
id1	foaf:made	paper-9	paper-12	...	paper-n
...	...				

Incoming relations					
Object	**Predicate**	**Subject 1**	**Subject 2**		**Subject n**
id1	foaf:knows	giovanni	nickolai	...	
id1	foaf:member	DERI	Ø	...	
...	...				

13.3.2 Implementation issues

Let's now explore how the structural information associated with a term can be transposed into Lucene. The data model is similar to the path-based model described in Proceedings of International Symposium on Digital Media Information Base, November 1997.[5] In this model, each term occurrence is associated with the following information: entity, tuple, cell, and position.

The content of a cell can be any kind of information (text, URI, integer, date, etc.) and is itself decomposed into a sequence of terms. These terms are indexed, similarly to a classical Lucene index, along with their position. In addition, we assign a cell identifier (cid) to each term occurrence. The cid is derived from the cell index in the tuple. For example, a term that occurs in the first cell will be labeled with cid=0. The tuple can be addressed using an internal identifier (tid) for each tuple within an entity. We assign to each entity a unique identifier (eid), which is in fact the internal document identifier assigned by Lucene.

The index format has been implemented using the Lucene payload feature (described in section 6.5). Each term payload contains the tuple and cell identifier. Therefore, a Lucene posting holds a sequence of term occurrences, in the following format:

```
Term            -> <eid, freq, TermPositions^freq>^tef
TermPositions   -> <pos, Payload>
Payload         -> <tid, cid>
```

The tef parameter is simply the number of entity descriptions that contains the term, and it's similar to the term document frequency in a normal document index. Those identifiers are stored efficiently using variable-byte encoding because they're generally small. In average, storing this information requires only 2 bytes per term.

13.3.3 Index schema

We designed a generic set of fields for Lucene documents that hold entities. The Lucene document schema is described in table 13.2. Some of the fields, such as subject, context, and content, are necessary for implementing the SIREn index. The field subject indexes and stores the subject (the resource identifier of the entity), whereas context indexes the provenance (URL) of the entity. Those fields are returned as search results but can also be used for restricting a query to a specific entity or context. The content field holds the tuple table—that is, the RDF statements describing the entity.

We chose the other fields for implementing additional features for the Sindice use case, such as query filter operators and faceted browsing. It's then possible to filter search results by ontology, domain, data source, or format.

---

[5] R. Sacks-Davis, T. Dao, J. A. Thom, and J. Zobel. Indexing documents for queries on structure, content and attributes. In *Proceedings of International Symposium on Digital Media Information Base (DMIB)*, pages 236–245. *World Scientific*, November 1997.

Table 13.2 The Lucene document schema used for the Sindice use case

Field name	Description
subject	URI of the entity (subject element of the statement).
context	URI of the data set containing the entity (context element of the statement) .
content	The list of tuples describing the entity. This field is using the SIREn data format presented earlier.
ontology	List of ontologies used in the entity description.
domain	The domain where the entity is published.
data-source	The source of the data: crawled, dumped, or pinged.
format	The original format of the data: RDF, RDFa, Microformats, etc.

13.3.4 *Data preparation before indexing*

Lucene documents are sent to the index server. The document is analyzed before indexing. We created our own Lucene analyzer for fields containing tuples. The field content, of type tuple, has a special syntax derived from the N-Triples syntax:

```
http://www.w3.org/1999/02/22-rdf-syntax-ns#type
➥   <http://xmlns.com/foaf/0.1/Person> .
<http://xmlns.com/foaf/0.1/name> "Renaud Delbru" .
<http://xmlns.com/foaf/0.1/knows> <http://g1o.net#me>
➥   _:node4321 .
```

URIs are enclosed in angle brackets, literals are written using double quotes, blank nodes are written as `_:nodeID`, and a dot signifies the end of a tuple.

A `TupleTokenizer`, a grammar-based tokenizer generated with JFlex, breaks text using the tuple syntax into tokens. It generates tokens of different types, such as `uri`, `bnode`, and `literal` for the elements of a tuple, but also `cell_delimiter` and `tuple_delimiter` to inform the `TupleAnalyzer` downstream of the ending of a tuple element or tuple (section 4.2.4 describes the token's type attribute). The `TupleTokenizer` embeds a Lucene analyzer for analysis of the literal tokens. Whenever a literal token is created, it's sent to this second analyzer in order to tokenize the literals. This offers the flexibility of reusing Lucene components for analyzing the textual information of the literals.

The `TupleAnalyzer` defines the `TokenFilters` that are applied to the output of the `TupleTokenizer`. We created two special filters for the SIREn extension: the `URINormalisationFilter` and the `SirenPayloadFilter`. Other original Lucene filters are used, such as `StopWordFilter` and `LowerCaseFilter`.

The `URINormalisationFilter` normalizes URIs by removing trailing slashes and by breaking down a URI into subwords and generating multiple variations; for example:

```
"http://xmlns.com/foaf/0.1/name" ->
    (position:token)
    0:"http"
```

```
1:"xmlns.com",
2:"foaf",
3:"0.1",
4:"name",
5:"http://xmlns.com/foaf/0.1/name"
```

These variations are useful for enabling full-text search on a URI. It's then possible to write queries like name, foaf AND name or http://xmlns.com/foaf/0.1/.

The class SirenPayloadFilter (shown in listing 13.1) assigns the structural information to each token and encodes them into the token payload. Note that the token filter uses the version 2.4 tokenizer APIs (for example, the next() method), which have been removed in Lucene as of version 3.0. Payloads are covered in section 6.5.

Listing 13.1 How `SirenPayloadFilter` processes the token stream

```
public class SirenPayloadFilter extends TokenFilter {
  protected int tuple, tupleElement = 0;

  @Override
  public Token next(final Token result) throws IOException {
    if ((result = input.next(result)) == null) return result;
    if (result.type().equals("<TUPLE_DELIMITER>")) {
      tuple++; tupleElement = 0;
    }
    else if (result.type().equals("<CELL_DELIMITER>"))
      tupleElement++;
    else
      result.setPayload(new SirenPayload(tupleID, cellID));
    return result;
  }
}
```

13.4   Searching entities with SIREn

Next we'll present a set of query operators, implemented into SIREn, for performing operations on the content and structure of the tuple table. Those query components are the building blocks for writing search queries for data sets and entities.

13.4.1 Searching content

SIREn includes primitive query operators that access the content of a tuple table. These query operators provide basic operations, such as term lookups (TermQuery, PhraseQuery) or more advanced functionality such as fuzzy or prefix operators. They can then be combined with higher-level operators such as Boolean operators (intersection, union, difference), proximity operators (phrase, near, before, after, etc.), or SIREn operators (cell, tuple).

These operators reproduce the same strategy as the original Lucene operators with the small difference that, during query processing, their scorers read tuple information from the payload and use them to filter out irrelevant matches. For example, the TermScorer scores a term and provides an iterator over the entity, tuple, cell, and position (eid, tid, cid, pos) of the term. In fact, all the SIREn Scorers implement the interface SirenIdIterator (shown in listing 13.2), which provides methods to skip entities, tuples, or cells during the iteration.

Listing 13.2 Interface of `SirenIdIterator`

```
public interface SirenIdIterator {
  public boolean skipTo(int entityID);                          ┐ Skips to
  public boolean skipTo(int entityID, int tupleID);             │ first match
  public boolean skipTo(int entityID, int tupleID, int cellID); ┘ after target

  public int dataset();
  public int entity();      ┐ Returns current
  public int tuple();       │ structural element
  public int cell();        │ identifier
  public int pos();         ┘
}
```

For operators performing a conjunction of multiple terms such as PhraseQuery, we use the following merge-join algorithm:

1 We retrieve the postings list of each term.
2 We walk through the postings lists simultaneously.
3 At each step, we compare the entity, tuple, and cell identifiers.
   - If a mismatch occurs, we discard the current entry.
   - If they are the same, the scorer performs the usual strategy of checking if each query term has valid positions (for example, adjacent positions). In case of a match, the scorer returns eid, tid, cid as results (which will be used by higher query components such as CellQuery) and advances the pointers to the next position in each postings list.

13.4.2 *Restricting search within a cell*

The CellQuery allows us to combine the primitive query components such as Term-Query or PhraseQuery with Boolean operations. The interface is similar to Lucene BooleanQuery but offers the ability to add multiple clauses using the addClause (PrimitiveSirenQuery c, Occur o) method.

The CellScorer scores a Boolean combination of primitive queries matching within a cell. The ConjunctionScorer, DisjunctionScorer, and ReqExclScorer implement the scoring mechanism of a conjunction, disjunction, or exclusion of terms inside a cell. They walk through the iterators of the scorers and perform joins using eid, tid, and cid, keeping only matches that occur inside a same cell. A CellScorer provides an iterator over the entities, tuples, and cells (eid, tid, cid) matching the query so that higher query components such as TupleQuery can filter matches per tuple.

A CellQuery provides an interface called CellQuery.setConstraint(int index), and, to add a cell index constraint cid=index. For example, imagine the cell index of a predicate is always 0. All matches that don't have a cid equal to 0 are discarded. The index constraint isn't hard, and can be represented as an interval using `CellQuery`. `setConstraint(int start, int end)` in order to search multiple cells where `cid` falls between `start` and `end`.

13.4.3 Combining cells into tuples

A `CellQuery` allows us to express a search over the content of a cell. Multiple cell query components can be combined to form a "tuple query" using the `TupleQuery` component. A tuple query retrieves tuples matching a Boolean combination of the cell queries. The `TupleQuery` provides a similar interface to `BooleanQuery` with the ability to add multiple clauses using the `addClause(CellQuery c, Occur o)` method.

The `TupleScorer` scores a Boolean combination of cells, and provides an iterator over the entities and tuples (`eid`, `tid`) matching the query. It's based on the `CellConjunctionScorer`, `CellDisjunctionScorer`, and `CellReqExclScorer` to score a conjunction, disjunction, or exclusion of cells inside a tuple. Each walks through the iterators of the underlying scorers (`CellScorer`) and perform joins over entities and tuples.

13.4.4 Querying an entity description

`TupleQuery`, `CellQuery`, and `TermQuery` can be combined using Lucene's `BooleanQuery`, allowing you to express rich queries for matching entities. The scoring is done by Lucene's `BooleanScorer` because each of the SIREn scorers complies with the Lucene `Scorer` class. Listing 13.3 shows how to build a query using the previously described operators. The query example will retrieve all entities related to `DERI` and that have a property labeled name or `fullname` with a value of `Renaud Delbru`.

Listing 13.3　Creation of an entity description query

```
CellQuery predicate = new CellQuery();                             ❶
predicate.addClause(new TermQuery(new Term("name")),
                    Occur.SHOULD);
predicate.addClause(new TermQuery(new Term("fullname")),
                    Occur.SHOULD);
predicate.setConstraint(0);

PhraseQuery q = new PhraseQuery();                                 ❷
q.add(new Term("renaud")); q.add(new Term("delbru"));

CellQuery object = new CellQuery();                                ❸
object.addClause(q, Occur.MUST);
object.setConstraint(1, Integer.MAX_VALUE);

TupleQuery tuple1 = new TupleQuery();                              ❹
tuple1.addClause(predicate, Occur.MUST);
tuple1.addClause(object, Occur.MUST);

BooleanQuery query = new BooleanQuery();                           ❺
query.addClause(tuple1, Occur.MUST);5
query.addClause(new TermQuery(new Term("DERI")),
                Occur.MUST);
```

① Matches the predicate `"name OR fullname"`.

② Matches the phrase `"renaud delbru"`.

③ Matches the object `"renaud delbru"`.

④ Matches `<"name OR fullname", "renaud delbru">`.

⑤ Matches `<"name OR fullname", "renaud delbru"> AND "DERI"`.

13.5 *Integrating SIREn in Solr*

Solr is an enterprise search server based on Lucene, developed within the same Apache Lucene top-level project as Lucene. It provides many useful features, such as faceted search, caching, replication, and distribution over shards. In this section we'll show you how easy it is to plug a new Lucene component into the Solr framework, and how Sindice is able to benefit from all features provided by Solr.

To connect SIREn to the Solr framework, we had to assign the `TupleAnalyzer` to the tuple field type in the Solr schema file, as shown in listing 13.4. We also created a parser for the SPARQL, the recommended RDF query language by the W3C.[6]

The first component of the query parser is the `SPARQLQueryAnalyzer` that processes the input SPARQL query into a stream of tokens. The second component is the `SPARQLParser`, which extends the `Solr.QParser` that invokes the `SPARQLQueryAnalyzer`, parses the stream of tokens, and builds the corresponding SIREn query.

To make the `SPARQLParser` available to the Solr front end, we created a `SPARQLParserPlugin` class that extends `Solr.QParserPlugin` and a modification of the Solr config file to register the plug-in; see listing 13.4.

> **Listing 13.4 Integration of SIREn through Solr schema.xml**

```
<fieldType name="tuple" class="solr.TextField">
  <analyzer type="index"
    class="org.sindice.solr.plugins.analysis.TupleAnalyzer"
    words="stopwords.txt"/>
  <analyzer type="query"
    class="org.sindice.solr.plugins.analysis.SPARQLQueryAnalyzer"
    words="stopwords.txt"/>
</fieldType>
...
<fields>
    <field name="content" type="tuple" indexed="true" stored="false"/>
    ... Other field definition ...
</fields>
```

13.6 *Benchmark*

We performed the following benchmark using synthetic datasets of RDF entities on a commodity server.[7] We varied the number of distinct predicates (fields) of these data

---

[6] See http://www.w3.org/TR/rdf-sparql-query/

[7] 8 GB of RAM, two-quad core Intel processors running at 2.23 GHz, 7200 RPM SATA disks, Linux 2.6.24-19, Java Version 1.6.0.06

Table 13.3 Comparison of size (in kb) of the main index files (synthetic data set with 128 fields)

Approach	TermInfoIndex (.tii)	TermInfoFile (.tis)	FreqFile (.frq)	ProxFile (.prx)	Total
Lucene	1627	113956	1179180	509815	1804578
SIREn	38	3520	769798	2697581	3470937
SIREn/Lucene	2%	3%	65%	529%	192%

sets between 8 and 128. To generate the values in one field (a field is generally multi-valued), we used a dictionary of 90,000 terms. We averaged the query time reported in this benchmark over 500 query executions. Each query contains two keywords randomly selected from the dictionary.

Table 13.3 shows that SIREn keeps a concise dictionary (the term dictionary is represented by two files per segment, the main file (*.tis) and the index file (*.tii)) whereas Lucene dictionary size increases linearly with the number of fields. With 128 fields, the size of the SIREn dictionary is 1.6 MB, whereas the size of the Lucene dictionary is 113 MB. In this case, SIREn is much more memory-efficient and lets us keep a larger part of the dictionary in memory. The file containing the posting lists (that is, the *.frq file that contains the lists of documents for each term, along with the frequency of the term in each document) is smaller using SIREn. Lucene has a different posting list for each term in each field; therefore, Lucene is creating more posting lists than SIREn, and this càuses storage overhead. But the file that contains the positional information (*.prx), which contains the lists of positions that each term occurs at within documents along with the payload associated with the current term position, becomes five times bigger than the Lucene one. This is due to the overhead of storing the structural information (tuple and cell identifier) in the payload, but the impact of this is limited because this file isn't usually kept in memory. The overall SIREn index size is below twice the size of Lucene index. Appendix B describes Lucene's index file format.

In tables 13.4 and 13.5, we can see that either for conjunction and disjunction Lucene performance decreases with the number of fields. To answer queries across a number of fields, Lucene expands the query by concatenating each field name to each keyword. For example, for a query with two keywords over 64 fields, the Lucene `MultiFieldQueryParser` (covered in section 5.4) will expand the query to 2 x 64 = 128 query terms. In SIREn, there's no query expansion. The worst case will be 2 (keyword terms) + 64 (field terms) = 66 query terms—and only 2 if search is performed across all fields (that is, when a field wildcard is used because no field terms have to be intersected with the keyword terms).

Similar performance for the field wildcard case could've been achieved with Lucene by using a catchall field, where all the values are concatenated together. In this case, doing so would duplicate information another time in the index (and in the dictionary), induce false positives, and be of no use when only a subset of fields has to be searched.

Table 13.4   Query time (in ms) for conjunction of two keywords across all fields (wildcard for field names)

Approach	8 fields	16 fields	32 fields	64 fields	128 fields
Lucene	100	356	659	1191	2548
SIREn	72	79	75	76	91

Table 13.5   Query time (in ms) for disjunction of two keywords across all fields (wildcard for field names)

Approach	8 fields	16 fields	32 fields	64 fields	128 fields
Lucene	85	144	287	599	1357
SIREn	45	59	62	74	109

Table 13.6 reports the execution time of keywords search over one, two, or three randomly selected required terms in a `BooleanQuery` on the synthetic data set of 64 fields. SIREn performs slightly worse than Lucene when search is restricted to one field. The reason is that SIREn intersects three posting lists (the posting list of the field and the posting lists of each keyword) whereas Lucene intersects only two (the posting list of each keyword). But when keyword search is performed over two or three fields, SIREn takes the advantage. The performance is similar in all the other cases, using disjunction or exclusion instead of conjunction. After profiling Lucene during query execution, we observed that 25 percent of the time is spent reading the dictionary (more precisely in the method `SegmentTermEnum.next()`).

Approach	Q-1F	Q-2F	Q-3F
Lucene	50	56	82
SIREn	77	53	58

Table 13.6   Query time (in ms) for keyword search in one, two, or three randomly selected fields

13.7   Summary

In this chapter, you learned about SIREn, a Lucene "extension" for efficient querying of large amounts of schema-free semistructured data. We say "extension" because SIREn is more like a whole purpose-built application running on top of Lucene with a set of custom Lucene components—Analyzers, Tokenizers, TokenFilters, and so on. SIREn enables Lucene and Solr to handle information directly coming from the "Web of Data," but can also be useful in enterprise data integration projects. The principal advantages that SIREn brings are as follows:

- It enables efficient search across a large number of fields.
- It is memory efficient with respect to the lexicon size.
- It enables flexible field names indexing (tokenized, wildcards, fuzzy matching on field names).
- It handles multivalued fields in an accurate way.

But when you expect to have data with a relatively small and fixed schema or when field values are distinct across fields, direct Lucene is a better choice; it will produce a smaller index and the query processing will be generally faster. In fact, SIREn isn't meant to replace Lucene features but to complement them. You can use Lucene fields for fixed and frequent properties in the data collection and use SIREn for the other properties or for to perform fast multifield queries.

SIREn is in use in the Sindice search engine, which currently indexes more than 50 million structured documents (for a total of 1 billion triples) and can serve thousands of queries per minutes on a commodity server machine.

Case study 3: LinkedIn

Adding facets and real-time search with Bobo Browse and Zoie

Contributed by JOHN WANG *and* JAKE MANNIX

LinkedIn.com is the largest social network for professionals in the world, with over 60 million users worldwide (as of March 2010), and has "people search" as a primary feature: users on the site have fully rich profiles that act as their public professional resume or curriculum vitae. A primary feature of the site is the ability to search for other users based on complex criteria, enabling use cases such as

- A hiring manager who wants to find potential employees
- Salespeople who want to find leads
- Tech-savvy executives of all levels who want to locate subject-matter experts for consultation

Search for people at LinkedIn is an extremely complex topic, complete with tremendous scalability issues, a distributed architecture, real-time indexing, and personalized search. Each search query is created by a registered user on the site who has his own individual subset of the full social network graph, which affects the relevance score of each hit differently for different searching users.

Lucene powers LinkedIn's searching. In this chapter we'll see two powerful extensions to Lucene developed and used at LinkedIn. The first, Bobo Browse (available as open source at http://sna-projects.com/bobo) provides faceting information for each search. Zoie, the second extension (available as open source at http://sna-projects.com/zoie), is a real-time search system built on top of Lucene.

14.1   *Faceted search with Bobo Browse*

The standard full-text search engine—and Lucene is no exception—is designed to quickly collect a few (say, 10) hits in the index that are the most relevant to the query provided, discarding the rest. If none of the "most relevant" documents are what the user wants, he must refine his query by adding further required terms. But the user has no guidance on what may be considered good terms for refinement, a process that's error-prone and adds a lot of work for the user. Sometimes the effort to refine goes too far: no results are found and the user must backtrack and try again. This is a common problem with search engines, not specific to Lucene.

With faceted search,[1] in addition to the top results, the user sees the distribution of field values for all documents in the result set. As an example, on LinkedIn each document is a person's profile; when a user searches for *java engineer*, she sees the top 10 of 177,878 people, but is also presented with the fact that *of all of those people*, IBM is the most popular value for the current company of the person with 2,090 hits; Oracle is the second-most popular value, with 1,938 people; Microsoft is the third, with 1,344; and so forth. The term *facet* is used to describe the field—current_company—for which we're returning these results, and *facet value* is the value of this field, such as IBM. *Facet count* is the number of hits on the particular facet value—2,090 for IBM. These are presented as links, and the user can refine her query by clicking IBM, which returns the 2,090 people matching the effective Lucene query of +java +engineer +current_company:IBM. Because the search engine will only return links for facet values with greater than 0 facet count, the user knows in advance how many hits she will get to her query, and in particular that it won't be 0. Figure 14.1 shows a LinkedIn facet search powered by Bobo Browse and Lucene.

14.1.1   *Bobo Browse design*

The Bobo Browse open source library is built on top of Lucene, and can add faceting to any Lucene-based project. A browsable index is simply a Lucene index with some declarations on how a field is used to support faceting. Such declaration can be defined in either the form of a Spring[2] configuration file added to the Lucene index directory with the name bobo.spring, as seen in table 14.1, or constructed programmatically while creating a BoboIndexReader. This architectural decision was made to allow for making a Lucene index facet browsable without reindexing. Each field in the declaration file is specified with a FacetHandler instance that loads a forward view of the data in a compressed form. Bobo Browse uses these FacetHandlers for counting, sorting, and field retrieval.

The Bobo Browse API follows closely with the Lucene search API, with structured selection and facet grouping specification as additional input parameters, and the output appended with facet information for each field. As with many software libraries, seeing example code linked against bobo-browse.jar will probably be more

---

[1]   See http://en.wikipedia.org/wiki/Faceted_search.
[2]   See http://www.springsource.org.

Figure 14.1   The LinkedIn.com search result page with facets, facet values, and their counts on the right

instructive than a couple of paragraphs. Let's walk through a simplified user profile example, where each document represents one person with the following fields:

- geo_region: One per document, formatted as a `String`. Examples: `New York City`, `SF BayArea`.
- industry_id: One per document, values of type integer greater than 0.
- locale: Multiple values per document. Examples: `en`, `fr`, `es`.
- company_id: Multiple values per document, each of type integer greater than 0.
- num_recommendations: One per document, values of type integer greater than or equal to 0; we'll facet on ranges [1 – 4], [5 – 10], [11 +].

Table 14.1 Bobo Browse allows you to configure facets declaratively through a Spring file.

Lucene document construction	Spring Beans specifying faceting information

geo_region:
• Store.No
• Index.NotAnalyzed-NoNorms
• omitTf
	``xml
	<bean id = "geo_region"
	➥class="com.browseengine.bobo.facets.impl.SimpleFacetHandler">
	  <constructor-arg value="geo_region">
	</bean>
	``

industry_id:
• Store.No
• Index.NotAnalyzed-NoNorms
• omitTf
• 10-digit 0 padding
	``xml
	<bean id = "industry_id"
	➥class="com.browseengine.bobo.facets.impl.SimpleFacetHandler">
	  <constructor-arg value="industry_id">
	  <constructor-arg>
	    <bean class=
	➥"com.browseengine.bobo.facets.data.PredefinedTermListFactory">
	       <constructor-arg value="java.lang.Integer" />
	       <constructor-arg value="0000000000"/>
	  </constructor-arg>
	</bean>
	``

locale:
• Store.No
• Indexed.Analyzed-NoNorms
• omitTf
	``xml
	<bean id = "locale" class=
	➥"com.browseengine.bobo.facets.impl.CompactMultiValueFacetHandler">
	  <constructor-arg value="locale">
	</bean>
	``

company_id:
• Store.No
• Indexed.Analyzed-NoNorms
• omitTf
• with 10-digit 0 padding
	``xml
	<bean id = "company_id"
	➥class=
	➥"com.browseengine.bobo.facets.impl.MultiValueFacetHandler">
	  <constructor-arg value="company_id">
	  <constructor-arg>
	    <bean class=
	➥"com.browseengine.bobo.facets.data.PredefinedTermListFactory">
	       <constructor-arg value="java.lang.Integer" />
	       <constructor-arg value="0000000000"/>
	  </constructor-arg>
	</bean>
	``

num_recommendations:
• Store.No
• Indexed.NotAnalyzed-NoNorms
• omitTf
• with 10-digit 0 padding
	``xml
	<bean id = "num_recommendations"
	➥class="com.browseengine.bobo.facets.impl.RangeFacetHandler">
	  <constructor-arg value="num_recommendations">
	  <constructor-arg>
	    <bean class=
	➥"com.browseengine.bobo.facets.data.PredefinedTermListFactory">
	       <constructor-arg value="java.lang.Integer" />
	       <constructor-arg value="0000000000"/>
	  </constructor-arg>
	  <constructor-arg>
	      <list>
	          <value>[1 TO 4]</value>
	          <value>[5 TO 10]</value>
	          <value>[11 TO *]</value>
	      </list>
	  </constructor-arg>
	</bean>
	``

To browse the Lucene index built with fields from table 14.1, we'll do something as simple as the following. First, let's assume that the application has a way of getting an `IndexReader` opened on the Lucene index at hand:

```
IndexReader reader = getLuceneIndexReader();
```

We then decorate it with Bobo Browse's index reader:

```
BoboIndexReader boboReader = BoboIndexReader.getInstance(reader);
```

Next we create a browse request:

```
// use setCount() and setOffset() for pagination:
BrowseRequest br = new BrowseRequest();
br.setCount(10);
br.setOffset(0);
```

One core component of a `BrowseRequest` is the driving query. Any subclass of Lucene's `Query` class works here, and all added facet constraints further restrict the driving query. In the extreme "pure browse" case, the application would use `Match-AllDocsQuery` as the driving query (see section 3.4.9).

```
QueryParser queryParser;
Query query = queryParser.parse("position_description:(software OR
    engineer)");
br.setQuery(query);
```

We could add on any Lucene `Filter` (see section 5.6) as well, with `Browse-Request.setFilter(Filter)`. We request facet information from this request by creating specific `FacetSpec`s, in which you specify the following:

- The maximum number of facets to return for each field.
- The ordering on the facets returned for each field: whether they're returned in the lexicographical order of the facet values or in the order of facets with the most associated hits. For example, imagine the color field has three facets returned: red(100), green(200), blue(30). We can either order them by lexicographical order:
  ```
  blue(30), green(200), red(100)
  ```
  or by hits:
  ```
  green(200), red(100), blue(30)
  ```
- That you only want to return a facet for a given field with a hit count greater than some value.

For the current example, we want to return not only the top 10 users with the term *software* or *engineer* in some of their position descriptions in their profiles, but we also want to find the top 20 company names out of the whole result set, and how many hits each company would have if you were to add it to the query, as in `"+company_name:<foo>"`:

```
FacetSpec companyNameSpec = new FacetSpec();
companyNameSpec.setOrderBy(          ❶
    FacetSortSpec.OrderHitsDesc);
```

```
companyNameSpec.setMaxCount(20);                    ◀── ❷
br.setFacetSpec("company_name", companyNameSpec);
```

We first request ❶ that the facets be sorted by facet count, descending, and then set ❷ the number of facets to be returned to 20. We may also want to find out something about the geographical distribution of the results:

```
FacetSpec geoRegionSpec = new FacetSpec();
geoRegionSpec.setMinHitCount(100);                  ◀── ❶
geoRegionSpec.setMaxCount(50);                       ◀── ❷
geoRegionSpec.setOrderBy(                                       ❸
    FacetSortSpec.OrderValueAsc);
br.setFacetSpec("geo_region", geoRegionSpec);
```

Instead of simply showing the top 20 regions, we get ❷ all the geo-regions (imagine that these were specifically the 50 US state abbreviations) that have ❶ at least 100 hits, and we order ❸ them in the usual alphabetical order.

Now we're ready to browse. With raw Lucene, we'd create an `IndexSearcher` wrapping an `IndexReader`. In the faceting world, we want a `BoboBrowser`—the analog of an `IndexSearcher`. In fact, `BoboBrowser` is a subclass of `IndexSearcher`, and implements the `Browsable` interface—which is the analog of Lucene's `Searchable` interface (which `IndexSearcher` implements). `Browsable` extends `Searchable` as well. This class mirroring and extending is common in Bobo Browse, and makes it easy for someone familiar with Lucene to quickly gain proficiency with Bobo Browse. The library is meant to extend all aspects of Lucene searching to the browsing paradigm. For example, this is how you create a browser:

```
Browseable browser = new BoboBrowser(boboReader);
```

Just as with `Searchable`, `Browsable` allows a high-level method for ease of use to just get your results:

```
BrowseResult result = browser.browse(br);
```

You can find out how many total results there were and get access to the hit objects:

```
int totalHits = result.getNumHits();
BrowseHit[] hits = result.getHits();
```

`BrowseHits` are like Lucene's `ScoreDocs`, but also contain facet values for all configured faceting fields, because there's essentially no cost to fill these in from the in-memory cache. The facet information is contained within a map whose keys are the field names and whose values are `FacetAccessible` objects. `FacetAccessible` contains a sorted `List<BrowseFacet>`, retrievable with `getFacets()`. Each `BrowseFacet` is a pair of value (a `String`) and count (an `int`).

```
Map<String, FacetAccessible> facetMap = result.getFacetMap();
```

Let's say the user's search matches a total of 1,299 hits, and that the top three companies were IBM, Oracle, and Microsoft. To narrow her search and look only at people who've worked at IBM or Microsoft but didn't work at Oracle, the user can take the same `BrowseRequest` she had before (or, more likely in a stateless web framework, a

recreated instance), and add to it a new `BrowseSelection` instance. A `BrowseSelec-`
`tion` corresponds to a SQL `WHERE` clause, which provides some structured filtering on
top of a text search query.

For example, in SQL, the clause `WHERE (company_id=1 OR company_id=2) AND`
`(company_id <> 3)` can be represented in a `BrowseSelection` as

```
BrowseSelection selection = new BrowseSelection("company_id");
selection.addValue("1");     // 1 = IBM
selection.addValue("2");     // 2 = Microsoft
selection.addNotValue("3"); // 3 = Oracle
selection.setSelectionOperation(ValueOperation.ValueOperationOr);
br.addSelection(selection);
```

14.1.2 Beyond simple faceting

Although Lucene provides access to the inverted index, Bobo Browse provides a forward view through `FacetHandlers`. Bobo Browse thus provides useful functionality
beyond faceting.

FAST FIELD RETRIEVAL

Bobo Browse can retrieve the field values for a specific document ID and field name.
With Lucene, a `Field` with the `Store.YES` attribute turned on can be stored:

```
doc.add(new Field("color","red",Store.YES,Index.NOT_ANALYZED_NO_NORMS));
```

then retrieved via the API:

```
Document doc = indexReader.document(docid);
String colorVal = doc.get("color");
```

We devised a test to understand performance better. We created an optimized index
of 1 million documents, each with one field named color with a value to be one of
eight color strings. This was a very optimized scenario for retrieval of stored data
because there was only one segment and much of the data could fit in memory. We
then iterated through the index and retrieved the field value for color. This took
1,250 milliseconds (ms).

Next, we did the same thing, but instead of creating a `BoboIndexReader` with a
`FacetHandler`, we built on the indexed data of the color field. We paid a penalty of 133
ms to load the `FacetHandler` once the index loads, and retrieval time took 41 ms. By
paying a 10 percent penalty once, we boosted the retrieval speed over 3,000 percent.

SORTING

One of the coolest parts of Lucene is sorting. Lucene cleverly leverages the field cache
and the fact that strings are indexed in a lexicographical order for fast sorting: the
comparison between string values of two documents can be reduced to comparing the
array indexes of these string values in the term table, and the cost of string comparison is reduced to integer arithmetic. Chapter 5 covers Lucene's sorting and its use of
the field cache.

Currently, Lucene sorting has a restriction that sort fields must not be tokenized:
every document in the index must have at most one value in a sortable field (see
section 2.4.6). While developing Bobo Browse, we devised a way of removing this

restriction: FieldCache is a forward view of the index. We extended the idea by incorporating FieldCache into FacetHandlers. Because we've made FacetHandlers pluggable, we started adding other powerful features into FacetHandlers, such as the ability to handle documents with multiple values in a given field. We're therefore able to facet and sort on multivalued fields (for example, any tokenized field).

We took a sample of our member profile index, about 4.6 million documents, sorted the entire index on a tokenized field (such as last name) and took the top 10 hits. The entire search/sort call on a development-type box took 300 ms.

Faceting need not be restricted to index-time-only content.

RUNTIME FACETHANDLERS

When we started designing the FacetHandler architecture, we realized that at index time we didn't have the data needed for faceting, such as personalized data or the searcher's social network. So we designed the framework to allow for *runtime* FacetHandlers. Such FacetHandlers are constructed at query time to support faceting on data provided at search time, such as a user's social graph and connection counts.

ZOIE INTEGRATION

Because of our scale both in terms of number of searchers as well as corpus size, along with our real-time requirement, we needed a distributed real-time solution for facet search. For this, we leveraged Zoie, an open source, real-time search and indexing system built on Lucene; we'll describe Zoie in section 14.2. Integration was easy: we created an IndexReaderDecorator that decorates a ZoieIndexReader into a BoboIndexReader:

```
class BoboIndexReaderDecorator<BoboIndexReader>
      implements IndexReaderDecorator{
  public BoboIndexReader decorate(ZoieIndexReader indexReader)
      throws IOException{
    return new BoboIndexReader(indexReader);
  }
}
```

and gave it to Zoie. In turn, Zoie acts as a BoboIndexReader factory that returns BoboIndexReaders in real time. In our search code, we simply do this:

```
List<BoboIndexReader> readerList = zoie.getIndexReaders();
Browsable[] browsers = new Browsable[readerList.size()];
for (int i = 0; i < readerList.size(); ++i){
  browsers[i] = new BoboBrowser(readerList.get(i));
}

Browsable browser = new MultiBoboBrowser(browsers);
```

Next we'll describe how LinkedIn achieves another important search capability: real-time search.

14.2 *Real-time search with Zoie*

A real-time search system makes it possible for queries to find a new document immediately (or almost immediately) after it's been updated. In the case of LinkedIn's people search, this means we want to make a member profile searchable as soon as the profile is created or updated.

NOTE   To be precise, as soon as the profile arrives at a node, the next search request that node receives can include the newly updated profile. In a distributed system, where indexing events are queued and delivered independently to each node, clients of the entire distributed system are only guaranteed to get results as up-to-date as the nodes they hit.

With Lucene's incremental update functionality, we believe we can extend Lucene to support real-time searching. A naïve solution would be to commit as often as possible while reopening the `IndexReader` for every search request. This poses a few scalability problems:

- The latency is relatively high. The cost of `IndexWriter.commit` on a disk-based index isn't negligible.
- The index would be fragmented heavily because each commit would create a new index segment, and index segment merge cost becomes significant if we commit per document.
- We may waste a lot of indexing work: the same member profile tends to be updated frequently in a short period of time. It ends up with a lot of deleted documents in the index, which affects search performance.
- We have to reload `IndexReader` frequently to make new documents available for search users. Opening an `IndexReader` per search request adds a significant amount of latency at search time.

An alternative is to keep the entire index in memory (for example, via a `RAMDirectory`, described in section 2.10). This alleviates the problems of high indexing latency and index fragmentation. But we'd still process wasteful indexing requests due to fast updates. Furthermore, even with the introduction of the `IndexReader.reopen()` API (see section 3.2.1), which improves the index reader load time, with customized `IndexReader` instances the cost of loading the index reader might be higher than what we'd be willing to pay. Here are some examples of extra data we're loading for our customized `IndexReader`:

- Zoie by default loads an array mapping Lucene `docID`s to application UIDs.
- Zoie loads data structures for faceted search (see the Bobo Browse study in section 14.1).
- Zoie loads static ranking, for example "people rank" from an external source. At LinkedIn, we use usage and search tracking data in combination with the social network to calculate a static people rank

It's clear that loading our custom `IndexReader` for each search request isn't feasible at scale. These problems motivated us to develop a real-time searching architecture at LinkedIn, and Zoie (http://sna-projects.com/zoie) is an open source project that's an offspring of this effort.

14.2.1 Zoie architecture

Let's look at the main Zoie components as well as some code. If you're impatient or just like pretty diagrams, jump to figure 14.2.

DATA PROVIDER AND DATA CONSUMER

When we started building Zoie, we imagined a constant stream of indexing requests flowing into our indexing system and our indexing system acting as a consumer of this stream. We abstracted this access pattern into a provider-consumer paradigm, and we defined *data provider* as the source of this stream and *data consumer* as our indexing system. A data provider in Zoie is just a marker interface to identify the concept; there's no contract defined in the interface.

Upon further abstraction, data providers can provide a stream of indexing requests from various sources, such as files, networks, and databases. A data consumer can be any piece of code that deals with the flow of indexing requests, and can even act as a data provider—by serving as an intermediate data massage or filtering layer to relay the indexing requests. With this abstraction, we give our system the flexibility to have our data arbitrarily massaged or aggregated before finally being consumed by the indexing system.

To have a fault-tolerant system, we need to be able to handle situations where the system is shut down ungracefully due a system crash or power outage. Although we're able to rely on the Lucene indexing mechanism to be solid so that our index isn't easily corrupted, we'd lose track of where we are in the stream of indexing requests. Having to reindex from scratch every time a system goes down isn't acceptable. Because of this, we have built into Zoie a versioning mechanism to persist the point in the stream where the last batch of indexing request was processed. From this version, a data provider can retrack so that the indexing requests can be regenerated. The version numbers are provided by the application; such version numbers can be timestamps or database commit numbers, for example.

Take a look at listing 14.1. We have data stored in a table in a relational database and we want to create a Lucene index for fast text search capabilities. In this table, there are three columns: id (long), content (String), and timestamp (long). The number of rows in this table is very large.

Listing 14.1   Indexing data events with Zoie

```
class Data {                              ❶ Hold
  long id;                                   indexing
  String content;                            data
}
                                          ❷ Filter out
class NoNullDataConsumer implements          null content
          DataConsumer<Data>, DataProvider {
  private DataConsumer<Data> _subConsumer;
  NoNullDataConsumer(DataConsumer<Data> subConsumer) {
    _subConsumer = subConsumer;
  }
```

```
public void consume(Collection<DataEvent<Data>> data) throws ZoieException
  {
  List<DataEvent<Data>> events = new LinkedList<DataEvent<Data>>();
  for (DataEvent<Data> evt : data){
    if (evt.content != null){
      events.add(evt);
    }
  }
  _subConsumer.consume(events);
}
}

ZoieSystem indexingSystem ... ;
indexingSystem.start();

ZoieSystemAdminMBean adminMBean =
    indexingSystem.getAdminMBean();
long lastVersion = adminMBean.getCurrentDiskVersion();

JDBCDataProvider dataProvider = new JDBCDataProvider(
  "SELECT id,content,tmstmp FROM newstable WHERE tmstmp >= "+lastVersion);
Collection<DataEvent<Data>> indexingRequests =
    dataProvider.getIndexingRequests();

NoNullDataConsumer consumer = new NoNullDataConsumer(indexingSystem);
consumer.consume(indexingRequests);
```

❸ Create, start Zoie

❹ Get last committed version

Retrieve ❺ indexing data

Create consumer chain ❻

Let's understand some Zoie internals. To implement real-time search, we decided to use multiple indexes: one main index on disk, plus two helper indexes in memory to handle transient indexing requests.

DISK INDEX

The disk index will grow to be rather large; therefore, indexing updates on disk will be performed in batches. Processing updates in batches allows us to merge updates of the same document to reduce redundant updates. Moreover, the disk index wouldn't be fragmented as the indexer wouldn't be thrashed by a large number of small indexing calls and requests. We keep a shared disk-based IndexReader to serve search requests. Once batch indexing is performed, we build and load a new IndexReader and then publish the new shared IndexReader. The cost of building and loading the IndexReader is thus hidden from the cost of search.

RAM INDEX(ES)

To ensure real-time behavior, the two helper memory indexes (MemA and MemB) alternate in their roles. One index, say MemA, accumulates indexing requests and serves real-time results. When a flush or commit event occurs, MemA stops receiving new indexing events, and indexing requests are sent to MemB. At this time search requests are served from all three indexes: MemA, MemB, and the disk index. These indexes are shown in figure 14.2.

Once the disk merge is completed, MemA is cleared and MemB and MemA get swapped. Until the next flush or commit, searches will be served from the new disk index, new MemA, and the now empty MemB.

Table 14.2 shows the states of different parts of the system as time (T) progresses.

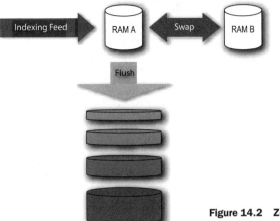

Figure 14.2   Zoie's three-index architecture: two in-memory indexes, and one disk-based index

Table 14.2   State of Zoie's indexes over time

Time	MemA	MemB	DiskIndex
T1: Request 1	Request 1 indexed	Empty	Empty
T2: Request 2	Request 1 and 2 indexed	Empty	Empty
T3: Request 3	Request 1 and 2 indexed	Request 3 indexed	Copying index data from MemA
T4: disk index published, memA and memB swaps	Request 3 indexed	Empty	Request 1 and 2 indexed
T5: Request 4	Request 3 and 4 indexed	Empty	Request 1 and 2 indexed
T5: Request 5	Request 3 and 4 indexed	Request 5 indexed	Request 1 and 2 indexed, Copying index data from MemA
T6: disk index published, memA and memB swaps	Request 5 indexed	Empty	Request 1, 2, 3, and 4 indexed

For each search request, we open and load a new `IndexReader` from each of the in-memory indexes, and along with the shared disk `IndexReader`, we build a list of `IndexReaders` for the user. See the following code snippet used in a simple search thread. The Zoie instance also implements the interface `proj.zoie.api.indexReaderFactory` (the explicit cast is used to make this clear):

```
static IndexReader buildIndexReaderFromZoie(ZoieSystem indexingSystem){
    IndexReaderFactory readerFactory = (IndexReaderFactory) indexingSystem;

    List<ZoieIndexReader> readerList = readerFactory.getIndexReaders();
```

```
    MultiReader reader = new MultiReader(readerList.toArray(
                        new IndexReader[readerList.size()]), false);
    return reader;
}

IndexSearcher searcher = new IndexSearcher(
    buildIndexReaderFromZoie(indexingSystem));
...
indexingSystem.returnIndexReaders(readerList);
```

Next, let's look at what knobs Zoie exposes to let us tune just how real-time we want
Zoie to be.

14.2.2 Real-time vs. near-real-time

With the helper in-memory index mechanism built into Zoie and the power of
Lucene's incremental update feature, we're able to achieve real-time search and
indexing. But there are applications where the real-time requirement may be relaxed
and near real time may be good enough. Say there's a small gap of time between when
a document is indexed or updated and when it or its new version is reflected in the
search result. Zoie can be configured either programmatically or at runtime via JMX
to support the relaxed real-time behavior by doing the following:

- Disabling real-time altogether (that is, don't use in-memory indexes)
- Adjusting the `batchSize` parameter, which is the number of indexing requests
  that should be in the queue before the queue is flushed and indexed to
  disk—only if this occurs before the `batchDelay` time condition is met
- Adjusting the `batchDelay` parameter, which is the amount of time Zoie should
  wait before the queue is flushed and indexed to disk—only if this occurs before
  the `batchSize` condition is met

With this configuration, Zoie becomes a one-disk index-based streaming search and
indexing system, with real-time or content freshness tuned with the `batchSize` and
`batchDelay` parameters. The Zoie managed beans (MBeans) exposed via Java Management Extensions (JMX) can be seen in figures 14.3 and 14.4.

14.2.3 Documents and indexing requests

In Zoie, each document is expected to have a unique long ID (UID). Zoie keeps track
of any document change such as creation, modification, or deletion by UID. It's the
application's responsibility to provide a UID for each document to be inserted into the
index. The UID is also used to perform duplicate removal of documents in both the
memory index as well as the disk index. We also benefit by having a quick mapping
between Lucene `docID`s to UIDs.

Any manipulation of a document (creation, modification, or deletion) is propa-
gated to Zoie as an indexing request. The indexing requests are transformed to
`proj.zoie.api.indexing.ZoieIndexable` instances via a `proj.zoie.api.index-`
`ing.ZoieIndexableInterpreter` that's provided to Zoie. The code in listing 14.2
demonstrates this.

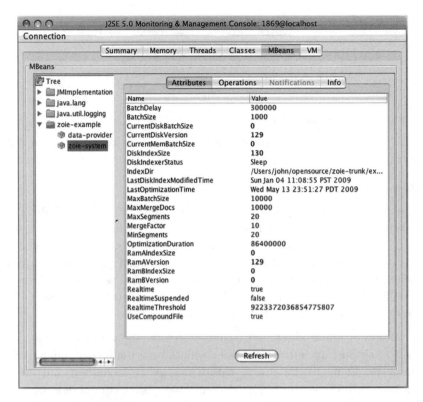

Figure 14.3   The read-only JMX view of Zoie's attributes, as rendered by JConsole

Listing 14.2   All indexing in Zoie is achieved through indexing requests

```java
class DataIndexable implements ZoieIndexable {
  private Data _data;
  public DataIndexable(Data data) {
      _data = data;
  }

  public long getUID() {
      return _data.id;
  }

  public IndexingReq[] buildIndexingReqs() {
      Document doc = new Document();
      doc.add(new Field("content",
                      _data.content,
                      Store.NO,
                      Index.ANALYZED));

      return new IndexingReq[]{new IndexingReq(doc)};
  }

  public boolean isDeleted() {
    return
      "_MARKED_FOR_DELETE".equals(_data.content);
  }
```

❶ Skip id field (Zoie manages it)

❷ Determine deleted, skipped at runtime

```
    public boolean isSkip() {
      return "_MARKED_FOR_SKIP".equals(_data.content);
    }
}

class DataIndexableInterpreter implements ZoieIndexableInterpreter<Data> {
    public ZoieIndexable interpret(Data src) {
        return new DataIndexable(src);
    }
}
```

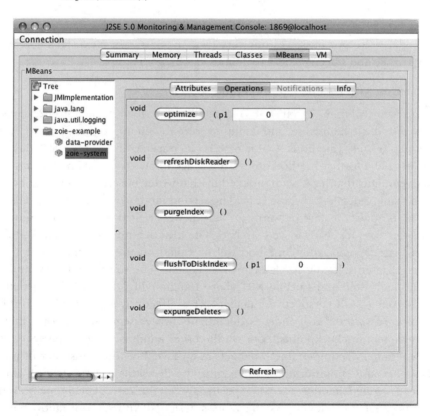

14.2.4 Custom IndexReaders

We find the ability to have application-specific `IndexReaders` very useful. In our case, we wanted to provide facet search capabilities through Bobo Browse in conjunction with Zoie for real-time search. So we've designed Zoie to pass on creating and loading custom `IndexReaders` if desired.

To do this, provide Zoie with a `proj.zoie.api.indexing.IndexReaderDecorator` implementation:

```
class MyDoNothingFilterIndexReader extends FilterIndexReader {
    public MyDoNothingFilterIndexReader(IndexReader reader) {
        super(reader);
```

Figure 14.4   Zoie exposes controls via JMX, allowing an operator to change its behavior at runtime.

```
    }
    public void updateInnerReader(IndexReader inner) {
        in = inner;
    }
}

class MyDoNothingIndexReaderDecorator implements
    IndexReaderDecorator<MyDoNothingFilterIndexReader> {
    public MyDoNothingIndexReaderDecorator decorate(
      ZoieIndexReader indexReader)
        throws IOException {
      return new MyDoNothingFilterIndexReader(indexReader);
    }
    public MyDoNothingIndexReaderDecorator redecorate(
      MyDoNothingIndexReaderDecorator decorated,
      ZoieIndexReader copy)
        throws IOException {
      decorated.updateInnerReader(copy);
      return decorated;
    }
}
```

Notice we're given a `ZoieIndexReader`, which is a Lucene `IndexReader` that can quickly map a Lucene `docID` to the application UID:

```
long uid = zoieReader.getUID(docid);
```

And voilà, we've got ourselves our very own `IndexReader`. Next, let's compare and contrast Zoie and Lucene's near-real-time search.

14.2.5 *Comparison with Lucene near-real-time search*

Lucene near-real-time search (NRT) capability, described in section 3.2.5, was introduced with the 2.9.0 release, and it aims to solve the same problem. Lucene NRT adds a couple of new methods to `IndexWriter`: `getReader()` and `setIndexReader-Warmer()`. The former method gives a reference to an `IndexReader` that has visibility into documents that have been indexed by that writer but that haven't yet been committed using `IndexWriter.commit()`. The second method, `setIndexReaderWarmer()`, lets callers specify a way to "warm up" the newly created `IndexReader` returned by `getReader()` so it's ready to be searched. The idea behind the `IndexReaderWarmer` is that its `warm(IndexReader)` method will be called on the `SegmentReader` for newly merged segments, letting you load any `FieldCache` state you need, for example.

Although Zoie and Lucene NRT share functionality, there are important differences. From an API perspective, Lucene NRT is effectively a private view on the internals of `IndexWriter` as it indexes documents, writes segments, merges them, and manages commit checkpoints. Zoie, on the other hand, is an indexing system on top of a real-time indexing engine. Zoie acts as an asynchronous consumer of incoming documents, and is optimized for managing the decisions to write to disk and make balanced segment merges for you, specifically for the case of real-time search. As a real time–enabled indexing system, Zoie is designed with smooth failover as well: if you're indexing too fast for Lucene to keep up with, Zoie buffers these documents into a batch, which it tries to empty as fast as it can. But if you reach the limit on how large that queue has been set to max out, the indexing system drops out of real-time mode and starts blocking on the consume() call, forcing clients who are trying to index too fast to slow down.

Another feature of Zoie's indexing system that's different from raw Lucene NRT is that Zoie keeps track of UID-to–internal docID mapping, for de-duplication of documents that have been modified in memory but that the disk directory doesn't know about yet. This UID can also be used for other things if your application keeps track of that UID (for example, many advanced search techniques involve scoring or filtering based on an external join with data that doesn't live in your index but that shares the same UID of the entities that become Lucene documents). Zoie's form of index reader warming is a little different than Lucene NRT, in that it allows you to plug in a "generified" decorator that can be whatever subclass of ZoieIndexReader your application needs, and it goes through whatever initialization and warming process you specify before being returned from the ZoieSystem. At LinkedIn, we do facet-based search with Bobo Browse (see section 14.1 for details), and this involves loading some in-memory uninverted field data before the facet-enabled reader can be used.

Lucene NRT took a different implementation approach to the concept of real-time search: because the IndexWriter has a full in-memory workspace that it uses for indexing, the idea was to clone whatever of that structure is needed for searching and return it for each getReader() call. The cost here is in choosing what in-memory state is cloned when callers ask for readers during heavy indexing. Zoie took the approach instead of trying to keep a RAMDirectory around to index into first, and keep it small enough that doing a completely fresh reopen() call was still inexpensive, even when done for each query request. Finally, as Zoie lives on top of Lucene without modifying any Lucene-internal code, Lucene NRT can in fact be plugged into Zoie as the real-time indexing engine. As of this writing, we have run some performance tests to compare Zoie with Lucene's NRT, but haven't yet run a comprehensive enough set of tests. We published our findings so far at http://code.google.com/p/zoie/wiki/ Performance_Comparisons_for_ZoieLucene24ZoieLucene29LuceneNRT, but we urge you to run comparison tests yourself. To help with that, we've put together a detailed recipe for running Zoie performance tests and published it on http:// code.google.com/p/zoie/wiki/Running_Performance_Test.

14.2.6 *Distributed search*

Zoie can be distributed easily by configuring the data provider to stream indexing requests for a given partition and by including brokering and merging logic on the result set. We assume documents are uniformly distributed across partitions, so we don't have a global IDF and we assume scores returned from different partitions are comparable. The diagram in figure 14.5 shows this setup.

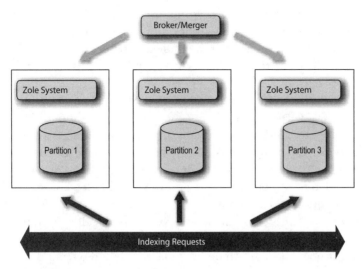

Figure 14.5 Distributed search with Zoie

The Broker/Merger in this case can be a separate service—for example, a servlet or simply a `MultiSearcher` instance with `RemoteSearchers` from each of the `Zoie-Systems`. Listing 14.3 shows an oversimplified example.

Listing 14.3 Distributed search with Zoie

```
ZoieSystem system1 ... ;                                        ⊲⎤ Create
IndexReader reader1 = buildIndexReaderFromZoie(system1);          ⎦ search node I
IndexSearcher searcher1 = new IndexSearcher(reader1);
Naming.bind("//localhost/Searchable1",new RemoteSearchable(searcher1));

ZoieSystem system2 ... ;                                        ⊲⎤ Create
IndexReader reader2 = buildIndexReaderFromZoie(system2);          ⎦ search node 2
IndexSearcher searcher2 = new IndexSearcher(reader2);
Naming.bind("//localhost/Searchable2",new RemoteSearchable(searcher2));

ZoieSystem system3 ... ;                                        ⊲⎤ Create
IndexReader reader3 = buildIndexReaderFromZoie(system3);          ⎦ search node 3
IndexSearcher searcher3 = new IndexSearcher(reader3);
Naming.bind("//localhost/Searchable3",new RemoteSearchable(searcher3));

Searchable s1 = (Searchable)Naming.lookup("//localhost/Searchable1");
Searchable s2 = (Searchable)Naming.lookup("//localhost/Searchable2");
Searchable s3 = (Searchable)Naming.lookup("//localhost/Searchable3");
MultiSearcher broker = new MultiSearcher(new Searchable[]{s1,s2,s3});
                                                Create broker/merger
```

We don't actually use RMI (remote method invocation) in production. We have search services running as servlets inside Jetty containers a remote procedure call (RPC) through Spring-RPC.

14.3 Summary

This chapter examined two powerful packages created on top of Lucene for Linke-dIn's substantial search needs. The first is Bobo Browse, a system that adds support for faceted search to Lucene. Bobo is a good example of a project that integrates well with Lucene, and can even make itself immediately useful through Spring-based configuration files, thus making it possible to add facets to an existing index and requiring no reindexing.

Zoie is a free and open source system for real-time indexing and searching that, like Bobo Browse, works on top of Lucene. Zoie is being used in the LinkedIn production search cluster serving search requests for people, jobs, companies, news, groups, forum discussions, and so forth. For people search, Zoie is deployed in distributed mode and is serving over 50 million documents in real time. As of this writing, LinkedIn runs Zoie on quad-core Solaris servers with 32 GB of RAM. Each server runs two JVMs, each with one Zoie instance managing about 5 million document partitions. In such a setup, Zoie handles about 5 million queries per day, per server with an average latency of only 50 ms, while also processing about 150,000 updates per day. Add to that the fact that some of the queries can be rather complex (such as 50 Boolean OR clauses containing phrase queries etc.), and it's clear that Zoie is a powerful system that you ought to consider when looking for real-time search solutions. Zoie can be downloaded from http://sna-projects.com/zoie/.

appendix A
Installing Lucene

The Java version of Lucene is just another JAR file, less than 1 MB in size. Using Lucene's API in your code requires only this single JAR file on your build and run-time classpath; it has no dependencies. This appendix provides the specifics of where to obtain Lucene, how to work with the distribution contents, and how to build Lucene directly from its source code. If you're using a port of Lucene in a language other than Java, refer to chapter 10 and the documentation provided with the port. If you're using a contrib module, chapter 8 describes how they're built. This appendix covers the core library of the Java version only.

A.1   *Binary installation*

To obtain the binary distribution of Lucene, follow these steps:

1   Download the latest binary Lucene release from the download area of the Apache Lucene website: http://lucene.apache.org/java. As of this writing, the latest version is 3.0.1; the subsequent steps assume this version. Download either the .zip or .tar.gz file, whichever format is more convenient for your environment.

2   Extract the binary file to the directory of your choice on your file system. The archive contains a top-level directory named lucene-3.0.1, so it's safe to extract to c:\ on Windows or your home directory on Unix. On Windows, if you have WinZip handy, use it to open the .zip file and extract its contents to c:\. If you're on Unix or you're using cygwin on Windows, unzip and untar (tar zxvf lucene-3.0.1.tar.gz) the .tar.gz file in your home directory.

3   Under the created lucene-3.0.1 directory, you'll find lucene-core-3.0.1.jar. This is the only file required to introduce Lucene into your applications. How you incorporate Lucene's JAR file into your application depends on your environment; there are numerous options. We recommend using Ant

to build your application's code. Be sure your code is compiled against the Lucene JAR using the classpath options of the `<javac>` task.

4 Include Lucene's JAR file in your application's distribution appropriately. For example, a web application using Lucene would include lucene-core-3.0.1.jar in the WEB-INF/lib directory. For command-line applications, be sure Lucene is on the classpath when launching the JVM.

The binary distribution includes a substantial amount of documentation, including Javadocs. The root of the documentation is docs/index.html, which you can open in a web browser. Lucene's distribution also ships two demonstration applications. We apologize in advance for the crude state of these demos—they lack polish when it comes to ease of use—but the documentation (found in docs/demo.html) describes how to use them step by step; we also cover the basics of running them here.

A.2 *Running the command-line demo*

The command-line Lucene demo consists of two command-line programs: one that indexes a directory tree of files and another that provides a simple search interface. They're contained in a separate JAR file, lucene-demos-3.0.1.jar, and are similar to the `Indexer` and `Searcher` examples we covered in chapter 1. To run this demo, set your current working directory to the directory where the binary distribution was expanded. Next, run `IndexFiles` like this:

```
java -cp lucene-core-3.0.1.jar;lucene-demos-3.0.1.jar
     ➥ org.apache.lucene.demo.IndexFiles docs
...
adding docs/queryparsersyntax.html
adding docs/resources.html
adding docs/systemproperties.html
adding docs/whoweare.html
9454 total milliseconds
```

This command indexes the entire docs directory tree into an index stored in the index subdirectory of the location where you executed the command.

NOTE Literally every file in the docs directory tree is indexed, including binary files such as *.png and *.jpg. None of the files are parsed; instead, each file is indexed by streaming its bytes into `StandardAnalyzer`.

To search the index just created, execute `SearchFiles` in this manner:

```
java -cp lucene-core-3.0.1.jar;lucene-demos-3.0.1.jar
            org.apache.lucene.demo.SearchFiles

Query: IndexSearcher AND QueryParser
Searching for: +indexsearcher +queryparser
10 total matching documents
0. docs/api/index-all.html
1. docs/api/allclasses-frame.html
2. docs/api/allclasses-noframe.html
3. docs/api/org/apache/lucene/search/class-use/Query.html
```

```
4. docs/api/overview-summary.html
5. docs/api/overview-tree.html
6. docs/demo2.html
7. docs/demo4.html
8. docs/api/org/apache/lucene/search/package-summary.html
9. docs/api/org/apache/lucene/search/package-tree.html
```

SearchFiles prompts interactively with Query:. QueryParser is used with StandardA-nalyzer to create a Query. A maximum of 10 hits are shown at a time; if there are more, you can page through them. Press Ctrl-C to exit the program.

Next, let's look at the web demo.

A.3   *Running the web application demo*

The web demo is slightly involved to set up and run properly. You need a web container; our instructions are for Tomcat 6.0.18. The docs/demo.html documentation provides detailed instructions for setting up and running the web application, but you can also follow the steps provided here.

The index used by the web application differs slightly from that in the command-line demo. First, it restricts itself to indexing only .html, .htm, and .txt files. Each file it processes (including .txt files) is parsed using a custom rudimentary HTML parser. To build the index initially, execute IndexHTML:

```
java -cp lucene-core-3.0.1.jar;lucene-demos-3.0.1.jar
  org.apache.lucene.demo.IndexHTML -create -index webindex docs
...
adding docs/resources.html
adding docs/systemproperties.html
adding docs/whoweare.html
Optimizing index...
7220 total milliseconds
```

The -index webindex switch sets the location of the index directory. In a moment, you'll need the full path to this directory to configure the web application. The final docs argument to IndexHTML is the directory tree to index. The -create switch creates an index from scratch. Remove this switch to update the index with files that have been added or changed since the last time the index was built.

Next, deploy luceneweb.war (from the root directory of the extracted distribution) into CATALINA_HOME/webapps. Start Tomcat, wait for the container to complete the startup routine, then edit CATALINA_HOME/webapps/lucene-web/configuration.jsp using a text editor (Tomcat should have expanded the .war file into a luceneweb directory automatically). Change the value of indexLocation appropriately, as in this example, specifying the absolute path to the index you built with IndexHTML:

```
String indexLocation =
     "/dev/LuceneInAction/install/lucene-3.0.1/webindex";
```

Now you're ready to try the web application. Visit http://localhost:8080/luceneweb in your web browser, and you should see "Welcome to the Lucene Template applica-tion…" (you can also change the header and footer text in configuration.jsp). If all is well with your configuration, searching for Lucene-specific words such as "Query-Parser AND Analyzer" should list valid results based on Lucene's documentation.

You may try to click on one of the search results links and receive an error. IndexHTML indexes a url field, which in this case is a relative path of docs/.... To make the result links work properly, copy the docs directory from the Lucene distribution to CATALINA_HOME/webapps/luceneweb.

NOTE Now that you've built two indexes, one for the command-line demo and the other for the web application demo, it's a perfect time to try Luke. See section 8.1 for details on using Luke. Point it at the index, and surf around a bit to get a feel for Luke and the contents of the index.

Next you'll see how to build Lucene from sources, which is useful if you'd like to start tinkering with your own changes to Lucene's source code.

A.4 *Building from source*

Lucene's source code is freely and easily available from Apache's Subversion repository. The prerequisites to obtain and build Lucene from source are Subversion client, Java Developer Kit (JDK), and Apache Ant. Follow these steps to build Lucene:

1 Check out the source code from Apache's Subversion repository. Follow the instructions at the Lucene Java website (http://lucene.apache.org/java) to access the repository using anonymous read-only access. This boils down to executing the following commands (from cygwin on Windows, or a Unix shell):

```
svn checkout https://svn.apache.org/repos/asf/lucene/dev/trunk/lucene
lucene-trunk
```

2 Build Lucene with Ant. At the command prompt, set your current working directory to the directory where you checked out the Lucene Subversion repository (C:\apache\lucene-trunk, for example). Type ant at the command line. Lucene's JAR will be compiled to the build subdirectory. The JAR filename is lucene-core-<*version*>.jar, where <*version*> depends on the current state of the code you obtained. It will typically be the next minor release, with a –dev attached, for example 3.1-dev.

3 Run the unit tests. If the Ant build succeeds, next run ant test (add JUnit's JAR to ANT_HOME/lib if it isn't already there) and ensure that all of Lucene's unit tests pass.

Lucene uses JFlex grammars for StandardTokenizer, and JavaCC grammars for QueryParser and the demo HTMLParser. The already-compiled .java version of the .jj files exists in the Subversion source code, so neither JFlex nor JavaCC are needed for compilation. But if you wish to modify the parser grammars, you need JFlex and JavaCC; you must also run the ant jflex or ant javacc target. You can find more details in the BUILD.txt file in the root directory of Lucene's Subversion repository.

A.5   *Troubleshooting*

We'd rather not try to guess what kinds of issues you may run into as you follow the steps to install Lucene, build Lucene, or run the demos. Checking the FAQ, searching the archives of the lucene-user email list, and using Lucene's issue-tracking system are good first steps when you have questions or issues. You'll find details at the Lucene website: http://lucene.apache.org/java.

appendix B
Lucene index format

In this book we've treated the Lucene index more or less as a black box and have concerned ourselves only with its logical view. Although you don't need to understand index structure details in order to use Lucene, you may be curious about the "magic." Lucene's index structure is a case study in itself of highly efficient data structures to maximize performance and minimize resource usage. You may see it as a purely technical achievement, or you can view it as a masterful work of art. There's something innately beautiful about representing rich structure in the most efficient manner possible. (Consider the information represented by fractal formulas or DNA as nature's proof.)

In this appendix, we'll first review the logical view of a Lucene index, where we've fed documents into Lucene and retrieved them during searches. Then, we'll expose the inner structure of Lucene's inverted index.

B.1   *Logical index view*

Let's first take a step back and start with a review of what you already know about Lucene's index. Consider figure B.1. From the perspective of a software developer using Lucene's API, an index can be considered a black box represented by the abstract `Directory` class. When indexing, you create instances of the Lucene `Document` class and populate it with `Fields` that consist of name and value pairs. The `Document` is then indexed by passing it to `IndexWriter.addDocument(Document)`. When searching, you again use the abstract `Directory` class to represent the index. You pass that `Directory` to the `IndexSearcher` class and then find `Documents` that match a given query by passing search terms encapsulated in the `Query` object to one of `IndexSearcher`'s search methods. The results are matching `Documents` represented by the `ScoreDoc` object.

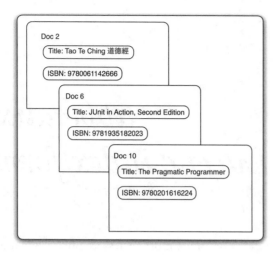

Figure B.1   The logical, black-box view of a Lucene index

B.2   About index structure

When we described Lucene's `Directory` class in section 1.5.2, we pointed out that one of its concrete subclasses, `SimpleFSDirectory`, stores the index in a file system directory. We've also used `Indexer`, a program for indexing text files, shown in listing 1.1. Recall that we specified several arguments when we invoked `Indexer` from the command line and that one of those arguments was the directory in which we wanted `Indexer` to create a Lucene index. What does that directory look like once `Indexer` is done running? What does it contain? In this section, we'll peek into a Lucene index and explain its structure.

Before we start, you should know that the index file format often changes between releases. It's free to change without breaking backward compatibility because the classes that access the index can detect when they're interacting with an older format index and act accordingly. The current format is always documented with each release, for example here, for the 3.0.1 release:

```
http://lucene.apache.org/java/3_0_1/fileformats.html
```

Lucene supports two index structures: multifile and compound. Multifile indexes use quite a few files to represent the index, whereas compound indexes use a special file, much like an archive such as a zip file, to hold multiple index files in a single file. Let's look at each type of index structure, starting with multifile.

B.2.1   Understanding the multifile index structure

If you look at the index directory created by our `Indexer`, you'll see a number of files whose names may seem random at first. These are index files, and they look similar to those shown here:

```
-rw-rw-rw- 1 mike users 12327579 Feb 29 05:29 _2.fdt
-rw-rw-rw- 1 mike users     6400 Feb 29 05:29 _2.fdx
-rw-rw-rw- 1 mike users       33 Feb 29 05:29 _2.fnm
```

```
-rw-rw-rw- 1 mike users  1036074 Feb 29 05:29 _2.frq
-rw-rw-rw- 1 mike users     2404 Feb 29 05:29 _2.nrm
-rw-rw-rw- 1 mike users  2128366 Feb 29 05:29 _2.prx
-rw-rw-rw- 1 mike users    14055 Feb 29 05:29 _2.tii
-rw-rw-rw- 1 mike users  1034353 Feb 29 05:29 _2.tis
-rw-rw-rw- 1 mike users     5829 Feb 29 05:29 _2.tvd
-rw-rw-rw- 1 mike users 10227627 Feb 29 05:29 _2.tvf
-rw-rw-rw- 1 mike users    12804 Feb 29 05:29 _2.tvx
-rw-rw-rw- 1 mike users       20 Feb 29 05:29 segments.gen
-rw-rw-rw- 1 mike users       53 Feb 29 05:29 segments_3
```

Notice that some files share the same prefix. In this example index, most of the files start with the prefix _2, followed by various extensions. This leads us to the notion of segments.

INDEX SEGMENTS

A Lucene index consists of one or more segments, and each segment is made up of several index files. Index files that belong to the same segment share a common prefix and differ in the suffix. In the previous example index, the index consisted of a single segment whose files started with _2.

The following example shows an index with two segments, _0 and _1:

```
-rw-rw-rw- 1 mike users 7743790 Feb 29 05:28 _0.fdt
-rw-rw-rw- 1 mike users    3200 Feb 29 05:28 _0.fdx
-rw-rw-rw- 1 mike users      33 Feb 29 05:28 _0.fnm
-rw-rw-rw- 1 mike users  602012 Feb 29 05:28 _0.frq
-rw-rw-rw- 1 mike users    1204 Feb 29 05:28 _0.nrm
-rw-rw-rw- 1 mike users 1337462 Feb 29 05:28 _0.prx
-rw-rw-rw- 1 mike users   10094 Feb 29 05:28 _0.tii
-rw-rw-rw- 1 mike users  737331 Feb 29 05:28 _0.tis
-rw-rw-rw- 1 mike users    2949 Feb 29 05:28 _0.tvd
-rw-rw-rw- 1 mike users 6294227 Feb 29 05:28 _0.tvf
-rw-rw-rw- 1 mike users    6404 Feb 29 05:28 _0.tvx
-rw-rw-rw- 1 mike users 4583789 Feb 29 05:28 _1.fdt
-rw-rw-rw- 1 mike users    3200 Feb 29 05:28 _1.fdx
-rw-rw-rw- 1 mike users      33 Feb 29 05:28 _1.fnm
-rw-rw-rw- 1 mike users  405527 Feb 29 05:28 _1.frq
-rw-rw-rw- 1 mike users    1204 Feb 29 05:28 _1.nrm
-rw-rw-rw- 1 mike users  790904 Feb 29 05:28 _1.prx
-rw-rw-rw- 1 mike users    7499 Feb 29 05:28 _1.tii
-rw-rw-rw- 1 mike users  548646 Feb 29 05:28 _1.tis
-rw-rw-rw- 1 mike users    2884 Feb 29 05:28 _1.tvd
-rw-rw-rw- 1 mike users 3933404 Feb 29 05:28 _1.tvf
-rw-rw-rw- 1 mike users    6404 Feb 29 05:28 _1.tvx
-rw-rw-rw- 1 mike users      20 Feb 29 05:28 segments.gen
-rw-rw-rw- 1 mike users      78 Feb 29 05:28 segments_3
```

You can think of a segment as a subindex, although each segment isn't a fully independent index.

As you'll see in the next section, each segment contains one or more Lucene Documents, the same ones we add to the index with the addDocument(Document) method in the IndexWriter class. By now you may be wondering what function segments serve in a Lucene index; what follows is the answer to that question.

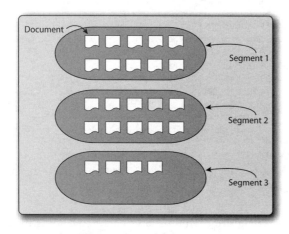

Figure B.2   Unoptimized index with three segments, holding 24 documents

INCREMENTAL INDEXING

Using segments lets you quickly add new Documents to the index by adding them to newly created index segments and only periodically merging them with other, existing segments. This process makes additions efficient because it minimizes physical index modifications. Figure B.2 shows an index that holds 24 Documents. This figure shows an unoptimized index—it contains multiple segments. If this index were to be optimized using the default Lucene indexing parameters, all 24 of its documents would be merged into a single segment.

One of Lucene's strengths is that it supports incremental indexing, which isn't something every IR library is capable of. Whereas some IR libraries need to reindex the whole corpus when new data is added, Lucene doesn't. After a document has been added to an index, its content is immediately made searchable. In IR terminology, this important feature is called incremental indexing. The fact that Lucene supports incremental indexing makes Lucene suitable for environments that deal with large bodies of information where complete reindexing would be unacceptable.

Because new segments are created as new Documents are indexed, the number of segments, and hence index files, varies while indexing is in progress. Once an index is fully built, the number of index files and segments remains steady.

A CLOSER LOOK AT INDEX FILES

Each index file carries a certain type of information essential to Lucene. If any index file is modified or removed by anything other than Lucene itself, the index becomes corrupted, and the only option is to run the CheckIndex tool (described in section 11.5.2) or perform a complete reindexing of the original data. On the other hand, you can add random files to a Lucene index directory without corrupting the index. For instance, if we add a file called random.txt to the index directory, as shown here, Lucene ignores that file, and the index doesn't become corrupted:

```
-rw-rw-rw- 1 mike users 12327579 Feb 29 05:29 _2.fdt
-rw-rw-rw- 1 mike users     6400 Feb 29 05:29 _2.fdx
-rw-rw-rw- 1 mike users       33 Feb 29 05:29 _2.fnm
```

```
-rw-rw-rw- 1 mike users  1036074 Feb 29 05:29 _2.frq
-rw-rw-rw- 1 mike users     2404 Feb 29 05:29 _2.nrm
-rw-rw-rw- 1 mike users  2128366 Feb 29 05:29 _2.prx
-rw-rw-rw- 1 mike users    14055 Feb 29 05:29 _2.tii
-rw-rw-rw- 1 mike users  1034353 Feb 29 05:29 _2.tis
-rw-rw-rw- 1 mike users     5829 Feb 29 05:29 _2.tvd
-rw-rw-rw- 1 mike users 10227627 Feb 29 05:29 _2.tvf
-rw-rw-rw- 1 mike users    12804 Feb 29 05:29 _2.tvx
-rw-rw-rw- 1 mike users       17 Mar 30 03:34 random.txt
-rw-rw-rw- 1 mike users       20 Feb 29 05:29 segments.gen
-rw-rw-rw- 1 mike users       53 Feb 29 05:29 segments_3
```

The secret to this is the segments file (segments_3). As you may have guessed from its name, the segments file stores the name and certain details of all existing index segments. Every time an `IndexWriter` commits a change to the index, the generation (the _3 in the previous code snippet) of the segments file is incremented. For example, a commit to this index would write segments_4 and remove segments_3 as well as any now unreferenced files. Before accessing any files in the index directory, Lucene consults this file to figure out which index files to open and read. Our example index has a single segment, _2, whose name is stored in this segments file, so Lucene knows to look only for files with the _2 prefix. Lucene also limits itself to files with known extensions, such as .fdt, .fdx, and other extensions shown in our example, so even saving a file with a segment prefix, such as _2.txt, won't throw Lucene off. Of course, polluting an index directory with non-Lucene files is strongly discouraged.

The exact number of files that constitute a Lucene index and each segment varies from index to index and depends how the fields were index (for example, indexing term vectors adds three files per segment). But every index contains one segments file per commit and a single segments.gen file. The segments.gen file is always 20 bytes and contains the suffix (generation) of the current segments as a redundant way for Lucene to determine the most recent commit.

CREATING A MULTIFILE INDEX

By now you should have a good grasp of the multifile index structure; but how do you use the API to instruct Lucene to create a multifile index and not the default compound-file index? Here's the answer:

```
IndexWriter writer = new IndexWriter(indexDir,
  new StandardAnalyzer(Version.LUCENE_30),
  true, IndexWriter.MaxFieldLength.UNLIMITED);
writer.setUseCompoundFile(false);
```

Because the compound-file index structure is the default, we disable it and switch to a multifile index by calling `setUseCompoundFile(false)` on an `IndexWriter` instance.

B.2.2 *Understanding the compound index structure*

A multifile index stores many separate files per segment. Furthermore, because new segments are created whenever documents are added to the index, there will be a variable and possibly large number of files in an index directory. Although the multifile index structure is straightforward and works for most scenarios, it can result in too many open files when an index has many segments, or when many indexes are open within a single JVM. Section 11.3.2 provides more details on understanding Lucene's use of file descriptors.

Modern OSs limit the number of files in the system, and per process, that can be opened at one time. Recall that Lucene creates new segments as new documents are added, and every so often it merges them to reduce the number of index files. But while the merge procedure is executing, the number of index files temporarily increases. If Lucene is used in an environment with lots of indexes that are being searched or indexed simultaneously, it's possible to hit the limit of open files set by the OS. This can also happen with a single Lucene index if the index isn't optimized or if other applications are running simultaneously and keeping many files open. Lucene's use of open file handles depends on the structure and state of an index. Section 11.3.2 describes approaches to control the number of open files.

COMPOUND INDEX FILES

The only visible difference between the compound and multifile indexes is the contents of an index directory. Here's an example of a compound index:

```
-rw-rw-rw-   1 mike    users   12441314 Mar 30 04:27 _2.cfs
-rw-rw-rw-   1 mike    users         15 Mar 30 04:27 segments_4
-rw-rw-rw-   1 mike    users         20 Mar 30 04:27 segments.gen
```

Instead of having to open and read 13 files from the index, as in the multifile index, Lucene must open only three files when accessing this compound index, thereby consuming fewer system resources. The compound index reduces the number of index files, but the concept of segments, documents, fields, and terms still applies. The difference is that a compound index contains a single .cfs file per segment, whereas each segment in a multifile index consists of seven different files. The compound structure encapsulates individual index files in a single .cfs file.

CREATING A COMPOUND INDEX

Because the compound index structure is the default, you don't have to do anything to specify it. But if you like explicit code, you can call the setUseCompoundFile(boolean) method, passing in true:

```
IndexWriter writer = new IndexWriter(indexDir,
   new StandardAnalyzer(Version.LUCENE_30),
   true, IndexWriter.MaxFieldLength.UNLIMITED);
writer.setUseCompoundFile(true);
```

You aren't locked into the multifile or compound format. After indexing, you can still switch from one format to another, although this will only affect newly written segments. But there is a trick!

B.2.3   *Converting from one index structure to the other*

It's important to note that you can switch between the two described index structures at any point during indexing. All you have to do is call the IndexWriter's setUseCompoundFiles(boolean) method at any time during indexing; the next time Lucene merges index segments, it will write the new segment in the format you specified.

Similarly, you can convert the structure of an existing index without adding more documents. For example, you may have a multifile index that you want to convert to a compound one, to reduce the number of open files used by Lucene. To do so, open your index with `IndexWriter`, specify the compound structure, optimize the index, and close it:

```
IndexWriter writer = new IndexWriter(indexDir,
  new StandardAnalyzer(Version.LUCENE_30),
  IndexWriter.MaxFieldLength.UNLIMITED);
writer.setUseCompoundFile(true);
writer.optimize();
writer.close();
```

We discussed optimizing indexes in section 2.9. Optimizing forces Lucene to merge index segments, thereby giving it a chance to write them in a new format specified via the `setUseCompoundFile(boolean)` method.

B.3   *Inverted index*

Lucene uses a well-known index structure called an *inverted index*. Quite simply, and probably unsurprisingly, an inverted index is an inside-out arrangement of documents in which terms take center stage. Each term refers to the documents that contain it. Let's dissect our sample book data index to get a deeper glimpse at the files in an index `Directory`.

Regardless of whether you're working with a `RAMDirectory`, an `FSDirectory`, or any other `Directory` implementation, the internal structure is a group of files. In a `RAMDirectory`, the files are virtual and live entirely within RAM. `FSDirectory` literally represents an index as a file system directory, as described earlier in this appendix.

The compound file mode adds an additional twist regarding the files in a `Directory`. When an `IndexWriter` is set for compound file mode, the "files" are written to a single .cfs file, which alleviates the common issue of running out of file handles. See section B.2.2 for more information on the compound file mode.

Our summary glosses over most of the intricacies of data compression used in the actual data representations. This extrapolation is helpful in giving you a feel for the structure instead of getting caught up in the minutiae (which, again, are detailed on the Lucene website).

Figure B.3 represents a slice of our sample book index. The slice is of a single segment (in this case, we had an optimized index with only a single segment). A segment is given a unique filename prefix (_c in this case).

The following sections describe each of the files shown in figure B.3 in more detail.

FIELD NAMES (.FNM)

The .fnm file contains all the field names used by documents in the associated segment. Each field is flagged to indicate options that were used while indexing:

- Is it indexed?
- Does it have term vectors enabled?

- Does it store norms?
- Does it have payloads?

The order of the field names in the .fnm file is determined during indexing and isn't necessarily alphabetical. Each field is assigned a unique integer, the field number, according to the order in this file. That field number, instead of the string name, is used in other Lucene files to save space.

TERM DICTIONARY (.TIS, .TII)

All terms (tuples of field name and value) in a segment are stored in the .tis file. Terms are ordered first alphabetically, according to the UTF 16 Java character, by field name and then by value within a field. Each term entry contains its *document frequency*: the number of documents that contain this term within the segment.

Figure B.3 shows only a sampling of the terms in our index, one or more from each field. Not shown is the .tii file, which is a cross-section of the .tis file designed to be kept in physical memory for random access to the .tis file. For each term in the .tis file, the .frq file contains entries for each document containing the term.

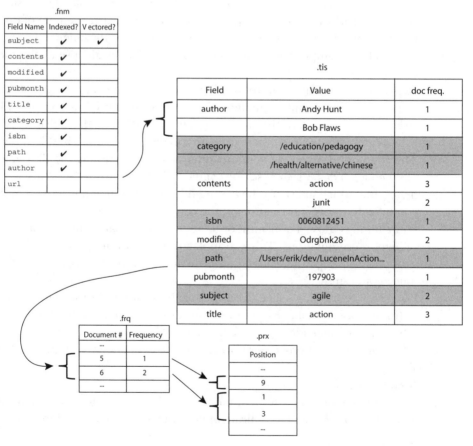

Figure B.3   Detailed look inside the Lucene index format

In our sample index, two books have the value "junit" in the contents field: JUnit in Action, Second Edition (document ID 6), and Ant in Action (document ID 5).

TERM FREQUENCIES

Term frequencies in each document are listed in the .frq file. In our sample index, Ant in Action (document ID 5) has the value `junit` once in the contents field. JUnit in Action, Second Edition has the value `junit` twice, provided once by the title field and once by the subject field. Our contents field is an aggregation of title, subject, and author. The frequency of a term in a document factors into the score calculation (see section 3.3) and typically boosts a document's relevance for higher frequencies.

For each document listed in the .frq file, the positions (.prx) file contains entries for each occurrence of the term within a document.

TERM POSITIONS

The .prx file lists the position of each term within a document. The position information is used when queries demand it, such as phrase queries and span queries. Position information for tokenized fields comes directly from the token position increments designated during analysis. This file also contains the payloads, if any.

Figure B.3 shows three positions, for each occurrence of the term `junit`. The first occurrence is in document 5 (Ant in Action) in position 9. In the case of document 5, the field value (after analysis) is `ant action apache jakarta ant build tool java development junit erik hatcher steve loughran`. We used the `StandardAnalyzer`; thus stop words (in in Ant in Action, for example) are removed. Document 6, JUnit in Action, Second Edition, has a contents field containing the value `junit` twice, once in position 1 and again in position 3: `junit action junit unit testing mock objects vincent massol ted husted`.[1]

STORED FIELDS

When you request that a field be stored (`Field.Store.YES`), it's written into two files: the .fdx file and the .fdt file. The .fdx file contains simple index information, which is used to resolve document number to exact position in the .fdt file for that document's stored fields. The .fdt file contains the contents of the fields that were stored.

TERM VECTORS

Term vectors are stored in three files. The .tvf file is the largest and stores the specific terms, sorted alphabetically, and their frequencies, plus the optional offsets and positions for the terms. The .tvd file lists which fields had term vectors for a given document and indexes byte offsets into the .tvf file so specific fields can be retrieved. Finally, the .tvx file has index information, which resolves document numbers into the byte positions in the .tvf and .tvd files.

NORMS

The .nrm file contains normalization factors that represent the boost information gathered during indexing. Each document has one byte in this file, which encodes the combination of the document's boost, that field's boost, and a normalization factor

---

[1] We're indebted to Luke, the fantastic index inspector, for allowing us to easily gather some of the data provided about the index structure.

based on the overall length of the content in that field. Section 2.5.3 describes norms in more detail.

DELETIONS

If any deletions have been committed to the index against documents contained in the segment, there will be a .del file present, named _X_N.del, where X is the name of the segment and N is an integer that increments every time new deletes are committed. This file contains a bit vector that's set for any deleted documents.

B.4   Summary

The rationale for the index structure is twofold: maximum performance and minimum resource utilization. For example, if a field isn't indexed it's a quick operation to dismiss it entirely from queries based on the indexed flag of the .fnm file. The .tii file, cached in RAM, allows for rapid random access into the term dictionary .tis file. Phrase and span queries need not look for positional information if the term itself isn't present. Streamlining the information most often needed, and minimizing the number of file accesses during searches is of critical concern. These are just some examples of how well thought out the index structure design is. If this sort of low-level optimization is of interest, refer to the Lucene index file format details on the Lucene website, where you'll find details we've glossed over here.

appendix C
Lucene/contrib benchmark

The contrib/benchmark module is a useful framework for running repeatable performance tests. By creating a short script, called an *algorithm* (file.alg), you tell the benchmark module what test to run and how to report its results. In chapter 11 we saw how to use benchmark for measuring Lucene's indexing performance. In this appendix we delve into more detail. Benchmark is quite new and will improve over time, so always check the Javadocs. The package-level Javadocs in the byTask subpackage have a good overview.

You might be tempted to create your own testing framework instead of learning how to use benchmark. Likely you've done so already many times in the past. But there are some important reasons to make the up-front investment and use benchmark instead:

- Because an algorithm file is a simple text file, it's easily and quickly shared with others so they can reproduce your results. This is vitally important in cases where you're trying to track down a performance anomaly and you'd like to isolate the source. Whereas for your own testing framework often there are numerous software dependencies and perhaps resources like local files or databases, that would have to be somehow transferred for someone else to run the test.

- The benchmark framework already has built-in support for common standard sources of documents (such as Reuters, Wikipedia, or TREC).

- With your own test, it's easy to accidentally create performance overhead in the test code itself (or even sneaky bugs!), which skews results. The benchmark package—because it's open source—is well debugged and well tuned, so it's less likely to suffer from this issue. And it only gets better over time!

- Thanks to a great many built-in tasks, you can create rich algorithms without writing any Java code. By writing a few lines (the algorithm file) you can craft nearly any test you'd like. You only have to change your script and rerun if you want to test something else. No compilation required!

- Benchmark has multiple extension points, to easily customize the source of documents, source of queries, and how the metrics are reported in the end. For advanced cases, you can also create and plug in your own tasks, as we did in section 11.2.1.
- Benchmark already gathers important metrics, like runtime, documents per second, and memory usage, saving you from having to instrument these in your custom test code.

Let's get started with a simple algorithm.

C.1   *Running an algorithm*

Save the following lines to a file, test.alg:

```
# The analyzer to use
analyzer=org.apache.lucene.analysis.standard.StandardAnalyzer

# Content source
content.source=org.apache.lucene.benchmark.byTask.feeds.ReutersContentSource

# Directory
directory=FSDirectory

# Turn on stored fields
doc.stored = true

# Turn on term vectors
doc.term.vectors = true

# Don't use compound-file format
compound = false

# Make only one pass through the documents
content.source.forever = false

# Repeat 3 times
{"Rounds"

  # Clear the index
  ResetSystemErase

  # Name the contained tasks "BuildIndex"
  {"BuildIndex"

  # Create a new IndexWriter
  -CreateIndex

  # Add all docs
  { "AddDocs" AddDoc > : *

  # Close the index
   -CloseIndex
  }

  # Start a new round
  NewRound
} : 3
```

```
# Report on the BuildIndex task
RepSumByPrefRound BuildIndex
```

As you can probably guess, this algorithm indexes the entire Reuters corpus, three times, and reports the performance of the BuildIndex step separately for each round. Those steps include creating a new index (opening an IndexWriter), adding all Reuters documents, and closing the index. Remember, when testing indexing performance it's important to include the time to close the index because necessary time-consuming tasks happen during close(). For example, Lucene waits for any still-running background merges to finish, then syncs all newly written files in the index. To run your algorithm, use this:

```
ant run-task -Dtask-alg=<file.alg> -Dtask.mem=512M
```

Note that if you've implemented any custom tasks, you'll have to include the classpath to your compiled sources by also adding this to the Ant command line:

```
-Dbenchmark.ext.classpath=/path/to/classes
```

Ant first runs a series of dependency targets—for example, making sure all sources are compiled and downloading, and unpacking the Reuters corpus. Finally, it runs your task and produces something like this under the run-task output:

```
Working Directory: /lucene/clean/contrib/benchmark/work
Running algorithm from: /lucene/clean/contrib/benchmark/eg1.alg
-----------> config properties:
analyzer = org.apache.lucene.analysis.standard.StandardAnalyzer
compound = false
content.source =
➡ org.apache.lucene.benchmark.byTask.feeds.ReutersContentSource
content.source.forever = false
directory = FSDirectory
doc.stored = true
doc.term.vectors = true
work.dir = work
----------------------------
-----------> algorithm:
Seq {
    Rounds_3 {
        ResetSystemErase
        BuildIndex {
            -CreateIndex
            AddDocs_Exhaust {
                AddDoc
            > * EXHAUST
            -CloseIndex
        }
        NewRound
    } * 3
    RepSumByPrefRound BuildIndex
}

    -----------> starting task: Seq
1.88 sec --> main added 1000 docs
4.04 sec --> main added 2000 docs
```

```
4.48 sec --> main added 3000 docs
…yada yada yada…
12.18 sec --> main added 21000 docs

--> Round 0-->1

------------> DocMaker statistics (0):
total bytes of unique texts:        17,550,748


0.2 sec --> main added 22000 docs
0.56 sec --> main added 23000 docs
0.92 sec --> main added 24000 docs
…yada yada yada…
8.02 sec --> main added 43000 docs

--> Round 1-->2

0.29 sec --> main added 44000 docs
0.63 sec --> main added 45000 docs
1.04 sec --> main added 46000 docs
…yada yada yada…
9.43 sec --> main added 64000 docs

--> Round 2-->3

-->Report sum by Prefix (BuildIndex) and Round (3 about 3 out of 14)
Operation round runCnt recsPerRun rec/s elapsedSec avgUsedMem avgTotalMem
BuildIndex    0     1      21578 1,682     12.83 26,303,608  81,788,928
BuildIndex -  1  -  1  -   21578 2,521  -   8.56 44,557,144  81,985,536
BuildIndex    2     1      21578 2,126     10.15 37,706,752  80,740,352
####################
### D O N E !!! ###
####################
```

The benchmark module first prints all the settings you're running with, under *config properties*. It's best to look this over and verify the settings are what you intended. Next it "pretty-prints" the steps of the algorithm. You should also verify this algorithm is what you expected. If you put a closing } in the wrong place, this is where you will spot it. Finally, benchmark runs the algorithm and prints the status output, which usually consists of

- The content source periodically printing how many documents it has produced
- The Rounds task printing whenever it finishes a new round

When this finishes, and assuming you have reporting tasks in your algorithm, the report is generated, detailing the metrics from each round.

The final report shows one line per round, because we're using a report task (Rep-SumByPrefRound) that breaks out results by round. For each round, it includes the number of records (added documents in this case), records per second, elapsed seconds, and memory usage. The average total memory is obtained by calling java.lang.Runtime.getRuntime().totalMemory(). The average used memory is computed by subtracting freeMemory() from totalMemory().

What exactly is a record? In general, most tasks count as +1 on the record count. For example, every call to AddDoc adds 1. Task sequences aggregate all records counts of their children. To prevent the record count from incrementing, you prefix the task with a hyphen (-) as we did earlier for `CreateIndex` and `CloseIndex`. This allows you to include the cost (time and memory) of creating and closing the index yet correctly amortize that total cost across all added documents.

So that was pretty simple, right? From this you could probably poke around and make your own algorithms. But to shine, you'll need to know the full list of settings and tasks that are available.

C.2 Parts of an algorithm file

Let's dig into the various parts of an algorithm file. This is a simple text file. Comments begin with the # character, and whitespace is generally not significant. Usually the settings, which bind global names to their values, appear at the top. Next comes the heart of the algorithm, which expresses the series of tasks to run, and in what order. Finally, there's usually one or more reporting tasks at the very end to generate the final summary. Let's look first at the settings.

Settings are lines that match this form:

```
name = value
```

where `name` is a known setting (the full list of settings is shown in tables C.1, C.2, and C.3). For example, `compound = false` tells the `CreateIndex` or `OpenIndex` task to create the `IndexWriter` with `setUseCompoundFile` set to `false`.

Often you want to run a series of rounds where each round uses different combinations of settings. Imagine you'd like to measure the performance impact of changing RAM buffer sizes during indexing. You can do this like so:

```
name = header:value1:value2:value3
```

For example, `ram.flush.mb = MB:2:4:8:16` would use a 2.0 MB, 4.0 MB, 8.0 MB, and 16.0 MB RAM buffer size in `IndexWriter` for each round of the test, and label the corresponding column in the report as "MB." Table C.1 shows the general settings, table C.2 shows settings that affect logging, and table C.3 shows settings that affect `IndexWriter`. Be sure to consult the online documentation for an up-to-date list. Also, your own custom tasks can define their own settings.

Table C.1 General settings

Name Default value	Description

`work.dir`
System property
`benchmark.work.dir` or `work.`
	Specifies the root directory for data and indexes.

`analyzer` `StandardAnalyzer`	Contains the fully qualified class name to instantiate as the analyzer for indexing and parsing queries.
`content.source` `SingleDocSource`	Specifies the class that provides the raw content.
`doc.maker` `DocMaker`	Specifies the class used to create documents from the content provided by the content source.

Table C.1 General settings *(continued)*

Name Default value	Description
content.source.forever true	Boolean. If `true`, the `content.source` will reset itself upon running out of content and keep producing the same content forever. Otherwise, it will stop when it has made one pass through its source.
content.source.verbose false	Specifies whether messages from the content source should be printed.
content.source.encoding null	Specifies the character encoding of the content source.
html.parser Not set	Contains the class name to filter HTML to text. The default is `null` (no HTML parsing is invoked). You can specify `org.apache.lucene.benchmark.byTask.feeds.DemoHTMLParser` to use the simple HTML parser included in Lucene's demo package.
doc.stored false	Boolean. If `true`, fields added to the document by the `doc.maker` are created with `Field.Store.YES`.
doc.tokenized true	Boolean. If `true`, fields added to the document by the `doc.maker` are created with `Field.Index.ANALYZED` or `Field.Index.ANALYZED_NO_NORMS`.
doc.tokenized.norms false	Specifies whether non-body fields in the document should be indexed with norms.
doc.body.tokenized.norms true	Specifies whether the body field should be indexed with norms.
doc.term.vector false	Boolean. If `true`, fields are indexed with term vectors enabled.
doc.term.vector.positions false	Boolean. If `true`, then term vectors positions are indexed.
doc.term.vector.offsets false	Boolean. If `true`, term vector offsets are indexed.
doc.store.body.bytes false	Boolean. If `true`, the document's fields are indexed with `Field.Store.YES` into the field docbytes.
doc.random.id.limit -1	Integer. If not equal to `-1` the `LineDocMaker` tasks will randomly pick IDs within this bound. This is useful with the `UpdateDoc` task for testing `IndexWriter`'s `updateDocument` performance
docs.dir Depends on document source	Contains the string directory name. Used by certain document sources as the root directory for finding document files in the file system.
docs.file Not set	Contains the string directory name. Used by certain document sources as the root filename. Used by `LineDocSource`, `WriteLineFile`, and `EnwikiContentSource` as the file for single-line documents.

Table C.1 General settings *(continued)*

Name Default value	Description
doc.index.props false	If `true`, the properties set by the content source for each document will be indexed as separate fields. Presently only `SortableSingleDocMaker` and any HTML content processed by the HTML parser set properties.
doc.reuse.fields true	Boolean. If `true`, a single shared instance of `Document` and a single shared instance of `Field` for each field in the document are reused. This gains performance by avoiding allocation and GC costs. But if you create a custom task that adds documents to an index using private threads, you'll need to turn this off. The normal parallel task sequence, which also uses threads, may leave this at `true` because the single instance is per thread.
query.maker SimpleQueryMaker	Contains the string class name for the source of queries. See section C.2.2 for details.
file.query.maker.file Not set	Specifies the string path to the filename used by `FileBasedQueryMaker`. This is the file that contains one text query per line
file.query.maker.default.field body	Specifies the field that `FileBasedQueryMaker` will issue its queries against.
doc.delete.step 8	When deleting documents in steps, this is the step that's added in between deletions. See the `DeleteDoc` task for more detail.

Table C.2 Settings that affect logging

Name Default value	Description
log.step 1000	Integer. Specifies how often to print the progress line for non-content-source tasks. You can also specify `log.step.<TASK>` (for example, `log.step.AddDoc`) to set a separate step per task. A value of `-1` turns off logging for that task.
content.source.log.step 0	Integer. Specifies how often to print the progress line, as measured by the number of docs created by the content source.
log.queries false	Boolean. If `true`, the queries returned by the query maker are printed.
task.max.depth.log 0	Integer. Controls which nested tasks should do any logging. Set this to a lower number to limit how many tasks log. `0` means to log only the top-level tasks.
writer.info.stream Not set	Enables `IndexWriter`'s `infoStream` logging. Use `SystemOut` for `System.out`; `SystemErr` for `System.err`; or a filename to direct the output to the specified file.

Table C.3   Settings that affect `IndexWriter`

Setting Default	Description
compound true	Boolean. `True` if the compound file format should be used.
merge.factor 10	Merge factor
max.buffered −1 (don't flush by doc count)	Max buffered docs
max.field.length 10000	Maximum field length
directory RAMDirectory	Directory
ram.flush.mb 16.0	RAM buffer size
merge.scheduler org.apache.lucene.index.ConcurrentMergeScheduler	Merge scheduler
merge.policy org.apache.lucene.index.LogByteSizeMergePolicy	Merge policy
deletion.policy org.apache.lucene.index.KeepOnlyLastCommitDeletionPolicy	Deletion policy

C.2.1   *Content source and document maker*

When running algorithms that index documents, you'll need to specify a source that creates documents. There are two settings:

- `content.source` specifies a class that provides the raw content to create documents from.
- `doc.maker` specifies a class that takes the raw content and produces Lucene documents.

The default `doc.maker`, `org.apache.lucene.benchmark.byTask.feeds.DocMaker`, is often sufficient. It will pull content from the content source, and based on the `doc.*` settings (for example, `doc.stored`) create the appropriate `Document`. The list of built-in `ContentSources` is shown in table C.4. In general, all content sources can decompress compressed bzip files on the fly and accept arbitrary encoding as specified by the `content.source.encoding` setting.

Each of these classes is instantiated once, globally, and then all tasks will pull documents from this source. Table C.4 describes the built-in ContentSource classes.

You can also create your own content source or doc maker by subclassing Content-Source or DocMaker. But take care to make your class thread-safe because multiple threads will share a single instance.

Table C.4 Built-in ContentSources

Name	Description
SingleDocSource	Provides a short (~150 words) fixed English text, for simple testing.
SortableSingleDocSource	Like SingleDocSource, but also includes an integer field, sort_field; a country field, country; and a random short string field, random_string. Their values are randomly selected per document to enable testing sort performance on the resulting index.
DirContentSource	Recursively visits all files and directories under a root directory (specified with the docs.dir setting), opening any file ending with the extension .txt, and yielding the file's contents. The first line of each file should contain the date, the second line should contain the title, and the rest of the document is the body.
LineDocSource	Opens a single file, specified with the docs.file setting, and reads one document per line. Each line should have title, date, and body, separated by the tab character. Generally this source has far less overhead than the others because it minimizes the I/O cost by working with only a single file.
EnwikiContentSource	Generates documents directly from the large XML export provided by http://wikipedia.org. The setting keep.image.only.docs, a Boolean setting that defaults to true, decides whether image-only (no text) documents are kept. Use docs.file to specify the XML file.
ReutersContentSource	Generates documents unpacked from the Reuters corpus. The Ant task get-files retrieves and unpacks the Reuters corpus. Documents are created as *.txt files under the output directory work/reuters-out. The setting docs.dir, defaulting to work/reuters-out, specifies the root location of the unpacked corpus.
TrecContentSource	Generates documents from the TREC corpus. This assumes you have already unpacked the TREC into the directory set by docs.dir.

C.2.2   *Query maker*

The `query.maker` setting determines which class to use for generating queries. Table C.5 describes the built-in query makers.

Table C.5   Built-in query makers

Name	Description
FileBasedQueryMaker	Reads queries from a text file one per line. Set `file.query.maker.default.field` (defaults to `body`) to specify which index field the parsed queries should be issued against. Set `file.query.maker.file` to specify the file containing the queries.
ReutersQueryMaker	Generates a small fixed set of 10 queries that roughly match the Reuters corpus.
EnwikiQueryMaker	Generates a fixed set of 90 common and uncommon actual Wikipedia queries.
SimpleQueryMaker	Used only for testing. Generates a fixed set of 10 synthetic queries.
SimpleSloppyPhraseQueryMaker	Takes the fixed document text from `SimpleDocMaker` and programmatically generates a number of queries with varying degrees of slop (from 0 to 7) that would match the single document from `SimpleDocMaker`.

C.3   *Control structures*

We've finished talking about settings, content sources, doc makers, and query makers. Now we'll talk about the available control structures in an algorithm, which is the all-important "glue" that allows you to take built-in tasks and combine them in interesting ways. Here are the building blocks:

- Serial sequences are created with { ... }. The enclosed tasks are run one after another, by a single thread. For example:

```
{CreateIndex AddDoc CloseIndex}
```

creates a new index, adds a single document pulled from the doc maker, then closes the index.

- Run a task in the background by appending &. For example:

```
OpenReader
{ Search > : * &
{ Search > : * &
Wait(30)
CloseReader
```

opens a reader, runs two search threads in the background, waits for 30 seconds, asks the background threads to stop, and closes the reader.

- Parallel sequences are created with [...]. A parallel sequence runs the enclosed tasks with as many threads as there are tasks, with each task running in its own thread. For example:

  ```
  [AddDoc AddDoc AddDoc AddDoc]
  ```

  creates four threads, each of which adds a single document, then stops.

- Repeating a task multiple times is achieved by appending :N to the end. For example:

  ```
  {AddDoc}: 1000
  ```

  adds the next 1,000 documents from the document source. Use * to pull all documents from the doc maker. For example:

  ```
  {AddDoc}: *
  ```

  adds all documents from the doc maker. When you use this, you must also set `content.source.forever` to `false`.

- Repeating a task for a specified amount of time is achieved by appending :Xs to the end. For example:

  ```
  {AddDoc}: 10.0s
  ```

  runs the `AddDoc` task for 10 seconds.

- Name a sequence like this:

  ```
  {"My Name" AddDoc} : 1000
  ```

  This defines a single `AddDoc` called "My Name," and runs that task 1,000 times. The double quotes surrounding the name are required even if the name doesn't have spaces. Your name will then be used in the reports.

- Some tasks optionally take a parameter string, in parentheses, after the task. For example, `AddDoc(1024)` will create documents whose body field consists of approximately 1,024 characters (an effort is made not to split words). If you try to pass a parameter to a task that doesn't take one, or the type isn't correct, you'll hit a "Cannot understand algorithm" error. Tables C.6 and C.7 detail the parameters accepted by each task.

- Turning off statistics of the child task requires the > character instead of } or]. This is useful for avoiding the overhead of gathering statistics when you don't require that level of detail. For example:

  ```
  { "ManyAdds" AddDoc > : 10000
  ```

  adds 10,000 docs and won't individually track statistics of each `AddDoc` call (but the 10,000 added docs are tracked by the outer sequence containing `"ManyAdds"`).

- In addition to specifying how many times a task or task sequence should be repeated, you can specify the target rate in count per second (default) or count per minute. Do this by adding : N : R after the task. For example:

  ```
  { AddDoc } : 10000 : 100/sec
  ```

  adds 10,000 documents at a rate of 100 documents per second. Or

  ```
  [ AddDoc ]: 10000: 3
  ```

adds 10,000 docs in parallel, spawning one thread for each added document, at a rate of three new threads per second.

- Each task contributes to the records count that's used for reporting at the end. For example, `AddDoc` returns 1. Most tasks return count 1, some return count 0, and some return a count greater than 1. Sometimes you don't want to include the count of a task in your final report. To do that, simply prepend a hyphen before your task. For example, if you use this:

```
{"BuildIndex"
   -CreateIndex
   {AddDoc}:10000
   -CloseIndex
 }
```

the report will record exactly 10,000 records, but if you leave the – out, it reports 10,002.

C.4   Built-in tasks

We've discussed the settings and the control structures, or glue, that allow you to combine tasks into larger sequences of tasks. Now, finally, let's review the built-in tasks. Table C.6 describes the built-in administration tasks, and table C.7 describes the tasks for indexing and searching

If the commands available for use in the algorithm don't meet your needs, you can add commands by adding a new task under the `org.apache.lucene.benchmark.byTask.tasks` package. You should extend the `PerfTask` abstract class. Make sure that your new task class name is suffixed by `Task`. For example, once you compile the class `SliceBreadTask.java` and ensure it's on the classpath that you specify to Ant, then you can invoke this task by using `SliceBread` in your algorithm.

Table C.6   Administration tasks

Task Name	Description
ClearStats	Clears all statistics. Report tasks run after this point will only include statistics from tasks run after this task.
NewRound	Begins a new round of a test. This command makes the most sense at the end of an outermost sequence. This increments a global "round counter." All tasks that start will record this new round count and their statistics would be aggregated under that new round count. For example, see the RepSumByNameRound reporting task. In addition, NewRound moves to the next setting if the setting specified different settings per round. For example, with setting merge.factor=mrg:10:100:10:100, merge.factor would change to the next value after each round. Note that if you have more rounds than number of settings, it simply wraps around to the first setting again.
ResetInputs	Reinitializes the document and query sources back to the start. For example, it's a good idea to insert this call after NewRound to make sure your document source feeds the exact same documents for each round. This is only necessary when you aren't running your content source to exhaustion.

Table C.6   Administration tasks *(continued)*

Task Name	Description
ResetSystemErase	Resets all index and input data, and calls System.gc(). This doesn't reset statistics. It also calls ResetInputs. All writers and readers are closed, nulled, and deleted. The index and directory are erased. You must call CreateIndex to create a new index after this call if you intend to add documents to an index.
ResetSystemSoft	Just like ResetSystemErase, except the index and work directory aren't erased. This is useful for testing performance of opening an existing index for searching or updating. You can use the OpenIndex task after this reset.

Table C.7   Built-in tasks for indexing and searching

Task Name / Description	Parameter
CreateIndex Creates a new index with IndexWriter. You can then use the AddDoc tand UpdateDoc tasks to make changes to the index.	
OpenIndex Opens an existing index with IndexWriter. You can then use the AddDoc and UpdateDoc tasks to change the index.	commitName A string label specifying which commit should be opened. This must match the commitName passed to a previous CommitIndex call.
OptimizeIndex Optimizes the index. This task optionally takes an integer parameter, which is the maximum number of segments to optimize. This calls the IndexWriter.optimize(int maxNumSegments) method. If there's no parameter, it defaults to 1. This requires that an IndexWriter be opened with either CreateIndex or OpenIndex.	maxNumSegments This is an integer, allowing you to perform a partial optimize if it's greater than 1.
CommitIndex Calls commit on the currently open IndexWriter. This requires that an IndexWriter be opened with either CreateIndex or OpenIndex.	commitName A string label that's recorded into the commit and can later be used by OpenIndex to open a specific commit.
RollbackIndex Calls IndexWriter.rollback to undo all changes done by the current IndexWriter since the last commit. This is useful for repeatable tests where you want each test to perform indexing but not commit any of the changes to the index so that each test always starts from the same index.	

Table C.7   Built-in tasks for indexing and searching *(continued)*

Task Name Description	Parameter
`CloseIndex` Closes the open index.	`doWait` `true` or `false`, passed to `IndexWriter.close`. If `false`, the `IndexWriter` will abort any running merges and forcefully close. This parameter is optional and defaults to `true`.
`OpenReader` Creates an `IndexReader` and `IndexSearcher`, available for the search tasks. If a `Read` task is invoked, it will use the currently open reader. If no reader is open, it will open its own reader, perform its task, and then close the reader. This enables testing of various scenarios: sharing a reader, searching with a cold reader, searching with a warm reader, etc.	`readOnly`, `commitName` `readOnly` is `true` or `false`. `commitName` is a string name of the specific commit point that should be opened.
`NearRealtimeReader` Creates a separate thread that periodically calls `getReader()` on the current `IndexWriter` to obtain a near-real-time reader, printing to `System.out` how long the reopen took. This task also runs a fixed `query body:1`, sorting by `docdate`, and reports how long the query took to run.	`pauseSec` A float that specifies how long to wait before opening each near-real-time reader.
`FlushReader` Flushes but doesn't close the currently open `IndexReader`. This is only meaningful if you've used one of the `Delete` tasks to perform deletions.	`commitName` A string name of the specific commit point that should be written.
`CloseReader` Closes the previously opened reader.	
`NewAnalyzer` Switches to a new analyzer. This task takes a single parameter, which is a comma-separated list of class names. Each class name can be shortened to just the class name, if it falls under the `org.apache.lucene.analysis` package; otherwise, it must be fully qualified. Each time this task is executed, it will switch to the next analyzer in its list, rotating back to the start if it hits the end.	
`Search` Searches an index. If the reader is already opened (with the `OpenReader` task), it's searched. Otherwise, a new reader is opened, searched, and closed. This task simply issues the search but doesn't traverse the results.	

Table C.7   Built-in tasks for indexing and searching *(continued)*

Task Name Description	Parameter
SearchWithSort Searches an index with a specified sort.	sortDesc A comma-separated list of field:type values. For example "country:string,sort_field:int". doc means to sort by Lucene's docID; noscore means to not compute scores; nomaxscore means to not compute the maximum score.
SearchTrav Searches an index and traverses the results. Like Search, except the top ScoreDocs are visited. This task takes an optional integer parameter, which is the number of ScoreDocs to visit. If no parameter is specified, the full result set is visited. This task returns as its count the number of documents visited.	traversalSize Integer count of how many ScoreDocs to visit.
SearchTravRet Searches an index and traverses and retrieves the results. Like SearchTrav, except for each ScoreDoc visited, the corresponding document is also retrieved from the index.	traversalSize Integer count of how many ScoreDocs to visit.
SearchTravRetLoadFieldSelector Search an index and traverse and retrieve only specific fields in the results, using FieldSelector. Like SearchTrav, except this task takes an optional comma-separated string parameter, specifying which fields of the document should be retrieved.	fieldsToLoad A comma-separated list of fields to load.
SearchTravRetHighlight Searches an index; traverses, retrieves, and highlights certain fields from the results using contrib/highlighter.	highlightDesc This task takes a comma-separated parameter list to control details of the highlighting. Please consult its Javadocs for the details.
SearchTravRetVectorHighlight Searches an index; traverses, retrieves, and highlights certain fields from the results using contrib/fast-vector-highlighter.	highlightDesc This task takes a comma-separated parameter list to control details of the highlighting. Please consult its Javadocs for the details.
SetProp Changes a property's value. Normally a property's value is set once when the algorithm is first loaded. This task lets you change a value midstream. All tasks executed after this one will see the new value.	propertyName,value Name and new value for the property.

Table C.7   Built-in tasks for indexing and searching (continued)

Task Name Description	Parameter
Warm Warms up a previously opened searcher by retrieving all documents in the index. Note that in a real application, this isn't sufficient as you'd also want to prepopulate the `FieldCache` if you're using it, and possibly issue initial searches for commonly searched for terms. Alternatively, you could create steps in your algorithm that simply run your own sequence of queries, as your custom warm-up.	
DeleteDoc Deletes a document by document ID, or by incrementing step size to compute the document ID to be deleted. Note that this task performs its deletions using `IndexReader`, so you must first open one using `OpenReader`.	`docID` An integer. If the parameter is negative, deletions are done by the `doc.delete.step` setting. For example, if the step size is 10, then each time this task is executed it will delete the document IDs in the sequence 0, 10, 20, 30, etc. If the parameter is non-negative, then this is a fixed document ID to delete.
DeleteByPercent Removes the specified percentage of all documents (`maxDoc()`). If the index has already removed more than this percentage, then first `undeleteAll` is called, and then the target percentage is deleted. Note that this task performs its deletions using `IndexReader`, so you must first open one using `OpenReader`.	`Percent` Double value (from 0 to 100) specifying what percentage of all docs should be deleted.
AddDoc Adds the next document to the index. `IndexWriter` must already be opened.	`docSize` A numeric parameter indicating the size of the added document, in characters. The body of each document from the content source will be truncated to this size, with the leftover being prepended to the next document. This requires that the doc maker support changing the document size.
UpdateDoc Calls `IndexWriter.updateDocument` to replace documents in the index. The docid field of the incoming document is passed as the `Term` to specify which document should be updated. The `doc.random.id.limit` setting, which randomly assigns `docID`s, is useful when testing `updateDocument`.	`docSize` Same meaning as `AddDoc`.

Table C.7 Built-in tasks for indexing and searching *(continued)*

Task Name Description	Parameter
ReadTokens This task tests the performance of just the analyzer's tokenizer. It simply reads the next document from the doc maker and fully tokenizes all its fields. As the count, this task returns the number of tokens encountered. This is a useful task to measure the cost of document retrieval and tokenization. By subtracting this cost from the time spent building an index, you can get a rough measure of what the actual indexing cost is.	
WriteLineDocTask Creates a line file that can then be used by LineDocMaker. See section C.4.1 for details.	docSize Same meaning as addDoc.
Wait Simply waits for the specified amount of time. This is useful when a number of prior tasks are running in the background (simply append &).	Time to wait. Append s for seconds, m for minutes, and h for hours.

C.4.1 Creating and using line files

Line files are simple text files that contain one document per line. Indexing documents from a line file incurs quite a bit less overhead than other approaches, such as opening and closing one file per document, pulling files from a database, or parsing an XML file. Minimizing such overhead is important if you're trying to measure performance of just the core indexing. If instead you're trying to measure indexing performance from a particular content source, then you should not use a line file.

The benchmark framework provides a simple task, WriteLineDoc, to create line files from any content source. Using this task, you can translate any source into a line file. The one limitation is that each document only has a date, title, and body field. The line.file.out setting specifies the file that's created. For example, use this algorithm to translate the Reuters corpus into a single-line file:

```
# Where to get documents from:
content.source=org.apache.lucene.benchmark.byTask.feeds.ReutersContentSource

# Stop after processing the document feed once:
content.source.forever=false

# Where to write the line file output:
line.file.out=work/reuters.lines.txt

# Process all documents, appending each one to the line file:
{WriteLineDoc}: *
```

Once you've done this, you can then use `reuters.lines.txt` and `LineDocSource` like this:

```
# Feed that knows how to process the line file format:
content.source=org.apache.lucene.benchmark.byTask.feeds.LineDocSource

# File that contains one document per line:
docs.file=work/reuters.lines.txt

# Process documents only once:
content.source.forever=false

# Create a new index, index all docs from the line file, close the
# index, produce a report.
CreateIndex
{AddDoc}: *
CloseIndex

RepSumByPref AddDoc
```

C.4.2   *Built-in reporting tasks*

Reporting tasks generate a summary report at the end of the algorithm, showing how many records per second were achieved, how much memory was used, showing one line per task or task sequence that gathered statistics. The reporting tasks themselves aren't measured or reported. Table C.8 describes the built-in reporting tasks. If needed, additional reports can be added by extending the abstract class `ReportTask` and by manipulating the statistics data in `Points` and `TaskStats`.

Table C.8   Reporting tasks

Task name	Description
RepAll	All (completed) tasks run.
RepSumByName	All statistics, aggregated by name. So, if AddDoc was executed 2,000 times, only one report line would be created for it, aggregating all those 2,000 statistic records.
RepSelectByPref prefix	All records for tasks whose name start with prefix.
RepSumByPref prefix	All records for tasks whose name start with prefix aggregated by their full task name.
RepSumByNameRound	All statistics, aggregated by name and by round. So, if AddDoc was executed 2,000 times in each of three rounds, three report lines would be created for it, aggregating all those 2,000 statistic records in each round. See more about rounds in the NewRound task description in table C.6.
RepSumByPrefRound prefix	Similar to RepSumByNameRound, except only tasks whose name starts with prefix are included.

C.5 *Evaluating search quality*

How do you test the relevance or quality of your search application? Relevance testing is crucial because, at the end of the day, your users won't be satisfied if they don't get relevant results. Many small changes to how you use Lucene, from the analyzer chain, to which fields you index, to how you build up a `Query`, to how you customize scoring, can have large impacts on relevance. Being able to properly measure such effects allows you to make changes that improve your relevance.

Yet, despite being the most important aspect of a search application, quality is devilishly difficult to pin down. There are certainly many subjective approaches. You can run a controlled user trial, or you can play with the application yourself. What do you look for? Besides checking if the returned documents are relevant, there are many other things to check: Are the excerpts accurate? Is the right metadata presented? Is the UI easily consumed on quick glance? No wonder so few applications are tuned for their relevance!

That said, if you'd like to objectively measure the relevance of returned documents, you're in luck: the `quality` package, under benchmark, allow you to do so. These classes provide concrete implementations based on the formats from the TREC corpus, but you can also implement your own. You'll need a "ground truth" transcribed set of queries, where each query lists the documents that are relevant to it. This approach is entirely binary: a given document from the index is deemed either relevant or not. From these we can compute precision and recall, which are the standard metrics in the information retrieval community for objectively measuring relevance of search results. Precision measures what subset of the documents returned for each query were relevant. For example, if a query has 20 hits and only one is relevant, precision is 0.05. If only one hit was returned and it was relevant, precision is 1.0. Recall measures what percentage of the relevant documents for that query was returned. So if the query listed eight documents as being relevant but six were in the result set, that's a recall of 0.75.

In a properly configured search application, these two measures are naturally at odds with each other. Let's say, on one extreme, you only show the user the very best (top 1) document matching his query. With such an approach, your precision will typically be high, because the first result has a good chance of being relevant, whereas your recall would be very low, because if there are many relevant documents for a given query you have only returned one of them. If we increase top 1 to top 10, then suddenly we'll be returning many documents for each query. The precision will necessarily drop because most likely you're now allowing some nonrelevant documents into the result set. But recall should increase because each query should return a larger subset of its relevant documents.

Still, you'd like the relevant documents to be higher up in the ranking. To account for this, average precision is computed. This measure computes precision at each of the N cutoffs, where N ranges from 1 to a maximum value, and then takes the average. So this measure is higher if your search application generally returns relevant documents earlier in the result set. Mean average precision (MAP) then measures the mean of average precision across a set of queries. A related measure, mean reciprocal rank (MRR), measures $1/M$, where M is the first rank that had a relevant document. You want both of these numbers to be as high as possible.

Listing C.1 shows how to use the `quality` package to compute precision and recall. Currently, in order to measure search quality, you must write your own Java code (there are no built-in tasks for doing so that would allow you to solely use an algorithm file). The queries to be tested are represented as an array of `QualityQuery` instances. The `TrecTopicsReader` knows how to read the TREC topic format into `QualityQuery` instances, but you could also implement your own. Next, the ground truth is represented with the simple `Judge` interface. The `TrecJudge` class loads *TREC*'s Qrel format and implements `Judge`. `QualityQueryParser` translates each `Quality-Query` into a real Lucene query. Finally, `QualityBenchmark` tests the queries by running them against a provided `IndexSearcher`. It returns an array of `QualityStats`, one each for each of the queries. The `QualityStats.average` method computes and reports precision and recall.

Listing C.1 Computing precision and recall statistics for your `IndexSearcher`

```java
public class PrecisionRecall {

  public static void main(String[] args) throws Throwable {

    File topicsFile = new File("src/lia/benchmark/topics.txt");
    File qrelsFile = new File("src/lia/benchmark/qrels.txt");
    Directory dir = FSDirectory.open(new File("indexes/MeetLucene"));
    Searcher searcher = new IndexSearcher(dir, true);

    String docNameField = "filename";

    PrintWriter logger = new PrintWriter(System.out, true);

    TrecTopicsReader qReader = new TrecTopicsReader();         // Read TREC topics
    QualityQuery qqs[] = qReader.readQueries(                  // as QualityQuery[]
        new BufferedReader(new FileReader(topicsFile)));

    Judge judge = new TrecJudge(new BufferedReader(            // Create Judge from
        new FileReader(qrelsFile)));                           // TREC Qrel file
                                                               // Verify query
    judge.validateData(qqs, logger);                          // and Judge match

    QualityQueryParser qqParser = new SimpleQQParser(          // Create
                        "title", "contents");                  // QueryParser

    QualityBenchmark qrun = new QualityBenchmark(qqs,
                qqParser, searcher, docNameField);
    SubmissionReport submitLog = null;
    QualityStats stats[] = qrun.execute(judge,                 // Run benchmark
        submitLog, logger);

    QualityStats avg =
      QualityStats.average(stats);                             // Print precision and
    avg.log("SUMMARY",2,logger, "   ");                        // recall measures
    dir.close();
  }
}
```

When you run the code in listing C.1 by entering ant `PrecisionRecall` at the command line within the book's source code directory, it will produce something like this:

```
SUMMARY
  Search Seconds:          0.015
  DocName Seconds:         0.006
  Num Points:             15.000
  Num Good Points:         3.000
  Max Good Points:         3.000
  Average Precision:       1.000
  MRR:                     1.000
  Recall:                  1.000
  Precision At  1:         1.000
  Precision At  2:         1.000
  Precision At  3:         1.000
  Precision At  4:         0.750
  Precision At  5:         0.600
  Precision At  6:         0.500
  Precision At  7:         0.429
  Precision At  8:         0.375
  Precision At  9:         0.333
  Precision At 10:         0.300
  Precision At 11:         0.273
  Precision At 12:         0.250
  Precision At 13:         0.231
  Precision At 14:         0.214
```

Note that this test uses the MeetLucene index, so you'll need to run ant `Indexer` if you skipped over that in chapter 1. This was a trivial test, because we ran on a single query that has exactly three correct documents (see the source files src/lia/benchmark/topics.txt for the queries and src/lia/benchmark/qrels.txt for the correct documents). You can see that the precision was perfect (1.0) for the top three results, meaning the top three results were in fact the correct answer to this query. Precision then gets worse beyond the top three results because any further document is incorrect. Recall is perfect (1.0) because all three correct documents were returned. In a real test you won't see perfect scores.

C.6   *Errors*

If you make a mistake in writing your algorithm, which is in fact very easy to do, you'll see a somewhat cryptic exception like this:

```
java.lang.Exception: Error: cannot understand algorithm!
    at org.apache.lucene.benchmark.byTask.Benchmark.<init>(Benchmark.java:63)
    at org.apache.lucene.benchmark.byTask.Benchmark.main(Benchmark.java:98)
Caused by: java.lang.Exception: colon unexpected: - Token[':'], line 6
    at org.apache.lucene.benchmark.byTask.utils.Algorithm.<init>
➥ (Algorithm.java:120)
    at org.apache.lucene.benchmark.byTask.Benchmark.<init>(Benchmark.java:61)
```

When this happens, simply scrutinize your algorithm. One common error is a misbalanced { or }. Try iteratively simplifying your algorithm to a smaller part and run that to isolate the error.

C.7 *Summary*

As you've seen, the benchmark package is a powerful framework for quickly creating indexing and searching performance tests and for evaluating your search application for precision and recall. It saves you tons of time because all the normal overhead in creating a performance test is handled for you. Combine this with the large library of built-in tasks for common indexing and searching operations, plus extensibility to add your own report, task, document, or query source, and you've got one very useful tool under your belt.

appendix D
Resources

Web search engines are your friends. Type `lucene` in your favorite web search engine and you'll find many interesting Lucene-related projects. Other good places to look are Source-Forge, Google Code, and GitHub; a search for `lucene` on any of those sites displays a number of open source projects written on top of Lucene.

D.1 Lucene knowledgebases

Search Lucene: http://search-lucene.com/

LucidFind: http://search.lucidimagination.com/

D.2 Internationalization

Unicode page in Wikipedia: http://en.wikipedia.org/wiki/Unicode

The Unicode Consortium: http://unicode.org

Bray, Tim, "Characters vs. Bytes": www.tbray.org/ongoing/When/200x/2003/04/26/UTF

Green, Dale, "Trail: Internationalization": http://java.sun.com/docs/books/tutorial/i18n/index.html

Lindenberg, Norbert, and Masayoshi Okutsu, "Supplementary Characters in the Java Platform": http://java.sun.com/developer/technicalArticles/Intl/Supplementary/

Peterson, Erik, "Chinese Character Dictionary—Unicode Version": www.mandarin-tools.com/chardict_u8.html

Spolsky, Joel, "The Absolute Minimum Every Software Developer Absolutely, Positively Must Know About Unicode and Character Sets (No Excuses!)": www.joelonsoftware.com/articles/Unicode.html

Davis, Mark, "Globalization Gotchas": http://macchiato.com/slides/GlobalizationGotchas.ppt

D.3   *Language detection*

Rosette Language Identifier, http://basistech.com/language-identification

Marr, Rich, "Creating a Language Detection API in 30 minutes": http://richmarr.word-press.com/2008/10/24/creating-a-language-detection-api-in-30-minutes/

Prager, John M., "Linguini: Language Identification for Multilingual Documents": ftp://ftp.software.ibm.com/software/globalization/documents/linguini.pdf

Java Text Categorization Library: http://textcat.sourceforge.net/

NGramJ: http://ngramj.sourceforge.net

Google Ajax Language API: http://code.google.com/apis/ajaxlanguage/documentation/

Sematext Language Identifier: www.sematext.com/products/language-identifier/index.html

Language identification on Wikipedia: http://en.wikipedia.org/wiki/Language_identification

D.4   *Term vectors*

Vector Space Model on Wikipedia: http://en.wikipedia.org/wiki/Vector_space_model

Latent Semantic Analysis on Wikipedia: http://en.wikipedia.org/wiki/Latent_semantic_analysis

The Latent Semantic Indexing home page: http://lsa.colorado.edu/

"Latent Semantic Indexing (LSI)": www.cs.utk.edu/~lsi

Stata, Raymie, Krishna Bharat, and Farzin Maghoul, "The Term Vector Database: Fast Access to Indexing Terms for Web Pages": www9.org/w9cdrom/159/159.html

D.5   *Lucene ports*

CLucene: www.sourceforge.net/projects/clucene/

Lucene.Net: http://incubator.apache.org/lucene.net/

KinoSearch: www.rectangular.com/kinosearch

Apache Lucy: http://lucene.apache.org/lucy/

PyLucene: http://lucene.apache.org/pylucene/

Ferret: http://ferret.davebalmain.com

PHP, (Zend_Search_Lucene, part of Zend Framework): http://framework.zend.com/

D.6   *Case studies*

Krugle: www.krugle.org/

DERI, SIREn: http://siren.sindice.com/

LinkedIn, Bobo-Browse: http://snaprojects.jira.com/browse/BOBO/

LinkedIn, Zoie: http://snaprojects.jira.com/browse/ZOIE

D.7   *Miscellaneous*

Manning, Christopher D., Prabhakar Raghavan, and Hinrich Schütze, *Introduction to Information Retrieval* (Cambridge University Press, 2008). See www-nlp.stanford.edu/IR-book/.

Calishain, Tara, and Rael Dornfest, *Google Hacks* (O'Reilly, 2003).

Gilleland, Michael, "Levenshtein Distance, in Three Flavors": www.merriampark.com/ld.htm

GNU Compiler for the Java Programming Language: http://gcc.gnu.org/java/

Google search results for Lucene: www.google.com/search?q=lucene

Apache Lucene Java: http://lucene.apache.org/java

Lucene Sandbox: http://lucene.apache.org/java/3_0_1/lucene-contrib/index.html

Suffix trees on Wikipedia: http://en.wikipedia.org/wiki/Suffix_tree

D.8   IR software

dmoz results for information retrieval: http://dmoz.org/Computers/Software/Information_Retrieval/

Egothor: www.egothor.org/

Minion: https://minion.dev.java.net/

Google Directory results for information retrieval: http://directory.google.com/Top/Computers/Software/Information_Retrieval/

ht://Dig: www.htdig.org

Managing Gigabytes for Java (MG4J): http://mg4j.dsi.unimi.it

Terrier: http://ir.dcs.gla.ac.uk/terrier

Namazu: www.namazu.org

Hounder: http://hounder.org

Search Tools for Web Sites and Intranets: www.searchtools.com

SWISH++: http://swishplusplus.sourceforge.net/

SWISH-E: http://swish-e.org/

Autonomy: www.autonomy.com

Aperture: http://aperture.sourceforge.net/

WebGlimpse: http://webglimpse.net

Xapian: www.xapian.org

The Lemur Toolkit: www.lemurproject.org

D.9   Doug Cutting's publications

Doug's official list of publications, from which this was derived, is available at http://lucene.sourceforge.net/publications.html.

D.9.1   Conference papers

"An Interpreter for Phonological Rules," coauthored with J. Harrington, Proceedings of Institute of Acoustics Autumn Conference, November 1986

"Information Theater versus Information Refinery," coauthored with J. Pedersen, P.-K. Halvorsen, and M. Withgott, AAAI Spring Symposium on Text-Based Intelligent Systems, March 1990

"Optimizations for Dynamic Inverted Index Maintenance," coauthored with J. Pedersen, Proceedings of SIGIR '90, September 1990

"An Object-Oriented Architecture for Text Retrieval," coauthored with J. O. Pedersen and P.-K. Halvorsen, Proceedings of RIAO '91, April 1991

"Snippet Search: A Single Phrase Approach to Text Access," coauthored with J. O. Pedersen and J. W. Tukey, Proceedings of the 1991 Joint Statistical Meetings, August 1991

"A Practical Part-of-Speech Tagger," coauthored with J. Kupiec, J. Pedersen, and P. Sibun, Proceedings of the Third Conference on Applied Natural Language Processing, April 1992

"Scatter/Gather: A Cluster-Based Approach to Browsing Large Document Collections," coauthored with D. Karger, J. Pedersen, and J. Tukey, Proceedings of SIGIR '92, June 1992

"Constant Interaction-Time Scatter/Gather Browsing of Very Large Document Collections," coauthored with D. Karger and J. Pedersen, Proceedings of SIGIR '93, June 1993

"Porting a Part-of-Speech Tagger to Swedish," Nordic Datalingvistik Dagen 1993, Stockholm, June 1993

"Space Optimizations for Total Ranking," coauthored with J. Pedersen, Proceedings of RIAO '97, Montreal, Quebec, June 1997

D.9.2   *U.S. Patents*

5,278,980: "Iterative technique for phrase query formation and an information retrieval system employing same," with J. Pedersen, P.-K. Halvorsen, J. Tukey, E. Bier, and D. Bobrow, filed August 1991

5,442,778: "Scatter-gather: a cluster-based method and apparatus for browsing large document collections," with J. Pedersen, D. Karger, and J. Tukey, filed November 1991

5,390,259: "Methods and apparatus for selecting semantically significant images in a document image without decoding image content," with M. Withgott, S. Bagley, D. Bloomberg, D. Huttenlocher, R. Kaplan, T. Cass, P.-K. Halvorsen, and R. Rao, filed November 1991

5,625,554 "Finite-state transduction of related word forms for text indexing and retrieval," with P.-K. Halvorsen, R.M. Kaplan, L. Karttunen, M. Kay, and J. Pedersen, filed July 1992

5,483,650 "Method of Constant Interaction-Time Clustering Applied to Document Browsing," with J. Pedersen and D. Karger, filed November 1992

5,384,703 "Method and apparatus for summarizing documents according to theme," with M. Withgott, filed July 1993

5,838,323 "Document summary computer system user interface," with D. Rose, J Bornstein, and J. Hatton, filed September 1995

5,867,164 "Interactive document summarization," with D. Rose, J. Bornstein, and J. Hatton, filed September 1995

5,870,740 "System and method for improving the ranking of information retrieval results for short queries," with D. Rose, filed September 1996

index

Q